The Bhagavad-Gītā

Select Other Books by the Authors

By Georg Feuerstein

The Deeper Dimension of Yoga

The Encyclopedia of Yoga and Tantra

The Path of Yoga

The Philosophy of Classical Yoga

Tantra: The Path of Ecstasy

Teachings of Yoga

Yoga Morality

The Yoga Tradition

By Georg Feuerstein and Brenda Feuerstein

Green Dharma

Green Yoga

The Bhagavad-Gītā

A NEW TRANSLATION

Georg Feuerstein

WITH BRENDA FEUERSTEIN

SHAMBHALA
BOSTON & LONDON
2011

Shambhala Publications, Inc.
Horticultural Hall
300 Massachusetts Avenue
Boston, Massachusetts 02115
www.shambhala.com

9 8 7 6 5 4 3 2 1

First Edition
Printed in the United States of America

♾ This edition is printed on acid-free paper that meets the American National Standards Institute Z39.48 Standard.
♻ This book is printed on 30% postconsumer recycled paper.
For more information please visit www.shambhala.com.

Distributed in the United States by Random House, Inc., and in Canada by Random House of Canada Ltd

Designed by Gopa & Ted2, Inc.

Library of Congress Cataloging-in-Publication Data

Bhagavadgita. English & Sanskrit.
The Bhagavad-Gita: a new translation / Georg Feuerstein with Brenda Feuerstein.—lst ed.
p. cm. Includes bibliographical references (p.) and index.
ISBN 978-1-59030-893-6 (pbk.: alk. paper)
I. Feuerstein, Georg. II. Feuerstein, Brenda. III. Title.
BL1138.62.E5 2011
294.5'92404521—dc22
2010051836

For Brenda, with my heartfelt thanks. She had the vision for the present version and maintained it right until completion. Without her encouragement and skillful assistance, this work would never have seen the light of day in its present form. Among other things, she shouldered the tedium of entering the Sanskrit text on the computer and found this task enjoyable at that.

Contents

Preface

yato dharmas tataḥ kṛṣṇaḥ
Where dharma is, there is Krishna.
—*Mahābhārata* 6.41.55

ALTHOUGH THE *Bhagavad-Gītā*—an episode in India's greatest epic, the *Mahābhārata*—was composed over two thousand years ago, its activist message is still relevant today, perhaps more so than ever—and not only to Hindus. We live in a time of great social and environmental upheaval, and the wisdom teachings of Krishna have, I propose, much to offer us all. Krishna imparted his activist Yoga to his disciple, Prince Arjuna, while he was poised on the battlefield, facing the immediate prospect of killing relatives and honored teachers who for various reasons had gathered on the enemy's side. Naturally, Arjuna found himself in a significant personal quandary—a struggle between right and wrong that is symbolic of all of life's great predicaments. Today, our battlefield is global, and what is at stake is the survival of our species and all higher life forms on planet Earth. We also are called to fight for the dignity and sustainability of the vast "underprivileged" section of the human population and the mental-emotional sanity of those who live in relative abundance.

Also, given the two world wars of the twentieth century, in which more than one hundred million people perished, and the numerous more or less local wars fought since then, the militaristic gospel of Krishna seems particularly pertinent. I would argue, however, that all war is an abomination and that, therefore, we must appropriately bracket the *Gītā*'s militaristic orientation and understand it in allegorical terms.

The Bharata war was probably a historical event long ago, which was remembered by generations of bards until Vyāsa Dvaipāyana ("Island-born

Editor")—whoever he may have been (more on this in chapter 6 of Part One)—artfully crafted a magnificent epic from which rural and, to some degree, also urban Indians still derive inspiration. Various dates for the war have been proposed—notably 3102 B.C.E. (the traditional beginning of the Age of Darkness, or *kali-yuga*), 2000 B.C.E., 1500 B.C.E., and 900 B.C.E.—which are all speculative. While the first date seems far too early, the last seems too late. Although there may well be numerous echoes of historical realities in Vyāsa's epic, it appears to be impossible to separate fact from fiction. In any case, chronology is not so important as the message of the *Mahābhārata.*

The gist of Krishna's teachings is that when the moral and spiritual welfare of a people are at stake, war is permissible. The epic and its *Gītā* episode revolve around the value of moral integrity—*dharma,* or the "law." It is no accident that the *Gītā* begins with the word *dharma.* In the first stanza, we find the phrase *dharma-kshetra* ("field of the law") juxtaposed with *kuru-kshetra* ("field of the Kurus"), the battlefield on which so many warriors lost their lives. We can readily understand this symbolically in the sense of life itself being a battlefield on which good and evil, or right and wrong, are at stake in every moment.

Admittedly, however, a literal interpretation seems also possible, whereby *dharma-kshetra* designates the culture area of the sacred land of the Vedic people who aspired to abide by civilized laws in consonance with the cosmic order (*rita*), as revealed by the great seers and sages of yore. See, for example, chapter 2, verse 19, of the *Mānava-Dharma-Shāstra* (popularly known as the Laws of Manu), which refers to the plain of the Kurus as the country of the brahmanical sages.

Whether we choose a metaphorical or a literal interpretation of the Bharata war as a whole, we can learn from—and faithfully translate—the *Gītā* even when we must question its militaristic morality. Thus, as a pacifist, I can still condone and applaud much of the *Gītā*'s wisdom. I have personally taken its warrior ethics as an occasion to once again reflect on my own preferred attitude to life and as a result have achieved greater clarity about my own sentiments and convictions.

We do not have to accept the *Gītā*'s—or any other traditional scripture's—teachings uncritically. In fact, this would prove unhelpful and even adverse for us. The only proper way to relate to any type of knowledge is with an open mind, which is by no means a sieve through which anything can pass freely, without critical inspection. The light of inspired reason (*buddhi*), which the *Gītā* holds in such high esteem, ought to be applied under all circumstances. I maintain that Krishna would not want us to abandon rationality. Even though he condoned and supported military action on the part of Prince Arjuna, who was a highly trained and incredibly skillful archer, Krishna left the final choice up to Arjuna, expecting that his disciple would consider his divine counsel carefully (that is, rationally).

I would even argue that the *Gītā* is constructive for us only to the degree that we engage this traditional scripture with a sensitive and empathetic but analytical mind. The popular notion that one ought to suspend reason in metaphysical matters and resort to belief is unsound. On the contrary, the ultimate concerns of metaphysics are so vitally important that we should ponder them with the most refined part of our mind, which is *buddhi.* As the grammatical root *budh* ("to be aware, awake") of this Sanskrit term suggests, *buddhi* is a mental faculty that is marked by alertness and lucidity—namely, wisdom.

The *Mahābhārata* epic, of which the *Gītā* can be said to be the ethical-philosophical essence, is reckoned to belong to both the category of *itihāsa,* or history, and *kāvya,* or the inspired literature of a poet-sage (*kavi*). We can look upon the *Gītā* in a similar way and appreciate both its historical and its symbolic-allegorical flavor. The latter perspective allows us to understand the central motif of the eighteen-day battle also in a figurative rather than a literal sense. In other words, the *Gītā*'s militaristic ethics need not be limited to a historical actuality but can readily be interpreted as symbolic of the larger struggle of life. Be that as it may, I propose that whether we understand the *Mahābhārata* war in literal or allegorical terms, the *Gītā*'s message has lost none of its vitality and relevance over the course of centuries.

The Sanskrit text of the *Gītā* in Part Two is from the well-known critical edition by Shripad Krishna Belvalkar (2nd reprint, 1968). I have included significant additional verses given in the critical apparatus of Dr. Belvalkar's text, which was first published in 1945.

In view of the large number of available *Gītā* translations, it has become customary to apologize for offering yet another rendering. I will refrain from doing so, for two reasons. I believe that my translation along with my commentary and notes has merit amid the spate of numerous popular paraphrases, which often cause discerning readers to rightly wonder about the accuracy of the translation before them. To give them an opportunity to check the fidelity of my own rendering, I have furnished a word-for-word translation highlighting my own interpretative preferences in Part Three.

The present rendering with commentarial notes represents a thoroughly revised version of my book *The Bhagavad-Gītā: Yoga of Contemplation and Action,* published in an Indian edition in 1980, which I withdrew from circulation shortly after its publication. The introductory essays in Part One were partly drawn from my out-of-print book *An Introduction to the Bhagavad-Gītā* (1974, republished 1995). For those wishing to delve still deeper than the present monograph affords, I have designed a distance-learning course, which is available through Traditional Yoga Studies (www.traditionalyogastudies.com), a company directed by my wife, Brenda Feuerstein, and registered in Canada.

For further comments on my translation, please see Part One, chapter 9, "On Translating the *Bhagavad-Gītā*." Information on the transliteration systems used and the pronunciation of Sanskrit follows this preface.

Of the numerous Sanskrit works on Yoga, two scriptures have become favorites of dedicated students of Yoga—the *Yoga-Sūtra* attributed to Patanjali and the *Bhagavad-Gītā* ascribed to Vyāsa. These can be considered foundational Yoga texts. While the former work addresses primarily ascetics, the latter is a gospel mainly for the *grihastha-yogin,* the spiritual practitioner who is a householder with a busy family life. Not surprisingly, the *Gītā* generally holds the stronger appeal for contemporary practitioners of Yoga, although Patanjali's text is more widely studied in yoga teacher trainings, perhaps because it is (wrongly) considered to be more accessible.

Unknowingly, the larger public in the Western hemisphere has come under the spell of this classic in the form of the Hollywood hit *The Legend of Bagger Vance* (2000), directed by Robert Redford, which demonstrated that the spiritual teachings of Krishna can be applied even on the "battlefield" of golf. The question is whether an unprepared movie audience can lastingly benefit from such a brief exposure to the *dharma* in the context of what is intended to be entertainment. Probably not.

There is, perhaps, a slightly better possibility of an enduring effect happening with the millions of practitioners of so-called Postural Yoga in the Western hemisphere, to the extent that they engage Yoga as a *spiritual discipline.* I hope that those few who have touched Yoga's spiritual dimension will explore the depth of the *Gītā*'s pristine spirituality. May this translation guide them in their studies.

Georg Feuerstein, Ph.D.

Acknowledgments

THIS WAS BY FAR my most challenging book to produce. I owe a profound thank-you to Peter Turner and David O'Neal for adopting this book and deciding to make it the best possible work on the subject. We all went the "extra mile" to realize this vision. My sincere thanks also go to the members of Shambhala's editorial and production staff, who made this book possible in its present elegant and pleasing version. I especially would like to extend heartfelt thanks to Ben Gleason for his meticulous work throughout the book, to Gopa & Ted2 for designing and typesetting the book, and to Kendra Crossen for her exceptional copyediting proficiency. Kendra diligently went over my manuscript with a fine-tooth comb and carefully removed a multitude of errors, ambiguities, and stylistic peculiarities. I feel fortunate that she was able to approach this task from a sturdy background of familiarity not only with the *Gītā* but also Hindu mythology.

The Transliteration and Pronunciation of Sanskrit

Transliteration

The following tables indicate the detailed transliteration of the Sanskrit alphabet as used in the transliterated sections on verso (left-hand) or even-numbered pages in Part Two (the *Bhagavad-Gītā* text). This system is also used in the word-for-word translation in Part Two. A less detailed system of transliteration, used elsewhere in the book, is described below.

Detailed Transliteration

Vowels

Simple Vowels

अ a short	आ ā long	इ i short	ई ī long	उ u short	ऊ ū long	ऋ ṛ semi-vowel	ॠ ṝ semi-vowel (long)	ऌ ḷ semi-vowel

Dipthongs

ए e	ऐ ai	ओ o	औ au

Consonants*

Gutturals	क ka	ख kha	ग ga	घ gha	ङ ṅa
Palatals	च ca	छ cha	ज ja	झ jha	ञ ña
Cerebrals	ट ṭa	ठ ṭha	ड ḍa	ढ ḍha	ण ṇa
Dentals	त ta	थ tha	द da	ध dha	न na
Labials	प pa	फ pha	ब ba	भ bha	म ma
Semivowels	य ya	र ra	ल la	व va	
Spirants	श śa	ष ṣa	स sa		
Aspirate	ह ha				
Visarga ("Discharge")	: ḥ				
Anusvāra ("Aftersound")	ँ ṃ				

*In Sanskrit, almost all consonants, unless modified, have an in-built *a* sound. The combination letters ज्ञ jña and क्ष kṣa are regarded as separate sound units in the system of Tantra.

Simplified Transliteration

A simplified system of transliteration is used in the essays of Part One and in the translation and footnotes on recto (right-hand) or odd-numbered pages of Part Two, so that readers unfamiliar with Sanskrit will not have to deal with the possible distraction of the more detailed scheme. In this simplified system, the long vowel sounds are indicated by macrons (*ā, ī, ū*). Other diacritics (such as underdot, tilde, and acute accent) have been omitted for all consonants. The spelling *sh* stands for both *ś* and *ṣ*. The letter *c* is retained for the sound *ch*.

Pronunciation

The vowels *a, i, u, ṛ*, and *ḷ* are short. The vowel sounds are open as in Italian; *ṛ* and *ḷ* are pronounced somewhat like *ri* and *li*, respectively. Many Sanskrit words—like योग *yoga*, त्याग *tyāga*, and राग *rāga*—end in a short *a*, which is vocalized. So, contrary to popular belief in Western and even Indian Yoga circles, such words are not pronounced (as in Hindi) *yog, tyāg,* or *rāg*.

The vowels *ā, ī,* and *ū,* and the four diphthongs are long. The diphthong *e* is pronounced as *ey* in *prey; ai* as in *my; o* as in *bone; au* as in *now*.

The letter *ṅ* has the sound of *ng* in *king; ca* is pronounced with *ch* in *church*; *ja* with *j* in *join*. *Cha* is aspirated *c*, distinct from *ch* as in *church*.

The cerebrals *ṭa, ṭha, ḍa, ḍha,* and *ṇa* are pronounced with the tongue curled back against the roof of the mouth.

The sound *va* is pronounced midway between *w* (as in *water*) and *v* (as in *very*).

The spirant *śa* is a *sh* sound between *sa* (as in *song*) and *ṣa*. The *ṣa* is pronounced like *sh* in *shun* (with the tongue curled back against the palate).

The *visarga* (*ḥ*) is pronounced as a hard *h* followed by a short echo of the preceding vowel, e.g., *yogaḥ*[a]; *samādhiḥ*[i]; *manuḥ*[u].

The nasal *ṃ* sounds rather like the French *n* in *bon*.

All aspirated consonants—namely, *kha, gha, cha, jha, ṭha, ḍha, tha, dha, bha,* and *pha*—are pronounced distinctly: *k-ha* (as in *ink-horn*); *t-ha* (as in *hot-head*), *p-ha* (as in *top-heavy*). The *th* is never pronounced like the *th* sound in the words *this* or *thing*. Nor is the *ph* sound pronounced as in *phone*.

The combination sound *jñ* (as in *jñāna*) is pronounced differently in different regions of India: in northern and eastern India, *gya* (without nasalization); in central and western India, *dnya;* in southern India, the nasalized *gna* is used.

Part One
Introductory Essays

yataḥ kṛṣṇas tato jayaḥ

Where Krishna is, there is victory.

—*Mahābhārata* (6.21.14)

I

The *Mahābhārata*

THE *Bhagavad-Gītā* as we know it today consists of eighteen chapters (23–40) of the sixth book of the *Mahābhārata*, one of India's two magnificent epics. The eighteen-book *Mahābhārata* is seven times as long as Greece's two great epics, the *Iliad* and *Odyssey*, combined, and almost three times as long as the Bible. It represents a detailed account of the events leading up to the devastating eighteen-day war between two closely connected royal lineages—the Kauravas (or Kurus) and the Pāndavas (or Pāndus)—and their many allies, the events of the war itself, and its sad consequences. The *Gītā* contains the profound spiritual-ethical teachings of Krishna, which seek to make sense of an atrocious war.

India's other great epic, the *Rāmāyana* ("Life of Rāma"), treats in 24,000 stanzas the legend of the divine hero Rāma, his combat with demonic forces, and the rescue of his wife, Sītā, who had been abducted by Rāvana, king of the netherworld Lankā (present-day Sri Lanka). The incredible wealth of episodes and stories, woven into this mammoth work like the colorful patterns of a carpet, continues to edify and delight the people of India to this day. Briefly, the core story of the *Rāmāyana* belongs to an earlier age than the Bharata war. But the text of the *Rāmāyana* was composed around the time of the *Mahābhārata*, probably by a single poet, named Vālmīki ("Ant").

Whereas the *Mahābhārata* insists on belonging to *smriti*, or conventional literary tradition, the *Rāmāyana* contends to be no more than poetry (*kāvya*). And as such it has served later generations of poets as a celebrated prototype for their own creations. The twentieth-century philosopher-sage Sri Aurobindo, who perhaps knew the life pulse of Indian spirituality better than any academic scholar, writes about Vālmīki's work:

> The *Rāmāyana* is a work of the same essential kind as the *Mahābhārata;* it differs only by a greater simplicity of plan, a more delicate ideal temperament and a finer glow of poetic warmth and color. The main bulk of the poem in spite of much accretion is evidently by a single hand and has a less complex and more obvious unity of structure. There is less of the philosophic, more of the purely poetic mind, more of the artist, less of the builder. (Aurobindo 1959, pp. 323–24)

If the *Rāmāyana* is compared to a superbly cut diamond, the *Mahābhārata* may be said to resemble a giant unpolished gem whose perfection and beauty lie in its very roughness and asymmetry. The character of the *Mahābhārata,* the "Great [Epic of the War] of the Bharata [Descendants]," is enormously complex. For it is, as Sri Aurobindo asserts,

> not only the story of the Bharatas, the epic of an early event which had become a national tradition, but on a vast scale the epic of the soul and religious and ethical mind and social and political ideals and culture and life of India. It is said popularly of it and with a certain measure of truth that whatever is in India is in the Mahabharata. The Mahabharata is the creation and expression not of a single individual mind, but of the mind of a nation; it is the poem of itself written by a whole people. (Aurobindo 1959, p. 326)

Aurobindo's remarks about this encyclopedic epic of the Bharatas are equally true of the *Gītā.* It is not so much the construction of an individual thinker with a bias for eclecticism as it is the work of a genius who endeavored, out of the very depths of his being, to give expression to the potentialities of the whole Indian soul.

As is stated in book 1, chapter 1, of the *Mahābhārata* itself (cited as 1.1), the sage Vyāsa bequeathed the great epic in two versions, one concise and the other more elaborate. Furthermore, the same section states that Vyāsa's original compilation comprised 24,000 verses and bore the title *Bhārata.* He is said to have written a summary in 150 verses, which is possibly what now stands as the introduction to the full version. Thereafter, the passage in chapter 1 continues, he worked out a second version consisting of altogether six million stanzas, of which three million are known only in the heavenly realm or world (*deva-loka*), one and a half million in the realm of the forefathers (*pitri-loka*), one million four hundred thousand in the world of the genii (*gandharva*), and only a hundred thousand in the human world. The last-mentioned figure is justified by the form in which the epic is extant today.

The *Mahābhārata*'s vast content is distributed over eighteen books (*parvan*). Although the plot of the *Gītā* can be understood on the basis of its own chapters, it may be useful to glance briefly at the contents of the chapters of the epic.

The Eighteen Books of the Epic

1. *Ādi-parvan* ("Book of Beginning"). In addition to its practical function as an introduction to the whole of the epic, this book depicts the childhood and career of the brothers Dhritarāshtra ("Firm Rule") and Pāndu ("Pale"). Dhritarāshtra is a blind king who has one daughter and one hundred sons—the Kuru princes, or Kauravas, who distinguish themselves by their bad character traits. Pāndu, by contrast, has five sons—the Pāndavas (Yudhishtira, Bhīma, Arjuna, Nakula, and Sahadeva)—who are outstanding for their many moral and other excellences. Upon the premature death of Pāndu, his five sons come under the care of Dhritarāshtra. Soon petty jealousies and quarrels developed between Dhritarāshtra's own sons and his protégés, which lay the foundation for the great war.

2. *Sabhā-parvan* ("Book of Assembly"). Here a lively description is given of one of the pivotal events of the epic: the stormy assembly (*sabhā*) in Hastināpura, the capital of the Kuru land, where Yudhishthira ("[He Who Is] Steadfast in Battle"), the eldest Pāndava, lost his entire kingdom in a game of dice, owing to despicable cheating by the Kauravas in conspiracy with their maternal uncle Shakuni ("Bird"). Having nothing left to gamble with, Yudhishthira stakes and loses his own brothers. Finally, there is nothing left to bet but the queen Draupadī (also known as Krishnā and as Pāncālī), the common wife of all five Pāndava brothers. Prince Duryodhana triumphantly summons her to the assembly hall for this ultimate humiliation of his opponents. When she refuses, she is dragged there by her long hair. When Dushshāsana, one of the Kaurava brothers, tries to rip off her sari as a sign of her servitude, the god Dharma, in response to her urgent prayer to Krishna, replaces it instantly and prevents her from being completely exposed. She eloquently and angrily defends her honor. The five Pāndavas, together with their joint wife, are sent into exile for a total of thirteen years. The thirteenth year is to be lived incognito. If their

identities were to be discovered, they would have to remain in exile for a further twelve years.

3. *Vana-parvan* ("Book of the Forest"). This book describes the life in the forest (*vana*) of the banished sons of Pāndu. It contains, among other outstanding passages, the often translated story of King Nala, who, like Yudhishthira, lost his kingdom through gambling. The legend of a faithful and devoted wife, Sāvitrī, is also related here. Princess Sāvitrī wandered throughout the country to find a pure husband for herself. She ended up finding him in a woodcutter's son by the name of Satyavant ("Truthful"). Her noble character inspired Sri Aurobindo to create his massive poetic work, *Sāvitrī.*

4. *Virāta-parvan* ("Book of Virāta"). This book describes the thirteenth year of exile, which the five brothers are forced to spend incognito in the service of King Virāta, the ruler of the Matsyas. The virile Arjuna disguises himself as a eunuch. In the end, Virāta offers his daughter Uttarā ("Supreme") in marriage to Arjuna, who accepts her hand on behalf of his son Abhimanyu ("Wrath"). They produce a son, the future emperor Parikshit ("Dwelling Around"), before Abhimanyu is slain on the thirteenth day of the great war.

5. *Udyoga-parvan* ("Book of Exertion"). This book shows the preparations for the great civil war. The Pāndavas raise seven armies and the Kauravas eleven. Yudhishthira appoints Dhrishtadyumna ("Bold Splendor") as generalissimo of the Pāndava armies. Chapters 33–40 of this book contain the moral teachings of Vidura ("Intelligent"), the wise uncle of both the Pāndavas and the Kauravas.

6. *Bhīshma-parvan* ("Book of Bhīshma"). This book gives a meticulously detailed account of the first encounters on the battlefield. It also contains the *Bhagavad-Gītā*, which summarizes the philosophy of the *Mahābhārata.* The *bhīshma-parvan* receives its title from the chief defender of the Kurus, Bhīshma ("Terrifying"), who advised the Pāndavas to fight him from behind the warrior Shikhandin ("Tufted"), whom he would not fight because Shikhandin had been born a female though raised as a son. Bhīshma was mortally wounded on the tenth day of the combat but delayed his actual death at will, owing to a divine boon he had received.

7. *Drona-parvan* ("Book of Drona"). Drona ("Tub"), who has a reputation for invincibility, succeeded Bhīshma as commander of the Kaurava forces. Despite his legendary power as a master of the arts of weaponry, he is promptly killed, owing to a deception that causes him to lay down his weapons.

8. *Karna-parvan* ("Book of Karna"). Karna ("Ear"), the new leader of the Kuru military, who would not fight while Bhīshma led the Kaurava forces, is slain by Arjuna after a long bout of combat. When Karna's chariot wheels get stuck in the ground, he reminds Arjuna to uphold the warrior ethic and wait until the chariot is righted. But Krishna—Arjuna's adviser—urges Arjuna to strike now while he can. When Karna is made commander (*senā-pati*), the Kauravas' fighting force numbers a mere five divisions.

9. *Shalya-parvan* ("Book of Shalya"). The war rages on. Among the Kurus, the commander-in-chief Shalya ("Sting") and Prince Duryodhana fall, which effectively ends the war. Duryodhana ascends to the realm of the sun god, Sūrya. Shalya fights with only three divisions against the Pāndavas' remaining one division.

10. *Sauptika-parvan* ("Book of the Nocturnal Attack"). The three surviving Kuru heroes—Kripa ("Pity"), Kritavarman ("Protector"), and Ashvatthāman ("Horse-stand")—unthinkably attack the encampment of the Pāndavas at night and slaughter the entire army while everyone is sleeping. Kripa objects that such a deed would be morally wrong by the agreed-on military standards, but Ashvatthāman, burning with hatred, overrules the objection, saying that the Pāndavas do not deserve such consideration because they themselves have engaged in foul play during the various battles. Only the five Pāndava brothers escape this ignoble carnage. Thus, the armies of both combatant parties are utterly destroyed. Ashvatthāman's fury even causes him to release magical weapons to render all Pāndava women barren. Through Krishna's divine intervention the child in Uttarā's womb, Parikshit, is saved, while Ashvatthāman is condemned to wander the earth in wretchedness for three thousand years.

11. *Strī-parvan* ("Book of Women"). This book is a moving description of the reconciliation between the blind Kaurava king Dhritarāshtra and the Pāndava princes. Funeral ceremonies are conducted by the survivors. Gāndharī, King Dhritarāshtra's wife, is furious with Krishna for allowing the slaughter to take place, and bitterly utters a curse that he and his tribe, the Vrishnis, should experience the same pain of grief.

12. *Shānti-parvan* ("Book of Peace"). Prince Yudhishthira is crowned. Bhīshma (who, as we saw in the *Bhīshma-parvan*, delayed his own death, though mortally wounded), relates at great length the path to the attainment of liberation (*moksha*)—the Self's realization of its eternal freedom. Because of this discourse, this *parvan* is considered one of the most important philosophical sections of the epic.

13. *Anushāsana-parvan* ("Book of Instruction"). Bhīshma's didactic talk about law, morals, and the value of ascetic practices is continued. Finally, with Krishna's permission, this great warrior and teacher expires.

14. *Ashvamedha-parvan* ("Book of the Horse Sacrifice"). King Yudhishthira stages a colossal horse sacrifice (*ashva-medha*) to consolidate his coronation and to bless the entire Bharata country. While the sacrificial horse is roaming freely, Arjuna follows and protects it for a full year. In the process, he fights many great battles.

15. *Āshramavasika-parvan* ("Book of Dwelling at the Hermitage"). After living at Yudhishthira's court in Hastināpura, the old king Dhritarāshtra and his queen, Gāndharī, withdraw into a forest hermitage (*āshrama*), and three years later they and Kuntī (the mother of the Pāndava princes) lose their lives in a forest conflagration.

16. *Mausala-parvan* ("Book of the Brawl"). This book is an account of Krishna's accidental death and his glorious ascension to heaven, as well as a description of the drunken brawl (*mausala,* "clubbing") that annihilates his dynasty and people. This misfortune, which happens thirty-six years after the war, is due to Queen Gāndharī's curse upon Krishna and the Vrishnis. At Krishna's funeral rites, Vyāsa tells the Pāndavas that for them the time to depart from the earth has come as well. Here Vyāsa is clearly beginning to wrap up his epic tale.

17. *Mahāprasthānika-parvan* ("Book of the Great Departure"). Deeply shocked by Krishna's death, the five sons of Pāndu renounce their kingdom and adopt a simple ascetic life in the wilderness. King Yudhishthira enthrones his nephew Parikshit, the son of Abhimanyu and Uttarā and the grandson of Arjuna. While ascending Mount Meru, the axis of the world, they fall dead one after the other.

18. *Svargārohanika-parvan* ("Book of Ascending to Heaven"). The five Pāndava brothers, who turn out actually to be divine beings, return to heaven. There they reunite with the Kaurava heroes, who have lost all enmity.

To these eighteen sections was appended in the third-fourth century C.E. the *Hari-Vamsha,* in which Krishna's birth and youth are narrated in great detail. Comprising more than 16,000 stanzas, this supplement served later generations of Krishna devotees as a prototype for other, more elaborate biographies of Krishna.

2

The Dramatic and Historical Setting of the *Bhagavad-Gītā*

The Dramatic Setting

To understand the *Bhagavad-Gītā* ("Lord's Song")[1]—often referred to simply as the *Gītā*—we must know something about its dramatic setting, which may or may not be based on historical actualities. The *Gītā* essentially consists in a dialogue between the God-man Krishna and his disciple Prince Arjuna. The dialogue takes place on the battlefield, the "Kuru field" (*kuru-kshetra*), or country of the Kauravas. Traditionally, this area is said to be located in a plain not far to the north of Delhi.

According to the *Gītā* itself (18.75), the dialogue was witnessed by Samjaya, minister to the blind Kaurava king, Dhritarāshtra. The sage Vyāsa had bestowed on Samjaya special paranormal powers to be able to report, blow by blow, the happenings on the distant battlefield, and thus his mind also captured the "wondrous" (*adbhuta*) private discourse between Krishna and Arjuna.

This dialogue takes place just as the two armies are on the verge of commencing the fight. The Kaurava princes, who are said to number one hundred (probably standing for a "multitude"), were cousins of the five

1. *Bhagavad,* or *bhagavat* (the grammatical stem), means "blessed one" and refers to the divine Person, specifically Krishna in the present context. The word is derived from *bhaga* ("dispenser," from the root *bhaj,* meaning "to participate, share"), which denotes "fortune, luck, dignity, loveliness, love" and also stands for the female genitals, which are dispensers of fortune in terms of bearing children perpetuating a family line. The suffix *vat* means "possessing." Thus, *Bhagavat* is he who possesses (or dispenses) good fortune. *Gītā* means "that which is sung/chanted," a feminine past participle from the root *gyai,* "to sing, chant," used as a noun.

Pāndava princes. The former were the sons of King Dhritarāshtra, whose capital was Hastināpura (modern Delhi). Ordinarily, the king's blindness would have prevented his ascension to the throne. Unfortunately, however, his half brother King Pāndu ("Pale One") had died prematurely, and his living brother, the sagely Vidura, was disqualified because his mother was from the lowest class, the servile estate (*shūdra*). Leaving the throne empty would have put an end to the great Lunar Dynasty of warrior-kings (*kshatriya*). Thus, by default Dhritarāshtra assumed the role of king until Pāndu's eldest son, Yudhishthira, was old enough to govern.

When that time arrived, Dhritarāshtra and his sons had a change of heart. In a rigged dice game, they ensured that the five Pāndava princes would not only forfeit their rightful kingdom but be exiled for thirteen years. In the final year, they had to live incognito or face another twelve-year exile. None of the Kauravas expected to see the sons of Pāndu again. However, against all odds and backed by King Drupada, the friendly ruler of the kingdom of the Pāncālas, and other neighboring tribal leaders—not least the God-man Krishna of the Yādavas—the five Pāndu princes returned from exile, demanding justice.

Thus, the stage was set for the colossal Bharata war, which is stated to have comprised eleven army divisions (*akshauhinī*) on the Kaurava side and seven on the Pāndava side. One division is, furthermore, said to have been composed of 21,870 elephants, 21,870 chariots, 65,610 horses, and 109,350 foot soldiers. All eighteen divisions would have consisted of nearly two million fighting men. These figures seem too large to be credible, but they convey the essential idea that the war involved most of the kingdoms of northern India. Could it have happened, though?

If we, speculatively, place the Bharata war (if ever it occurred) about 2000 B.C.E., the population of India is estimated to have been around four million people. This would not have allowed a large army of some two million able-bodied men to be mobilized for combat, but conceivably, a total of over one million men could have participated in the Bharata war, which would match Vyāsa's account better. Of course, the population of northern India might have been larger than conventionally assumed. But this still leaves us with the bard's inordinate figures for elephants, horses, and chariots. Such speculations, fascinating as they may be, in any case do not contribute to our understanding of the contents of the *Mahābhārata*.

More relevant is the fact that the aforementioned figures are based on the prominent epic number symbolism of 18—all figures are multiples of 18! Interestingly, there are 18 books in the *Mahābhārata*; 18 chapters in the

Gītā; the Bharata war was fought over a period of 18 days; Krishna lived for 18 more years after the war, and so on.[2]

Bearing various contexts in mind, the number 18 is suggestive of the notion of self-sacrifice—the ideal kind of sacrifice, which is reminiscent of the archetypal self-immolation of the Primordial Man (*purusha*) of the Vedas, who divided himself into countless forms to create the universe. Through the willing self-sacrifice of the noble warriors on the battlefield, life was thought to be able to continue in an orderly fashion.

The ancient *Brihadāranyaka-Upanishad* (1.1) likens the world to a sacrificial horse (*ashva*) and the process of world creation to the elaborate horse sacrifice (*ashva-medha*) that was conducted to benefit a great king and his country. In the old *Chāndogya-Upanishad* (3.16.1), we find this significant declaration: "Man, verily, is sacrifice."

On the morning of the first day of battle, Prince Arjuna had a sudden change of heart: He no longer wished to win his kingdom back if this meant the death of family, friends, and beloved teachers. This was the critical moment at which he received Krishna's activist teachings.

The epic narrative has many twists and turns. Notably, in the end, the five Pāndava princes turn out to be the sons of deities rather than of the mortal King Pāndu, and they, as befits heroes, appropriately ascend to heaven. Yudhishthira, the eldest and noblest, was fathered by the god Dharma ("Law"); the extremely skilled archer Arjuna by Indra (the leader of the host of deities); the extraordinarily powerful Bhīma (also known as Bhīmasena) by the god Vāyu ("Wind"); while the twins Nakula and Sahadeva were sired by the two Ashvins (the celestial physicians).

On a more mundane level, the five Pāndavas were married to the same woman, the lovely Pāncālī, also called Draupadī after her father King Drupada, the ruler of the Pāncāla tribe. Vyāsa explained this unorthodox polyandric arrangement as follows: Arjuna had won Draupadī's hand in marriage when of all the suitors he alone succeeded in stringing a mighty bow and then shooting five arrows in succession at a remote target and through the middle of a revolving disk. The royal maiden gladly accepted Arjuna as her husband. At the time, the five Pāndava brothers were living incognito after escaping a murderous attack by the Kauravas. When Arjuna revealed his true identity, King Drupada was overjoyed. Upon returning home, the Pāndavas' beloved mother, Kuntī, heard their

2. For more on the symbolism of number 18, see Georg Feuerstein, "108: A Symbol-Laden Number," at www.traditionalyogastudies.com/108.pdf.

footsteps outside their simple dwelling and, thinking that her sons had returned from their daily round of begging for alms, called out to them to share among them what they had received. She was ignorant of the fact that destiny had brought Princess Draupadī into their lives, but literally respecting their mother's innocent wish, the five brothers resolved to share Draupadī, who agreed. Formal ceremonies were held to sanction this unusual marriage.

Furthermore, Arjuna discovered that he had been in close association with the God-man Krishna, the most illustrious ruler of the Lunar Dynasty, throughout many previous lives.

It supposedly took Vyāsa two and a half years to compose the entire epic, which he dictated to the elephant-headed god Ganesha, the only scribe who could keep up with the bard's dictation. What strikes one as a singularly ingenious contrivance, worthy of a Shakespeare, is that Vyāsa, the reputed author of both the *Mahābhārata* and the *Gītā,* wrote himself indelibly into the epic drama as the father of the blind king Dhritarāshtra. Truly, it would have been difficult to find a more poignant illustration of the interwoven complexities of the finite world of change, *samsāra*, governed by the invisible and impartial karmic law of action and reaction from which only spiritual liberation (*moksha*) will grant respite.

The *Bhagavad-Gītā* purports to be both *dharma-shāstra* (a textbook on law and morality) and *moksha-shāstra* (a textbook on liberation). It is a creative reflection on the relationship between the two grand ideals of morality and liberation. On the one hand, the *Gītā* shows how morality is essential to a spiritual life; on the other hand, it argues that in order to attain spiritual freedom, we must *ultimately* jettison all *dharmas.*

What better circumstance to explore these issues than the Bharata war, Arjuna's vacillation, the Kauravas' all-too-human attitudes, the Pāndavas' semidivine bravery (securing them a place in heaven), and Krishna's divine influence throughout the entire drama?

The Historical Setting

The *Mahābhārata* is a vast, ingenious and boldly constructed edifice whose epic kernel, the enmity between the Pāndavas and Kauravas, is hidden—rather like the inmost doll in a set of nested Russian dolls—beneath a bulky mass of secondary narratives, minor episodes, religious discourses, and philosophical, cosmogonic, and theological reflections. The actual nucleus of the epic consists of little more than perhaps 20,000 verses—

that is, about one-fifth of the total mass of the extant epic—and the rest reads like footnotes or appendices.

Academics have in the past tended to evaluate the *Gītā* as an interesting but not particularly indispensable footnote. There is little justification for this derogatory view. Anyone who contends that it is highly improbable that Krishna should have initiated Arjuna into the secrets of his Yoga by holding a lengthy discourse just before the battle fails to recognize the fact that the epic is not only a blow-by-blow account of the conflict between two dynastic contenders but also a spiritual-moral "history."

When looked at exclusively from a purely historical point of view, there is little in the epic that is convincing and tangible. On the other hand, the reader who leaves aside the question of historical validity and concerns himself only with the spiritual content of the *Mahābhārata* is quickly convinced that Vyāsa was recording not objective history so much as ahistoric realities clothed either in symbols and myths or in the language of philosophy. Both extremist positions are lopsided. To be sure, the *Gītā* cannot be divorced from the main theme of the epic, which is the Bharata war. On the contrary, it contains, as it were, the spiritual-moral raison d'être for the war.

The *external* circumstances leading to the great war—stripped of all unnecessary detail—are the following: After the premature death of Pāndu, the king of the Bharatas, his blind brother, Dhritarāshtra, temporarily ascended the throne until his own sons would come of age. There was an immediate enmity between the hundred sons of Dhritarāshtra and the five orphaned children of Pāndu, especially because the supernaturally strong Bhīmasena was fond of teasing his cousins. As they were growing up, the jealousies and quarrels deepened into solid hatred on the part of the hundred Kaurava progenies. Dhritarāshtra's children decided to rid themselves of their unwanted cousins. Their murderous plot miscarried, and the five Pāndava princes fled into the forest and roamed the country disguised as *brāhmanas*.

One day they heard that Drupada, the ruler of the Pancālas, intended to give away his daughter in marriage and that all noblemen of the North were invited to the festivities. They decided to go. King Drupada announced that he would give his daughter to that suitor who could hit a distant target through a high-mounted revolving ring with an immense bow he himself had made. Of all contenders, only Arjuna accomplished this task and thus won the hand of the princess. At this contest the sons of Pāndu also met Krishna, leader of the Vrishni tribe, who from then on became their inseparable friend and counselor. The unexpected alliance with the kingdom of the Pancālas and the Yādava dynasty of Krishna militarily enabled the Pāndavas to return to their homeland and claim their share of the paternal kingdom.

Dhritarāshtra agreed to parcel out the Kuru land, and the descendants of Pāndu were allocated the country along the river Yamunā, whereas the sons of the blind king kept the stretch of land along the upper Ganges. Dhritarāshtra's numerous sons were displeased and contrived a rather different pathway for themselves and their Pāndava cousins.

In the rigged game of dice described earlier, Yudhishthira lost his entire kingdom, bringing ruin to the newly founded dynasty. Only by the intervention of the old king, Dhritarāshtra, were the Pāndavas able to escape literal enslavement. Instead, they were sent into exile for thirteen long years full of remarkable adventures. As soon as the thirteenth year had elapsed, the Pāndavas demanded the restoration of their kingdom. However, the hateful and power-mad Duryodhana rejected their claim outright. Krishna, the king of the Vrishnis, tried to negotiate between both parties, but his intercession remained fruitless. Finally, the Pāndavas thought of war as the only solution left to them. As leaders of the two military forces, Arjuna and Duryodhana independently approached Krishna for his support. Krishna himself pledged not to fight but offered them a choice between his powerful army and his personal counsel. Duryodhana decided for Krishna's massive troops, whereas Arjuna was keen to secure Krishna's personal aid.

This is the situation as we find it at the outset of the *Gītā,* when the two clans confront each other on the *kuru-kshetra,* the country or "field" of the Kurus. (The accompanying diagram is provided as an aid to visualizing the scene.) The name Kuru goes back to a member of the large tribe of the Bharatas. It applies equally to the hundred sons of King Dhritarāshtra and the five sons of his deceased brother, Pāndu, but to make distinction easier, the five princes are better known as the Pāndavas.

Dating the *Gītā*

In its current form, the vulgate *Gītā*—as it was known already to Shankara—can be placed in c. 400–300 B.C.E. Its teachings, however, point back to an even earlier period in which the Bharata war would have taken place.

Possibly because of the *Gītā*'s monotheism, some authorities have

Kauravas

11 divisions (akshauhinī) =
240,570 chariots + 240,570 elephants + 721,710 horses + 1,202,850 foot soldiers

Duryodhana

Commander: Bhīshma

Subsequent Kaurava Commanders

1. Drona 2. Karna 3. Shalya 4. Duryodhana

KURU-KSHETRA

Commander: Bhīmasena

Arjuna with Krishna

7 divisions (akshauhinī) =
153,090 chariots + 153,090 elephants + 501,270 horses + 765,450 foot soldiers

Pāndavas

unconvincingly argued for a post-Christian date for this work. There is no question about the pre-Christian origin of the Pāncarātra tradition to which the *Gītā* loosely belongs.

However, the claim by Hindu traditionalists that the *Gītā* is a product of the third to fourth millennium B.C.E. cannot be taken seriously. First, such an early date would conflict with the Puranic chronologies and also with a plausible date for the *Rig-Veda* and the culture that created it. Second, the date of 3102 B.C.E. for the beginning of the present *kali-yuga* is first mentioned in the Purānas. The problem is that on conceptual and linguistic grounds the epic's origin has been determined as being later than the Buddha (563–483 B.C.E.).

Besides, the *Gītā* (4.7–8) itself mentions that Krishna taught Arjuna an age-old Yoga that had been lost, and also that he re-embodies from age to age (*yuge yuge*) whenever the sacred order (*dharma*)—the moral and spiritual law—is in decline. Thus, it would in any case be more accurate to regard the moment of Krishna's instruction to Prince Arjuna as the beginning of a new age (*yuga*)—that is, the ongoing *kali-yuga* of moral and spiritual decline. But Krishna does not, of course, furnish us with a specific date for the new age, and we can only arrive at a date by inference, as indeed did Puranic authors when giving 3102 B.C.E. as the starting date for the present *kali-yuga.* Their dating, however, appears to be based on questionable astronomical data.

Linguistic and Archaeological Truth

In vocabulary, style, and content, the *Gītā* manifestly belongs to the early philosophical portions of the *Mahābhārata* and is somewhat later than the *Katha-Upanishad* and the *Shvetāshvatara-Upanishad,* which offer similar yogic teachings. The Indian scholar K. N. Upadhyaya (1971, p. 29) placed the *Gītā* in the fifth century B.C.E., which is a ballpark figure, though most authorities favor between 400 and 300 B.C.E. It is important to acknowledge that the present text of the *Gītā* must not be confused with its source theme—the Bharata war, which could have happened very much earlier.

Subhash Kak (2003) and other researchers, basing themselves on a revised dating of the dynastic chronologies found in the Purānas, have fixed the Bharata war to c. 1900 B.C.E., which, curiously, coincides with the assumed demise of the Vedic-Indus-Sarasvatī civilization.

Hard-core Western Indologists have rejected even this early date and argued for c. 900 B.C.E. for the great war—a date derived from the so-called Aryan invasion theory of the nineteenth century. This theory has been proven wrong, and thus any chronology based on it must be immediately suspect. (See, e.g., Colin Renfrew, *Archaeology & Language* 1987, and G. Feuerstein, et al., *In Search of the Cradle of Civilization* 1995.)

With the 1998 discovery of a submerged city off the coast of modern Dwarka in northwestern India, which has been tentatively identified as Krishna's royal city of Dvārakā and dated c. 1450 B.C.E., the tantalizing possibility of dating the Bharata war to roughly that time has presented itself. It is at least conceivable that this war, if it ever happened, gave rise to all sorts of ballads that in due course led to the *Mahābhārata* and thus also the *Gītā* as we know it. At the end of Professor Kak's paper, he admits that the date of 1900 B.C.E. is as conjectural as any other. With this admission, we are free to opt for 1500 B.C.E., which at least has the tentative support of archaeology. The port city of Dvārakā ("Gate") may yet prove an important chronological marker, a gate that brings a certain structure to the course of events surrounding Krishna and the great war.

Chronology

The following chronology is partly based on recent research and thinking (especially by native Indian scholars) rather than the highly conservative ideas found in scholarly textbooks (which largely are inherited from nineteenth-century Western scholarship). The academic establishment is only slowly beginning to accept that we must completely reconsider the history of ancient India.

Two historical pivots, which recent researchers have established and which have been taken fully into account in the chronology below, are (a) the date of 1900 B.C.E. for the disappearance of the large Sarasvatī River celebrated in the *Rig-Veda* and (b) the date of 1450 B.C.E. for the submergence of the walled city of Dvārakā.

Timeline of Key Scriptures, Events, and People

Date	Scripture/Event/Person
6500 B.C.E.	The beginnings of the town of Mehrgarh (in modern Afghanistan). Evidence of Mother Goddess worship. Astonishing cultural continuity with later Hinduism.
4000–2000 B.C.E.	Period indicated for the *Rig-Veda* based on astronomical data and general historical reasoning.
3300 B.C.E.	Possible date for Manu Vaivasvata, the seventh Manu and the first great ruler after the Great Flood mentioned in various Sanskrit scriptures.
3102, Feb. 18 B.C.E.	Traditional but improbable date for the beginning of the *kali-yuga*, supposedly coinciding with the end of the Bharata war.
3000 B.C.E.	Beginning of the urban centers along the Indus River, which were part of the Indus-Sarasvatī civilization.
2600–1900 B.C.E.	The "Harappan phase" of the Indus-Sarasvatī civilization. The mature phase of the Indus-Sarasvatī civilization, called the "Harappan phase" after the first of its cities unearthed by archaeologists. (See, e.g., G. Possehl, ed. 1982.)
1900 B.C.E.	Approx. time of drying-up of the mighty Sarasvatī River that meanders through the Thar Desert toward the Indian Ocean.
2450 B.C.E.	Approx. date for King Bharata of the Pauravas (Purus), after whom India is named.
2050 B.C.E.	Approx. date for King Dasharatha of Ayodhyā, father of Rāma, hero of the later *Rāmāyana*.

1550 B.C.E.	Possible date for composition of the last hymns of the *Rig-Veda.*
1500–1200 B.C.E.	Conservative date for the invasion of the Indo-Aryan tribes from the Russian steppes. Conjectural date for composition of the voluminous *Shatapatha-Brāhmana.*
1450 B.C.E.	Date of the submergence of Krishna's capital Dvārakā (in modern Gujarat), determined by underwater archaeology to have been later than the Bharata war. Based on this date, the war could be dated c. 1500 B.C.E.
1350 B.C.E.	Approx. date for Kapila, legendary founder of the Sāmkhya school.
563–483 B.C.E.	Lifetime of Gautama, the Buddha.
400–300 B.C.E.	Likely date for composition of the extant *Bhagavad-Gītā.*
150 C.E.	Probable date for Patanjali, compiler of the *Yoga-Sūtra.*
300 C.E.	Possible date for the *Hari-Vamsha*, 16,000-verse appendix to the *Mahābhārata,* giving a version of Krishna's legendary life story.
300–400 C.E.	Composition of the earliest extant Purānas. Final redaction of the *Mahābhārata.*
400–450 C.E.	Approx. date for composition of Īshvara Krishna's *Sāmkhya-Kārikā,* the authoritative text for Sāmkhya as a philosophical system.
400–1200 C.E.	Era of the composition of the Pāncarātra-Samhitās, the *Sātvata-Samhitā* being the oldest scripture of this genre.

788–820 C.E.	Traditional dates for Shankara, who wrote the earliest extant commentary on the *Gītā,* though he probably lived over a century earlier.
900 C.E.	Possible date for the composition of the *Bhāgavata-Purāna.*
1017–1123 C.E.	Lifetime of Rāmānuja, who wrote an authoritative commentary on the *Gītā.*
1050 C.E.	Approx. date for Abhinavagupta, a great Kashmiri guru and scholar of the Shaiva tradition, who wrote a commentary on the *Gītā.*
1190–1276 C.E. or 1199–1278 C.E.	Estimated dates for Madhva, founder of the dualist branch of Vedānta, who wrote a commentary on the *Gītā.*
1275–1296 C.E.	Jnānadeva, Maharashtra's most renowned adept and the youthful author of the famous *Jnāneshvarī* commentary on the *Gītā.*
1479–1531 C.E.	Lifetime of Vallabha, an important teacher of *bhakti-yoga.*
1485–1533 C.E.	Lifetime of Caitanya, one of the foremost medieval Vaishnava teachers of Bengal.
1500 C.E.	Approx. date for translation of the *Gītā* into Persian.
1785 C.E.	Publication of Charles Wilkins's English rendering of the *Gītā*
1820 C.E.	Latin translation of the *Gītā* by Otto Frank.
1863–1902 C.E.	Lifetime of Swami Vivekananda, chief disciple of Sri Ramakrishna (1836–1886 C.E.), and largely (but not exclusively) responsible for introducing spiritual Yoga to

	the West. Author of four influential books on the various Yogas, he wrote on *karma-* and *bhakti-yoga*.
1869–1948 C.E.	Lifetime of Mohandas K. Gandhi, advocate of the principle of nonharming (*ahimsā*), who held the *Gītā* in the highest esteem.
1883–1896 C.E.	English rendering of the *Mahābhārata* by K. M. Ganguli (12 vols.).
1933–1959 C.E.	Publication of the critical edition of the *Mahābhārata* under the editorship of V. S. Sukthankar (19 vols.).
1966 C.E.	Founding of the International Society for Krishna Consciousness ("Hare Krishnas") by A. C. Bhaktivedanta Swami, who translated, among other texts, the *Gītā* and *Bhāgavata-Purāna* into English.

3

Dramatis Personae of the *Gītā*

Krishna

The central figure of the *Gītā* and the *Mahābhārata* epic as a whole is the God-man Krishna, who is deemed a human incarnation of the Divine, called Vishnu. In many ways, the great epic as we know it today is the creation of the Vaishnava tradition of devotion to Vishnu. Other religio-cultural traditions, notably Shaivism (revolving around Shiva), have of course contributed to the present version as well, but Vaishnaivism seems written into the epic story itself.

The name Krishna has two possible etymologies. The first is "Black," a reference to Krishna's dark skin color. The second is "Attractor," which stems from the verbal root *krish* ("to draw, pull") and refers to Krishna's effect on his devotees.

Was Krishna a historical person or merely a figure of myth? Whether or not we believe that the figure of Krishna entered the epic at a later time, as some scholars assume, we need not doubt his historicity. There is good evidence for Krishna's existence in antiquity. The *Chāndogya-Upanishad* (3.17.6), which antedates the extant *Mahābhārata,* already mentions Krishna as the son of Devakī. We know from the epic and other texts that Devakī was the wife of Vāsudeva, who is first mentioned as a divinity in the *Taittirīya-Āranyaka* (10.16), which is even earlier than the *Chāndogya-Upanishad.*

The same Upanishadic passage also mentions that Krishna was a pupil of Ghora Angirasa and even refers to a particular teaching according to which one should ponder the following thoughts at one's final hour:

> You are indestructible (*akshita*). You are unwavering (*acyuta*). You are the essence of life (*prāna*).

This instruction is reminiscent of the final-hour Yoga given by Krishna in the *Bhagavad-Gītā* (8.11), where the term "imperishable" (*akshara*) is used, which stems from the same verbal root as the past participle *akshita,* here rendered as "indestructible."

Little is known of Krishna's teacher, although India's former president Sarvepalli Radhakrishnan, who was also a noted scholar, states in a footnote to his translation of the *Gītā* (1948, p. 28, n. 7) that Ghora Angirasa is also called Krishna Angirasa in the *Kaushītaki-Brāhmana* (30.9), and that he possibly composed hymn 8.74 of the *Rig-Veda,* which is a warm eulogy to the sacrificial fire.

In his celebrated work *Ashtādhyāyī* (4.3.98), the renowned Sanskrit grammarian Pānini mentions Vāsudeva (i.e., Krishna) and Arjuna as objects of religious devotion. This suggests that both are likely to have been at least several generations prior to Pānini's time, since the divinization of heroes seldom happens overnight. Arjuna was one of the god Indra's names, and Pānini's reference might have been to the deity rather than the deified warrior Arjuna. Pānini is generally assigned to c. 400–300 B.C.E.

The *Mahābhārata* clearly identifies Krishna as the ruler of the Vrishni tribe and of the proud city of Dvārakā, which was submerged in the ocean, very probably owing to a substantial earthquake, a phenomenon not uncommon in that region of northwestern India. This event is in fact mentioned in the great epic, and the ruins of a city, which was identified by a leading Indian archaeologist as the ancient Dvārakā, have been found offshore in the area that is customarily assigned to the Vrishnis.

Dvārakā must be distinguished from the modern town Dwarka in the Saurashtra region of Gujarat. The submerged port city is identified with underwater structures discovered at the island Bet Dwarka, which is also known as Shankhoddhāra, or Shankhodhara, where conchs (*shankha*) can still be found abundantly. It is located approximately nineteen miles north of modern Dwarka and was also known as Kushasthalī. At the time of Krishna, the island was still a peninsula before rising sea levels turned it into an island. Under his leadership, the citizens of Kushasthalī fortified the town and made it impregnable. Kushasthalī existed already prior to the occupation by Krishna's tribe.

Overpopulation caused the Vrishnis to also settle near what is now the modern town of Dwarka, and their settlement was known as Dvārāvatī. As the ocean claimed the land, both Vrishni sites were abandoned and remained unoccupied for a millennium.

In the *Gītā* (10.37), Krishna declares: "I am Vāsudeva among the Vrishnis." Elsewhere (*Gītā* 7.19), he states: "Vāsudeva is all," which is explained as the realization of those sages who, after many lifetimes, recognize that Krishna is the Divine Lord.

Vrishni was an important king of the Yadu dynasty. He is said to have descended from Vishnu, meaning that he belonged to the Vaishnava tradition. The Yadu rulers (Yādavas) were also known as Sātvatas, which means that they believed in Vishnu/Vāsudeva as the Divine Lord (*bhāgavat*). In other words, their faith was Bhāgavatism, as specified in the *Bhāgavata-Purāna*.

The God-man Krishna was born into the Yadu dynasty and seems to have commanded so much respect that he was deemed and worshipped as a divine incarnation. At the same time, his teachings connected divinity with the Sun. In the *Gītā* (4.1), Krishna states unequivocally that, as the Divine, he proclaimed this "immutable Yoga" to Vivasvat (the Sun), who imparted it to Manu, who in turn taught it to Ikshvāku, the founder of India's Solar Dynasty (which, along with the Lunar Dynasty, was one of the great lineages of ancient India).

There is also a strong solar connection through Krishna's teacher Gora Angirasa, who belonged to the Bhārgavas. The lineage of the Bhārgavas was founded by the mighty seer Bhrigu, a son of the creator-deity Brahma.

One time, the seers were wondering who the Godhead was among the trinity Brahma-Vishnu-Shiva. Bhrigu was dispatched to help them discover the truth. He went to Brahma, who was sitting in assembly. When Bhrigu disrespectfully sat down on a chair, Brahma became very angry. The seer left without saying a word. He next went to Shiva. When Shiva wanted to welcome him with an embrace, Bhrigu took a step back and said, "Don't touch me!" Shiva was about to lance the seer with his trident when his divine spouse, Pārvatī, intervened on Bhrigu's behalf, sparing his life.

He next went to Vishnu, who was asleep. Bhrigu kicked the deity in the chest. Vishnu awoke abruptly, but when he saw Bhrigu before him, he begged the seer's pardon, touching his foot. Bhrigu's footprint is still imprinted on Vishnu's chest. He and the other great seers of yore concluded from Vishnu's behavior that he was the true Godhead among the deities forming the grand triad (*trimūrti*), and they started to worship him more intensely. Not surprisingly, Krishna declares in the *Gītā* (10.25) that he is "Bhrigu among the great seers."

It is clear from the *Mahābhārata* and more specifically the *Gītā* (3.32, 9.11, 18.67) that Krishna's divinity did not remain unchallenged. From the epic and its *Gītā* episode, however, it is also self-evident that his status as a divine incarnation had nothing to do with the dubious claim of a haughty or mad ruler. Krishna was no Caesar or Pharaoh. At least the Hindu scriptures treat Krishna with the utmost respect.

To return to Vrishni's story: According to the *Brahmānda-Purāna* (3. 71.1), King Vrishni was hostile toward Krishna because he thought that Krishna had stolen the divine jewel Syamantaka, which was given to Satrājit by the god Sūrya ("Sun") himself. Krishna had shown an interest in purchasing the jewel at whatever price, which was enough to arouse Vrishni's suspicion. Hearing the rumor, Krishna retrieved the jewel from a lion's den and restored it to Satrājit. Satrājit's brother Prasena had borrowed the priceless jewel to wear while hunting when he was killed by a lion. Vrishni's father was King Madhu, one of the five sons of a king named Kārttavīrya Arjuna.

A great deal of information about Krishna is given in the *Mahābhārata* and its appendix, the *Hari-Vamsha,* as well as the extensive Purāna literature, although most of it is bound to be mythological rather than historical. The *Hari-Vamsha,* which appears to have been appended to the great epic around 300 C.E., tells Krishna's childhood story in enormous detail and fills in the blatant gap in the story as related in the great epic.

Even though the epic does not say much about Krishna's early life, it acknowledges his pastoral background and his having been brought up by foster parents. Possibly, the lack of detail in the *Mahābhārata* led to the creation of the 24,000 verses of the *Hari-Vamsha,* which can be seen as the earliest extant Purāna. Subsequently, Krishna's life story was further developed, or related, in the *Bhāgavata-Purāna,* which is generally placed c. 900 C.E.

When Krishna's father Vasudeva, who was the son of King Shūrasena of Mathurā, renounced the throne and became a humble cowherd, Ugrasena became king. His son Kamsa, who was an incarnation of the antigod (*asura*) Kālanemi, imprisoned his father and arrogated the throne. A soothsayer told him he would be killed by the eighth son of his sister Devakī, the wife of Vasudeva, who had left Mathurā to raise cows.

To prevent Kamsa's killing Devakī, Vasudeva had to swear they would hand all their children over to Kamsa as soon as they were born. Kamsa killed six of their sons by smashing them against the ground. The seventh child was aborted.

The eighth child was Krishna, whose life was saved when Vishnu magically transferred him to the womb of Yashodā, and Yashodā's child to Devakī. When Kamsa came to kill what he believed was Devakī's newborn, the child slipped through his fingers, rose into the air, and told him that his slayer had already been born elsewhere. Panicked, Kamsa ordered a countrywide search for Krishna, to have him murdered. All his demonic ambassadors of death were easily killed by Krishna instead. In the end, Krishna destroyed King Kamsa himself.

Later in his life, Krishna had to flee from the vengeance of King Jarāsandha, the father of the slain Kamsa's two wives, who were mourning his death. Krishna left Mathurā with his people and established a new city—Dvārakā—on the Gulf of Kutch. While the Pāndavas were in exile, Krishna busied himself with travels and multiple marriages. Among his wives were Rukminī, the daughter of King Bhīshmaka of Vidarbha; Jāmbavatī, sister of a Yādava royal; the female ascetic Kālindī, who gave birth to ten sons; his niece Kaikeyī; Lakshmanā, a daughter of the king of Madra; three other women; and not least the innocent 16,000 daughters of Naraka, a demon king whom he later on destroyed. Wondering how Krishna managed to keep such a large harem satisfied, the sage Nārada (who perhaps should have had more pious thoughts) visited the house of each of the 16,008 wives and found Krishna dwelling in each.

When the Kaurava princes refused to restore the kingdom to their Pāndava cousins, Krishna intervened and became a major visible and invisible player in the preparations of the war. Although he did not actually take up arms against the Kauravas, Krishna was an indefatigable counselor, consoler, and magician. He created darkness in order for Arjuna to be able to kill his enemy Jayadratha; looked after the horses on the battlefield; took in his own invincible chest a weapon intended for Arjuna; prevented Arjuna from committing suicide, and prompted Pāndava heroes to fight and kill specific leaders of the enemy army.

Queen Gāndharī, the wife of Dhritarāshtra, had lost all her sons in the war and blamed Krishna for it. She cursed him, saying that in thirty-six years he, too, would be witnessing the death of his relations. It so passed. While Krishna was on a pilgrimage, the Vrishnis along with members of the Yadu dynasty, under the influence of alcohol, started to fight with one another. Upon his return, Krishna was furious to see so much death and destruction, and he annihilated the remainder of his ill-fated race.

Krishna himself was inadvertently killed by the arrow of an *asura* called Jara ("Old Age"). It was left to grieving Arjuna to bury his teacher, who, we might gather from this myth, died of old age. After shedding his mortal coil, Krishna resumed his immortal form as Vishnu/Nārāyana.

The archaeologist S. S. Rao, who surveyed the submerged city of Dvārakā, said of Krishna that he "is the embodiment of intellectual and spiritual glory. No other single individual or idea has so much influenced the course of India's religion, philosophy, art and literature as the life and personality of Krishna" (1999, p. 13).

According to Vaishnava theology, Vishnu is not merely a transcendental Reality but a loving Supreme Person who cares deeply for his creation. His caring, or grace (*prasāda*), is made particularly obvious by the fact that Vishnu projects himself repeatedly into the world in order to restore cosmic and moral order (*rita* or *dharma*). Thus, Krishna was the ninth of ten divine incarnations or "descents" (*avatāra*). (See chapter 4, "Divine Incarnations of Vishnu," for more on the *avatāra* concept.)

Epithets of Krishna Used in the Gītā

An epithet is a descriptive word or phrase used in place of the name of a person or thing. The following twenty-one epithets of Krishna are found in the *Gītā:*

Acyuta: Unfallen/Unwavering
Anantarūpa: [He who is of] Endless/Infinite Form
Arisūdana: Enemy-Slayer
Bhagavat/Bhagavān: Blessed One
Deva: God
Devesha: Lord of the Gods
Govinda: Cow-Finder
Hari: Remover [of Suffering]; or Stealer of Hearts
Hrishīkesha: [He Whose] Hair Stands Up [from Thrill]; or Lord of the Senses
Janārdana: He Who Agitates [Sinful] People
Keshava: Hairy One
Keshinisūdana: Slayer of [the Demon] Keshin
Mādhava: Relating to [the Slayer of the Demon] Madhu; or Descendant of Madhu (see Part Two, note 4 for 1.14)
Madhusūdana: Destroyer of [the Demon] Madhu (see Part Two, note 4 for 1.14)

Prabhu: Lord
Purushottama: Supreme Person or Supreme Spirit
Vārshneya: Descendent-of-the-Vrishnis
Vāsudeva: Son-of-Vasudeva (see Part Two, note 58 for 10.37)
Vishnu: [All-]Pervasive
Yādava: Descendent-of-Yadu (see Part Two, note 43 for 11.41)
Yogeshvara: Lord of Yoga

Arjuna

Next to Krishna, Prince Arjuna ("White") is the second most important individual in the *Gītā*. He is the great friend and devotee of Krishna and in the *Mahābhārata* is often also referred to as Krishna.

Arjuna is listed as the third son of King Pāndu and Queen Draupadī (Kuntī), but the situation is, predictably, far more complex. While still residing at the palace of King Kuntibhoja, Kuntī had for four months served the great sage Durvāsas so splendidly that he wanted to acknowledge her service. He gave her a special mantra, which she could use five times. He instructed her that by repeating the mantra, she would beget a child by whatever person she thought of during her mantric recitation. He also assured her that she would not have to worry about losing her virginity. King Pāndu was under a troubling spell that made it impossible for him to even touch his two wives, as this would mean his instant death. The sage Durvāsas's gift allowed Kuntī to ensure the continuity of the royal lineage.

Wanting to test the mantra first, Kuntī chose to think of the god Sūrya ("Sun"), who promptly appeared to her. Soon she gave birth to Karna ("Ear"), who was born wearing armor and earrings. As long as he wore these, he was invincible. Yet, he generously gave them to Indra, even though he knew that Indra was somehow plotting against him.

Kuntī placed Karna in a box and set him adrift on the river Ashvā ("Horse"). The box drifted all the way to the distant capital Campāpurī of the kingdom of Anga, which was renowned for its charioteers (*sūta*). Karna was found in the river and adopted by the charioteer Adhiratha. Although Kuntī knew from spies about Karna's life in Adhiratha's house, she kept his birth secret from her other sons, but just before the Bharata war she disclosed to Karna that she was his mother and the Pāndavas were his brothers. The Pāndavas did not learn of Karna's true identity until the war was over and he was dead. Karna promised that he would not kill any of his brothers but would take Arjuna's life in the upcoming war. He was destined to fail in his attempted fratricide.

Then, more seriously, Kuntī repeated the mantra again and got Dharmaputra (i.e., Yudhishthira) from the god Dharma ("Law"). The third child was Arjuna, begotten by Indra, the warlike leader of the host of deities, while the fourth child was Bhīmasena, who was begotten by the god Vāyu ("Wind").

The remaining mantric wish she gave to her co-wife Mādrī, who thought of the celestial twins, the Ashvins, and promptly gave birth to the twins Nakula and Sahadeva. When King Pāndu died at young Yudhishthira's ceremony that invested him with the traditional sacred thread of a twice-born member of society, Mādrī opted to have herself immolated on her husband's funeral pyre (in the ancient custom known as *sāti,* known in English as *suttee*). Kuntī chose to bring up all five Pāndava princes.

Even though Yudhishthira was to succeed his human father, Pāndu, his kingship was more ritual than actual. It was Arjuna whose military skills and enormous strength made him de facto king. His alliance with Krishna enabled him to militarily oppose the Kauravas, win the dreadful war, and secure Yudhishthira's rule.

Arjuna and his brothers were brought up at the court of Hastināpura along with their Kaurava cousins. Arjuna learned the art of war (*dhanurveda,* "knowledge of the bow") first under Shuka, then under Kripa, and finally under Drona. Noticing how easily his hand could find his mouth even in the dark, Arjuna taught himself to use the bow in complete darkness.

One time, when they were bathing in the Ganges, a whale gripped Drona's leg and he was saved from certain death by a well-aimed arrow from Arjuna's bow. Drona was deeply grateful and initiated Arjuna into the secret of *brahma-shirāstra* ("Brahma's-head missile"), on condition that he would never use this terrible weapon (which had the power to tear off one of the heads of the god Brahma).

During a competition organized by the blind King Dhritarāshtra, Arjuna proved as competent an archer as his teacher Karna. When the king wanted to declare Karna the victor nonetheless, Arjuna became angry and insulted Karna by saying he was too lowborn to participate in a royal contest. Instantly, Dhritarāshtra's oldest son Duryodhana, who had always been jealous of Arjuna, intervened. He settled the matter by proclaiming Karna as the ruler of Anga. This incident served to greatly fan the fire of enmity between the Kauravas and the Pāndavas.

When the time came to pay Drona his fee (a ritual offering) for his patient instruction in archery, Drona asked Drupada, the ruler of Pāncāla, to be brought before him in fetters. The Pāndavas fulfilled their weapons guru's desire, which effectively ended Drona's hatred toward Drupada. The king of Pāncāla offered Drona half his large kingdom. On that occasion, Drona advised Arjuna not to hesitate fighting him, if ever Drona were to oppose him. The two heroes did indeed fight in the war, but it was Dhrishtadyumna, the son of King Drupada and brother of Pāncālī, who cut off Drona's head after the latter had entered deep meditation during one of the battles.

Once the Pāndavas had grown up, King Drupada wished for his daughter Krishnā to be married, and he permitted her to select her own husband in an open archery competition. King Drupada had a large bow installed and, at a great distance, a machine with a revolving ring in front of the target. All kinds of suitors arrived at the ceremony, including Karna and Duryodhana, but none could even lift the large bow. Only Arjuna managed to pick it up and with a single arrow hit the difficult target.

King Drupada, who had secretly hoped for Arjuna to marry his daughter, was extremely pleased. He had received false news earlier that the Pāndavas had perished in the conflagration of a palace made of shellac (the result of a conspiracy against them), and seeing Arjuna alive and victorious made him especially joyous.

When the five princes arrived back at their makeshift home in the forest, Kuntī called out to them to enjoy among themselves whatever they had received that day. They had been collecting food for their mother and themselves while they were in hiding from the Kauravas. Kuntī had no idea that Arjuna had won the hand of Drupada's daughter. She thus could not have foreseen that her words would have a far-reaching outcome: obeying their mother's words to the letter, the five Pāndavas shared Krishnā as their common wife, to which the young princess consented. At the sage Nārada's advice, each one of them could spend a whole year with her without being disturbed by the other brothers.

In addition to his marriage with Krishnā/Pāncālī/Draupadī, Arjuna was also married to several other women, including Ulūpikā (daughter of a king of the Nāgas, a serpent race), Citrāngadā (daughter of the king of Manalur), and Subhadrā (Krishna's sister).

During the eighteen-day war, Arjuna served as generalissimo. He fought numerous combats and destroyed the Kaurava army. He killed Bhīshma and Karna, as well as many other great warriors.

After the war, Arjuna and his brothers went to Hastināpura of the Pāndava kingdom to assume governance of the whole country under the formal leadership of Yudhishthira. After many years of courtly life, Arjuna was killed by his son Babhruvāhana, who acted in fulfillment of a curse uttered against Arjuna by the eight Vasus (deities of the elements) and the river-goddess Gangā (Ganges). His death, these deities felt, would redeem Arjuna's unrighteous act of killing the mighty Bhīshma while the latter was fighting another combatant. Arjuna, instigated by Krishna, committed several such offenses during the war and was chastised for them by the other fighters.

Arjuna was revived from death at his son's hand by his wife Ulūpikā, the Nāga princess. Old age, however, was creeping up on him. Upon Krishna's death, which greatly saddened Arjuna, he felt deprived of all his strength. Collectively, the Pāndava princes went on a long pilgrimage to the Himalayas.

On their way, Pāncālī died first. Then followed Sahadeva and Nakula. Arjuna was fourth. Yudhishthira (Dharmaputra) refused to ascend to heaven until he was assured of the fact that his brothers were already there. He even insisted on taking his faithful dog with him to heaven.

Epithets of Arjuna Used in the Gītā

Like Krishna, Arjuna is given many epithets in the *Gītā* (and many more in the *Mahābhārata* as a whole):

Anagha: Sinless One
Bharata: Descendant-of-Bharata (King Bharata, the first ruler of the Bharata tribe and a predecessor of the famous king Kuru)
Bharatarshabha: Bull of Bharata.
Bharatasattama: Foremost of the Bharatas
Bharatashreshtha: Best of the Bharatas
Dhanamjaya: Winner of [Spiritual] Wealth
Gudākesha: [He Whose] Hair Is in a Ball (or Topknot); or, esoterically, He Who Has Conquered Sleep
Kaunteya: Son-of-Kuntī
Kirītin: [He Who Wears a] Diadem
Kurunandana: Joy of the Kurus
Kurupravīra: Hero of the Kurus
Kurusattama: Foremost of the Kurus
Kurushreshtha: Best of the Kurus

Pāndava: Descendant-of-Pāndu or Son-of-Pāndu
Paramtapa: Scorcher of Foes
Pārtha: Son-of-Prithā
Purusharishabha: Bull among Men
Purushavyāghra: Man-Tiger
Savyasācin: [He Who Is] Skilled with the Left [Hand]

Yudhishthira

Yudhishthira ("[He Who Is] Steadfast in Battle)," also called Dharmaputra ("son of Dharma"), the eldest of the five Pāndavas, is a major figure in the great epic. He stands for lawfulness, righteousness, truthfulness, and integrity. His behavior is more like a *brāhmana*'s than a warrior's. Yudhishthira found violence abhorrent and did his utmost to prevent the war. Yet, once the Kauravas firmly declined to return to the Pāndavas even an acre of their kingdom, he accepted martial support from his own family and friendly rulers. He also had no difficulty enlisting his brother Bhīmasena's brute strength and his brother Arjuna's more sophisticated deployment of power. The unusual relationship between these three has been ably analyzed by Ruth Cecily Katz (1989).

Dharmaputra, a son of the god Dharma, possessed many virtues, but he had one serious flaw: a predilection for gambling. Thus, in a rigged dice game, he lost his kingdom, wife, and family to the cheating Kauravas. To a fault, he accepted the dire consequences even when he learned that he had been cheated. He was so upright that, upon death, he refused entry into heaven until his dog was admitted as well. (The dog turned out to have been a manifestation of his father, Dharma, all along.)

There was one major incident during the Bharata war where, on Krishna's stipulation, Yudhishthira bent his own moral rectitude. Drona, a formidable warrior, was the principal weapons instructor to both the Kauravas and the Pāndavas, but because of financial entanglements he fought on the side of the Kauravas. He greatly doted on his only son, Ashvatthāman. When Drona and Ashvatthāman caused devastation in the rank and file of the Pāndava alliance, his enemies employed a trick to at least temporarily distract Drona. He was told that Ashvatthāman had been killed. An elephant by that name had indeed just been killed, but Drona of course thought of his son. He asked Yudhishthira to confirm this, which Yudhishthira did, muttering "the elephant" under his breath.

Overwhelmed by grief, Drona dropped down to the ground and entered into deep meditation in order to end his life. Ignoring all the rules of honorable battle, Dhrishtadyumna, the son of the ruler of Pāncāla, rushed forward and cut off Drona's head. Yudhishthira's half-truth spared, at least for now, the lives of many Pāndava warriors and ended the war more quickly.

Boiling with anger, Ashvatthāman took revenge with Shiva's help by storming the encampment of his enemies by night, killing numerous seasoned warriors, including Dhristhadyumna.

Although Yudhishthira has no dialogue in the *Gītā,* he—like Bhīmasena, Nakula, Sahadeva, Dhritarāshtra, and Bhīshma—deserves to be singled out, as he is an important figure in the drama of the *Mahābhārata.*

Bhīmasena

Bhīmasena, or simply Bhīma, was famous for his extraordinary strength. As a ten-day-old baby, he fell off his mother's lap on hard rock. There was not a scratch on him from the accident, but the rock was crushed to powder. Later, when he was undergoing military training, he learned to master the mace.

As a child and then a young man, Bhīma would regularly defeat and hurt his Kaurava cousins during games. The resentful Kauravas poisoned him and dumped him in the Ganges. As he sank down to the river bottom, a member of the Nāga race bit him, which happened to antidote the Kauravas' poison. While Bhīma rested in the underworld of the Nāgas, the serpent king Vāsuki gave him a magical potion that boosted his strength to that of ten thousand elephants. He returned to the human world on the ninth day, when his mother and siblings had all but abandoned hope that he might still be alive.

After their shellac residence was consumed by fire and Pāncālī and the five Pāndava princes had to flee into the forest, Bhīmasena carried them all on his broad shoulders when their own feet failed them. Subject to angry outbursts, he shouted at the top of his lungs that Yudhishthira should have his hands burned for gambling away his kingdom and family and for exposing their joint wife, Pāncālī, to the coarseness and indecency of the Kauravas.

Bhīma was an inveterate demon slayer and even dared to tackle the aged monkey king Hanumān but could not overcome him. Hanumān, King

Rāma's devotee and dedicated helper, congratulated Bhīma and assisted him with good counsel.

At one point in the great war, Bhīma annihilated the entire elephant division of the Kauravas and single-handedly killed 25,000 infantry. In various battles, he managed to kill most of Dhritarāshtra's sons. He broke Duryodhana's thigh, as he had sworn he would. When Bhīmasena, as he also had vowed, killed Dushshāsana, he triumphantly drank the blood bubbling from the warrior's chest. It was Dushshāsana who had dishonored Pāncālī by ripping off her outer garments.

When Bhīmasena's siblings praised the God-man Krishna for ensuring their victory in the war, Bhīmasena haughtily claimed that all success was due to his prowess. To teach him a lesson, Krishna good-naturedly invited Bhīma to mount the divine bird Garuda with him. They flew to a huge lake near Lankā where Rāma had once fought the demon king Rāvana. Krishna asked Bhīma to locate on foot the source of the lake, but the warrior failed to do so. In the process, he was attacked by local warriors. To his horror, he lacked the power to defend himself and anxiously ran back to Krishna for protection.

Making the lake disappear with a motion of his hand, the God-man explained to the proud Pāndava that his attackers were lake-protecting *asuras* and the lake itself was the skull of the demon Kumbhakarna ("Pot-Ear"), killed by Rāma. Shaken up, Bhīmasena humbly apologized to Krishna.

Nakula

One of the twin sons of the Ashvins, Nakula was deemed the most handsome of the Pāndavas. He studied archery under Drona and in the war fought against him but did not gain victory over his teacher.

On ascending the throne, Yudhishthira sent his brother to the west, and Nakula's booty from conquered regions was carried to Hastināpura on ten thousand camels. During the Pāndavas' exile, Nakula was killed by a demon but restored to life by Yudhishthira's fervent prayer to the god Dharma.

After the great war, Nakula was given the palace of Durmarshana, one of King Dhritarāshtra's sons. He had a son named Shatānīka by Pāncālī and a son named Niramitra by Karenumatī, the daughter of the king of Cedi.

Sahadeva

Almost as handsome as his twin brother, Sahadeva ("With God"), the last-born Pāndava, was married to both Pāncālī and Vijayā, the daughter of King Dyutimān of Madra. From the former marriage, he had a son called Shrutasena ("[He Who Is] Dependent on What Has Been Heard"), who was killed by Ashvatthāman; from the latter marriage, he had a son named Suhotra ("Good Invocation").

Sahadeva was fond of serving others, and during the Pāndavas' year of exile in disguise, he donned the role of the king's overseer of the cattle and sustained his mother and siblings with milk and buttermilk. He was a skilled fighter and during the war eliminated the entire Kaurava cavalry. As he had sworn, he also killed Shakuni, the uncle of the Kaurava princes, who tricked Yudhishthira during the game of dice that lost the Pāndavas their kingdom and thus started a devastating family feud.

Dhritarāshtra

King Dhritarāshtra ("Firm Rule"), the blind brother of Pāndu, was the son of the sage Vyāsa and Ambikā. He was born blind as a result of Ambikā's keeping her eyes shut while the fearsome-looking Vyāsa was making love to her. Brought up alongside Pāndu and Vidura under the benign guidance of their much older half brother, Bhīshma, Dhritarāshtra turned into a cultured young man.

He had one hundred sons and a single daughter by Gāndhārī, daughter of the king of Gāndhāra. The eldest son was Duryodhana, who seems to have suffered from an inbuilt aversion to his Pāndava cousins.

Unfortunately, Prince Duryodhana was King Dhritarāshtra's great weakness, and the blind ruler was constantly outsmarted and outmaneuvered by his evil son until it was too late to avert the war.

Dhritarāshtra appears as a speaker in the *Gītā* only in the opening verse, where he bids his loyal minister Samjaya to narrate the events of the battle to him, since he could not see. Many times during the narration, Dhritarāshtra experienced great despair and even fainted.

At the end of the war, Dhritarāshtra embraced the Pāndavas and requested Yudhishthira to guide the offering ceremony for the dead. Then he, Gāndhārī, and Kuntī (mother of the Pāndavas) opted together to retire to the forest in order to do penance. They were killed by a wildfire.

Duryodhana

The eldest and worst son of King Dhritarāshtra, Duryodhana ("Bad Fighting") is the *Mahābhārata*'s arch villain. He was born under many evil omens, but Dhritarāshtra could not, as advised, bring himself to kill his first-born. When Kuntī, Pāndu's widow, sought shelter at the palace in Hastināpura, King Dhritarāshtra gladly extended his protection to them.

Duryodhana, however, managed to turn childhood squabbles into ruthless attacks on his Pāndava cousins' lives and in due course into a monumental war that destroyed his own race and millions of other combatants.

Even when the Pāndavas had braved their exile of thirteen years, Duryodhana refused to render them even as small a piece of their land as would hold a pin.

When Krishna offered both warring parties either a powerful army of one million fighters or himself in a position of adviser, Duryodhana—dismissing Krishna's spiritual power—was only too happy to get such an army.

While Duryodhana fought fiercely in the Bharata war, he also ran away from the battlefield a few times, and one time immersed himself in a still lake to hide out. His thigh was smashed by Bhīmasena, who after Duryodhana's death occupied the latter's palace.

Speaking verses 3–11 in Chapter 1 of the *Gītā,* Duryodhana is integral to the entire Bharata story.

Bhīshma

Bhīshma ("Terrifying"), the son of King Shantanu and Queen Gangā, took a "terrifying" vow of life-long celibacy so that his father could marry the fisher maid Satyavatī. Since Satyavatī's father had agreed to give away his daughter only on condition that her sons would one day rule, Bhīshma on the spot decided to renounce his right of succession. His father was overjoyed and granted him the power to die at will. When badly wounded in the great war, the hero used yogic means to postpone his death for fifty-eight days to wait for the auspicious moment. In the meantime, he imparted many ethical and philosophical teachings to Yudhishthira.

Bhīshma served as the general-in-chief of the Kauravas, although he dearly loved Yudhishthira and his brothers. Even though Bhīshma had the strength to destroy the Pāndava armies, he declared that he would never kill the Pāndava princes, who were like sons to him. To ensure the Pāndavas' victory, he told Yudhishthira how he, Bhīshma, could be fought successfully. He would not fight Shikhandin, who was born a woman but had changed gender with a tree spirit. She had hated Bhīshma for several lifetimes, because he slighted her.

While Shikhandin was attacking Bhīshma in the battle on the eighth day of the war, Arjuna fired arrows at Bhīshma from behind Shikhandin's back. This represented a serious breach of fighting etiquette, but since Bhīshma had envisioned and even desired a positive outcome for the Pāndavas, Arjuna was blamed less than perhaps he should have.

After Bhīshma was wounded by Arjuna's arrows, his supreme command of the Kaurava armies went to Drona, then Karna, and finally Shalya. In the end, Duryodhana had to take charge of his forces himself and was fatally wounded by Bhīmasena.

Although Bhīshma does not appear in the *Gītā* as a speaker, he is mentioned several times in Chapter 1, once in Chapter 2, and twice in Chapter 11 of our text, which indicates his importance.

Samjaya

King Dhritarāshtra's faithful minister Samjaya ("Full Victory"), though a noncombatant, directly participates in the *Gītā* as the narrator. As the narrative begins, he is asked by the king to describe the happenings of the war to him. The sage Vyāsa had bestowed divine sight upon Samjaya so that he could report to Dhritarāshtra absolutely everything, blow by blow, that took place on the distant battlefield. Even though in the employ of the blind Kaurava ruler, Samjaya was a remarkably neutral observer. He lost the "divine eye" the moment Duryodhana fell, which marked the end of the terrible war.

At one point, the Vrishni hero Sātyaki (Yuyudhāna) took Samjaya captive, but he set him free again on Vyāsa's advice. Toward the end of the war, he joined King Dhritarāshtra and Queen Gāndharī in their forest penance, the traditional end-of-life practice.

4

Divine Incarnations of Vishnu

THE CONCEPT OF *avatāra,* "descent" or divine incarnation, has become familiar in the West with the absorption of the term *avatar* into the English language. In Indian mythology it usually refers specifically to incarnations of Vishnu, the second deity (along with Brahma and Shiva) in the trinity of Creator-Preserver-Destroyer. In his essay "Indian Mythology" in volume 2 of *The Cultural Heritage of India*, the influential Indologist R. N. Dandekar (2002) identified "faint traces" of the concept of *avatāra* in the ancient *Rig-Veda,* which describes how Vishnu crossed the entire world in "three strides" and went beyond it. In one stanza, he is said to have "planted his steps in three places." We can understand these images as meaning that Vishnu left his benign imprint upon creation. Similarly, the *avatāras* are also imprints by which Vishnu ensures that the creation conforms to his divine idea and unfolds harmoniously. In fact, Vishnu incarnates whenever the world has, for whatever reason, moved away from the Creator's original intention and become subject to chaos or delusion.

Vaishnava theology recognizes ten major *avatāras*:

1. Matsya ("Fish")
2. Kūrma ("Turtle")
3. Varāha ("Boar")
4. Vāmana ("Dwarf")
5. Nara-Simha ("Man-Lion")
6. Parashu-Rāma ("Rāma with the Ax")
7. Rāmacandra ("Moonlike Rāma")
8. Krishna ("Black" or "Attractor")
9. Buddha ("Awakened")
10. Kalkin ("[He Who] Pulverizes [the World]")

Here is a brief description of each divine incarnation following the details given in the Puranic literature:

1. *Matsya,* the first incarnation, appeared when the world was covered by water. In the form of a giant fish, Vishnu saved the first human being, Manu, by tying his ark to Matsya's "horn." In due course, sea levels dropped and safe land became visible. If we want to pin history to this myth, we can see in it a reference to the great deluge reported in many ancient cultures.

2. In another age, when the world was again threatened with extinction, Vishnu incarnated as *Kūrma,* the Turtle. On his hard shell he balanced Mount Mandara, the world axis, while gods and antigods were churning the world ocean. This primordial churning with the aid of the cosmic serpent Vasuki, whose giant body served as a rope, yielded fourteen precious substances: (1) the moon, (2) Lakshmī, goddess of good fortune, (3) wine, or the goddess of wine, Surā, (4) *kaustubha,* a jewel of inestimable value, (5) the eight-headed horse Uccaihshravas, (6) the wishfulfilling tree Parijātā, (7) the all-bountiful cow Surabhi, (8) the divine physician Dhanvantara, (9) Indra's elephant Iravat, (10) the conch of victory, (11) the unerring bow Dhanusha, (12) miraculous herbs, (13) the beautiful nymph Rhambā, and (14) the nectar of immortality (*amrita*), the most precious of all substances.

3. Vishnu's third incarnation was *Varāha,* the Boar, also associated with a deluge. According to one account, the demon Hiranyāksha ("Gold Eye") had dragged the Earth to the bottom of the ocean, and Varāha slew the demon and brought it back to the top.

4. In his fourth incarnation, as the dwarf *Vamāna,* Vishnu specifically sought to punish the arrogant King Bali, whose asceticism had won him rulership over the entire world, including the realm of the deities. He had stopped the ritual worship of the deities and thus was a bad example for all humanity. Vamāna appeared to him as a dwarfish priest begging for the space of three steps to construct a hut. Bali granted the *brāhmana*'s wish, and Vamāna took three steps to claim his ground. His first step covered the material realm, the second step encompassed the divine realm, and with the third step, he stomped King Bali into the underworld.

5. *Nara-Simha* was part human and part beast. Vishnu assumed this strange form in order to slay the demon Hiranyakashipu, who was invincible to deities, humans, and animals. Only a creature like Nara-Simha was capable of destroying the demonic ruler of the Daitya race. Vishnu incarnated in order to avenge and save his faithful devotee Prahlāda, the son of Hiranyakashipu.

6. In the *tretā-yuga* (the third of the world ages), the members of the ruling class (*kshatriya,* the warrior class) had gained such power that they began to oppress all other classes, especially the *brāhmanas* (the priestly class). Vishnu incarnated as *Parashu-Rāma* in order to rectify their wrongs. His fierceness was such that he eradicated all the *kshatriya* males. The *Mahābhārata* (3.118.9) states that he filled the five Samanta lakes with their blood. His indomitable ax was a gift from Shiva, and he also was the military instructor of Karna. In a fight with Ganesha (also known as Ganapati), the ax was broken, and in an outburst of anger, Parashu-Rāma broke one of Ganesha's tusks, which is why the elephant-headed deity is commonly depicted with only one tusk intact.

7. His successor, Rāmacandra—"moonlike" or gentle (*candra*) Rāma—was born with the specific purpose of ridding the earth of the demon Rāvana. His exploits, which also belong to the *tretā-yuga,* are related in the *Rāmāyana* epic, which comprises 76,000 verses. Rāma inherited the throne of the city-kingdom of Ayodhyā. A good part of the *Rāmāyana* deals with Rāma's rescue of his wife Sītā in Lankā, where she was held captive by Rāvana. When Rāma finally became ruler of Ayodhyā, he governed in an exemplary fashion—upholding both justice and the happiness and welfare of all.

8. *Krishna* is discussed separately above, in addition to further remarks below.

9. The inclusion of the historical *Buddha* (c. 563–483 B.C.E.) among the *avatāras* of Vishnu may seem curious, considering that Buddhism, once predominant in India, eventually all but disappeared from the land of its birth, at least partly because of Hindu hostility to Buddhism. If it is true, as the French Indologist Alain Daniélou (1991, 180) remarked, that "Buddhism has left but few traces in the mythology and the religion of India," then surely the Buddha's incorporation into Vaishnavism must be one of the most significant traces. Indeed, owing to his great influence, the Vaishnavas could not ignore the Buddha but instead absorbed him into their belief system. They held that Vishnu incarnated as the Buddha in order to spread false teachings that would delude the unpious away from the true faith, leading them to hell—a rather sectarian view. On the positive side, the Buddha's simple lifestyle and his exceptional rational lucidity, as recorded in the Buddhist literature, convinced many Hindus to convert to the Buddha Dharma—most notably, in the twentieth century, the "untouchables" who, under the leadership of Dr. B. R. Ambedkar, became Buddhists in order to free themselves from the oppressive caste system.

10. *Kalkin,* or *Kalki,* is the prophesied future incarnation of Vishnu, who will come at the end of the *kali-yuga*—the present age of decline—riding on a white steed and brandishing a fiery sword. Sometimes visualized simply as a white horse, Kalkin is thought to usher in a new golden age, or *krita-yuga* (or *satya-yuga*).

Five of the ten incarnations are human—Vamāna, Parashu-Rāma, Rāmacandra, Krishna, and Buddha—and five belong to the realm of theology and myth. Moreover, the series of ten incarnations belongs to the later world of the Purānas. The *Mahābhārata* is not yet familiar with it, though it mentions several of the *avatāras.*

The only complete (*pūrna*), or perfect, incarnation of Vishnu is thought to be Krishna, the divine teacher of Arjuna. As such he can claim to speak with the authority of the Divine. As is clear from his self-testimony (see 15.17–18 and other stanzas), he *is* the supreme Reality.

Under the impact of the overwhelming theophany described so vividly in Chapter 11 of the *Gītā,* Arjuna is overawed by Krishna's multidimensional reality. Shaken to his core, he begs Krishna's pardon for having regarded him in the past as a mere human being and having carelessly addressed him as friend and comrade (see 11.41–42), while in actuality, Krishna is the unrivaled lord of the universe.

Divine incarnations must be clearly distinguished from the numerous "deities" (*deva, sura*) inhabiting the heavenly worlds. Although the word "god" is commonly used to translate *deva,* these are akin to the angelic beings of the Judeo-Christian and Muslim religions, who also are stationed far below God. The deities are unquestionably "higher" or "subtler" entities than human beings, but they are without any important mission. Like all other creatures, they belong to the realm of conditioned existence (*samsāra*) and are subject to the law of karma. The Divine is called the beginning of all the deities (see 10.2), the Primordial God (11.38), and God of gods (11.13).

5

The *Gītā*'s Syncretism and Holistic Orientation

Syncretism: Reconciling the Opposites

The most outstanding characteristic of the *Bhagavad-Gītā* is its overall *syncretistic* orientation, which governs all domains of the complex doctrinal structure of this celebrated Sanskrit work—its metaphysical, theological, psychological, and ethical teachings. According to *The New Shorter Oxford English Dictionary*, syncretism is the "attempted union or reconciliation of diverse or opposite tenets or practices, esp. in philosophy or religion." This characteristic has led some scholars to assume that the text is a composite with numerous interpolations, which is probably the case. Efforts to identify the alleged subtexts and interpolations, however, have been rather unconvincing.

Nowadays, the term *syncretism* is often used in a pejorative sense. This is not the case here. Syncretism seems to be a natural tendency of the human mind whenever it is confronted with many cultural or philosophical strands. The *Gītā* represents an attempt to integrate Sāmkhya-Yoga ontology and ethics, Pāncarātra metaphysics, the devotionalism of the Krishna-Vāsudeva tradition (Bhāgavatism), and the kind of panentheistic nondualism first encountered in the Upanishads. (More on these various traditions in chapter 8 of Part One, "The *Gītā* in Hindu Thought and Culture.") Note that panentheism ("All is in God") is not the same as pantheism ("All is God"). While the latter sees the world and nature as identical with God, the former sees the world as only part of the incomprehensible vastness of the Divine, or Ultimate Reality.

The *Gītā*'s syncretism is not entirely successful. Over the years, many researchers have pointed to apparent discrepancies. Some of these, however, are based on a misunderstanding of the text; others are actual discrepancies. As the philosopher Eliot Deutsch (1968, pp. 159ff.) put it, the *Gītā* is "neither a systematic philosophical treatise nor a mere 'poem,'" but it represents an attempt to integrate diverse religio-philosophical values and ideas, "with mixed results." He saw this as the interpretative "middle way" between the view that regards the teachings of the *Gītā* as absolutely uniform and coherent and the view that it throws together many opinions without even an attempt to integrate them.

Arvind Sharma (1986) of McGill University made a study of alleged contradictions in the *Gītā.* He distinguished among several categories: theological contradiction, soteriological ambiguity, metaphysical antinomy, liturgical inconsistency, canonical ambivalence, ethical dilemma, yogic *embarras de richesses,* and interpretive difference.

Theological contradiction relates to four questions that seem to be answered differently in different passages of the *Gītā:*

1. Is the Divine personal or impersonal?
2. Is the Divine active or passive?
3. Is the Divine immanent or transcendent?
4. Is the Divine wishing humans well, or is it chastising or indifferent to them?

The answer to the first question is that the Divine, as we will see later on, is both personal and impersonal. This question presupposes a discrepancy between the two, which does not really exist. The situation is the same with the other questions.

Because, according to the *Gītā,* the Divine has a higher *and* a lower nature—one composed of the primary qualities (*guṇa*) and one beyond them—it can be said to be both active *and* passive, immanent *and* transcendent, as well as indifferent (at the highest level) *and* engaged with humanity (mainly in the form of the divine incarnations, or *avatāras*). This disposes of alleged discrepancies implied in questions 2 to 4.

Soteriological ambiguity refers to the *Gītā*'s apparently contradictory explanation about how liberation is achieved. According to Professor Sharma, verses 8.5 and 8.13 preach the ideal of disembodied liberation (*videha-mukti*), which means that liberation can be accomplished only posthumously, whereas verse 5.19 is in favor of living liberation (*jīvan-mukti*) here and now. A careful reading of these verses shows that they are *not* mutually contradictory but refer to distinct *phases* in the process of liberation, where *jīvan-mukti* precedes *videha-mukti.*

Metaphysical antinomy suggests that there is more than one answer to the question: Is the world real or unreal? Arvind Sharma himself is not sure whether the *Gītā* offers contradictory views. In my reading of it, it does not.

Liturgical inconsistency refers to alleged contradictions about ritualism, which is simultaneously "sharply criticized" (see 2.42–43) and "strongly favored" (see 4.31). On closer inspection, the *Gītā* criticizes specifically Vedic ritualism and not ritualism in general. The Pāncarātra tradition is known to have been critical of the Vedic tradition, which is why the Vedic priesthood has in general rejected Pāncarātrism.

What we can call the strained relationship between Vedism and Pāncarātrism would also explain the so-called *canonical ambivalences.*

The *Gītā*'s *ethical dilemma* is at the heart of Arjuna's dilemma: Is it right to kill under any circumstances? On the one hand the God-man Krishna convinced his disciple Arjuna to engage in the Bharata war, and on the other hand he preached nonharming. This ethical dilemma led, among other things, to Mohandas Gandhi's resisting the British Raj in a *nonviolent* manner, while N. Godse, his assassin—leaning on the same *Gītā*—found Gandhi's murder morally justifiable. This is in fact a crucial issue, which every student of the *Gītā* must confront.

Yogic embarras de richesses is a category that, according to Arvind Sharma, consists in the fact that the *Gītā* champions multiple yogic approaches. At the most fundamental level, the *Gītā* distinguishes between the orientation of Sāmkhya and that of Yoga. Even Arjuna was greatly confused, and so the perplexity of the modern interpreter is understandable.

Interpretive difference refers to the fact that many ancient (and modern) authorities have explained the teachings of the *Gītā* differently. Thus, there are the interpretations by Shankara (radical nondualism), Rāmānuja (qualified nondualism), and Mādhva (dualism), and others. All these interpreters claim to have the most authentic interpretation of the *Gītā.* Many scholars think that Rāmānuja (1017–1137 C.E.) came closest to the actual intention of the *Gītā*. He views the world as the "body" of the Divine, not as a mere illusion.

Holism: An Integrative Worldview

Closely related to the *Gītā*'s syncretism is its holism. Holism is an intellectual orientation that looks at the whole of something rather than at mere particulars, or parts. The philosophical term *holism* stems from the Greek word *holon* ("whole"). While the *Gītā* takes a broad, integrative view of life, it does not pretend to propound a fully developed philosophical system in which each and every component is well defined and demarcated from the rest. The inclusion of this Sanskrit text into an epic suggests that it was intended for popular consumption rather than the edification of learned pundits. Because of the *Gītā*'s relatively syncretistic approach, some scholars—notably Franklin Edgerton (1944)—have proposed that it propounds a compromise philosophy. This is not the case, however. It is more likely that the *Gītā* offers an early genuine creative synthesis. Its worldview (*darshana*) is intrinsically coherent and meaningful. Its teachings represent philosophy in the broadest sense, as love of wisdom.

The *Gītā* is one of those remarkable accomplishments that add vivid color to the proliferating history of philosophy by refusing to settle for a one-dimensional interpretation of reality and instead probing deeper into the mysteries of life. It addresses the great, important things that modern, science-oriented thought tends to shun, caught up as it is in a confusing maze of empirical research data and fixated on the ideal of objectivity. The *Gītā* concerns itself with the vital issues of existence, such as the meaning of life and death, the significance of ignorance, knowledge, wisdom, doubt, faith, immortality, virtue, and not least the unimaginable potential of the human mind—all issues that are as relevant today as they were in antiquity.

Considering the organic interconnectedness of its ideas, it seems hardly rewarding to study the *Gītā* by slicing up its teachings into watertight compartments. Apparent inconsistencies in the text, which are supposed to evince the work's composite nature, can readily be explained either as arising from its multilayered approach or as a function of its syncretism. While the *Gītā* cannot be classified as a strictly systematic exposition, its materials are nevertheless organized in a logical manner.

So, it is perfectly possible to present the *Gītā*'s philosophical tenets in a systematic way, using familiar Western philosophical categories, such as ontology, epistemology, theology, cosmology, anthropology, eschatology, ethics, and mysticism. This is, of course, merely a convenient device, and as long as we remain aware of the tentative nature of all such divisions, we will not do injury to the basic unity of Krishna's teachings.

The *Gītā* shows a holistic approach, which it shares with many other Indian and non-Indian gnostic teachings.[1] The holistic orientation finds expression, among other things, in the *Gītā*'s adopted methodology of systematic introspection leading to transcendental insight (i.e., mystical awareness). One might even argue that it is this particular methodology that has significantly overdetermined the *Gītā*'s doctrinal syncretism and terminology.

The *Gītā*, it is important to remember, is both a textual entity and the voice of a spiritual tradition. It can be looked upon as a poem, a popular philosophical-ethical-religious tract, and not least as a vade mecum for the student of Yoga.

This many-sidedness makes this scripture a real touchstone of Sanskrit scholarship. It is composed in mostly simple, melodious Sanskrit verse; the real hurdle for the translator/interpreter lies in the density of Krishna's concepts, which are not fully explicated. It seems, moreover, that the conceptual world of the *Gītā* can be effectively deciphered only when we adopt the kind of holistic approach that is so distinctive of it. In other words and more specifically, we will succeed in penetrating Krishna's teachings only to the degree that we can empathize with the interconnectedness of all things. This is a fundamental notion of Indic thought and thus also of the *Gītā*, and is being rediscovered in our own time through disciplines like ecology and quantum theory.

1. I have availed myself of the Greek-based term *gnostic* to refer to the teachings that emphasize knowledge, or wisdom, as a means to spiritual liberation.

6

Vyāsa—Bard and Sage

Who Was Vyāsa?

Tradition credits the legendary Vyāsa Dvaipāyana ("Island-born Editor") with having compiled the *Gītā*'s present seven hundred verses. It is important to know that the Sanskrit word *vyāsa* is not so much a personal name as a profession, for the word means literally "separator" and designates an "arranger," "collator," "compiler," or "editor" (from *vi* + *as*, "to throw, cast"). As the name suggests, a *vyāsa* was someone who "separated out," or sifted through, various traditions and arranged existing lore into a cohesive whole.

Undoubtedly, there were many such *vyāsas* who contributed to the formation of the ancient world's longest text, and a certain Vyāsa Dvaipāyana was ostensibly the most important or best remembered of these individuals. For the sake of convenience, however, I will ignore historical accuracy at times and refer to the *vyāsa* designated as Dvaipāyana ("Island-born") as the "author" of the *Gītā.*

Popular Hindu tradition has done a disservice to history by conflating the various *vyāsas* throughout India's history into a single individual, who is credited with compiling not only the Vedas but also the *Mahābhārata* and the *Gītā,* as well as the Purānas and other Sanskrit works. This one Vyāsa would have had to live hundreds of years!

Vyāsa Dvaipāyana, whose childhood name was Krishna (not to be confused with the God-man Krishna), has the hermit Parāshara for his father and the fisherwoman Kālī for his mother. The story of how a hermit and a fisherwoman came to be Vyāsa's parents is related in the *Mahābhārata* itself (1.60–63).

One day King Uparicaravasu ("Vasu Who Travels Above") of the Cedi tribe was out hunting in the forest. Witnessing the copulation of wild animals, his lust was so aroused that he experienced a spontaneous seminal emission. He had his semen couriered to his waiting wife. It so happened that the semen fell into the River Kālindī and a fish swallowed it. Now, that fish was in actuality a celestial nymph by the name of Adrikā, who had been cursed to spend a lifetime as a fish. In due course, the fish was caught by a fisherman, who cut it open. In the fish's belly he found a male and a female child. The boy was handed over to the king himself, while the fisherman kept and brought up the girl, whom he named Kālī. Because her skin smelled of fish, she came to be called Matsyagandhī, or "She-who-smells-of-fish."

The fisherman was also the local ferryman. One day, the sage Parāshara ("Destroyer," from the verbal root *shrī*) asked to be ferried across the waters. The ferryman, who was having his midday meal, asked his foster daughter to deliver the sage to the other shore. Parāshara became enamored of the beautiful maiden who was rowing the boat. She politely fended off his advances, begging him not to violate her. His passion grew stronger, and he magically created a fog around the boat, which transformed her fishy smell to a fragrance of musk. Next he created an artificial island in the river, where—unseen by anyone—they made love. Kālī became pregnant but was assured by Parāshara that even after giving birth she would continue to be a virgin. He prophesied that a son would be born to her who was a portion of the god Vishnu and who would achieve great fame for his erudition and wisdom.

Kālī instantly felt her belly grow and immediately gave birth to a radiant boy, who at once grew into a young man named Krishna (the future Vyāsa). He begged his mother not to worry about him and promised her to appear whenever she wished to see him. After bidding goodbye to his mother, Krishna departed, following the age-old track of ascetics living in isolation in the forest.

Kālī resumed her life with her ferryman father. Then, one day, King Shamtanu ("Peaceful Body") was hunting in the forest near their dwelling and was drawn to the maiden by her musky scent. When he saw her beauty and grace, he promptly fell in love with her. Although the king already had a wife, he asked for Kālī's hand in marriage, which her father granted.

Kālī, now called Satyavatī ("Truthful"), gave birth to two royal sons. Both met with misfortune and died. Grief-stricken, Satyavatī thought of her hidden son, Vyāsa, who promptly manifested to her. She requested that he sire children to the two wives of her childless son Vicitravīrya

("[He Who Is] Brilliantly Heroic"). Vyāsa consented. The first wife, called Ambālikā (meaning perhaps "Mother Bee"), gave birth to Pāndu ("Pale"); the other, known as Ambikā ("Little Mother"), gave birth to the blind Dhritarāshtra ("Firm Rule"). The Bharata war unfolded between the feuding sons of these two kingly half brothers—the Pāndavas and the Kauravas.

While at Shamtanu's palace, Vyāsa fell in love with a maid and fathered yet another son, the sagely Vidura ("Intelligent"), whose teachings are recorded in the *Mahābhārata* (1.199ff.). Vidura became renowned for his intelligence throughout the country. He served the blind King Dhritarāshtra as adviser. Because he was dedicated to righteousness, however, he was strongly partial to the sons of Pāndu. The birth of Dhritarāshtra's oldest son, Duryodhana ("Bad Fighting"), was surrounded by many ill omens. Interpreting the omens, Vidura advised the king to abandon the child, but Dhritarāshtra ignored this suggestion. Vidura also was instrumental in saving the lives of the Pāndavas when Duryodhana conspired to burn them alive in a specially built house made of highly flammable shellac. The Pāndavas burned down the mansion themselves, hoping that Duryodhana would conclude that they all had died in the conflagration. They in fact managed to escape the inferno through a secret underground passage, which Vidura had ordered to be secretly constructed.

King Dhritarāshtra had some pangs of conscience about sending his deceased brother Pāndu's sons into exile. Mostly, however, he was afraid of how the people would react, because the Pāndavas were hugely popular. Vidura advised him to disown his own sons and restore the kingdom to the Pāndavas. The military teachers Bhīshma and Drona were favoring a compromise: to give half the kingdom to the Pāndavas and retain the other half for his own Kaurava sons. Dhritarāshtra responded by dismissing Vidura, who then followed the Pāndavas into exile. Before long, the king had a change of heart and invited Vidura back to the palace and even apologized to him respectfully.

Vidura did his best to prevent the war, and his failure to do so caused him great grief. When the preparations for the war were under way, Vidura went on a pilgrimage. When, in due course, he heard from Maitreya, a disciple of Parāshara, that the war was over, the Kauravas had been exterminated, and Yudhishthira, the eldest of the five Pāndava sons, had been installed as the rightful king, he returned to the capital.

After advising Yudhishthira for a period of time, Vidura retired to the forest along with the blind Dhritarāshtra and his wife Gāndharī,

Kuntī (wife of the deceased king Pāndu and the mother of Arjuna), and others.

Grieving Satyavatī likewise resolved to retire to the forest in order to do penance. As is recorded in the *Mahābhārata* (1.119.13), her exertions were successful and, after many years, she attained heaven.

In the meantime, Vyāsa's life went in the opposite direction. He frequently abandoned the isolation of his forest hermitage and periodically lived at the royal court at the capital Hastināpura. It helped that he could travel over long distances in an instant. He advised the Pāndavas, anointed Yudhishthira as king after the war, bestowed on Samjaya the divine vision enabling him to witness the dialogue between Krishna and Arjuna, and instructed Yudhishthira to perform the elaborate horse sacrifice to ritually secure the kingdom.

Toward the end of his earthly life, Vyāsa retired to the Himalaya. In his contemplations, he saw the events of his life unfold, not least the complex circumstances culminating in the Bharata war. Wanting to write down the details of this story, he petitioned the creator god Brahma to find him a competent scribe. The choice fell upon the elephant-headed deity Ganesha, who alone was able to follow the sage's nonstop dictation, which lasted for two and a half or, alternatively, in another version of the narrative, three years.

It was Vyāsa's great disciples, notably Vaishampāyana and Jaimini, who recited the *Mahābhārata* around India. Vyāsa's only son, Shuka ("Parrot"), recited the epic to the host of semidivine beings, including *gandharvas*, *yakshas*, and *rākshasas*. Shuka, or Shukadeva, was destined to become an accomplished adept (*siddha*) who, like a radiant star, rose from the peak of the sacred Mount Kailāsha, Shiva's home, into the sky.

Twenty-eight Vyāsas

According to the *Mahābhārata* itself (1.1), Vyāsa composed both a detailed and an abridged version of his epic poem. As we have seen, he first created a version comprising 24,000 stanzas, which was known as the *Bhārata*. Vyāsa himself condensed his original composition to a mere 150 verses. Next, he produced an expanded version of 600,000 verses.

Of these, only 100,000 stanzas are known in the realm of humans, while the remainder of the *Mahābhārata* was heard by subtle beings of various kinds. The extant version is just over 100,000 verses if we include the appendix called the *Hari-Vamsha*. It should also be mentioned that only roughly twenty thousand verses deal with the actual war and the myths surrounding it. Much of the other material relates to the education of Yudhishthira, who represents the ideal king. Many of the remaining sections do not relate to the war at all and are like fascinating "fillers," which tell about the history of sages, deities, or demons, or provide teachings on morality, asceticism, renunciation, and so on.

These references in the great epic suggest very strongly that the text underwent various transformations, which is also what modern scholarship has found, though the layers of accretions (interpolations) have not yet been determined convincingly. This may never be possible.

In the first section of the opening chapter of the *Mahābhārata,* we learn that when the deities weighed Vyāsa's epic against the four Vedas, the former weighed heavier than the latter. One verse (1.56.15) clearly states: "This [work] is unexcelled, pure, and equal to the Vedas. This Purāna, praised by seers, is unexcelled [among things that] are heard."

Specifically, Vyāsa's epic was known as "Krishna's Veda" (*kārshna-veda*), so named after the omniscient sage Vyāsa's birth name. Hence it came to be thought (1.119.1) that "he who knows the *Mahābhārata*'s purport is saved from all sins." The omniscience ascribed to Vyāsa puts him beyond the human realm and simultaneously permitted the popular claim that his epic also was divine in origin, as is traditionally claimed of the Vedic revelation (*shrūti*). (For more on the revealed tradition, see chapter 8 of Part One, "The *Gītā* in Hindu Thought and Culture.")

The *Vishnu-Purāna* (3.3), one of the oldest texts of this genre, provides a list of twenty-eight names, beginning with Brahma himself. The other Vyāsas are either lesser deities or great sages, who have the status of a deity and thus are, like Vyāsa Dvaipāyana, endowed with omniscience.

Each Manu Age (*manvantara*)—the span of life of a *manu,* or First Man—has its own Veda-Vyāsa, that is, a being who in a sense becomes the long-lived reservoir of sacred knowledge for humanity at the time. Perhaps this is one way of saying that the human species is protected and always has access to the spiritual dimension of existence.

7

The Hindu Concept of Cyclic Time

WE MUST SAY something here about the Hindu notion of chronological cycles, since the *Gītā* (4.8 and 8.17) mentions the concept of *yuga* ("age"). According to some traditions a *yuga* consists of one thousand "divine" years, but (in other contexts) can also stand for a span of five years. Together a set of four *yugas* amounts to twelve thousand "divine" years, which is the equivalent of 432,000 (or 12,000 x 360) human years. One thousand *yugas* constitute one *kalpa*, or aeon, which is a single divine day of the creator-deity Brahma! He lives for 100 "divine" years, which is 3,110.4 billion human years. At the end of this unimaginable period, Brahma dies and the universe is destroyed before a new Brahma appears and gives rise to the universe again. (The timeless transcendental Reality, *brahman*, is unaffected by this time process.)

One Day of Brahma, which is one *kalpa*, entails fourteen Manu Ages or *manvantaras* (from *manu* "thinker" + *antara* "period"). That is, there are fourteen successive worlds inhabited by humanity. They last as long as the life span of the ancestral human in each *manvantara*, who is called Manu. At the end of a Brahmic Day, when Brahma falls asleep, the human world is destroyed—a condition called *pralaya*—until the deity reawakens and re-creates the world. At the end of Brahma's life, the universe blinks out of existence until the eventual rebirth of Brahma. The disappearance of the universe is not tantamount to its nonexistence. Just as after each Brahmic Day, the final cosmic dissolution at the death of Brahma (*mahā-pralaya*) is merely a transition into sheer potentiality within the vastness of the Supreme Being.

Each Brahmic Day and each Brahmic Night also comprise a single set of four *yugas*, which is known as one *catur-yuga* or *mahā-yuga* ("great age").

The word *yuga* can be found as early as the archaic *Rig-Veda,* where it is used thirty-three times in two significantly distinct senses: one is a five-year period, the other an unspecified rather long period (see Kane 1994, pp. 486ff.). Both usages are also known to the *Mahābhārata,* and the *Gītā* (8.17) even makes a point of mentioning that a *kalpa* is equal to one thousand (divine) years. Here we are concerned with *yuga* as a protracted stretch of time.

From the perspective of humanity, the *yugas* are regarded as being of special significance because they represent a cyclic decline affecting not only spirituality and morality but also the sociocultural and even anatomical aspects of human existence. Thus, in the opening *yuga*—known as *krita-yuga* ("age of what is [well-]done") or *satya-yuga* ("age of truth")—humanity is blessed with a state of excellent physical, emotional, and mental health, as well as sociocultural and environmental harmony. In the next *yuga*—called *tretā-yuga,* or "age of thrice"—life conditions are less optimal. The third *yuga*—referred to as *dvāpara-yuga*, or "age of dual [markings]"—confronts humanity with still more inner and outer deterioration. But the worst of all is the *kali-yuga.* The term *kali* does not denote the goddess Kālī, but the most unfavorable cast of a die. In fact, the names of all four *yugas* are derived from the game of dice. It is generally said that in the *kali-yuga,* the *dharma* has so greatly declined that it is barely manifest.

The four *yugas* are typically arranged in the following manner:

1. *Krita-yuga*: dawn, 400 divine years + proper period, 4,000 divine years + dusk, 400 divine years = total, 4,800 divine years; *dharma* is fully intact.
2. *Tretā-yuga:* dawn, 300 divine years + proper period, 3,000 divine years + dusk, 300 divine years = total, 3,600 divine years; *dharma* is three-quarters of its full strength.
3. *Dvāpara-yuga:* dawn, 200 divine years + proper period, 2,000 divine years + dusk, 200 divine years = total, 2,400 divine years; *dharma* is at half strength.
4. *Kali-yuga:* dawn, 100 divine years + proper period, 1,000 divine years + dusk, 100 divine years = total, 1,200 divine years; *dharma* is at one-quarter of its full power.

The grand total is 12,000 divine years, or 4,320,000 human years.

Each *yuga* has its own distinct spiritual orientation, as follows:

1. *Krita-yuga: tapas,* or asceticism
2. *Tretā-yuga: jnāna,* or metaphysical knowledge
3. *Dvāpara-yuga: yajna,* or ritual sacrifice
4. *Kali-yuga: dāna,* or charity

It is easy to see in the above schema the historical progression between the asceticism of the Vedas, the gnosis of the Upanishads, the sacrificialism of the Mīmāmsā school, and our contemporary approach, which would indeed benefit from a more prominent practice of charity in order to benefit all the millions of fellow humans who lack food, water, and proper shelter.

It is said that in the *kali-yuga,* human beings are no longer capable of properly following the appropriate paths of asceticism, metaphysical knowledge, and ritual sacrifice. This appears to be the case nowadays, as any genuine spiritual teacher can verify. It also seems that we find it difficult even to practice charity, the prescribed approach of the *kali-yuga,* in the right way.

The *kali-yuga,* or present-day dark age, supposedly started on February 18, 3102 B.C.E., when the Bharata war began or, according to another explanation, when Krishna dropped his human form (thirty-six years after the war was launched). Other traditional explanations for the beginning of the *kali-yuga* exist. The main idea is that we are denizens of this harsh age, which spans a total of 1,200 x 360 = 432,000 human years. So, contrary to Western New Age thinking, the next golden age is a long way removed from us.

By no means all Hindu thinkers are in agreement with the above *yuga* model, which leaves many cosmological questions unanswered. One of the best-known authorities of modern times is Sri Yukteswar, the guru of the world-renowned Paramahansa Yogananda. Sri Yukteswar (1984) connected the *yugas* with the Earth's precessional cycle, which is normally thought to be 25,800 years but in Yukteswar's system is shortened to 24,000 years. He also assumed that the *kali-yuga* is not followed directly by another golden age but in ascending order by another *kali-yuga, dvāpara-yuga, tretā-yuga,* and then *satya-yuga.* Thus, according to him, we are now in the middle of a *dvāpara-yuga,* which David Frawley (1991) calculated as having started in 1699 C.E. and continuing until 4099 C.E.

What many Hindus and Western writers miss is the fact that the *yuga* model has since the time of the Purānas been deemed to be specific to India, and therefore does not have relevance for the rest of the world. Be that as it may, we can also follow those Hindus who, like the wise lawgiver Manu in his *Manu-Smriti* (10.301), do not regard the four eras as perpetually fixed. Thus, Manu thought that by proper conduct, a ruler could bring about the benign conditions of the *krita-yuga*. In other words, whatever the prevailing conditions may be, collective action can change them for the better.

8

The *Gītā* in Hindu Thought and Culture

Revealed or Remembered?

TRADITIONAL HINDU LITERATURE is divided into revealed works (*shrūti*) and "remembered" works (*smriti*). The *shrūti* comprise the four Vedas (*Rig-, Yajur-, Sāma-,* and *Atharva-Veda*) and their respective Brāhmanas (ritual texts), Āranyakas (ritual texts for forest-dwelling ascetics), and Upanishads (gnostic scriptures focusing on *jnāna-yoga*). The Sanskrit word *shrūti* is a feminine noun derived from the past participle *shrūta,* meaning "heard." The early Sanskrit literature was transmitted by way of mouth and was faithfully memorized by listening to it. These Sanskrit scriptures were originally orally transmitted and are said to have been "seen" by highly realized adepts, who passed them on to their disciples in an initiatory setting. These works form the very core of Brāhmanism, the tradition of the priestly estate (*brāhmana*), though the early and most revered Upanishads also are associated with the warrior estate (*kshatriya*). It should be noted that the various religious communities, such as the Vaishnavas, Shaivas, and Shāktas, have their own revealed literature in the form of the Samhitās, Āgamas, and Tantras, respectively.

While the *Gītā* is not formally part of the Vedic revelatory literature, it has long been honored as a revealed scripture. As a part of the *Mahābhārata*, the *Gītā* belongs formally to the category of "remembered" (*smriti*) or traditional literature. Yet, according to its colophons (verses appearing at the ends of chapters, formally stating the close of each chapter), it claims independent authority as a secret doctrine (*upanishad*).[1]

1. It is doubtful that the colophons were originally part of the *Gītā*. Also, the word *upanishad* ("secret doctrine" or "secret") is used in the plural locative qualifying the term *gītā* in the opening words of each colophon: *iti shrīmad-bhagavad-gītāsu upanishatsu*, literally: "thus, in the sung

These colophons are clearly a later addition and are part of an attempt to place the *Gītā* firmly in the stream of Hindu orthodoxy—that is, Brāhmanism. The *Gītā*'s association with Vaishnavism and more specifically Krishnaism (Bhāgavatism), however, rendered this attempt futile. For the Vaishnava-Pāncarātra-Bhāgavata tradition essentially developed in circles that were at the margins of Brāhmanism, the orthodox Vedic nucleus of Hindu civilization, and that were gesturing toward promoting their own revelation rather than that of the Vedas.

Brāhmanism

To appreciate what it means that the Vaishnava tradition is unorthodox, we must know that Brāhmanism looks upon the four Vedas as canonical. They are seen as the eternal "Word" of the Divine itself; there can be no other revelation. Vaishnavism, like Shaivism, is a religio-cultural tradition that has its own revelation. In both traditions, the monotheistic worship of God (as Vishnu or Shiva, respectively) is demanded. This goes against the grain of orthodox Brāhmanism, which is not monotheistic but is more appropriately called monistic or nondualistic: *brahman* (the Absolute) is beyond all form, beyond all deities, and impersonal.

Unlike other scriptures, the Vedas are deemed to be of "nonhuman" (*apaurusheya*), or "transhuman" origin. Every word in the unauthored Vedas is sacred, which is why for the longest time the *brāhmanas* kept the Vedas concealed from the eyes and ears of non-*brāhmanas*, whom they considered spiritually unworthy. Even though ordinary Hindus apart from outcastes are allowed to attend religious ceremonies during which the Vedas are recited by qualified priests, the difficult archaic Sanskrit language in which they are couched makes it virtually impossible for noninitiates to understand them, just as ancient Latin was a sealed book for the uneducated masses of medieval Europe. The German theologian and mystic Meister Eckhart was the first to preach in the vernacular, i.e., German, rather than in Latin, thus opening up Christian teachings to the illiterate and the half-educated.

The reason for the exclusivism and elitism of the priestly specialists in India has often been attributed to their desire for power. Social power

---

secrets of the Blessed Lord . . ." To give an example, the colophon of the first chapter reads "Thus, in the sung secrets of the Blessed Lord, in the Knowledge of the Absolute, in the Scripture of Yoga, in the dialogue between Shrī Krishna and Arjuna, [this] is the first chapter, named the Yoga of Arjuna's Despondency."

may well have been a motivating factor, as has been the case with the priestly class of other societies. But the *brāhmanas* also have felt that the spiritual knowledge contained in the Vedas ought to be protected against corruption. They rightly feared that the disclosure of essentially spiritual teachings to all and sundry would only lead to misinterpretation (by those without adequate training), confusion, and abuse, as it does today with the easy availability of the Vedas in paperback versions.

As we can see from the *Gītā,* even Krishna felt protective of his spiritual heritage. He calls his instruction of Prince Arjuna "more secret than [any other] secret" (18.63). We would say "top secret." He advised his disciple not to disclose his teachings to anyone who lacks asceticism, has no devotion to him (Krishna), is bereft of obedience, or speaks ill of him (18.67).

The Vedic Canon (*Shrūti*)

The Vedic canonical literature is more comprehensive than any other religious canon on earth. According to a recent revised chronology, the Vedas were collected by *brāhmanas* some five thousand years ago. Since these scriptures were regarded as revealed to the highly refined minds of great "seers" (*rishi*), they were in need of interpretation for the benefit of more ordinary mortals. Thus, the Vedas (or Samhitās, "Collections" of Vedic hymns) gave rise to a large exegetical (explanatory) literature.

This body of exegetical works comprises the various Brāhmanas (ritual texts) and Āranyakas (ritual texts for forest-dwelling ascetics), as well as the over two hundred gnostic scriptures called Upanishads. All these secondary works are also regarded as revealed and sacred, just like the Vedas.

Understanding the *Gītā* in a Wider Context

The *Bhagavad-Gītā*—often simply referred to as the *Gītā*—is the most popular religio-spiritual scripture of Hinduism. This was not always so. Although the *Gītā* is composed in relatively simple Sanskrit, it was largely a sealed book to the illiterate masses of India. Thus, it cannot be said to have been very popular until modernity, even though the learned have long regarded it as an authority, despite the fact that it does not belong to the group of texts deemed to be "Vedic revelation," or *shrūti.* Its rise to widespread popularity coincided with the emergence of Neo-Hinduism[2]

2. "Neo-Hinduism" refers to religio-political reformist movements like the Brahmo Samaj

in the late nineteenth century and the popular translations of the *Gītā* into vernacular languages like Hindi, Bengali, and English.

In status and in its placement within the body of Hindu literature, it has been compared to the New Testament within Christianity. This seems not entirely fitting. If the ancient Vedas—the *Rig-*, *Yajur-*, *Sāma-*, and *Atharva-Veda*—can be compared to the Old Testament, then the Upanishads could be said to correspond to the New Testament. These gnostic scriptures, of which there are over two hundred individual texts (belonging to diverse eras), are continuous with the Vedic revelation but at the same time strike a new note. The *Gītā* is traditionally said to be the "essence" (*rasa*) of the Upanishadic teachings.

Similarly, the Sermon on the Mount has often been looked upon as containing the essence of the teachings of Jesus, which are clearly based on the Old Testament but also go beyond the old religio-moral code of Moses. Many New Testament scholars regard the influential Sermon on the Mount as an assemblage of some of the best teachings of Jesus given on various occasions and in different locations. Thus, it would perhaps be more appropriate to correlate the *Bhagavad-Gītā* with the Sermon on the Mount, which famously begins with a discourse on the beatitudes (see Luke 6:20–23 and, in more generalized form, Matthew 5:3–12).

Vishnu and Vaishnavism

Within the Indian context, the *Gītā* is a key text of the ancient Vaishnava tradition, the religio-cultural complex that developed around the worship of Vishnu ("Pervader").[3] According to most Indologists, Vishnu was a "minor" deity of the Vedic pantheon, because he has only five of the over one thousand hymns dedicated to him in the esteemed *Rig-Veda* of the *brāhmanas*. By contrast, Indra has over two hundred and fifty hymns, Agni about two hundred, and Soma over one hundred. The paucity of

(founded by Raja Ram Mohan Roy in 1828), the Arya Samaj (founded by Dayananda Sarasvati in 1875), and Bal Gangadhar Tilak's more militaristic movement in Maharashtra, as well as related missionary efforts, notably Swami Vivekananda's vigorous export of Hinduism to the West from 1893 on. Among the creators of the "Hindu Renaissance" also belongs Aurobindo Ghose, the founder of Integral Yoga, who, among many other writings, also published interpretative works on the *Bhagavad-Gītā*. During a one-year prison sentence in 1907–1908 for an alleged politically motivated terrorist act, Sri Aurobindo had a vision of Krishna placing a copy of the *Gītā* into his hands. It turned this political reformer into a philosophical sage.

3. For a historical treatment, see Jan Gonda 1970, 1993. See also Siddhantashastree 1985 and Jaiswal 1981.

Rig-Vedic hymns addressed to Vishnu may, however, not be a reliable indicator of this deity's importance in early Vedic times. It is quite likely that Vishnu was at the center of a religious cult that thrived at the margins of the brahmanical orthodoxy that was responsible for the creation of the *Rig-Veda* and that had no reason to devote much space to Vishnu.

We know so little about the beginnings of the Vedic culture that it is best not to indulge in bold conjectures. What we do know about Vishnu is that by the Vedic era he was already regarded as an especially benign deity. He is said to have crossed the universe in three strides (a hint at his solar character), with the highest and invisible stride taking him into the heavenly realm. All three strides are said to be for the benefit of humanity. This mythological or symbolic motif is reiterated in the Brāhmanas and subsequent Indian literature, including the *Rāmāyana* and *Mahābhārata* epics.

As a matter of fact, the extant *Mahābhārata* is a Vaishnava document of the first rank and unmistakably evinces the dominance of Vishnu worship among the various religious strands flourishing in that era. Although Shiva is mentioned in the great epic more frequently than Vishnu, the latter—through the essential role of Krishna—has the greater importance of the two.

It is, however, also true that Shiva is not an incidental figure in the *Mahābhārata.* The epic is a highly syncretistic work, and both Shiva and Vishnu have an instrumental role to play in it, though the relationship between these two deities is by no means uniform. Sometimes they are portrayed as alternate manifestations of the Divine; at other times they are treated in a sectarian way, as being mutually exclusive. The differences between them are most marked in their iconographic depictions.

Although the name Shiva means "Good," Shiva is most often portrayed as a fierce ascetic, in contrast to Vishnu, who is depicted as an exceptionally benign deity. For both, the epic claims the status of Supreme Godhead. Thus, the *Mahābhārata* promulgates an extraordinary kind of monotheism in which the two deities are both granted ultimacy. We can see in this the ongoing struggle between the epic's syncretist strand on the one side and sectarianism on the other.

The Pāncarātra Tradition

Remarkably, Vishnu retained his benign solar character throughout his long history. When the Pāncarātra tradition came into focus in the early post-Buddhist era, its votaries must have been able to look back upon a long and rich history of development, though its earliest beginnings are shrouded in darkness. From the moment of its clear emergence, the Pāncarātra tradition centered on Vishnu, especially in the form of the god Nārāyana.

Some scholars think of the Pāncarātra tradition as a relatively late offshoot of the Bhāgavata tradition (discussed below). This idea, however, fails to take into account that the idea of the archetypal self-sacrifice of the Primordial Man (*purusha*), as first enunciated in the *Rig-Veda* (10.90), is fundamental to the theology constructed around Nārāyana, who is the central object of worship of the Pāncarātra adherents.

The term *pāncarātra* ("five nights") and the name Nārāyana appear together for the first time in the *Shatapatha-Brāhmana* (13.6.1), a late Brāhmana that can be dated back to perhaps c. 1500 B.C.E. It is here that we find the explanation that the sage Nārāyana achieved divine status by means of a five-day sacrificial ritual (*sattra*). In other words, this is a clear statement about a human being having become divinized.

This is followed by a long pause in the available historical record before Nārāyana and the Pāncarātra tradition are mentioned again in the *Nārayanīya* section of the *Mahābhārata* (12.31–39). At least such is the scholarly consensus on this matter, which ignores the fact that there is the *Mahānārāyana-Upanishad*, which, because of its obvious syncretism, is generally placed in c. 300 B.C.E. but could well include more ancient materials. In this scripture, which belongs to the *Krishna-Yajur-Veda* and is also traditionally known as the *Yājnikī-Upanishad* ("Secret Teaching on the Sacrificial [Act]"), we find the following prayer (1.29):

> May we know Nārāyana. For that purpose, may we contemplate Vāsudeva. In that contemplation (*dhyāna*), may Vishnu impel us.

This prayer makes a close association between Nārāyana, Vāsudeva, and Vishnu. The three deities mentioned here are not separate entities but aspects of the same great Being, or even just three distinct names for the ultimate Singularity (*eka*).

Here mention must be made of the *Vishnu-Purāna,* one of the earliest works of the Puranic genre. This scripture is generally assigned to c. 300–400 C.E. and has been characterized as a Pāncarātra text preceding the Pāncarātra-Samhitā literature (see below). It seems to belong to the same age as the aforementioned *Nārayanīya* section of the *Mahābhārata.*

The Pāncarātra tradition is markedly monotheistic, and its followers are therefore commonly referred to as *ekāntins.* They are said to be able to enter directly into the Supreme—Vāsudeva—without having to first "realize" the various manifestations of the Divine known as *vyūhas,* or "emanations." Sometimes, this feature is taken to be a distinguishing characteristic, which demarcates the Pāncarātra tradition from Bhāgavatism and other Vaishnava schools of a "mixed type" of worship. Thus, one could say that the Pāncarātra avows radical monotheism.

The Pāncarātra philosophy entails important cosmological concepts of the Sāmkhya tradition, which, in conjunction with the theological *vyūha* model, are used to explain the process of world creation. Although the Ultimate is formless, it becomes accessible through its diverse emanations and manifestations. Activity, notably the dynamics of spiritual growth, is made possible through the Power (*shakti*) of Vishnu, the Divine. Thus, there is a pronounced Shakti element in the Pāncarātra system.

The four "forms" (*mūrti*) of God are Vāsudeva, Sankarshana (or Baladeva or Balarāma), Pradyumna, and Aniruddha, who, in turn, have many secondary emanations (or *vibhāva*). The first is the highest aspect, which gives rise to Sankarshana (sometimes equated with Shiva); Sankarshana gives birth to Pradyumna, who is responsible for the separation between the principle of awareness (*purusha*) and the principle of materiality (*prakriti*). Then emerges Aniruddha, who protects creation and guides humanity to enlightenment through wisdom.

In addition, the Divine has a number of "descents" (*avatāra*) into human form, notably Rāma and Krishna.

In the ritual dimension, the Pāncarātra tradition distinguishes itself from Vedic Brāhmanism by disallowing animal sacrifices and favoring the iconic worship of the Divine by means of harmless flower and water offerings. The influence of the Pāncarātra system can be seen by the prevalence of *pūjā* (ritual worship of a chosen deity) over the Vedic *yajna* (ritual sacrifice) in Hinduism.

As, for instance, the *Ahirbudhnya-Samhitā* makes clear, the Yoga method of the Pāncarātra system consists essentially in the devotee's total self-surrender to the Divine, as first taught in the *Bhagavad-Gītā.* In later Vaishnavism, this devotional practice is known as *prapatti* ("resignation").

It is a remarkable paradox that despite the *Gītā*'s emphasis on *ahimsā* (nonharming), it teaches a martial ethics. We will examine this peculiar teaching in detail later on.

Pāncarātra-Samhitās. In the period between perhaps 400 and 1200

C.E., the Pāncarātra adherents created, it is said, 108 Samhitās ("Collections")—in actual fact, over two hundred of them. The oldest, most esteemed, and most important are the *Sātvata-*, the *Paushkara-*, and the *Jayākhya-Samhitā*, which are known as the "Three Jewels" (*ratna-traya*). They were inscribed on birch bark and, because of this, appear to have been created in the Himalayan area of Kashmir, where writing on birch bark was common.

Among the slightly later Pāncarātra scriptures, the *Ahirbudhnya* (perhaps c. 800 C.E.) has a special place because of its detailed explication of Pāncarātra theology-philosophy. Portions of it have been translated into English, first by Otto Schrader (1916) and subsequently also by the Japanese scholar Mitsunori Matsubara (1994), a professor of Indology at Koyasan University.

The Sātvata Tradition

The *Mahābhārata* (6.66) refers to a *sātvata-vidhi*, or Sātvata method. Sātvata is also one of the names of Krishna, which refers to his royal lineage. We know that the Sātvatas were an important branch of the Yadu dynasty, which traced its origin back to Vishnu. It would appear that the Sātvatas were especially associated with two principal branches of Vaishnavism, Pāncarātra and Bhāgavata.

In his path-breaking book *Introduction to the Pāncarātra and the Ahirbudhnya-Samhitā* (1916), the German scholar F. Otto Schrader, who was the director of the well-known Adyar Library (near Chennai, India) at the time of publication, thought that *sātvata-vidhi* must refer to one of the Pāncarātra-Samhitās, which evolved in northern India. There is in fact a highly authoritative Pāncarātra scripture known under the title of *Sātvata-Samhitā*, and the extant text does indeed belong to the oldest group of scriptures of this genre. It has been dated to c. 400 C.E., which is one or two centuries later than the *Nārāyanīya* section of the *Mahābhārata*, placed about 200–300 B.C.E. The date 400 C.E., however, is purely conjectural. It is conceivable that this Samhitā contains material that is far older.

Vishnu is prominent in many parts of the *Mahābhārata* and also in the similarly dated *Rāmāyana* epic, which suggests the growing popularity of this deity. Many of the myths surrounding Vishnu were shaped at that time, though versions of at least some of them might have been in vogue long before then.

Bhāgavatism

The unorthodox Pāncarātra tradition, as witnessed prominently in the *Nārāyanīya* section of the *Mahābhārata,* is not the only religio-cultural current revolving around the worship of Vishnu/Nārāyana.

In addition to the Pāncarātra tradition, which can be found in both North and South India, Vishnu worship and lore are also endemic to the Bhāgavata tradition, with which the *Bhagavad-Gītā* is closely associated. The Bhāgavatas particularly focused on the worship of Vishnu in his manifestation or descent as Krishna. Bhāgavatism possibly originated with the cultic worship of an enlightened master named Krishna, mentioned as the son of Devakī in the old *Chāndogya-Upanishad,* but considered by some scholars to be different from the Krishna, also the son of Devakī, whose life is told in the *Bhāgavata-Purāna.*

The historical connection between the Bhāgavatas and the Pāncarātras is not entirely clear, but it appears that the two religious traditions have had multiple mutual influences from pre-Buddhist times (that is, prior to c. 500 B.C.E.) and that somehow the Sātvata/Yadu dynasty to which Krishna belonged played an instrumental role in their development.

As is apparent from the teachings of Krishna in the *Mahābhārata,* including the *Gītā,* this teacher had a somewhat uneasy relationship with the orthodox brahmanical community. The thrust of his teachings in fact favors the warrior (*kshatriya*) rather than the priestly class. For instance, in the *Bhagavad-Gītā* (2.42) Krishna critically mentions those "undiscerning [people who], delighting in the lore of the Vedas (*veda-vāda-rata*), utter flowery speech," which merely earns them reincarnation rather than liberation.

In verses 9.20–21, Krishna points to the knowers of the three Vedas (*Rig-*, *Yajur-*, and *Sāma-Veda*) who, by drinking their beloved *soma* concoction, are cleansed of sin but only arrive in the pleasurable heavenly region of Indra yet are still not liberated and must return to the world of mortals again and again.

In verse 9.11, Krishna hints at a controversy over himself even while he was still embodied. He refers to those who despise him in his human form because they are ignorant of his transcendental nature. To resolve Prince Arjuna's doubts, Krishna grants him—in Chapter 11—a mind-blowing mystical vision of his macrocosmic, or divine, nature ("cosmic consciousness"). Afterward, Krishna makes it clear (11.48) that study of the Vedas cannot possibly lead to such a supreme vision. Only love or utter devotion (*bhakti*) to him as the ultimate Being or Reality can guide a spiritual seeker to this sublime revelation.

Such is the testimony of a God-realized master, who traditionally is regarded as the Divine in human form. Krishna presented his teachings not as an innovation but as a revival of an age-old tradition, which originated with Krishna (4.1ff.), who imparted it to Vivasvat, the Sun. In claiming that he imparted these teachings from the most ancient times, Krishna identifies himself with Vishnu, as he does explicitly elsewhere (10.21): "Of the Ādityas [solar deities descended from Aditi or "Boundless," the mother of all deities], I am Vishnu."

The Bhāgavatas saw Krishna as previously having been incarnated as the great adept Nārāyana, and Arjuna as having been Nārāyana's disciple Nāra ("Human"). So there has been a long karmic link between Krishna and Arjuna, which is hinted at in the *Bhagavad-Gītā* (4.5) where Krishna affirms that while he is aware of all his incarnations, Arjuna is not aware of his own.

Bhāgavata-Purāna. Roughly about 900 C.E., the Bhāgavatas created the incredibly influential *Bhāgavata-Purāna,* also called *Shrīmad-Bhāgavata,* which is full of Krishnaite theology, mythology, and ritual. In a total of 335 chapters distributed over twelve books, it elaborates on the earthly life of Krishna as a cowherd. It stands out for its philosophical sophistication and refined Sanskrit. This scripture was made famous in the West by the Hare Krishna devotees from the International Society for Krishna Consciousness (ISKCON) under the spiritual leadership of A. C. Bhaktivedanta Swami (also known by the honorific Śrila Prabhupāda). The importance of this work can be judged from the huge number of Sanskrit commentaries on it. One of the finest sections of the *Bhāgavata-Purāna* (11.7–29) is the *Uddhava-Gītā,* which consists of an instructional dialogue between Krishna and the sage Uddhava.

Trimūrti

In medieval India, Vishnu came to be represented as one of the three aspects of the brahmanical theological construct of *trimūrti* ("triple form" or simply "trinity," from *tri* + *mūrti*). Benign Vishnu is given the role of Preserver of the universe, while Brahma is its Creator and Shiva its Destroyer. This is a core motif of classical (Puranic) Hinduism. Even though the trinity of Brahma-Vishnu-Shiva is often iconographically depicted—either with three heads on one neck or three faces on one head—it never achieved prominence in actual ritual worship.

This artificial construct must have had a certain appeal in specific periods, as India's great Sanskrit poet Kālidāsa, who has been compared to England's Shakespeare, composed a hymn in celebration of this triad.

The concept of *trimūrti* is first hinted at in the *Maitrāyanīya-Upanishad* (4.5–6 and 5.2), a later work composed perhaps in c. 300 B.C.E. Its appearance in the great epic is considered to be a late interpolation. Generally, the *Mahābhārata* treats the deities Brahma, Vishnu, and Shiva in rather fluid relationship, which would suggest that the mythological character of these three principal deities vis-à-vis each other was still in a process of definition.

The *trimūrti* can be understood as the end result of a long and convoluted process of synthesis between Vaishnavism, Shaivism, and Brāhmanism. It should not come as a surprise that early Western scholars of Hinduism, who tended to approach India with a Christian bias, should have been struck by the vague parallel between the Hindu triad of deities and the Christian Trinity.

Hari-Vamsha

Although Vishnu as Krishna is integral to the *Mahābhārata,* the epic recounts Krishna's elaborate life story only in a 16,000-verse appendix, the *Hari-Vamsha* ("Lineage of Hari [Krishna]"), which was composed perhaps c. 300 C.E. and has the quality of a Purāna. It stimulated the subsequent creation of the multivolume *Bhāgavata-Purāna,* which is entirely devoted to Krishna.

The Ārvārs

In the seventh to eighth century C.E., Vaishnavism took root in South India, where it was represented by the Ārvārs or Ālvārs—Tamil poets who advocated the great ideal of spiritual love-devotion (*bhakti*) to the divine Singularity in the form of Vishnu. As defined by the scholar Surendranath Dasgupta (1952, 68): "The word Ārvār means one who has a deep intuitive knowledge of God and one who is immersed in the contemplation of Him. The works of the Ārvārs are full of intense and devoted love for Visnu." The earliest of these honored figures are Saroyogin (Tamil: Poygaiy), Pūtayogin (Tamil: Bhūtatt'), Mahadyogin (Tamil: Pēy), and Bhaktisāra (Tamil: Tirumarisai Pirān). The best known are Nāmm, Periy, and the female saint Āndāl.

The Shrī-Vaishnava Tradition

In the eleventh century C.E., Vaishnavism experienced a major upswing at the hands of the long-lived teacher Rāmānuja (1017–1137 C.E.), the founder of the Shrī-Vaishnava tradition. He was a vigorous champion of Pāncarātra teachings and rituals. Wherever this widely traveled teacher went, he sought to replace existing orthodox Vaikhānasa liturgy with the unorthodox Pāncarātra forms of worship, which were considered odious by the orthodox Vedic priesthood. The term *vaikhānasa* refers to a forest-dwelling ascetic and his lifestyle, as stipulated by the Vedic orthodoxy.

The Kashmiri Recension of the *Gītā*

There are two main recensions of the *Gītā*: the vulgate and the Kashmiri. The vulgate version as adopted and passed down by the famous philosopher Shankarācārya, or Shankara (author of the earliest extant commentary on the *Gītā*), consists of 700 stanzas (*shloka*). There is also a recension current in Kashmir that was commented upon, for example, by the Shaiva master and scholar Abhinavagupta (born mid-eleventh century C.E.), which contains fifteen additional verses not present in the vulgate; it has been translated into English by Boris Marjanovic (2006). That the *Gītā,* a work of Vaishnavism, had become very popular by c. 1050 C.E. can be seen from Abhinavagupta's commentary, which is written from the perspective of Kashmir Shaivism rather than Vaishnavism.

Unlike the preceptors of Advaita Vedānta (Absolute Nondualism), Abhinavagupta believed that the universe is not illusory but real, and in this respect he reflects the *Gītā* more faithfully than other interpreters.

Also, from the perspective of Advaita Vedānta, action (*kriyā*) is part of the illusory universe and utterly absent from the ultimate Reality. By contrast, Kashmir Shaivism affirms that action is not an imperfection but inherent in the ultimate Reality. Therefore, action is not contrary to enlightenment.

Abhinavagupta commented only on certain stanzas, focusing on those on which he could offer deeper insights or practical esoteric instructions.

Traditional "Imitation" *Gītās* and Translations

The great popularity of the *Gītā* within premodern Hinduism can be gauged from the number of "imitations," which include the *Anu-Gītā*

(*Mahābhārata* 6.13–40, presented as a recapitulation of Krishna's teachings given on the battlefield), the *Uddhāva-Gītā* (*Bhāgavata-Purāna* 11.6–29), the *Shiva-Gītā* (*Padma-Purāna* 5, consisting of sixteen chapters with a total of 806 verses), the *Ganesha-Gītā* (*Ganesha-Purāna* 1.138–148), and the *Brahma-Gītā* (*Yoga-Vāsishtha* 6.53–58).

Early on, the *Gītā* was translated into Sanskrit-derived vernacular Indian languages along with the rest of the *Mahābhārata,* and from there the *Gītā*'s teachings found their way into other languages and cultures.

Some five hundred years ago the *Mahābhārata,* including the *Gītā,* was translated into Persian, and some one hundred years ago the *Gītā* was translated into Arabic. In the mid-twentieth century the Makhan Lal Roy Choudhury, a professor of Islamic history and culture at the University of Calcutta, prepared a new Arabic translation.[4]

Since the seventeenth century, Hindu wisdom has found its way into the hands of Westerners. The very first rendering into a European language (English) was prepared by Sir Charles Wilkins and published as early as 1785. Wilkins started out as a "writer" in the Bengal service and was the first to cast types in the Bengali and Persian scripts. He has been deemed the first European to really understand Sanskrit. His rendering influenced the growing class of English-speaking Indians.

A Greek translation was made in 1802 (but not printed until 1849) by Demetrios Galanos, a scholar who lived in India for many years.

A Latin rendering of selections from the *Gītā* was undertaken by the German linguist Otto Frank in 1820. Three years later, the renowned philosopher and poet August Wilhelm von Schlegel brought out his complete Latin rendering of the *Gītā.* He spoke of this work as "a sublime mixture of poetic and philosophical genius." In 1834, C. R. S. Peiper translated the *Gītā* into German, and Christian Lassen rendered it into French in 1846. These efforts were followed by many others.

The important point to appreciate is that this text, written in what is now an obscure language, has won an appreciative worldwide readership. Perhaps the peak of its dissemination outside of India was reached when copies of the English translation by Śrila Prabhupāda, founder of the ISKCON movement, were distributed by Hare Krishna monastics at Western airports and other public venues. The ISKCON movement, though reckoned among the so-called New Religions, is really an offshoot

4. M. L. R. Choudhury, *Al-Kitab* (Calcutta: Thacker Spink, 1951).

of the theistic Vedānta school of Caitanya, a saintly Hindu ecstatic of the fifteenth century.

The Influence of the *Gītā* on Buddhism

Although Hinduism's Krishna devotees claim the *Gītā* as an authoritative scripture for their own tradition, the influence of this comparatively small work—only 700 verses—has extended far beyond the boundaries of Vaishnavism and has even left its mark on some schools of Mahāyāna Buddhism. According to Sarvepalli Radhakrishnan (1948, p. 11n), the *Gītā* influenced both the *Saddharma-Pundarīka* ("Lotus of the True Law"),[5] which is part of the Prajnā-Pāramitā ("Perfection of Wisdom") literature and may date back to c. 100 B.C.E., and the *Mahāyāna-Shraddhā-Utpatti* (*Mahāyānashraddhotpatti,* "Awakening of Faith in the Great Vehicle), attributed to Ashvaghosha, who lived c. 100 C.E.[6]

There also is a curious parallelism between the *Gītā* and the popular Pali Buddhist text *Dhamma-Pada* (Sanskrit: *Dharma-Pāda*), which belongs to the early Buddhist corpus of writings and is assigned to c. 400 B.C.E. Some authorities have argued that Buddhism inspired some of the thinking found in the *Gītā.*[7] They typically refer to the fact that the *Gītā* employs the word *nirvāna,* which is said to belong exclusively to the vocabulary and philosophy of Buddhism. This need not necessarily be so, however. It is at least equally likely that the term *nirvāna* was current in Indian philosophical circles at the time of the Buddha, and he simply availed himself of it and gave it its unique Buddhist flavor. As I explain in my translation of the *Gītā,* the concept of *brahma-nirvāna* found in four places in this scripture (2.72; 5.24–26) has a specific non-Buddhist (Sāmkhya-Yoga) meaning. Perhaps the *Gītā* and the *Dhamma-Pada* are best regarded as springing from the same fertile intellectual soil, the former more particularly articulating the Vaishnava heritage and the latter the Buddhist legacy.

5. For an early English rendering, see Kern 1963.
6. The attribution of this influential scripture to Ashvaghosha has been challenged by several scholars, notably from Japan. The absence of the Sanskrit text makes it difficult to settle the question, and it is conceivable that the original text was written in Chinese. See Aśvaghoṣa 1908 (trans. Richard); see also Aśvaghosha 1967 (trans. Hakeda).
7. Recently, John Clifford Holt argued that the ethical dialogue between Krishna and Arjuna "is, no doubt, of Buddhist inspiration." *The Buddhist Viṣṇu: Religious Transformation, Politics, and Culture* (New York: Columbia University Press, 2004), p. 11. As Holt acknowledged (p. 19), this point was made long ago by Swami Vivekananda, the great Hindu "missionary," whose presentation on Hinduism at the 1893 Parliament of Religions in Chicago was a great success.

To be sure, the Sāmkhya-Yoga tradition, which is captured in the *Gītā,* was at one time the most formidable opponent of Buddhism, but we may with reasonable certainty assume that the former preceded the latter. We can detect the beginnings of Sāmkhya-Yoga already in certain hymns of the *Rig-Veda* (especially 10.90 and 10.129), which date back to the third millennium B.C.E. The Pāncarātra tradition, which contained basic Sāmkhya-Yoga ideas, was probably widespread at the time of the Buddha, one of whose two major teachers, Ārāda Kālāpa (Ālāro Kālāmo in Pali), is thought to have belonged to the (Sāmkhya-)Yoga tradition, as presented especially in Chapter 2 of the *Gītā.*

9

On Translating the *Bhagavad-Gītā*

THE *Bhagavad-Gītā* is a fairly short Sanskrit scripture composed in preclassical Sanskrit between 400 and 300 B.C.E. Many of its seven hundred melodious verses are straightforward, but not a few are neither linguistically simple nor philosophically readily comprehended. It is undoubtedly the simple verses and the overall dramatic setting of this scripture that allowed this text to enjoy growing popularity over the centuries. To be sure, some stanzas are downright problematic for any translator and call for deeper study. Popular translations tend to gloss over these difficulties and often end up misrepresenting the Sanskrit original.

The present rendering of the *Bhagavad-Gītā* is based on Shripad Krishna Belvalkar's (1947) critical edition of the *Mahābhārata* epic, and it includes interesting variant verses found in some of the Sanskrit manuscripts collated by Belvalkar and his team of scholars.

This translation differs from most others in at least one important respect: it is far more literal than previous renderings in order to preserve as much of the idiosyncrasies and intended meanings of the original as possible. Some translators have argued that literalness obscures rather than illuminates the meaning of the Sanskrit text and that its intent is better preserved by a free rendering. This objection, however, merely seems to have served as an excuse for bypassing a critical examination of both text and context.

Glancing at the vast available literature on the *Bhagavad-Gītā*, one can distinguish several major approaches in the translation/interpretation of this ancient scripture.

1. The earliest attempt to make the *Bhagavad-Gītā* accessible to the English public was the 1785 rendering by Charles Wilkins (which was translated into French by Abbé M. Parraud in 1787). Wilkins's translation has

all the shortcomings of a first-time rendering. He left many Sanskrit terms untranslated or poorly transliterated (e.g., "moonee" for *muni*), and he also chose something of a biblical style, peppered with Latin words, which are unlikely to be familiar to the modern Western reader. This translation in a way gave rise to three distinct but often overlapping approaches: (1) the philological/antiquarian approach, (2) the spiritual/hortatory orientation, and (3) the poetic approach.

2. Characteristic of the first category, which is chiefly concerned with grammatical accuracy and scholarly minutiae, are the early translations by August Wilhelm von Schlegel (1823), Christian Lassen (1846), Kashinath Trimbak Telang (1882; included as volume 8 in F. Max Müller's famous *Sacred Books of the East* series), Richard Garbe (1905), and Franklin Edgerton (1925). Here also belong the twentieth-century translations, among others, by Sarvepalli Radhakrishnan (1948), R. C. Zaehner (1966), J. A. B. van Buitenen (1973–1975), Kees Bolle (1979), and Richard Gotshalk (1985).

3. Representative of the second group are renderings like those of Swami Prabhavananda and Christopher Isherwood (1944) and Bhaktivedanta Swami (1983). To this category belong also many of the translations that retain a more traditionalist outlook and are far less sensitive to the textual and semantic complexities of the *Gītā*. An exceptional work in this group is the study by Krishna Prem (1938). The central weakness of the spiritual/hortatory approach is its distinct disinterest in philological/historical matters.

4. Largely in response to the philological/antiquarian approach, which was felt to downplay the *Gītā*'s aesthetic beauty, some students of the *Gītā* launched into a poetic treatment of the text. The generally defective linguistic and philosophical treatment found in such works is due to the uncompromising subjugation of the criteria of meaning and accuracy to principles of meter, rhyme, and rhythm. The best-known poetic paraphrase is that by Edwin Arnold (1939). More recent attempts are those by Geoffrey Parrinder (1974) and Juan Mascaró (1962).

5. Still further removed from the original meaning of the *Bhagavad-Gītā* is the spawning popular literature, which is lacking in interpretative power, accuracy, and beauty. This could almost be thought of as constituting a separate approach were it not for its defectiveness.

To demonstrate the weakness of emphatically poetic translations, I wish to single out Juan Mascaró's (1962) rendering. See, for instance, his translation of verse 2.47:

> Set thy heart upon thy work, but never on the reward thereof.
> Work not for a reward; but never cease to do thy work.

This does not at all reflect the profound spirit of the original. The Sanskrit text literally says:

> In action alone is your rightful-interest, never in [its] fruit. Let not your motive be the fruit of action; nor let your attachment be to inaction.

Mascaró gets the first half right, providing we do not ask what specifically is meant by "reward." But he misses the point of the second hemistich. The phrase "never cease to do thy work" should properly be rendered as "nor let your attachment be to inaction"—which is somewhat different. For the *Bhagavad-Gītā* is primarily interested in our *attitude* toward the performance of actions. It is concerned with our attachment or nonattachment to things. Inaction may be appropriate under certain conditions, just as action may prove to be the right course (which it frequently is). This does not come across in Mascaró's version.

Another example is verse 7.30, which Mascaró misinterprets thus:

> They know me in earth and in heaven, and in the fire of sacrifice. Their souls are pure, in harmony, and even when their time to go comes they see me.

As opposed to this, Krishna's actual words are:

> Those yoked-minded [*yogins*] who know Me [as] the elemental-basis, [as] the divine-basis, along with the sacrificial-basis, and [who know] Me also at the time of going-forth [i.e., at death]—[they indeed] know.

The important and undoubtedly difficult Sanskrit terms *adhibhūta, adhidaiva,* and *adhiyajna* cannot simply be equated with "earth," "heaven" and "fire of sacrifice" respectively. No straightforward equivalent renderings are possible in English, and so I am using admittedly awkward circumscriptions, such as "elemental-basis," "divine-basis," and "sacrificial-basis." Also, the phrase "their souls are pure" cannot be found in the Sanskrit original at all. Such instances of textual misrepresentation could easily be multiplied, also from other renderings.

With hundreds of *Gītā* translations into English and other languages in existence (if not all in print), it would be foolhardy to think that any one translation could possibly be final. Therefore, the most I can claim for my own rendering is that it is based on my earnest effort to capture as much as possible of the spirit of this time-honored work and also to do justice to its language as best I could, though realizing that my approach of textual and contextual fidelity cannot also at the same time reflect the *Gītā*'s melodious quality.

Devices Used in the Translation

In an attempt to do justice to the message of the *Gītā*, I have introduced several devices that will enable readers to judge for themselves where the dividing line is between translation and interpretation.

Thus, I have made extensive use of hyphens, parentheses, and brackets:

Whenever a Sanskrit word has implied meanings that I felt deserved spelling out, I have availed myself of hyphenated phrases, such as "own-law" for *svadharma,* "own-being" for *svabhāva,* "basis-of-self" (*adhyātman*), "elemental-basis" (*adhibhūta*), "divine-basis" (*adhidaiva*), "sacrificial-basis" (*adhiyajna*), "primary-quality" (*guna*), "world-ground" (*brahman*), "son-of-Pāndu" (*pāndava*), "descendant-of-Bharata" (*bhārata*), "all-that-is-born" (*jāta*), "what-is-all-too-human" (*mānushya*), and so forth. The parsed transliterated and explained text forming Part Three allows readers to follow my reasoning for such constructs and my translation in general.

Sanskrit terms added to clarify the translation appear in parentheses.

Words enclosed in square brackets are mainly interpolations: words that are not actually found in the Sanskrit original but are required in translation in order to convey the meaning of the habitually concise Sanskrit sentences. This method provides the reader with a reliable yardstick against which to check other translations. In a few instances, the bracketed words are purely explanatory.

For their convenience, readers may simply ignore the brackets used in the present rendering. They are intended to give those with an interest in Sanskrit a clearer sense of which words—apart from grammatically required words like "is," "the," or "of"—are not actually present in the original text. Ignoring the brackets, though not the words within them, yields grammatically correct as well as meaningful sentences.

I capitalize words such as *Self* or *Reality* to indicate where such words suggest transcendence. I extend this practice to the personal pronouns *Me* and *Mine* when the God-man Krishna refers to himself.

Word Choices

Sanskrit has a remarkably vast vocabulary, and an abundance especially of psychological terms. Thus, although I have endeavored to use the same English equivalent for a given Sanskrit term, this has not always been possible or even advisable. For instance, I have translated the term *kāraṅa* as "cause," "instrument," "means," or "sake" to make sense of the context. Also, I have used "mind" for the following terms: *manas, cetas, citta, mānasa.* Another instance is *prakriti,* which most of the time has the sense of "Cosmos" but in some stanzas (e.g., 3.33) must be assigned the general meaning of "nature."

There are some semantically less charged words for which I have used the same English term to avoid awkwardness. For instance, *apajāyate* (2.65), *bhavati* (additional verse after 3.37), and *prabhavati* (8.19) have all been given the meaning of "it arises" when that seemed best.

The important term *dharma* I have uniformly translated as "law," allowing the context to color each particular instance of use. On occasion, I have even allowed the Sanskrit term to stand untranslated.

Regarding the frequent terms *ātman* and *purusha,* I have for the sake of convenience used "Self" for the former and "Spirit" for the latter, unless *purusha* clearly stands for "person," "man," or "Primordial Man." The term *ātman* involves the additional difficulty that it can refer either to the transcendental "Self" or to the empirical "self," as well as stand for the reflexive pronoun "oneself," "itself," and so on. Moreover, I have as much as possible retained the use of plural or singular in accordance with the Sanskrit original, even at the risk of allowing the rendering to sound a little awkward at times. Although words like *eva* are perhaps mostly used in order to meet metric requirements, they may occasionally serve to emphasize a point, but this is not always clear. I have rendered *eva* variously as "verily," or "indeed." Similarly, I have translated the indeclinable *tu* as "but" as well as "indeed." At times these words have been omitted from the translation, as indicated in the word-for-word section in Part Three.

Part Two

Bhagavad-Gītā

TRANSLATION, WITH SANSKRIT TEXT
AND TRANSLITERATION

satyaṃ vada dharmaṃ cara

Speak the truth; cultivate virtue.

—*Taittirīya-Upaniṣad* 1.2.1

धृतराष्ट्र उवाच
धर्मक्षेत्रे कुरुक्षेत्रे समवेता युयुत्सवः ।
मामकाः पाण्डवाश्चैव कमकुर्वत संजय ॥ १—१ ॥
संजय उवाच
दृष्ट्वा तु पाण्डवानीकं व्यूढं दुर्योधनस्तदा ।
आचार्यमुपसंगम्य राजा वचनमब्रवीत् ॥ १—२ ॥
पश्यैतां पाण्डुपुत्राणामाचार्य महतीं चमूम् ।
व्यूढां द्रुपदपुत्रेण तव शिष्येण धीमता ॥ १—३ ॥
अत्र शूरा महेष्वासा भीमार्जुनसमा युधि ।
युयुधानो विराटश्च द्रुपदश्च महारथः ॥ १—४ ॥
धृष्टकेतुश्चेकितानः काशिराजश्च वीर्यवान् ।
पुरुजित्कुन्तिभोजश्च शैब्यश्च नरपुङ्गवः ॥ १—५ ॥
युधामन्युश्च विक्रान्त उत्तमौजाश्च वीर्यवान् ।
सौभद्रो द्रौपदेयाश्च सर्व एव महारथाः ॥ १—६ ॥
अस्माकं तु विशिष्टा ये तान्निबोध द्विजोत्तम ।
नायका मम सैन्यस्य संज्ञार्थं तान्ब्रवीमि ते ॥ १—७ ॥

dhṛtarāṣṭra uvāca

1. dharmakṣetre kurukṣetre samavetā yuyutsavaḥ
   māmakāḥ pāṇḍavāś caiva kim akurvata saṃjaya

   saṃjaya uvāca

2. dṛṣṭvā tu pāṇḍavānīkaṃ vyūḍhaṃ duryodhanas tadā
   ācāryam upasaṃgamya rājā vacanam abravīt
3. paśyaitāṃ pāṇḍuputrāṇām ācārya mahatīṃ camūm
   vyūḍhāṃ drupadaputreṇa tava śiṣyeṇa dhīmatā
4. atra śūrā maheṣvāsā bhīmārjunasamā yudhi
   yuyudhāno virāṭaś ca drupadaś ca mahārathaḥ
5. dhṛṣṭaketuś cekitānaḥ kāśirājaś ca vīryavān
   purujit kuntibhojaś ca śaibyaś ca narapuṃgavaḥ
6. yudhāmanyuś ca vikrānta uttamaujaś ca vīryavān
   saubhadro draupadeyāś ca sarva eva mahārathāḥ
7. asmākaṃ tu viśiṣṭā ye tān nibodha dvijottama
   nāyakā mama sainyasya saṃjñārthaṃ tān bravīmi te

CHAPTER I

The Yoga of Arjuna's Despondency

[The blind king] Dhritarāshtra said:

1.1 On the *dharma* field, the Kuru field, my [men] and the [five] sons-of-Pāndu were assembled, eager to fight. What did they do, Samjaya?

Samjaya [minister to the blind king] said:

1.2 Seeing the ranks of the sons-of-Pāndu lined up, Prince Duryodhana [of the Kauravas] approached his preceptor [Drona] and spoke these words:

1.3 Preceptor, behold this vast army of the sons-of-Pāndu arrayed by the son of Drupada [Drishtadyumna], your wise disciple.

1.4 Here are heroes, great archers, equal in battle (*yudha*) to Bhīma and Arjuna—Yuyudhāna, Virāta, and Drupada, the grand chariot-warrior;

1.5 Dhrishtaketu, Cekitāna, and the valiant king of the Kāshis, Purujit, Kuntibhoja and Shaibya, a bull among men;

1.6 the courageous Yudhāmanyu and the valiant Uttamaujas, the son-of-Subhadrā [named Abhimanyu] and the [five] sons-of-Draupadī, all great chariot-warriors.[1]

1.7 Learn also, O best of the twice-born,[2] of those who are [most] excellent among us, the leaders of my army. I name them for you by [their] proper names.

1. Here the phrase *mahā-rathāh* (lit. "great chariots") refers not to a chariot but to the skillful master of a chariot (*ratha-īsha*). He is not the same as the charioteer (*rathin*). Thus, Arjuna was the master of a chariot, while Krishna, who did not actually fight in the Bharata war, served as his charioteer. The warriors—heroes one and all—mentioned in the following stanzas have their own stories and are discussed in the distance-learning course on the *Bhagavad-Gītā* administered by Traditional Yoga Studies, www.traditionalyogastudies.com.

2. "Twice-born" (*dvija*)—from *dvi* ("twice") and *ja* ("born")—refers to the higher classes of traditional India's class hierarchy: *brāhmanas* (priestly elite), *kshatriyas* (military estate), and *vaishyas* (merchants/artisans/peasants). These are deemed "born" a second time through the formal process of investiture with the sacred thread. The class of the *shūdras* (servile estate) is exempted from this privilege.

भवान्भीष्मश्च कर्णश्च कृपश्च समितिंजयः ।
अश्वत्थामा विकर्णश्च सौमदत्तिस्तथैव च ॥ १—८ ॥
अन्ये च बहवः शूरा मदर्थे त्यक्तजीविताः ।
नानाशस्त्रप्रहरणाः सर्वे युद्धविशारदाः ॥ १—९ ॥
अपर्याप्तं तदस्माकं बलं भीष्माभिरक्षितम् ।
पर्याप्तं त्विदमेतेषां बलं भीमाभिरक्षितम् ॥ १—१० ॥
अयनेषु च सर्वेषु यथाभागमवस्थिताः ।
भीष्ममेवाभिरक्षन्तु भवन्तः सर्व एव हि ॥ १—११ ॥
तस्य संजनयन्हर्षं कुरुवृद्धः पितामहः ।
सिंहनादं विनद्योच्चैः शङ्खं दध्मौ प्रतापवान् ॥ १—१२ ॥
ततः शङ्खाश्च भेर्यश्च पणवानकगोमुखाः ।
सहसैवाभ्यहन्यन्त स शब्दस्तुमुलोऽभवत् ॥ १—१३ ॥
ततः श्वेतैर्हयैर्युक्ते महति स्यन्दने स्थितौ ।
माधवः पाण्डवश्चैव दिव्यौ शङ्खौ प्रदध्मतुः ॥ १—१४ ॥

8. bhavān bhīṣmaś ca karṇaś ca kṛpaś ca samitiṃjayaḥ
aśvatthāmā vikarṇaś ca saumadattis tathaiva ca
9. anye ca bahavaḥ śūrā madarthe tyaktajīvitāḥ
nānāśastrapraharaṇāḥ sarve yuddhaviśāradāḥ
10. aparyāptaṃ tad asmākaṃ balaṃ bhīṣmābhirakṣitam
paryāptaṃ tv idam eteṣāṃ balaṃ bhīmābhirakṣitam
11. ayaneṣu ca sarveṣu yathābhāgam avasthitāḥ
bhīṣmam evābhirakṣantu bhavantaḥ sarva eva hi
12. tasya saṃjanayan harṣaṃ kuruvṛddhaḥ pitāmahaḥ
siṃhanādaṃ vinadyocchaiḥ śaṅkhaṃ dadhmau pratāpavān
13. tataḥ śaṅkhāś ca bheryaś ca paṇavānakagomukhāḥ
sahasaivābhyahanyanta sa śabdas tumulo'bhavat
14. tataḥ śvetair hayair yukte mahati syandane sthitau
mādhavaḥ pāṇḍavaś caiva divyau śaṅkhau pradadhmatuḥ

1.8 Yourself, Bhīshma, Karna, and Kripa, victorious in combat, Ashvatthāman, Vikarna, and also the son-of-Somadatta,

1.9 and many other heroes who [are ready to] lay down their life for my sake. Various are their assailing weapons, and all are skilled in battle.

1.10 Unlimited is this our force guarded by Bhīshma, yet that force of theirs, guarded by Bhīma, [appears] limited.[3]

1.11 [Addressing all warriors, Prince Duryodhana continued:] In all maneuvers positioned as appointed, verily, every one of you guard Bhīshma!

1.12 [Samjaya said:] To give him [Duryodhana] joy, the aged grandsire of the Kurus [Bhīshma] powerfully blew his conch, raising on high [a sound like] a lion's roar.

1.13 Then suddenly conches, kettledrums, cymbals, trumpets, and drums were sounded; the uproar was tumultuous.

1.14 Then, standing in their great chariot yoked to white steeds, Mādhava[4] [Krishna] and the son-of-Pāndu [Arjuna] also blew their divine conchs.

3. The vulgate reading of this verse is problematic, because it implies that the Kauravas' huge army under Bhīshma is smaller (more "limited") than the Pāndavas' under Bhīma, which, according to other epic passages, is incorrect. I have therefore opted for an available alternate reading, which was already known to the post-Shankara commentator Bhāskara (ninth century): *aparyāpta tad asmākam balam bhīma-abhirakshitam / paryāptam tv idam eteshām balam bhīshma-abhirakshitam.* This reading was also accepted by the great Kashmiri scholar and master Abhinavagupta.

4. The name Mādhava can be understood either as "descendant-of-Madhu" or "relating to [the slayer of the demon called] Madhu." Madhu was a king of the lunar lineage to which Krishna belonged. In regard to the latter meaning, compare Krishna's epithet Madhusūdana (see, e.g., 1.35), which means literally "slayer of [the demon] Madhu": Here it means Krishna.

पाञ्चजन्यं हृषीकेशो देवदत्तं धनंजयः ।
पौण्ड्रं दध्मौ महाशङ्खं भीमकर्मा वृकोदरः ॥ १—१५ ॥
अनन्तविजयं राजा कुन्तीपुत्रो युधिष्ठिरः ।
नकुलः सहदेवश्च सुघोषमणिपुष्पकौ ॥ १—१६ ॥
काश्यश्च परमेष्वासः शिखण्डी च महारथः ।
धृष्टद्युम्नो विराटश्च सात्यकिश्चापराजितः ॥ १—१७ ॥
द्रुपदो द्रौपदेयाश्च सर्वशः पृथिवीपते ।
सौभद्रश्च महाबाहुः शङ्खान्दध्मुः पृथक्पृथक् ॥ १—१८ ॥

15. pāñcajanyaṃ hṛṣīkeśo devadattaṃ dhanaṃjayaḥ
    pauṇḍraṃ dadhmau mahāśaṅkhaṃ bhīmakarmā vṛkodaraḥ
16. anantavijayaṃ rājā kuntīputro yudhiṣṭhiraḥ
    nakulaḥ sahadevaś ca sughoṣamaṇipuṣpakau
17. kāśyaś ca parameṣvāsaḥ śikhaṇḍī ca mahārathaḥ
    dhṛṣṭadyumno virāṭaś ca sātyakiś cāparājitaḥ
18. drupado draupadeyāś ca sarvaśaḥ pṛthivīpate
    saubhadraś ca mahābāhuḥ śaṅkhān dadhmuḥ pṛthak-pṛthak

1.15 Hrishīkesha[5] [Krishna] blew Pāncajanya,[6] Dhanamjaya[7] [Arjuna] [blew] Devadatta;[8] the wolf-bellied[9] doer-of-fearful-deeds [Bhīma] blew the great conch Paundra.[10]

1.16 [The conch called] Anantavijaya[11] [was sounded by] the son-of-Kuntī, Yudhishthira the [rightful] king; Nakula and Sahadeva [blew] Sughosha[12] and Manipushpaka.[13]

1.17 And the Kāshi-king, supreme archer, and Shikhandin,[14] the grand chariot-warrior, and Dhrishtadyumna, Virāta, and Sātyaki, the unconquered,

1.18 Drupada and the sons-of-Draupadī, O Lord of the Earth, as well as the mighty-armed son-of-Subhadrā—all together they each blew [his own] conch.

5. Some of the ancient commentators derive the name Hrishīkesha from *hrishīka-īsha* or "lord of the senses," but this etymology is more esoteric than literal. The literal meaning is "[he whose] hair (*kesha*) is bristling [from excitement or ecstatic thrill]," that is, "he whose hair stands on end."
6. The importance of conchs can be seen from the fact that they were given individual names. *Pāncajanya* literally means "relating to Pancajana." After killing the demon Pancajana, who lived inside a conch, Krishna appropriated the conch.
7. This epithet of Arjuna means literally "conqueror of wealth" (*dhanam-jaya*), referring either to material or spiritual booty.
8. The conch named Devadatta ("God-given") was Indra's present to Prince Arjuna.
9. The phrase "wolf-bellied" refers to brawny Bhīma's enormous appetite.
10. Bhīma's conch, Paundra, derives its name from a tribe that fought on the side of the Pāndavas.
11. *Ananta-vijaya* means "endless victory." One can see this as a hidden reference to *dharma,* which is always victorious and which is the very essence of Yudhishthira, who, as noted earlier, was sired by the god Dharma. (See Part One, chapter 3, "Dramatis Personae of the *Gītā*").
12. *Sughosha* derives from "good" (*su*) and "sound," and can be rendered as "good-sounding" or, more poetically, "sweet-toned."
13. *Mani-pushpaka* means "gem-flowered."
14. Shikhandin accomplished the feat of killing the otherwise invincible Bhīshma, because Bhīshma would not fight a woman. In his immediately preceding life, the valiant male warrior Shikhandin was Ambā, a daughter of the ruler of Kāshi (modern Varanasi). In that lifetime, she was supposed to marry Bhīshma but he declined, because he had vowed never to marry. The one with whom she was in love also rejected her. She took to the forest and practiced severe austerities. All the while she was irrationally resentful of Bhīshma and was intend on destroying him. When, as a result of her ascetic practices, Shiva manifested in front of her and prophesied that she would be reborn as a man and then kill Bhīshma, she promptly immolated herself. On the tenth day of the war, Ambā reborn as Shikhandin managed to pierce Bhīshma's chest with ten arrows. To the end, Bhīshma thought of Shikhandin as a woman and taunted that warrior as such. He yogically delayed his inevitable death from the severe wounds by ten days to ensure that he would leave this earth at an auspicious moment.

स घोषो धार्तराष्ट्राणां हृदयानि व्यदारयत् ।
नभश्च पृथिवीं चैव तुमुलो व्यनुनादयन् ॥ १—१९ ॥
अथ व्यवस्थितान्दृष्ट्वा धार्तराष्ट्रान्कपिध्वजः ।
प्रवृत्ते शस्त्रसंपाते धनुरुद्यम्य पाण्डवः ॥ १—२० ॥
हृषीकेशं तदा वाक्यमिदमाह महीपते ।
सेनयोरुभयोर्मध्ये रथं स्थापय मेऽच्युत ॥ १—२१ ॥
यावदेतान्निरीक्षेऽहं योद्धुकामानवस्थितान् ।
कैर्मया सह योद्धव्यमस्मिन् रणसमुद्यमे ॥ १—२२ ॥
योत्स्यमानानवेक्षेऽहं य एतेऽत्र समागताः ।
धार्तराष्ट्रस्य दुर्बुद्धेर्युद्धे प्रियचिकीर्षवः ॥ १—२३ ॥
एवमुक्तो हृषीकेशो गुडाकेशेन भारत ।
सेनयोरुभयर्मध्ये स्थापयित्वा रथोत्तमम् ॥ १—२४ ॥
भीष्मद्रोणप्रमुखतः सर्वेषां च महीक्षिताम् ।
उवाच पार्थ पश्यैतान्समवेतान्कुरूनिति ॥ १—२५ ॥
तत्रापश्यत्स्थितान्पार्थः पितॄनथ पितामहान् ।
आचार्यान्मातुलान्भ्रातॄन्पुत्रान्पौत्रान्सखींस्तथा ॥ १—२६ ॥

19. sa ghoṣo dhārtarāṣṭrāṇāṃ hṛdayāni vyadārayat
    nabhaś ca pṛthivīṃ caiva tumulo vyanunādayan
20. atha vyavasthitān dṛṣṭvā dhārtarāṣṭrān kapidhvajaḥ
    pravṛtte śastrasaṃpāte dhanur udyamya pāṇḍavaḥ
21. hṛṣīkeśaṃ tadā vākyam idam āha mahīpate
    senayor ubhayor madhye rathaṃ sthāpaya me'cyuta
22. yāvad etān nirīkṣe'haṃ yoddhukāmān avasthitān
    kair mayā saha yoddhavyam asmin raṇasamudyame
23. yotsyamānān avekṣe'haṃ ya ete'tra samāgatāḥ
    dhārtarāṣṭrasya durbuddher yuddhe priyacikīrṣavaḥ
    [saṃjaya uvāca]
24. evam ukto hṛṣīkeśo guḍākeśena bhārata
    senayor ubhayor madhye sthāpayitvā rathottamam
25. bhīṣmadroṇapramukhataḥ sarveṣāṃ ca mahīkṣitām
    uvāca pārtha paśyaitān samavetān kurūn iti
26. tatrāpaśyat sthitān pārthaḥ pitṛn atha pitāmahān
    ācāryān mātulān bhrātṛn putrān pautrān sakhīṃs tathā

1.19 That uproar pierced the hearts of the sons-of-Dhritarāshtra, making sky and earth resound tumultuously.

1.20 Then, beholding the sons-of-Dhritarāshtra in array, the ape-bannered[15] son-of-Pāndu [Arjuna] took up his bow at the clash of weapons.

1.21 Then, O Lord of the Earth, he addressed Hrishīkesha [Krishna] with these words:

Halt my chariot in the middle between both armies, O Acyuta,[16]

1.22 so that I may survey those who are assembled, eager for battle, [and see] with whom I must fight in this enterprise of combat (*rāna*).

1.23 I behold those here assembled, ready to fight and desirous to please the evil-minded sons-of-Dhritarāshtra in battle (*yuddha*).

[Samjaya said:]

1.24 Thus addressed by Gudākesha[17] [Arjuna], Hrishīkesha brought that excellent chariot to a halt between both armies, O descendant-of-Bharata.

1.25 In front of Bhīshma, Drona, and all the [other] rulers of the earth, he said:

O son-of-Prithā,[18] behold these Kurus assembled [here].

1.26 Standing there, the son-of-Prithā saw fathers, grandfathers, preceptors, uncles, brothers, sons, grandsons, as well as comrades,

15. Arjuna's banner depicted an ape (*kapi*), more specifically the ape king Hanumat (nominative: Hanumān). Hanumat is a son of the God of Wind. Thus, symbolically, Hanumat represents the breath, which Krishna asked Arjuna to master in order to control his mind (see, e.g., 5.28).
16. Acyuta, another epithet of Krishna, means "unfallen," that is, unwavering and imperishable.
17. Gudākesha means "[he whose] hair [is twisted into] a ball," that is, "he who is wearing a top-knot." The esoteric meaning is "[he who has] conquered sleep."
18. In Arjuna's epithet "son-of-Prithā" (Pārtha), Prithā is another name for Kuntī, the mother of the five Pāndavas. See also note 19 for 1.27.

श्वशुरान्सुहृदश्चैव सेनयोरुभयोरपि ।
तान्समीक्ष्य स कौन्तेयः सर्वान्बन्धूनवस्थितान् ॥ १—२७ ॥
कृपया परयाविष्टो विषीदन्निदमब्रवीत् ।
दृष्ट्वेमान्स्वजनान्कृष्ण युयुत्सून्समवस्थितान् ॥ १—२८ ॥
सीदन्ति मम गात्राणि मुखं च परिशुष्यति ।
वेपथुश्च शरीरे मे रोमहर्षश्च जायते ॥ १—२९ ॥
गाण्डीवं स्रंसते हस्तात्त्वक्चैव परिदह्यते ।
न च शक्नोम्यवस्थातुं भ्रमतीव च मे मनः ॥ १—३० ॥
निमित्तानि च पश्यामि विपरीतानि केशव ।
न च श्रेयोऽनुपश्यामि हत्वा स्वजनमाहवे ॥ १—३१ ॥
न काङ्क्षे विजयं कृष्ण न च राज्यं सुखानि च ।
किं नो राज्येन गोविन्द किं भोगैर्जीवितेन वा ॥ १—३२ ॥
येषामर्थे काङ्क्षितं नो राज्यं भोगाः सुखानि च ।
त इमेऽवस्थिता युद्धे प्राणांस्त्यक्त्वा धनानि च ॥ १—३३ ॥
आचार्याः पितरः पुत्रास्तथैव च पितामहाः ।
मातुलाः श्वशुराः पौत्राः श्यालाः संबन्धिनस्तथा ॥ १—३४ ॥

27. śvaśurān suhṛdaś caiva senayor ubhayor api
tān samīkṣya sa kaunteyaḥ sarvān bandhūn avasthitān
28. kṛpayā parayāviṣṭo viṣīdann idam abravīt
dṛṣṭvemān svajanān kṛṣṇa yuyutsūn samavasthitān
29. sīdanti mama gātrāṇi mukhaṃ ca pariśuṣyati
vepathuś ca śarīre me romaharṣaś ca jāyate
30. gāṇḍīvaṃ sraṃsate hastāt tvak caiva paridahyate
na ca śaknomy avasthātuṃ bhramatīva ca me manaḥ
31. nimittāni ca paśyāmi viparītāni keśava
na ca śreyo'nupaśyāmi hatvā svajanam āhave
32. na kāṅkṣe vijayaṃ kṛṣṇa na ca rājyaṃ sukhāni ca
kiṃ no rājyena govinda kiṃ bhogair jīvitena vā
33. yeṣām arthe kāṅkṣitaṃ no rājyaṃ bhogāḥ sukhāni ca
ta ime'vasthitā yuddhe prāṇāṃs tyaktvā dhanāni ca
34. ācāryāḥ pitaraḥ putrās tathaiva ca pitāmahāḥ
mātulāh śvaśurāḥ pautrāḥ śyālāḥ saṃbandhinas tathā

1.27 fathers-in-law, good-hearted [friends], in both armies, and seeing them—all his kinsmen—standing [in array], the son-of-Kuntī[19] [Arjuna]

1.28 was filled with deep pity. Despondent, he spoke thus:

O Krishna, seeing these, my own people, standing [before me] eager to fight,

1.29 my limbs fail, my mouth is parched, trembling [lays hold upon] my body, and [my] hair is caused to bristle [with distress].

1.30 [My bow] Gāndīva[20] slips from [my] hand, and also [my] skin is completely afire; I am also not able to stand, and my mind seems to reel.

1.31 Moreover, I see adverse omens, O Keshava;[21] nor can I foresee good (*shreya*) in slaying [my] own people in combat.

1.32 I do not hanker after victory, O Krishna, nor yet the kingdom [that I lost], or pleasures. Of what [use] is the kingdom to us, O Govinda?[22] Of what [avail are] enjoyments, or [for that matter] life?

1.33 Those for whose sake we hanker after the kingdom, enjoyments, and pleasures, stand [here ready] for combat, surrendering [their] lives and riches—

1.34 preceptors, fathers, sons as well as grandfathers, [maternal] uncles, fathers-in-law, grandsons, brothers-in-law, as well as [other] relatives.

19. "Son-of-Kuntī" (Kaunteya) is another frequent epithet for Arjuna. Kuntī, whose birthname was Prithā, was the sister of Vasudeva, Krishna's father. Her father, King Shūrasena, had long ago promised to give his firstborn daughter to his issueless nephew Kuntibhoja. Thus, Prithā became the adopted daughter of her cousin Kuntibhoja and from then on was known as Kuntī.

20. Like other cultures, the Indians typically named the weapons of heroes. The word *gāndīva* (also spelled *gāndiva*) is the name of Arjuna's bow, which was given to him by Agni, the fire deity.

21. *Keshava* means "hairy one," referring to Krishna's long hair.

22. *Govinda* means literally "cow finder," an old epithet of Indra in the *Rig-Veda*, here applied to Krishna. The word *go* can denote either the masculine "bull" or the feminine "cow." Esoterically, it refers to spiritual treasure. The word *go* can also stand for the senses and for the earth.

एतान्न हन्तुमिच्छामि घ्नतोऽपि मधुसूदन ।
अपि त्रैलोक्यराज्यस्य हेतोः किं नु महीकृते ॥ १—३५ ॥
निहत्य धार्तराष्ट्रान्नः का प्रीतिः स्याज्जनार्दन ।
पापमेवाश्रयेदस्मान्हत्वैतानाततायिनः ॥ १—३६ ॥
तस्मान्नार्हा वयं हन्तुं धार्तराष्ट्रान्स्वबान्धवान् ।
स्वजनं हि कथं हत्वा सुखिनः स्याम माधव ॥ १—३७ ॥
यद्यप्येते न पश्यन्ति लोभोपहतचेतसः ।
कुलक्षयकृतं दोषं मित्रद्रोहे च पातकम् ॥ १—३८ ॥
कथं न ज्ञेयमस्माभिः पापादस्मान्निवर्तितुम् ।
कुलक्षयकृतं दोषं प्रपश्यद्भिर्जनार्दन ॥ १—३९ ॥
कुलक्षये प्रणश्यन्ति कुलधर्माः सनातनाः ।
धर्मे नष्टे कुलं कृत्स्नमधर्मोऽभिभवत्युत ॥ १—४० ॥
अधर्माभिभवात्कृष्ण प्रदुष्यन्ति कुलस्त्रियः ।
स्त्रीषु दुष्टासु वार्ष्णेय जायते वर्णसंकरः ॥ १—४१ ॥
संकरो नरकायैव कुलघ्नानां कुलस्य च ।
पतन्ति पितरो ह्येषां लुप्तपिण्डोदकक्रियाः ॥ १—४२ ॥

35. etān na hantum icchāmi ghnato'pi madhusūdana
api trailokyarājyasya hetoḥ kiṃ nu mahīkṛte
36. nihatya dhārtarāṣṭrān naḥ kā prītiḥ syāj janārdana
pāpam evāśrayed asmān hatvaitān ātatāyinaḥ
37. tasmān nārhā vayaṃ hantuṃ dhārtarāṣṭrān svabāndhavān
svajanaṃ hi kathaṃ hatvā sukhinaḥ syāma mādhava
38. yady apy ete na paśyanti lobhopahatacetasaḥ
kulakṣayakṛtaṃ doṣaṃ mitradrohe ca pātakam
39. kathaṃ na jñeyam asmābhiḥ pāpād asmān nivartitum
kulakṣayakṛtaṃ doṣaṃ prapaśyadbhir janārdana
40. kulakṣaye praṇaśyanti kuladharmāḥ sanātanāḥ
dharme naṣṭe kulaṃ kṛtsnam adharmo 'bhibhavaty uta
41. adharmābhibhavāt kṛṣṇa praduṣyanti kulastriyaḥ
strīṣu duṣṭāsu vārṣṇeya jāyate varṇasaṃkaraḥ
42. saṃkaro narakāyaiva kulaghnānāṃ kulasya ca
patanti pitaro hy eṣāṃ luptapiṇḍodakakriyāḥ

1.35 I do not wish to kill them, O Madhusūdana,[23] even if they should slay [me]; not even for the sake of rulership over the triple world,[24] how [much less] for the sake of the earth?

1.36 If we kill the sons-of-Dhritarāshtra, what delight could be ours, O Janārdana?[25] Only sin would cling to us should we slay those [offenders]-whose-bows-are-strung.

1.37 Therefore we are not allowed to kill the sons-of-Dhritarāshtra [who are, after all, our] own kin. For, how could we be happy, O Mādhava,[26] if we slay our own people?

1.38 Even if they, [with their] minds corrupted by greed, cannot see that to destroy the family is flawed, and treachery toward a friend is a transgression,

1.39 how should we not be wise [enough] to turn away from this sin, [we who] behold the flaw in the destruction of the family,[27] O Janārdana?

1.40 Upon the destruction of the family, the everlasting family laws collapse. Once the law has perished, lawlessness (*adharma*) befalls the whole family.

1.41 Through the prevalence of lawlessness, O Krishna, the family's women are corrupted; once the women are defiled, O descendant-of-Vrishni,[28] intermixing of the classes[29] occurs.

1.42 [This] intermixing [leads] to hell the family and the family destroyers. Also, their ancestors fall[30] [when] the ritual-offerings (*kriyā*) of rice-balls and water are discontinued.

23. On the epithet Madhusūdana, see note 4 for 1.14.
24. The compound word *trailokya* ("triple world") refers to earth, midheaven (atmosphere), and heaven, which is the home of the deities.
25. Krishna's epithet Janārdana means "[he who] agitates (*ardana*) people," referring to evil folk.
26. On Mādhava, see note 4 for 1.14.
27. The word *kula,* here rendered as "family," can also stand for "community," or "society." From a traditional perspective, society is one large family under one spiritual law. It thrives when that law is upheld, and it falters when it is not observed.
28. *Vārshneya* means literally "descendant-of-Vrishni." Vrishni, who succeeded Madhu, was a great king of the Yadu dynasty, to which Krishna belonged.
29. *Varna* is often mistranslated as "caste," but the term (which literally means "color") denotes "social estate" or "class." Indian society distinguishes between four social classes or estates—that of the *brāhmanas* (priests), the *kshatriyas* (warriors), the *vaishyas* (merchants/artisans/peasants), and the *shūdras* (servants). The notion of "color" here has generally been taken to have racial overtones, but this need not inevitably be the case. A psychological-spiritual interpretation is possible. Thus, a "dark" individual is spiritually or morally dark.
30. The condition of the ancestors (*pitri*) in the hereafter is thought to depend on the daily food offerings. Neglect of this duty results in their "falling" to lower and less and less pleasant strata of postmortem existence.

दोषैरेतैः कुलघ्नानां वर्णसंकरकारकैः ।
उत्साद्यन्ते जातिधर्माः कुलधर्माश्च शाश्वताः ॥ १—४३ ॥
उत्सन्नकुलधर्माणां मनुष्याणां जनार्दन ।
नरके नियतं वासो भवातीत्यनुशुश्रुम ॥ १—४४ ॥
अहो बत महत्पापं कर्तुं व्यवसिता वयम् ।
यद्राज्यसुखलोभेन हन्तुं स्वजनमुद्यताः ॥ १—४५ ॥
यदि मामप्रतीकारमशस्त्रं शस्त्रपाणयः ।
धार्तराष्ट्रा रणे हन्युस्तन्मे क्षेमतरं भवेत् ॥ १—४६ ॥
एवमुक्त्वार्जुनः संख्ये रथोपस्थ उपाविशत् ।
विसृज्य सशरं चापं शोकसंविग्नमानसः ॥ १—४७ ॥

43. doṣair etaiḥ kulaghnānāṃ varṇasaṃkarakārakaiḥ
    utsādyante jātidharmāḥ kuladharmāś ca śāśvatāḥ
44. utsannakuladharmāṇāṃ manuṣyāṇāṃ janārdana
    narake niyataṃ vāso bhavatīty anuśuśruma
45. aho bata mahat pāpaṃ kartuṃ vyavasitā vayam
    yad rājyasukhalobhena hantuṃ svajanam udyatāḥ
46. yadi māṃ apratīkāram aśastraṃ śastrapāṇayaḥ
    dhārtarāṣṭrā raṇe hanyus tan me kṣemataraṃ bhavet
47. evam uktvārjunaḥ saṃkhye rathopastha upāviśat
    visṛjya saśaraṃ cāpaṃ śokasaṃvignamānasaḥ

1.43 By these flaws of the family destroyers, by the class minglers, the caste laws and the eternal family law are destroyed.

1.44 For the men who have destroyed the family law, O Janārdana, there is a sure abode in hell; thus have we heard.

1.45 Ah! Alas! We [are indeed determined to] commit a great sin, as we are prepared to slay our own people out of greed for royal pleasures.

1.46 If in [the imminent] combat, the sons-of-Dhritarāshtra, arms in hand, should slay me, unarmed and unresisting, this would be more agreeable to me.

1.47 Having thus spoken in the [midst of] conflict (*samkhya*), Arjuna sank down on the chariot seat, casting down bow and arrow, [his] mind agitated with grief.[31]

31. The presence of both pity (*kripā*)—see 1.28—and grief (*shoka*) in Arjuna's mind indicates that his despondency was not conventional—such as being triggered by mere attachment or cowardice. It was a genuine moral and spiritual crisis.

संजय उवाच
तं तथा कृपयाविष्टमश्रुपूर्णाकुलेक्षणम् ।
विषीदन्तमिदं वाक्यमुवाच मधुसूदनः ॥ २—१ ॥
श्रीभगवानुवाच
कुतस्त्वा कश्मलमिदं विषमे समुपस्थितम् ।
अनार्यजुष्टमस्वर्ग्यमकीर्तिकरमर्जुन ॥ २—२ ॥
क्लैब्यं मा स्म गमः पार्थ नैतत्त्वय्युपपद्यते ।
क्षुद्रं हृदयदौर्बल्यं त्यक्त्वोत्तिष्ठ परंतप ॥ २—३ ॥
अर्जुन उवाच
कथं भीष्महं संख्ये द्रोणं च मधुसूदन ।
इषुभिः प्रतियोत्स्यामि पूजार्हावरिसूदन ॥ २—४ ॥
गुरूनहत्वा हि महानुभावा
ञ्श्रेयो भोक्तुं भैक्ष्यमपीह लोके ।
हत्वार्थकामांस्तु गुरूनिहैव
भुञ्जीय भोगान् रुधिरप्रदिग्धान् ॥ २—५ ॥

saṃjaya uvāca

1. taṃ tathā kṛpayā viṣṭam aśrupūrṇākulekṣaṇam
   viṣīdantam idaṃ vākyam uvāca madhusūdanaḥ

   śrībhagavān uvāca

2. kutas tvā kaśmalam idaṃ viṣame samupasthitam
   anāryajuṣṭam asvargyam akīrtikaram arjuna
3. klaibyaṃ mā sma gamaḥ pārtha naitat tvayy upapadyate
   kṣudraṃ hṛdayadaurbalyaṃ tyaktvottiṣṭha paraṃtapa

   arjuna uvāca

4. kathaṃ bhīṣmam ahaṃ saṃkhye droṇaṃ ca madhusūdana
   iṣubhiḥ pratiyotsyāmi pūjārhāv arisūdana
5. gurūn ahatvā hi mahānubhāvāñ
   śreyo bhoktuṃ bhaikṣyam apīha loke
   hatvārthakāmāṃs tu gurūn ihaiva
   bhuñjīya bhogān rudhirapradigdhān

CHAPTER 2

The Yoga of Knowledge

Samjaya said:

2.1 To him thus overcome with pity [and] despairing, [his] downcast eyes filled with tears, Madhusūdana[1] [Krishna] spoke this word:

[The Blessed Lord said:]

2.2 Whence comes this weakness over you in [such] difficulty [as the present one]? [This attitude] befitting a non-*ārya*[2] is not-conducive-to-heaven (*asvargya*) and brings disrepute, O Arjuna.

2.3 Do not adopt unmanliness,[3] O son-of-Prithā,[4] for this becomes you not. Give up this base faint-heartedness! Rise, O Paramtapa![5]

Arjuna said:

2.4 How [can] I attack Bhīshma and Drona in combat with arrows, O Madhusūdana? [They are] worthy of reverence, O Arisūdana.[6]

2.5 For, [it would be] better here in [this] world even to eat alms-food than to slay greatly dignified teachers. Although they are desirous of gain, they are my leaders, [and] were I to slay them, I should enjoy here [on earth] but blood-smeared pleasures.[7]

1. On Krishna's epithet Madhusūdana, see note 4 for 1.14.
2. The Vedic people differentiated themselves from others by their "noble" (*ārya*) as opposed to barbarian conduct. Their self-designation as Āryans has commonly been overinterpreted along racial lines, and this notion has been brought into disrepute by the ideologists and warmongers of the Third Reich. The long-held idea that the Āryans invaded the North of India about 1500 B.C.E., displacing or subjugating the indigenous population, has been seriously challenged, so that doubt has also been cast on racial interpretations of the word *ārya*.
3. The word *klaibya* ("unmanliness") is derived from the adjective *klība* = "emasculated," "unmanly," or "cowardly."
4. On Arjuna's epithet son-of-Prithā (Pārtha), see note 18 for 1.25.
5. Arjuna's epithet Paramtapa denotes "assailer of another" [i.e., a foe].
6. Arisūdana means "slayer of the enemy (*ari*)."
7. This and the following three stanzas are in the *trishtubh* meter, which usually has 44 syllables (4 lines x 11 syllables), rather than the 16-syllable *shloka* meter in which most of the *Gītā* is composed. Here, however, the first two lines of stanza 6 have an extra syllable each (which is allowable in this meter).

न चैतद्विद्मः कतरन्नो गरीयो
यद्वा जयेम यदि वा नो जयेयुः ।
यानेव हत्वा न जिजीविषाम
स्तेऽवस्थिताः प्रमुखे धार्तराष्ट्राः ॥ २—६ ॥
कार्पण्यदोषोपहतस्वभावः
पृच्छामि त्वां धर्मसंमूढचेताः ।
यच्छ्रेयः स्यान्निश्चितं ब्रूहि तन्मे
शिष्यस्तेऽहं शाधि मां त्वां प्रपन्नम् ॥ २—७ ॥
न हि प्रपश्यामि ममापनुद्या
द्यच्छोकमुच्छोषणमिन्द्रियाणाम् ।
अवाप्य भूमावसपत्नमृद्धं
राज्यं सुराणामपि चाधिपत्यम् ॥ २—८ ॥
संजय उवाच
एवमुक्त्वा हृषीकेषं गुडाकेशः परंतप ।
न योत्स्य इति गोविन्दमुक्त्वा तूष्णीं बभूव ह ॥ २—९ ॥
तमुवाच हृषीकेषः प्रहसन्निव भारत ।
सेनयोरुभयोर्मध्ये विषीदन्तमिदं वचः ॥ २—१० ॥

6. na caitad vidmaḥ kataran no garīyo
yad vā jayema yadi vā no jayeyuḥ
yān eva hatvā na jijīviṣāma
ste'vasthitāḥ pramukhe dhārtarāṣṭrāḥ
7. kārpaṇyadoṣopahatasvabhāvaḥ
pṛcchāmi tvāṃ dharmasaṃmūḍhacetāḥ
yac chreyaḥ syān niścitaṃ brūhi tan me
śiṣyas te 'haṃ śadhi māṃ tvāṃ prapannam
8. na hi prapaśyāmi mamāpanudyā
dyac chokam ucchoṣaṇam indriyāṇām
avāpya bhūmāv asapatnaṃ ṛddhaṃ
rājyaṃ surāṇām api cādhipatyam

saṃjaya uvāca
9. evam uktvā hṛṣīkeśaṃ guḍākeśaḥ paraṃtapaḥ
na yotsya iti govindam uktvā tūṣṇīṃ babhūva ha
10. tam uvāca hṛṣīkeṣaḥ prahasann iva bhārata,
senayor ubhayor madhye viṣīdantam idaṃ vacaḥ

2.6 Nor do we know which is important for us, whether we should be victorious or that they should conquer us. Having slain the sons-of-Dhritarāshtra arrayed facing [us], we would not wish to live.

2.7 My own-being[8] is corrupted by the fault of [misplaced] pity.[9] With [my] mind (*cetas*) confused (*sammūdha*) about the law, I ask you which is the better [course of action]. Tell me for certain. I am approaching you as a pupil. Instruct [me].

2.8 For I cannot see what would dispel the grief [that] dries up [my] senses, [even if I were] to win unrivaled, prosperous rulership on earth or even sovereignty over the deities.

Samjaya said:

2.9 Thus spoke Gudākesha,[10] Scorcher of Foes, to Hrishīkesha,[11] [and then] having declared to Govinda[12] "I will not fight," he lapsed into silence.

2.10 [While they were standing] between the two armies, O descendant-of-Bharata [i.e., Dhritarāshtra], Hrishīkesha laughingly, as it were, spoke this word to him, the dejected [Arjuna]:

8. *Svabhāva,* here rendered as "own-being," is one of the most important concepts of the *Mahābhārata* and the *Gītā*. It is more than "inner nature" or "psyche." It also stands for the felt sense of duty arising from one's station in life into which one is born. Thus, a warrior like Prince Arjuna—when he is not perplexed or otherwise corrupted—would see it as his unfailing duty to protect the people and the moral and spiritual law of the country. In other words, Arjuna's *svabhāva* is intimately connected with his destiny as a warrior.

9. The term *kārpanya,* translated here as "pity," is derived from the same verbal root as *kripā*. It seems to suggest a sentiment somewhat less than serene compassion (*karunā*).

10. On Arjuna's epithet Gudākesha, see note 17 for 1.24.

11. On Krishna's epithet Hrishīkesha, see note 5 for 1.15.

12. On Krishna's epithet Govinda, see note 22 for 1.32.

श्रीभगवानुवाच
अशोच्यानन्वशोचस्त्वं प्रज्ञावादांश्च भाषसे ।
गतासूनगतासूंश्च नानुशोचन्ति पण्डिताः ॥ २—११ ॥

« त्वं मानुष्येणोपहतान्तरात्मा
विषादमोहाभिभवाद्विसंज्ञः ।
कृपागृहीतः समवेक्ष्य बन्धू
नभिप्रपन्नान्मुखमन्तकस्य ॥»

न त्वेवाहं जातु नासं न त्वं नेमे जनाधिपाः ।
न चैव न भविष्यामः सर्वे वयमतः परम् ॥ २—१२ ॥
देहिनोऽस्मिन्यथा देहे कौमारं यौवनं जरा ।
तथा देहान्तरप्राप्तिर्धीरस्तत्र न मुह्यति ॥ २—१३ ॥
मात्रास्पर्शास्तु कौन्तेय शीतोष्णसुखदुःखदाः ।
आगमापायिनोऽनित्यास्तांस्तितिक्षस्व भारत ॥ २—१४ ॥
यं हि न व्यथयन्त्येते पुरुषर्षभ ।
समदुःखसुखं धीरं सोऽमृतत्वाय कल्पते ॥ २—१५ ॥

śrībhagavān uvāca
11. aśocyān anvaśocas tvaṃ prajñāvādāṃś ca bhāṣase
gatāsūn agatāsūṃś ca nānuśocanti paṇḍitāḥ

« tvaṃ mānuşyeṅopahatāntarātmā viṣādamohābhibhavād visaṃjñaḥ
kṛpāgṛhītaḥ samavekṣya bandhūn abhiprapannān mukham
antakasya »

12. na tv evāhaṃ jātu nāsaṃ na tvaṃ neme janādhipāḥ
na caiva na bhaviṣyāmaḥ sarve vayam ataḥ param
13. dehino'smin yathā dehe kaumāraṃ yauvanaṃ jarā
tathā dehāntaraprāptir dhīras tatra na muhyati
14. mātrāsparśās tu kaunteya śītoṣṇasukhaduḥkhadāḥ
āgamāpāyino'nityās tāṃs titikṣasva bhārata
15. yaṃ hi na vyathayanty ete puruṣaṃ puruṣarṣabha
samaduḥkhasukhaṃ dhīraṃ so'mṛtatvāya kalpate

The Blessed Lord said:

2.11 You grieve[13] [for those who are] not to be grieved for, and [yet] you speak words of wisdom. The learned (*pandita*) do not sorrow for the dead or the living.[14]

« Overpowered by dejection and delusion, your inner self, assailed by what-is-all-too-human (*mānushya*), lacks understanding. [You are] seized by pity on seeing [your] kinsmen fall into the jaws of death.[15] »

2.12 Verily, never was I not, were you not, or were these rulers not, nor will any one of us not be henceforth.

2.13 Just as in this body the body-essence[16] [experiences] childhood, youth, and old age, so too it obtains another body [after death]. A thoughtful [man] is not confused by this.

2.14 Material[17] contacts [i.e., sensations], O son-of-Kuntī,[18] give rise indeed to heat and cold, pleasure and pain; [they] come and go [and thus are] impermanent. Endure them [patiently], O descendant-of-Bharata!

2.15 For, the man whom these [pairs-of-opposites][19] do not distress, the wise one (*dhīra*) [for whom] pain and pleasure are the same,[20] O Purusharshabha[21]—he is fit for immortality.[22]

13. The Sanskrit text has "you have grieved" (*anvashocas tvam*).

14. The Sanskrit text reads *gata-asūn-agata-asūn*, "gone the life-breaths, not gone the life-breaths." The word *asu,* here used in the plural, is a synonym for *prāna,* meaning "life-force" or "breath."

15. This additional stanza is in the *trishtubh* meter.

16. The body-essence (*dehin*), or simply the "embodied one," is the Self in its immanent aspect as the spirit or life-principle (*jīva*) of the living being. Elsewhere in the *Gītā* it is also called *dehabhrit* ("body-wearer") and *shārīrin* ("embodied").

17. In his commentary on this verse, Shankara interprets *mātrā* ("measure/matrix"; here "material") in the specific sense of *tanmātra* (from *tad* "that" + *mātrā*), or "subtle-element," namely the sensory functions of sound, touch, form, taste, and smell.

18. On Arjuna's epithet "son-of-Kuntī" (Kaunteya), see note 19 for 1.27.

19. The pairs-of-opposites (*dvandva*) are opposites like heat/cold, dry/wet, which are apt to cause distress.

20. *Sama* is an important term in the philosophy of Krishna. In 2.48, Yoga is actually defined as *samatva,* "evenness," "equability," or "equanimity," and the crowning experience of all Yoga is the "vision of sameness" (*sama-darshana*), which looks upon all things and beings—great or small—as the same One and therefore as being of equal value. The vision of sameness is a matter of deep equanimity and contentment, which allows the Yoga practitioner to encounter both pleasant and unpleasant experiences without agitation or karmically charged reaction.

21. Arjuna's epithet Purusharshabha (from *purusha* + *rishabha*) means literally "Bull [among] Men."

22. Immortality here stands for spiritual liberation (*moksha*). As Sarvepalli Radhakrishnan (1948) remarks in his fine commentary on this verse: "Eternal life is different from survival of death which is given to every embodied being. It is the transcendence of life and death."

नासतो विद्यते भावो नाभावो विद्यते सतः ।
उभयोरपि दृष्टोऽन्तस्त्वनयोस्तत्त्वदर्शिभिः ॥ २—१६ ॥
अविनाशि तु तद्विद्धि येन सर्वमिदं ततम् ।
विनाशमव्ययस्यास्य न कश्चित्कर्तुमर्हति ॥ २—१७ ॥
अन्तवन्त इमे देहा नित्यस्योऽक्ताः शरीरिणः ।
अनाशिनोऽप्रमेयस्य तस्माद्युध्यस्व भारत ॥ २—१८ ॥
य एनं वेत्ति हन्तारं यश्चैनं मन्यते हतम् ।
उभौ तौ न विजानीतो नायं हन्ति न हन्यते ॥ २—१९ ॥
न जायते मृयते वा कदाचि
न्नायं भूत्वा भविता वा न भूयः ।
अजो नित्यः शाश्वतोऽयं पुराणो
न हन्यते हन्यमाने शरीरे ॥ २—२० ॥
वेदाविनाशिनं नित्यं य एनमजमव्ययम् ।
कथं स पुरुषः पार्थ कं घातयति हन्ति कम् ॥ २—२१ ॥
वासांसि जीर्णानि यथा विहाय
नवानि गृह्णाति नरोऽपराणि ।
तथा शरीराणि विहाय जीर्णा
न्यन्यानि संयाति नवानि देही ॥ २—२२ ॥

16. nāsato vidyate bhāvo nābhāvo vidyate sataḥ
ubhayor api dṛṣto'ntas tv anayos tattvadarśibhiḥ
17. avināśi tu tad viddhi yena sarvam idaṃ tatam
vināśam avyayasyāsya na kaścit kartum arhati
18. antavanta ime dehā nityasyo'ktāḥ śarīriṇaḥ
anāśino'prameyasya tasmād yudhyasva bhārata
19. ya enaṃ vetti hantāraṃ yaś cainaṃ manyate hatam
ubhau tau na vijānīto nāyaṃ hanti na hanyate
20. na jāyate mriyate vā kadāci
nnāyaṃ bhūtvā bhavitā vā na bhūyaḥ
ajo nityaḥ śāśvato'yaṃ purāṇo na hanyate hanyamāne śarīre
21. vedāvināśinaṃ nityaṃ ya enam ajam avyayam
kathaṃ sa puruṣaḥ pārtha kaṃ ghātayati hanti kam
22. vāsāṃsi jīrṇāni yathā vihāya
navāni gṛhnāti naro'parāṇi
tathā śarīrāṇi vihāya jīrṇā nyanyāni saṃyāti navāni dehī

2.16 Of the nonexistent (*asat*) there is no coming-into-being; of the existent (*sat*) there is no disappearance. Moreover, the "end"[23] of both is seen by the seers-of-Reality.[24]

2.17 Yet, know as indestructible that by which this entire [world] is spread out.[25] No one is able to accomplish the destruction of this immutable (*avyaya*) [Reality].

2.18 Finite are said [to be] these bodies of the eternal embodied [Self, *ātman*], the Indestructible, the Incommensurable. Hence fight, O descendant-of-Bharata!

2.19 He who thinks of this [Self] as slayer and he who thinks [of this Self] as slain—they both do not know. This [Self] does not slay nor is it slain.

2.20 This [Self] is not born nor [does it] ever die, nor having-come-to-be shall it again cease-to-be. This unborn, eternal, everlasting, primordial [Self] is not slain when the body is slain.[26]

2.21 The man (*purusha*) who knows this Indestructible, Eternal, Unborn, Immutable [One]—how and whom can he cause-to-be slain [or] slay, O son-of-Prithā?

2.22 As a man, [after] discarding worn-out garments, seizes other, new ones, so does the embodied [Self], [after] discarding worn-out bodies, enter other, new ones.[27]

23. The meaning of *anta* ("end") here requires clarification. Neither Shankara nor Abhinavagupta comments specifically on this word. Radhakrishnan (1948) uses "conclusion"; Sargeant (1984) gives "certainty," while Hill (1928/1966) and van Buitenen (1981) give "boundary." The end of both propositions—in the sense of their final justification—is the actual realization of utter freedom. Those who are liberated truly know. They "see," firsthand, that whatever exists always exists. For everyone else, the two propositions—that the nonexistent cannot come to be and the existent cannot cease to be—can be little more than opinions.

24. The word *tattva* literally means "thatness" (what Immanuel Kant called the *Ding an sich*, or "thing in itself") and refers to the nature of a thing as it really is. A *tattva-darshin,* or "seer-of Reality," is one whose knowledge is "truth-bearing" (*ritambhara*), as Patanjali puts it in his *Yoga-Sūtra* (1.48). The "thing" in question is the ultimate "thing," which is no-thing at all, the permanent Reality that, short of enlightenment, we can grasp only piecemeal.

25. On "spread out," see note 33 for 4.32.

26. This stanza is in the *trishtubh* meter.

27. This stanza is also in the *trishtubh* meter.

नैनं छिन्दन्ति शस्त्राणि नैनं दहति पावकः ।
न चैनं क्लेदयन्त्यापो न शोषयति मारुतः ॥ २—२३ ॥
अच्छेद्योऽयमदाह्योऽयमक्लेद्योऽशोष्य एव च ।
नित्यः सर्वगतः स्थाणुरचलोऽयं सनातनः ॥ २—२४ ॥
अव्यक्तोऽयमचिन्त्योऽयमविकार्योऽयमुच्यते ।
तस्मादेवं विदित्वैनं नानुशोचितुमर्हसि ॥ २—२५ ॥
अथ चैनं नित्यजातं नित्यं वा मन्यसे मृतम् ।
तथापि त्वं महाबाहो नैनं शोचितुमर्हसि ॥ २—२६ ॥
जातस्या हि ध्रुवो मृत्युर्ध्रुवं जन्म मृतस्य च ।
तस्मादपरिहार्येऽर्थे न त्वं शोचितुमर्हसि ॥ २—२७ ॥
अव्यक्तादिनि भूतानि व्यक्तमध्यानि भारत ।
अव्यक्तनिधनान्येव तत्र का परिदेवना ॥ २—२८ ॥
आश्चर्यवत्पश्यति कश्चदेन
माश्चर्यवद्वदति तथैव चान्यः ।
आश्चर्यवच्चैनमन्यः शृणोति
श्रुत्वाप्येनं वेद न चैव कश्चित् ॥ २—२९ ॥

23. nainaṃ chindanti śastrāṇi nainaṃ dahati pāvakaḥ
na cainaṃ kledayanty āpo na śoṣayati mārutaḥ
24. acchedyo'yam adāhyo'yam akledyo'śoṣya eva ca
nityaḥ sarvagataḥ sthāṇur acalo'yaṃ sanātanaḥ
25. avyakto'yam acintyo'yam avikāryo'yam ucyate
tasmād evaṃ viditvainaṃ nānuśocitum arhasi
26. atha cainaṃ nityajātaṃ nityaṃ vā manyase mṛtam
tathāpi tvaṃ mahābāho nainaṃ śocitum arhasi
27. jātasya hi dhruvo mṛtyur dhruvaṃ janma mṛtasya ca
tasmād aparihārye'rthe na tvaṃ śocitum arhasi
28. avyaktādini bhūtāni vyaktamadhyāni bhārata
avyaktanidhanāny eva tatra kā paridevanā
29. āścaryavat paśyati kaścid ena
māścaryavad vadati tathaiva cānyaḥ
āścaryavac cainam anyaḥ śṛṇoti
śrutvāpy enaṃ veda na caiva kaścit

2.23 Weapons do not cleave this [Self]. Fire does not burn this [Self]. Water does not wet this [Self]. The wind does not dry [it].[28]

2.24 This [Self] is uncuttable; [this] is unburnable, unwettable, and undryable. This ever-lasting [Reality] is eternal, omnipresent, stable, unmoving.

2.25 This [Self] is called unmanifest (*avyakta*), unthinkable, unchangeable. Hence knowing this [Self] thus, you should not grieve!

2.26 Moreover, [even if] you deem this [Self] eternally born and eternally dying [with the body], you should not grieve for it, O mighty-armed [Arjuna].

2.27 For, certain is the death of all-that-is-born and certain the birth of all-that-dies. Therefore, in [regard to this] inevitable matter, you should not grieve.

2.28 Beings, O descendant-of-Bharata, are unmanifest in [their] beginnings, manifest (*vyakta*) in [their] middle-states, and unmanifest indeed in their ends. What [reason is there] for lamenting over this?

2.29 Someone sees this [Self as] a marvel;[29] another similarly speaks of this [Self as] a marvel; and [yet] another hears of this [Self as] a marvel. Yet, having heard, [seen, or spoken of it thus], no one, verily [really] knows this [Self].[30]

28. This stanza is in the *trishtubh* meter. See note 7 for 2.5.

29. Abhinavagupta (in whose commentary this stanza is numbered 2.30) asks: "If this Self is thus indestructible, why then is [this truth] not apprehended by everyone?" He answers his own question by stating that only some people actually realize the Self, which is what is required to perceive its wondrous or awe-inspiring nature.

30. This stanza is again in the *trishtubh* meter but has an extra syllable in the second line.

देही नित्यमवध्योऽयं देहे सर्वस्य भारत ।
तस्मात्सर्वाणि भूतानि न त्वं शोचितुमर्हसि ॥ २—३० ॥
स्वधर्ममपि चावेक्ष्य न विकम्पितुमर्हसि ।
धर्म्याद्धि युद्धाच्छ्रेयोऽन्यत्क्षत्रियस्य न विद्यते ॥ २—३१ ॥
यदृच्छया चोपपन्नं स्वर्गद्वारमपावृतम् ।
सुखिनः क्षत्रियाः पार्थ लभन्ते युद्धमीदृशम् ॥ २—३२ ॥
अथ चेत्त्वमिमं धर्म्यं संग्रामं न करिष्यसि ।
ततः स्वधर्मं कीर्तिं च हित्वा पापमवाप्स्यसि ॥ २—३३ ॥
अकीर्तिं चापि भूतानि कथयिष्यन्ति तेऽव्ययाम् ।
संभावितस्य चाकीर्तिर्मरणादतिरिच्यते ॥ २—३४ ॥
भयाद्रणादुपरतं मंस्यन्ते त्वां महारथाः ।
येषां च त्वं बहुमतो भूत्वा यास्यसि लाघवम् ॥ २—३५ ॥

30. dehī nityam avadhyo'yaṃ dehe sarvasya bhārata
tasmāt sarvāṇi bhūtāni na tvaṃ śocitum arhasi
31. svadharmam api cāvekṣya na vikampitum arhasi
dharmyādd hi yuddhāc chreyo'nyat kṣatriyasya na vidyate
32. yadṛcchayā copapannaṃ svargadvāram apāvṛtam
sukhinaḥ kṣatriyāḥ pārtha labhante yuddham īdṛśam
33. atha cet tvam imaṃ dharmyaṃ saṃgrāmaṃ na kariṣyasi
tataḥ svadharmaṃ kīrtiṃ ca hitvā pāpam avāpsyasi
34. akīrtiṃ cāpi bhūtāni kathayiṣyanti te 'vyayām
saṃbhāvitasya cākīrtir maraṇād atiricyate
35. bhayād raṇād uparataṃ maṃsyante tvāṃ mahārathāḥ
yeṣāṃ ca tvaṃ bahumato bhūtvā yāsyasi lāghavam

2.30 This body-essence (*dehin*) is eternally inviolable, [although residing] in the body of all [beings], O descendant-of-Bharata. Therefore, you should not grieve for any being.[31]

2.31 Further, considering your own-law,[32] you should not waver. For there is nothing better for a warrior than a lawful[33] war.

2.32 [Moreover,] happy the warriors, O son-of-Prithā, [who] encounter such a battle (*yuddha*), occurring by chance[34] and opening the gate to heaven [for the brave fighter].

2.33 Now, if you will not engage this lawful combat (*samgrāma*), then, by disregarding [both] own-law and honor, you will incur sin.

2.34 Furthermore, [all] beings will recount your dishonor forever. And for the honorable [man], dishonor surpasses death.[35]

2.35 They, the great chariot-warriors, will regard you [as one who] withdrew from combat (*rāna*) out of fear. You will become [an object of] levity for those who [now] hold [you in] great esteem.

31. Literally: "Therefore, you should not grieve for all beings (*sarvāni bhūtāni*)."

32. Like the concept of *svabhāva* ("own-being"), its correlate *svadharma* ("own-law") is a vitally important notion in the ethics of the *Mahābhārata*. In brief, it is the normative behavior arising from one's *svabhāva*. In Arjuna's case, his birth into the warrior estate afforded him all sorts of privileges but also a good many obligations, notably the protection of the people and the preservation of the spiritually based law of his society.

33. The phrase *dharmya-yuddha* has frequently been rendered as "just war." The term *dharmya*, however, implies much more, because the concept of *dharma* is more profound than mere "justice." *Dharma* ties in with the cosmic order (*rita*) that is responsible for the orderly procession of the stars and seasons. On the human level, *dharma* does what *rita* does on the larger, environmental level.

34. The term *yadricchā* ("chance") is used rather loosely here, because in a universe governed by the iron law of karma, there really are no chance events. Some translators have rendered the word as "good fortune." How fortunate, one may ask, can it be to be killed and go to heaven when heaven is traditionally deemed to fall far short of spiritual liberation? The literal meaning of *yadricchā* (from *yad,* "which," + *ricchā*) is "that which is inflicted" or, more colloquially, "what goes."

35. The phrase "surpasses death" (*maranād atiricyate*) means "is worse than death."

अवाच्यवादांश्च बहून्वदिष्यन्ति तवाहिताः ।
निन्दन्तस्तव सामर्थ्यं ततो दुःखतरं नु किम् ॥ २—३६ ॥
हतो वा प्राप्स्यसि स्वर्गं जित्वा वा भोक्ष्यसे महीम् ।
तस्मादुत्तिष्ठ कौन्तेय युद्धाय कृतनिश्चयः ॥ २—३७ ॥
सुखदुःखे समे कृत्वा लाभालाभौ जयाजयौ ।
ततो युद्धाय युज्यस्व नैवं पापमवाप्स्यसि ॥ २—३८ ॥
एषा तेऽभिहिता सांख्ये बुद्धिर्योगे त्विमां शृणु ।
बुद्ध्या युक्तो यया पार्थ कर्मबन्धं प्रहास्यसि ॥ २—३९ ॥
नेहाभिक्रमनाशोऽस्ति प्रत्यवायो न विद्यते ।
स्वल्पमप्यस्य धर्मस्य त्रायते महतो भयात् ॥ २—४० ॥
व्यवसायात्मिका बुद्धिरेकेह कुरुनन्दन ।
बहुशाखा ह्यनन्ताश्च बुद्धयोऽव्यवसायिनाम् ॥ २—४१ ॥

36. avācyavādāṃś ca bahūn vadiṣyanti tavāhitāḥ
nindantas tava sāmarthyaṃ tato duḥkhataraṃ tu kim
37. hato vā prāpsyasi svargaṃ jitvā vā bhokṣyase mahīm
tasmād uttiṣṭha kaunteya yuddhāya kṛtaniścayaḥ
38. sukhaduḥkhe same kṛtvā lābhālābhau jayājayau
tato yuddhāya yujyasva naivaṃ pāpam avāpsyasi
39. eṣā te'bhihitā sāṃkhye buddhir yoge tv imāṃ śṛṇu
buddhyā yukto yayā pārtha karmabandhaṃ prahāsyasi
40. nehābhikramanāśo'sti pratyavāyo na vidyate
svalpam apy asya dharmasya trāyate mahato bhayāt
41. vyavasāyātmikā buddhir ekeha kurunandana
bahuśākhā hy anantāś ca buddhayo'vyavasāyinām

2.36 And many abusive words will your ill-wishers speak, denouncing your prowess. What [could be] more painful (*duhkha*) than that?

2.37 [Should you be] slain, you will reach heaven. [Should you be] victorious, you will enjoy [dominion over] the earth. Therefore, O son-of-Kuntī, arise resolute [to fight in] the battle![36]

2.38 Holding pleasure and pain, profit and loss, victory and defeat as alike, gird yourself for the battle! Thus you will not incur sin.

2.39 This is wisdom[37] [as] revealed to you according to Sāmkhya.[38] Hear [now] about this [as employed] in Yoga. Yoked by the wisdom-faculty, you will transcend the binding [effect of] action, O son-of-Prithā.

2.40 Here no effort is lost; there is no slipping back. Even a little of this law rescues [a person] from great fear.

2.41 The wisdom-faculty [that is] of the essence of determination[39] is [indeed] single, O Kurunandana.[40] However, many-branched and endless are the wisdom-faculties [of those who are] devoid of determination.

36. It might seem that in this group of stanzas, Krishna is "laying a guilt trip" on his disciple. The divine teacher does indeed use conventional arguments to get his disciple motivated. But we must remember the important qualifying remark of 2.10 that Hrishīkesha imparted his teachings "laughingly, as it were" (*prahasann iva*). We could understand this easily in the sense that he was benignly mocking Arjuna. In order to create a mind of clarity (*sattva*) in a student, the teacher first has to dynamize a lethargic mind by introducing the quality of *rajas* into it. The progression, then, is *tamas→rajas→sattva.* Ultimately, of course, all three primary-qualities (*guna*) must be transcended in order to bring about spiritual liberation. From the highest perspective, even *sattva,* the principle of lucidity, represents a limitation. (On the *gunas*, see note 44 for 2.45.)

37. *Buddhi* is a key term of Yoga and Sāmkhya. It has a wide range of meanings, including "mind," "cognition," "understanding," "wisdom," and "wisdom-faculty" (or higher mind). In the Yoga and Sāmkhya traditions, it stands for a particular aspect of the mind, namely that faculty which is responsible for discernment between what is real and what is unreal—the kind of wisdom without which there can be no spiritual growth. Although the notion of "mental faculties" is no longer popular among psychologists, it seems appropriate to use this concept in regard to the ontology and psychology of Yoga and Sāmkhya. Thus, *buddhi* is here rendered as both "wisdom" and "wisdom-faculty."

38. The Sāmkhya tradition, closely related to Yoga, is concerned with the enumeration (hence *samkhya,* "number") of the basic categories of existence (*tattva*), such as Spirit (*purusha*) and Matter (*prakriti,* lit. "procreatrix"). While the former has no subdivisions, the latter has a number of evolutes that yield the universe as we know it, namely the higher mind or wisdom-faculty (*buddhi*), the lower mind (*manas*), the principle of individuation or ego-sense (*ahamkāra*), the ten senses (*indriya*), the five subtle elements (*tanmātra*), and the five elements (*bhūta*).

39. *Vyavasāya,* here rendered as "determination," has also been translated as "resolution" or "will."

40. Arjuna's epithet Kurunandana means "joy or delight (*nandana*) of the Kurus." Here the word *Kuru* is used broadly and refers not just to the descendants of King Dhritarāshtra but to the dynastic descendants of the old king Kuru, which includes both Dhritarāshtra's hundred sons and also the five sons of King Pāndu and their predecessors; the Kuru dynasty originated with the god Brahma and went through many kings, including Yayāti (see Krishna Yadu lineage, in note 43 for 11.41) but then to Puru, thirteen other kings, Bharata, ten other kings, and then to Kuru.

यामिमां पुष्पितां वाचं प्रवदन्त्यविपश्चितः ।
वेदवादरताः पार्थ नान्यदस्तीति वादिनः ॥ २—४२ ॥
कामात्मानः स्वर्गपरा जन्मकर्मफलप्रदाम् ।
क्रियाविशेषबहुलां भोगैश्वर्यगतिं प्रति ॥ २—४३ ॥
भोगैश्वर्यप्रसक्तानां तयापहृतचेतसाम् ।
व्यवसायात्मिका बुद्धिः समाधौ न विधीयते ॥ २—४४ ॥
त्रैगुण्यविषया वेदा निस्त्रैगुण्यो भवार्जुन ।
निर्द्वन्द्वो नित्यसत्त्वस्थो निर्योगक्षेम आत्मवान् ॥ २—४५ ॥
यावानर्थ उदपाने सर्वतः संप्लुतोदके ।
तावान्सर्वेषु वेदेषु ब्राह्मणस्य विजानतः ॥ २—४६ ॥
कर्मण्येवाधिकारस्ते मा फलेषु कदाचन ।
मा कर्मफलहेतुर्भूर्मा ते सङ्गोऽस्त्वकर्मणि ॥ २—४७ ॥

42. yām imāṃ puṣpitāṃ vācaṃ pravadanty avipaścitaḥ
vedavādaratāḥ pārtha nānyad astīti vādinaḥ
43. kāmātmānaḥ svargaparā janmakarmaphalapradām
kriyāviśeṣabahulāṃ bhogaiśvaryagatiṃ prati
44. bhogaiśvaryaprasaktānāṃ tayāpahṛtacetasām
vyavasāyātmikā buddhiḥ samādhau na vidhīyate
45. traiguṇyaviṣayā vedā nistraiguṇyo bhavārjuna
nirdvandvo nityasattvastho niryogakṣema ātmavān
46. yāvān artha udapāne sarvataḥ saṃplutodake
tāvān sarveṣu vedeṣu brāhmaṇasya vijānataḥ
47. karmaṇy evādhikāras te mā phaleṣu kadācana
mā karmaphalahetur bhūr mā te saṅgo'stv akarmaṇi

2.42 Undiscerning [people], delighting in the lore of the Veda,[41] O son-of-Prithā, utter flowery speech, saying there is nothing else.[42]

2.43 Having desire [as their] essence (*ātman*), intent on heaven, claim that [a good re-]birth is the fruit of [ritual] action, [and have] many special rites for the attainment of enjoyment and lordship.

2.44 Of [those who are] attached to enjoyment and lordship [and have] "carried-away" minds—[their] wisdom-faculty, [which is of] the essence of determination, is not settled in ecstasy.[43]

2.45 The triad of primary-qualities[44] [of the manifested universe] is the subject-matter of the Vedas. Become free of the triple primary-qualities, free of the pairs-of-opposites,[45] and, O Arjuna, abide always in *sattva,*[46] without [trying to] gain or keep [anything]. [Be] Self-possessed![47]

2.46 As much use [as is] a water-reservoir flooded with water all-round, so much [use is there] in all the Vedas for the knowing Brahmin.[48]

2.47 In action alone is your rightful-interest (*adhikāra*), never in [its] fruit.[49] Let not your motive be the fruit of action; nor let your attachment be to inaction (*akarman*).

41. *Veda* stands here for the Vedic revelation as embodied in the four collections—*Rig-Veda, Yajur-Veda, Sāma-Veda,* and *Atharva-Veda*—and their associated ancient explanatory scriptures.
42. Here Krishna's comments need not necessarily be taken as a condemnation of the Vedic revelatory tradition itself, but rather of those who have a fundamentalist attitude toward it. But see 2.46.
43. The ecstatic mind is a fully concentrated mind. Thus, the term *samādhi* could here appropriately be rendered as "concentration."
44. *Traigunya,* or "triad of primary-qualities," refers to the three fundamental qualities (*guna*) of cosmic existence (*prakriti*): the principle of lucidity (*sattva*), the principle of dynamism (*rajas*), and the principle of inertia (*tamas*). Through endless combinations, these three qualities—*guna* means "strand"—make up the myriad of phenomena in the manifest world.
45. On the term *dvandva* ("pairs-of-opposites"), see note 19 for 2.15.
46. The compound *nitya-sattva-stha* can mean either "abiding in the eternal *sattva*" or "abiding always in *sattva*." The latter seems more likely. The word *sattva* may in this particular context be translated as "truth" or "reality," since it can hardly refer to the *guna* called *sattva*, given that Arjuna was told to step beyond the *gunas*, if only by way of implication. The exhortation to always abide in *sattva* means to cultivate equanimity, which is a manifestation of a sattvic state of mind. When the mind is soaked with *sattva,* it can make the leap into Self-realization, or spiritual liberation. *Sattva* is a common synonym for *buddhi*.
47. Note the initial capital in "Self-possessed" (*ātmavat*). The ordinary worldling is self-possessed, that is, "full of ego." But the spiritual practitioner is intent on identifying with the transcendental Self or, rather, on allowing the Self to become the identity of his or her mind and personality.
48. This stanza has sometimes been interpreted as a denigration of the Vedas, but a careful reading of it shows that this is not the case. What Krishna is saying is that for a Self-realized person, all the knowledge in the world, even the great wisdom found in the Vedic revelation, has lost its usefulness, because the ultimate goal of life, namely liberation, has been accomplished.
49. The technical term *phala,* or "fruit," implies more than "result." It is a karmic consequence.

योगस्थः कुरु कर्माणि सङ्गं त्यक्त्वा धनंजय ।
सिद्ध्यसिद्ध्योः समो भूत्वा समत्वं योग उच्यते ॥ २—४८ ॥
दूरेण ह्यवरं कर्म बुद्धियोगाद्धनंजय ।
बुद्धौ शरणमन्विच्छ कृपणाः फलहेतवः ॥ २—४९ ॥
बुद्धियुक्तो जहातिह उभे सुकृतदुष्कृते ।
तस्माद्योगाय युज्यस्व योगः कर्मसु कौशलम् ॥ २—५० ॥
कर्मजं बुद्धियुक्ता हि फलं त्यक्त्वा मनीषिणः ।
जन्मबन्धविनिर्मुक्ताः पदं गच्छन्त्यनामयम ॥ २—५१ ॥
यदा ते मोहकलिलं बुद्धिर्व्यतितरिष्यति ।
तदा गन्तासि निर्वेदं श्रोतव्यस्य श्रुतस्य च ॥ २—५२ ॥
श्रुतिविप्रतिपन्ना ते यदा स्थास्यति निश्चला ।
समाधावचला बुद्धिस्तदा योगमवाप्स्यसि ॥ २—५३ ॥

48. yogasthaḥ kuru karmāṇi saṅgaṃ tyaktvā dhanaṃjaya
siddhyasiddhyoḥ samo bhūtvā samatvaṃ yoga ucyate
49. dūreṇa hy avaraṃ karma buddhiyogād dhanaṃjaya
buddhau śaraṇam anviccha kṛpaṇāḥ phalahetavaḥ
50. buddhiyukto jahātiha ubhe sukṛtaduṣkṛte
tasmād yogāya yujyasva yogaḥ karmasu kauśalam
51. karmajaṃ buddhiyuktā hi phalaṃ tyaktvā manīṣiṇaḥ
janmabandhavinirmuktāḥ padaṃ gacchanty anāmayam
52. yadā te mohakalilaṃ buddhir vyatitariṣyati
tadā gantāsi nirvedaṃ śrotavyasya śrutasya ca
53. śrutivipratipannā te yadā sthāsyati niścalā
samādhāv acalā buddhis tadā yogam avāpsyasi

2.48 Steadfast in Yoga, perform actions abandoning attachment, O Dhanamjaya,[50] [always] remaining the same in success and failure. Yoga is called equanimity.

2.49 Far inferior indeed is [mere] action than *buddhi-yoga*, O Dhanamjaya. Seek refuge in the wisdom-faculty! Pitiful are those whose motive is the fruit [of action].

2.50 The *buddhi*-yoked leaves behind here [in this world] both well-done and ill-done [actions]. Hence yoke yourself to Yoga. Yoga is skill in [the performance of] actions.

2.51 The wise [who are] *buddhi* yoked, who have renounced action-born fruit, who are liberated from the bondage of birth [and death]—they go to the region [that is] free from ill.

2.52 When your wisdom-faculty has traversed the thicket of delusion, then you will acquire disinterest in what will be heard and what has been heard [i.e., mundane knowledge].

2.53 When your wisdom-faculty, diverted[51] by revealed-tradition (*shrūti*) will stand motionless and still in ecstasy, then you will attain to [the sublime state of] Yoga.

50. On Arjuna's epithet Dhanamjaya, see note 7 for 1.15.

51. The word *vipratipannā,* here rendered as "diverted," suggest a mind that is distracted. The word is derived from the root *pad* ("to fall") + *vi* ("dis-") + *prati* ("toward/in regard to"). It has variously been translated as "disregarding" (Sargeant 1984), "averse" (Edgerton 1944), and "not disturbed" (Bhaktivedanta Swami 1983).

अर्जुन उवाच

स्थितप्रज्ञस्य का भाषा समाधिस्थस्य केशव ।
स्थितधीः किं प्रभाषेत किमासीत व्रजेत किम् ॥ २—५४ ॥

श्रीभगवानुवाच

प्रजहाति यदा कामान्सर्वान्पार्थ मनोगतान् ।
आत्मन्येवात्मना तुष्टः स्थितप्रज्ञस्तदोऽच्यते ॥ २—५५ ॥
दुःखेष्वनुद्विग्नमनाः सुखेषु विगतस्पृहः ।
वीतरागभयक्रोधः स्थितधीर्मुनिरुच्यते ॥ २—५६ ॥
यः सर्वत्रानभिस्नेहस्तत्तत्प्राप्य शुभाशुभम् ।
नाभिनन्दति न द्वेष्टि तस्य प्रज्ञा प्रतिष्ठिता ॥ २—५७ ॥

arjuna uvāca

54. sthitaprajñasya kā bhāṣā samādhisthasya keśava
sthitadhīḥ kiṃ prabhāṣeta kim āsīta vrajeta kim

śrībhagavān uvāca

55. prajahāti yadā kāmān sarvān pārtha manogatān
ātmany evātmanā tuṣṭaḥ sthitaprajñas tado'cyate
56. duḥkheṣv anudvignamanāḥ sukheṣu vigataspṛhaḥ
vītarāgabhayakrodhaḥ sthitadhīr munir ucyate
57. yaḥ sarvatrānabhisnehas tattat prāpya śubhāśubham
nābhinandati na dveṣṭi tasya prajñā pratiṣṭhitā

Arjuna said:

2.54 What, O Keshava,[52] is the definition of the [*yogin* who is] steadied in gnosis,[53] abiding in ecstasy? How does [he who is] steadied in vision[54] speak? How sit? How move about?

The Blessed Lord said:

2.55 When [a man] relinquishes all desires [that] enter the mind, O son-of-Prithā, and is content with the Self in the Self, then is he called steadied in gnosis.

2.56 [A man whose] mind is unagitated in sorrow (*duhkha*), [who is] devoid of longing in [his contact with] pleasure (*sukha*), and free from passion (*rāga*), fear (*bhaya*), and anger (*krodha*)—he is called a sage[55] steadied in vision.

2.57 He who is unattached all-round [and who] neither rejoices nor dislikes [when] encountering this [or] that auspicious [or] inauspicious [experience]—his gnosis is well established.

52. On Krishna's epithet Keshava, see note 21 for 1.31.

53. The Sanskrit *prajnā* corresponds to the Greek *gnosis*, which is a higher kind of ("mystical") knowledge. To use the Greek equivalent seemed more appropriate here than to repeat "wisdom," which goes well with *buddhi*.

54. The word *dhī* is an old Vedic word designating the inspired vision of a seer (*rishi*). Thus, *sthita-dhī* denotes "[he whose] vision is steadied/settled." It is a synonym of the compound *sthita-prajnā* ("steadied in gnosis"), found in the same stanza.

55. *Muni* is a common appellation for a "sage." More specifically, the word hints at a prominent ascetic practice among sages, which is the voluntary cultivation of silence (*mauna*).

यदा संहरते चायं कूर्मोऽङ्गानीव सर्वशः ।
इन्द्रियाणीन्द्रियार्थेभ्यस्तस्य प्रज्ञा प्रतिष्ठिता ॥ २—५८ ॥
विषया विनिवर्तन्ते निराहारस्य देहिनः ।
रसवर्जं रसोऽप्यस्य परं दृष्ट्वा निवर्तते ॥ २—५९ ॥
यततो ह्यपि कौन्तेय पुरुषस्य विपश्चितः ।
इन्द्रियाणि प्रमाथीनि हरन्ति प्रसभं मनः ॥ ॥ २—६० ॥
तानि सर्वाणि संयम्य युक्त आसीत मत्परः ।
वशे हि यस्येन्द्रियाणि तस्य प्रज्ञा प्रतिष्ठिता ॥ २—६१ ॥
ध्यायतो विषयान्पुंसः सङ्गस्तेषूपजायते ।
सङ्गात्संजायते कामः कामात्क्रोधोऽभिजायते ॥ २—६२ ॥
क्रोधाद्भवति संमोहः संमोहात्स्मृतिविभ्रमः ।
स्मृतिभ्रम्शाद्बुद्धिनाशो बुद्धिनाशात्प्रणश्यति ॥ २—६३ ॥
रागद्वेषवियुक्तैस्तु विषयानिन्द्रयैश्चरन् ।
आत्मवश्यैर्विधेयात्मा प्रसादमधिगचछति ॥ २—६४ ॥

58. yadā saṃharate cāyaṃ kūrmo'ṅgānīva sarvaśaḥ
indriyāṇīndriyārthebhyas tasya prajñā pratiṣṭhitā
59. viṣayā vinivartante nirāhārasya dehinaḥ
rasavarjaṃ raso'pyasya paraṃ dṛṣtvā nivartate
60. yatato hy api kaunteya puruṣasya vipaścitaḥ
indriyāṇi pramāthīni haranti prasabhaṃ manaḥ
61. tāni sarvāṇi saṃyamya yukta āsīta matparaḥ
vaśe hi yasyendriyāṇi tasya prajñā pratiṣṭhitā
62. dhyāyato viṣayān puṃsaḥ saṅgas teṣūpajāyate
saṅgāt saṃjāyate kāmaḥ kāmāt krodho'bhijāyate
63. krodhād bhavati saṃmohaḥ saṃmohāt smṛtivibhramaḥ
smṛtibhramśād buddhināśo buddhināśāt praṇaśyati
64. rāgadveṣaviyuktais tu viṣayān indriyaiś caran
ātmavaśyair vidheyātmā prasādam adhigacchati

2.58 And when he withdraws from every side his senses from the objects of the senses as a tortoise [draws in its] limbs, his gnosis is well established.

2.59 For the non-eating[56] embodied (*dehin*) [Self] the objects disappear, except for the relish. [Upon] seeing the Supreme, the relish also disappears for him.

2.60 Yet, even of the striving, discerning man, the agitated senses forcibly carry away the mind, O son-of-Kuntī.

2.61 Controlling all these [senses], yoked [and] intent on Me, let him sit [in an easeful posture]. For he whose senses are under control, his gnosis is well established.

2.62 [When] a man contemplates objects, direct-contact with them is born. From direct-contact springs desire; from desire, anger is produced.

2.63 From anger comes confusion; from confusion, disorder of the memory;[57] from disorder of the memory, the destruction of the wisdom-faculty. On the destruction of the wisdom-faculty, [a person] is lost.

2.64 [Although] moving with the senses among objects, the well-governed self, disjoined from passion and aversion [and] with [all] self-restraints[58] [applied], approaches serenity-grace.[59]

56. The qualifying adjective "non-eating" (*nirāhāra*) refers to the nongrasping attitude of a spiritual practitioner culminating in the nonperception of objects.

57. The word *smriti,* or "memory," is here used in a specific way, namely in the sense of "present-mindedness" or even "awareness." Hence the expression *smrti-vibhrama,* or "memory disorder," can be equated with cognitive disorder. The compound *buddhi-nāsha,* or "destruction of *buddhi,*" on the other hand, may *in extremis* well be interpreted in terms of a "nervous breakdown," as R. C. Zaehner (1966) suggests, though there are deeper connotations to it. For the loss of *buddhi* implies a deep-level disorganization of the human personality, rendering a person incapable of the kind of discernment that is instrumental to inner growth and the attainment of spiritual liberation.

58. The Sanskrit original uses the plural in the instrumental case ("by restraints," *vashyaih*).

59. The word *prasāda* refers to the complete inner stillness in which a person becomes qualified for the grace (*prasāda*) of the Divine. The author of the *Bhagavad-Gītā* was no doubt aware of this double connotation.

प्रसादे सर्वदुःखानां हानिरस्योऽपजायते ।
प्रसन्नचेतसो ह्याशु बुद्धिः पर्यवतिष्ठते ॥ २—६५ ॥
नस्ति बुद्धिरयुक्तस्य न चायुक्तस्य भावना ।
न चाभावयतः शान्तिरशान्तस्य कुतः सुखम् ॥ २—६६ ॥
इन्द्रियाणां हि चरतां यन्मनोऽनुविधीयते ।
तदस्य हरति प्रज्ञां वायुर्नावमिवाम्भसि ॥ २—६७ ॥
तस्माद्यस्य महाबाहो निगृहीतानि सर्वशः ।
इन्द्रियाणीन्द्रियार्थेभ्यस्तस्य प्रज्ञा प्रतिष्ठिता ॥ २—६८ ॥

65. prasāde sarvaduḥkhānāṃ hānir asyo'pajāyate
prasannacetaso hy āśu buddhiḥ paryavatiṣṭhate
66. nāsti buddhir ayuktasya na cāyuktasya bhāvanā
na cābhāvayataḥ śāntir aśāntasya kutaḥ sukham
67. indriyāṇāṃ hi caratāṃ yan mano'nuvidhīyate
tad asya harati prajñāṃ vāyur nāvam ivāmbhasi
68. tasmād yasya mahābāho nigṛhītāni sarvaśaḥ
indriyāṇīndriyārthebhyas tasya prajñā pratiṣṭhitā

2.65 [On reaching] serenity-grace, there arises for him the cessation of all sorrow. For the clear-minded, the wisdom-faculty is at once firmly grounded.

2.66 There is no wisdom-faculty for the unyoked.[60] And for the unyoked there is also no becoming-whole.[61] [For him who does] not become-whole there is no peace.[62] Whence [comes] happiness to an unpeaceful [man]?

2.67 When the mind is governed by the roaming senses, then it carries away gnosis as the wind [carries away] a ship on the sea.

2.68 Hence, O mighty-armed [Arjuna], he whose senses are all-round withheld from the things of the senses, his gnosis is [well] established.

60. The person who fails to control the senses lacks the single *buddhi* spoken of in 2.41.

61. *Bhāvanā* is a tricky term to translate into English. The usual translations such as "development" or "meditation" seem inadequate. The word is formed from the grammatical root *bhū* ("to become").

62. If gnosis (*prajnā*) is the cognitive aspect of the ecstatic experience (*samādhi*), then peace is its emotive aspect. True, lasting peace comes only with spiritual liberation.

या निशा सर्वभूतानां तस्यां जागर्ति संयमी ।
यस्यां जाग्रति भुतानि सा निशा पश्यतो मुनेः ॥ २—६९ ॥
आपूर्यमाणमचलप्रतिष्ठं समुद्रमापः प्रविशन्ति यद्वत् ।
तद्वत्कामा यं प्रविशन्ति सर्वे स शान्तिमाप्नोति न कामकामी ॥ २—७० ॥
विहाय कामान्यः सर्वान्पुमांश्चरति निःस्पृहः ।
निर्ममो निरहंकारः स शान्तिमधिगच्छति ॥ २—७१ ॥
एषा ब्राह्मी स्थितिः पार्थ नैनां प्राप्य विमुह्यति ।
स्थित्वास्यमन्तकालेऽपि ब्रह्मनिर्वाणमृच्छति ॥ २—७२ ॥

69. yā niśā sarvabhūtānāṃ tasyāṃ jāgarti saṃyamī
    yasyāṃ jāgrati bhūtāni sā niśā paśyato muneḥ
70. āpūryamāṇam acalapratiṣṭhaṃ samudram āpaḥ praviśanti yadvat
    tadvat kāmā yaṃ praviśanti sarve sa śāntim āpnoti na kāmakāmī
71. vihāya kāmān yaḥ sarvān pumāṃś carati niḥspṛhaḥ
    nirmamo nirahaṃkāraḥ sa śāntim adhigacchati
72. eṣā brāhmī sthitiḥ pārtha naināṃ prāpya vimuhyati
    sthitvāsyām antakāle'pi brahmanirvāṇam ṛcchati

2.69 That which is night for all beings, therein is the [self-]controlled awake. That wherein beings are awake, that is night for the seeing sage.[63]

2.70 Just as the waters enter the ocean, full [yet having] unmoving ground, so all desires enter him; he attains peace [but] not the desirer of desires.[64]

2.71 That man (*pumān*) who, forsaking all desires, moves about devoid of longing, devoid of [the thought of] "mine," without ego-sense—he approaches peace.[65]

2.72 This is the brahmic state, O son-of-Prithā. Attaining this, [a person] is no [longer] deluded. Abiding therein also at the end-time [i.e., at death], he attains extinction in the world-ground (*brahma-nirvāna*).[66]

63. This verse can be interpreted psychoanalytically: "Night" symbolizes the unconscious, which the *yogin* transmutes into supraconsciousness. On the other hand, when he is in the ecstatic state, the empirical space-time consciousness becomes "night" for him, since it lies below the threshold of his awareness

64. Detachment does not mean repression but rather the "superlimation" (not merely sublimation) of all desires; they are molten into one single dynamic volition directed toward self-transcendence. See *Brihadāranyaka-Upanishad* 4. 3.21. I introduced the distinction between sublimation and superlimation in G. Feuerstein, *Sacred Sexuality: The Erotic Spirit in the World's Great Religions* (Rochester, Vt.: Inner Traditions, 2003), p. 197.

65. The attainment of peace (*shānti*) presupposes a complete reorganization of the psychic structure, as a result of which a person is not reborn but becomes merged with the world-ground (the *brahma-nirvāna* of 2.72). However, this condition of liberation does not involve the desired higher awakening in the eternal body of God taught by Krishna.

66. This verse hints at the two types, or stages, of spiritual liberation. The first is *jīvanmukti* ("living liberation"), emancipation while retaining the physical body. The second is *videhamukti* ("disembodied liberation"), which occurs upon the complete disintegration of the individual's psychosomatic structures. *Videhamukti* is mergence with the world-ground, which is the cosmic form of *brahman*, otherwise called *prakriti-pradhāna,* or "cosmic foundation."

अर्जुन उवाच
ज्यायसी चेत्कर्मणस्ते मता बुद्धिर्जनार्दन ।
तत्किं कर्मणि घोरे मां नियोजयसि केशव ॥ ३—१ ॥
व्यामिश्रेणेव वाक्येन बुद्धिं मोहयसीव मे ।
तदेकं वद निश्चित्य येन श्रेयोऽहमाप्नुयाम् ॥ ३—२ ॥
श्रीभगवानुवाच
लोकेऽस्मिन्द्विविधा निष्ठा पुरा प्रोक्ता मयानघ ।
ज्ञानयोगेन सांख्यानां कर्मयोगेन योगिनाम् ॥ ३—३ ॥
न कर्मणामनारम्भान्नैष्कर्म्यं पुरुषोऽश्नुते ।
न च संन्यसनादेव सिद्धिं समाधिगच्छति ॥ ३—४ ॥

arjuna uvāca

1. jyāyasī cet karmaṇas te matā buddhir janārdana
   tat kiṃ karmaṇi ghore māṃ niyojayasi keśava
2. vyāmiśreṇaiva vākyena buddhiṃ mohayasīva me
   tad ekaṃ vada niścitya yena śreyo'ham āpnuyām

śrībhagavān uvāca

3. loke'smin dvividhā niṣṭhā purā proktā mayānāgha
   jñānayogena sāṃkhyānāṃ karmayogena yoginām
4. na karmaṇām anārambhān naiṣkarmyaṃ puruṣo'śnute
   na ca saṃnyasanād eva siddhiṃ samādhigacchati

CHAPTER 3

The Yoga of Action

Arjuna said:

3.1 O Janārdana,[1] if you [are of] the conviction that wisdom is superior to action, then why, O Keshava,[2] do you urge me into [this] dreadful deed?

3.2 You apparently confuse my wisdom-faculty with ambiguous speech.[3] Tell me for sure the one [means] by which I should [be able to] attain the [highest] good.

The Blessed Lord said:

3.3 Long ago, I proclaimed a twofold way-of-life (*nishthā*) in this world, O Anagha[4]— Jnāna-Yoga[5] for the Sāmkhyas,[6] and Karma-Yoga[7] for *yogins*.

3.4 Not by the non-initiation[8] of actions [does] a man enjoy action-transcendence,[9] nor by renunciation alone [does] he approach perfection.[10]

1. On Krishna's epithet Janārdana, see note 25 for 1.36.
2. On the epithet Keshava, see note 21 for 1.31.
3. Here Arjuna audaciously tells his guru that he is confusing him with contradictory statements. At least he has the decency of qualifying his criticism by saying "apparently" (*iva*).
4. The epithet Anagha means "blameless" or "sinless." Arjuna is without sin insofar as he is a partial manifestation of the god Indra.
5. Jnāna-Yoga is the path of self-transcendence through discriminative wisdom.
6. Here the word *sāmkhya* (used in the plural) refers not to the Sāmkhya tradition but to its adherents.
7. Karma-Yoga is Krishna's unique path of self-transcending action.
8. The term *anārambha*, here rendered as "non-initiation," means literally "nonbeginning." It is generally translated as "abstention."
9. *Naishkarmya*, or "action-transcendence," is a difficult word to capture in English. Words like "actionlessness" or "freedom from action," which are often used, do not convey the sense of the original. Perhaps "freedom-in-action" would be a better way of conveying the implied meaning of *naishkarmya*, which involves no egoic agency.
10. "Perfection" (*siddhi*) refers to the ultimate accomplishment on the spiritual path, which is liberation.

न हि कश्चित्क्षणमपि जातु तिष्ठत्यकर्मकृत् ।
कार्यते ह्यवशः कर्म सर्वः प्रकृतिजैर्गुणैः ॥ ३—५ ॥
कर्मेन्द्रियाणि संयम्य य आस्ते मनसा स्मरन् ।
कर्मेन्द्रियैः कर्मयोगमसक्तः स विशिष्यते ॥ ३—६ ॥
इन्द्रियार्थान्विमूढात्मा मिथ्याचारः स उच्यते ।
यस्त्विन्द्रियाणि मनसा नियम्यारभतेऽर्जुन ॥ ३—७ ॥
नियतं कुरु कर्म त्वं कर्म ज्यायो ह्यकर्मणः ।
शरीरयात्रापि च ते न प्रसिध्येदकर्मणः ॥ ३—८ ॥
यज्ञार्थात्कर्मणोऽन्यत्र लोकोऽयं कर्मबन्धनः ।
तदर्थं कर्म कौन्तेय मुक्तसङ्गः समाचर ॥ ३—९ ॥
सहयज्ञाः प्रजाः सृष्ट्वा पुरोऽवाच प्रजापतिः ।
अनेन प्रसविष्यध्वमेष वोऽस्त्विष्टकामधुक् ॥ ३—१० ॥

5. na hi kaścit kṣaṇam api jātu tiṣṭhaty akarmakṛt
kāryate hy avaśaḥ karma sarvaḥ prakṛtijair guṇaiḥ
6. karmendriyāṇi saṃyamya ya āste manasā smaran
indriyārthān vimūḍhātmā mithyācāraḥ sa ucyate
7. yas tv indriyāṇi manasā niyamyārabhate'rjuna
karmendriyaiḥ karmayogam asaktaḥ sa viśiṣyate
8. niyataṃ kuru karma tvaṃ karma jyāyo hy akarmaṇaḥ
śarīrayātrāpi ca te na prasidhyed akarmaṇaḥ
9. yajñārthāt karmaṇo'nyatra loko'yaṃ karmabandhanaḥ
tadarthaṃ karma kaunteya muktasaṅgaḥ samācara
10. sahayajñāḥ prajāḥ sṛṣṭvā puro'vāca prajāpatiḥ
anena prasaviṣyadhvam eṣa vo'stv iṣṭakāmadhuk

3.5 For, not even for a moment [can] anyone ever remain without performing action. Every [being] is indeed unwittingly (*avasha*) made to perform action by the primary-qualities[11] born of the cosmos.[12]

3.6 The confounded self, who, [while] restraining the action senses,[13] sits remembering the sense objects with the mind—he is called a hypocrite.[14]

3.7 But [more] excellent is he, O Arjuna, who, controlling the [cognitive] senses[15] with the mind, embarks unattached on Karma-Yoga with the action senses.

3.8 You must do the necessary[16] action, for action is superior to inaction; not even your body's processes[17] can be accomplished by inaction.

3.9 This world is bound by action save when this action is intended as sacrifice.[18] With that purpose [in mind], O son-of-Kuntī[19] [Arjuna], engage in action devoid of attachment.

3.10 Prajāpati[20] of old said, emanating creatures together with sacrifice: "By this shall you procreate; let this [sacrifice] be this wish-fulfilling cow[21] [of your] desires."

11. The three primary-qualities (*guna*) are *sattva, rajas,* and *tamas.*

12. Usually, *prakriti* is translated as "nature," but the term really conveys all of cosmic existence, as opposed to the transcendental Spirit (*purusha*). The compound *prakriti-ja* ("Cosmos-born") refers to the cosmic matrix, the world-ground of conditioned existence or what in the Sāmkhya tradition is called *prakriti-pradhāna* ("cosmic foundation").

13. The five conative senses, or "action senses" (*karma-indriya*, written *karmendriya*), are voice (voice box), hands, feet, anus, and genitals.

14. The compound *mithyā-ācāra,* or "[he whose] conduct is false," is here rendered as "hypocrite."

15. The five cognitive senses (*jnāna-indriya*, written *jnānendriya*) are eyes, ears, nose, tongue, and skin. These, together with the five conative senses and the lower mind (*manas*), make eleven senses in all.

16. Shankara explains *niyata* quite rightly in a psychological way as work for which one is fitted (*adhikrita*). It does not mean primarily the moral duties prescribed by the sacred canon, as was maintained, for instance, by Franklin Edgerton (1944, p. 59) and others. Hence the translation of *niyata* as "obligatory" is too limited and easily gives rise to the mistaken notion that it implies some kind of compulsion exerted on the individual by the traditional mores. "Necessary," which is my proposed translation, suggests that an action is deemed necessary in a particular context.

17. *Yātrā* (in the plural) means literally "goings-on"; hence the present rendering as "processes."

18. Sacrifice (*yajna*) plays an all-important role in Hinduism. Symbolically, it implies the surrendering of the lower to the higher, that is, of the ego-self to the transcendental Self.

19. See note 19 for 1.27.

20. Prajāpati—lit. "lord (*pati*) of creatures"—is a synonym for Brahma, the Creator.

21. The mythological wish-fulfilling cow (*kāma-dhuk*) is said to grant all one's desires. See also 10.28.

देवान्भावयतानेन ते देवा भावयन्तु वः ।
परस्परं भावयन्तः श्रेयः परमवाप्स्यथ ॥ ३—११ ॥
इष्टान्भोगान्हि वो देवा दास्यन्ते यज्ञभाविताः ।
तैर्दत्तानप्रदायैभ्यो यो भुङ्क्ते स्तेन एव सः ॥ ३—१२ ॥
यज्ञशिष्टाशिनः सन्तो मुच्यन्ते सर्वकिल्बिषैः ।
भुञ्जते ते त्वघं पापा ये पचन्त्यात्मकारणात् ॥ ३—१३ ॥
अन्नाद्भवन्ति भूतानि पर्जन्यादन्नसंभवः ।
यज्ञाद्भवति पर्जन्यो यज्ञः कर्मसमुद्भवः ॥ ३—१४ ॥
कर्म ब्रह्मोद्भवं विद्धि ब्रह्माक्षरसमुद्भवम् ।
तस्मात्सर्वगतं ब्रह्म नित्यं यज्ञे प्रतिष्ठितम् ॥ ३—१५ ॥
एवं प्रवर्तितं चक्रं नानुवर्तयतीह यः ।
अघायुरिन्द्रियारामो मोघं पार्थ स जीवति ॥ ३—१६ ॥

11. devān bhāvayatānena te devā bhāvayantu vaḥ
parasparaṃ bhāvayantaḥ śreyaḥ param avāpsyatha
12. iṣṭān bhogān hi vo devā dāsyante yajñabhāvitaḥ
tair dattān apradāyaibhyo yo bhuṅkte stena eva saḥ
13. yajñaśiṣṭāśinaḥ santo mucyante sarvakilbiṣaiḥ
bhuñjate te tv aghaṃ pāpā ye pacanty ātmakāraṇāt
14. annād bhavanti bhūtāni parjanyād annasaṃbhavaḥ
yajñād bhavati parjanyo yajñaḥ karmasamudbhavaḥ
15. karma brahmodbhavaṃ viddhi brahmākṣarasamudbhavam
tasmāt sarvagataṃ brahma nityaṃ yajñe pratiṣṭhitam
16. evaṃ pravartitaṃ cakraṃ nānuvartayatīha yaḥ
aghāyur indriyārāmo moghaṃ pārtha sa jīvati

3.11 With this may you sustain the deities[22] so that the deities may sustain you. Sustaining one another, you shall obtain the supreme good (*shreya*).

3.12 For, sustained by sacrifice, the deities will give you the desired "food."[23] He who enjoys their gifts without giving [something in return] is but a thief.

3.13 Good [men], consuming the sacrificial leavings, are released from all guilt, but those who cook for their own sake[24] are evil and "eat" [the karmic fruit of] wickedness.

3.14 From food, beings come-into-being. Food is produced from rain. From sacrifice, the rain comes-into-being. Sacrifice is born from [ritual] action.[25]

3.15 Know that [all] action arises from the world-ground. The world-ground is born from the Imperishable.[26] Therefore the omnipresent world-ground is ever established in sacrifice.

3.16 Thus, he who does not turn the rotating wheel[27] [of action as sacrifice] lives a wicked life, in vain, [attached to] sensual delight, O son-of-Prithā[28] [Arjuna].

22. The word *deva* means lit. "shining one." The gods and goddesses of Hinduism are similar to the angels of the Judeo-Christian belief system. The traditional notion is that these deities are sustained by the subtle essence of sacrificial offerings. By way of extension, this term is also sometimes used as an epithet for the Supreme Being itself, also designated as "God of gods" (*deva-deva*) in verse 10.15.

23. The word *bhoga* means both "enjoyment" and "eating." This verse expresses very clearly the reciprocity that is thought to exist between gods and humans, which is part of the cosmic order (*rita*).

24. Those who cook for themselves without making any sacrificial offerings to the deities are deemed extremely self-centered, and their sinful attitude reaps them only negative karmic reward. According to Krishna Prem (1938/1969, p. 24), the gods symbolize consciousness nourishing the manifested form. This psychological interpretation is possibly true, though not exclusive of other meanings.

25. Again, this verse describes the reciprocal linkage between humans and gods, in which the performance of sacrifice is central. This obscure verse recalls an archaic "ecological" doctrine first formulated in the *Taittirīya-Upanishad* 2.2 and 3.10.

26. Here "Imperishable" refers to the *akshara-purusha,* or supreme Godhead.

27. The motif of the "wheel" suggests the idea of conscious participation in life through ego-transcending (self-sacrificing) action.

28. See note 18 for 1.25.

यस्त्वात्मरतिरेव स्यादात्मतृप्तश्च मानवः ।
आत्मन्येव च संतुष्टस्तस्य कार्यं न विद्यते ॥ ३—१७ ॥
नैव तस्य कृतेनार्थो नाकृतेनेह कश्चन ।
न चास्य सर्वभूतेषु कश्चिदर्थव्यपाश्रयः ॥ ३—१८ ॥
तस्मादसक्तः सततं कार्यं कर्म समाचर ।
असक्तो ह्याचरन्कर्म परमाप्नोति पूरुषः ॥ ३—१९ ॥
कर्मणैव हि संसिद्धिमास्थिता जनकादयः ।
लोकसंग्रहमेवापि संपश्यन्कर्तुमर्हसि ॥ ३—२० ॥
यद्यदाचरति श्रेष्ठस्तत्तदेवेतरो जनः ।
स यत्प्रमाणं कुरुते लोकस्तदनुवर्तते ॥ ३—२१ ॥
न मे पार्थास्ति कर्तव्यं त्रिषु लोकेषु किंचन ।
नानवाप्तमवाप्तव्यं वर्त एव च कर्मणि ॥ ३—२२ ॥
यदि ह्यहं न वर्तेयं जातु कर्मण्यतन्द्रितः ।
मम वर्त्मानुवर्तन्ते मनुष्याः पार्थ सर्वशः ॥ ३—२३ ॥

17. yas tv ātmaratir eva syād ātmatṛptaś ca mānavaḥ
ātmany eva ca saṃtuṣṭas tasya kāryaṃ na vidyate
18. naiva tasya kṛtenārtho nākṛteneha kaścana
na cāsya sarvabhūteṣu kaścid arthavyapāśrayaḥ
19. tasmād asaktaḥ satataṃ kāryaṃ karma samācara
asakto hy ācaran karma param āpnoti pūruṣaḥ
20. karmaṇaiva hi saṃsiddhim āsthitā janakādayaḥ
lokasaṃgraham evāpi saṃpaśyan kartum arhasi
21. yad-yad ācarati śreṣṭhas tat-tad evetaro janaḥ
sa yat pramāṇaṃ kurute lokas tad anuvartate
22. na me pārthāsti kartavyaṃ triṣu lokeṣu kiṃcana
nānavāptam avāptavyaṃ varta eva ca karmaṇi
23. yadi hy ahaṃ na varteyaṃ jātu karmaṇy atandritaḥ
mama vartmānuvartante manuṣyāḥ pārtha sarvaśaḥ

3.17 Yet, for a human-being [who] should have enjoyment only [in] the Self, [who should be] satisfied with the Self, and [who should be] content in the Self, there is nothing [left] to be done.[29]

3.18 For him indeed there is no purpose in any [action] done or not done here [on earth]. And he [has] no dependence on any being for any purpose.

3.19 Therefore, always perform unattached the deed to be done,[30] for the man (*purusha*) performing action [while being] unattached attains the Supreme.

3.20 By action indeed [King] Janaka and others attained [spiritual] consummation. Even considering only the world's welfare,[31] you ought to act.

3.21 Whatever indeed the best does, that verily other people [will do as well]. What[ever] standard he sets, that the world follows.[32]

3.22 For me, O son-of-Prithā, [there is] no [action] to be done in the three worlds,[33] nor [anything] ungained to be gained—and yet I engage in action.

3.23 For, if I should not untiringly engage in action at all, humans [would], O son-of-Prithā, follow everywhere My "track."[34]

29. The Self-realized adept may or may not act. Where all actions are performed out of "spontaneity" (*sahaja*) springing from wisdom, there is no sense of "duty" (*dharma*). This is also why Krishna can say: "Relinquishing all *dharmas*, come to Me alone for shelter" (18.66).

30. The word *kārya* ("to be done") is the future passive participle of *kri* "to do." It is the ethical "ought."

31. The rare compound *loka-samgraha,* here translated as "world's welfare," appears in the *Gītā* only in this verse and in 3.25. Swami Tripurari's (2001) rendering, "[considering] people in general," is too weak, while Radhakrishnan's (1948) rendering of the compound as "maintenance of the world" is a bit too vague. Van Buitenen's (1981) "[looking to] what holds the world together" is literal but also vague. Edgerton (1944) wrongly interprets the term as "control of the world." In his book *The Ethics of the Gītā* (1971), G. W. Kaveeshwar explains the term as "guidance of the masses"; we may ask, guidance toward what? In their commentaries, Rāmānuja, Shankara, and Abhinavagupta leave the word *loka-samgraha* unexplained, as if it required no explanation. Nataraja Guru (1973) gives "integration of the world." He insightfully observes: "The word *lokasamgraham* (keeping the world together) does not imply any social service or uplift work of closed groups or communities. It refers to human interest or welfare in a globally comprehensive sense" (p. 193). The ancient king Janaka was apparently fully Self-realized but kept up with the affairs of state in order to benefit people.

32. Curiously, Krishna's statement does not seem to apply to the *kali-yuga*, which is traditionally thought to have begun around the end of the Bharata war. It is definitely not true of our own era, where people seem to emulate the worst examples rather than the best and where the foolish tend to willingly follow the blind.

33. On the three worlds, or realms (*loka*), see note 24 for 1.35.

34. The Sanskrit word used for "track" is *vartman* in the sense of "example."

उत्सीदेयुरिमे लोका न कुर्यां कर्म चेदहम् ।
संकरस्य च कर्ता स्यामुपहन्यामिमाः प्रजाः ॥ ३—२४ ॥
सक्ताः कर्मण्यविद्वांसो यथा कुर्वन्ति भारत ।
कुर्याद्विद्वांस्तथासक्तश्चिकीर्षुर् लोकसंग्रहम् ॥ ३—२५ ॥
न बुद्धिभेदं जनयेदज्ञानां कर्मसङ्गिनाम् ।
जोषयेत्सर्वकर्माणि विद्वान्युक्तः समाचरन् ॥ ३—२६ ॥
प्रकृतेः क्रियमाणानि गुणैः कर्माणि सर्वशः ।
अहंकारविमूढात्मा कर्ताहमिति मन्यते ॥ ३—२७ ॥
तत्त्ववित्तु महाबाहो गुणकर्मविभागयोः ।
गुणा गुणेषु वर्तन्त इति मत्वा न सज्जते ॥ ३—२८ ॥
प्रकृतेर्गुणसंमूढाः सज्जन्ते गुणकर्मसु ।
तानकृत्स्नविदो मन्दान्कृत्स्नविन्नविचालयेत् ॥ ३—२९ ॥

24. utsīdeyur ime lokā na kuryāṃ karma ced aham
    saṃkarasya ca kartā syām upahanyām imāḥ prajāḥ
25. saktāḥ karmaṇy avidvāṃso yathā kurvanti bhārata
    kuryād vidvāṃs tathāsaktaś cikīrṣur lokasaṃgraham
26. na buddhibhedaṃ janayed ajñānāṃ karmasaṅginām
    joṣayet sarvakarmāṇi vidvān yuktaḥ samācaran
27. prakṛteḥ kriyamāṇāni guṇaiḥ karmāṇi sarvaśaḥ
    ahaṃkāravimūḍhātmā kartāham iti manyate
28. tattvavit tu mahābāho guṇakarmavibhāgayoḥ
    guṇā guṇeṣu vartanta iti matvā na sajjate
29. prakṛter guṇasaṃmūḍhāḥ sajjante guṇakarmasu
    tān akṛtsnavido mandān kṛtsnavin na vicālayet

3.24 If I were not to perform action, these worlds would perish,[35] and I would be the author of chaos[36] and would destroy [all] these creatures.

3.25 Just as the unwise perform [their deeds] attached to action, O descendant-of-Bharata, so the wise should act thus unattached, desiring to accomplish the world's welfare.

3.26 Let not [the wise] generate a *buddhi*-breach[37] in ignorant, action-attached [people]. Let the wise, yoked [and] performing [actions], cause [others] to rejoice in all actions.

3.27 Actions are everywhere performed by the primary-qualities (*guna*) of the Cosmos (*prakriti*). [Yet, he whose] self is deluded by the ego-sense[38] thinks: "I am the doer."

3.28 But, O mighty-armed [Arjuna], the knower-of-Reality [understands] the apportionment[39] of the primary-qualities and actions, realizing that the primary-qualities act upon primary-qualities, is not attached.

3.29 [Those] fooled by the primary-qualities of the Cosmos [become] attached to the actions of the primary-qualities. The knower of the Whole should not upset those dull-witted knowers of the non-Whole.[40]

35. The Sanskrit original has the optative *utsīdeyuh,* derived from the prefix *ud-* ("up/out of") and the verbal root *sad* ("to sit"), meaning "they should go away."
36. The term *samkara* denotes the opposite of "law" or "order" implied in the word *dharma.*
37. The Sanskrit term *buddhi-bheda,* here rendered as "*buddhi*-breach," signifies a break in the capacity for organized cognition, leading to conceptual confusion. It also has an emotional ingredient, suggesting a psychic state of collapse similar to a nervous breakdown.
38. The term *ahamkāra* means literally "I-maker."
39. The phrase *guna-karma-vibhāga,* or "apportionment of the primary-qualities and action," probably finds its explanation in 4.13 where Krishna speaks of the four estates, whose members are distinguished by their distinct emotional-mental qualities, depending on the function of the *gunas* in their natures. The word *vibhāgayoh* ("of apportionment" is in the genitive dual. Van Buitenen (1981) and Hill (1928/1966) have "distribution," while Edgerton (1944) has "separation."
40. Most translators understand the terms *kritsna-vid* and *akritsna-vid* in the sense of "complete knower" and "incomplete knower" respectively, but I feel that possibly something deeper is implied. Thus, I have chosen to take *kritsna* as referring to the Ultimate, the Whole, rather than as qualifying the knower. The ignorant person, in other words, does not see the total picture but has only a partial perspective, whereas the sage sees the Whole (*pūrna*) as it is.

मयि सर्वाणि कर्माणि संन्यस्याध्यात्मचेतसा ।
निराशिर्निर्ममो भूत्वा युध्यस्व विगतज्वरः ॥ ३—३० ॥
ये मे मतमिदं नित्यमनुतिष्ठन्ति मानवाः ।
श्रद्धावन्तोऽनसूयन्तो मुच्यन्ते तेऽपि कर्मभिः ॥ ३—३१ ॥
ये त्वेतदभ्यसूयन्तो नानुतिष्ठन्ति मे मतम् ।
सर्वज्ञानविमूढांस्तान्विद्धि नष्टानचेतसः ॥ ३—३२ ॥
सदृशं चेष्टते स्वस्याः प्रकृतेर्ज्ञानवानपि ।
प्रकृतिं यन्ति भूतानि निग्रहः किं करिष्यति ॥ ३—३३ ॥
इन्द्रियस्येन्द्रियस्यार्थे रागद्वेषौ व्यवास्थितौ ।
तयोर्न वशमागच्छेत्तौ ह्यस्य परिपन्थिनौ ॥ ३—३४ ॥
श्रेयान्स्वधर्मो विगुणः परधर्मात्स्वनुष्ठितात् ।
स्वधर्मे निधनं श्रेयः परधर्मो भयावहः ॥ ३—३५ ॥
अर्जन उवाच
अथ केन प्रयुक्तोऽयं पापं चरति पूरुषः ।
अनिच्छन्नपि वार्ष्णेय बलादिव नियोजितः ॥ ३—३६ ॥

30. mayi sarvāṇi karmāṇi saṃnyasyādhyātmacetasā
nirāśīr nirmamo bhūtvā yudhyasva vigatajvaraḥ
31. ye me matam idaṃ nityam anutiṣṭhanti mānavāḥ
śraddhāvanto'nasūyanto mucyante te'pi karmabhiḥ
32. ye tv etad abhyasūyanto nānutiṣṭhanti me matam
sarvajñānavimūḍhāṃs tān viddhi naṣṭān acetasaḥ
33. sadṛśaṃ ceṣṭate svasyāḥ prakṛter jñānavān api
prakṛtiṃ yanti bhūtāni nigrahaḥ kiṃ kariṣyati
34. indriyasyendriyasyārthe rāgadveṣau vyavāsthitau
tayor na vaśam āgacchet tau hy asya paripanthinau
35. śreyān svadharmo viguṇaḥ paradharmāt svanuṣṭhitāt
svadharme nidhanaṃ śreyaḥ paradharmo bhayāvahaḥ

arjuna uvāca
36. atha kena prayukto'yaṃ pāpaṃ carati pūruṣaḥ
anicchann api vārṣṇeya balād iva niyojitaḥ

3.30 Renouncing all actions in Me, with the mind [turned toward] the basis-of-self,[41] [and] having become without hope,[42] without [the sense of] "mine," [with your] fever-of-anxiety departed—fight!

3.31 Those human-beings who ever practice this My teaching, firm-in-faith and uncomplaining, they, too, are liberated from [the bondage of] actions.

3.32 But those who, complaining, do not follow this My teaching—know them as [people who are] fooled by all knowledge, lost [and] mindless.

3.33 Even the knowledgeable [man] behaves in accordance with his innate nature (*prakriti*). [All] beings follow [their own] nature. What will repression accomplish?

3.34 Passion and hatred are directed toward the objects of [their] respective senses. Let none come under their power, for both are waylayers on his [path].

3.35 Better is [one's] own-law imperfectly [carried out] than another's law well performed. [It is] better [to find] death in [the performance of one's] own-law, for another's law is fear instilling.[43]

Arjuna said:

3.36 Now, by what is this [earthly] man impelled to commit a sin, even unwittingly, O descendant-of-Vrishni?[44] As though constrained by force?

41. *Adhyātman,* "basis-of-self," is difficult to translate. It can refer both to the highest Self and to the inner self. In the present context, the phrase *adhyātma-cetasā* ("with the mind [directed toward] the inner-self") probably means something like "with the mind turned to the inner self." This is supported by 8.3, where the term is defined as "own-being" (*svabhāva*).

42. In Christian theology much has been made of the positive function of hope—the hope that in the end all will be made whole. Yoga, by contrast, emphasizes the negative side of hope (*āshis*) as a state of mind that merely keeps a person attached to the sensory world and thus implicated in the karmic nexus.

43. This is one of the most important verses of the *Gītā,* for it makes profound sense psychologically and ethically. Psychologically, because to follow someone else's moral course may do violence to one's own conscience (consider, for example, a soldier's *blind* obedience to a superior's orders) and therefore to one's sense of psychological integrity. Ethically, because someone else's moral sense may not correspond to our own and therefore can cause us to engender karma that is alien to our own mind and unfavorable to us. In any case, we are bound to feel ill at ease by adopting another person's course. See also 18.47.

44. On the epithet Vārshneya ("descendant-of-Vrishni"), see note 28 for 1.41.

श्रीभगवानुवाच
काम एष क्रोध एष रजोगुणसमुद्भवः ।
महाशनो महापाप्मा विद्ध्येनमिह वैरिणम् ॥ ३—३७ ॥

«अर्जुन उवाच
भवत्येष कथं कृष्ण कथं चैव विवर्धते ।
किमात्मकः किमाचारस्तन्मामाचक्ष्य पृच्छतः ॥
श्रीभगवानुवाच
एष सूक्ष्मः परः शत्रुर्देहिनामिन्द्रियैः सह ।
सुखतन्त्र इवासिनो मोहयन्पार्थ तिष्ठति ॥
कामक्रोधमयो घोरः स्तम्भहर्षसमुद्भवः ।
अहंकारोऽभिमानात्म दुस्तरः पापकर्मभिः ॥
हर्षमस्य निवर्त्यैष शोकमस्य ददाति च ।
भयं चास्य करोत्येष मोहयंस्तु मुहुर्मुहुः ॥
स एष कलुषः क्षुद्रश्छिद्रप्रेक्षी धनंजय ।
रजःप्रवृत्तो मोहात्मा मनुष्याणामुपद्रवः»

śrībhagavān uvāca
37. kāma eṣa krodha eṣa rajoguṇasamudbhavaḥ
mahāśano mahāpāpmā viddhy enam iha vairiṇam

« arjuna uvāca
bhavatyeṣa kathaṃ kṛṣṇa kathaṃ caiva vivardhate
kimātmakaḥ kimācārastanmamācakṣya pṛcchataḥ

śrībhagavān uvāca
eṣa sūkṣmaḥ paraḥ śatrurdehinām indriyaiḥ saha
sukhatantra ivāsino mohayan pārtha tiṣṭhati
kāmakrodhamayo ghoraḥ stambhaharṣasamudbhavaḥ
ahaṃkāro'bhimānātmā dustaraḥ pāpakarmabhiḥ
harṣamasya nivartyaiṣa śokamasya dadāti ca
bhayaṃ cāsya karotyeṣa mohayaṃstu muhurmuhuḥ
sa eṣa kaluṣaḥ kṣudraśchidraprekṣī dhanaṃjaya
rajaḥ pravṛtto mohātmā manuṣyāṇām upadravaḥ.»

The Blessed Lord said:

3.37 It is desire; it is anger born of *rajo-guna,*[45] all-devouring, greatly evil—know this [as] the enemy here [on earth]!

«Arjuna said:

How does it arise, O Krishna, and how increase? What is [its] essence, what [its] form-of-expression? This tell me [who] asks.

The Blessed Lord said:

This [desire] is the subtle supreme foe of [all] the body-essences (*dehin*) together with [their] senses. It persists, seated seemingly (*iva*) in a web of pleasure, deluding [everyone], O son-of-Prithā. Made of desire [and] anger, [this enemy is] terrible; causing paralyzing exhilaration, [it is] the ego-sense of the essence (*ātman*) of infatuation difficult-to-transcend by sinful actions.
[Quickly] it deprives him of exhilaration and gives him grief.
And, again and again stupefying [all], it brings him fear.
It is turbid, [something that causes a person to] peep into keyholes, O Dhanamjaya,[46] propelled by *rajas,* of the essence (*ātman*) of delusion, the distress of human beings.»

45. *Rajo-guna* is *rajas,* the primary-quality (*guna*) of activity. See note 44 for 2.45.
46. On the epithet Dhanamjaya, see note 7 for 1.15.

धूमेनाव्रियते वह्निर्यथादर्शो मलेन च ।
यथोल्बेनावृतो गर्भस्तथा तेनेदमावृतम् ॥ ३—३८ ॥
आवृतं ज्ञानमेतेन ज्ञानिनो नित्यवैरिणा ।
कामरूपेण कौन्तेय दुष्पूरेणानलेन च ॥ ३—३९ ॥
इन्द्रियाणि मनो बुद्धिरस्याधिष्ठानमुच्यते ।
एतैर्विमोहयत्येष ज्ञानमावृत्य देहिनम् ॥ ३—४० ॥
तस्मात्त्वमिन्द्रियाण्यादौ नियम्य भरतर्षभ ।
पाप्मानं प्रजहि ह्येनं ज्ञानविज्ञाननाशनम् ॥ ३—४१ ॥
इन्द्रियाणि पराण्याहुरिन्द्रियेभ्यः परं मनः ।
मनसस्तु परा बुद्धिर्यो बुद्धेः परतस्तु सः ॥ ३—४२ ॥
एवं बुद्धेः परं बुद्ध्वा संस्तभ्यात्मानमात्मना ।
जहि शत्रुं महाबाहो कामरूप दुरासदम् ॥ ३—४३ ॥

38. dhūmenāvriyate vahnir yathādarśo malena ca
yatholbenāvṛto garbhas tathā tenedam āvṛtam
39. āvṛtaṃ jñānam etena jñānino nityavairiṇā
kāmarūpeṇa kaunteya duṣpūreṇānalena ca
40. indriyāṇi mano buddhir asyādhiṣṭhānam ucyate
etair vimohayaty eṣa jñānam āvṛtya dehinam
41. tasmāt tvam indriyāṇy ādau niyamya bharatarṣabha
pāpmānaṃ prajahi hy enaṃ jñānavijñānanāśanam
42. indriyāṇi parāṇy āhur indriyebhyaḥ paraṃ manaḥ
manasas tu parā buddhir yo buddheḥ paratas tu saḥ
43. evaṃ buddheḥ paraṃ buddhvā saṃstabhyātmānam ātmanā
jahi śatruṃ mahābāho kāmarūpaṃ durāsadam

3.38 As fire is enveloped by smoke and a mirror [obscured] by dust; as an embryo is concealed by a membrane, so is this [world] covered over by that [desire].

3.39 Knowledge is concealed by this perpetual enemy of the knower, this insatiable fire in the form of desire, O son-of-Kuntī.[47]

3.40 Senses, mind, and wisdom-faculty are called the hiding-places of this [enemy of wisdom]. Through these it fools the body-essence (*dehin*), concealing knowledge.

3.41 Therefore, O Bharatarshabha,[48] restrain the senses first, strike down this evil [that is] destroying [both true] knowledge (*jnānā*) and world-knowledge (*vijnāna*).[49]

3.42 Superior, they say, are the senses; superior to the senses is the mind; [even more] superior than the mind is the wisdom-faculty; what is superior to the wisdom-faculty is verily He.[50]

3.43 Thus having awakened to[51] [Him who is] superior to the wisdom-faculty, stabilizing the self by the Self,[52] slay, O mighty-armed [Arjuna], the enemy in the form of desire, difficult-to-conquer.

47. On son-of-Kuntī (Kaunteya), see note 19 for 1.27.

48. The epithet Bharatarshabha means "Bharata Bull."

49. The word *vijnāna* generally refers to the kind of differentiating knowledge by which we come to know the world. This meaning is epitomized by the prefix *vi-*. By contrast, *jnāna* here stands for gnosis, true knowledge.

50. Rāmānuja insists that the masculine pronoun *sah* ("he") here refers to "desire" (*kāma,* which is a masculine noun), but this is unconvincing. It is far more likely that it denotes the transcendental Self (*ātman*). Compare *Katha-Upanishad* 3.10 and 6.7.

51. The original has the Sanskrit gerund *buddhvā,* derived from the same root as *buddhi*, namely, *budh,* "to know/be awake."

52. Since Sanskrit has no capital letters, the phrase *samstabhyātmānam ātmanā* could also be translated simply as "stabilizing oneself by oneself." The context, however, suggests that it is one's realization of the Self that helps stabilize the lower self, or mind.

श्रीभगवानुवाच
इमं विवस्वते योगं प्रोक्तवानहमव्ययम् ।
विवस्वान्मनवे प्राह मनुरिक्ष्वाकवेऽब्रवीत् ॥ ४—१ ॥
एवं परंपराप्राप्तमिमं राजर्षयो विदुः ।
स कालेनेह महता योगो नष्टः परंतप ॥ ४—२ ॥
स एवायं मया तेऽद्य योगः प्रोक्तः पुरातनः ।
भक्तोऽसि मे सखा चेति रहस्यं ह्येतदुत्तमम् ॥ ४—३ ॥
अर्जुन उवाच
अपरं भवतो जन्म परं जन्म विवस्वतः ।
कथमेतद्विजानीयां त्वमादौ प्रोक्तवानिति ॥ ४—४ ॥
श्रीभगवानुवाच
बहूनि मे व्यतीतानि जन्मानि तव चार्जुन ।
तान्यहं वेद सर्वाणि न त्वं वेत्थ परंतप ॥ ४—५ ॥

śrībhagavān uvāca

1. imaṃ vivasvate yogaṃ proktavān aham avyayam
   vivasvān manave prāha manur ikṣvākave'bravīt
2. evaṃ paraṃparāprāptam imaṃ rājarṣayo viduḥ
   sa kāleneha mahatā yogo naṣṭaḥ paraṃtapa
3. sa evāyaṃ mayā te'dya yogaḥ proktaḥ purātanaḥ
   bhakto'si me sakhā ceti rahasyaṃ hy etad uttamam
   arjuna uvāca
4. aparaṃ bhavato janma paraṃ janma vivasvataḥ
   katham etad vijānīyāṃ tvam ādau proktavān iti

   śrībhagavān uvāca

5. bahūni me vyatītāni janmāni tava cārjuna
   tāny ahaṃ veda sarvāṇi na tvaṃ vettha paraṃtapa

CHAPTER 4

The Yoga of Wisdom

The Blessed Lord said:

4.1 This immutable Yoga I proclaimed to Vivasvat.[1] Vivasvat told it to Manu,[2] and Manu declared it to Ikshvāku.[3]

4.2 Thus received from one to another, it was learned by the royal seers. [However], in the long course-of-time this Yoga was lost here [on earth], O Paramtapa.[4]

4.3 This ancient Yoga, verily I proclaim to you today, [for] you are My devotee[5] and friend. Truly, this is the unexcelled secret.[6]

Arjuna said:

4.4 Later is Your[7] birth, earlier is Vivasvat's birth; how should I understand this [statement of yours that] You proclaimed [this Yoga] in the beginning?

The Blessed Lord said:

4.5 Many are My past births, and so are yours, O Arjuna. I know them all, [but] you do not know [yours], O Paramtapa.

1. Vivasvat (nominative: Vivasvān) is the name of the Sun as the chief solar deity.
2. Manu is the mythological progenitor of the human race, India's "Adam." Each age (*yuga*) is said to have its own Manu.
3. Ikshvāku was the royal founder of the Solar Dynasty in India.
4. On the epithet Paramtapa, see note 5 for 2.3.
5. A *bhakta* is a person endowed with *bhakti,* or "devotion/love."
6. The word *rahasya* ("secret") may contain a hidden reference to the fact that in its colophons, the *Gītā* is described as an Upanishad, which is a secret teaching. It's whispered outside the village.
7. The word *bhavatah* ("of You") is the formal equivalent to the familiar *tava* ("of you"), indicated here by capitalizing "Your."

अजोऽपि सन्नव्यात्मा भूतानामीश्वरोऽपि सन् ।
प्रकृतिं स्वामधिष्ठाय संभवाम्यात्ममायया ॥ ४—६ ॥
यदा यदा हि धर्मस्य ग्लानिर्भवति भारत ।
अभ्युत्थानमधर्मस्य तदात्मानं सृजाम्यहम् ॥ ४—७ ॥
परित्राणाय साधूनां विनाशाय च दुष्कृताम् ।
धर्मसंस्थापनार्थाय संभवामि युगे युगे ॥ ४—८ ॥
जन्म कर्म च मे दिव्यमेवं यो वेत्ति तत्त्वतः ।
त्यक्त्वा देहं पुनर्जन्म नैति मामेति सोऽर्जुन ॥ ४—९ ॥
वीतरागभयक्रोधा मन्मया मामुपाश्रिताः ।
बहवो ज्ञानतपसा पूता मद्भावमागताः ॥ ४—१० ॥
ये यथा मां प्रपद्यन्ते तांस्तथैव भजाम्यहम् ।
मम वर्त्मानुवर्तन्ते मनुष्याः पार्थ सर्वशः ॥ ४—११ ॥

6. ajo'pi sann avyayātmā bhūtānām īśvaro'pi san
prakṛtiṃ svām adhiṣṭhāya saṃbhavamy ātmamāyayā
7. yadā yadā hi dharmasya glānir bhavati bhārata
abhyutthānam adharmasya tadātmānaṃ sṛjāmy aham
8. paritrāṇāya sādhūnāṃ vināśāya ca duṣkṛtām
dharmasaṃsthāpanārthāya saṃbhavāmi yuge yuge
9. janma karma ca me divyam evaṃ yo vetti tattvataḥ
tyaktvā dehaṃ punarjanma naiti mām eti so'rjuna
10. vītarāgabhayakrodhā manmayā mām upāśritāḥ
bahavo jñānatapasā pūtā madbhāvam āgatāḥ
11. ye yathā māṃ prapadyante tāṃs tathaiva bhajāmy aham
mama vartmānuvartante manuṣyāḥ pārtha sarvaśaḥ

4.6 Although [I am] unborn, the immutable Self, [and] although being the Lord of [all] beings—[yet] by governing My own nature (*prakriti*), I come-to-be through the creative-power (*māyā*)[8] of Myself.

4.7 For, whenever there is a diminution of the law, O descendant-of-Bharata, and an upswing of lawlessness, then I create Myself [in manifest form].[9]

4.8 For the protection of good [people], for the destruction of wrongdoers, for the sake of establishing the law, I come-into-being from age to age.[10]

4.9 He who thus really knows My divine birth and action, abandoning the body, never [again] undergoes rebirth; he comes to Me, O Arjuna.

4.10 Many [people] free from passion, fear, [and] anger, filled by Me, resorting to Me, purified by the austerity[11] of knowledge—[they all] come to My state-of-existence (*bhāva*).

4.11 Just as these [*yogins*] resort to Me, so do I love them [in turn]. Everywhere, O son-of-Prithā, humans follow My "track."[12]

8. The word *māyā* is not employed here in the sense of "illusion" but is intended to denote the dynamic force that constitutes the "lower nature" of God, by which his will is made manifest in the created universe. See 7.4–7.5 for the notion of a "lower" and a "higher" nature of God.
9. This is the first time in the *Gītā* that the teaching of divine incarnations (*avatāra*) is broached. This notion belongs particularly to Vaishnavism.
10. Age = *yuga*. See Part One, chapter 7, "The Hindu Concept of Cyclic Time."
11. Here knowledge as wisdom is understood as austerity, or asceticism (*tapas*).
12. The term *vartman* ("track") can also be rendered as "path."

काङ्क्षन्तः कर्मणां सिद्धिं यजन्त इह देवताः ।
क्षिप्रं हि मानुषे लोके सिद्धिर्भवति कर्मजा ॥ ४—१२ ॥
चातुर्वर्ण्यं मया सृष्टं गुणकर्मविभागशः ।
तस्य कर्तारमपि मां विद्ध्यकर्तारमव्ययम् ॥ ४—१३ ॥
न मां कर्माणि लिम्पन्ति न मे कर्मफले स्पृहा ।
इति मां योऽभिजानाति कर्मभिर्न स बध्यते ॥ ४—१४ ॥
एवं ज्ञात्वा कृतं कर्म पूर्वैरपि मुमुक्षुभिः ।
कुरु कर्मैव तस्मात्त्वं पूर्वैः पूर्वतरं कृतम् ॥ ४—१५ ॥
किं कर्म किमकर्मेति कवयोऽप्यत्र मोहिताः ।
तत्ते कर्म प्रवक्ष्यामि यज्ज्ञात्वा मोक्ष्यसेऽशुभात् ॥ ४—१६ ॥
कर्मणो ह्यपि बोद्धव्यं बोद्धव्यं च विकर्मणः ।
अकर्मणश्च बोद्धव्यं गहना कर्मणो गतिः ॥ ४—१७ ॥
कर्मण्यकर्म यः पश्येदकर्मणि च कर्म यः ।
स बुद्धिमान्मनुष्येषु स युक्तः कृत्स्नकर्मकृत् ॥ ४—१८ ॥

12. kāṅkṣantaḥ karmaṇāṃ siddhiṃ yajanta iha devatāḥ
    kṣipraṃ hi mānuṣe loke siddhir bhavati karmajā
13. cāturvarṇyaṃ mayā sṛṣṭaṃ guṇakarmavibhāgaśaḥ
    tasya kartāram api māṃ viddhy akartāram avyayam
14. na māṃ karmāṇi limpanti na me karmaphale spṛhā
    iti māṃ yo'bhijānāti karmabhir na sa badhyate
15. evaṃ jñātvā kṛtaṃ karma pūrvair api mumukṣubhiḥ
    kuru karmaiva tasmāt tvaṃ pūrvaiḥ pūrvataraṃ kṛtam
16. kiṃ karma kim akarmeti kavayo'py atra mohitāḥ
    tat te karma pravakṣyāmi yaj jñātvā mokṣyase'śubhāt
17. karmaṇo hy api boddhavyaṃ boddhavyaṃ ca vikarmaṇaḥ
    akarmaṇaś ca boddhavyaṃ gahanā karmaṇo gatiḥ
18. karmaṇy akarma yaḥ paśyed akarmaṇi ca karma yaḥ
    sa buddhimān manuṣyeṣu sa yuktaḥ kṛtsnakarmakṛt

4.12 Hankering after success in their [ritual] actions, they sacrifice here [on earth] to the deities; for in the human world, success born of [ritual] action comes swiftly.

4.13 The quartet-of-classes[13] was created by Me, [with] primary-qualities and actions [appropriately] apportioned.[14] Although I am the author of this [creation], know Me [as] the immutable nondoer.[15]

4.14 Actions do not defile Me. [There is] for Me no hankering for action's fruit. He who recognizes Me [as the nondoer] thus is not bound by actions.

4.15 Knowing thus, the ancients desirous-of-liberation, too, performed action. Therefore, indeed, you [should likewise] perform action [as] was done by the ancients of old.

4.16 "What is action? What is inaction?" About this even the bards[16] are confused. I shall declare to you that action, having known which, you will be freed from ill.

4.17 Indeed, one ought to understand [the nature] of action; one ought to understand wrong-action (*vikarman*), and one ought to understand inaction (*akarman*). Impenetrable[17] is the course of action.

4.18 He who sees inaction in action and action in inaction is wisdom-endowed among humans; [he is] yoked, performing whole action.[18]

13. On the four classes, or estates, see note 29 to 1.41.
14. On the term *vibhāga,* see note 39 for 3.28.
15. Verses like this one bring grist to the mill of Shankara's radical nondualist philosophy. However, this stanza's actual intention is quite in contrast with any such extreme stance. For, there is nothing illusory (*māyikā*) about Krishna's authorship of the world. He is both transcendent and immanent, and thus his incommensurable being defies all logical categories. Logic only admits of an either/or but is oblivious to the both/and of mystical experience.
16. The term *kavi* ("bard") is frequently used as a synonym for *muni* ("sage").
17. The term *gahanā* ("impenetrable") seems to be related to (though not directly derived from) the verbal root *guh*, which means "to cover/conceal/keep secret."
18. The phrase *kritsna-karma-krit* ("performing whole action") plays on the idea of wholeness, as discussed in connection with note 40 for 3.29. "Whole" (*kritsna*) deeds are actions that preserve and bear out the Whole, i.e., which are spontaneous in the sense that it is the structure of the Whole that asserts itself in one's doings. These doings are naturally good because they reflect the universal order (*rita*).

यस्य सर्वे समारम्भाः कामसंकल्पवर्जिताः ।
ज्ञानाग्निदग्धकर्माणं तमाहुः पण्डितं बुधाः ॥ ४—१९ ॥
त्यक्त्वा कर्मफलासङ्गं नित्यतृप्तो निराश्रयः ।
कर्मण्यभिप्रवृत्तोऽपि नैव किंचित्करोति सः ॥ ४—२० ॥
निराशीर्यतचित्तात्मा त्यक्तसर्वपरिग्रहः ।
शारीरं केवलं कर्म कुर्वन्नाप्नोति किल्बिषम् ॥ ४—२१ ॥
यदृच्छालाभसंतुष्टो द्वन्द्वातीतो विमत्सरः ।
समः सिद्धावसिद्धौ च कृत्वापि न निबध्यते ॥ ४—२२ ॥
गतसङ्गस्य मुक्तस्य ज्ञानावस्थितचेतसः ।
यज्ञायाचरतः कर्म समग्रं प्रविलीयते ॥ ४—२३ ॥
ब्रह्मार्पणं ब्रह्म हविर्ब्रह्माग्नौ ब्रह्मणा हुतम् ।
ब्रह्मैव तेन गन्तव्यं ब्रह्मकर्मसमाधिना ॥ ४—२४ ॥

19. yasya sarve samārambhāḥ kāmasaṃkalpavarjitāḥ
jñānāgnidagdhakarmāṇaṃ tam āhuḥ paṇḍitaṃ budhāḥ
20. tyaktvā karmaphalāsaṅgaṃ nityatṛpto nirāśrayaḥ
karmaṇy abhipravṛtto'pi naiva kiṃcit karoti saḥ
21. nirāśīr yatacittātmā tyaktasarvaparigrahaḥ
śārīraṃ kevalaṃ karma kurvan nāpnoti kilbiṣam
22. yadṛcchālābhasaṃtuṣṭo dvandvātīto vimatsaraḥ
samaḥ siddhāv asiddhau ca kṛtvāpi na nibadhyate
23. gatasaṅgasya muktasya jñānāvasthitacetasaḥ
yajñāyācarataḥ karma samagraṃ pravilīyate
24. brahmārpaṇaṃ brahma havir brahmāgnau brahmaṇā hutam
brahmaiva tena gantavyaṃ brahmakarmasamādhinā

4.19 [That man] whose every enterprise is free from desire and motive,[19] [whose] action is burned in the fire of knowledge—him the wise call [truly] "learned" (*pandita*).

4.20 Having relinquished [all] attachment to the fruit of actions, ever content and independent, though engaged in [right] action—he does not act at all.[20]

4.21 Hoping-for-nothing,[21] self [and] thought restrained, abandoning all possessions and performing action only [with] the body[22]—he does not incur guilt.

4.22 Content with what is chance obtained,[23] transcending the pairs-of-opposites,[24] without envy, the same in success and failure, though performing [actions]—he is not bound.

4.23 [For him whose] attachment is gone, [who is] liberated, [whose] mind is established in knowledge [while] performing action for sacrifice, [the consequence of karma] is entirely dissolved.

4.24 The world-ground[25] is the offering. The world-ground is the oblation offered by the world-ground into the world-ground's fire. The world-ground, verily, is to be reached by him through concentration[26] [upon] action, [which is of the nature of] the world-ground.

19. The word *samkalpa*, which usually stands for "intention/volition/resolution/purpose," is here employed in the sense of "motive." The consideration of the world's welfare (*loka-samgraha*) asked for in 3.20 would not count as a motive in the ordinary sense of the word, since it is essentially an expression of the cosmic order (*rita*) within the mind of an attuned Yoga practitioner. See also 6.2.

20. Truly unselfish (or self-transcending) deeds are considered to be of the nature of sacrifice, or action-transcendence (*naishkarmya*). On this, see note 9 for 3.4.

21. On the yogic take on hope (*āshis*), see note 42 for 3.30.

22. The phrase *sharīram kevalam karma kurvan* ("performing action only [with] the body") can also mean "performing action only [for the maintenance of] the body." Compare 3.8.

23. For the term *yadricchā* ("chance"), see note 34 for 2.32.

24. On the term *dvandva* ("pairs-of-opposites"), see note 19 for 2.15.

25. In my opinion, the term *brahman* stands here for the world-ground, God's lower nature, rather than the Ultimate, as, for example, in the Upanishads. See note 66 for 2.72.

26. On the term *samādhi*, here given as "concentration," see note 43 for 2.44.

दैवमेवापरे यज्ञं योगिनः पर्युपासते ।
ब्रह्माग्नावपरे यज्ञं यज्ञेनैवोपजुह्वति ॥ ४—२५ ॥
श्रोत्रादीनीन्द्रियाण्यन्ये संयमाग्निषु जुह्वति ।
शब्दादीन्विषयानन्य इन्द्रियाग्निषु जुह्वति ॥ ४—२६ ॥
सर्वाणीन्द्रियकर्माणि प्राणकर्माणि चापरे ।
आत्मसंयमयोगाग्नौ जुह्वति ज्ञानदीपिते ॥ ४—२७ ॥
द्रव्ययज्ञास्तपोयज्ञा योगयज्ञास्तथापरे ।
स्वाध्यायज्ञानयज्ञाश्च यतयः संशितव्रताः ॥ ४—२८ ॥
अपाने जुह्वति प्राणं प्रणेऽपानं तथापरे ।
प्राणापानगती रुद्ध्वा प्राणायामपरायणाः ॥ ४—२९ ॥
अपरे नियताहाराः प्राणान्प्राणेषु जुह्वति ।
सर्वेऽप्येते यज्ञविदो यज्ञक्षपितकल्मषाः ॥ ४—३० ॥
यज्ञशिष्टामृतभुजो यान्ति ब्रह्म सनातनम् ।
नायं लोकोऽस्त्ययज्ञस्य कुतोऽन्यः कुरुसत्तम ॥ ४—३१ ॥

25. daivam evāpare yajñaṃ yoginaḥ paryupāsate
brahmāgnāv apare yajñaṃ yajñenaivopajuhvati
26. śrotrādīnīndriyāṇy anye saṃyamāgniṣu juhvati
śabdādīn viṣayān anya indriyāgniṣu juhvati
27. sarvāṇīndriyakarmāṇi prāṇakarmāṇi cāpare
ātmasaṃyamayogāgnau juhvati jñānadīpite
28. dravyayajñās tapoyajñā yogayajñās tathāpare
svādhyāyajñānayajñāś ca yatayaḥ saṃśitavratāḥ
29. apāne juhvati prāṇaṃ prāṇe'pānaṃ tathāpare
prāṇāpānagatī ruddhvā prāṇāyāmaparāyaṇāḥ
30. apare niyatāhārāḥ prāṇān prāṇeṣu juhvati
sarve'py ete yajñavido yajñakṣapitakalmaṣāḥ
31. yajñaśiṣṭāmṛtabhujo yānti brahma sanātanam
nāyaṃ loko'sty ayajñasya kuto'nyaḥ kurusattama

4.25 Some *yogins,* verily, conduct a god-related (*daiva*) sacrifice; by means of sacrifice, others offer [directly] into the fire of the world-ground.

4.26 Others offer hearing and the other senses in the fire of restraint, [while] others offer sound and the other objects [of the senses] in the fire of the senses.

4.27 Still others offer all the actions of the senses and the actions of the life-force[27] in the fire of the Yoga of self-restraint, kindled by knowledge.[28]

4.28 Some [again]—ascetics of severe vows—[offer] material-objects as sacrifice, austerity (*tapas*) as sacrifice, Yoga as sacrifice, and knowledge [gained from] study[29] as sacrifice.

4.29 Yet others [who are] intent on breath control[30] offer the in-breath into the out-breath [and] the out-breath into the in-breath by controlling the flow of the in-breath and out-breath.[31]

4.30 Others [who are] restricting [their] diet offer breaths into breaths. All these are indeed knowers of [the true] sacrifice, [whose] defilements are removed by sacrifice.

4.31 Enjoying the nectarine (*amrita*) sacrificial remains, they enter the ever-lasting world-ground. This world is not for the nonsacrificer—how [much less] the other [world], O Kurusattama?[32]

27. The life-force (*prāna*) is the *élan vital* sustaining the somatic processes. See *Chāndogya-Upanishad* 7.15.1: "Or just as spokes are fastened in the hub (*nābhi*), so in this vital-force all is fastened. Life moves by the vital-force; the vital-force gives life, gives [life] to a living [being]" (*yathā vā arā nābhau samarpitāḥ evam asmin prāṇe sarvaṃ samarpitam prāṇaḥ prāṇena yāti prāṇaḥ prāṇaṃ dadāti praṇāya dadāti*).

28. This Yoga is a symbolic enactment of the well-known fire sacrifice (*agni-hotra*) described in the *Chāndogya-Upanishad* 5.19–24.

29. The compound *svādhyāya-jnāna,* here given as "knowledge [gained from] study," could possibly be translated as "book knowledge," but the phrase could also mean "knowledge and study."

30. The practice of *prānāyāma* (*prāna* + *āyāma,* lit. "breath extension"), here rendered as "breath control," belongs to the oldest techniques of Yoga. It consists in controlling the vital-force by means of breath regulation.

31. The word *prāna* ("breath") is frequently used both as a generic term (in the sense of "vital force") and as the designation of a particular type of vital energy. The Upanishadic tradition distinguishes five types of *prāna:* (1) *prāna,* or "in-breath," (2) *apāna,* or "out-breath," (3) *vyāna,* or "diffused breath," (4) *udāna,* or "up-breath," and (5) *samāna,* or "central-breath." See, e.g., *Brihadāranyaka-Upanishad* 1.5.3. In this stanza (4.29), *prāna* has the sense of "in-breath."

32. The epithet Kurusattama means "Foremost of the Kurus."

एवं बहुविधा यज्ञा वितता ब्रह्मणो मुखे ।
कर्मजान्विद्धि तान्सर्वानेवं ज्ञात्वा विमोक्ष्यसे ॥ ४—३२ ॥
श्रेयान्द्रव्यमयाद्यज्ञाज्ज्ञानयज्ञः परंतप ।
सर्वं कर्माखिलं पार्थ ज्ञाने परिसमाप्यते ॥ ४—३३ ॥
तद्विद्धि प्रणिपातेन परिप्रश्नेन सेवया ।
उपदेक्ष्यन्ति ते ज्ञानं ज्ञानिनस्तत्त्वदर्शिनः ॥ ४—३४ ॥
यज्ज्ञात्वा न पुनर्मोहमेवं यास्यसि पाण्डव ।
येन भूतान्यशेषेण द्रक्ष्यस्यात्मन्यथो मयि ॥ ४—३५ ॥
अपि चेदसि पापेभ्यः सर्वेभ्यः पापकृत्तमः ।
सर्वं ज्ञानप्लवेनैव वृजिनं संतरिष्यसि ॥ ४—३६ ॥
यथैधांसि समिद्धोऽग्निर्भस्मसात्कुरुतेऽर्जुन ।
ज्ञानाग्निः सर्वकर्माणि भस्मसात्कुरुते तथा ॥ ४—३७ ॥
न हि ज्ञानेना सदृशं पवित्रमिह विद्यते ।
तत्स्वयं योगसंसिद्धः कालेनात्मनि विन्दति ॥ ४—३८ ॥
श्रद्धावाँल्लभते ज्ञानं तत्परः संयतेन्द्रियः ।
ज्ञानं लब्ध्वा परां शान्तिमचिरेणाधिगच्छति ॥ ४—३९ ॥

32. evaṃ bahuvidhā yajñā vitatā brahmaṇo mukhe
karmajān viddhi tān sarvān evaṃ jñātvā vimokṣyase
33. śreyān dravyamayād yajñāj jñānayajñaḥ paraṃtapa
sarvaṃ karmākhilaṃ pārtha jñāne parisamāpyate
34. tad viddhi praṇipātena paripraśnena sevayā
upadekṣyanti te jñānaṃ jñāninas tattvadarśinaḥ
35. yaj jñātvā na punar moham evaṃ yāsyasi pāṇḍava
yena bhūtāny aśeṣeṇa drakṣyasy ātmany atho mayi
36. api ced asi pāpebhyaḥ sarvebhyaḥ pāpakṛttamaḥ
sarvaṃ jñānaplavenaiva vṛjinaṃ saṃtariṣyasi
37. yathaidhāṃsi samiddho'gnir bhasmasāt kurute'rjuna
jñānāgniḥ sarvakarmāṇi bhasmasāt kurute tathā
38. na hi jñānena sadṛśaṃ pavitram iha vidyate
tat svayaṃ yogasaṃsiddhaḥ kālenātmani vindati
39. śraddhāvāṃl labhate jñānaṃ tatparaḥ saṃyatendriyaḥ
jñānaṃ labdhvā parāṃ śāntim acireṇādhigacchati

4.32 Thus, manifold are the sacrifices spread out[33] in the presence of the world-ground.[34] Know that all these are born of [ritual] action. Knowing thus, you will be released.

4.33 Better than the material sacrifice is the sacrifice of knowledge, O Paramtapa. All action, O son-of-Prithā, is completely consummated in knowledge.

4.34 [Learn to] know this by reverence, inquiry, and service. The knowers [who] behold Reality[35] will teach you knowledge—

4.35 having known which, you will not again succumb to confusion, O son-of-Pāndu, [and] by which, you will behold all beings in the Self and then in Me.[36]

4.36 Even if you were the most sinful among all sinners, you will indeed cross all crookedness with the raft of knowledge.

4.37 As a kindled fire reduces its [wood] fuel to ashes, O Arjuna, so the fire of knowledge reduces all actions to ashes.

4.38 For there is here [on earth] no purifier like knowledge; and [one who is] perfected in Yoga will find this by himself in time within [him]self.

4.39 The faith-filled[37] [*yogin*] intent on That, [with] senses restrained, attains knowledge. Having attained knowledge, he will quickly attain supreme peace.

33. The word *vitata* ("spread out"), which is derived from the verbal root *tan* ("to expand"), refers to the sacrificial practice of setting out one's oblations at the fire altar to be offered into the fire.

34. The world-ground (*brahman*) is omnipresent, and hence its presence (*mukha*, literally "mouth" or "face") is also wherever sacrifices are conducted. From another perspective, the "mouth" of the Absolute is the sacrificial fire. Zaehner (1966) translates: "spread out athwart the mouth of *brahman*." This is yet another reference to the close relation existing between *brahman* and *yajna*. See 3.15.

35. The word *tattva* literally means "thatness."

36. This verse anticipates 6.29–32.

37. Krishna Prem (1938/1969, p. 36) remarks about faith that it is "not the blind belief of the sectarian creeds-men, but the firm aspiration of the soul which seeks to give itself an aspiration which is itself a reflection of the Wisdom that it precludes."

अज्ञश्चाश्रद्दधानश्च संशयात्मा विनश्यति ।
नायं लोकोऽस्ति न परो न सुखं संशयात्मनः ॥ ४—४० ॥
योगसंन्यस्तकर्माणं ज्ञानसंछिन्नसंशयम् ।
आत्मवन्तं न कर्माणि निबध्नन्ति धनंजय ॥ ४—४१ ॥
तस्मादज्ञानसंभूतं हृत्स्थं ज्ञानासिनात्मनः ।
छित्त्वैनं संशयं योगमातिष्ठोत्तिष्ठ भारत ॥ ४—४२ ॥

40. ajñaś cāśraddadhānaś ca saṃśayātmā vinaśyati
nāyaṃ loko'sti na paro na sukhaṃ saṃśayātmanaḥ
41. yogasaṃnyastakarmāṇaṃ jñānasaṃchinnasaṃśayam
ātmavantaṃ na karmāṇi nibadhnanti dhanaṃjaya
42. tasmād ajñānasaṃbhūtaṃ hṛtsthaṃ jñānāsinātmanaḥ
chittvainaṃ saṃśayaṃ yogam ātiṣṭhottiṣṭha bhārata

4.40 [The person who is] unknowing and without faith and of doubting self will perish. For the doubting self, there is no happiness either in this world or the next.

4.41 [He who has] renounced action through Yoga, [whose] doubt is dispelled by knowledge, [who is] self-possessed—[him] actions do not bind, O Dhanamjaya.[38]

4.42 Therefore, severing with the sword of knowledge this doubt, born of ignorance, seated in your heart: Resort to Yoga, O descendant-of-Bharata! Arise![39]

38. On the epithet Dhanamjaya, see note 7 for 1.15. The adjective "self-possessed" (*ātmavanta*) means "self-controlled" rather than "egocentric."

39. Nataraja Guru (1973) offers the following interesting comment: "The sword of wisdom is to be found in the Self and the doubt is found in the heart, i.e., they are both located at two poles within the psychological make-up of the person. A change of heart is effected by a dose of wisdom, as it were, and vice-versa." Here Krishna does not yet directly tell Arjuna to fight, as he does subsequently, once he sees that his disciple has made up his mind to engage in the battle. His argument is more subtle, bringing out the spiritual aspect of his teaching. In resorting to Yoga, to spirituality, Arjuna is bound to do the right thing.

अर्जुन उवाच
संन्यासं कर्मणां कृष्ण पुनर्योगं च शंससि ।
यच्छ्रेय एतयोरेकं तन्मे ब्रूहि सुनिश्चितम् ॥ ५—१ ॥
श्रीभगवानुवाच
संन्यासः कर्मयोगश्च निःश्रेयसकरावुभौ ।
तयोस्तु कर्मसंन्यासात्कर्मयोगो विशिष्यते ॥ ५—२ ॥
ज्ञेयः स नित्यसंन्यासी यो न द्वेष्टि न काङ्क्षति ।
निर्द्वन्द्वो हि महाबाहो सुखं बन्धात्प्रमुच्यते ॥ ५—३ ॥
सांख्ययोगौ पृथग्बालाः प्रवदन्ति न पण्डिताः ।
एकमप्यास्थितः सम्यगुभयोर्विन्दते फलम् ॥ ५—४ ॥
यत्सांख्यैः प्राप्यते स्थानं तद्योगैरपि गम्यते ।
एकं सांख्यं च योगं च यः पश्यति स पश्यति ॥ ५—५ ॥
संन्यासस्तु महाबाहो दुःखमाप्तुमयोगतः ।
योगयुक्तो मुनिर्ब्रह्म नचिरेणाधिगच्छति ॥ ५—६ ॥
योगयुक्तो विशुद्धात्मा विजितात्मा जितेन्द्रियः ।
सर्वभूतात्मभूतात्मा कुर्वन्नपि न लिप्यते ॥ ५—७ ॥

arjuna uvāca
1. saṃnyāsaṃ karmaṇāṃ kṛṣṇa punar yogaṃ ca śaṃsasi
   yac chreya etayor ekaṃ tan me brūhi suniścitam

   śrībhagavān uvāca
2. saṃnyāsaḥ karmayogaś ca niḥśreyasakarāv ubhau
   tayos tu karmasaṃnyāsāt karmayogo viśiṣyate
3. jñeyaḥ sa nityasaṃnyāsī yo na dveṣṭi na kāṅkṣati
   nirdvandvo hi mahābāho sukhaṃ bandhāt pramucyate
4. sāṃkhyayogau pṛthag bālāḥ pravadanti na paṇḍitāḥ
   ekam apy āsthitaḥ samyag ubhayor vindate phalam
5. yat sāṃkhyaiḥ prāpyate sthānaṃ tad yogair api gamyate
   ekaṃ sāṃkhyaṃ ca yogaṃ ca yaḥ paśyati sa paśyati
6. saṃnyāsas tu mahābāho duḥkham āptum ayogataḥ
   yogayukto munir brahma nacireṇādhigacchati
7. yogayukto viśuddhātmā vijitātmā jitendriyaḥ
   sarvabhūtātmabhūtātmā kurvann api na lipyate

CHAPTER 5

THE YOGA OF THE RENUNCIATION OF ACTION

Arjuna said:

5.1 You praise, O Krishna, the renunciation (*samnyāsa*) of actions and then again Yoga. Which one is the better of these two? That tell me for certain!

The Blessed Lord said:

5.2 Renunciation and Karma-Yoga—both lead to the greatest-fortune.[1] But of the two, the Karma-Yoga is better than [mere] renunciation of action.

5.3 He who does not hate or hanker after [anything] is to be known as a perpetual renouncer. For, without [the influence of] the pairs-of-opposites, he is easily released from bondage, O mighty-armed [Arjuna].

5.4 "Sāmkhya[2] and Yoga are different," declare the simpletons, not the learned. Resorting properly to even one [method], [a practitioner] finds the fruit of both.

5.5 That state which is attained by the [followers-of-] Sāmkhya is also reached by the [followers-of-] Yoga. He who sees Sāmkhya and Yoga as one, sees [correctly].

5.6 But renunciation, O mighty-armed [Arjuna], is difficult to attain without Yoga. The sage yoked in Yoga quickly approaches the world-ground (*brahman*).

5.7 [He who is] yoked in Yoga, [who has] purified the self, subdued the self, conquered the senses, [and whose] self has become the Self of all beings—even though performing [actions], he is not defiled.

1. The greatest fortune is liberation, the summum bonum of life.

2. Sāmkhya here means not the well-known classical system devised by Īshvara Krishna (c. 400–450 C.E.) but simply the life of renunciation and contemplation, as opposed to Yoga, which signifies the active life of unselfish deeds.

नैव किंचित्करोमीति युक्तो मन्येत तत्त्ववित् ।
पश्यञ्शृण्वन्स्पृशञ्जिघ्रन्नश्नन्गच्छन्स्वपञ्श्वसन् ॥ ५—८ ॥
प्रलपन्विसृजन्गृह्णन्नुन्मिषन्निमिषन्नपि ।
इन्द्रियाणीन्द्रियार्थेषु वर्तन्त इति धारयन् ॥ ५—९ ॥
ब्रह्मण्याधाय कर्माणि सङ्गं त्यक्त्वा करोति यः ।
लिप्यते न स पापेन पद्मपत्त्रमिवाम्भसा ॥ ५—१० ॥
कायेन मनसा बुद्ध्या केवलैरिन्द्रियैरपि ।
योगिनः कर्म कुर्वन्ति सङ्गं त्यक्त्वात्मशुद्धये ॥ ५—११ ॥
युक्तः कर्मफलं त्यक्त्वा शान्तिमाप्नोति नैष्ठिकीम् ।
अयुक्तः कामकारेण फले सक्तो निबध्यते ॥ ५—१२ ॥
सर्वकर्माणि मनसा संन्यस्यास्ते सुखं वशी ।
नवद्वारे पुरे देही नैव कुर्वन्न कारयन् ॥ ५—१३ ॥
न कर्तृत्वं न कर्माणि लोकस्य सृजति प्रभुः ।
न कर्मफलसंयोगं स्वभावस्तु प्रवर्तते ॥ ५—१४ ॥
नादत्ते कस्यचित्पापं न चैव सुकृतं विभुः ।
अज्ञानेनावृतं ज्ञानं तेन मुह्यन्ति जन्तवः ॥ ५—१५ ॥

8. naiva kiṃcit karomīti yukto manyate tattvavit
paśyañ śṛṇvan spṛśañ jighrann aśnan gacchan svapañ śvasan
9. pralapan visṛjan gṛhṇann unmiṣan nimiṣann api
indriyāṇīndriyārtheṣu vartanta iti dhārayan
10. brahmaṇy ādhāya karmāṇi saṅgaṃ tyaktvā karoti yaḥ
lipyate na sa pāpena padmapattram ivāmbhasā
11. kāyena manasā buddhyā kevalair indriyair api
yoginaḥ karma kurvanti saṅgaṃ tyaktvātmaśuddhaye
12. yuktaḥ karmaphalaṃ tyaktvā śāntim āpnoti naiṣṭhikīm
ayuktaḥ kāmakāreṇa phale sakto nibadhyate
13. sarvakarmāṇi manasā saṃnyasyāste sukhaṃ vaśī
navadvāre pure dehī naiva kurvan na kārayan
14. na kartṛtvaṃ na karmāṇi lokasya sṛjati prabhuḥ
na karmaphalasaṃyogaṃ svabhāvas tu pravartate
15. nādatte kasyacit pāpaṃ na caiva sukṛtaṃ vibhuḥ
ajñānenāvṛtaṃ jñānaṃ tena muhyanti jantavaḥ

5.8 "I do nothing"—thus reflects [the *yogin* who is] yoked, the knower of Reality, [while he is] seeing, hearing, touching, smelling, eating, walking, sleeping, breathing,

5.9 talking, excreting, grasping, opening as well as closing [the eyes], and maintaining: "The senses abide in the sense objects."

5.10 He who acts, assigning [all] actions to the world-ground, and having abandoned attachment, is not defiled by sin, as a lotus leaf [is not stained] by water [surrounding it].

5.11 Having abandoned [all] attachment, the *yogins* perform action for self-purification with body, mind, wisdom-faculty, and even merely with the senses.

5.12 [He who is] yoked, having relinquished the fruit of action, attains ultimate peace. The unyoked [individual], acting from desire and attached to the fruit [of action], is bound [by karma].

5.13 Renouncing all actions with the mind, sitting happily and [as the] ruler—the body-essence (*dehin*) within the nine-gated city [i.e., the body], verily neither acts nor causes-to-act.

5.14 The lord [of the body] neither creates agency nor world's actions, nor the union [between] action and [its] fruit. It is the own-being [of the world-ground that] stimulates-to-action.

5.15 The all-pervading [lord of the body] does not take on anyone's good or sinful [deeds]. Knowledge is covered by ignorance; thereby are people deluded.

ज्ञानेन तु तदज्ञानं येषां नाशितमात्मनः ।
तेषामादित्यवज्ज्ञानं प्रकाशयति तत्परम् ॥ ५—१६ ॥
तद्बुद्धयस्तदात्मानस्तन्निष्ठास्तत्परायणाः ।
गच्छन्त्यपुनरावृत्तिं ज्ञाननिर्धूतकल्मषाः ॥ ५—१७ ॥

«स्मरन्तोऽपि मुहुस्त्वेतत्स्पृशन्तोऽपि स्वकर्मणि ।
सक्ता अपि न सज्जन्ति पङ्के रविकरा इव ॥»

विद्याविनयसंपन्ने ब्राह्मणे गवि हस्तिनि ।
शुनि चैव श्वपाके च पण्डिताः समदर्शिनः ॥ ५—१८ ॥
इहैव तैर्जितः सर्गो येषां साम्ये स्थितं मनः ।
निर्दोषं हि समं ब्रह्म तस्माद्ब्रह्मणि ते स्थिताः ॥ ५—१९ ॥
न प्रहृष्येत्प्रियं प्राप्य नोद्विजेत्प्राप्य चाप्रियम् ।
स्थिरबुद्धिरसंमूढो ब्रह्मविद्ब्रह्मणि स्थितः ॥ ५—२० ॥
बाह्यस्पर्शेष्वसक्तात्मा विन्दत्यात्मनि यत्सुखम् ।
स ब्रह्मयोगयुक्तात्मा सुखमक्षयमश्नुते ॥ ५—२१ ॥
ये हि संस्पर्शजा भोगा दुःखयोनय एव ते ।
आद्यन्तवन्तः कौन्तेय न तेषु रमते बुधः ॥ ५—२२ ॥

16. jñānena tu tad ajñānaṃ yeṣāṃ nāśitam ātmanaḥ
tesām ādityavaj jñānaṃ prakāśayati tat param
17. tadbuddhayas tadātmānas tanniṣṭhās tatparāyaṇāḥ
gacchanty apunarāvṛttiṃ jñānanirdhūtakalmaṣāḥ

« smaranto'pi muhus tv etat spṛśanto'pi svakarmaṇi
saktā api na sajjanti paṅke ravikarā iva »

18. vidyāvinayasaṃpanne brāhmaṇe gavi hastini
śuni caiva śvapāke ca paṇḍitāḥ samadarśinaḥ
19. ihaiva tair jitaḥ sargo yeṣāṃ sāmye sthitaṃ manaḥ
nirdoṣaṃ hi samaṃ brahma tasmād brahmaṇi te sthitāḥ
20. na prahṛṣyet priyaṃ prāpya nodvijet prāpya cāpriyam
sthirabuddhir asaṃmūḍho brahmavid brahmaṇi sthitaḥ
21. bāhyasparśeṣv asaktātmā vindaty ātmani yat sukham
sa brahmayogayuktātmā sukham akṣayam aśnute
22. ye hi saṃsparśajā bhogā duḥkhayonaya eva te
ādyantavantaḥ kaunteya na teṣu ramate budhaḥ

5.16 But for those whose ignorance of the self [has been] destroyed by knowledge, their knowledge, like the sun, illumines that Supreme.

5.17 [Those who have their] wisdom-faculties [focused on] That, [their] selves [immersed in] That, [who have] That as basis, That as supreme-goal—they go [to the Supreme], never again [to experience] rebirth, [because all their] defilements are cast off through knowledge.

«Though remembering this repeatedly and coming-in-touch with [the fruit of their] own action, although attached, they adhere not [really], like the sun's rays in a puddle. »

5.18 The learned see the same[3] in a *brāhmana* endowed with understanding and culturedness, in a cow, an elephant, even a dog or a "dog-cooker."[4]

5.19 Even here [on earth], those whose mind is established in sameness have conquered creation. For the world-ground is devoid-of-faults [and ever] the same. Hence they are established in the world-ground.

5.20 [The *yogin*] should not rejoice on gaining a cherished [thing], nor should he become agitated on gaining a noncherished [i.e., unpleasant thing]. With steadied wisdom-faculty, the knower-of-*brahman,* devoid-of-confusion, is established in the world-ground.

5.21 [He whose] self is unattached to external contacts—he finds joy in the Self [and he whose] self is yoked in Yoga to the world-ground[5]—he attains immutable joy.

5.22 For, contact-born enjoyments are indeed wombs of sorrow, having a beginning and an end. In these, O son-of-Kuntī,[6] the sage does not delight.

3. See note 18 for 2.15.

4. The *shva-pāka* ("dog-cooker") is one of the lowest types of outcaste described in the lawgiver Manu's *Dharma-Shāstra* (10.51–56).

5. The phrase *brahma-yoga-yukta-ātma* could also be rendered thus: "the self is yoked in the Yoga of Brahman."

6. On son-of-Kuntī (Kaunteya), see note 19 for 1.27.

शक्नोतीहैव यः सोढुं प्राक्शरीरविमोक्षणात् ।
कामक्रोधोद्भवं वेगं स युक्तः स सुखी नरः ॥ ५—२३ ॥
योऽन्तःसुखोऽन्तरारामस्तथान्तर्ज्योतिरेव यः ।
स योगी ब्रह्मनिर्वाणं ब्रह्मभूतोऽधिगच्छति ॥ ५—२४ ॥
लभन्ते ब्रह्मनिर्वाणमृषयः क्षीणकल्मषाः ।
छिन्नद्वैधा यतात्मानः सर्वभूतहिते रताः ॥ ५—२५ ॥
कामक्रोधवियुक्तानां यतीनां यतचेतसाम् ।
अभितो ब्रह्मनिर्वाणं वर्तते विदितात्मनाम् ॥ ५—२६ ॥
स्पर्शान्कृत्वा बहिर्बाह्यांश्चक्षुश्चैवान्तरे भ्रुवोः ।
प्राणापानौ समौ कृत्वा नासाभ्यन्तरचारिणौ ॥ ५—२७ ॥
यतेन्द्रियमनोबुद्धिर्मुनिर्मोक्षपरायणः ।
विगतेच्छाभयक्रोधो यः सदा मुक्त एव सः ॥ ५—२८ ॥
भोक्तारं यज्ञतपसां सर्वलोकमहेश्वरम् ।
सुहृदं सर्वभुतानां ज्ञात्वा मां शान्तिमृच्छति ॥ ५—२९ ॥

23. śaknotīhaiva yaḥ soḍhuṃ prāk śarīravimokṣaṇāt
kāmakrodhodbhavaṃ vegaṃ sa yuktaḥ sa sukhī naraḥ
24. yo'ntaḥsukho'ntarārāmas tathāntarjyotir eva yaḥ
sa yogī brahmanirvāṇaṃ brahmabhūto'dhigacchati
25. labhante brahmanirvāṇam ṛṣayaḥ kṣīṇakalmaṣāḥ
chinnadvaidhā yatātmānaḥ sarvabhūtahite ratāḥ
26. kāmakrodhaviyuktānāṃ yatīnāṃ yatacetasām
abhito brahmanirvāṇaṃ vartate viditātmanām
27. sparśān kṛtvā bahir bāhyāṃś cakṣuś caivāntare bhruvoḥ
prāṇāpānau samau kṛtvā nāsābhyantaracāriṇau
28. yatendriyamanobuddhir munir mokṣaparāyaṇaḥ
vigatecchābhayakrodho yaḥ sadā mukta eva saḥ
29. bhoktāraṃ yajñatapasāṃ sarvalokamaheśvaram
suhṛdaṃ sarvabhūtānāṃ jñātvā māṃ śāntim ṛcchati

5.23 He, verily, who is able to bear here [on earth], before [he finds] release from the body, the shock arising from desire and anger—he is yoked, he is a happy man.

5.24 He who has inner joy, inner rejoicing, and hence inner light is indeed a *yogin*. Having become the world-ground,[7] he approaches extinction in the world-ground (*brahma-nirvāna*).

5.25 The seers [whose] defilements have dwindled, [whose] dualities are destroyed, [whose] selves are controlled, [and who] delight in the good of all beings—they reach extinction in the world-ground.

5.26 For [those] Self-knowing ascetics [who are] freed from desire and anger [and whose] mind is controlled, extinction in the world-ground is close.

5.27 Shutting out [all] external contacts [and fixing] the sight in the middle of the eyebrows, making the in-breath and out-breath move evenly in the nose,

5.28 the sage [whose] senses, mind, and wisdom-faculty are controlled, [who is] intent on liberation and ever devoid of longing, fear, [and] anger—he is truly liberated.

5.29 Knowing Me as the enjoyer of sacrificial austerities, the great Lord of all the worlds, the kind-hearted [friend] of all beings—he attains peace.

7. Zaehner (1966/1969, pp. 214–15) wrongly suggested that the term *brahma-bhūta*, here translated as "having become the world-ground," has the same meaning as in the Buddhist literature. The Buddhist concept of "extinction" (*nirvāna*) must be properly understood in the context of the unique teaching on dependent origination (*pratītya-samutpada*) and emptiness (*shūnyatā*).

श्रीभगवानुवाच
अनाश्रितः कर्मफलं कार्यं कर्म करोति यः ।
स संन्यासी च योगी च न निरग्निर्न चाक्रियः ॥ ६—१ ॥
यं संन्यासमिति प्राहुर्योगं तं विद्धि पाण्डव ।
न ह्यसंन्यस्तसंकल्पो योगी भवति कश्चन ॥ ६—२ ॥
आरुरुक्षोर्मुनेर्योगं कर्म कारणमुच्यते ।
योगारूढस्य तस्यैव शमः कारणमुच्यते ॥ ६—३ ॥
यदा हि नेन्द्रियार्थेषु न कर्मस्वनुषज्जते ।
सर्वसंकल्पसंन्यासी योगारूढस्तदोच्यते ॥ ६—४ ॥
उद्धरेदात्मनात्मानं नात्मानमवसादयेत् ।
आत्मैव ह्यात्मनो बन्धुरात्मैव रिपुरात्मनः ॥ ६—५ ॥
बन्धुरात्मात्मनस्तस्य येनात्मैवात्मना जितः ।
अनात्मनस्तु शत्रुत्वे वर्तेतात्मैव शत्रुवत् ॥ ६—६ ॥
जितात्मनः प्रशान्तस्य परमात्मा समाहितः ।
शीतोष्णसुखदुःखेषु तथा मानापमानयोः ॥ ६—७ ॥

śrībhagavān uvāca

1. anāśritaḥ karmaphalaṃ kāryaṃ karma karoti yaḥ
   sa saṃnyāsī ca yogī ca na niragnir na cākriyaḥ
2. yaṃ saṃnyāsam iti prāhur yogaṃ taṃ viddhi pāṇḍava
   na hy asaṃnyastasaṃkalpo yogī bhavati kaścana
3. ārurukṣor muner yogaṃ karma kāraṇam ucyate
   yogārūḍhasya tasyaiva śamaḥ kāraṇam ucyate
4. yadā hi nendriyārtheṣu na karmasv anuṣajjate
   sarvasaṃkalpasaṃnyāsī yogārūḍhas tadocyate
5. uddhared ātmanātmānaṃ nātmānam avasādayet
   ātmaiva hy ātmano bandhur ātmaiva ripur ātmanaḥ
6. bandhur ātmātmanas tasya yenātmaivātmanā jitaḥ
   anātmanas tu śatrutve vartetātmaiva śatruvat
7. jitātmanaḥ praśāntasya paramātmā samāhitaḥ
   śītoṣṇasukhaduḥkheṣu tathā mānāpamānayoḥ

CHAPTER 6

The Yoga of Meditation

The Blessed Lord said:

6.1 He who performs the action to be done,[1] regardless[2] of action's fruit, is a renouncer and a *yogin*; not [so is he who is] without the [sacrificial] fire and is inactive.[3]

6.2 What they call "renunciation," know this to be Yoga, O son-of-Pāndu. For, without renouncing [selfish] motive,[4] no one becomes a *yogin*.

6.3 For a sage desiring-to-ascend [to the heights of] Yoga, action is said to be the means. For him who has ascended [to the apex of] Yoga, quiescence (*shama*) is said to be the means.[5]

6.4 When indeed [the sage] clings neither to the sense objects nor to actions, renouncing all motive—then he is said [to have] indeed ascended in Yoga (*yoga-ārūdha*).

6.5 He should raise the self by the Self; he should not let the self sink; for, [as] the self is indeed the friend of the Self, [so also] is the self indeed Self's enemy.[6]

6.6 The self is the friend of the Self of him whose self is conquered by the Self; but for [him who is] bereft-of-Self, the self is like an enemy in enmity.

6.7 The supreme Self of the self-conquered and tranquil [*yogin*] is [as it were] concentrated in [experiencing] cold [and] heat, pleasure [and] pain, as well as in honor and dishonor.

1. That one's actions should also be appropriate (or "to be done") is a vitally important aspect of right action according to Karma-Yoga. It is not enough to be merely indifferent to results.
2. The word *anāshrita,* here rendered as "regardless," means "not dependent," that is, "independent of."
3. This stanza again epitomizes the ideal of inner or symbolic renunciation, i.e., renunciation *in* action rather than *of* action.
4. See also 4.19.
5. Here a contrast is made between the fully accomplished adept, who always rests in quiescence, and the still-active practitioner. The sage who has "arrived" has no further task to fulfill. His Karma-Yoga is his constant state of tranquil being.
6. See my remarks about the challenge of translating the term *ātman* as "self/Self" in note 52 for 3.43.

ज्ञानविज्ञानतृप्तात्मा कूटस्थो विजितेन्द्रियः ।
युक्त इत्युच्यते योगी समलोष्टाश्मकाञ्चनः ॥ ६—८ ॥
सुहृन्मित्रार्युदासीनमध्यस्थद्वेष्यबन्धुषु ।
साधुष्वपि च पापेषु समबुद्धिर्विशिष्यते ॥ ६—९ ॥
योगी युञ्जीत सततमात्मानं रहसि स्थितः ।
एकाकी यतचित्तात्मा निराशीरपरिग्रहः ॥ ६—१० ॥
शुचौ देशे प्रतिष्ठाप्य स्थिरमासनमात्मनः ।
नात्युच्छ्रितं नातिनीचं चैलाजिनकुशोत्तरम् ॥ ६—११ ॥
तत्रैकाग्रं मनः कृत्वा यतचित्तेन्द्रियक्रियः ।
उपविश्यासने युञ्ज्याद्योगमात्मविशुद्धये ॥ ६—१२ ॥
समं कायशिरोग्रीवं धारयन्नचलं स्थिरः ।
संप्रेक्ष्य नासिकाग्रं स्वं दिशश्चानवलोकयन् ॥ ६—१३ ॥
प्रशान्तात्मा विगतभीर्ब्रह्मचारिव्रते स्थितः ।
मनः संयम्य मच्चित्तो युक्त आसीत मत्परः ॥ ६—१४ ॥
युञ्जन्नेवं सदात्मानं योगी नियतमानसः ।
शान्तिं निर्वाणपरमां मत्संस्थामधिगच्छति ॥ ६—१५ ॥

8. jñānavijñānatṛptātmā kūṭastho vijitendriyaḥ
yukta ity ucyate yogī samaloṣṭāśmakāñcanaḥ
9. suhṛnmitrāryudāsīnamadhyasthadveṣyabandhuṣu
sādhuṣv api ca pāpeṣu samabuddhir viśiṣyate
10. yogī yuñjīta satatam ātmānaṃ rahasi sthitaḥ
ekākī yatacittātmā nirāśīr aparigrahaḥ
11. śucau deśe pratiṣṭhāpya sthiram āsanam ātmanaḥ
nātyucchritaṃ nātinīcaṃ cailājinakuśottaram
12. tatraikāgraṃ manaḥ kṛtvā yatacittendriyakriyaḥ
upaviśyāsane yuñjyād yogam ātmaviśuddhaye
13. samaṃ kāyaśirogrīvaṃ dhārayann acalaṃ sthiraḥ
saṃprekṣya nāsikāgraṃ svaṃ diśaś cānavalokayan
14. praśāntātmā vigatabhīr brahmacārivrate sthitaḥ
manaḥ saṃyamya maccitto yukta āsīta matparaḥ
15. yuñjann evaṃ sadātmānaṃ yogī niyatamānasaḥ
śāntiṃ nirvāṇaparamāṃ matsaṃsthām adhigacchati

6.8 The *yogin* [whose] self is satisfied with knowledge and worldly-knowledge, [who is] summit-abiding[7] [and with his] senses conquered is said [to be] yoked (*yukta*): [to him] a clod-of-earth, a stone, and a [piece of] gold are the same.

6.9 [That *yogin*] is distinguished [whose] wisdom-faculty is the same toward[8] companions, good-hearted friends, enemies, the indifferent, the hateful, as well as among good and sinful [people].

6.10 The *yogin* should continually yoke himself, [while] remaining in privacy, alone, [with] mind and self restrained, free-from-hope[9] and without grasping [for sense objects].

6.11 Establishing a stable seat for himself in a pure place, neither too high nor too low, [with] a cloth, deerskin, or *kusha*-grass [for] covering,[10]

6.12 there making the mind one-pointed, [with] the activity of mind and senses controlled, he should, seated on the seat, yoke [himself in] Yoga for [the purpose of] self-purification.

6.13 Holding trunk, head, and neck even, motionless, and steady, gazing [relaxedly] at the tip of his nose, and without looking round about,

6.14 [with] tranquil self, devoid of fear, steadfast in the vow of chastity, controlling the mind, [with his] attention on Me, yoked—he should sit, intent on Me.

6.15 Thus ever yoking himself, the *yogin* of controlled mind approaches peace: the supreme extinction (*nirvāna*),[11] [which has its] subsistence in Me.

7. Shankara and Rāmānuja take the term *kuta-stha* ("summit-abiding") to be equivalent to "cessation [from action]," but this is not the case. Although the "method" of a fully Self-realized adept is said to be quietude (*shama*), he still has to act while he is embodied. This is the whole point of Krishna's teaching. S. Radhakrishnan (1948) flatly translates *kuta-stha* as "unchanging." Zaehner (1966), again, renders this word as "sublime, aloof," which captures one aspect of the state involved. But Bhaktivedanta Swami (1983) more correctly gives it as "situated in transcendence," which is a good description of the condition.

8. Here the locative is used to yield the meaning of "toward" or "in regard to."

9. On hope, see note 42 for 3.30.

10. The word *shuci,* often translated as "clean," surely implies not just physical cleanliness but also ritual purity. Also, *kusha* is a type of grass considered especially sacred by the Hindus.

11. "Extinction in the world-ground" (*brahma-nirvāna*) is the lower form of spiritual realization. It is superseded by the realization of the personal God.

नात्यश्नतस्तु योगोऽस्ति न चैकान्तमनश्नतः ।
न चातिस्वप्नशीलस्य जाग्रतो नैव चार्जुन ॥ ६—१६ ॥
युक्ताहारविहारस्य युक्तचेष्टस्य कर्मसु ।
युक्तस्वप्नावबोधस्य योगो भवति दुःखहा ॥ ६—१७ ॥
यदा विनियतं चित्तमात्मन्येवावतिष्ठते ।
निःस्पृहः सर्वकामेभ्यो युक्त इत्युच्यते तदा ॥ ६—१८ ॥
यथा दीपो निवातस्थो नेङ्गते सोपमा स्मृता ।
योगिनो यतचित्तस्य युञ्जतो योगमात्मनः ॥ ६—१९ ॥
यत्रोपरमते चित्तं निरुद्धं योगसेवया ।
यत्र चैवात्मनात्मानं पश्यन्नात्मनि तुष्यति ॥ ६—२० ॥
सुखमात्यन्तिकं यत्तद्बुद्धिग्राह्यमतीन्द्रियम् ।
वेत्ति यत्र न चैवायं स्थितश्चलति तत्त्वतः ॥ ६—२१ ॥
यं लब्ध्वा चापरं लाभं मन्यते नाधिकं ततः ।
यस्मिन्स्थितो न दुःखेन गुरुणापि विचाल्यते ॥ ६—२२ ॥
तं विद्याद्दुःखसंयोगवियोगं योगसंज्ञितम् ।
स निश्चयेन योक्तव्यो योगोऽनिर्विण्णचेतसा ॥ ६—२३ ॥

16. nātyaśnatas tu yogo'sti na caikāntam anaśnataḥ
    na cātisvapnaśīlasya jāgrato naiva cārjuna
17. yuktāhāravihārasya yuktaceṣṭasya karmasu
    yuktasvapnāvabodhasya yogo bhavati duḥkhahā
18. yadā viniyataṃ cittam ātmany evāvatiṣṭhate
    niḥspṛhaḥ sarvakāmebhyo yukta ity ucyate tadā
19. yathā dīpo nivātastho neṅgate sopamā smṛtā
    yogino yatacittasya yuñjato yogam ātmanaḥ
20. yatroparamate cittaṃ niruddhaṃ yogasevayā
    yatra caivātmanātmānaṃ paśyann ātmani tuṣyati
21. sukham ātyantikaṃ yat tad buddhigrāhyam atīndriyam
    vetti yatra na caivāyaṃ sthitaś calati tattvataḥ
22. yaṃ labdhvā cāparaṃ lābhaṃ manyate nādhikaṃ tataḥ
    yasmin sthito na duḥkhena guruṇāpi vicālyate
23. taṃ vidyād duḥkhasaṃyogaviyogaṃ yogasaṃjñitam
    sa niścayena yoktavyo yogo'nirviṇṇacetasā

6.16 But [this] Yoga is not for the overeater nor for [him who] eats not at all, nor yet for [him who has] the habit of excessive sleep, nor even for [him who is constantly] awake, O Arjuna.

6.17 [Rather this] Yoga dispels the suffering of [him who is] yoked in food [i.e., diet] and recreation, [who is] yoked in the execution of deeds, [who is] yoked [in regard to] sleep and waking.

6.18 When the mind is restrained [and] abides in the Self alone, [and is] devoid-of-longing for all [objects of] desire—then [the *yogin*] is called "yoked" (*yukta*).

6.19 "As a lamp standing in a windless [place] flickers not"—that simile is recalled [when] a *yogin* of yoked mind practices the Yoga of the self.

6.20 When the mind is curbed, controlled by the service of Yoga, and when the Self is beheld by the self in the Self—[then he] is content.

6.21 That is the utmost joy which is extrasensory (*atīndriya*) [and which can be] grasped by the wisdom-faculty [alone]. And when he knows this, standing [still], he moves not from Reality;[12]

6.22 having obtained which he thinks [that there] is no other, greater gain than that, and abiding in which, he is not shaken even by heavy suffering.

6.23 This he should know as [that which is] named "Yoga": the disunion of the union with suffering. That Yoga is to be practiced with determination and with an undejected mind.

12. The word *tattvatas* is clearly used here in the sense of "from Reality."

संकल्पप्रभवानकामांस्त्यक्त्वा सर्वानशेषतः ।
मनसैवेन्द्रियग्रामं विनियम्य समन्ततः ॥ ६—२४ ॥
शनैः शनैरुपरमेद्बुद्ध्या धृतिगृहीतया ।
आत्मसंस्थं मनः कृत्वा न किंचिदपि चिन्तयेत् ॥ ६—२५ ॥
यतो यतो निश्चरति मानश्चञ्चलमस्थिरम् ।
ततस्ततो नियम्यैतदात्मन्येव वशं नयेत् ॥ ६—२६ ॥
प्रशान्तमनसं ह्येनं योगिनं सुखमुत्तमम् ।
उपैति शान्तरजसं ब्रह्मभूतमकल्मषम् ॥ ६—२७ ॥
युञ्जन्नेवं सदात्मानं योगी विगतकल्मषः ।
सुखेन ब्रह्मसंस्पर्शमत्यन्तं सुखमश्नुते ॥ ६—२८ ॥
सर्वभूतस्थमातमानं सर्वभूतानि चात्मनि ।
ईक्षते योगयुक्तात्मा सर्वत्र समदर्शनः ॥ ६—२९ ॥
यो मां पश्यति सर्वत्र सर्वं च मयि पश्यति ।
तस्याहं न प्रणश्यामि स च मे न प्रणश्यति ॥ ६—३० ॥
सर्वभूतस्थितं यो मां भजत्येकत्वमास्थितः ।
सर्वथा वर्तमानोऽपि स योगी मयि वर्तते ॥ ६—३१ ॥

24. saṃkalpaprabhavān kāmāṃs tyaktvā sarvān aśeṣataḥ
    manasaivendriyagrāmaṃ viniyamya samantataḥ
25. śanaiḥ śanair uparamed buddhyā dhṛtigṛhītayā
    ātmasaṃsthaṃ manaḥ kṛtvā na kiṃcid api cintayet
26. yato yato niścarati manaś cañcalam asthiram
    tatastato niyamyaitad ātmany eva vaśaṃ nayet
27. praśāntamanasaṃ hy enaṃ yoginaṃ sukham uttamam
    upaiti śāntarajasaṃ brahmabhūtam akalmaṣam
28. yuñjann evaṃ sadātmānaṃ yogī vigatakalmaṣaḥ
    sukhena brahmasaṃsparśam atyantaṃ sukham aśnute
29. sarvabhūtastham ātmānaṃ sarvabhūtāni cātmani
    īkṣate yogayuktātmā sarvatra samadarśanaḥ
30. yo māṃ paśyati sarvatra sarvaṃ ca mayi paśyati
    tasyāhaṃ na praṇaśyāmi sa ca me na praṇaśyati
31. sarvabhūtasthitaṃ yo māṃ bhajaty ekatvam āsthitaḥ
    sarvathā vartamāno'pi sa yogī mayi vartate

6.24 Abandoning entirely all desires arising from motive [and], verily, completely restraining the host of senses by the mind,

6.25 little by little he should come to rest. Making the mind settled in the Self by holding the wisdom-faculty steadfast, he should not think of anything.

6.26 Wherever the fickle, unsteady mind roves about, from there, restraining it, he should bring it under the control of the Self.

6.27 For the supreme joy comes to that *yogin* [whose] mind is tranquil, [whose] passion is appeased, [who has] become [one with] the world-ground [and who is] free-from-defilement.

6.28 Thus always yoking the self, the *yogin* [whose] defilements are gone, with ease attains endless joy [through] contact[13] with the world-ground.

6.29 He [whose] self is yoked through Yoga [and who] everywhere beholds the same (*sama-darshana*) sees the Self abiding in all beings and all beings in the Self.

6.30 He who sees Me everywhere and sees all in Me, to him I am not lost, nor is he lost to Me.

6.31 He who is established in oneness [and] worships Me abiding in all beings, howsoever indeed he exists—that *yogin* dwells in Me.

13. Here "contact" (*samsparsha*) is used metaphorically. It is quite distinct from the kind of "touch" (*sparsha*) which is purely sensory. "Contact" is suprasensory and mediated by the wisdom-faculty (*buddhi*), which is immersed in the world-ground.

आत्मौपम्येन सर्वत्र समं पश्यति योऽर्जुन ।
सुखं वा यदि वा दुःखं स योगी परमो मतः ॥ ६—३२ ॥
अर्जुन उवाच
योऽयं योगस्त्वया प्रोक्तः साम्येन मधुसूदन ।
एतस्याहं न पश्यामि चञ्चलत्वात्स्थितिं स्थिराम् ॥ ६—३३ ॥
चञ्चलं हि मनः कृष्ण प्रमाथि बलवद्दृढम् ।
तस्याहं निग्रहं मन्ये वायोरिव सुदुष्करम् ॥ ६—३४ ॥
श्रीभगवानुवाच
असंशयं महाबाहो मनो दुर्निग्रहं चलम् ।
अभ्यासेन तु कौन्तेय वैराग्येण च गृह्यते ॥ ६—३५ ॥
असंयतात्मना योगो दुष्प्राप ईति मे मतिः ।
वश्यात्मना तु यतता शक्योऽवाप्तुमुपायतः ॥ ६—३६ ॥
अर्जुन उवाच
अयतिः श्रद्धयोपेतो योगाच्चलितमानसः ।
अप्राप्य योगसंसिद्धं कां गतिं कृष्ण गचछति ॥ ६—३७ ॥

32. ātmaupamyena sarvatra samaṃ paśyati yo'rjuna
sukhaṃ vā yadi vā duḥkhaṃ sa yogī paramo mataḥ

arjuna uvāca

33. yo'yaṃ yogas tvayā proktaḥ sāmyena madhusūdana
etasyāhaṃ na paśyāmi cañcalatvāt sthitiṃ sthirām

34. cañcalaṃ hi manaḥ kṛṣṇa pramāthi balavad dṛḍham
tasyāhaṃ nigrahaṃ manye vāyor iva suduṣkaram

śrībhagavān uvāca

35. asaṃśayaṃ mahābāho mano durnigrahaṃ calam
abhyāsena tu kaunteya vairāgyeṇa ca gṛhyate

36. asaṃyatātmanā yogo duṣprāpa iti me matiḥ
vaśyātmanā tu yatatā śakyo'vāptum upāyataḥ

arjuna uvāca

37. ayatiḥ śraddhayopeto yogāc calitamānasaḥ
aprāpya yogasaṃsiddhiṃ kāṃ gatiṃ kṛṣṇa gacchati

6.32 He who sees by [reason of] the Self's identity the same everywhere,[14] O Arjuna, whether [it be] joy or suffering—he is deemed a supreme *yogin.*

Arjuna said:

6.33 This Yoga which has been proclaimed by You [to be achieved] through sameness, O Madhusūdana[15]—I cannot see a steady state [by which it could be realized], because of [the mind's] fickleness.

6.34 The mind is indeed fickle, O Krishna, impetuous, strong, and obstinate.[16] Its control, I think, is very-difficult-to-achieve, like [that of] of the wind.

The Blessed Lord said:

6.35 Undoubtedly, O mighty-armed [Arjuna], the mind is difficult-to-restrain [and] fickle. But by practice and dispassion,[17] O son-of-Kuntī, it can be seized.

6.36 [For him whose] self is unsubdued, Yoga is difficult to obtain; this is My conviction. But [for him whose] self is under control, it is possible by striving to attain [it] by the [appropriate] means.[18]

Arjuna said:

6.37 The undisciplined [whose] mind has deviated from [the process of] Yoga, [and who consequently does] not attain the consummation of Yoga, [but who has] arrived at faith—what course does he take, O Krishna?

14. Zaehner (1966) translates this term as "by analogy with self," and Radhakrishnan (1948) as "equality of others with oneself," but surely what is intended here is the mystical realization of the Self's omnipresence in everything.

15. On Madhusūdana, see note 4 for 1.14.

16. Zaehner (1966) prefers to translate *balavad-dridha* as "exceedingly strong."

17. *Abhyāsa* ("practice") and *vairāgya* ("dispassion") are the two complementary poles of every kind of spiritual path.

18. The text uses the word *upāya* ("means"), which is a major term in Buddhism (where it is often translated as "skillful means").

«लिप्समानः सतां मार्गं प्रमूढो ब्रह्मणः पथि ।
अनेकाचित्तो विभ्रान्तो मोहस्यैव वशं गतः ॥»

कच्चिन्नोभयविभ्रष्टश्छिन्नाभ्रमिव नश्यति ।
अप्रतिष्ठो महाबाहो विमूढो ब्रह्मणः पथि ॥ ६–३८ ॥
एतन्मे संशयं कृष्ण छेत्तुमर्हस्यशेषतः ।
त्वदन्यः संशयस्यास्य छेत्ता न ह्युपपद्यते ॥ ६–३९ ॥
श्रीभगवानुवाच
पार्थ नैवेह नामुत्र विनाशस्तस्य विद्यते ।
न हि कल्याणकृत्कश्चिद्दुर्गतिं तात गच्छति ॥ ६–४० ॥
प्राप्य पुण्यकृताँल्लोकानुषित्वा शाश्वतीः समाः ।
शुचीनां श्रीमतां गेहे योगभ्रष्टोऽभिजायते ॥ ६–४१ ॥
अथवा योगिनामेव कुले भवति धीमताम् ।
एतद्धि दुर्लभतरं लोके जन्म यदीदृशम् ॥ ६–४२ ॥
तत्र तं बुद्धिसंयोगं लभते पौर्वदेहिकम् ।
यतते च ततो भूयः संसिद्धौ कुरुनन्दन ॥ ६–४३ ॥

« lipsamānaḥ satāṃ mārgaṃ pramūḍho brahmaṇaḥ pathi,
anekacitto vibhrānto mohasya eva vaśaṃ gatah »

38. kaccin nobhayavibhraṣṭaś chinnābhram iva naśyati
apratiṣṭḥo mahābāho vimūḍho brahmaṇaḥ pathi
39. etan me saṃśayaṃ kṛṣṇa chettum arhasy aśeṣataḥ
tvadanyaḥ saṃśayasyāsya chettā na hy upapadyate

śrībhagavān uvāca
40. pārtha naiveha nāmutra vināśas tasya vidyate
na hi kalyāṇakṛt kaścid durgatiṃ tāta gacchati
41. prāpya puṇyakṛtāṃl lokān uṣitvā śāśvatīḥ samāḥ
śucīnāṃ śrīmatāṃ gehe yogabhraṣṭo'bhijāyate
42. athavā yoginām eva kule bhavati dhīmatām
etaddhi durlabhataraṃ loke janma yad īdṛśam
43. tatra taṃ buddhisaṃyogaṃ labhate paurvadehikam
yatate ca tato bhūyaḥ saṃsiddhau kurunandana

« [The *yogin* who,] desirous of the road of the virtuous, [but] confused on the path to Brahman, [becomes] of dis-united (*an-eka*) mind, [becomes] distracted, [and] comes under the power of delusion. »

6.38 Does he [who is] unsuccessful in both [practice and dispassion] not perish like a riven cloud, without foundation, deluded on the path to the world-ground, O mighty-armed [Krishna]?

6.39 This doubt of mine You can completely dispel, O Krishna. None other than You steps forward to dispel this doubt.

The Blessed Lord said:

6.40 O son-of-Prithā, neither here [on earth] nor in the [world] above [i.e., in the next world] is there destruction for him, because no doer of good takes a bad-course, O son.

6.41 Reaching the worlds of doers of virtuous [deeds] and having dwelled [there] for endless[19] years, [he who has] failed in Yoga[20] is born [again] into the home of pure, auspicious [people].

6.42 Or else, he is born into a family of wise *yogins;* yet such a birth is very difficult to obtain in [this] world.

6.43 There he achieves union with the wisdom-faculty [as it matured in his] previous embodiment; and once again he strives for consummation [in Yoga], O Kurunandana.[21]

19. "Endless" (*shāshvatī*) is meant figuratively here, for even the most sublime worlds, or realms, are finite. The span of life in the subtle realms may extend over many ages, possibly an entire *kalpa* or more, as with Brahma, who lives for one hundred *kalpas* (more than fifteen billion years).
20. A Yoga practitioner who has "failed in Yoga" (*yoga-brashta*) is essentially someone who has failed to attain liberation. This compound is often understood as "fallen from Yoga," but that implies that a *yogin* has somehow strayed from the path, which need not be the case.
21. On Kurunandana, see note 40 for 2.41.

पूर्वाभ्यासेन तेनैव ह्रियते ह्यवशोऽपि सः ।
जिज्ञासुरपि योगस्य शब्दब्रह्मातिवर्तते ॥ ६—४४ ॥
प्रयत्नाद्यतमानस्तु योगी संशुद्धकिल्बिषः ।
अनेकजन्मसंसिद्धस्ततो याति परां गतिम् ॥ ६—४५ ॥
तपस्विभ्योऽधिको योगी ज्ञानिभ्योऽपि मतोऽधिकः ।
कर्मिभ्यश्चाधिको योगी तस्माद्योगी भवार्जुन ॥ ६—४६ ॥
योगिनामपि सर्वेषां मद्गतेनान्तरात्मना ।
श्रद्धावान्भजते यो मां स मे युक्ततमो मतः ॥ ६—४७ ॥

44. pūrvābhyāsena tenaiva hriyate hy avaśo'pi saḥ
jijñāsur api yogasya śabdabrahmātivartate
45. prayatnād yatamānas tu yogī saṃśuddhakilbiṣaḥ
anekajanmasaṃsiddhas tato yāti parāṃ gatim
46. tapasvibhyo'dhiko yogī jñānibhyo'pi mato'dhikaḥ
karmibhyaś cādhiko yogī tasmād yogī bhavārjuna
47. yoginām api sarveṣāṃ madgatenāntarātmanā
śraddhāvān bhajate yo māṃ sa me yuktatamo mataḥ

6.44 By [virtue of his] practice in the previous [life], he is carried [forward] even against [his] will. [If he] is even desirous to know Yoga, he transcends the sonar world-ground (*shabda-brahman*).[22]

6.45 But the *yogin*, striving with effort, cleansed of guilt, perfected through many a birth, thence goes the supreme course.[23]

6.46 The *yogin* is greater than ascetics. [He is] thought even greater than knowers, and the *yogin* is greater than the performers-of-ritual-actions. Therefore, be a *yogin*, O Arjuna!

6.47 Of all the *yogins*, moreover, he who worships Me [endowed] with faith, [and whose] inner self[24] is absorbed in Me, is deemed [to be] most yoked to Me.

22. *Shabda-brahman* ("sonar world-ground") refers to the transcendental matrix, which manifests to the clairvoyant *yogin* as the sacred sound OM, which symbolizes the Ultimate (Brahman).
23. The "supreme course" (*parām gatim*) is final liberation in the higher nature of God, which is the Supreme Person (*purushottama*)—i.e., Krishna. See also note 15 for 7.18.
24. By "inner self" (*antarātman*) is meant the deepest (or highest) aspect of the human mind, which is the *buddhi*. When the wisdom-faculty is thoroughly trained on God, the *yogin* enters into a special relationship with God, on whose grace he may count for the remainder of the self-transcending journey.

श्रीभगवानुवाच

मय्यासक्तमनाः पार्थ योगं युञ्जन्मदाश्रयः ।
असंशयं समग्रं मां यथा ज्ञास्यसि तच्छृणु ॥ ७—१ ॥
ज्ञानं तेऽहं सविज्ञानमिदं वक्ष्याम्यशेषतः ।
यज्ज्ञात्वा नेह भूयोऽन्यज्ज्ञातव्यमवशिष्यते ॥ ७—२ ॥
मनुष्याणां सहस्रेषु कश्चिद्यतति सिद्धये ।
यततामपि सिद्धानां कश्चिन्मां वेत्ति तत्त्वतः ॥ ७—३ ॥
भुमिरापोऽनलो वायुः खं मनो बुद्धिरेव च ।
अहंकार इतीयं मे भिन्ना प्रकृतिरष्टधा ॥ ७—४ ॥
अपरेयमितस्त्वन्यां प्रकृतिं विद्धि मे पराम् ।
जीवभूतां महाबाहो ययेदं धार्यते जगत् ॥ ७—५ ॥

śrībhagavān uvāca

1. mayy āsaktamanāḥ pārtha yogaṃ yuñjan madāśrayaḥ
   asaṃśayaṃ samagraṃ māṃ yathā jñāsyasi tac chṛṇu
2. jñānaṃ te'haṃ savijñānam idaṃ vakṣyāmy aśeṣataḥ
   yaj jñātvā neha bhūyo'nyaj jñātavyam avaśiṣyate
3. manuṣyāṇāṃ sahasreṣu kaścid yatati siddhaye
   yatatām api siddhānāṃ kaścin māṃ vetti tattvataḥ
4. bhūmir āpo'nalo vāyuḥ khaṃ mano buddhir eva ca
   ahaṃkāra itīyaṃ me bhinnā prakṛtir aṣṭadhā
5. apareyam itas tv anyāṃ prakṛtiṃ viddhi me parām
   jīvabhūtāṃ mahābāho yayedaṃ dhāryate jagat

CHAPTER 7

The Yoga of Wisdom and Knowledge

The Blessed Lord said:

7.1 Hear [now], O son-of-Prithā, how, [with] the mind attached to Me, engaged in Yoga, [with] Me as refuge, you may know Me fully, without doubt.[1]

7.2 I will declare to you, without reserve, this knowledge together with world-knowledge, knowing which nothing more remains to be known here [on earth].

7.3 Among thousands of humans, [scarcely] anyone strives for perfection. Even among the striving adepts, [scarcely] anyone knows Me truly.

7.4 Earth, water, fire, air, ether, mind, wisdom-faculty, and the ego-sense[2]—this is the eightfold division of My [lower] nature (*prakriti*).

7.5 This is [My] lower [nature]. But know My higher nature to be other than this: the life-element (*jīva-bhūta*)[3] by which this universe is supported,[4] O mighty-armed [Arjuna].

1. Full knowledge of God means the ecstatic realization of the Supreme Person (*purushottama*), God-as-Supraperson, who is beyond the world-ground (*brahman*) and also beyond the conglomeration of transcendental subjects (*purusha*) called "life-element" (*jīva-bhūta*) in verse 7.5. To be attached (*āsakta*) to the Divine is not a karmic attachment. According to the *Gītā,* it is really the only way to transcend the Cosmos in all its levels and to attain transcendental oneness with the Supreme Person.

2. The term *ahamkāra* ("I-maker") belongs to the stock vocabulary of the Yoga and Sāmkhya traditions—here perhaps macrocosmically, as an ontic category, rather than microcosmically, as the feeling of individuality.

3. The term *jīva-bhūta* refers to the collectivity of transcendental "monads" of pure Awareness, God's "higher nature."

4. In what sense, we may ask, can the "life-element" (*jīva-bhūta*) be said to "support" (*dhāryate*) the universe? In his commentary on this stanza, Swami Tripurari (2001) explains that the "life-principle," which he circumscribes as *jīva-shakti* (power of life), is "God's intermediate power." He continues: "It is similar in nature to God and dissimilar to matter. It is at the same time dissimilar to God in that it is prone to being deluded by the influence of material nature." But can a transcendental reality like *jīva-bhūta,* which is beyond the "I-maker" and other psychomental faculties, be subject to delusion? Only individual beings (*jīva*), or personalities, can become deluded by matter. The transcendental collectivity of Selves, however, can be said to "support" the universe inasmuch as life (*jīva*) is foundational to the myriad of living beings, or forms, that make up the Cosmos.

एतद्योनीनि भूतानि सर्वाणीत्युपधारय ।
अहं कृत्स्नस्य जगतः प्रभवः प्रलयस्तथा ॥ ७—६ ॥
मत्तः परतरं नान्यत्किंचिदस्ति धनंजय ।
मयि सर्वमिदं प्रोतं सूत्रे मणिगणा इव ॥ ७—७ ॥
रसोऽहमप्सु कौन्तेय प्रभास्मि शशिसूर्ययोः ।
प्रणवः सर्ववेदेषु शब्दः खे पौरुषं नृषु ॥ ७—८ ॥
पुण्यो गन्धः पृथिव्यां च तेजश्चास्मि विभावसौ ।
जीवनं सर्वभूतेषु तपश्चास्मि तपस्विषु ॥ ७—९ ॥
बीजं मां सर्वभूतानां विद्धि पार्थ सनातनम् ।
बुद्धिर्बुद्धिमतामस्मि तेजस्तेजस्विनामहम् ॥ ७—१० ॥
बलं बलवतां चाहं कामरागविवर्जितम् ।
धर्माविरुद्धो भूतेषु कामोऽस्मि भरतर्षभ ॥ ७—११ ॥
ये चैव सात्त्विका भावा राजसास्तामसाश्च ये ।
मत्त एवेति तान्विद्धि न त्वहं तेषु ते मयि ॥ ७—१२ ॥
त्रिभिर्गुणमयैर्भावैरेभिः सर्वमिदं जगत् ।
मोहितं नाभिजानाति मामेभ्यः परमव्ययम् ॥ ७—१३ ॥

6. etadyonīni bhūtāni sarvāṇīty upadhāraya
aham kṛtsnasya jagataḥ prabhavaḥ pralayas tathā
7. mattaḥ parataraṃ nānyat kiṃcid asti dhanaṃjaya
mayi sarvam idaṃ protaṃ sūtre maṇigaṇā iva
8. raso'ham apsu kaunteya prabhāsmi śaśisūryayoḥ
praṇavaḥ sarvavedeṣu śabdaḥ khe pauruṣaṃ nṛṣu
9. puṇyo gandhaḥ pṛthivyāṃ ca tejaś cāsmi vibhāvasau
jīvanaṃ sarvabhūteṣu tapaś cāsmi tapasviṣu
10. bījaṃ māṃ sarvabhūtānāṃ viddhi pārtha sanātanam
buddhir buddhimatām asmi tejas tejasvinām aham
11. balaṃ balavatāṃ cāhaṃ kāmarāgavivarjitam
dharmāviruddho bhūteṣu kāmo'smi bharatarṣabha
12. ye caiva sāttvikā bhāvā rājasās tāmasāś ca ye
matta eveti tān viddhi na tv ahaṃ teṣu te mayi
13. tribhir guṇamayair bhāvair ebhiḥ sarvam idaṃ jagat
mohitaṃ nābhijānāti mām ebhyaḥ param avyayam

7.6 Understand that this [My higher nature] is the womb of all beings. I am the origin and the dissolution of this whole[5] world.

7.7 Higher than I there is nothing whatsoever, O Dhanamjaya.[6] On Me all this [universe] is strung like clusters of jewels upon a thread.

7.8 I am the flavor of water, O son-of-Kuntī.[7] I am the radiance of sun and moon, the *pranava*[8] of all the Vedas, the sound in and of space, [and] the manhood of men.[9]

7.9 And [I am] the pure fragrance of earth, and I am the glow of fire, the life of all beings, and I am the austerity of ascetics.

7.10 Know Me [as] the eternal seed of all beings, O son-of-Prithā.[10] I am the wisdom-faculty of the wisdom-endowed, [and] I am the radiance of [those who are] radiant.

7.11 And I am the power of the powerful, devoid of desire and passion. In beings I am desire [that is] not opposed to the law (*dharma*), O Bharatarshabha.[11]

7.12 Moreover, know that [all] those luminous (*sāttvika*), dynamic (*rājasa*), and obscuring (*tāmasa*) states [found in the world], verily, [proceed] from Me. Yet, I am not in them; they are in Me.[12]

7.13 By these three states-of-existence formed by the primary-qualities (*guna*), this entire universe is deluded, [and it does] not recognize Me [as] immutable [and as abiding] beyond them.

5. On the word *kritsna,* see note 40 for 3.29.
6. On the epithet Dhanamjaya, see note 7 for 1.15.
7. On son-of-Kuntī (Kaunteya), see note 19 for 1.27.
8. The "humming sound" (*pranava*) is the sacred monosyllable OM.
9. To make better sense in English, I have treated all locatives as genitives.
10. On son-of-Prithā (Pārtha), see note 18 for 1.25.
11. On Bharatarshabha, see note 48 for 3.41.
12. According to the ontology of Yoga and Sāmkhya, everything in the universe is composed of the three primary-qualities (*guna*): *sattva, rajas,* and *tamas.* That which lies beyond the Cosmos, or creation, is *nirguna* ("beyond-the-three-primary-qualities").

दैवी ह्येषा गुणमयी मम माया दुरत्यया ।
मामेव ये प्रपद्यन्ते मायामेतां तरन्ति ते ॥ ७—१४ ॥
न मां दुष्कृतिनो मूढाः प्रपद्यन्ते नराधमाः ।
माययापहृतज्ञाना आसुरं भावमाश्रिताः ॥ ७—१५ ॥
चतुर्विधा भजन्ते मां जनाः सुकृतिनोऽर्जुन ।
आर्तो जिज्ञासुरर्थार्थी ज्ञानी च भरतर्षभ ॥ ७—१६ ॥
तेषं ज्ञानी नित्ययुक्त एकभक्तिर्विशिष्यते ।
प्रियो हि ज्ञानिनोऽत्यर्थमहं स च मम प्रियः ॥ ७—१७ ॥
उदाराः सर्व एवैते ज्ञानी त्वात्मैव मे मतम् ।
आस्थितः स हि युक्तात्मा मामेवानुत्तमां गतिम् ॥ ७—१८ ॥
बहूनां जन्मनामन्ते ज्ञानवान्मां प्रपद्यते ।
वासुदेवः सर्वमिति स महात्मा सुदुर्लभः ॥ ७—१९ ॥
कामैस्तैस्तैर्हृतज्ञानाः प्रपद्यन्तेऽन्यदेवताः ।
तं तं नियममास्थाय प्रकृत्या नियताः स्वया ॥ ७—२० ॥
यो यो यां यां तनुं भक्तः श्रद्धयार्चितुमिच्छति ।
तस्य तस्याचलां श्रद्धां तामेव विदधाम्यहम् ॥ ७—२१ ॥

14. daivī hy eṣā guṇamayī mama māyā duratyayā
mām eva ye prapadyante māyām etāṃ taranti te
15. na māṃ duṣkṛtino mūḍhāḥ prapadyante narādhamāḥ
māyayāpahṛtajñānā āsuraṃ bhāvam āśritāḥ
16. caturvidhā bhajante māṃ janāḥ sukṛtino'rjuna
ārto jijñāsur arthārthī jñānī ca bhāratarṣabha
17. teṣaṃ jñānī nityayukta ekabhaktir viśiṣyate
priyo hi jñānino'tyartham ahaṃ sa ca mama priyaḥ
18. udārāḥ sarva evaite jñānī tv ātmaiva me matam
āsthitaḥ sa hi yuktātmā mām evānuttamāṃ gatim
19. bahūnāṃ janmanām ante jñānavān māṃ prapadyate
vāsudevaḥ sarvam iti sa mahātmā sudurlabhaḥ
20. kāmais tais tair hṛtajñānāḥ prapadyante'nyadevatāḥ
taṃ taṃ niyamam āsthāya prakṛtyā niyatāḥ svayā
21. yo yo yāṃ yāṃ tanuṃ bhaktaḥ śraddhayārcitum icchati
tasya tasyācalāṃ śraddhāṃ tām eva vidadhāmy aham

7.14 For, this [entire universe] is My divine creative-power (*māyā*),[13] composed of the primary-qualities, difficult-to-transcend.[14] Those who resort to Me alone transcend this creative-power [of Mine].

7.15 The wrongdoers, confounded, lowest of men, do not resort to Me; deprived of knowledge by [My] creative-power, [they] have recourse to a demonic (*āsura*) condition.

7.16 Four kinds of good-doing people worship Me, O Arjuna: the afflicted, the desirous-of-knowledge, [he whose] object is the welfare [of the world], and the knower, O Bharatarshabha.

7.17 Of these [four], the knower [who is] ever yoked [and] of single devotion is excellent, because to the knower I am exceedingly dear; and he is dear to Me.

7.18 All these are indeed exalted, but the knower I deem [to be] My Self indeed, for [with] yoked self he is established in Me alone, the supreme course.[15]

7.19 At the end of many births, the knowledge-endowed resort to Me. "Vāsudeva is all"—thus [realizes] that great self, [which is] very-difficult-to-find.

7.20 [Those who are] deprived of knowledge by whatever[16] desires resort to other deities, having recourse to this or that rule, constrained by their own nature.[17]

7.21 Whatever form[18] whichever devotee desires to worship with faith, that very[19] immovable faith of his do I grant.

13. On the term *māyā*, see note 8 for 4.6.

14. The femine word *duratyayā* (from *ati* "beyond" + *i* "to go") is here used as a qualifier of *māyā*.

15. We know from verse 6.45 that the "supreme course" is none other than Krishna. The word *gati* can mean either "state" or "course." I prefer the latter, because this suggests that the process of liberation in God is dynamic rather than static.

16. The phrase *tais-tair* ("these [or] those") qualifying the word "desires" is here translated as "whatever."

17. The expression *prakrityā niyatāh svayā*, here rendered as "constrained by their own nature," implies a reference to the fundamental idea of *svabhāva*.

18. The commentator Madhva of the Dvaita or Dualist school thinks that the choice of the word *tanu*, often employed to denote "body," is highly significant in this context. He relates it to the idea that all the various deities constitute, as it were, the body (i.e., the lower mode) of God's eternal Being.

19. The duplicate phrase *tasya tasya* ("of him") is grammatically required by the preceding *yo yah*.

स तया श्रद्धया युक्तस्तस्याराधनमीहते ।
लभते च ततः कामान्मयैव विहितान्हि तान् ॥ ७—२२ ॥
अन्तवत्तु फलं तेषां तद्भवत्यल्पमेधसाम् ।
देवान्देवयजो यान्ति मद्भक्ता यान्ति मामपि ॥ ७—२३ ॥
अव्यक्तं व्यक्तिमापन्नं मन्यन्ते मामबुद्धयः ।
परं भावमजानन्तो ममाव्ययमनुत्तमम् ॥ ७—२४ ॥
नाहं प्रकाशः सर्वस्य योगमायासमावृतः ।
मूढोऽयं नाभिजानाति लोको मामजमव्ययम् । ७—२५ ॥
वेदाहं समतीतानि वर्तमानानि चार्जुन ।
भविष्याणि च भूतानि मां तु वेद न कश्चन ॥ ७—२६ ॥
इच्छाद्वेषसमुत्थेन द्वन्द्वमोहेन भारत ।
सर्वभूतानि संमोहं सर्गे यान्ति परंतप ॥ ७—२७ ॥
येषां त्वन्तगतं पापं जनानां पुण्यकर्मणाम् ।
ते द्वन्द्वमोहनिर्मुक्ता भजन्ते मां दृढव्रताः ॥ ७—२८ ॥
जरामरणमोक्षाय मामाश्रित्य यतन्ति ये ।
ते ब्रह्म तद्विदुः कृत्स्नमध्यात्मं कर्म चाखिलम् ॥ ७—२९ ॥

22. sa tayā śraddhayā yuktas tasyārādhanam īhate
labhate ca tataḥ kāmān mayaiva vihitān hi tān
23. antavat tu phalaṃ teṣāṃ tad bhavaty alpamedhasām
devān devayajo yānti madbhaktā yānti mām api
24. avyaktaṃ vyaktim āpannaṃ manyante mām abuddhayaḥ
paraṃ bhāvam ajānanto mamāvyayam anuttamam
25. nāhaṃ prakāśaḥ sarvasya yogamāyāsamāvṛtaḥ
mūḍho'yaṃ nābhijānāti loko mām ajam avyayam
26. vedāhaṃ samatītāni vartamānāni cārjuna
bhaviṣyāṇi ca bhūtāni māṃ tu veda na kaścana
27. icchādveṣasamutthena dvandvamohena bhārata
sarvabhūtāni saṃmohaṃ sarge yānti paraṃtapa
28. yeṣāṃ tv antagataṃ pāpaṃ janānāṃ puṇyakarmaṇāṃ
te dvandvamohanirmuktā bhajante māṃ dṛḍhavratāḥ
29. jarāmaraṇamokṣāya mām āśritya yatanti ye
te brahma tad viduḥ kṛtsnam adhyātmaṃ karma cākhilam

7.22 Yoked by that faith, he seeks to reverence that [adopted deity] and thence obtains [his] desires [which are in reality] dispensed by Me indeed.

7.23 But finite is the fruit of those of little intelligence. Deity worshippers go to [their respective] deities. My devotees, however, come to Me.

7.24 The unwise think of Me as the unmanifest (*avyakta*) [having] fallen into manifestation. [They are] ignorant of My higher state-of-existence (*bhāva*), [which is] immutable and unsurpassed.

7.25 Veiled by the creative-power [of My] Yoga, I am not visible-light to all; this deluded universe knows Me not, the Unborn, Immutable.

7.26 I know [all] beings, past and present, and those-to-come; but, O Arjuna, no one [truly] knows Me.

7.27 Deluded by the pairs-of-opposites[20] arising from longing[21] and aversion, O descendant-of-Bharata, all beings succumb to delusion in [this] creation, O Paramtapa.[22]

7.28 But the men [who perform] meritorious (*punya*) actions, for whom evil has come to an end—they, released from the delusion of the pairs-of-opposites [and who are] of steadfast vows, worship Me.

7.29 Those who strive toward release from old age and death by taking refuge in Me, they [come to] know wholly (*kritsna*) that world-ground, the basis-of-self,[23] and the entire [mystery of] action.

20. On the term *dvandva* ("pairs-of-opposites"), see note 19 for 2.15.

21. Here "longing" (*icchā*) stands for "attachment" (*rāga*).

22. On Arjuna's epithet Paramtapa, see note 5 for 2.3.

23. On the term *adhyātman*, see note 41 for 3.30.

साधिभूताधिदैवं मां साधियज्ञं च ये विदुः ।
प्रयाणकालेऽपि च मां ते विदुर्युक्तचेतसः ॥ ७—३० ॥

30. sādhibhūtādhidaivaṃ māṃ sādhiyajñaṃ ca ye viduḥ
prayāṇakāle'pi ca māṃ te vidur yuktacetasaḥ

7.30 Those yoked-minded [*yogins*] who know Me [as] the basis-of-being, [as] the divine-basis, along with the basis-of-sacrifice, and [who know] Me also at the time of going-forth[24]—[they indeed] know.

24. The Sanskrit compound *prayāna-kāla*, derived from the prefix *pra* and the verbal root *i* ("to go"), means literally "going-forth" and stands for "the time of death." The death process is considered very important in Yoga, as is explained below, in Chapter 8.

अर्जुन उवाच
किं तद्ब्रह्मकिमध्यात्मं किं कर्म पुरुषोत्तम ।
अधिभूतं च किं प्रोक्तमधिदैवं किमुच्यते ॥ ८—१ ॥
अधियज्ञः कथं कोऽत्र देहेऽस्मिन्मधुसूदन ।
प्रयाणकाले च कथं ज्ञेयोऽसि नियतात्मभिः ॥ ८—२ ॥
श्रीभगवानुवाच
अक्षरं ब्रह्म परमं स्वभावोऽध्यात्ममुच्यते ।
भूतभावोद्भवकरो विसर्गः कर्मसंज्ञितः ॥ ८—३ ॥
अधिभूतं क्षरो भावः पुरुषश्चाधिदैवतम् ।
अधियज्ञोऽहमेवात्र देहे देहाभृतां वर ॥ ८—४ ॥
अन्तकाले च मामेव स्मरन्मुक्त्वा कलेवरम् ।
यः प्रयाति स मद्भावं याति नास्त्यत्र संशयः ॥ ८—५ ॥

arjuna uvāca
1. kiṃ tad brahma kim adhyātmaṃ kiṃ karma puruṣottoma
adhibhūtaṃ ca kiṃ proktam adhidaivaṃ kim ucyate
2. adhiyajñaḥ kathaṃ ko'tra dehe'smin madhusūdana
prayāṇakāle ca kathaṃ jñeyo'si niyatātmabhiḥ

śrībhagavān uvāca
3. akṣaraṃ brahma paramaṃ svabhāvo'dhyātmam ucyate
bhūtabhāvodbhavakaro visargaḥ karmasaṃjñitaḥ
4. adhibhūtaṃ kṣaro bhāvaḥ puruṣaś cādhidaivatam
adhiyajño'ham evātra dehe dehabhṛtāṃ vara
5. antakāle ca mām eva smaran muktvā kalevaram
yaḥ prayāti sa madbhāvaṃ yāti nāsty atra saṃśayaḥ

CHAPTER 8

The Yoga of the Imperishable Absolute

Arjuna said:

8.1 What is that world-ground (*brahman*)? What is the basis-of-self? What is action, O Purushottama?[1] And what is proclaimed [to be] the elemental-basis? What is [that which] is said [to be] the divine-basis?

8.2 Who is here in this body [as] the sacrificial-basis, and how, O Madhusūdana?[2] And how are You to be known at the time of going-forth by [those who are of] restrained self?[3]

The Blessed Lord said:

8.3 The Imperishable is the supreme Brahman. The own-being (*svabhāva*) is called the basis-of-self. The creativity[4] originating the state-of-existence of beings is designated as action.

8.4 The elemental-basis is the perishable state-of-existence, and the divine-basis is Spirit.[5] I am the sacrificial-basis here in the body, O best of body-wearers.

8.5 And he who in the last hour, having released the body[6] [while] remembering Me alone, goes forth—he goes to My state-of-existence; there is no doubt of this.

1. Krishna's epithet Purushottama is composed of *purusha* ("person") and *uttama* ("supreme, unexcelled"), commonly translated as Supreme Person or Supreme Spirit.
2. On Madhusūdana, see note 4 for 1.14.
3. It would appear that in his commentary on this stanza, Abhinavagupta miscounted the number of Arjuna's questions as nine rather than as eight; an honest mistake.
4. The term *visarga,* which means something like "discharge," is here used in a more philosophical sense. I have rendered it as "creativity." Rāmānuja, an inveterate ascetic, takes *visarga* to refer to procreation at the human level. While Shankara's comments on this remain somewhat obscure, Abhinavagupta has this explanation: "Creativity (*visarga*) is the gradual (*kramena*) [creation] of beings." For him the Ultimate is intrinsically endowed with power (*shakti*), which gives rise to creation.
5. Spirit (*purusha*) is the transcendental witnessing Self, which exists in untold numbers and makes up the transcendental "collectivity" that in 7.5 is referred to as the "life-element" (*jīva-bhūta*).
6. The word *kalevara* ("body"; lit. "best of forms") denotes the corpse. This rare term is employed again in the next verse.

यं यं वापि स्मरन्भावं त्यजत्यन्ते कलेवरम् ।
तं तमेवैति कौन्तेय सदा तद्भावभावितः ॥ ८—६ ॥
तस्मात्सर्वेषु कालेषु मामनुस्मर युध्य च ।
मय्यर्पितमनोबुद्धिर्मामेवैष्यस्यसंशयः ॥ ८—७ ॥
अभ्यासयोगयुक्तेन चेतसा नान्यगामिना ।
परमं पुरुषं दिव्यं याति पार्थानुचिन्तयन् ॥ ८—८ ॥
कविं पुराणमनुशासितार
मणोरणीयांसमनुस्मरेद्यः ।
सर्वस्य धातारमचिन्त्यरूप
मादित्यवर्णं तमसः परस्तात् ॥ ८—९ ॥
प्रयाणकाले मानसाचलेन
भक्त्या युक्तो योगबलेन चैव ।
भ्रुवोर्मध्ये प्राणमावेश्य साम्य
क्स तं परं पुरुषमुपैति दिव्यम् ॥ ८—१० ॥

6. yaṃ yaṃ vāpi smaran bhāvaṃ tyajaty ante kalevaram
tam tam evaiti kaunteya sadā tadbhāvabhāvitaḥ
7. tasmāt sarveṣu kāleṣu mām anusmara yudhya ca
mayy arpitamanobuddhir mām evaiṣyasy asaṃśayaḥ
8. abhyāsayogayuktena cetasā nānyagāminā
paramaṃ puruṣaṃ divyaṃ yāti pārthānucintayan
9. kaviṃ purāṇam anuśāsitāra
maṇor aṇīyāṃsam anusmared yaḥ
sarvasya dhātāram acintyarūpa
māḍityavarṇaṃ tamasaḥ parastāt
10. prayāṇakāle manasācalena
bhaktyā yukto yogabalena caiva
bhruvor madhye prāṇam āveśya samya
ksa taṃ paraṃ puruṣam upaiti divyam

8.6 Also, whatever state-of-existence [a person may be] remembering [when] in the end he abandons the body, even to that [state] does he go, O son-of-Kuntī,[7] always forced-to-become that state-of-existence.[8]

8.7 Therefore, remember Me at all times and fight! [When] mind and wisdom-faculty are fixed on Me, you will undoubtedly come to Me.

8.8 [With] the mind yoked by the Yoga of practice and not going astray—[the yogin] goes to the supreme divine Spirit (*purusha*),[9] contemplating [Him], O son-of-Prithā.[10]

8.9 He who remembers the ancient Bard, Governor [of all], smaller than an atom, Supporter of all, of inconceivable form, sun-colored [and abiding] beyond darkness—

8.10 that [*yogin*], at the time of going-forth, with unmoving mind, yoked by devotion and by the power of Yoga, directing the life-force properly to the middle of the eyebrows, comes to that supreme divine Spirit.[11]

7. On son-of-Kuntī (Kaunteya), see note 19 for 1.27.

8. This verse has been widely misunderstood. It does not state that the last thought on the deathbed determines the subsequent condition in the afterlife, which, in turn, shapes the next embodiment. Rather it is the totality of one's being that is responsible for the succeeding state-of-being, the last thought merely being a particularization of one's essential nature.

9. The "supreme divine Person" (*paramam purusham divyam*) is none other than the Purushottama, that is, the Godhead known as Krishna/Vishnu/Nārāyana/Vāsudeva.

10. On son-of-Prithā (Pārtha), see note 18 for 1.25.

11. Verses 9 to 11 are in the *trishtubh* meter, with the last line of verse 10 being one syllable too long.

यदक्षरं वेदविदो वदन्ति
विशन्ति यद्यतयो वीतरागाः ।
यदिच्छन्तो ब्रह्मचर्यं चरन्ति
तत्ते पदं संग्रहेण प्रवक्ष्ये ॥ ८—११ ॥
सर्वद्वाराणि संयम्य मनो हृदि निरुध्य च ।
मूर्ध्न्याधायात्मनः प्राणमास्थितो योगधारणाम् ॥ ८—१२ ॥
ओमित्येकाक्षरं ब्रह्म व्याहरन्मामनुस्मरन् ।
यः प्रयाति त्यजन्देहं स याति परमां गतिम् ॥ ८—१३ ॥
अनन्यचेताः सततं यो मां स्मरति नित्यशः ।
तस्याहं सुलभः पार्थ नित्ययुक्तस्य योगिनः ॥ ८—१४ ॥
मामुपेत्य पुनर्जन्म दुःखालयमशाश्वतम् ।
नाप्नुवन्ति महात्मानः संसिद्धिं परमां गताः ॥ ८—१५ ॥
आ ब्रह्मभुवनाल्लोकाः पुनरावर्तिनोऽर्जुन ।
मामुपेत्य तु कौन्तेय पुनर्जन्म न विद्यते ॥ ८—१६ ॥
सहस्रयुगपर्यन्तमहर्यद्ब्रह्मणो विदुः ।
रात्रिं युगसहस्रान्तां तेऽहोरात्रविदो जनाः ॥ ८—१७ ॥

11. yad akṣaraṃ vedavido vadanti
    viśanti yad yatayo vītarāgāḥ
    yad icchanto brahmacaryaṃ caranti
    tat te padaṃ saṃgraheṇa pravakṣye
12. sarvadvārāṇi saṃyamya mano hṛdi nirudhya ca
    mūrdhny ādhāyātmanaḥ prāṇam āsthito yogadhāraṇām
13. om ity ekākṣaraṃ brahma vyāharan mām anusmaran
    yaḥ prayāti tyajan dehaṃ sa yāti paramāṃ gatim
14. ananyacetāḥ satataṃ yo māṃ smarati nityaśaḥ
    tasyāhaṃ sulabhaḥ pārtha nityayuktasya yoginaḥ
15. mām upetya punarjanma duḥkhālayam aśāśvatam
    nāpnuvanti mahātmānaḥ saṃsiddhiṃ paramāṃ gatāḥ
16. ā brahmabhuvanāl lokāḥ punarāvartino'rjuna
    mām upetya tu kaunteya punarjanma na vidyate
17. sahasrayugaparyantam ahar yad brahmaṇo viduḥ
    rātriṃ yugasahasrāntāṃ te'horātravido janāḥ

8.11 [That] of which the Veda-knowers speak as the Imperishable (*akshara*), into which the ascetics enter devoid of passion, and desiring which they pursue chastity—that state[12] I will declare to you briefly.

8.12 Controlling all the gates[13] [of the body], confining the mind in the heart, placing one's life-force within the head and established in the concentration (*dhāranā*) of Yoga,

8.13 reciting OM, the monosyllable[14] [signifying] Brahman, remembering Me—he who [thus] departs, abandoning the body, goes the supreme course.[15]

8.14 By him [who is] always of undiverted (*ananya*) mind, [by] whoever remembers Me constantly—by the *yogin* [who is] continually yoked, I am easily attained, O son-of-Prithā.

8.15 Coming to Me, [these] great selves, having gone to supreme consummation, do not undergo rebirth into [this] impermanent abode [i.e., world] of suffering.

8.16 The worlds, up to the realm of Brahma,[16] repeatedly evolve [out of the world-ground], O Arjuna. [For those] having come to Me, however, O son-of-Kuntī, there is no [further] rebirth.

8.17 [Those] who know that a Day of Brahma lasts a thousand [divine] aeons (*yuga*)[17] and a Night ends after a thousand aeons—these people are knowers [of the cosmic meaning of] day and night.

12. The word *pada* means literally "step" and hence can also be rendered as "path."

13. The "gates" (*dvāra*) of the body are usually given as nine: eyes, ears, nostrils, mouth, genitals, and anus.

14. The Sanskrit word *eka-akshara,* here meaning "monosyllable" (i.e., OM), can also mean "the one Imperishable."

15. On the "supreme course," see note 23 for 6.45.

16. Brahma, also called Prajāpati ("Lord of Creatures"), is the firstborn of creation.

17. On the *yugas* and other time periods, see Part One, chapter 7, "The Hindu Concept of Cyclic Time."

अव्यक्ताद्व्यक्तयः सर्वाः प्रभवन्त्यहरागमे ।
रात्र्यागमे प्रलीयन्ते तत्रैवाव्यक्तसंज्ञके ॥ ८—१८ ॥
भूतग्रामः स एवायं भूत्वा भूत्वा प्रलीयते ।
रात्र्यागमेऽवशः पार्थ प्रभवत्यहरागमे ॥ ८—१९ ॥
परस्तस्मात्तु भावोऽन्योऽव्यक्तोऽव्यक्तात्सनातनः ।
यः स सर्वेषु भूतेषु नश्यत्सु न विनश्यति ॥ ८—२० ॥
अव्यक्तोऽक्षर इत्युक्तस्तमाहुः परमां गतिम् ।
यं प्राप्य न निवर्तन्ते तद्धाम परमं मम ॥ ८—२१ ॥
पुरुषः स परः पार्थ भक्त्या लभ्यस्त्वनन्यया ।
यस्यान्तःस्थानि भूतानि येन सर्वमिदं ततम् ॥ ८—२२ ॥
यत्र काले त्वनावृत्तिमावृत्तिं चैव योगिनः ।
प्रयाता यान्ति तं कालं वक्ष्यामि भरतर्षभ ॥ ८—२३ ॥
अग्निर्ज्योतिरहः शुक्लः षण्मासा उत्तरायणम् ।
तत्र प्रयाता गचछन्ति ब्रह्म ब्रह्मविदो जनाः ॥ ८—२४ ॥

18. avyaktād vyaktayaḥ sarvāḥ prabhavanty aharāgame
rātryāgame pralīyante tatraivāvyaktasaṃjñake
19. bhūtagrāmaḥ sa evāyaṃ bhūtvā bhūtvā pralīyate
rātryāgame'vaśaḥ pārtha prabhavaty aharāgame
20. paras tasmāt tu bhāvo'nyo'vyakto'vyaktāt sanātanaḥ
yaḥ sa sarveṣu bhūteṣu naśyatsu na vinaśyati
21. avyakto'kṣara ity uktas tam āhuḥ paramāṃ gatim
yaṃ prāpya na nivartante tad dhāma paramaṃ mama
22. puruṣah sa paraḥ pārtha bhaktyā labhyas tv ananyayā
yasyāntaḥsthāni bhūtāni yena sarvam idaṃ tatam
23. yatra kāle tv anāvṛttim āvṛttiṃ caiva yoginaḥ
prayātā yānti taṃ kālaṃ vakṣyāmi bhāratarṣabha
24. agnir jyotir ahaḥ śuklaḥ ṣaṇmāsā uttarāyaṇam
tatra prayātā gacchanti brahma brahmavido janāḥ

8.18 From the unmanifest [world-ground], all manifest [things] spring forth at the coming of a [cosmic] Day; at the coming of a [cosmic] Night, they dissolve [back] indeed into that [state] designated as the unmanifest.

8.19 This same aggregation of beings, [which] comes-into-being again and again, dissolves involuntarily at the coming of the [cosmic] Night, O son-of-Prithā. At the coming of the [cosmic] Day, it springs forth [again].

8.20 But beyond that, [there is] another state-of-being; [beyond] the unmanifest, [there is yet another] Unmanifest, the everlasting [Supreme Person]—He who on the destruction of all beings is not destroyed.

8.21 The Unmanifest is called Imperishable (*akshara*). Him they call the supreme course from which, when attained, they do not return [to the perishable world]—this is My supreme abode.

8.22 That Supreme Spirit, O son-of-Prithā, is attainable through devotion [directed to] none other [than Me], in whom all beings abide [and] by whom this entire [universe] is spread out [like a spider's web].

8.23 The time at which the *yogins* [who have] gone-forth[18] go to [the path of] no-return or return [respectively]—that time I will [now] declare [to you], O Bharatarshabha.[19]

8.24 Fire, luminosity, day, the bright [fortnight], the six months of the [sun's] northern course—going-forth in these, the people [who are] knowers of Brahman go to Brahman.[20]

18. "Gone-forth" (*prayāta*) means "left the body," that is, died.

19. On Bharatarshabha, see note 48 for 3.41.

20. In the Upanishads, this "bright course" is also called the "path of the gods" (*deva-yāna*), because it leads to subtle, celestial realms, the dwelling places of the deities.

धूमो रात्रिस्तथा कृष्णः षण्मासा दक्षिणायनम् ।
तत्र चान्द्रमसं ज्योतिर्योगी प्राप्य निवर्तते ॥ ८—२५ ॥
शुक्लकृष्णे गती ह्येते जगतः शाश्वते मते ।
एकया यात्यनावृत्तिमन्ययावर्तते पुनः ॥ ८—२६ ॥
नैते सृती पार्थ जानन्योगी मुह्यति कश्चन ।
तस्मात्सर्वेषु कालेषु योगयुक्तो भवार्जुन ॥ ८—२७ ॥
वेदेषु यज्ञेषु तपःसु चैव
दानेषु यत्पुण्यफलं प्रदिष्टम् ।
अत्येति तत्सर्वमिदं विदित्वा
योगी परं स्थानमुपैति चाद्यम् ॥ ८—२८ ॥

25. dhūmo rātris tathā kṛṣṇaḥ ṣaṇmāsā dakṣiṇāyanam
tatra cāndramasaṃ jyotir yogī prāpya nivartate
26. śuklakṛṣṇe gatī hy ete jagataḥ śāśvate mate
ekayā yāty anāvṛttim anyayāvartate punaḥ
27. naite sṛtī pārtha jānan yogī muhyati kaścana
tasmāt sarveṣu kāleṣu yogayukto bhavārjuna
28. vedeṣu yajñeṣu tapaḥsu caiva
dāneṣu yat puṇyaphalaṃ pradiṣṭam
atyeti tat sarvam idaṃ viditvā
yogī paraṃ sthānam upaiti cādyam

8.25 Smoke, night, the dark [fortnight], the six months of the southern course [of the sun]—in these the *yogin* attains to the lunar luminosity [and thereafter] returns [to the phenomenal world].[21]

8.26 Verily, these two courses, the bright and the dark, are considered to be eternal in [this] universe. By one [course] he goes to [the state of] no-return, by the other he returns again.

8.27 Knowing these [two] pathways, O son-of-Prithā, no *yogin* whatever is deluded. Hence at all times be yoked in Yoga, O Arjuna!

8.28 Whatever meritorious fruit is assigned to [the study of] the *Vedas*, to sacrifices, austerities or gifts—the *yogin*, knowing this [teaching], transcends all this and reaches the supreme and primal state.[22]

21. This "dark course" is the "path of the ancestors" (*pitri-yāna*), leading to rebirth.
22. This verse is in the *trishtubh* meter.

श्रीभगवानुवाच
इदं तु ते गुह्यतमं प्रवक्ष्याम्यनसूयवे ।
ज्ञानं विज्ञानसहितं यज्ज्ञात्वा मोक्ष्यसेऽशुभात् ॥ ९—१ ॥
रजविद्या रजगुह्यं पवित्रमिदमुत्तमम् ।
प्रत्यक्षावगमं धर्म्यं सुसुखं कर्तुमव्ययम् ॥ ९—२ ॥
अश्रद्दधानाः पुरुषा धर्मस्यास्य परंतप ।
अप्राप्य मां निवर्तन्ते मृत्युसंसारवर्त्मनि ॥ ९—३ ॥
मया ततमिदं सर्वं जगदव्यक्तमूर्तिना ।
मत्स्थानि सर्वभूतानि न चाहं तेष्ववस्थितः ॥ ९—४ ॥
न च मत्स्थानि भूतानि पश्य मे योगमैश्वरम् ।
भूतभृन्न च भूतस्थो ममात्मा भूतभावनः ॥ ९—५ ॥

śrībhagavān uvāca

1. idaṃ tu te guhyatamaṃ pravakṣyāmy anasūyave
   jñānaṃ vijñānasahitaṃ yaj jñātvā mokṣyase'śubhāt
2. rājavidyā rājaguhyaṃ pavitram idam uttamam
   pratyakṣāvagamanaṃ dharmyaṃ susukhaṃ kartum avyayam
3. aśraddadhānāḥ puruṣā dharmasyāsya paraṃtapa
   aprāpya māṃ nivartante mṛtyusaṃsāravartmani
4. mayā tatam idaṃ sarvaṃ jagad avyaktamūrtinā
   matsthāni sarvabhūtāni na cāhaṃ teṣv avasthitaḥ
5. na ca matsthāni bhūtāni paśya me yogam aiśvaram
   bhūtabhṛn na ca bhūtastho mamātmā bhūtabhāvanaḥ

CHAPTER 9

The Yoga of the Royal Wisdom and the Royal Secret

The Blessed Lord said:

9.1 To you [who are] non-grumbling,[1] I will [now] declare this most secret knowledge together with world-knowledge (*vijnāna*), knowing which you shall be freed from [all] inauspicious [karma].

9.2 This is the royal science,[2] the royal secret, a supreme purifier, evident-to-one's-understanding,[3] lawful (*dharmya*), very easy to apply—[and yet] immutable.

9.3 Men (*purusha*) [who] have no faith in this law, O Paramtapa[4], return to the course of the death cycle[5] without reaching Me.

9.4 By Me, unmanifest in form, this entire universe was spread out. All beings abide in Me, but I do not subsist in them.[6]

9.5 And [yet] beings are not abiding in Me.[7] Behold My lordly (*aishvara*) Yoga: My Self sustains [all] beings, yet, not abiding in beings, causes beings to be.[8]

1. The adjective *anasūya*, here rendered as "non-grumbling," implies an ungrudging quality. In his time, Krishna must have encountered a certain amount of resistance, because his teaching was unorthodox from the perspective of the brahmanical mainstream (see 9.11).

2. Here the term "royal" (*rāja*) either suggests a quality of specialness or can refer to the fact that the kind of teaching imparted by Krishna has been passed along within royal circles. Krishna himself was a king (*rāja*) of the Lunar Dynasty within the Vrishni tribe.

3. The phrase *pratyakshāvagamanam* is composed of *prati* + *aksha* ("before the eyes") and *avagamana* ("understanding"). What this verse indicates is that the royal science of Krishna's Yoga is self-evident.

4. On the epithet Paramtapa, see note 5 for 2.3.

5. The compound *mrityu-samsāra,* here translated as "death cycle," refers to the empirical world, which is of a cyclic nature, since karma leads all being from life to death to rebirth, and so on.

6. See 7.7.

7. The phrase "abiding in Me" is *mat-sthāni* ("My places") in the original, which is meant to qualify the plural *bhūtāni* ("beings").

8. The word *bhāvana* means literally "causing-to-be."

«सर्वगः सर्वश्चाद्यः सर्वकृत्सर्वदर्शनः ।
सर्वज्ञः सर्वदर्शी च सर्वात्मा सर्वतोमुखः»

यथाकाशस्थितो नित्यं वायुः सर्वत्रगो महान् ।
तथा सर्वाणि भूतानि मत्स्थानीत्युपधारय ॥ ९—६ ॥

«एवं हि सर्वभूतेषु चराम्यनभिलक्षितः ।
भूतप्रकृतिमात्स्थाय सहैव च विनैव च»

सर्वभूतानि कौन्तेय प्रकृतिं यान्ति मामिकाम् ।
कल्पक्षये पुनस्तानि कल्पादौ विसृजाम्यहम् ॥ ९—७ ॥
प्रकृतिं स्वामवष्टभ्य विसृजामि पुनः पुनः ।
भूतग्राममिमं कृत्स्नमवशं प्रकृतेर्वशात् ॥ ९—८ ॥
न च मां तानि कर्माणि निबध्नन्ति धनंजय ।
उदासीनवदासीनमसक्तं तेषु कर्मसु ॥ ९—९ ॥
मयाध्यक्षेन प्रकृतिः सूयते सचाराचरम् ।
हेतुनानेन कौन्तेय जगद्विपरिवर्तते ॥ ९—१० ॥
अवजानन्ति मां मूढा मानुषीं तनुमाश्रितम् ।
परं भावमजानन्तो मम भूतमहेश्वरम् ॥ ९—११ ॥

« sarvagaḥ sarvaś cādyaḥ sarvakṛtsarvadarśanaḥ
sarvajñaḥ sarvadarśī ca sarvātmā sarvatomukhaḥ»

6. yathākāśasthito nityaṃ vāyuḥ sarvatrago mahān
tathā sarvāṇi bhūtāni matsthānīty upadhāraya

« evaṃ hi sarvabhūteṣu carāmyanabhilakṣitaḥ
bhūtaprakṛtimāt sthāya sahaiva ca vinaiva ca»

7. sarvabhūtāni kaunteya prakṛtiṃ yānti māmikām
kalpakṣaye punas tāni kalpādau visṛjāmy aham
8. prakṛtiṃ svām avaṣṭabhya visṛjāmi punaḥ punaḥ
bhūtagrāmam imaṃ kṛtsnam avaśaṃ prakṛter vaśāt
9. na ca māṃ tāni karmāṇi nibadhnanti dhanaṃjaya
udāsīnavad āsīnam asaktaṃ teṣu karmasu
10. mayādhyakṣeṇa prakṛtiḥ sūyate sacarācaram
hetunānena kaunteya jagad viparivartate
11. avajānanti māṃ mūḍhā mānuṣīṃ tanum āśritam
paraṃ bhāvam ajānanto mama bhūtamaheśvaram

«Omnipresent, whole, primordial, all-doing, all-seeing, all-knowing [is] the Seer-of-all, the Self-of-all, facing everywhere. »

9.6 As the mighty wind, [moving] ever and everywhere, abides in space,[9] so understand [that] all beings abide in Me.

«Thus indeed I move unrecognized in all beings, adopting the nature (*prakriti*) of beings; [thus I am as it were] with and without [them].»

9.7 All beings, O son-of-Kuntī,[10] come to My nature at the end (*kshaya*) of an aeon;[11] then I emit them again at the beginning of a [new] aeon.

9.8 Supported by [My] own [lower] nature,[12] I emit again and again this whole (*kritsna*) powerless aggregation of beings by the power (*vasha*) of [My] nature.

9.9 And these actions [of Mine] do not bind me, O Dhanamjaya.[13] Unattached, I behave[14] in these actions like [someone who is completely] disinterested.

9.10 Under My supervision, [My lower] nature produces [things] moving and unmoving. For this reason, O son-of-Kuntī, the universe revolves.

9.11 Fools scorn[15] Me in the human body [which I have] assumed, ignorant [as they are] of My higher state-of-existence: [as] the Great Lord[16] of [all] beings.

9. The technical term *ākāsha* denotes the fifth element, ether, here translated as "space." In the present context, it could also be rendered as "ether-space."

10. On son-of-Kuntī (Kaunteya), see note 19 for 1.27.

11. On *kalpa* ("aeon"), see Part One, chapter 7, "The Hindu Concept of Cyclic Time." The word *kshaya,* here rendered as "end," means literally "destruction."

12. God's "lower nature" (*apara-prakriti*) refers to his "lower" (*apara*) nature, which is manifestation. See 7.4–5.

13. On the epithet Dhanamjaya, see note 7 for 1.15.

14. The Sanskrit original has "[I am] seated" (*āsīnam*).

15. See note 1 for 9.1.

16. Here the compound *maheshvara*, derived from *mahā* ("great") and *īshvara* ("lord"), means Purushottama, or God as the Supreme Person.

मोघाशा मोघकर्माणो मोघज्ञाना विचेतसः ।
राक्षसीमासुरीं चैव प्रकृतिं मोहिनीं श्रिताः ॥ ९—१२ ॥
महात्मानस्तु मां पार्थ दैवीं प्रकृतिमाश्रिताः ।
भजन्त्यनन्यमनसो ज्ञात्वा भूतादिमव्ययम् ॥ ९—१३ ॥
सततं कीर्तयन्तो मां यतन्तश्च दृढव्रताः ।
नमस्यन्तश्च मां भक्त्या नित्ययुक्ता उपासते ॥ ९—१४ ॥
ज्ञानयज्ञेन चाप्यन्ये यजन्तो मामुपासते ।
एकत्वेन पृथक्त्वेन बहुधा विश्वतोमुखम् ॥ ९—१५ ॥
अहं क्रतुरहं यज्ञः स्वधाहमहमौषधम् ।
मन्त्रोऽहमहमेवाज्यमहमग्निरहं हुतम् ॥ ९—१६ ॥
पिताहमस्य जगतो माता धाता पितामहः ।
वेद्यं पवित्रमोंकार ऋक्साम यजुरेव च ॥ ९—१७ ॥
गतिर्भर्ता प्रभुः साक्षी निवासः शरणं सुहृत् ।
प्रभवः प्रलयः स्थानं निधानं बीजमव्ययम् ॥ ९—१८ ॥
तपाम्यहमहं वर्षं निगृह्णाम्युत्सृजामि च ।
अमृतं चैव मृत्युश्च सदसच्चाहमर्जुन ॥ ९—१९ ॥

12. moghāśā moghakarmāṇo moghajñānā vicetasaḥ
    rākṣasīm āsurīṃ caiva prakṛtiṃ mohinīṃ śritāḥ
13. mahātmānas tu māṃ pārtha daivīṃ prakṛtim āśritāḥ
    bhajanty ananyamanaso jñātvā bhūtādim avyayam
14. satataṃ kīrtayanto māṃ yatantaś ca dṛḍhavratāḥ
    namasyantaś ca māṃ bhaktyā nityayuktā upāsate
15. jñānayajñena cāpy anye yajanto mām upāsate
    ekatvena pṛthaktvena bahudhā viśvatomukham
16. ahaṃ kratur ahaṃ yajñaḥ svadhāham aham auṣadham
    mantro'ham aham evājyam aham agnir ahaṃ hutam
17. pitāham asya jagato mātā dhātā pitāmahaḥ
    vedyaṃ pavitram oṃkāra ṛk sāma yajur eva ca
18. gatir bhartā prabhuḥ sākṣī nivāsaḥ śaraṇaṃ suhṛt
    prabhavaḥ pralayaḥ sthānaṃ nidhānaṃ bījam avyayam
19. tapāmy aham ahaṃ varṣaṃ nigṛhṇāmy utsṛjāmi ca
    amṛtaṃ caiva mṛtyuś ca sad asac cāham arjuna

9.12 Vain are the hopes, vain the actions, vain the "knowledge"[17] [of those who are] bereft-of-sense. [They] resort to a delusive nature (*prakriti*) [that is] monstrous and demonic.[18]

9.13 But the great selves, O son-of-Prithā,[19] taking refuge in [My] divine nature, worship Me with [their] minds [intent] on no other [deity], knowing [Me to be] the immutable beginning of [all] beings.

9.14 Always glorifying Me and striving, steadfast [in their] vows, and bowing down, ever yoked, they worship Me with devotion.

9.15 And others worship Me by offering the sacrifice of knowledge [and by regarding Me as] unity [in] diversity, manifold [and] facing everywhere.

9.16 I am the rite. I am the sacrifice. I am the oblation. I am the herb. I am the mantra. I am the clarified-butter. I am the fire. I am the offering.

9.17 I am the father of this universe, the mother, the supporter, the grandsire, [all that is] to-be-known, the purifier, the syllable OM, and the *Rig-*, *Sāma-* and *Yajur-*[*Veda*].[20]

9.18 [I am] the course, the sustainer, the Lord, the witness (*sākshin*), the home and refuge, the friend, the origin, dissolution and ultimate state, the receptacle, the immutable seed [in all beings].

9.19 I burn [like the sun]. I hold back and pour forth the rain. I am immortality and death, the existent and the nonexistent, O Arjuna.

17. I have placed "knowledge" (*jnāna*) in quotation marks because those who are "bereft-of-sense" (*vicetas*) cannot be expected to have real knowledge.

18. Sargeant (1984) makes the valid observation that the term *prakriti* is used in this verse not to mean God's lower nature (as in the next verse) but in a more general sense.

19. On son-of-Prithā (Pārtha), see note 18 for 1.25.

20. The *Atharva-Veda* is omitted here, presumably for metric reasons. Often only the three principal Vedic collections (*samhitā*) are mentioned. See, e.g., 9.20.

त्रैविद्या मां सोमपाः पूतपापा
यज्ञैरिष्ट्वा स्वर्गतिं प्रार्थयन्ते ।
ते पुण्यमासाद्य सुरेन्द्रलोक
मश्नन्ति दिव्यान्दिवि देवभोगान् ॥ ९—२० ॥
ते तं भुक्त्वा स्वर्गलोकं विशालं
क्षीणे पुण्ये मर्त्यलोकं विशन्ति ।
एवं त्रयीधर्ममनुप्रपन्ना
गतागतं कामकामा लभन्ते ॥ ९—२१ ॥
अनन्याश्चिन्तयन्तो मां ये जनाः पर्युपासते ।
तेषां नित्याभियुक्तानां योगक्षेमं वहाम्यहम् ॥ ९—२२ ॥
येऽप्यन्यदेवता भक्ता यजन्ते श्रद्धयान्विताः ।
तेऽपि मामेव कौन्तेय यजन्त्यविधिपूर्वकम् ॥ ९—२३ ॥
अहं हि सर्वयज्ञानां भोक्ता च प्रभुरेव च ।
न तु मामभिजानन्ति तत्त्वेनातश्च्यवन्ति ते ॥ ९—२४ ॥
यान्ति देवव्रता देवान्पितॄन्यान्ति पितृव्रताः ।
भूतानि यान्ति भूतेज्या यान्ति मद्याजिनोऽपि माम् ॥ ९—२५ ॥

20. traividyā māṃ somapāḥ pūtapāpā
yajñair iṣṭvā svargatiṃ prārthayante
te puṇyam āsādya surendraloka
maśnanti divyān divi devabhogān
21. te taṃ bhuktvā svargalokaṃ viśālaṃ
kṣīṇe puṇye martyalokaṃ viśanti
evaṃ trayīdharmam anuprapannā
gatāgataṃ kāmakāmā labhante
22. ananyāś cintayanto māṃ ye janāḥ paryupāsate
teṣāṃ nityābhiyuktānāṃ yogakṣemaṃ vahāmy aham
23. ye'py anyadevatābhaktā yajante śraddhayānvitāḥ
te'pi mām eva kaunteya yajanty avidhipūrvakam
24. ahaṃ hi sarvayajñānāṃ bhoktā ca prabhur eva ca
na tu mām abhijānanti tattvenātaś cyavanti te
25. yānti devavratā devān pitṛn yānti pitṝvratāḥ
bhūtāni yānti bhūtejyā yānti madyājino'pi mām

9.20 [Those] *soma* drinkers [who know] the triple science,[21] purged of sin and having worshipped Me with sacrifices, wish for the course to heaven (*svar*); attaining the meritorious world of the lord-of-gods,[22] they taste the gods' divine pleasures in heaven (*div*).[23]

9.21 Having enjoyed that vast heavenly world[24] [and with] their merit exhausted, they enter [again] the world of mortals. Thus, [those who] follow the triple law,[25] desiring [objects of] desire, gain [but the world of] coming-and-going.[26]

9.22 For those men who, reflecting on Me, [with] undiverted (*ananya*) [mind], worship [Me], ever yoked, I bring security in Yoga.[27]

9.23 Even those who are devoted to other deities and worship [them] endowed with faith—they, verily, worship Me, O son-of-Kuntī, [although] not according to [established] ordinance.

9.24 For, I am the enjoyer of all sacrifices and indeed the [supreme] Lord. But they do not know Me in truth. Hence they fall [back into the state of conditioned existence].

9.25 The god-vowed go to the gods; the ancestor-vowed go to the ancestors; to the lower-beings[28] go [those who] worship lower-beings, but to Me go [all who] sacrifice to Me.[29]

21. The expression *traividyā* ("triple science") denotes the three Vedas mentioned in 9.17.
22. The compound *surendra* ("lord-of-gods") refers to the leader of the celestial host, namely Indra.
23. This verse is in the *trishtubh* meter.
24. The "heavenly world" (*svarga-loka*) is the subtle realm inhabited by the deities.
25. All classical commentators and modern translators understand the compound "triple law" (*trayī-dharma*) as referring to the three principal Vedas.
26. This verse is in the *trishtubh* meter.
27. The phrase *yoga-kshema* ("security in Yoga") stands not for ordinary comfort but for spiritual succor.
28. Here the word *bhūta* denotes elemental spirit.
29. The modes of worship, again, depend on the innate (karmic) character (*svabhāva,* "own-being") of a person. See 17.4.

पत्रं पुष्पं फलं तोयं यो मे भक्त्या प्रयच्छति ।
तदहं भक्त्युपहृतमश्नामि प्रयतात्मनः ॥ ९—२६ ॥
यत्करोषि यदश्नासि यज्जुहोषि ददासि यत् ।
यत्तपस्यसि कौन्तेय तत्कुरुष्व मदर्पणम् ॥ ९—२७ ॥
शुभाशुभफलैरेवं मोक्ष्यसे कर्मबन्धनैः ।
संन्यासयोगयुक्तात्मा विमुक्तो मामुपैष्यसि ॥ ९—२८ ॥
समोऽहं सर्वभूतेषु न मे द्वेष्योऽस्ति न प्रियः ।
ये भजन्ति तु मां भक्त्या मयि ते तेषु चाप्यहम् ॥ ९—२९ ॥
अपि चेत्सुदुराचारो भजते मामनन्यभाक् ।
साधुरेव स मन्तव्यः सम्यग्व्यवसितो हि सः ॥ ९—३० ॥
क्षिप्रं भवति धर्मात्मा शश्वच्छान्तिं निगच्छति ।
कौन्तेय प्रतिजानीहि न मे भक्तः प्रणश्यति ॥ ९—३१ ॥
मां हि पार्थ व्यपाश्रित्य येऽपि स्युः पापयोनयः ।
स्त्रियो वैश्यस्तथा शूद्रास्तेऽपि यान्ति परां गतिम् ॥ ९—३२ ॥
किं पुनर्ब्राह्मणाः पुण्या भक्ता राजर्षयस्तथा ।
अनित्यमसुखं लोकमिमं प्राप्य भजस्व माम् ॥ ९—३३ ॥

26. pattraṃ puṣpaṃ phalaṃ toyaṃ yo me bhaktyā prayacchati
tad ahaṃ bhaktyupahṛtam aśnāmi prayatātmanaḥ
27. yat karoṣi yad aśnāsi yaj juhoṣi dadāsi yat
yat tapasyasi kaunteya tat kuruṣva madarpaṇam
28. śubhāśubhaphalair evaṃ mokṣyase karmabandhanaiḥ
saṃnyāsayogayuktātmā vimukto māṃ upaiṣyasi
29. samo'haṃ sarvabhūteṣu na me dveṣyo'sti na priyaḥ
ye bhajanti tu māṃ bhaktyā mayi te teṣu cāpy aham
30. api cet sudurācāro bhajate mām ananyabhāk
sādhur eva sa mantavyaḥ samyag vyavasito hi saḥ
31. kṣipraṃ bhavati dharmātmā śaśvacchāntiṃ nigacchati
kaunteya pratijānīhi na me bhaktaḥ praṇaśyati
32. māṃ hi pārtha vyapāśritya ye'pi syuḥ pāpayonayaḥ
striyo vaiśyās tathā śūdrās te'pi yānti parāṃ gatim
33. kiṃ punar brāhmaṇāḥ puṇyā bhaktā rājarṣayas tathā
anityam asukhaṃ lokam imaṃ prāpya bhajasva mām

9.26 He who offers Me an offering out of devotion [and] with an exerting self[30]—[be it] a leaf, flower, fruit, [or] water—[that] I [will] eat.[31]

9.27 Whatever you do, whatever you eat, whatever you sacrifice, whatever you give, whatever austerities-you-perform—do that, O son-of-Kuntī, [as] an offering to Me.

9.28 Thus you will be freed from the bonds of action, [whose] fruits are auspicious [or] inauspicious. Released, [with] the self yoked by the Yoga of renunciation, you will come to Me.

9.29 I am the same[32] in all beings. To Me there is none hateful or dear. But those who worship Me with devotion, they are in Me and I am also in them.

9.30 Even if [a person of] very evil conduct worships Me, devoted to no other, he should, verily, be considered good, for he is rightly resolved.[33]

9.31 Swiftly he becomes a self [established in] the law (*dharma*) [and] attains everlasting peace, O son-of-Kuntī. Understand [that] no devotee of Mine is lost!

9.32 For, even those, O son-of-Prithā, who take refuge in Me, though [they be born] of sinful wombs, [as well as] women, merchants, and even serfs—they [all] go the supreme course.[34]

9.33 How [much more], then, meritorious *brāhmanas* and devoted royal seers? [Since you have] attained [birth in] this transient and joyless world, worship Me!

30. The ablative compound *prayatātmanah* ("by exerting self"), here translated as "with an exerting self," refers to the *yogin* who is deeply dedicated to the process of spiritual self-transformation.
31. Here Krishna reiterates the age-old belief that the deities—and the God of gods—"eats" sacrificial offerings, that is, consumes the subtle aspect of an oblation. Another way of putting this is to say that he accepts an offering made with devotion.
32. The term "same" (*sama*) refers to the idea of sameness (*samatva*); see note 18 for 2.15.
33. The capacity for resolution (*vyavasāya*) is innate to the wisdom-faculty (*buddhi*).
34. On the "supreme course," see note 23 for 6.45.

मन्मना भव मद्भक्तो मद्याजी मां नमस्कुरु ।
मामेवैष्यसि युक्त्वैवमात्मानं मत्परायणः ॥ ९—३४ ॥

34. manmanā bhava madbhakto madyājī māṃ namaskuru
mām evaiṣyasi yuktvaivam ātmānaṃ matparāyaṇaḥ

9.34 Be Me-minded, My devotee. My sacrificer! To Me make obeisance! Thus, having yoked the self, you will, intent on Me, verily come to Me.

श्रीभगवानुवाच
भूय एव महाबाहो शृणु मे परमं वचः ।
यत्तेऽहं प्रीयमाणाय वक्ष्यामि हितकाम्यया ॥ १०—१ ॥
न मे विदुः सुरगणाः प्रभवं न महर्षयः ।
अहमादिर्हि देवानां महर्षीणां च सर्वशः ॥ १०—२ ॥
यो मामजमनादिं च वेत्ति लोकमहेश्वरम ।
असंमूढः स मर्त्येषु सर्वपापैः प्रमुच्यते ॥ १०—३ ॥
बुद्धिर्ज्ञानमसंमोहः क्षमा सत्यं दमः शमः ।
सुखं दुःखं भवोऽभावो भयं चाभयमेव च ॥ १०—४ ॥
अहिंसा समता तुष्टिस्तपो दानं यशोऽयशः ।
भवन्ति भावा भूतानां मत्त एव पृथग्विधाः ॥ १०—५ ॥
महर्षयः सप्त पूर्वे चत्वारो मनवस्तथा ।
मद्भावा मानसा जाता येषां लोक इमाः प्रजाः ॥ १०—६ ॥
एतां विभूतिं योगं च मम यो वेत्ति तत्त्वतः ।
सोऽविकम्पेन योगेन युज्यते नात्र संशयः ॥ १०—७ ॥

śrībhagavān uvāca

1. bhūya eva mahābāho śṛṇu me paramaṃ vacaḥ
   yat te'haṃ prīyamāṇāya vakṣyāmi hitakāmyayā
2. na me viduḥ suragaṇāḥ prabhavaṃ na maharṣayaḥ
   aham ādir hi devānāṃ maharṣīṇāṃ ca sarvaśaḥ
3. yo māṃ ajam anādiṃ ca vetti lokamaheśvaram
   asaṃmūḍhaḥ sa martyeṣu sarvapāpaiḥ pramucyate
4. buddhir jñānam asaṃmohaḥ kṣamā satyaṃ damaḥ śamaḥ
   sukhaṃ duḥkhaṃ bhavo'bhāvo bhayaṃ cābhayam eva ca
5. ahiṃsā samatā tuṣṭis tapo dānaṃ yaśo'yaśaḥ
   bhavanti bhāvā bhūtānāṃ matta eva pṛthagvidhāḥ
6. maharṣayaḥ sapta pūrve catvāro manavas tathā
   madbhāvā mānasā jātā yeṣāṃ loka imāḥ prajāḥ
7. etāṃ vibhūtiṃ yogaṃ ca mama yo vetti tattvataḥ
   so'vikampena yogena yujyate nātra saṃśayaḥ

CHAPTER 10

The Yoga of [Divine] Manifestation

The Blessed Lord said:

10.1 Moreover, O mighty-armed [Arjuna], hear My supreme word, which I will declare to you [who are My] beloved [friend], out of a desire for [your] welfare.

10.2 Neither the hosts of gods nor the great seers know My origin. For I am the beginning of the gods and of the great seers [and of all other entities] everywhere.

10.3 He who knows Me, the world's Great Lord, as unborn and beginningless, is not bewildered among mortals [but] is released from all sins.

10.4 [Control of the] wisdom-faculty, knowledge, nonbewilderment, patience, truthfulness, restraint, tranquillity, pleasure, pain, becoming, nonbecoming, fear and also fearlessness;

10.5 nonharming (*ahimsā*), sameness, contentment, austerity, charity, dignity and indignity—[such are] the states-of-existence (*bhāva*) of the beings [who] arise [in all their] diversity from Me indeed.

10.6 The seven great seers of old,[1] as also the four Manus[2] [sharing in] My state-of-existence, were born of My mind; from them [sprung] the world [with all] these creatures.

10.7 He who knows in truth this My power-of-manifestation[3] and Yoga, is yoked by unshaking Yoga. Of this there is no doubt.

1. The seven great seers are usually identified as Kashyapa, Atri, Vasishtha, Vishvāmitra, Gautama, Jamadagni, and Bharadvāja.

2. The four Manus (see note 2 for 4.1) are part of a sequence of fourteen Manus: Svāyambhuva (the original Manu), Svārocisha, Auttama, Tāmasa, Raivata, Cākshusha, and in seventh place Manu Vaivasvata (the progenitor of the present human species and the ruler of the current *manvantara,* or Manu Age) whose reign will come to an end in another two million years or so. After him there will be seven more Manus before the universe will vanish entirely upon the demise of the present creator-deity Brahma. (Svāyambhuva is the lawgiver of note 4 for 5.18.)

3. Zaehner (1966) translates *vibhūti* as "far-flung power"; Nataraja Guru (1973) as "unique value"; Radhakrishnan (1948) as "glory," while Edgerton (1944) has "supernal-manifestation." Hill (1928/1966) rightly remarks that this word "contains an idea of 'power' or 'lordship' and also an idea of 'pervasion' or 'immanence.'"

अहं सर्वस्य प्रभवो मत्तः सर्वं प्रवर्तते ।
इति मत्वा भजन्ते मां बुधा भावसमन्विताः ॥ १०—८ ॥
मच्चित्ता मद्गतप्राणा बोधयन्तः परस्परम् ।
कथयन्तश्च मां नित्यं तुष्यन्ति च रमन्ति च ॥ १०—९ ॥
तेषां सततयुक्तानां भजतां प्रीतिपूर्वकम् ।
ददामि बुद्धियोगं तं येन मामुपयान्ति ते ॥ १०—१० ॥
तेषामेवानुकम्पार्थमहमज्ञानजं तमः ।
नाशयाम्यात्मभावस्थो ज्ञानदीपेन भास्वता ॥ १०—११ ॥
अर्जुन उवाच
परं ब्रह्म परं धाम पवित्रं परमं भवान् ।
पुरुषं शाश्वतं दिव्यमादिदेवमजं विभुम् ॥ १०—१२ ॥
आहुस्त्वामृषयः सर्वे देवर्षिर्नारदस्तथा ।
असितो देवलो व्यासः स्वयं चैव ब्रवीषि मे ॥ १०—१३ ॥

8. ahaṃ sarvasya prabhavo mattaḥ sarvaṃ pravartate
iti matvā bhajante māṃ budhā bhāvasamanvitāḥ
9. maccittā madgataprāṇā bodhayantaḥ parasparam
kathayantaś ca māṃ nityaṃ tuṣyanti ca ramanti ca
10. teṣāṃ satatayuktānāṃ bhajatāṃ prītipūrvakam
dadāmi buddhiyogaṃ taṃ yena mām upayānti te
11. teṣām evānukampārtham aham ajñānajaṃ tamaḥ
nāśayāmy ātmabhāvastho jñānadīpena bhāsvatā

arjuna uvāca
12. paraṃ brahma paraṃ dhāma pavitraṃ paramaṃ bhavān
puruṣaṃ śāśvataṃ divyam ādidevam ajaṃ vibhum
13. āhus tvām ṛṣayaḥ sarve devarṣir nāradas tathā
asito devalo vyāsaḥ svayaṃ caiva bravīṣi me

10.8 I am the origin of all. From Me everything emerges. Considering this, the wise endowed with [the appropriate] state-of-existence[4] worship Me.

10.9 Me-minded, the life-force dissolved[5] in Me, enlightening each other and constantly talking of Me—they are content and they rejoice.

10.10 To these [wise men who are] ever yoked and worship [Me] with delight, I give that *buddhi-yoga*[6] by which they approach Me.

10.11 Out of compassion (*anukampā*) for those [sages], I dispel the nescience-born darkness with the bright lamp of knowledge, [while] abiding in [My] Self's state-of-existence.

Arjuna said:

10.12 You are the supreme Brahman, supreme abode, supreme purifier, the eternal divine Spirit, primordial God, unborn, all-pervading.

10.13 [In this way] speak of You all the seers and also the divine seer Nārada,[7] Asita Devala,[8] and Vyāsa;[9] and [You] Yourself tell me so.

4. Zaehner (1966) translates the term *bhāva* ("state-of-existence") here as "warm affection," while Bhaktivedanta Swami (1983) renders it as "with all their hearts." Shankara explains it as *bhāvanā paramārthatattvābhiniveśah,* or "cultivation: intentness on the transcendental Reality." If understood as "state-of-existence," the term *bhāva* denotes the psychological condition of openness to the ultimate Reality, which is fundamental to Yoga.

5. The word *gata* (lit. "gone"), here rendered as "dissolved," can also be given as "absorbed [in Me]." A more devotional translation of the entire phrase would be "the life-force [or: their life] surrendered to Me."

6. The compound *buddhi-yoga,* here left untranslated, has many connotations. It refers to the yogic capacity for wisdom, or the ability to exercise one's innate wisdom-faculty, thanks to Krishna's grace.

7. Nārada, one of the most famous sages of the Purānas, is said in the epic to have had seven prominent births. As the son of King Drumila and Queen Kalāvatī, he received the teachings of Bhāgavatism directly from Vishnu.

8. Asita Devala is the name of a sage mentioned elsewhere in the *Mahābhārata* as one of the disciples of Vyāsa. He was instrumental in disseminating the epic to the general public. Edgerton (1944) wrongly thought that Asita and Devala were two different sages.

9. This is an instance where Vyāsa, the composer of the entire *Mahābhārata,* has cleverly written himself into his own composition.

सर्वमेतदृतं मन्ये यन्मां वदसि केशव ।
न हि ते भगवन्व्यक्तिं विदुर्देवा न दानवाः ॥ १०—१४ ॥
स्वयमेवात्मनात्मानं वेत्थ त्वं पुरुषोत्तम ।
भूतभावन भूतेश देवदेव जगत्पते ॥ १०—१५ ॥
वक्तुमर्हस्यशेषेण दिव्या ह्यात्मविभूतयः ।
याभिर्विभूतिभिर्लोकानिमांस्त्वं व्याप्य तिष्ठसि ॥ १०—१६ ॥
कथं विद्यामहं योगिंस्त्वां सदा परिचिन्तयन् ।
केषु केषु च भावेषु चिन्त्योऽसि भगवन्मया ॥ १०—१७ ॥
विस्तरेणात्मनो योगं वभूतिं च जनार्दन ।
भूयः कथय तृप्तिर्हि शृण्वतो नास्ति मेऽमृतम ॥ १०—१८ ॥
श्रीभगवानुवाच
हन्त ते कथयिष्यामि दिव्या ह्यात्मविभूतयः ।
प्राधान्यतः कुरुश्रेष्ठ नास्त्यन्तो विस्तरस्य मे ॥ १०—१९ ॥

14. sarvam etad ṛtaṃ manye yan māṃ vadasi keśava
na hi te bhagavan vyaktiṃ vidur devā na dānavāḥ
15. svayam evātmanātmanaṃ vettha tvaṃ puruṣottama
bhūtabhāvana bhūteśa devadeva jagatpate
16. vaktum arhasy aśeṣeṇa divyā hy ātmavibhūtayaḥ
yābhir vibhūtibhir lokān imāṃs tvaṃ vyāpya tiṣṭhasi
17. kathaṃ vidyām ahaṃ yogiṃs tvāṃ sadā paricintayan
keṣu keṣu ca bhāveṣu cintyo'si bhagavan mayā
18. vistareṇātmano yogaṃ vibhūtiṃ ca janārdana
bhūyaḥ kathaya tṛptir hi śṛṇvato nāsti me'mṛtam

śrībhagavān uvāca
19. hanta te kathayiṣyāmi divyā hy ātmavibhūtayaḥ
prādhānyataḥ kuruśreṣtha nāsty anto vistarasya me

10.14 All this that You tell me I deem to be true (*rita*), O Keshava.[10] Indeed, O Blessed One, neither the gods nor the demons know [this] manifest [form of] Yours.

10.15 By [Your] Self You Yourself know [Your] Self, O Supreme Spirit generating beings, Lord of beings, God of gods, ruler of the universe.

10.16 You should tell [me], without reservation, [of Your] divine Self's powers-of-manifestation, by which powers-of-manifestation (*vibhūti*) You abide in these worlds, pervading [them].

10.17 [Though] ever reflecting on You, how am I to know [You], a *yogin*? And in various states-of-existence ought I to think of You, O Blessed One?

10.18 Tell me again extensively, O Janārdana,[11] about Yoga and the power-of-manifestation of [Your] Self. For I am not satiated [with] hearing the nectar [of Your speech].

The Blessed Lord said:

10.19 Lo! I will tell you the principal of [My] divine Self's powers-of-manifestation, Kurushreshtha,[12] [because] there is no end to My extent.

10. On the epithet Keshava, see note 21 for 1.31.
11. On Janārdana, see note 25 for 1.36.
12. Kurushreshtha is an epithet of Arjuna meaning "Best of the Kurus."

अहमात्मा गुडाकेश सर्वभूताशयस्थितः ।
अहमादिश्च मध्यं च भूतानामन्त एव च ॥ १०—२० ॥
अदित्यानामहं विष्णुर्ज्योतिषां रविरंशुमान् ।
मरीचिर्मरुतामस्मि नक्षत्राणामहं शशी ॥ १०—२१ ॥
वेदानां सामवेदोऽस्मि देवानामस्मि वासवः ।
इन्द्रियाणां मनश्चास्मि भूतानामस्मि चेतना ॥ १०—२२ ॥

20. aham ātmā guḍākeśa sarvabhūtāśayasthitaḥ
aham ādiś ca madhyaṃ ca bhūtānām anta eva ca
21. ādityānām ahaṃ viṣṇur jyotiṣāṃ ravir aṃśumān
marīcir marutām asmi nakṣatrāṇām ahaṃ śaśī
22. vedānāṃ sāmavedo'smi devānām asmi vāsavaḥ
indriyāṇāṃ manaś cāsmi bhūtānām asmi cetanā

10.20 I am the Self, Gudākesha,[13] abiding in the resting-place[14] of all beings. [And] I am the beginning, the middle, and the end of [all] beings.

10.21 Of the Ādityas[15] I am Vishnu; of lights, the radiant sun. Among the Maruts,[16] I am Marīci.[17] Among the lunar mansions,[18] I am the moon.

10.22 I am the *Sāma-Veda* of the *Vedas*. I am Vāsava[19] of the gods, and I am the mind among the senses.[20] I am sentience (*cetanā*) among beings.

13. On Gudākesha, an epithet of Arjuna, see note 17 for 1.24.

14. The word *āshaya*, here rendered as "resting-place," is derived from the verbal root *shī* ("to recline"). Esoterically, it refers to the heart.

15. From one perspective, Vishnu is a great solar deity and the leader of the Ādityas. The Ādityas, the sons of Aditi (who represents boundless space), are the Vedic solar deities Varuna, Mitra, Aryamat, Bhaga, Daksha, and Amsha. Sometimes twelve Ādityas are named.

16. The Maruts, the twenty-one warlike sons of the Vedic god Rudra ("Howler"), are associated with the wind. In the *Hari-Vamsha* ("Hari's [Krishna's] Lineage"), the voluminous traditional appendix to the *Mahābhārata*, twenty-four Maruts are mentioned by name, and in other texts an even greater number is given for them.

17. Marīci, the leader of the Maruts, is connected with lightning storms.

18. The term *nakshatra*, usually rendered as "constellation," here refers to the 27 (later 28) lunar mansions (divisions of the moon's path in Vedic astrology) corresponding to as many stellar constellations.

19. Vāsava is another name for Indra.

20. The mind (*manas*) is generally called the eleventh sense (*indriya*) because it processes all the sensory input.

रुद्राणां शंकरश्चास्मि वित्तेशो यक्षरक्षसाम् ।
वसूनां पावकश्चास्मि मेरुः शिखरिणामहम् ॥ १०—२३ ॥
पुरोधसां च मुख्यं मां विद्धि पार्थ बृहस्पतिम् ।
सेनानीनामहं स्कन्दः सरसामस्मि सागरः ॥ १०—२४ ॥
महर्षीणां भृगुरहं गिरामस्म्येकमक्षरम् ।
यज्ञानां जपयज्ञोऽस्मि स्थावराणां हिमालयः ॥ १०—२५ ॥

23. rudrāṇāṃ śaṃkaraś cāsmi vitteśo yakṣarakṣasām
vasūnāṃ pāvakaś cāsmi meruḥ śikhariṇām aham
24. purodhasāṃ ca mukhyaṃ māṃ viddhi pārtha bṛhaspatim
senānīnām ahaṃ skandaḥ sarasām asmi sāgaraḥ
25. maharṣīṇāṃ bhṛgur ahaṃ girām asmy ekam akṣaram
yajñānāṃ japayajño'smi sthāvarāṇāṃ himālayaḥ

10.23 And I am Shamkara[21] among the Rudras, Lord of Riches among the Yakshas[22] and Rākshasas,[23] and I am fire among the Vasus.[24] I am Meru[25] among the [seven sacred] mountain peaks.

10.24 And know Me to be Brihaspati[26] [to be] chief among the domestic-priests, O son-of-Prithā.[27] I am Skanda[28] among commanders. I am the ocean among watery-expanses.

10.25 I am Bhrigu[29] among the great seers. I am the monosyllable[30] among utterances. I am the sacrifice of recitation among sacrifices, and the Himalaya among immovable [objects].

21. Shamkara ("Peace-maker") is foremost among the Rudras, who are usually numbered as eleven, though the *Mahābhārata* (13.984) gives their number as eleven hundred. They are sometimes equated with the Maruts. Shamkara is also one of the epithets of Shiva. See also note 7 for 11.6.

22. The Yakshas are nature spirits who are typically depicted as large-bellied dwarfs. The lord of riches (*vittesha*) is better known as Kubera.

23. The Rākshasas are destructive ogres that particularly like to interrupt sacrifices and other sacred activities.

24. The eight Vasus ("Dwellers") are deities who are associated with space and the elements. According to the *Mahābhārata,* they are Dharā (the earth), Dhruva (the pole star, standing for the lunar mansions, or constellations), Soma (the moon), Aha (waters), Anila (wind), Anala (fire), Pratyūsha (the sun), and Prabhāsa (the sky).

25. According to mythology, Mount Meru is the sacred mountain at the center of Jambudvīpa (the inhabited world-island, or earth), the *axis mundi,* made entirely of gold. Jampudvīpa is one of seven "continents" that make up the known universe. In yogic symbolism, Meru represents the spinal axis along which the "serpent power" (*kundalinī-shakti*) must rise to the top in order for a practitioner to attain enlightenment.

26. Brihaspati ("Great Father/Lord") is the chief priest of the deities and is associated with the planet Jupiter.

27. On son-of-Prithā (Pārtha), see note 18 for 1.25.

28. Skanda is one of the sons of Shiva. A warlike deity, Skanda is associated with the planet Mars.

29. Bhrigu is among the most renowned sages of ancient times. According to mythology, this powerful sage dared to kick Vishnu in order to awaken him. When Vishnu, instead of getting angry, lovingly embraced the offending foot, Bhrigu became converted into a faithful worshipper of Vishnu.

30. On the monosyllable om, or aum, see note 14 for 8.13.

अश्वत्थः सर्ववृक्षाणां देवर्षीणां च नारदः ।
गन्धर्वाणां चित्ररथः सिद्धानां कपिलो मुनिः ॥ १०—२६ ॥
उच्चैःश्रवसमश्वानां विद्धि माममृतोद्भवम् ।
ऐरावतं गजेन्द्राणां नराणां च नराधिपम् ॥ १०—२७ ॥
आयुधानामहं वज्रं धेनूनामस्मि कामधुक् ।
प्रजनश्चास्मि कन्दर्पः सर्पाणामस्मि वासुकिः ॥ १०—२८ ॥
अनन्तश्चास्मि नागानां वरुणो यादसामहम् ।
पितॄणामर्यमा चास्मि यमः संयमतामहम् ॥ १०—२९ ॥

26. aśvatthaḥ sarvavṛkṣāṇāṃ devarṣīṇāṃ ca nāradaḥ
gandharvāṇāṃ citrarathaḥ siddhānāṃ kapilo muniḥ
27. uccaiḥśravasam aśvānāṃ viddhi mām amṛtodbhavam
airāvataṃ gajendrāṇāṃ narāṇāṃ ca narādhipam
28. āyudhānām ahaṃ vajraṃ dhenūnām asmi kāmadhuk
prajanaś cāsmi kandarpaḥ sarpāṇām asmi vāsukiḥ
29. anantaś cāsmi nāgānāṃ varuṇo yādasām aham
pitṝṇām aryamā cāsmi yamaḥ saṃyamatām aham

10.26 [I am] the *ashvattha* [-tree][31] among all trees, and Nārada among the divine seers, Citraratha[32] among the Gandharvas,[33] the sage Kapila[34] among the perfected.

10.27 Among horses, know Me to be Uccaihshravas[35] born from nectar, Airavata[36] among lordly elephants, and the human ruler among men.

10.28 Among weapons, I am the thunderbolt (*vajra*).[37] Among cows, I am the wish-fulfilling cow,[38] and I am procreating Kandarpa.[39] I am Vāsuki[40] among serpents.

10.29 And among the Nāgas,[41] I am Ananta.[42] Among the water-dwellers, I am Varuna,[43] and among the ancestors, I am Aryaman.[44] Among subjugators, I am Yama.[45]

31. The *ashvattha* tree is the *Ficus religiosa*, better known as the pipal tree. See the extensive note by Hill (1928/1966, p. 185f.) on stanza 15.1 (quoted in part below, in note 1 for 15.1). The *ashvattha* symbolizes the world of change (*samsāra*).

32. Citraratha is the chief of the Gandharvas.

33. The Gandharvas ("Fragrances") are sky-dwelling male spirits associated with the Sun God, who is often called a Gandharva. They are virile and, according to Puranic mythology, mostly benevolent spirits and "guardian angels" of music, song, and dance.

34. Kapila is traditionally celebrated as the founder of the Sāmkhya tradition.

35. Uccaihshravas is Indra's horse.

36. Airavata is Indra's elephant, who, like Uccaihshravas, emerged when the world ocean was churned by the gods and anti-gods.

37. The thunderbolt (*vajra*) has since the time of the Vedas been considered Indra's weapon.

38. The mythological wish-fulfilling cow (*kāma-dhuk*), which grants all one's desires.

39. Kandarpa, a mind-born son of Brahma, is one of the many names of the god Kāma ("Desire/Lust"). Popular legend has it that immediately after he was born, he asked Brahma: "Whom should I make proud?" (*kam darpayāmi*), and Brahma turned the question into his newborn son's name. The phrase *prajanashcāsmi kandarpah* is possibly defective. At least one manuscript has *prajaneshvapi kandarpah*, "of [or among] creatures I am Kandarpa."

40. Vāsuki, the great serpent, was used as a rope during the churning of the world ocean, with the gods holding one end of the rope and the anti-gods the other.

41. The Nāgas are the human-headed serpents who are said to dwell underground or in the waters and who guard the treasures of the earth, or what's left of them.

42. Ananta ("Endless"), also known as Shesha ("Remainder"), is the thousand-headed king of the Nāgas. He serves as Vishnu's bed of repose.

43. Varuna, a major deity in early Vedic times, was worshipped in the Puranic era as the lord of the waters.

44. Aryaman ("comrade") is one of the Ādityas (see note 15 for 10.21) and also the chief of the ancestors (*pitri*).

45. Yama ("Controller") is the God of Death.

प्रह्लादश्चास्मि दैत्यानां कालः कलयतामहम् ।
मृगाणां च मृगेन्द्रोऽहं वैनतेयश्च पक्षिणाम् ॥ १०—३० ॥
पवनः पवतामस्मि रमः शस्त्रभृतामहम ।
झषाणां मकरश्चास्मि स्रोतसामस्मि जाह्नवी ॥ १०—३१ ॥
सर्गाणामादिरन्तश्च मध्यं चैवाहमर्जुन ।
अध्यात्मविद्या विद्यानां वादः प्रवदतामहम् ॥ १०—३२ ॥
अक्षराणामकारोऽस्मि द्वन्द्वः सामासिकस्य च ।
अहमेवाक्षयः कालो धाताहं विश्वतोमुखः ॥ १०—३३ ॥
मृत्युः सर्वहरश्चाहमुद्भवश्च भविष्यताम् ।
कीर्तिः श्रीर्वाक्च नारीणां स्मृतिर्मेधा धृतिः क्षमा ॥ १०—३४ ॥
बृहत्साम तथा साम्नां गायत्री छन्दसामहम् ।
मासानां मार्गशीर्षोऽहमृतूनां कुसुमाकरः ॥ १०—३५ ॥

30. prahlādaś cāsmi daityānāṃ kālaḥ kalayatām aham
    mṛgāṇāṃ ca mṛgendro'haṃ vainateyaś ca pakṣiṇām
31. pavanaḥ pavatām asmi rāmaḥ śastrabhṛtām aham
    jhaṣāṇāṃ makaraś cāsmi srotasām asmi jāhnavī
32. sargāṇām ādir antaś ca madhyaṃ caivāham arjuna
    adhyātmavidyā vidyānāṃ vādaḥ pravadatām aham
33. akṣarāṇām akāro'smi dvandvaḥ sāmāsikasya ca
    aham evākṣayaḥ kālo dhātāhaṃ viśvatomukhaḥ
34. mṛtyuḥ sarvaharaś cāham udbhavaś ca bhaviṣyatām
    kīrtiḥ śrīr vāk ca nārīṇāṃ smṛtir medhā dhṛtiḥ kṣamā
35. bṛhatsāma tathā sāmnāṃ gāyatrī chandasām aham
    māsānāṃ mārgaśīrṣo'ham ṛtūnāṃ kusumākaraḥ

10.30 And I am Prahlāda[46] among the Daityas.[47] I am Time among reckoners, and I am lord of the beasts [i.e., the lion] among beasts, and Vainateya[48] among birds.

10.31 I am the wind among purifying [things]. I am Rāma[49] among weapon-bearers, and I am the crocodile among water-monsters. I am Jānhavī[50] among streams.

10.32 Also, O Arjuna, I am the beginning, the middle, and the end of [all] creations. [I am] the science of the basis-of-self among [all] sciences. Among speakers, I am [their] speech.

10.33 I am the letter *a* among letters, and the *dvandva*[51] among the system-of-[grammatical]-compounds. Verily, I am imperishable time. I am the supporter, facing everywhere.

10.34 I am also all-seizing death, and the origin of future-events. And among feminine [words I am] *fame, fortune, speech, memory, intelligence, steadfastness,* and *patience.*

10.35 Again, among chants, I am the great chant;[52] of meters, the *gāyatrī* [-meter];[53] of months, I am *mārgashīrsha;*[54] among seasons, the "flower mine."[55]

46. Prahlāda, a son of the demon-king Hiranyakashipu, became famous because of his exemplary devotion to his father's enemy, Vishnu.
47. The Daityas are the descendents of Diti, the daughter of Daksha Prajāpati (the Creator) and one of the wives of Sage Kashyapa. All her children are antigods (*asura*), who were conceived from sheer lust and at an inauspicious time, while her sister Aditi's children are all deities (*sura*). The word *diti* suggest restriction, or boundedness.
48. Vainateya, a prominent son of Vinatā (one of the wives of Kashyapa), is better known as Vishnu's mount Garuda, who is half-man, half-eagle.
49. Rāma is here Rāmacandra, one of Vishnu's divine incarnations and the hero of the *Rāmāyana* epic.
50. Jāhnavī ("Jahnu's descendant") is the river Gangā (Ganges).
51. On *dvandva* ("pairs-of-opposites"), see note 19 for 2.15.
52. The "great chant" (*brihat-sāma*) consists of verses of the *Sāma-Veda* that are written in the *brihatī* meter of 36 syllables (4 lines = 8 + 8 + 12 + 8 syllables).
53. The *gāyatrī* meter (3 lines x 8 syllables = 24 syllables) is the meter employed in the most famous verse of the *Rig-Veda* (3.62.10)—famous because it is even now recited daily by pious Brahmins.
54. The season of *mārgashīrsha* (November-December) is named after the constellation *mriga-shiras* ("deer head").
55. The poetic expression *kusuma-ākara* means literally "flower mine," i.e., abundance of flowers, and refers to springtime.

द्यूतं छलयतामस्मि तेजस्तेजस्विनामहम् ।
जयोऽस्मि व्यवसायोऽस्मि सत्त्वं सत्त्ववतामहम् ॥ १०—३६ ॥
वृष्णीनां वासुदेवोऽस्मि पाण्डवानां धनंजयः ।
मुनीनामप्यहं व्यासः कवीनामुशना कविः ॥ १०—३७ ॥
दण्डो दमयतामस्मि नीतिरस्मि जिगीषताम् ।
मौनं चैवास्मि गुह्यानां ज्ञानं ज्ञानवतामहम् ॥ १०—३८ ॥
«ओषधीनां यवश्चास्मि धातूनामस्मि काञ्चनम् ।
सौरभेयो गवामस्मि स्नेहानां सर्पिरप्यहम् ।
सर्वासां तृणजतीनां दर्भोऽहं पाण्डुनन्दन ॥»

36. dyūtaṃ chalayatām asmi tejas tejasvinām aham
jayo'smi vyavasāyo'smi sattvaṃ sattvavatām aham
37. vṛṣṇīnāṃ vāsudevo'smi pāṇḍavānāṃ dhanaṃjayaḥ
munīnām apy ahaṃ vyāsaḥ kavīnām uśanā kaviḥ
38. daṇḍo damayatām asmi nītir asmi jigīṣatām
maunaṃ caivāsmi guhyānāṃ jñānaṃ jñānavatām aham

« oṣadhīnāṃ yavaś cāsmi dhātūnām asmi kāñcanam,
saurabheyo gavām asmi snehānāṃ sarpir apy aham,
sarvāsāṃ tṛṇajatīnāṃ darbho'haṃ pāṇḍunandana »

10.36 I am the gambling of tricksters. I am the splendor of the splendid, I am victory, I am resolution,[56] I am the *sattva*[57] of [those who are] *sattva*-endowed.

10.37 I am Vāsudeva[58] among the Vrishnis,[59] Dhanamjaya[60] among the sons-of-Pāndu.[61] Also, I am Vyāsa among the sages, the bard Ushanas[62] among bards.

10.38 I am the rod-of-punishment of the chastisers. I am the statecraft of [those who are] eager-for-conquest. I am, moreover, the silence of secrets. I am the knowledge of the knowledge-endowed.

«I am barley among herbs. I am gold among metals. I am the descendant-of-Surabhī[63] among cows. I am butter among fats. I am the *darbha* [-grass] among all species of grasses, O delight-of-Pāndu.[64]

56. *Vyavasāya,* here translated as "resolution," may also be rendered as "determination" (as in 2.41) or "will."
57. On *sattva,* see note 36 for 2.37.
58. *Vāsudeva* means "son-of-Vasudeva." *Vasudeva* means "God [of All] Things," the name of Krishna's father.
59. The Vrishnis are a tribe of the solar dynasty to which Krishna belonged. Vrishni was the name of a famous ruler of this dynasty, which traces itself back to Vishnu himself.
60. On Dhanamjaya, see note 7 for 1.15. Here Krishna affirms that he is Arjuna.
61. The Pāndavas are the five sons—Arjuna and his brothers—of King Pāndu, who was their "official" human father, married to Queen Kuntī. The Pāndavas' actual fathers were five deities.
62. Ushanas, a son of the sage Bhrigu (see 10.25), is mentioned as early as the *Rig-Veda* (8.23.17).
63. Surabhī is the wish-fulfilling cow (see above, 10.28), whose daughter is Saubhadrā, who might here be confused with Krishna's sister of the same name.
64. Pāndunandana ("Delight of Pāndu") is an epithet on the model of Kurunandana, used in 2.41 (see note 40). This extra verse differs from the rest in that it has 3 lines x 16 syllables.

यच्चापि सर्वभूतानां बीजं तदहमर्जुन ।
न तदस्ति विना यत्स्यान्मया भूतं चराचरम् ॥ १०—३९ ॥
नान्तोऽस्ति मम दिव्यानां विभूतीनां परंतप ।
एष तूद्देशतः प्रोक्तो विभूतेर्विस्तरो मया ॥ १०—४० ॥
यद्यद्विभूतिमत्सत्त्वं श्रीमदूर्जितमेव वा ।
तत्तदेवावगच्छ त्वं मम तेजोंऽशसंभवम् ॥ १०—४१ ॥
अथ वा बहुनैतेन किं ज्ञातेन तवार्जुन ।
विष्टभ्याहमिदं कृत्स्नमेकांशेन स्थितो जगत् ॥ १०—४२ ॥

39. yac cāpi sarvabhūtānāṃ bījaṃ tad aham arjuna
na tad asti vinā yat syān mayā bhūtaṃ carācaram
40. nānto'sti mama divyānāṃ vibhūtīnāṃ paraṃtapa
eṣa tūddeśataḥ prokto vibhūter vistaro mayā
41. yad yad vibhūtimat sattvaṃ śrīmad ūrjitam eva vā
tat tad evāvagaccha tvaṃ mama tejo'ṃśasaṃbhavam
42. atha vā bahunaitena kiṃ jñātena tavārjuna
viṣṭabhyāham idaṃ kṛtsnam ekāṃśena sthito jagat

10.39 And I am also that which is the seed [of perfection] in all beings, O Arjuna. There is no being, moving or unmoving, that can exist apart from Me.

10.40 There is no end to My divine powers-of-manifestation, O Paramtapa.[65] [What] I have proclaimed about the extent of [My] powers-of-manifestation was by-way-of-example.

10.41 Whatever power-charged (*vibhūtimat*), prosperous, or vigorous entity (*sattva*) [there is]—that you [must] recognize [as a] fragmentary birth of My [divine] splendor.

10.42 But of what [use is it] for you, O Arjuna, to know so many [details]? Having established this whole universe with a single fragment [of Myself], I abide [as the Ever-Immovable].

65. On Paramtapa, see note 5 for 2.3.

अर्जुन उवाच
मदनुग्रहाय परमं गुह्यमध्यात्मसंज्ञितम् ।
यत्त्वयोक्तं वचस्तेन मोहोऽहं विगतो मम ॥ ११—१ ॥
भवाप्ययौ हि भूतानां श्रुतौ स्तिरशो मया ।
त्वत्तः कमलपत्राक्ष माहात्म्यमपि चव्ययम् ॥ ११—२ ॥
एवमेतद्यथात्थ त्वमात्मानं परमेश्वर ।
द्रष्टुमिच्छामि ते रूपमैश्वरं पुरुषोत्तम ॥ ११—३ ॥
मन्यसे यदि तच्छक्यं मया द्रष्टुमिति प्रभो ।
योगेश्वर ततो मे त्वं दर्शयात्मानमव्ययम् ॥ ११—४ ॥
श्रीभगवानुवाच
पश्य मे पार्थ रूपाणि शतशोऽथ सहस्रशः ।
नानाविधानि दिव्यानि नानावर्णाकृतीनि च ॥ ११—५ ॥
पश्यादित्यान्वसून्रुद्रानश्विनौ मरुतस्तथा ।
बहून्यदृष्टपूर्वाणि पश्याश्चर्याणि भारत ॥ ११—६ ॥

arjuna uvāca
1. madanugrahāya paramaṃ guhyam adhyātmasaṃjñitam
   yat tvayoktaṃ vacas tena moho'yaṃ vigato mama
2. bhavāpyayau hi bhūtānāṃ śrutau vistaraśo mayā
   tvattaḥ kamalapattrākṣa māhātmyam api cāvyayam
3. evam etad yathāttha tvam ātmānaṃ parameśvara
   draṣṭum icchāmi te rūpam aiśvaraṃ puruṣottama
4. manyase yadi tac chakyaṃ mayā draṣṭum iti prabho
   yogeśvara tato me tvaṃ darśayātmānam avyayam

śrībhagavān uvāca
5. paśya me pārtha rūpāṇi śataśo'tha sahasraśaḥ
   nānāvidhāni divyāni nānāvarṇākṛtīni ca
6. paśyādityān vasūn rudrān aśvinau marutas tathā
   bahūny adṛṣṭapūrvāṇi paśyāścaryāṇi bhārata

CHAPTER 11

The Yoga of the Vision of [the Lord's] All-Form

Arjuna said:

11.1 As a favor to me, You have uttered this speech [about] the supreme mystery called the basis-of-self[1] by which this confusion of mine is dispelled.

11.2 For I have heard of the emergence and the dissolution of beings from You in detail, O lotus-eyed [Krishna], as well as of [Your] immutable glory.[2]

11.3 Even as you have described [Your] Self, O Supreme Lord, thus do I desire to see Your lordly form, O Supreme Spirit.[3]

11.4 If, Lord, You think it possible for me to see that [form of Yours], O Lord of Yoga, then do reveal to me [Your] immutable Self.

The Blessed Lord said:

11.5 O son-of-Prithā,[4] behold My forms, [which are] a hundredfold, a thousandfold, of varied kinds, divine, many-colored and many-shaped.

11.6 Behold the Ādityas,[5] the Vasus,[6] Rudras,[7] Ashvins,[8] as also the Maruts.[9] Behold, O descendant-of-Bharata, [all the] many wonders never seen before.

1. On the term *adhyātman,* see note 41 for 3.30.
2. The first line of this verse has one extra syllable. This could easily be rectified by writing *param* for *paramam*.
3. Krishna's epithet Purushottama is composed of *purusha* ("person") and *uttama* ("supreme, unexcelled"), commonly translated as Supreme Person or, as here, Supreme Spirit.
4. On son-of-Prithā (Pārtha), see note 18 for 1.25.
5. On the Ādityas, see note 15 for 10.21.
6. On the Vasus, see note 24 for 10.23.
7. The eleven Rudras ("Howlers"), like the Maruts, belong to the midspace (*antarīksha*), which is the external atmosphere and the internal mental space. They symbolize the life-force (*prāna*). See also note 21 for 10.23.
8. The two Ashvins are divine horse-headed twins, the Vedic patron gods of healing and agriculture. They are the forerunners of dawn and are depicted as seated in a golden chariot pulled by birds or horses.
9. On the Maruts, see note 16 for 10.21.

इहैकस्थं जगत्कृत्स्नं पश्याद्य सचराचरम् ।
मम देहे गुडाकेश यच्चान्यद्द्रष्टुमिच्छसि ॥ ११—७ ॥
न तु मां शक्ष्यसे द्रष्टुमनेनैव स्वचक्षुषा ।
दिव्यं ददामि ते चक्षुः पश्य मे योगमैश्वरम् ॥ ११—८ ॥
संजय उवाच
एवमुक्त्वा ततो राजन्महायोगेश्वरो हरिः ।
दर्शयामास पार्थाय परमं रूपमैश्वरम् ॥ ११—९ ॥
अनेकवक्त्रनयनमनेकाद्भुतदर्शनम् ।
अनेकदिव्याभरधरं दिव्यानेकोद्यतायुधम् ॥ ११—१० ॥
दिव्यमाल्यामबरधरं दिव्यगन्धानुलेपनम् ।
सर्वाश्चर्यमयं देवमनन्तं विश्वतोमुखम् ॥ ११—११ ॥
दिवि सूर्यसहस्रस्य भवेद्युगपदुत्थिता ।
यदि भाः सदृशी सा स्याद्भासस्तस्य महात्मनः ॥ ११—१२ ॥
तत्रैकस्थं जगत्कृत्स्नं प्रविभक्तमनेकधा ।
अपश्यद्देवदेवस्य शरीरे पाण्डवस्तदा ॥ ११—१३ ॥

7. ihaikastham̩ jagat kr̥tsnam̩ paśyādya sacarācaram
mama dehe guḍākeśa yac cānyad draṣṭum icchasi
8. na tu mām̩ śakṣyase draṣṭum anenaiva svacakṣuṣā
divyam̩ dadāmi te cakṣuḥ paśya me yogam aiśvaram

sam̩jaya uvāca
9. evam uktvā tato rājan mahāyogeśvaro hariḥ
darśayām āsa pārthāya paramam̩ rūpam aiśvaram
10. anekavaktranayanam anekādbhūtadarśanam
anekadivyābharaṇam̩ divyānekodyatāyudham
11. divyamālyāmbaradharam̩ divyagandhānulepanam
sarvāścaryamayam̩ devam anantam̩ viśvatomukham
12. divi sūryasahasrasya bhaved yugapad utthitā
yadi bhāḥ sadr̥śī sā syād bhāsas tasya mahātmanaḥ
13. tatraikastham̩ jagat kr̥tsnam̩ pravibhaktam anekadhā
apaśyad devadevasya śarīre pāṇḍavas tadā

11.7 Behold now, O Gudākesha,[10] the whole universe, [with all] moving and unmoving [things], abiding as one here in My [cosmic] body, and whatever else you desire to see.
11.8 Yet, you will not be able to see Me with this your own [physical] eye. I will give you the divine eye. Behold My lordly Yoga.

Samjaya said [to King Dhritarāshtra]:
11.9 Having spoken thus, O king, the great Lord of Yoga, Hari, then revealed, [His] supreme lordly form to the son-of-Prithā.
11.10 [His form has] many mouths and eyes, many wondrous appearances (*darshana*), many divine adornments, many divine upraised weapons,
11.11 wearing divine garlands and garments, anointed with divine fragrances, all-wonderful. [Behold] God, infinite [and] omnipresent.
11.12 If the splendor of a thousand suns were to arise at once in the sky (*div*), that would be like the splendor of that Great Self.[11]
11.13 Then the son-of-Pāndu saw the whole universe, divided manifold, abiding in the One, there in the body of the God of gods.

10. On the epithet Gudākesha, see note 17 for 1.24.

11. This verse, as well as 11.32, was made famous in the West by the American physicist J. Robert Oppenheimer, the "father of the atomic bomb," who as a young man had studied the *Gītā* in the original Sanskrit. He reported that upon witnessing the mushroom cloud at the first nuclear weapons test on July 16, 1945, he recalled the line "If the radiance of a thousand suns were to burst forth at once in the sky, that would be like the splendor of the Mighty One" (11.10 in the 1944 translation by Swami Nikhilananda). In addition, he recalled verse 11.32, which in that translation was: "Now I am become Death, the destroyer of worlds."

ततः स विस्मयाविष्टो हृष्टरोमा धनंजयः ।
प्रणम्य प्राणम्या शिरसा कृताञ्जलिरबषत ॥ ११—१४ ॥
अर्जुन उवाच
पश्यामि देवांस्तव देव देहे
सर्वास्तथा भूतविशेषसंघान् ।
ब्रह्माणमीशं कमलासनस्थ।
मृषींश्च सर्वानुरगांश्च दिव्यान् ॥ ११—१५ ॥
अनेकबाहूदरवक्त्रनेत्रं
पश्यामि त्वा सर्वतोऽनन्तरूपम् ।
नान्त न मध्यं न पुनस्तवादिं
पश्यामि विश्वेश्वर विश्वरूप ॥ ११—१६ ॥
किरीटिनं गदिनं चक्रिणं च
तेजोराशिं सर्वतो दीप्तिमन्तम ।
पश्यामि त्वां दुर्निरीक्ष्यं समन्ता
द्दीप्तानलार्कद्युतिमप्रमेयम् ॥ ११—१७ ॥
त्वमक्षरं परमं वेदितव्यं
त्वमस्य विश्वस्य परं निधानम् ।
त्वमव्ययः शाश्वतधर्मगोप्ता
सनातनस्त्वं पुरुषो मतो मे ॥ ११—१८ ॥

14. tataḥ sa vismayāviṣṭo hṛṣṭaromā dhanaṃjayaḥ
praṇamya śirasā devaṃ kṛtāñjalir abhāṣata

arjuna uvāca

15. paśyāmi devāṃs tava deva dehe sarvāṃs tathā bhūtaviśeṣasaṃghān
brahmāṇam īśaṃ kamalāsanastha mṛṣīṃś ca sarvān uragāṃś ca divyān

16. anekabāhūdaravaktranetraṃ paśyāmi tvāṃ sarvato'nantarūpam
nāntaṃ na madhyaṃ na punas tavādiṃ paśyāmi viśveśvara viśvarūpa

17. kirīṭinaṃ gadinaṃ cakriṇaṃ ca tejorāśiṃ sarvato dīptimantam
paśyāmi tvāṃ durnirīkṣyaṃ samantād dīptānalārkadyutim aprameyam

18. tvam akṣaraṃ paramaṃ veditavyaṃ tvam asya viśvasya paraṃ nidhānam
tvam avyayaḥ śāśvatadharmagoptā sanātanas tvaṃ puruṣo mato me

11.14 Then Dhanamjaya,[12] [Arjuna] filled with astonishment, his hair bristling, bowing his head before God [Krishna], and saluting with *anjali,*[13] spoke [thus]:

Arjuna said:

11.15 O God, in Your body I behold the gods and all the [various] kinds of beings, Lord Brahma seated on the lotus seat,[14] and all the seers and divine serpents.[15]

11.16 Everywhere, I behold You [who are] of endless form, [with] many arms, bellies, mouths, [and] eyes. I see in You no end, no middle, and also no beginning, O All-Lord, All-Form![16]

11.17 I behold You [with] diadem, mace, and discus—a mass of brilliance, flaming all-around. [Yet You are] hard-to-see completely, [for You are] an immeasurable blazing radiance of sun-fire.

11.18 You ought to be known as the supreme Imperishable. You are the supreme receptacle of all this. You are the Immutable, the Guardian of the eternal law. You are the everlasting Spirit. [This] is my conviction.

12. On the epithet Dhanamjaya, see note 7 for 1.15.

13. *Anjali* is the gesture of folded hands (palms joined with fingers extended) raised to the forehead. It suggests respectful salutation.

14. According to Shankara, Brahma's lotus seat, or throne (*kamala-āsana*), is Mount Meru, the axis of the universe.

15. This and all stanzas until and including 11.50 are composed in the *trishtubh* meter.

16. The expression "All-Form" (*vishva-rūpa*) refers to Krishna's universal or cosmic aspect.

अनादिमध्यान्तमनन्तवीर्य
मनन्तबाहुं शशिसूर्यनेत्रम् ।
पश्यामि त्वा दीप्तहुताशवक्त्रं
स्वतेजसा विश्वमिदं तपन्तम् ॥ ११—१९ ॥
द्यावापृथिव्योरिदमन्तरं हि
व्याप्तं त्वयैकेन दिशश्च सर्वाः ।
दृष्ट्वाद्भुतं रूपमिदं तवोग्रं
लोकत्रयं प्रव्यथितं महात्मन् ॥ ११—२० ॥
अमी हि त्वा सुरसंघा विशन्ति
केचिद्भीताः प्राञ्जलयो गृणन्ति ।
स्वस्तीत्युक्त्वा महर्षिसिद्धसंघाः
स्तुवन्ति त्वा स्तुतिभिः पुष्कलाभिः ॥ ११—२१ ॥
रुद्रादित्या वसवो ये च साध्या
विश्वेऽश्विनौ मरुतश्चोष्मपाश्च ।
गन्धर्वयक्षासुरसिद्धसंघा
वीक्षन्ते त्वा विस्मिताश्चैव सर्वे ॥ ११—२२ ॥

19. anādimadhyāntam anantavīrya manantabāhuṃ śaśisūryanetram paśyāmi tvāṃ dīptahutāśavaktraṃ svatejasā viśvam idaṃ tapantam
20. dyāvāpṛthivyor idam antaraṃ hi vyāptaṃ tvayaikena diśaś ca sarvāḥ dṛṣṭvādbhutaṃ rūpam idaṃ tavograṃ lokatrayaṃ pravyathitaṃ mahātman
21. amī hi tvā surasaṃghā viśanti kecid bhītāḥ prāñjalayo gṛṇanti svastīty uktvā maharṣisiddhasaṃghāḥ stuvanti tvāṃ stutibhiḥ puṣkalābhiḥ
22. rudrādityā vasavo ye ca sādhyā viśve'śvinau marutaś coṣmapāś ca gandharvayakṣāsurasiddhasaṃghā vīkṣante tvā vismitāś caiva sarve

11.19 Without beginning, middle, or end, of infinite vitality, [with] infinite arms [and with] moon and sun [as] eyes: I behold You—[Your] blazing mouth[s] eating [everything as an] oblation—burning up all this with Your own brilliance.

11.20 By You alone is this [space][17] between heaven and earth pervaded, and all the quarters [too]. Seeing this wondrous,[18] terrifying form of Yours, the triple world shudders, O Great Self.

11.21 Yonder, these hosts of deities enter into You. Some, terrified, praise [You] with *anjali* [-gesture]. Crying out "Hail [to You]!" the multitude of great seers and perfected-ones laud You with plenteous hymns-of-praise.

11.22 Rudras, Ādityas, Vasus and Sādhyas,[19] the Vishve[-devas],[20] the [two] Ashvins, the Maruts and the quaffers-of-steam,[21] and the hosts of the Gandharvas,[22] Yakshas,[23] Asuras,[24] and perfected-ones—[they] all behold You, [utterly] astounded.

17. The space between sky (heaven) and earth is known as *antarīksha* ("[that which is] seen between").

18. Krishna's cosmic form strikes Arjuna as wondrous because within it all things are seen simultaneously (*coincidentia oppositorum*). At the same time, this cosmic vision is terrifying, undoubtedly because the Divine includes within its scope also all those things that frighten ordinary mortals, notably the reality of suffering and death. This expresses Arjuna's encounter with God as the *mysterium tremendum et fascinosum* (a Latin phrase coined by the theologian Rudolf Otto for the experience of the sacred as a "fearful and fascinating mystery").

19. The sky-dwelling Sādhyas are deities who are connected with the sun and who, as their designation suggests, are means of realization for those aspiring to reach the solar spirit.

20. The ten or thirteen Vishvedevas ("All-Gods") are deities who are associated with primarily psychological principles, such as truth (*satya*), will (*kratu*), pleasantness (*rocaka*), forbearance (*dhriti*), and so on.

21. The "quaffers-of-steam" (*ushma-pa*) are the ancestral spirits (*pitri*), who are thought to feed on the steam of hot food offerings. To make daily offerings to these spirits of the dead is an important obligation for pious Hindus.

22. On the Gandharvas, see note 33 for 10.26.

23. On the Yakshas, see note 22 for 10.23.

24. The Asuras are anti-gods. See note 47 for 10.30.

रूपं महत्ते बहुवक्त्रनेत्रं
महाबाहो बहुबाहूरुपादम् ।
बहूदरं बहुदंष्ट्राकरालं
दृष्ट्वा लोकाः प्रव्यथितास्तथाहम् ॥ ११—२३ ॥
नभःस्पृशं दीप्तमनेकवर्णं
व्यात्ताननं दीप्तविशालनेत्रम ।
दृष्ट्वा हि त्वां प्रव्यथितान्तरात्मा
धृतिं न विन्दामि शमं च विष्णो ॥ ११—२४ ॥
दंष्ट्राकरालानि च ते मुखानि
दृष्ट्वैव कालानलसंनिभानि ।
दिशो न जाने न लभे च शर्म
प्रसीद देवेश जगन्निवास ॥ ११—२५ ॥
अमी च त्वां धृतराष्ट्रस्य पुत्राः
सर्वे सहैवावनिपालसंघैः ।
भीष्मो द्रोणः सूतपुत्रस्तथासौ
सहास्मदीयैरपि योधमुख्यैः ॥ ११—२६ ॥

23. rūpaṃ mahat te bahuvaktranetraṃ
mahābāho bahubāhūrupādam
bahūdaraṃ bahudaṃṣṭrākarālaṃ
dṛṣṭvā lokāḥ pravyathitās tathāham
24. nabhaḥspṛśaṃ dīptam anekavarṇaṃ
vyāttānanaṃ dīptaviśālanetram
dṛṣṭvā hi tvāṃ pravyathitāntarātmā
dhṛtiṃ na vindāmi śamaṃ ca viṣṇo
25. daṃṣṭrākarālāni ca te mukhāni
dṛṣṭvaiva kālānalasaṃnibhāni
diśo na jāne na labhe ca śarma
prasīda deveśa jagannivāsa
26. amī ca tvāṃ dhṛtarāṣṭrasya putrāḥ
sarve sahaivāvanipālasaṃghaiḥ
bhīṣmo droṇaḥ sūtaputras tathāsau
sahāsmadīyair api yodhamukhyaiḥ

11.23 Beholding [that] great form of Yours, [with its] many mouths and eyes, O mighty-armed [Krishna], [its] many arms, thighs, feet, many bellies, many formidable fangs—the worlds shudder; so [do] I.

11.24 Touching the world-sky,[25] flaming many-colored, [with] gaping mouths and flaming vast eyes—beholding You [thus], [my] inmost self[26] quakes, and I [can] find no fortitude or tranquillity, O Vishnu.

11.25 And seeing Your [many] mouths [studded with] formidable fangs resembling the fire [at the end] of time, I know not where-to-turn,[27] and I find no shelter. Be gracious [unto me], O Lord of the gods, O Home of the universe!

11.26 And all these sons of Dhritarāshtra together with hosts of protectors of the earth—Bhīshma, Drona, as well as the son of the charioteer [i.e., Karna] and also our leading warriors—

25. Rāmānuja offers a detailed explanation of the term *nabhas,* here translated as "world-sky," which he equates with the transcendental "space" of the Ultimate Being beyond the world-ground. This is doubtful, however, because Arjuna's cosmic vision is necessarily related to the Cosmos. The transcendental Reality is formless and "beyond-the-three-primary-qualities" (*nirguna*).
26. The term *antarātman,* here rendered as "inmost self," refers to the deepest aspect of the human personality. It is not equivalent to the transcendental Self, as suggested by Zaehner (1966). For Shankara and Rāmānuja, it clearly signifies the mind. It is probably a synonym for *buddhi* (see note 24 for 6.47).
27. The Sanskrit text reads *disho na jāne,* lit. "I don't know the [four] quarters [of space]."

वक्त्राणि ते त्वरमाणा विशन्ति
दंष्ट्राकरालानि भयानकानि ।
केचिद्विलग्ना दशनान्तरेषु
संदृश्यन्ते चूर्णितैरुत्तमाङ्गैः ॥ ११—२७ ॥

« नानरूपैः पुरुषैर्वध्यमना
विशन्ति ते वक्त्रमचिन्त्यरूपम् ।
यौधिष्ठिरा धार्तरष्ट्राश्च योधाः
शास्त्रैः कृत्ता विविधैः सर्वैव ।
त्वत्तेजसा निहता नूनमेते
तथा हीमे त्वच्छरीरं प्रविष्टाः ॥»

यथा नदीनां बहवोऽम्बुवेगाः
समुद्रमेवाभिमुखा द्रवन्ति ।
तथा तवामी नरलोकवीरा
विशिन्ति वक्त्राण्यभिविज्वलन्ति ॥ ११—२८ ॥
यथा प्रदीप्तं ज्वलनं पतङ्गा
विशन्ति नाशाय समृद्धवेगाः ।
तथैव नाशाय विशन्ति लोका
स्तवापि वक्त्राणि समृद्धवेगाः ॥ ११—२९ ॥

27. vaktrāṇi te tvaramāṇā viśanti daṃṣṭrākarālāni bhayānakāni
kecid vilagnā daśanāntareṣu saṃdṛśyante cūrṇitair uttamāṇgaiḥ

« nānarūpaiḥ puruṣairvadhyamanā viśanti te vaktram acintyarūpam
yaudhiṣṭhirā dhārtarāṣṭrāś ca yodhāḥ śāstraiḥ kṛttā vividhaiḥ sarvaiva
tvat tejasā nighatā nūnam ete tathā hīme tvaccharīraṃ praviṣṭaḥ»

28. yathā nadīnāṃ bahavo'mbuvegāḥ samudram evābhimukhā dravanti
tathā tavāmī naralokavīrā viśanti vaktrāṇy abhivijvalanti
29. yathā pradīptaṃ jvalanaṃ pataṅgā viśanti nāśāya samṛddhavegāḥ
tathaiva nāśāya viśanti lokā stavāpi vakrāṇi samṛddhavegāḥ

11.27 they swiftly enter Your mouths with formidable fear-instilling fangs. Some are seen with pulverized heads sticking in between [Your] teeth.

«Slain by various kinds of men, they enter Your mouth[s] of inconceivable form—all the fighting followers-of-Yudhishtira and the followers-of-Dhritarāshtra are cut down by diverse weapons and all are surely annihilated by your radiance: thus these [men] presently enter Your body.[28] »

11.28 As many rivers and water torrents flow headlong into the ocean, so do these heroes of the world of men enter Your flaming mouths.

11.29 As moths in profuse streams enter a blazing flame to [their own] destruction, so do the worlds in profuse streams enter Your mouths for [their utter] destruction.

28. This additional stanza is not in the *trishtubh* meter like the rest of the passage, which marks it as an interpolation.

लेलिह्यसे ग्रसमानः समन्ता
ल्लोकान्समग्रान्वदनैर्ज्वलद्भिः ।
तेजोभिरापूर्य जगत्समग्रं
भासस्तवोग्राः प्रतपन्ति विष्णो ॥ ११—३० ॥
आख्याहि मे को भवानुग्ररूपो
नमोऽस्तु ते देववर प्रसीद ।
विज्ञातुमिच्छामि भवन्तमाद्यं
न हि प्रजानामि तव प्रवृत्तिम् ॥ ११—३१ ॥
श्रीभगवानुवाच
कालोऽस्मि लोकक्षयकृत्प्रवृद्धो
लोकान्समाहर्तुमिह प्रवृत्तः ।
ऋतेऽपि त्वा न भविष्यन्ति सर्वे
येऽवस्थिताः प्रत्यनीकेषु योधाः ॥ ११—३२ ॥
तस्मात्त्वमुत्तिष्ठ यशो लभस्व
जित्वा शत्रून्भुङ्क्ष्व राज्यं समृद्धम् ।
मयैवैते निहताः पूर्वमेव
निमित्तमात्रं भव सव्यसाचिन् ॥ ११—३३ ॥

30. lelihyase grasamānaḥ samantāl lokān samagrān vadanair jvaladbhiḥ
tejobhir āpūrya jagat samagraṃ bhāsas tavogrāḥ pratapanti viṣṇo
31. ākhyāhi me ko bhavān ugrarūpo namo'stu te devavara prasīda
vijñātum icchāmi bhavantam ādyaṃ na hi prajānāmi tava pravṛttim

śrībhagavān uvāca
32. kālo'smi lokakṣayakṛt pravṛddho lokān samāhartum iha pravṛttaḥ
ṛte'pi tvā na bhaviṣyanti sarve ye'vasthitāḥ pratyanīkeṣu yodhāḥ
33. tasmāt tvām uttiṣṭha yaśo labhasva jitvā śatrūn bhuṅkṣva rājyaṃ samṛddham
mayaivaite nihatāḥ pūrvam eva nimittamātraṃ bhava savyasācin

11.30 With flaming mouths, You lick up, devouring, all the worlds entirely. Filling the entire universe with [Your] brilliance, Your dreadful rays scorch [all], O Vishnu.

11.31 Tell me who You are of dreadful form. May salutation be to You! O Best of gods, have mercy! I wish to know You [as You were in] the beginning. For I [do] not comprehend Your [divine] creativity.

The Blessed Lord said:

11.32 I am time, mighty wreaker of the world's destruction, engaged here in annihilating the worlds. Except for you, all these warriors arrayed in the opposing armies shall not be [alive after this battle].

11.33 Therefore, you arise [and] win glory! Conquering the enemies, enjoy a prosperous kingdom! Verily, they are [all] slain already by Me. Be [My] mere instrument, O Savyasācin![29]

29. The epithet Savyasācin ("[He who is] skilled with the left [hand]") refers to Arjuna's exceptional ambidextrous capacity as an archer.

द्रोणं च भीष्मं च जयद्रथं च
कर्णं तथान्यानपि योधवीरान् ।
मया हतांस्त्वं जहि मा व्यथिष्ठा
युध्यस्व जेतासि रणे सपत्नान् ॥ ११—३४ ॥
संजय उवाच
एतच्छ्रुत्वा वचनं केशवस्य
कृताञ्जलिर्वेपमानः किरीटी ।
नमस्कृत्वा भूय एवाह कृष्णं
सगद्गदं भीतभीतः प्रणम्य ॥ ११—३५ ॥
अर्जुन उवाच
स्थाने हृषीकेश तव प्रकीर्त्या
जगत्प्रहृष्यत्यनुरज्यते च ।
रक्षांसि भीतानि दिशो द्रवन्ति
सर्वे नमस्यन्ति च सिद्धसंघाः ॥ ११—३६ ॥

34. droṇaṃ ca bhīṣmaṃ ca jayadrathaṃ ca karṇaṃ tathānyān api yodhavīrān
mayā hatāṃs tvaṃ jahi mā vyathiṣṭhā yudhyasva jetāsi raṇe sapatnān

saṃjaya uvāca
35. etac chrutvā vacanaṃ keśavasya kṛtāñjalir vepamānaḥ kirīṭī
namaskṛtvā bhūya evāha kṛṣṇaṃ sagadgadaṃ bhītabhītaḥ praṇamya

arjuna uvāca
36. sthāne hṛṣīkeśa tava prakīrtyā jagat prahṛṣyaty anurajyate ca
rakṣāṃsi bhītāni diśo dravanti sarve namasyanti ca siddhasaṃghāḥ

11.34 Drona[30] and Bhīshma[31] and Jayadratha[32] and Karna,[33] as well as [all] the other warrior heroes, are [already] slain by Me. You [must] strike [them]! Do not hesitate. Fight! You will conquer [your] rivals in battle.

Samjaya said:

11.35 Hearing these words of Keshava,[34] Kirītin[35] [Arjuna], saluting with the *anjali* [-gesture], trembling, saluting again and bowing down, said to Krishna, with stammering [voice], very frightened:

Arjuna said:

11.36 Rightly, O Hrishīkesha,[36] the universe rejoices and is enraptured with Your praise. The Rākshasas[37] flee, terrified, in [all] directions, and all the hosts of perfected ones salute [You].

30. Drona ("Tub"), mentioned in the early chapters of the *Gītā*, was the military instructor of both the Kauravas and the Pāndavas but opted to fight on the side of the former party.
31. On Bhīshma, see Part One, chapter 3, "Dramatis Personae of the *Gītā*," and note 14 for 1.17.
32. Jayadratha, king of Sindhu, fought on the Kaurava side and had behaved ignominiously toward Draupadī, the Pāndava brothers' shared wife.
33. Karna ("Ear"), a formidable Kaurava warrior, was a half brother to Arjuna.
34. On Keshava, see note 21 for 1.31.
35. The epithet Kirītin means "[He Who Wears a] Diadem"—that is, he who is crowned as a Pāndava prince.
36. On Hrishīkesha, see note 5 for 1.15.
37. On the Rākshasas, see note 23 for 10.23.

कस्माच्च ते न नमेरन्महात्म
न्गरीयसे ब्रह्मणोऽप्यादिकर्त्रे ।
अनन्त देवेश जगन्निवास
त्वमक्षरं सदसत्तत्परं यत् ॥ ११—३७ ॥
त्वमादिदेवः पुरुषः पुराण
स्त्वमस्य विश्वस्य परं निधानम् ।
वेत्तासि वेद्यं च परं च धाम
त्वया ततं विश्वमनन्तरूप ॥ ११—३८ ॥
वायुर्यमोऽग्निर्वरुणः शशाङ्कः
प्रजापतिस्त्वं प्रपितामहश्च ।
नमो नमस्तेऽस्तु सहस्रकृत्वः
पुनश्च भूयोऽपि नमो नमस्ते ॥ ११—३९ ॥
नमः पूरस्तादथ पृष्ठतस्ते
नमोऽस्तु ते सर्वत एव सर्व ।
अनन्तवीर्यामितविक्रमस्त्वं
सर्वं समाप्नोषि ततोऽसि सर्वः ॥ ११—४० ॥

37. kasmāc ca te na nameran mahātman garīyase brahmaṇo'py ādikartre
ananta deveśa jagannivāsa tvam akṣaraṃ sad asat tatparaṃ yat
38. tvam ādidevaḥ puruṣaḥ purāṇas tvam asya viśvasya paraṃ nidhānam
vettāsi vedyaṃ ca paraṃ ca dhāma tvayā tataṃ viśvam anantarūpa
39. vāyur yamo'gnir varuṇaḥ śaśāṅkaḥ prajāpatis tvaṃ prapitāmahaś ca
namo namas te'stu sahasrakṛtvaḥ punaś ca bhūyo'pi namo namas te
40. namaḥ purastād atha pṛṣṭhatas te namo'stu te sarvata eva sarva
anantavīryāmitavikramas tvaṃ sarvaṃ samāpnoṣi tato'si sarvaḥ

11.37 And why should they not salute [You], O Great Self, [You who are] greater even than Brahma, the primordial creator? O Infinite Lord of the gods, O Home of the universe, You are the Imperishable, existence and nonexistence and what is beyond that.

11.38 You are the Primordial God, the ancient Spirit (*purusha*). You are the supreme receptacle of all this. You are the knower and [what-is]-to-be-known and the supreme abode. By You all this is spread out, O [You of] infinite form!

11.39 You are Vāyu,[38] Yama,[39] Agni,[40] Varuna,[41] the moon, and Prajāpati,[42] the great-grandsire. Salutation, salutation be to You a thousandfold; and again and again salutation, salutation to You!

11.40 Salutation to You from in front and from behind! Salutation to You from all-around, O All! You are of infinite vitality [and] immeasurable might. You complete all, hence You are all.

38. Vāyu is the God of Wind.
39. Yama is the God of Death.
40. Agni is the God of Fire, the most prominent deity in the Vedic era.
41. Varuna is the God of the Waters. See note 43 for 10.29.
42. Prajāpati, or "Lord of Creatures," is the first creator, who is superior even to the creator deity Brahma.

सखेति मत्वा प्रसभं यदुक्तं
हे कृष्ण हे यादव हे सखेति ।
अजानता महिमानं तवेदं
मया प्रमादात्प्रणयेन वापि ॥ ११—४१ ॥
यच्चावहासार्थमसत्कृतोऽसि
विहारशय्यासनभोजनेषु ।
एकोऽथ वाप्यच्युत तत्समक्षं
तत्क्षामये त्वामहमप्रमेयम् ॥ ११—४२ ॥
पितासि लोकस्य चराचरस्य
त्वमस्य पूज्यश्च गुरुर्गरीयान् ।
न त्वत्समोऽस्त्यभ्यधिकः कुतोऽन्यो
लोकत्रयेऽप्यप्रतिमप्रभाव ॥ ११—४३ ॥
तस्मात्प्रणम्य प्रणिधाय कायं
प्रसादये त्वामहमीशमीड्यम् ।
पितेव पुत्रस्य सखेव सख्युः
प्रियः प्रियायार्हसि देव सोढुम् ॥ ११—४४ ॥

41. sakheti matvā prasabhaṃ yad uktaṃ he kṛṣṇa he yādava he sakheti
ajānatā mahimānaṃ tavedaṃ mayā pramādāt praṇayena vāpi
42. yac cāvahāsārtham asatkṛto'si vihāraśayyāsanabhojaneṣu
eko'tha vāpy acyuta tatsamakṣaṃ tat kṣāmaye tvām aham aprameyam
43. pitāsi lokasya carācarasya tvam asya pūjyaś ca gurur garīyān
na tvatsamo'sty abhyadhikaḥ kuto'nyo lokatraye'py apratimaprabhāva
44. tasmāt praṇamya praṇidhāya kāyaṃ prasādaye tvām aham īśam īḍyam
piteva putrasya sakheva sakhyuḥ priyaḥ priyāyārhasi deva soḍhum

11.41 That [I], ignorant of Your majesty, through my heedlessness or perhaps out of fondness and thinking importunately [that You are my] friend, saying [impolitely] "Hey, Krishna! Hey, Yādava![43] Hey, friend!"[44]

11.42 and that in jest [I showed] disrespect to You, [while] playing, reposing, sitting, or eating, [either] alone or in the presence [of others]—[for] that, O Acyuta,[45] I beg Your pardon, [you who are] unfathomable!

11.43 You are the father of the world, [which contains] moving and unmoving [things]. You are worship-worthy and [the world's] very venerable teacher. None is equal to You—how [is there anything] greater in the triple world, O [You of] matchless might?

11.44 Therefore bowing-down and bending-low [my] body, I seek indulgence from you, the praiseworthy Lord. You should bear [with me], O God, as a father with [his] son, as a friend with a friend or a lover with the beloved.

43. The epithet Yādava means "Descendant of Yadu." Yadu was a great ruler of the solar dynasty to which Krishna belonged as well. On the human level, Krishna was a king of the Yadu dynasty, with the lineage going from the god Brahma to Atri, Candra, Budha, Purūravas, Āyus, Nahusha, Yayāti, and then to Kuru.

44. Stanzas 11.41–44 are in the *trishtubh* meter.

45. On Acyuta, see note 16 for 1.21.

«दिव्यानि कर्माणि तवाद्भुतानि
पूर्वाणि पूर्वेऽप्यृषयः स्मरन्ति ।
नान्योऽस्ति कर्ता जगतस्त्वमेको
धाता विधाता च विभुर्भवश्च ॥
तवाद्भुतं किं नु भवेदसह्यं
किं वाशक्यं परतः कीर्तयिष्ये ।
कर्तासि सर्वस्य यतः स्वयं वै
विभो ततः सर्वमिदं त्वमेव ॥
अत्यद्भुतं कर्म न दुष्करं ते
कर्मोपमानं न हि विद्यते ते ।
न ते गुणानां परिमाणमस्ति
न तेजसो नापि बलस्य नर्द्धेः ॥»

अदृष्टपूर्वं हृषितोऽस्मि दृष्ट्वा
भयेन च प्रव्यथितं मनो मे ।
तदेव मे दर्शय देव रूपं
प्रसीद देवेश जगन्निवास ॥ ११—४५ ॥
किरीटिनं गदिनं चक्रहस्त
मिच्छामि त्वां द्रष्टुमहं तथैव ।
तेनैव रूपेण चतुर्भुजेन
सहस्रबाहो भव विश्वमूर्ते ॥ ११—४६ ॥

« divyāni karmāṇi tavādbhūtāni pūrvāṇi pūrve'py ṛṣayaḥ smaranti
nānyo'sti kartā jagatas tvam eko dhātā vidhātā ca vibhur bhavaś ca
tavādbhūtaṃ kiṃ nu bhaved asahyaṃ kiṃ vāśakyaṃ parataḥ kīrtayiṣye
kartāsi sarvasya yataḥ svayaṃ vai vibho tataḥ sarvam idaṃ tvameva
atyadbhutaṃ karma na duṣkaraṃ te karmopamānaṃ na hi vidyate te
na te guṇānāṃ parimāṇam asti na tejaso nāpi balasya narddheḥ»

45. adṛṣṭapūrvaṃ hṛṣito'smi dṛṣṭvā bhayena ca pravyathitaṃ mano me
tad eva me darśaya deva rūpaṃ prasīda deveśa jagannivāsa
46. kirīṭinaṃ gadinaṃ cakrahastam icchāmi tvāṃ draṣṭum ahaṃ tathaiva
tenaiva rūpeṇa caturbhujena sahasrabāho bhava viśvamūrte

«The seers of old recall Your divine, wondrous ancient deeds. There is no other creator of the universe. You are the one [who is] the originator, dispenser, almighty, and becoming [i.e., the unfolding universe].

Indeed, what wonder could there be [that is] impossible for You? Or what further [wonder] could I praise [that] is impossible [for You]? Since You Yourself are the maker of all, O Almighty, You are verily all this.

No action, [however] wondrous, is difficult for You, for there is no parallel to Your deeds. There is no measure to Your qualities, nor [to Your] brilliance, or strength, or prosperity.[46]»

11.45 I am thrilled at having seen [what] has not been seen before. But my mind is distressed with fear. [Therefore], O God, show me that [human] form [of Yours again]. Be gracious, O Lord of the gods, O Home of the universe![47]

11.46 I wish to see You even as [You were before], [with Your] crown, [holding] the mace and discus-in-hand. Assume that four-armed form [of Yours again], O Thousand-armed All-form!

46. This extra passage is found in some of the manuscripts used by Belvalkar and is brought here only to give the reader a sense of the kind of elaboration that is possible for any traditional Sanskrit scripture.
47. This and the next stanza are in the *trishtubh* meter.

श्रीभगवानुवाच
मया प्रसन्नेन तवार्जुनेदं
रूपं परं दर्शितमात्मयोगात् ।
तेजोमयं विश्वमनन्तमाद्यं
यन्मे त्वदन्येन न दृष्टपूर्वम् ॥ ११—४७ ॥
न वेदयज्ञाध्ययनैर्न दानै
र्न च क्रियाभिर्न तपोभिरुग्रैः ।
एवंरूपः शक्य अहं नृलोके
द्रष्टुं त्वदन्येन कुरुप्रवीर ॥ ११—४८ ॥
मा ते व्यथा मा च विमूढभावो
दृष्ट्वा रूपं घोरमीदृङ्ममेदम् ।
व्यपेतभीः प्रीतमनाः पुनस्त्वं
तदेव मे रूपमिदं प्रपश्य ॥ ११—४९ ॥
संजय उवाच
इत्यर्जुनं वासुदेवस्तथोक्त्वा
स्वकं रूपं दर्शयामास भूयः ।
आश्वासयामास च भीतमेनं
भूत्वा पुनः सौम्यवपुर्महात्मा ॥ ११—५० ॥

śrībhagavān uvāca

47. mayā prasannena tavārjunedaṃ rūpaṃ paraṃ darśitam ātmayogāt tejomayaṃ viśvam anantam ādyaṃ yan me tvadanyena na dṛṣṭapūrvam

48. na vedayajñādhyayanair na dānair na ca kriyābhir na tapobhir ugraiḥ evaṃrūpaḥ śakya ahaṃ nṛloke draṣṭuṃ tvadanyena kurupravīra

49. mā te vyathā mā ca vimūḍhabhāvo dṛṣtvā rūpaṃ ghoram īdṛṇ mamedam vyapetabhīḥ prītamanāḥ punas tvaṃ tad eva me rūpam idaṃ prapaśya

saṃjaya uvāca

50. ity arjunaṃ vāsudevas tathoktvā svakaṃ rūpaṃ darśayām āsa bhūyaḥ āśvāsayām āsa ca bhītam enaṃ bhūtvā punaḥ saumya vapur mahātmā

The Blessed Lord said:

11.47 Out of My kindness for you, O Arjuna, [I have] shown [to You] this supreme form by [My] Self's Yoga—this brilliant, all[-comprising], infinite, and primordial [form] of Mine that has not been seen before by anyone [but] you.[48]

11.48 Neither by the Vedas, sacrifices, nor study, nor by charity, nor by rituals, nor by fierce austerity can I be seen thus-formed in the world of men by anyone [but] you, O Kurupravīra![49]

11.49 You [need] not tremble. Do not [succumb to] a bewildered condition at seeing that horrifying form of Mine. Freed from [all] fear and glad minded, behold again this My [familiar physical] form, the very [form which you know so well].

Samjaya said:

11.50 Having thus spoken to Arjuna, Vāsudeva[50] revealed again [His] own [human] form, and having assumed again [His] pleasant [human] body, the Great Self comforted the terrified [Arjuna].

48. Stanzas 11.47–50 are in the *trishtubh* meter.

49. The epithet Kurupravīra means "Hero of the Kurus."

50. On Vāsudeva, see note 58 for 10.37.

अर्जुन उवाच
दृष्ट्वेदं मानुषं रूपं तव सौम्यं जनार्दन ।
इदानीमस्मि संवृत्तः सचेताः प्रकृतिं गतः ॥ ११—५१ ॥
श्रीभगवान उवाच
सुदुर्दर्शमिदं रूपं दृष्टवानसि यन्मम ।
देवाप्यस्य रूपस्य नित्यं दर्शनकाङ्क्षिणः ॥ ११—५२ ॥
नाहं वेदैर्न तपसा न दानेन न चेज्यया ।
शक्य एवंविधो द्रष्टुं दृष्टवानसि मां यथा ॥ ११—५३ ॥
भक्त्या तवनन्यया शक्याहमेवंविधोऽर्जुन ।
ज्ञातुं द्रष्टुं च तत्त्वेन प्रवेष्टुं च परंतप ॥ ११—५४ ॥
मत्कर्मकृन्मत्परमो मद्भक्तः सङ्गवर्जितः ।
निर्वैरः सर्वभूतेषु यः स मामेति पाण्डव ॥ ११—५५ ॥

arjuna uvaca
51. dṛṣṭvedaṃ mānuṣaṃ rūpaṃ tava saumyaṃ janārdana
idānīm asmi saṃvṛttaḥ sacetāḥ prakṛtiṃ gataḥ
śrībhagavān uvāca
52. sudurdarśam idaṃ rūpaṃ dṛṣṭavān asi yan mama
devā apy asya rūpasya nityaṃ darśanakāṇkṣiṇaḥ
53. nāhaṃ vedair na tapasā na dānena na cejyayā
śakya evaṃvidho draṣṭuṃ dṛṣṭavān asi māṃ yathā
54. bhaktyā tv ananyayā śakya aham evaṃvidho'rjuna
jñātuṃ draṣṭuṃ ca tattvena praveṣṭuṃ ca paraṃtapa
55. matkarmakṛn matparamo madbhaktaḥ saṅgavarjitaḥ
nirvairaḥ sarvabhūteṣu yaḥ sa mām eti pāṇḍava

Arjuna said:

11.51 Beholding [again] this pleasant human form of Yours, O Janārdana,[51] I have now regained [a state in which my] consciousness has returned [to its normal] nature.[52]

The Blessed Lord said:

11.52 Very-difficult-to-see is this My form which you have seen. Even the gods are forever hankering after a glimpse of this form.

11.53 In the shape in which you have seen Me, I cannot be seen by [means of] the Vedas, nor by austerity, nor by gifts, nor by sacrifice.

11.54 But, O Arjuna, by devotion [directed to] no other, I can be known in this shape and be seen and, in reality, entered into, O Paramtapa.[53]

11.55 He who does My work, [with] Me [as his] supreme [intent], [who is] devoted to Me [with all ordinary] attachment abandoned, free-from-enmity toward all beings—he comes to Me, O son-of-Pāndu.

51. On Janārdana, see note 25 for 1.36.
52. With this stanza, the *shloka* meter is resumed.
53. On Paramtapa, see note 5 for 2.3.

अर्जुन उवाच
एवं सततयुक्ता ये भक्तास्त्वां पर्युपासते ।
ये चाप्यक्षरमव्यक्तं तेषां के योगवित्तमाः ॥ १२—१ ॥
श्रीभगवानुवाच
मय्यावेश्य मनो ये मां नित्ययुक्ता उपासते ।
श्रद्धया परयोपेतास्ते मे युक्ततमा मताः ॥ १२—२ ॥
ये त्वक्षरमनिर्देश्यमव्यक्तं पर्युपासते ।
सर्वत्रगमचिन्त्यं च कूटस्थमचलं ध्रुवम् ॥ १२—३ ॥
संनियम्येन्द्रियग्रामं सर्वत्र समबुद्धयः ।
ते प्राप्नुवन्ति मामेव सर्वभूतहिते रताः ॥ १२—४ ॥
क्लेशोऽधिकतरस्तेषामव्यक्तासक्तचेतसाम् ।
अव्यक्ता हि गतिर्दुःखं देहवद्भिरवाप्यते ॥ १२—५ ॥
ये तु सर्वाणि कर्माणि मयि संन्यस्य मत्पराः ।
अनन्येनैव योगेन मां ध्यायन्ता उपासते ॥ १२—६ ॥

arjuna uvāca

1. evaṃ satatayuktā ye bhaktās tvāṃ paryupāsate
   ye cāpy akṣaram avyaktaṃ teṣāṃ ke yogavittamāḥ
   śrībhagavān uvāca
2. mayy āveśya mano ye māṃ nityayuktā upāsate
   śraddhayā parayopetās te me yuktatamā matāḥ
3. ye tv akṣaram anirdeśyam avyaktaṃ paryupāsate
   sarvatragam acintyaṃ ca kūṭastham acalaṃ dhruvam
4. saṃniyamyendriyagrāmaṃ sarvatra samabuddhayaḥ
   te prāpnuvanti mām eva sarvabhūtahite ratāḥ
5. kleśo'dhikataras teṣām avyaktāsaktacetasām
   avyaktā hi gatir duḥkhaṃ dehavadbhir avāpyate
6. ye tu sarvāṇi karmāṇi mayi saṃnyasya matparāḥ
   ananyenaiva yogena māṃ dhyāyanta upāsate

CHAPTER 12

The Yoga of Devotion

Arjuna said:

12.1 Devotees who are thus ever yoked [and] worship You, or [those] who [worship] the Imperishable Unmanifest—which of these are the best knowers of Yoga?

The Blessed Lord said:

12.2 Those I deem [to be] most yoked who, fixing [their] mind on Me, worship Me, ever yoked and endowed with supreme faith.

12.3 But [those] who worship the imperishable, indefinable Unmanifest, [which is] omnipresent, inconceivable, summit-abiding,[1] unmoving, [and] firm,

12.4 [and who], restraining the hosts of senses, [having their] wisdom-faculty [remain] the same in everything [and] delighting in the welfare of all beings—they, verily, attain Me.

12.5 [Much] greater is the struggle[2] of those [whose] mind is attached to the Unmanifest. For, the Unmanifest is reached by embodied [beings along] a troubled course.[3]

12.6 But those who are renouncing all actions in Me, [who are] intent on Me—[they] worship [Me] by contemplating Me through no other[4] [means than] Yoga.

1. The expression *kūtastha* (from *kūta,* "summit, peak," and *stha,* "abiding") means literally "summit-abiding," which is frequently translated into English as "unchanging," though Hill (1928/1966) gives "Immovably Exalted."

2. The Sanskrit text has *klesha,* or "affliction," here rendered as "struggle."

3. The phrase *avyaktā hi gatir duhkham* can also be translated as "for the Unmanifest [is a] difficult goal."

4. Sargeant (1984) translates *ananyenaiva yogena* as "with undistracted Yoga," while Hill (1928/1966) has "with undivided control."

तेषामहं समुद्धर्ता मृत्युसंसारसागरात् ।
भवामि नचिरात्पार्थ मय्यावेशितचेतसाम् ॥ १२—७ ॥
मय्येव मन आधत्स्व मयि बुद्धिं निवेशय ।
निवसिष्यसि मय्येव अत ऊर्ध्वं न संशयः ॥ १२—८ ॥
अथ चित्तं समाधातुं न शक्नोषि मयि स्थिरम् ।
अभ्यासयोगेन ततो मामिच्छाप्तुं धनंजय ॥ १२—९ ॥
अभ्यासेऽप्यसमर्थोऽसि मत्कर्मपरमो भव ।
मदर्थमपि कर्माणि कुर्वन्सिद्धिमवाप्स्यसि ॥ १२—१० ॥
अथैतदप्यशक्तोऽसि कर्तुं मद्योगमाश्रितः ।
सर्वकर्मफलत्यागं ततः कुरु यतात्मवान् ॥ १२—११ ॥
श्रेयो हि ज्ञानमभ्यासाज्ज्ञानाद्ध्यानं विशिष्यते ।
ध्यानात्कर्मफलत्यागस्त्यागाच्छान्तिरनन्तरम् ॥ १२—१२ ॥
अद्वेष्टा सर्वभूतानां मैत्रः करुण एव च ।
निर्ममो निरहंकारः समदुःखसुखः क्षमी ॥ १२—१३ ॥

7. teṣām ahaṃ samuddhartā mṛtyusaṃsārasāgarāt
bhavāmi nacirāt pārtha mayy āveśitacetasām
8. mayy eva mana ādhatsva mayi buddhiṃ niveśaya
nivasiṣyasi mayy eva ata ūrdhvaṃ na saṃśayaḥ
9. atha cittaṃ samādhātuṃ na śaknoṣi mayi sthiram
abhyāsayogena tato mām icchāptuṃ dhanaṃjaya
10. abhyāse'py asamartho'si matkarmaparamo bhava
madartham api karmāṇi kurvan siddhim avāpsyasi
11. athaitad apy aśakto'si kartuṃ madyogam āśritaḥ
sarvakarmaphalatyāgaṃ tataḥ kuru yatātmavān
12. śreyo hi jñānam abhyāsāj jñānād dhyānaṃ viśiṣyate
dhyānāt karmaphalatyāgas tyāgāc chāntir anantaram
13. adveṣṭā sarvabhūtānāṃ maitraḥ karuṇa eva ca
nirmamo nirahaṃkāraḥ samaduḥkhasukhaḥ kṣamī

12.7 For those [whose] mind is fixed on Me, O son-of-Prithā,[5] I become, before long, the uplifter from the ocean of the cycle of death.[6]

12.8 Place [your] mind in Me alone. Settle [your] wisdom-faculty (*buddhi*) in Me. Henceforth[7] you shall dwell in Me alone. [Of this there is] no doubt.

12.9 Now, [if] you are unable to concentrate the mind firmly on Me, then seek to attain Me through Yoga practice,[8] O Dhanamjaya.[9]

12.10 And [if] you are unable [to apply yourself to yogic] practice, [then] be[10] My supreme work. For even performing actions for My sake, you shall attain perfection.

12.11 Now, [if] you are unable to do even this, then, resorting to My Yoga [through devotion and] relinquishing all actions' fruit, perform [actions with] controlled self.[11]

12.12 For better than [ritual] practice is knowledge. Superior to knowledge is meditation. From meditation [comes] the relinquishment of actions' fruit. From relinquishment [results] immediate peace.[12]

12.13 [He who feels] no hatred for any being [is] friendly and compassionate, devoid of [the idea of] "mine," without ego-sense, the same in pleasure and pain, [and] patient.

5. On son-of-Prithā (Pārtha), see note 18 for 1.25.

6. The expression *mrityu-samsāra-sāgara* ("ocean of the cycle of death") refers to conditional existence with its repeated deaths and rebirths.

7. Some translators logically connect "henceforth" (*ata ūrdhvam*) with *na samshaya* ("no doubt").

8. The Sanskrit text has *abhyāsayogena,* here translated as "through Yoga practice."

9. On Dhanamjaya, see note 7 for 1.15.

10. The imperative "be" is a literal translation of *bhava*. The justification and explanation for this rendering are found in 11.33, where Arjuna is asked to be Krishna's "instrument" or "tool" (*nimitta*). Zaehner's (1966) translation of *mat-karma-paramo bhava* reads "work-and-act for Me"; Radhakrishnan's (1948) is "be as one whose supreme aim is My service"; and Hill's (1928/1966) is "make work for me thine aim."

11. In my rendering of this stanza I follow Rāmānuja, who equates "My Yoga" with Bhakti-Yoga. Some manuscripts give *udyogam* ("effort") for *madyogam* ("My Yoga").

12. Usually this stanza is understood differently: "For better is wisdom than [mere] effort, better than wisdom meditation; and [better] than meditation to renounce the fruits of works: renunciation leads straightaway to peace" (Zaehner 1966). Translated in this manner, the verse, as Zaehner notes, indeed "does not seem to fit in naturally with what has gone before." But this difficulty can be resolved if one takes the expression *dhyānāt* of the line *dhyānāt karma-phala-tyāgah* to be an ablative, which indicates direction rather than comparison. More important, one must read on and appreciate Krishna's gospel of devotion. As Hill (1928/1966) observes, the traditional commentators "vainly grappled" with this stanza's message while many contemporary commentators "preserve a discreet silence." Hill, too, resolves the apparent paradox by pointing to Krishna's Bhakti-Yoga.

संतुष्टः सततं योगी यतात्मा दृढनिश्चयः ।
मय्यर्पितमनोबुद्धिर्यो मद्भक्तः स मे प्रियः ॥ १२—१४ ॥
यस्मान्नोद्विजते लोको लोकान्नोद्विजते च यः ।
हर्षामर्षभयोद्वेगैर्मुक्तो यः स च मे प्रियः ॥ १२—१५ ॥
अनपेक्षः शुचिर्दक्ष उदासीनो गतव्यथः ।
सर्वारम्भपरित्यागी यो मद्भक्तः स मे प्रियः ॥ १२—१६ ॥
यो न हृष्यति न द्वेष्टि न शोचति न काङ्क्षति ।
शुभाशुभपरित्यागी भक्तिमान्यः स मे प्रियः ॥ १२—१७ ॥
समः शत्रौ च मित्रे च तथा मानावमानयोः ।
शीतोष्णसुखदुःखेषु समः सङ्गविवर्जितः ॥ १२—१८ ॥
तुल्यनिन्दास्तुतिर्मौनी संतुष्टो येन केनचित् ।
अनिकेतः स्थिरमतिर्भक्तिमान्मे प्रियो नरः ॥ १२—१९ ॥
ये तु धर्म्यामृतमिदं यथोक्तं पर्युपासते ।
श्रद्धधाना मत्परमा भक्तास्तेऽतीव मे प्रियाः ॥ १२—२० ॥

14. saṃtuṣṭaḥ satataṃ yogī yatātmā dṛḍhaniścayaḥ
mayy arpitamanobuddhir yo madbhaktaḥ sa me priyaḥ
15. yasmān nodvijate loko lokān nodvijate ca yaḥ
harṣāmarṣabhayodvegair mukto yaḥ sa ca me priyaḥ
16. anapekṣaḥ śucir dakṣa udāsīno gatavyathaḥ
sarvārambhaparityāgī yo madbhaktaḥ sa me priyaḥ
17. yo na hṛṣyati na dveṣṭi na śocati na kāṅkṣati
śubhāśubhaparityāgī bhaktimān yaḥ sa me priyaḥ
18. samaḥ śatrau ca mitre ca tathā mānāvamānayoḥ
śītoṣṇasukhaduḥkheṣu samaḥ saṅgavivarjitaḥ
19. tulyanindāstutir maunī saṃtuṣṭo yena kenacit
aniketaḥ sthiramatir bhaktimān me priyo naraḥ
20. ye tu dharmyāmṛtam idaṃ yathoktaṃ paryupāsate
śraddadhānā matparamā bhaktās te'tīva me priyāḥ

12.14 [That] *yogin,* [who is] ever content, self-controlled, of firm resolve, [with] mind and wisdom-faculty offered up in Me, who is devoted to Me—he is [truly] dear to Me.

12.15 [He] from whom the world does not shrink and who does not shrink from the world, and who is free from exultation, anger, fear, and agitation[13]—he is dear to Me.

12.16 [He] who is impartial, pure, skilled, indifferent, [whose] disquiet has gone, [who has] relinquished all [selfish] undertaking [and who is] devoted to Me—he is dear to Me.

12.17 [He] who neither rejoices nor hates, nor grieves, nor hankers after [anything], [and who has fully] relinquished pleasant and unpleasant [things], who is [thus] filled-with-devotion—he is dear to Me.

12.18 [He who is] the same toward friend and enemy, as also toward honor and dishonor, [who is] the same in cold and heat, pleasure and sorrow (*duhkha*), [and who is] devoid of attachment,

12.19 [who holds] equal blame and praise,[14] [who is] silent, content with whatever [comes his way], [who is] homeless, [who is] of steady mind and filled-with-devotion—[that] man is dear to Me.

12.20 But those [who] worship this lawful (*dharmya*) nectar-of-immortality[15] as declared [by Me], [who] have faith, [who make] Me the supreme [goal and] are devoted to [Me]—they are exceedingly dear to Me.

13. The word *udvega,* here rendered as "agitation," has many possible meanings. Some translators give it as "distress," others as "anxiety."

14. See also 6.7. Some manuscripts and editions have the variant *mānāpmānayoh.*

15. The phrase *dharmyāmritam,* here reproduced as "lawful nectar-of-immortality," has also been rendered as "wisdom nectar" (Sargeant 1984), "holy law of deathlessness" (Hill 1928/1966), "imperishable path of devotional service" (Bhaktivedanta Swami 1983), and "righteous immortal value" (Nataraja Guru 1973). My own translation is based on the notion that the *Gītā*'s author may have had in mind that there are teachings (such as alchemy) that promise a kind of ambrosia (*amrita*) that fall shorts of the nectar held out by Krishna's teaching. As in many other instances, the *yogin*-commentator Nataraja Guru perhaps comes closest to the intended meaning. On the meaning of *dharmya* ("lawful"), see note 33 for 2.31.

अर्जुन उवाच
प्रकृतिं पुरुषं चैव क्षेत्रं क्षेत्रज्ञमेव च ।
एतद्वेदितुमिच्छामि ज्ञानं ज्ञेयं च केशव ॥ १३—० ॥
श्रीभगवानुवाच
इदं शरीरं कौन्तेय क्षेत्रमित्यभिधीयते ।
एतद्यो वेत्ति तं प्राहुः क्षेत्रज्ञ इति तद्विदः ॥ १३—१ ॥
क्षेत्रज्ञं चापि मां विद्धि सर्वक्षेत्रेषु भारत ।
क्षेत्रक्षत्रज्ञयोर्ज्ञानं यत्तज्ज्ञानं मतं मम ॥ १३—२ ॥
तत्क्षेत्रं यच्च यादृक्च यद्विकारि यतश्च यत् ।
स च यो यत्प्रभावश्च तत्समासेन मे शृणु ॥ १३—३ ॥
ऋषिभिर्बहुधा गीतं छन्दोभिर्विविधैः पृथक् ।
ब्रह्मसूत्रपदैश्चैव हेतुमद्भिर्विनिश्चितैः ॥ १३—४ ॥

arjuna uvāca

0. prakṛtiṃ puruṣaṃ caiva kṣetraṃ kṣetrajñam eva ca
   etad veditum icchāmi jñānaṃ jñeyaṃ ca keśava
   śrībhagavān uvāca
1. idaṃ śarīraṃ kaunteya kṣetram ity abhidhīyate
   etad yo vetti taṃ prāhuḥ kṣetrajña iti tadvidaḥ
2. kṣetrajñaṃ cāpi māṃ viddhi sarvakṣetreṣu bhārata
   kṣetrakṣetrajñayor jñānaṃ yat taj jñānaṃ mataṃ mama
3. tat kṣetraṃ yac ca yādṛk ca yadvikāri yataś ca yat
   sa ca yo yatprabhāvaś ca tat samāsena me śṛṇu
4. ṛṣibhir bahudhā gītaṃ chandobhir vividhaiḥ pṛthak
   brahmasūtrapadaiś caiva hetumadbhir viniścitaiḥ

CHAPTER 13

The Yoga of the Distinction between the Field and the Field-Knower

Arjuna said:

13.0 Cosmos (*prakriti*) and Spirit (*purusha*), "field" and "field-knower," knowledge and what-is-to-be-known (*jneya*): this, O Keshava,[1] I desire to know.[2]

The Blessed Lord said:

13.1 This body [and mind], O son-of-Kuntī,[3] is designated as the "field"; he who knows this [body and mind] is called the "field-knower" by [those who] know it.[4]

13.2 And [you should] also know Me as the "field-knower" in all "fields," O descendant-of-Bharata. The knowledge of "field" and the "field-knower"—that, I deem [real] knowledge.

13.3 What that "field" is and what [it is] like and what [its] modifications are and whence [it comes], as well as who he [i.e., the "field-knower"] is and what [his] might is—hear that [now] from Me briefly.

13.4 [It has been] sung by seers in many ways [and] distinctly in various hymns and also in well-reasoned and conclusive aphoristic expressions[5] about the world-ground (*brahman*).

1. On the epithet Keshava, see note 21 for 1.31.
2. This stanza is missing in some manuscripts (thus it is numbered 13.0). "What-is-to-be-known" (*jneya*) refers to the multitude of objects.
3. On son-of-Kuntī (Kaunteya), see note 19 for 1.27.
4. This stanza furnishes the esoteric meaning of *kshetra*, which also sheds new light on the *Gītā*'s opening verse. God is the field-knower of all the individual fields *simultaneously*. Any one Self-monad is a field-knower only with respect to the particular psychosomatic organism with which it is associated. By implication, God also "knows" the various Selves composing the *jīva-bhūta* of his total Being.
5. Traditional commentators understand this reference to mean the *Brahma-Sūtra* ascribed to Bādarāyana. Most contemporary scholars think that this is very unlikely and that the aphorisms on *brahman* mentioned here represent another, earlier work.

महाभूतान्यहंकारो बुद्धिरव्यक्तमेव च ।
इन्द्रियाणि दशैकं च पञ्च चेन्द्रियगोचराः ॥ १३—५ ॥
इच्छा द्वेषः सुखं दुःखं संघातश्चेतना धृतिः ।
एतत्क्षेत्रं समासेन सविकारमुदाहृतम् ॥ १३—६ ॥
अमानित्वमदम्भित्वमहिंसा क्षान्तिरार्जवम् ।
आचार्योपासनं शौचं स्थैर्यमात्मविनिग्रहः ॥ १३—७ ॥
इन्द्रियार्थेषु वैराग्यमनहंकार एव च ।
जन्ममृत्युजराव्याधिदुःखदोषानुदर्शनम् ॥ १३—८ ॥
असक्तिरनभिष्वङ्गः पुत्रदारगृहादिषु ।
नित्यं च समचित्तत्वमिष्टानिष्टोपपत्तिषु ॥ १३—९ ॥

5. mahābhūtāny ahaṃkāro buddhir avyaktam eva ca
   indriyāṇi daśaikaṃ ca pañca cendriyagocarāḥ
6. icchā dveṣaḥ sukhaṃ duḥkhaṃ saṃghātaś cetanā dhṛtiḥ
   etat kṣetraṃ samāsena savikāram udāhṛtam
7. amānitvam adambhitvam ahiṃsā kṣāntir ārjavam
   ācāryopāsanaṃ śaucaṃ sthairyam ātmavinigrahaḥ
8. indriyārtheṣu vairāgyam anahaṃkāra eva ca
   janmamṛtyujarāvyādhiduḥkhadoṣānudarśanam
9. asaktir anabhiṣvaṅgaḥ putradāragṛhādiṣu
   nityaṃ ca samacittatvam iṣṭāniṣṭopapattiṣu

13.5 The great elements,[6] the ego-sense, the wisdom-faculty and the unmanifest,[7] the eleven senses[8] [including the lower mind] and the five "cow-pastures"[9] of the senses,

13.6 desire (*icchā*), aversion, pleasure, pain, confusion,[10] consciousness, [and] "holding"[11]—these in brief are described as the "field" with [its] modifications.

13.7 Lack-of-pride, unpretentiousness, nonharming, patience, uprightness, reverence for the preceptor, purity, steadiness, self-restraint,

13.8 dispassion toward sense objects and indeed absence-of-ego-sense (*anahamkāra*), insight[12] into the defects of birth, death, old age, illness and suffering,

13.9 nonattachment, absence-of-clinging to son, wife, home and the like, and a constant same-mindedness[13] in desirable [and] undesirable happenings,

6. The "great elements" (*mahābhūta*) are earth, water, fire, air, and ether-space. These compose all material things, including the body.

7. The "unmanifest" (*avyakta*) is the previously mentioned dimension of existence that is undifferentiated, sheer potential.

8. On the eleven senses, see note 13 for 3.6 and note 15 for 3.7.

9. The "cow-pastures" (*gocara*) are the range of sensory objects presenting themselves to the senses (*indriya*).

10. The Sanskrit text uses the term *samghāta,* which generally has the meaning of "aggregation," "compression," "density." Sargeant (1984) curiously translates this as "organic whole" (meaning the physical body), which makes little sense in the present context. Hill (1928/1966) rightly observes that "the appearance of this word—*saṃghāta*—among the modifications of mind is not easy to explain." Rejecting previous renderings, he opts to render it as "association" but admits that even this is obscure. Basing myself on the connotation "density," I think that "confusion" is just as likely.

11. The term *dhriti* in this catalogue of mental faculties has been translated in a variety of ways—as "constancy" (Hill 1928/1966), "conviction" (Bhaktivedanta Swami 1983), "firmness" (Nataraja Guru 1973), and "steadfastness" (Edgerton 1944; Radhakrishnan 1948; Sargeant 1984). Because memory is such an important mental faculty, my own educated guess is that *dhriti* is used here in the sense of "holding" or "retaining."

12. The term *darshana* means "seeing/viewing" and has been translated as "perception" and "keeping in view," but in the present context, "insight" seems a preferable rendering.

13. The Sanskrit text has *sama-cittatva.* On the notion of *sama,* see note 18 for 2.15.

मयि चानन्ययोगेन भक्तिरव्यभिचारिणी ।
विविक्तदेशसेवित्वमरतिर्जनसंसदि ॥ १३—१० ॥
अध्यात्मज्ञाननित्यत्वं तत्त्वज्ञानार्थदर्शनम् ।
एतज्ज्ञानमिति प्रोक्तमज्ञानं यदतोऽन्यथा ॥ १३—११ ॥
ज्ञेयं यत्तत्प्रवक्ष्यामि यज्ज्ञात्वामृतमश्नुते ।
अनादिमत्परं ब्रह्म न सत्तन्नासदुच्यते ॥ १३—१२ ॥
सर्वतःपाणिपादं तत्सर्वतोऽक्षिशिरोमुखम् ।
सर्वतःश्रुतिमल्लोके सर्वमावृत्य तिष्ठति ॥ १३—१३ ॥
सर्वेन्द्रियगुणाभासं सर्वेन्द्रियविवर्जितम् ।
असक्तं सर्वभृच्चैव निर्गुणं गुणभोक्तृ च ॥ १३—१४ ॥
बहिरन्तश्च भूतानामचरं चरमेव च ।
सूक्ष्मत्वात्तदविज्ञेयं दूरस्थं चान्तिके च तत् ॥ १३—१५ ॥
अविभक्तं च भूतेषु विभक्तमिव च स्थितम् ।
भूतभर्तृ च तज्ज्ञेयं ग्रसिष्णु प्रभविष्णु च ॥ १३—१६ ॥

10. mayi cānanyayogena bhaktir avyabhicāriṇī
    viviktadeśasevitvam aratir janasaṃsadi
11. adhyātmajñānanityatvaṃ tattvajñānārthadarśanam
    etaj jñānam iti proktam ajñānaṃ yad ato'nyathā
12. jñeyaṃ yat tat pravakṣyāmi yaj jñātvāmṛtam aśnute
    anādimat paraṃ brahma na sat tan nāsad ucyate
13. sarvataḥpāṇipādaṃ tat sarvato'kṣiśiromukham
    sarvataḥśrutimal loke sarvam āvṛtya tiṣṭhati
14. sarvendriyaguṇābhāsaṃ sarvendriyavivarjitam
    asaktaṃ sarvabhṛc caiva nirguṇaṃ guṇabhoktṛ ca
15. bahir antaś ca bhūtānām acaraṃ caram eva ca
    sūkṣmatvāt tad avijñeyaṃ dūrasthaṃ cāntike ca tat
16. avibhaktaṃ ca bhūteṣu vibhaktam iva ca sthitam
    bhūtabhartṛ ca taj jñeyaṃ grasiṣṇu prabhaviṣṇu ca

13.10 and unswerving devotion to Me, with no other [means than] Yoga,[14] resorting to a solitary place, and a dislike [of being in] the company of people,

13.11 constancy in the knowledge of the basis-of-self[15] and insight[16] into the purpose of knowledge of Reality—[all] this is proclaimed [to be genuine] knowledge. Nescience is what is otherwise.

13.12 I shall [now] declare what-is-to-be-known, knowing which [a *yogin*] attains to immortality. The beginningless supreme world-ground[17] is called neither existence nor nonexistence.

13.13 That [world-ground] is present (*tishtati*) in the world, [with] hands and feet everywhere, eyes, heads, and mouths everywhere, ears everywhere, enveloping all.

13.14 Appearing [to possess] all the sense qualities, [it is] devoid of all the senses.[18] [It is] unattached and yet all-supporting, beyond the primary-qualities[19] and [yet] the enjoyer of the primary-qualities.

13.15 [That world-ground] is without and within [all] beings, unmoving and yet moving.[20] That cannot be known because [of its] subtleness. That is standing afar and [yet is] near.

13.16 And undivided, [it] abides in beings, seeming divided. That [*brahman*] is to be known as the supporter of beings, [their] devourer, and [their] generator (*prabhavishnu*).

14. On the expression *ananya* in connection with Yoga, see also note 4 for 12.6.

15. On *adhyātman* ("basis-of-self"), see note 41 for 3.30.

16. See note 12 for 13.8.

17. On *brahman,* here given as "world-ground," see note 66 for 2.72.

18. Compare 11.37, which states that Krishna is both *sat* ("existence") and *asat* ("nonexistence") and yet abides beyond them. (Elsewhere, e.g., 13.21, *sat* and *asat* are translated as "good" and "bad.") See also *Shvetāshvatara-Upanishad* 4.18 and *Rig-Veda* 10.129.

19. On the primary-qualities (*guna*), see note 44 for 2.45.

20. The Sanskrit expression *carācara* does not usually have this metaphysical significance but mostly refers to mobile and immobile things. Compare 13.26, where the words *sthāvara* ("motionless") and *jangama* ("moving") are employed to denote the same.

ज्योतिषामपि तज्ज्योतिस्तमसः परमुच्यते ।
ज्ञानं ज्ञेयं ज्ञानगम्यं हृदि सर्वस्य विष्ठितम् ॥ १३—१७ ॥
इति क्षेत्रं तथा ज्ञानं ज्ञेयं चोक्तं समासतः ।
मद्भक्त एतद्विज्ञाय मद्भावायोपपद्यते ॥ १३—१८ ॥
प्रकृतिं पुरुषं चैव विद्ध्यनादी उभावपि ।
विकारांश्च गुणांश्चैव विद्धि प्रकृतिसंभवान् ॥ १३—१९ ॥
कार्यकारणकर्तृत्वे हेतुः प्रकृतिरुच्यते ।
पुरुषः सुखदुःखानां भोक्तृत्वे हेतुरुच्यते ॥ १३—२० ॥
पुरुषः प्रकृतिस्थो हि भुङ्क्ते प्रकृतिजान्गुणान् ।
कारणं गुणसङ्गोऽस्य सदसद्योनिजन्मसु ॥ १३—२१ ॥
उपद्रष्टानुमन्ता च भर्ता भोक्ता महेश्वरः ।
परमात्मेति चाप्युक्तो देहेऽस्मिन्पुरुषः परः ॥ १३—२२ ॥
य एवं वेत्ति पुरुषं प्रकृतिं च गुणैः सह ।
सर्वथा वर्तमानोऽपि न स भूयोऽभिजायते ॥ १३—२३ ॥
ध्यानेनात्मनि पश्यन्ति केचिदात्मानमात्मना ।
अन्ये सांख्येन योगेन कर्मयोगेन चापरे ॥ १३—२४ ॥

17. jyotiṣām api taj jyotis tamasaḥ param ucyate
jñānaṃ jñeyaṃ jñānagamyaṃ hṛdi sarvasya viṣṭhitam
18. iti kṣetraṃ tathā jñānaṃ jñeyaṃ coktaṃ samāsataḥ
madbhakta etad vijñāya madbhāvāyopapadyate
19. prakṛtiṃ puruṣaṃ caiva viddhy anādī ubhāv api
vikārāṃś ca guṇāṃś caiva viddhi prakṛtisaṃbhavān
20. kāryakāraṇakartṛtve hetuḥ prakṛtir ucyate
puruṣaḥ sukhaduḥkhānāṃ bhoktṛtve hetur ucyate
21. puruṣaḥ prakṛtistho hi bhuṅkte prakṛtijān guṇān
kāraṇaṃ guṇasaṅgo'sya sadasadyonijanmasu
22. upadraṣṭānumantā ca bhartā bhoktā maheśvaraḥ
paramātmeti cāpy ukto dehe'smin puruṣaḥ paraḥ
23. ya evaṃ vetti puruṣaṃ prakṛtiṃ ca guṇaiḥ saha
sarvathā vartamāno'pi na sa bhūyo'bhijāyate
24. dhyānenātmani paśyanti kecid ātmānam ātmanā
anye sāṃkhyena yogena karmayogena cāpare

13.17 That [world-ground] is also called the Light of lights beyond darkness. [It is] knowledge, what-is-to-be-known,[21] accessible to knowledge, seated in the heart of all [beings].

13.18 Thus the "field," likewise knowledge [and] what-is-to-be-known, is briefly explained. Knowing this, My devotee approaches My state-of-being.

13.19 Know both Cosmos (*prakriti*) and Spirit (*purusha*) [to be] beginningless, and know also that the modifications and the primary-qualities arise from the Cosmos.

13.20 Cosmos is called the cause (*hetu*) in [regard to] the agency [underlying the evolutionary] instruments [and] effects. The Spirit is called the cause [inasmuch as it is] the enjoyership of pleasure and pain.

13.21 The Spirit, abiding in the Cosmos, enjoys the primary-qualities (*guna*) born of the Cosmos. Attachment to the primary-qualities is the cause of its birth in good (*sat*) and bad (*asat*) wombs.

13.22 The highest Spirit in this body is called supervisor and permitter, supporter, enjoyer, great lord, and also supreme Self.

13.23 He who thus knows the Spirit and the Cosmos together with the primary-qualities—in whatever way he exists, he is not born again.

13.24 Some perceive through meditation the Self in the Self by the Self; others through the Sāmkhya [type of] Yoga, and [yet] others through the Yoga of action (*karma-yoga*).

21. The term *jneya* ("what-is-to-be-known") refers to the object of cognition.

अन्ये त्वेवमजानन्तः श्रुत्वान्येभ्य उपासते ।
तेऽपि चातितरन्त्येव मृत्युं श्रुतिपरायणाः ॥ १३—२५ ॥
यावत्संजायते किंचित्सत्त्वं स्थावरजङ्गमम् ।
क्षेत्रक्षेत्रज्ञसंयोगात्तद्विद्धि भरतर्षभ ॥ १३—२६ ॥
समं सर्वेषु भूतेषु तिष्ठन्तं परमेश्वरम् ।
विनश्यत्स्वविनश्यन्तं यः पश्यति स पश्यति ॥ १३—२७ ॥
समं पश्यन्हि सर्वत्र समवस्थितमीश्वरम् ।
न हिनस्त्यात्मनात्मानं ततो याति परां गतिम् ॥ १३—२८ ॥
प्रकृत्यैव च कर्माणि क्रियमाणानि सर्वशः ।
यः पश्यति तथात्मानमकर्तारं स पश्यति ॥ १३—२९ ॥
यदा भूतपृथग्भावमेकस्थमनुपश्यति ।
तत एव च विस्तारं ब्रह्म संपद्यते तदा ॥ १३—३० ॥
अनादित्वान्निर्गुणत्वात्परमात्मायमव्ययः ।
शरीरस्थोऽपि कौन्तेय न करोति न लिप्यते ॥ १३—३१ ॥

25. anye tv evam ajānantaḥ śrutvānyebhya upāsate
    te'pi cātitaranty eva mṛtyuṃ śrutiparāyaṇāḥ
26. yāvat saṃjāyate kiṃcit sattvaṃ sthāvarajaṅgamam
    kṣetrakṣetrajñasaṃyogāt tad viddhi bharatarṣabha
27. samaṃ sarveṣu bhūteṣu tiṣṭhantaṃ parameśvaram
    vinaśyatsv avinaśyantaṃ yaḥ paśyati sa paśyati
28. samaṃ paśyan hi sarvatra samavasthitam īśvaram
    na hinasty ātmanātmānaṃ tato yāti parāṃ gatim
29. prakṛtyaiva ca karmāṇi kriyamāṇāni sarvaśaḥ
    yaḥ paśyati tathātmānam akartāraṃ sa paśyati
30. yadā bhūtapṛthagbhāvam ekastham anupaśyati
    tata eva ca vistāraṃ brahma saṃpadyate tadā
31. anāditvān nirguṇatvāt paramātmāyam avyayaḥ
    śarīrastho'pi kaunteya na karoti na lipyate

13.25 But others, ignorant of this, hearing [about it] from others, worship [it]—they, too, transcend death [by being] dedicated to [what they have] heard.

13.26 Whatever entity (*sattva*) is born, motionless or moving, know this [to have sprung] from the union of the "field" and the "field-knower," O Bharatarshabha.[22]

13.27 He who sees the supreme Lord present in all beings [as] the same, not perishing upon [their eventual] perishing—he sees; he sees [indeed].

13.28 For, seeing the Lord abiding everywhere [as] the same, he cannot hurt [him]self by [him]self and hence treads the highest course.

13.29 And he who sees that actions are performed exclusively by the Cosmos [and that] the Self is thus inactive—he sees [indeed].

13.30 When he perceives the diverse states-of-existence of [all] beings as abiding in the One [and when he understands their] spreading-forth from that—then he attains to the world-ground.

13.31 Because this immutable supreme Self is beginningless and beyond the primary-qualities, although abiding in the body [and mind], [it] neither acts nor is defiled, O son-of-Kuntī.

22. On the epithet Bharatarshabha, see note 48 for 3.41.

यथा सर्वगतं सौक्ष्म्यादाकाशं नोपलिप्यते ।
सर्वत्रावस्थितो देहे तथात्मा नोपलिप्यते ॥ १३—३२ ॥
यथा प्रकाशयत्येकः कृत्स्नं लोकमिमं रविः ।
क्षेत्रं क्षेत्री तथा कृत्स्नं प्रकाशयति भारत ॥ १३—३३ ॥
क्षेत्रक्षेत्रज्ञयोरेवमन्तरं ज्ञानचक्षुषा ।
भूतप्रकृतिमोक्षं च ये विदुर्यान्ति ते परम् ॥ १३—३४ ॥

32. yathā sarvagataṃ saukṣmyād ākāśaṃ nopalipyate
sarvatrāvasthito dehe tathātmā nopalipyate
33. yathā prakāśayaty ekaḥ kṛtsnaṃ lokam imaṃ raviḥ
kṣetraṃ kṣetrī tathā kṛtsnaṃ prakāśayati bhārata
34. kṣetrakṣetrajñayor evam antaraṃ jñānacakṣuṣā
bhūtaprakṛtimokṣaṃ ca ye vidur yānti te param

13.32 As the omnipresent ether-space because [of its] subtleness is not polluted, so the Self, [although] abiding everywhere in a body, is not defiled.

13.33 As the sun singly illuminates this whole world, so the "field-owner" (*kshetrin*) illuminates the "field," O descendant-of-Bharata.

13.34 Those who with the eye of knowledge thus know the difference [between] the "field" and the "field-knower" and [also] the [path of] liberation [from] the elemental (*bhūta*) Cosmos[23]—they go to the Supreme.

23. Edgerton (1944) understands the phrase *bhūtaprakritimoksham* as "release from the material nature of beings." By "elemental Cosmos" is meant cosmic existence made up of the elements (*bhūta*).

श्रीभगवानुवाच
परं भूयः प्रवक्ष्यामि ज्ञानानां ज्ञानमुत्तमम् ।
यज्ज्ञात्वा मुनयः सर्वे परां सिद्धिमितो गताः ॥ १४—१ ॥
इदं ज्ञानमुपाश्रित्य मम साधर्म्यमागताः ।
सर्गेऽपि नोपजायन्ते प्रलये न व्यथन्ति च ॥ १४—२ ॥
मम योनिर्महद्ब्रह्म तस्मिन्गर्भं दधाम्यहम् ।
संभवः सर्वभूतानां ततो भवति भारत ॥ १४—३ ॥
सर्वयोनिषु कौन्तेय मूर्तयः संभवन्ति याः ।
तासां ब्रह्म महद्योनिरहं बीजप्रदः पिता ॥ १४—४ ॥
सत्त्वं रजस्तम इति गुणाः प्रकृतिसंभवाः ।
निबध्नन्ति महाबाहो देहे देहिनमव्ययम् ॥ १४—५ ॥
तत्र सत्त्वं निर्मलत्वात्प्रकाशकमनामयम् ।
सुखसङ्गेन बध्नाति ज्ञानसङ्गेन चानघ ॥ १४—६ ॥
रजो रागात्मकं विद्धि तृष्णासङ्गसमुद्भवम् ।
तन्निबध्नाति कौन्तेय कर्मसङ्गेन देहिनम् ॥ १४—७ ॥

śrībhagavān uvāca

1. paraṃ bhūyaḥ pravakṣyāmi jñānānāṃ jñānam uttamam
   yaj jñātvā munayaḥ sarve parāṃ siddhim ito gatāḥ
2. idaṃ jñānam upāśritya mama sādharmyam āgatāḥ
   sarge'pi nopajāyante pralaye na vyathanti ca
3. mama yonir mahad brahma tasmin garbhaṃ dadhāmy aham
   saṃbhavaḥ sarvabhūtānāṃ tato bhavati bhārata
4. sarvayoniṣu kaunteya mūrtayaḥ saṃbhavanti yāḥ
   tāsāṃ brahma mahad yonir ahaṃ bījapradaḥ pitā
5. sattvaṃ rajas tama iti guṇāḥ prakṛtisaṃbhavāḥ
   nibadhnanti mahābāho dehe dehinam avyayam
6. tatra sattvaṃ nirmalatvāt prakāśakam anāmayam
   sukhasaṅgena badhnāti jñānasaṅgena cānagha
7. rajo rāgātmakaṃ viddhi tṛṣṇāsaṅgasamudbhavam
   tan nibadhnāti kaunteya karmasaṅgena dehinam

CHAPTER 14

The Yoga of the Distinction between the Triple Qualities

The Blessed Lord said:

14.1 I shall again proclaim the unexcelled knowledge, best of [all] kinds-of-knowledge, knowing which all the sages have gone hence to highest perfection.

14.2 Having resorted to this knowledge and reached identity[1] with Me, they are not born [again] even at [the time of a new] creation, nor [need] they tremble at [the time of] dissolution [of the Cosmos].

14.3 The great world-ground[2] is My womb. In it I plant the fetus; from that comes the birth of all beings, O descendant-of-Bharata.

14.4 Whatever forms are born in any womb, O son-of-Kuntī,[3] of those [forms] the great world-ground is the womb, and I am the father [who] gives the seed.

14.5 *Sattva, rajas,* and *tamas*[4]—the [three] primary-qualities born of the Cosmos, fasten the immutable body-essence (*dehin*) to the body, O mighty-armed [Arjuna].

14.6 Of these, *sattva* because of its immaculateness is illuminating [and] without ill. It binds, [however,] by [subtle] attachment to joy and by attachment to knowledge, O Anagha.[5]

14.7 Know that *rajas* is of the nature of passion, produced from thirst[6] and attachment. It binds, O son-of-Kuntī, the body-essence by attachment to action.

1. The term *sādharmya,* here rendered as "identity," means more literally "that-which-is-with-the-[same]-law."
2. On "*brahman*" designating the world-ground, see note 66 for 2.72.
3. On son-of-Kuntī (Kaunteya), see note 19 for 1.27.
4. On the primary-qualities (*guna*), see note 44 for 2.45.
5. On Arjuna's epithet Anagha, see note 4 for 3.3.
6. "Thirst" (*trishnā*) is another term for craving for sensual pleasure, or *kāma*.

तमस्त्वज्ञानजं विद्धि मोहनं सर्वदेहिनाम् ।
प्रमादालस्यनिद्राभिस्तन्निबध्नाति भारत ॥ १४—८ ॥
सत्त्वं सुखे सञ्जयति रजः कर्मणि भारत ।
ज्ञानमावृत्य तु तमः प्रमादे सञ्जयत्युत ॥ १४—९ ॥
रजस्तमश्चाभिभूय सत्त्वं भवति भारत ।
रजः सत्त्वं तमश्चैव तमः सत्त्वं रजस्तथा ॥ १४—१० ॥
सर्वद्वारेषु देहेऽस्मिन्प्रकाश उपजायते ।
ज्ञानं यदा तदा विद्याद्विवृद्धं सत्त्वमित्युत ॥ १४—११ ॥
लोभः प्रवृत्तिरारम्भः कर्मणामशमः स्पृहा ।
रजस्येतानि जायन्ते विवृद्धे भरतर्षभ ॥ १४—१२ ॥
अप्रकाशोऽप्रवृत्तिश्च प्रमादो मोह एव च ।
तमस्येतानि जायन्ते विवृद्धे कुरुनन्दन ॥ १४—१३ ॥
यदा सत्त्वे प्रवृद्धे तु प्रलयं याति देहभृत् ।
तदोत्तमविदां लोकानमलान्प्रतिपद्यते ॥ १४—१४ ॥

8. tamas tv ajñānajaṃ viddhi mohanaṃ sarvadehinām
pramādālasyanidrābhis tan nibadhnāti bhārata
9. sattvaṃ sukhe sañjayati rajaḥ karmaṇi bhārata
jñānam āvṛtya tu tamaḥ pramāde sañjayaty uta
10. rajas tamaś cābhibhūya sattvaṃ bhavati bhārata
rajaḥ sattvaṃ tamaś caiva tamaḥ sattvaṃ rajas tathā
11. sarvadvāreṣu dehe'smin prakāśa upajāyate
jñānaṃ yadā tadā vidyād vivṛddhaṃ sattvam ity uta
12. lobhaḥ pravṛttir ārambhaḥ karmaṇām aśamaḥ spṛhā
rajasy etāni jāyante vivṛddhe bharatarṣabha
13. aprakāśo'pravṛttiś ca pramādo moha eva ca
tamasy etāni jāyante vivṛddhe kurunandana
14. yadā sattve pravṛddhe tu pralayaṃ yāti dehabhṛt
tadottamavidāṃ lokān amalān pratipadyate

14.8 But know that *tamas* is born of [spiritual] ignorance, deluding all body-essences. It binds, O descendant-of-Bharata, by heedlessness, indolence, and sleep.

14.9 *Sattva* attaches [a person] to joy; *rajas* to action; but knowledge-veiling *tamas* attaches [him] to heedlessness, O descendant-of-Bharata.

14.10 [When] *rajas* and *tamas* are overpowered, *sattva* becomes [strong], O descendant-of-Bharata. And thus also *rajas* [when] *sattva* and *tamas* [are overpowered], as well as *tamas* [when] *sattva* and *rajas* [are overpowered].

14.11 [When] luminosity, [which is] knowledge,[7] appears at all gates of this body, then [a *yogin*] should know that *sattva* has increased.

14.12 Greed, activity, [selfish] undertaking of actions, unrest, and desire—these arise from *rajas* [when it] increases, O Bharatarshabha.[8]

14.13 Lack-of-luminosity and inactivity, [as well as] heedlessness and also delusion—these arise from *tamas* [when it] increases, O Kurunandana.[9]

14.14 But when the body-wearer goes to [personal] dissolution [i.e., experiences death] when *sattva* has increased, then he enters the undefiled worlds of the knowers of the Supreme.

7. Many translators interpret the phrase *prakāsha upajāyate jñānam yadā* as "when the light of knowledge . . ." Edgerton (1944) gives "an illumination . . . which is knowledge." Hill (1928/1966) gives "When . . . knowledge is as light. . . ."

8. On Bharatarshabha, see note 48 for 3.41.

9. On Kurunandana, see note 40 for 2.41.

रजसि प्रलयं गत्वा कर्मसङ्गिषु जायते ।
तथा प्रलीनस्तमसि मूढयोनिषु जायते ॥ १४—१५ ॥
कर्मणः सुकृतस्याहुः सात्त्विकं निर्मलं फलम् ।
रजसस्तु फलं दुःखमज्ञानं तमसः फलम् ॥ १४—१६ ॥
सत्त्वात्संजायते ज्ञानं रजसो लोभ एव च ।
प्रमादमोहौ तमसो भवतोऽज्ञानमेव च ॥ १४—१७ ॥
ऊर्ध्वं गच्छन्ति सत्त्वस्था मध्ये तिष्ठन्ति राजसाः ।
जघन्यगुणवृत्तिस्था अधो गच्छन्ति तामसाः ॥ १४—१८ ॥
नान्यं गुणेभ्यः कर्तारं यदा द्रष्टानुपश्यति ।
गुणेभ्यश्च परं वेत्ति मद्भावं सोऽधिगच्छति ॥१४—१९ ॥
गुणानेतानतीत्य त्रीन्देही देहसमुद्भवान् ।
जन्ममृत्युजरादुःखैर्विमुक्तोऽमृतमश्नुते ॥ १४—२० ॥
अर्जुन उवाच
कैर्लिङ्गैस्त्रीन्गुणानेतानतीतो भवति प्रभो ।
किमाचारः कथं चैतांस्त्रीन्गुणानतिवर्तते ॥ १४—२१

15. rajasi pralayaṃ gatvā karmasaṅgiṣu jāyate
tathā pralīnas tamasi mūḍhayoniṣu jāyate
16. karmaṇaḥ sukṛtasyāhuḥ sāttvikaṃ nirmalaṃ phalam
rajasas tu phalaṃ duḥkham ajñānaṃ tamasaḥ phalam
17. sattvāt saṃjāyate jñānaṃ rajaso lobha eva ca
pramādamohau tamaso bhavato'jñānam eva ca
18. ūrdhvaṃ gacchanti sattvasthā madhye tiṣṭhanti rājasāḥ.
jaghanyaguṇavṛttisthā adho gacchanti tāmasāḥ
19. nānyaṃ guṇebhyaḥ kartāraṃ yadā draṣṭānupaśyati
guṇebhyaś ca paraṃ vetti madbhāvaṃ so'dhigacchati
20. guṇān etān atītya trīn dehī dehasamudbhavān
janmamṛtyujarāduḥkhair vimukto'mṛtam aśnute

arjuna uvāca
21. kair liṅgais trīn guṇān etān atīto bhavati prabho
kimācāraḥ kathaṃ caitāṃs trīn guṇān ativartate

14.15 [When the body-wearer] meets with dissolution [i.e., death] when *rajas* [is dominant, then he] is born among [those who are] action-attached. Similarly, [when the body-wearer] is dissolved [i.e., dies] when *tamas* [is prevalent, then he] is born in the wombs [of those who are] deluded.

14.16 The fruit of well-done action, they say, [is] *sattva*-natured [and] undefiled. But the fruit of *rajas* is suffering, and the fruit of *tamas* is ignorance.

14.17 From *sattva* arises knowledge and from *rajas* greed, [while] heedlessness, delusion, as well as ignorance come from *tamas*.

14.18 [Those who] abide in *sattva* go upward. The rajasic stay in the middle, and the tamasic, [who are] established in the lowest mode of the primary-qualities, go downward.

14.19 When the seer [i.e., the witnessing aspect of the mind] sees [that there is] no agent other than the primary-qualities and [when the *yogin*] knows [that which is] beyond the primary-qualities—[then] he attains to My state-of-being.

14.20 Transcending these three primary-qualities, [which] produce the body, the body-essence (*dehin*)—freed from birth, death, old age, and suffering—gains immortality.[10]

Arjuna said:

14.21 By what signs is he-who-transcends these primary-qualities [recognized], O Lord? What [is his] behavior? How does he pass beyond these three primary-qualities?

10. The body-essence (*dehin*), or Self, is already immortal. This stanza is therefore often regarded as one of the *Gītā*'s self-contradictory statements, but we have here simply an instance of popular language.

श्रीभगवानुवाच
प्रकाशं च प्रवृत्तिं च मोहमेव च पाण्डव ।
न द्वेष्टि संप्रवृत्तानि न निवृत्तानि काङ्क्षति ॥ १४—२२ ॥
उदासीनवदासीनो गुणैर्यो न विचाल्यते ।
गुणा वर्तन्त इत्येव योऽवतिष्ठति नेङ्गते ॥ १४—२३ ॥
समदुःखसुखः स्वस्थः समलोष्टाश्मकाञ्चनः ।
तुल्यप्रियाप्रियो धीरस्तुल्यनिन्दात्मसंस्तुतिः ॥ १४—२४ ॥
मानावमानयोस्तुल्यस्तुल्यो मित्रारिपक्षयोः ।
सर्वारम्भपरित्यागी गुणातीतः स उच्यते ॥ १४—२५ ॥
मां च योऽव्यभिचारेण भक्तियोगेन सेवते ।
स गुणान्समतीत्यैतान्ब्रह्मभूयाय कल्पते ॥ १४—२६ ॥
ब्रह्मणो हि प्रतिष्ठाहममृतस्याव्ययस्य च ।
शाश्वतस्य च धर्मस्य सुखस्यैकान्तिकस्य च ॥ १४—२७ ॥

śrībhagavān uvāca
22. prakāśaṃ ca pravṛttiṃ ca moham eva ca pāṇḍava
na dveṣṭi saṃpravṛttāni na nivṛttāni kāṅkṣati
23. udāsīnavad āsīno guṇair yo na vicālyate
guṇā vartanta ity eva yo'vatiṣṭhati neṅgate
24. samaduḥkhasukhaḥ svasthaḥ samaloṣṭāśmakāñcanaḥ
tulyapriyāpriyo dhīras tulyanindātmasaṃstutiḥ
25. mānāvamānayos tulyas tulyo mitrāripakṣayoḥ
sarvārambhaparityāgī guṇātītaḥ sa ucyate
26. māṃ ca yo'vyabhicāreṇa bhaktiyogena sevate
sa guṇān samatītyaitān brahmabhūyāya kalpate
27. brahmaṇo hi pratiṣṭhāham amṛtasyāvyayasya ca
śāśvatasya ca dharmasya sukhasyaikāntikasya ca

The Blessed Lord said:

14.22 Illumination and activity and delusion—[when they] arise, he hates [them] not; [when they] cease, he hankers not after [them], O son-of-Pāndu.[11]

14.23 He who is seated like an indifferent[12] [person] is not perturbed by the primary-qualities. "The primary-qualities revolve [of their own accord]"—thus [thinks he] who stands-aloof and does not stir.

14.24 [He is] the same in pleasure [and] pain, self-reliant, the same [toward] a clod-of-earth, stone or gold, equal [-minded] toward dear and unpleasant [things], steadfast, equal [-minded] toward blame or praise [showered on] him.

14.25 Equal [-minded] in honor and dishonor; equal [-minded] toward the sides of friend or enemy; a renouncer of all undertakings—he is called [one who has] transcended the primary-qualities (*gunātīta*).

14.26 And he who serves Me with the unfailing Yoga of devotion, having transcended these primary-qualities, is fit to become the world-ground.

14.27 For, I am the foundation of the world-ground, of the immortal and immutable, of the everlasting law, and of singular joy.[13]

11. On son-of-Pāndu (Pāndava), see note 61 for 10.37.

12. This attitude is one of spiritual indifference rather than noncaring. See also 9.9.

13. Here Krishna reiterates his earlier statement that he is above the world-ground (*brahman*). See also note 66 for 2.72.

श्रीभगवानुवाच
ऊर्ध्वमूलमधःशाखमश्वत्थं प्राहुरव्ययम् ।
छन्दांसि यस्य पर्णानि यस्तं वेद स वेदवित् ॥ १५—१ ॥
अधश्चोर्ध्वं प्रसृतस्तस्य शाखा
गुणप्रवृद्धा विषयप्रवालाः ।
अधश्च मूलान्यनुसंततानि
कर्मानुबन्धीनि मनुष्यलोके ॥ १५—२ ॥
न रूपमस्येह तथोपलभ्यते ।
नान्तो न चादिर्न च संप्रतिष्ठा
अश्वत्थमेनं सुविरूढमूल
मसङ्गशस्त्रेण दृढेन छित्त्वा ॥ १५—३ ॥
ततः पदं तत्परिमार्गितव्यं
यस्मिन्गता न विर्तन्ति भूयः ।
तमेव चाद्यं पुरुषं प्रपद्ये
यतः प्रवृत्तिः प्रसृता पुराणी ॥ १५—४ ॥

śrībhagavān uvāca

1. ūrdhvamūlam adhaḥśākham aśvatthaṃ prāhur avyayam
   chandāṃsi yasya parṇāni yas taṃ veda sa vedavit
2. adhaś cordhvaṃ prasṛtas tasya śākhā
   guṇapravṛddhā viṣayapravālāḥ
   adhaś ca mūlāny anusaṃtatāni
   karmānubandhīni manuṣyaloke
3. na rūpam asyeha tathopalabhyate
   nānto na cādir na ca saṃpratiṣṭhā
   aśvattham enaṃ suvirūḍhamūla-
   masaṅgaśastreṇa dṛḍhena chittvā
4. tataḥ padaṃ tat parimārgitavyaṃ
   yasmin gatā na nivartanti bhūyaḥ
   tam eva cādyaṃ puruṣaṃ prapadye
   yataḥ pravṛttiḥ prasṛtā purāṇī

CHAPTER 15

The Yoga of the Supreme Person

The Blessed Lord said:

15.1 The immutable *ashvattha* [tree],[1] they say, [has its] roots above and [its] branches below, and its leaves are the [Vedic] hymns—he who knows this, he is a Veda-knower.

15.2 Its branches, spreading out below and above, are nourished by the primary-qualities; the objects [are] the twigs, and below in the human world the roots proliferate, action-linked.[2]

15.3 Its form is not thus perceived here [in the world], nor [its] end, nor [its] beginning, nor [its] foundation. Having felled this *ashvattha* [tree] of well-developed roots with the firm weapon of nonattachment,[3]

15.4 then that state is to be tracked from which [those who have] reached [it] do not return again. And I go-for-refuge verily to that primordial Spirit whence flowed forth the ancient creativity.

1. The *ashvattha* tree, mentioned earlier, in 10.26 (see note 31 to that verse), is an ancient symbol of the world of change, *samsāra*. See *Rig-Veda* 1.24.7 and *Katha-Upanishad* 6.1. Compare *Chāndogya-Upanishad* 6.11. Hill (1928/1966) makes some interesting remarks on this tree: "It does not, like its cousin the banyan, drop aerial rootlets to take fresh root in the earth. Why, then, is it said to have roots above and branches below? [See *Gītā* 15.1.] The formation of the tree is peculiar, in that its roots (which often stand in part above the ground) do not altogether, as in other trees, lose themselves in a central rounded trunk, but to a great extent retaining their separate form, climb up in a cluster, each to spread out into a separate branch. Each root is thus continuous with its own branch; and therefore, root and branch being inseparably one, it is possible to speak of the branch as descending to the earth, and of the root as rising aloft."
2. The expression "action-linked" (*karma-anubandhīni*) refers to the fact that the root of *samsāra* is karmic interconnectedness. Stanzas 15.2–5 are in the *trishtubh* meter.
3. The first line of this stanza has an extra syllable.

निर्मानमोह जितासङ्गदोषा
अध्यात्मनित्या विनिवृत्तकामाः ।
द्वन्द्वैर्विमुक्ताः सुखदुःखसंज्ञै
र्गच्छन्त्यमूढाः पदमव्ययं तत् ॥ १५—५ ॥
न तद्भासयते सूर्यो न शशाङ्को न पावकः ।
यद्गत्वा न निवर्तन्ते तद्धाम परमं मम ॥ १५—६ ॥
ममैवांशो जीवलोके जीवभूतः सनातनः ।
मनःषष्ठानीन्द्रियाणि प्रकृतिस्थानि कर्षति ॥ १५—७ ॥
शरीरं यदवाप्नोति यच्चाप्युत्क्रामतीश्वरः ।
गृहीत्वैतानि संयाति वायुर्गन्धानिवाशयात् ॥ १५—८ ॥
श्रोत्रं चक्षुः स्पर्शनं च रसनं घ्राणमेव च ।
अधिष्ठाय मनश्चायं विषयानुपसेवते ॥ १५—९ ॥
उत्क्रामन्तं स्थितं वापि भुञ्जानं वा गुणान्वितम् ।
विमूढा नानुपश्यन्ति पश्यन्ति ज्ञानचक्षुषः ॥ १५—१० ॥
यतन्तो योगिनश्चैनं पश्यन्त्यात्मन्यवस्थितम् ।
यतन्तोऽप्यकृतात्मानो नैनं पश्यन्त्यचेतसः ॥ १५—११ ॥

5. nirmānamohā jitasaṅgadoṣā
adhyātmanityā vinivṛttakāmāḥ
dvandvair vimuktāḥ sukhaduḥkhasaṃjñai-
rgacchanty amūḍhāḥ padam avyayaṃ tat
6. na tad bhāsayate sūryo na śaśāṅko na pāvakaḥ
yad gatvā na nivartante tad dhāma paramaṃ mama
7. mamaivāṃśo jīvaloke jīvabhūtaḥ sanātanaḥ
manaḥṣaṣṭhānīndriyāṇi prakṛtisthāni karṣati
8. śarīraṃ yad avāpnoti yac cāpy utkrāmatīśvaraḥ
gṛhītvaitāni saṃyāti vāyur gandhān ivāśayāt
9. śrotraṃ cakṣuḥ sparśanaṃ ca rasanaṃ ghrāṇam eva ca
adhiṣṭhāya manaś cāyaṃ viṣayān upasevate
10. utkrāmantaṃ sthitaṃ vāpi bhuñjānaṃ vā guṇānvitam
vimūḍhā nānupaśyanti paśyanti jñānacakṣuṣaḥ
11. yatanto yoginaś cainaṃ paśyanty ātmany avasthitam
yatanto'py akṛtātmāno nainaṃ paśyanty acetasaḥ

15.5 [Those who are] without pride and delusion, [who have] vanquished [all] blemish of attachment, ever [abiding in] the basis-of-self, [who have] stilled [all] desires, [and who are] freed from the pairs-of-opposites known as pleasure and pain—they go, undeluded, to that immutable state.

15.6 The sun does not illuminate that [state], nor the moon,[4] nor fire. That is My supreme abode from which, once reached, they do not return.

15.7 Only a fragment of Myself, the everlasting life-element in the world of the living, attracts [to itself a particular set of] senses, [of which] the mind [is] the sixth,[5] abiding in the Cosmos (*prakriti*).

15.8 Whatever body the lord[6] takes on and from whatever [body] he rises [again]—having seized these [senses together with the mind], he moves about [with them] even as the wind [carries] scents from [their] place-of-origin [to elsewhere].

15.9 Employing hearing, seeing, touch, taste, and smell as well as the mind—this [embodied Self] indulges in the objects [of the senses].

15.10 Endowed with the primary-qualities (*guna*), [the embodied Self] rises [from the body], or abides [in it], or enjoys [objects]—[this] the deluded do not see, [but] the knowledge-eyed[7] see [it].

15.11 And the striving *yogins* behold him [the lord of the body] as established in the Self, but the unintelligent of unperfected self, though striving, see him not.[8]

4. The term used here for the moon is "rabbit-marked" (*shashānka*). What in the West is called "the man in the moon," Indians (and other Asians) regard as a rabbit.

5. The expression *jīva-bhūta*, here rendered as "life element," is the Self immanent in the manifested world. It is an aspect of the Divine that is higher than the world-ground (Brahman). See note 3 for 7.5.

6. Sometimes the lower mind (*manas*) is regarded as the eleventh sense, depending on whether the five conative senses (*karmendriya*) are included in the enumeration. See note 13 for 3.6.

7. Here the term "lord" (*īshvara*) appears to refer to the embodied Self, not the Ultimate Person (*purushottama*), or the Divine.

8. The expression *jnāna-cakshushah* ("knowledge-eyed") characterizes those who are endowed with Yoga's wisdom. The phrase is identical with *divya-cakshus* (the "divine eye" in 11.8).

यदादित्यगतं तेजो जगद्भासयतेऽखिलम् ।
यच्चन्द्रमसि यच्चाग्नौ तत्तेजो विद्धि मामकम् ॥ १५—१२ ॥
गामाविश्य च भूतानि धारयाम्यहमोजसा ।
पुष्णामि चौषधीः सर्वाः सोमो भूत्वा रसात्मकः ॥ १५—१३ ॥
अहं वैश्वानरो भूत्वा प्राणिनां देहमाश्रितः ।
प्राणापानसमायुक्तः पचाम्यन्नं चतुर्विधम् ॥ १५—१४ ॥
सर्वस्य चाहं हृदि संनिविष्टो
मत्तः स्मृतिर्ज्ञानमपोहनं च ।
वेदैश्च सर्वैरहमेव वेद्यो
वेदान्तकृद्वेदविदेव चाहम् ॥ १५—१५ ॥
द्वाविमौ पुरुषौ लोके क्षरश्चाक्षर एव च ।
क्षरः सर्वाणि भूतानि कूटस्थोऽक्षर उच्यते ॥ १५—१६ ॥
उत्तमः पुरुषस्त्वन्यः परमात्मेत्युदाहृतः ।
यो लोकत्रयमाविश्य बिभर्त्यव्यय ईश्वरः ॥ १५—१७ ॥
यस्मात्क्षरमतीतोऽहमक्षरादपि चोत्तमः ।
अतोऽस्मि लोके वेदे च प्रथितः पुरुषोत्तमः ॥ १५—१८ ॥

12. yad ādityagataṃ tejo jagad bhāsayate'khilam
yac candramasi yac cāgnau tat tejo viddhi māmakam
13. gām āviśya ca bhūtāni dhārayāmy aham ojasā
puṣṇāmi cauṣadhīḥ sarvāḥ somo bhūtvā rasātmakaḥ
14. ahaṃ vaiśvānaro bhūtvā prāṇināṃ deham āśritaḥ
prāṇāpānasamāyuktaḥ pacāmy annaṃ caturvidham
15. sarvasya cāhaṃ hṛdi saṃniviṣṭo
mattaḥ smṛtir jñanam apohanaṃ ca
vedaiś ca sarvair aham eva vedyo
vedāntakṛd vedavid eva cāham
16. dvāv imau puruṣau loke kṣaraś cākṣara eva ca
kṣaraḥ sarvāṇi bhūtāni kūṭastho'kṣara ucyate
17. uttamaḥ puruṣas tv anyaḥ paramātmety udāhṛtaḥ
yo lokatrayam āviśya bibharty avyaya īśvaraḥ
18. yasmāt kṣaram atīto'ham akṣarād api cottamaḥ
ato'smi loke vede ca prathitaḥ puruṣottamaḥ

15.12 The brilliance which has entered the sun [and] which illuminates the entire universe, which is in the moon, and which is in fire—that brilliance know as Mine.

15.13 And penetrating the earth,[9] I support [all] beings by [My] vitality, and becoming *soma*[10] of the nature of ambrosial-rain, I nourish all herbs.

15.14 Becoming the *vaishvānara*[11] [fire] situated in the body of living [beings], I, conjoined with the in-breath (*prāna*) and out-breath (*apāna*), "cook"[12] the fourfold food.[13]

15.15 And I am lodged in the heart of all [beings]. From Me [come] memory, knowledge, and reasoning, and I am [that which is] to be known by all the Vedas. I am [also] the maker of Vedas'-end[14] and the Veda-knower.[15]

15.16 Two Spirits (*purusha*) are in this world, the perishable and the imperishable. The perishable [Spirit] is all beings; the imperishable [Spirit] is called "summit-abiding."[16]

15.17 But other [than these two] is the unexcelled Spirit named the supreme Self who, penetrating the three worlds, supports [them] as the immutable Lord.

15.18 Since I transcend the perishable and am even higher than the imperishable, therefore I am extolled in the world and in the *Vedas* as Purushottama.[17]

9. Here the rare word *gā* is used for the Earth, which Shankara equates with *prithivī*.

10. Following Shankara, I take the word *soma* to refer not to the soma plant, which played a key role in Vedic ritualism, but to the moon, which is traditionally believed to be associated with rain and fertility. Thus, the moon's "essence" (*rasa*) would be rain. Shankara speaks of the moon as being of the "form of all essences" (*sarvarasānām ākārah*).

11. The *vaishvānara* is the digestive "fire" of the stomach.

12. Here the expression "I cook" (*pacāmi*) has the meaning of "I digest."

13. According to Hill (1928/1966), the four kinds of food are nourishment that is masticated, swallowed or drunk, sucked, or licked.

14. Hill (1928/1966) notes that the term *vedānta*, here rendered as "Vedas'-end," probably refers to the Upanishads. Some scholars think that this verse is an interpolation. In any case, the reference cannot be to the full-fledged Vedānta system as we know it from Shankara and others.

15. This stanza is in the *trishtubh* meter.

16. On the term *kutastha* ("summit-abiding"), see note 7 for 6.8.

17. On Purushottama, see note 3 for 11.3.

यो मामेवमसंमूढो जानाति पुरुषोत्तमम् ।
स सर्वविद्भजति मां सर्वभावेन भारत ॥ १५—१९ ॥
इति गुह्यतमं शास्त्रमिदमुक्तं मयानघ ।
एतद्बुद्ध्वा बुद्धिमान्स्यात्कृतकृत्यश्च भारत ॥ १५—२० ॥

19. yo mām evam asaṃmūḍho jānāti puruṣottamam
sa sarvavid bhajati māṃ sarvabhāvena bhārata
20. iti guhyatamaṃ śāstram idam uktaṃ mayānagha
etad buddhvā buddhimān syāt kṛtakṛtyaś ca bhārata

15.19 Who thus knows Me, undeluded, as Purushottama—he,
all-knowing, worships Me with all [his] being (*bhāva*),
O descendant-of-Bharata.

15.20 Thus, this most secret teaching was declared by Me, O Anagha.[18]
Knowing this, [a person] will become wise and work-fulfilled,[19]
O descendant-of-Bharata.

18. On Arjuna's epithet Anagha, see note 4 for 3.3.

19. The expression *krita-kritya* ("work-fulfilled") describes a person who has discharged all obligations. This implies that the *yogin* transcends the realm of "ought" and "ought not" and performs all actions out of spontaneity. See 3.22.

श्रीभगवानुवाच
अभयं सत्त्वसंशुद्धिर्ज्ञानयोगव्यवस्थितिः ।
दानं दमश्च यज्ञश्च स्वाध्यायस्तप आर्जवम् ॥ १६—१ ॥
अहिंसा सत्यमक्रोधस्त्यागः शान्तिरपैशुनं ।
दया भूतेष्वलोलुप्त्वं मार्दवं ह्रीरचापलम् ॥ १६—२ ॥
तेजः क्षमा धृतिः शौचमद्रोहो नातिमानिता ।
भवन्ति संपदं दैवीमभिजातस्य भारत ॥ १६—३ ॥
दम्भो दर्पोऽतिमानश्च क्रोधः पारुष्यमेव च ।
अज्ञानं चाभिजातस्य पार्थ संपदमासुरीम् ॥ १६—४ ॥
दैवी संपद्विमोक्षाय निबन्धायासुरी मता ।
मा शुचः संपदं दैवीमभिजातोऽसि पाण्डव ॥ १६—५ ॥
द्वौ भूतसर्गौ लोकेऽस्मिन्दैव आसुर एव च ।
दैवो विस्तरशः प्रोक्त आसुरं पार्थ मे शृणु ॥ १६—६ ॥
प्रवृत्तिं च निवृत्तिं च जना न विदुरासुराः ।
न शौचं नापि चाचारो न सत्यं तेषु विद्यते ॥ १६—७ ॥

śrībhagavān uvāca

1. abhayaṃ sattvasaṃśuddhir jñānayogavyavasthitiḥ
   dānaṃ damaś ca yajñaś ca svādhyāyas tapa ārjavam
2. ahiṃsā satyam akrodhas tyāgaḥ śāntir apaiśunaṃ
   dayā bhūteṣv aloluptvaṃ mārdavaṃ hrīr acāpalam
3. tejaḥ kṣamā dhṛtiḥ śaucam adroho nātimānitā
   bhavanti saṃpadaṃ daivīm abhijātasya bhārata
4. dambho darpo'timānaś ca krodhaḥ pāruṣyam eva ca
   ajñānaṃ cābhijātasya pārtha saṃpadam āsurīm
5. daivī saṃpad vimokṣāya nibandhāyāsurī matā
   mā śucaḥ saṃpadaṃ daivīm abhijāto'si pāṇḍava
6. dvau bhūtasargau loke'smin daiva āsura eva ca
   daivo vistaraśaḥ prokta āsuraṃ pārtha me śṛṇu
7. pravṛttiṃ ca nivṛttiṃ ca janā na vidur āsurāḥ
   na śaucaṃ nāpi cācāro na satyaṃ teṣu vidyate

CHAPTER 16

The Yoga of the Distinction between the Divine and Demoniac Destiny

The Blessed Lord said:

16.1 Fearlessness, purity of *sattva*, steadfastness in the Yoga of knowledge, charity, restraint and sacrifice, study (*svādhyāya*), austerity, uprightness,

16.2 nonharming, truthfulness, absence-of-anger, relinquishment, peace, nonslandering, kindness toward [all] beings, nongreediness, gentleness, modesty, absence-of-haste,

16.3 vigor (*tejas*), patience, fortitude, purity, absence-of-malice, [and having] no excessive-pride—[these] are [the endowments] of [him who] is born to a divine destiny, O descendant-of-Bharata.

16.4 Ostentation, arrogance and excessive-conceit, anger as well as harshness and ignorance—[these are] the endowment of [him who] is born to a demonic destiny, O son-of-Prithā.[1]

16.5 The divine destiny is considered [to lead] to liberation, the demonic [destiny] to bondage. Do not grieve! You are born to a divine destiny, O son-of-Pāndu.[2]

16.6 Two [types of] beings have been created in this world—the divine and also the demonic. The divine [I have already] proclaimed extensively. Hear from Me [now] about the demonic [beings], O son-of-Prithā.

16.7 The demonic people do not know [the paths of] activity and cessation.[3] Neither purity nor good-conduct nor truthfulness is found in them.

1. On son-of-Prithā (Pārtha), see note 18 for 1.25.

2. On son-of-Pāndu (Pāndava), see note 61 for 10.37.

3. The terms *pravritti* ("activity") and *nivritti* ("cessation") together usually refer to mundane activity and withdrawal from life respectively. (See also 18.30.) But they can also have a cosmological significance, namely, "creation" and "dissolution."

असत्यमप्रतिष्ठं ते जगदाहुरनीश्वरम् ।
अपरस्परसंभूतं किमन्यत्कामहैतुकम् ॥ १६—८ ॥
एतां दृष्टिमवष्टभ्य नष्टात्मानोऽल्पबुद्धयः ।
प्रभवन्त्युग्रकर्माणः क्षयाय जगतोऽहिताः ॥ १६—९ ॥
काममाश्रित्य दुष्पूरं दम्भमानमदान्विताः ।
मोहाद्गृहीत्वाऽसद्ग्राहान्प्रवर्तन्तेऽशुचिव्रताः ॥ १६—१० ॥
चिन्तामपरिमेयां च प्रलयान्तामुपाश्रिताः ।
कामोपभोगपरमा एतावदिति निश्चिताः ॥ १६—११ ॥
आशापाशशतैर्बद्धाः कामक्रोधपरायणाः ।
ईहन्ते कामभोगार्थमन्यायेनार्थसंचयान् ॥ १६—१२ ॥
इदमद्य मया लब्धमिमं प्राप्स्ये मनोरथम् ।
इदमस्तीदमपि मे भविष्यति पुनर्धनम् ॥ १६—१३ ॥
असौ मया हतः शत्रुर्हनिष्ये चापरानपि ।
ईश्वरोऽहमहं भोगी सिद्धोऽहं बलवान्सुखी ॥ १६—१४ ॥
आढ्योऽभिजनवानस्मि कोऽन्योऽस्ति सदृशो मया ।
यक्ष्ये दास्यामि मोदिष्य इत्यज्ञानविमोहिताः ॥ १६—१५ ॥

8. asatyam apratiṣṭhaṃ te jagad āhur anīśvaram
aparasparasaṃbhūtaṃ kim anyat kāmahaitukam
9. etāṃ dṛṣṭim avaṣṭabhya naṣṭātmāno'lpabuddhayaḥ
prabhavanty ugrakarmāṇaḥ kṣayāya jagato'hitāḥ
10. kāmam āśritya duṣpūraṃ dambhamānamadānvitāḥ
mohād gṛhītvā'sadgrāhān pravartante'śucivratāḥ
11. cintām aparimeyāṃ ca pralayāntām upāśritāḥ
kāmopabhogaparamā etāvad iti niścitāḥ
12. āśāpāśaśatair baddhāḥ kāmakrodhaparāyaṇāḥ
īhante kāmabhogārtham anyāyenārthasaṃcayān
13. idam adya mayā labdham imaṃ prāpsye manoratham
idam astīdam api me bhaviṣyati punar dhanam
14. asau mayā hataḥ śatrur haniṣye cāparān api
īśvaro'ham ahaṃ bhogī siddho'haṃ balavān sukhī
15. āḍhyo'bhijanavān asmi ko'nyo'sti sadṛśo mayā
yakṣye dāsyāmi modiṣya ity ajñānavimohitāḥ

16.8 They say: "The universe is without truth, without foundation, without a lord, not produced in sequence; what else [is it but] caused by desire?"

16.9 Holding this view, [these] lost selves of little wisdom (*buddhi*) and cruel deeds, come forth as enemies for the destruction of the world.

16.10 Depending on insatiable desire, possessed of ostentation, pride, [and] intoxication, holding untrue conceptions through delusion, they practice impure vows.

16.11 And obsessed with innumerable cares ending [only] with dissolution [at death], [having] the gratification of desires as [their] supreme [goal]—[they are] convinced that this [is all].

16.12 Bound by hundreds of cords of hope, addicted to desire [and] anger, they seek to amass riches by unjust means, with the [sole] purpose of gratifying [their] desires.

16.13 "This has been gained by me today"—"I shall fulfill this 'mind-chariot'"[4]—"This is [now] mine, and this wealth shall also [be mine]"—

16.14 "That enemy is slain by me, and I shall slay [many] others"—"I am the lord"—"I am the enjoyer"—"I am the perfected-one, mighty and happy"—

16.15 "I am rich, well born"—"Who else is like me?"—"I shall sacrifice, I shall be charitable, and I shall rejoice!"—Thus [say those who are] deluded by ignorance.

4. The expression *manoratha* ("mind-chariot") stands for "fancy" or "fantasy."

अनेकचित्तविभ्रान्ता मोहजालसमावृताः ।
प्रसक्ताः कामभोगेषु पतन्ति नरकेऽशुचौ ॥ १६—१६ ॥
आत्मसंभाविताः स्तब्धा धनमानमदान्विताः ।
यजन्ते नामयज्ञैस्ते दम्भेनाविधिपूर्वकम् ॥ १६—१७ ॥
अहंकारं बलं दर्पं कामं क्रोधं च संश्रिताः ।
मामात्मपरदेहेषु प्रद्विषन्तोऽभ्यसूयकाः ॥ १६—१८ ॥
तानहं द्विषतः क्रूरान्संसारेषु नराधमान् ।
क्षिपाम्यजस्रमशुभानासुरीष्वेव योनिषु ॥ १६—१९ ॥
आसुरीं योनिमापन्ना मूढा जन्मनि जन्मनि ।
मामप्राप्यैव कौन्तेय ततो यान्त्यधमां गतिम् ॥ १६—२० ॥
त्रिविधं नरकस्येदं द्वारं नाशनमात्मनः ।
कामः क्रोधस्तथा लोभस्तस्मादेतत्त्रयं त्यजेत् ॥ १६—२१ ॥
एतैर्विमुक्तः कौन्तेय तमोद्वारैस्त्रिभिर्नरः ।
आचरत्यात्मनः श्रेयस्ततो याति परां गतिम् ॥ १६—२२ ॥
यः शास्त्रविधिमुत्सृज्य वर्तते कामकारतः ।
न स सिद्धिमवाप्नोति न सुखं न परां गतिम् ॥ १६—२३ ॥

16. anekacittavibhrāntā mohajālasamāvṛtāḥ
prasaktāḥ kāmabhogeṣu patanti narake'śucau
17. ātmasaṃbhāvitāḥ stabdhā dhanamānamadānvitāḥ
yajante nāmayajñais te dambhenāvidhipūrvakam
18. ahaṃkāraṃ balaṃ darpaṃ kāmaṃ krodhaṃ ca saṃśritāḥ
mām ātmaparadeheṣu pradviṣanto'bhyasūyakāḥ
19. tān ahaṃ dviṣataḥ krūrān saṃsāreṣu narādhamān
kṣipāmy ajasram aśubhān āsurīṣv eva yoniṣu
20. āsurīṃ yonim āpannā mūḍhā janmani janmani
mām aprāpyaiva kaunteya tato yānty adhamāṃ gatim
21. trividhaṃ narakasyedaṃ dvāraṃ nāśanam ātmanaḥ
kāmaḥ krodhas tathā lobhas tasmād etat trayaṃ tyajet
22. etair vimuktaḥ kaunteya tamodvārais tribhir naraḥ
ācaraty ātmanaḥ śreyas tato yāti parāṃ gatim
23. yaḥ śāstravidhim utsṛjya vartate kāmakārataḥ
na sa siddhim avāpnoti na sukhaṃ na parāṃ gatim

16.16 Led astray by many thoughts, entangled in a net of delusion, addicted to the gratification of desires—they fall into an impure hell.

16.17 Self-conceited, obstinate, full of intoxication [and] pride of wealth—they perform [merely] nominal (*nāma*) sacrifices with deceit [and] without following [proper] rules.

16.18 Clinging to the ego-sense, force, arrogance, desire, and anger—[these] detractors hate Me [who abide] in [their] own (*ātman*) [and] other bodies.

16.19 These cruel haters, lowest of men [and] inauspicious, I hurl incessantly [back] into the cycle [of birth and death and force them to take birth] in demonic wombs.

16.20 Fallen into demonic wombs, birth after birth deluded [and], verily, not reaching Me—[these unfortunate beings] thence tread the lowest course,[5] O son-of-Kuntī.[6]

16.21 Threefold is this gate of hell [leading to] self-destruction: desire, anger, as well as greed. Therefore one should abandon this triad.

16.22 The man [who is] released from these three gates of darkness pursues [what is] best for [him]self and thence treads the supreme course [to liberation].

16.23 He who, discarding the scriptural ordinance,[7] follows the prompting of [his] desires does not reach perfection, nor joy, nor the supreme course.

5. The lowest course is hell, as opposed to emancipation.

6. On son-of-Kuntī (Kaunteya), see note 19 for 1.27.

7. This term probably refers to both the Vedas and the Dharma-Shāstra (moral-legal) literature.

तस्माच्छास्त्रं प्रमाणं ते कार्याकार्यव्यवस्थितौ ।
ज्ञात्वा शास्त्रविधानोक्तं कर्म कर्तुमिहार्हसि ॥ १६—२४ ॥

24. tasmāc chāstraṃ pramāṇaṃ te kāryākāryavyavasthitau
jñātvā śāstravidhānoktaṃ karma kartum ihārhasi

16.24 Therefore, the standard of scripture [should guide] you in determining right[8] [and] wrong. Knowing [what is] said by scriptural injunction, you ought to perform [the allotted] action here [in this world].

8. The term *kārya* ("right") means literally "[what is] to be done."

अर्जुन उवाच
ये शास्त्रविधिमुत्सृज्य यजन्ते श्रद्धयान्विताः ।
तेषां निष्ठा तु का कृष्ण सत्त्वमाहो रजस्तमः ॥ १७—१ ॥
श्रीभगवानुवाच
त्रिविधा भवति श्रद्धा देहिनां सा स्वभावजा ।
सात्त्विकी राजसी चैव तामसी चेति तां श्रृणु ॥ १७—२ ॥
सत्त्वानुरूपा सर्वस्य श्रद्धा भवति भारत ।
श्रद्धामयोऽयं पुरूषो यो यच्छ्रद्धः स एव सः ॥ १७—३ ॥
यजन्ते सत्त्विका देवान्यक्षरक्षांसि राजसाः ।
प्रेतान्भूतगणांश्चान्ये यजन्ते तामसा जनाः ॥ १७—४ ॥

arjuna uvāca

1. ye śāstravidhim utsṛjya yajante śraddhayānvitāḥ
   teṣāṃ niṣṭhā tu kā kṛṣṇa sattvam āho rajas tamaḥ

   śrībhagavān uvāca

2. trividhā bhavati śraddhā dehināṃ sā svabhāvajā
   sāttvikī rājasī caiva tāmasī ceti tāṃ śṛṇu
3. sattvānurūpā sarvasya śraddhā bhavati bhārata
   śraddhāmayo'yaṃ puruṣo yo yacchraddhaḥ sa eva saḥ
4. yajante sāttvikā devān yakṣarakṣāṃsi rājasāḥ
   pretān bhūtagaṇāṃś cānye yajante tāmasā janāḥ

CHAPTER 17

The Yoga of Distinction between the Triple Faith

Arjuna said:

17.1 [Those] who sacrifice, discarding scriptural ordinance [yet are] endowed with faith—what is their way-of-life,[1] O Krishna? *Sattva, rajas,* or *tamas*?

The Blessed Lord said:

17.2 The faith of the body-essences (*dehin*) is threefold, born of [their] own-being: *sattva*-natured, *rajas*-natured, or *tamas*-natured. Hear [more about] this.

17.3 The faith of every [being] corresponds to his essence,[2] O descendant-of-Bharata. This [mortal] person (*purusha*) is of the form of faith. Whatever his faith is, that, verily, is he.

17.4 [Those who are] *sattva*-natured worship the gods. The *rajas*-natured [worship] the Yakshas[3] and Rākshasas.[4] And the others, the *tamas*-natured people, worship the departed[5] and the hosts of elementals.

1. The word *nishthā* also occurs in stanzas 3.3 and 18.50 (see note 30).

2. The Sanskrit text has *sattva,* here given as "essence." According to Abhinavagupta, the word is synonymous with *svabhāva.*

3. On the Yakshas, see note 22 for 10.23.

4. On the Rākshasas, see note 23 for 10.23.

5. The *pretas,* here rendered as "the departed," are what we might call "ghosts." Hill (1928/1966) gives this illuminating note: "A *preta* is generally supposed to be a departed spirit whose funeral ceremonies have not been properly completed or performed, and who consequently cannot become a *pitri* [ancestral spirit]; he is said to enter dead bodies and to haunt cemeteries and other place of ill-omen."

अशास्त्रविहितं घोरं तप्यन्ते ये तपो जनाः ।
दम्भाहंकारसंयुक्ताः कामरागबलान्विताः ॥ १७—५ ॥
कर्शयन्तः शरीरस्थं भूतग्राममचेतसः ।
मां चैवान्तःशरीरस्थं तान्विद्ध्यासुरनिश्चयान् ॥ १७—६ ॥
आहारस्त्वपि सर्वस्य त्रिविधो भवति प्रियः ।
यज्ञस्तपस्तथा दानं तेषां भेदमिमं शृणु ॥ १७—७ ॥
आयुःसत्त्वबलारोग्यसुखप्रीतिविवर्धनाः ।
रस्याः स्निग्धाः स्थिरा हृद्या आहाराः सात्त्विकप्रियाः ॥ १७—८ ॥
कट्वम्ललवणात्युष्णतीक्ष्णरूक्षविदाहिनः ।
आहारा राजसस्येष्टा दुःखशोकामयप्रदाः ॥ १७—९ ॥
यातयामं गतरसं पूति पर्युषितं च यत् ।
उच्छिष्टमपि चामेध्यं भोजनं तामसप्रियम् ॥ १७—१० ॥
अफलाकाङ्क्षिभिर्यज्ञो विधिदृष्टो य इज्यते ।
यष्टव्यमेवेति मनः समाधाय स सात्त्विकः ॥ १७—११ ॥
अभिसंधाय तु फलं दम्भार्थमपि चैव यत् ।
इज्यते भरतश्रेष्ठ तं यज्ञं विद्धि राजसम् ॥ १७—१२ ॥

5. aśāstravihitaṃ ghoraṃ tapyante ye tapo janāḥ
dambhāhaṃkārasaṃyuktāḥ kāmarāgabalānvitāḥ
6. karśayantaḥ śarīrasthaṃ bhūtagrāmam acetasaḥ
māṃ caivāntaḥśarīrasthaṃ tān viddhy āsuraniścayān
7. āhāras tv api sarvasya trividho bhavati priyaḥ
yajñas tapas tathā dānaṃ teṣāṃ bhedam imaṃ śṛṇu
8. āyuḥsattvabalārogyasukhaprītivivardhanāḥ
rasyāḥ snigdhāḥ sthirā hṛdyā āhārāḥ sāttvikapriyāḥ
9. kaṭvamlalavaṇātyuṣṇatīkṣṇarūkṣavidāhinaḥ
āhārā rājasasyeṣṭā duḥkhaśokāmayapradāḥ
10. yātayāmaṃ gatarasaṃ pūti paryuṣitaṃ ca yat
ucchiṣṭam api cāmedhyaṃ bhojanaṃ tāmasapriyam
11. aphalākāṅkṣibhir yajño vidhidṛṣṭo ya ijyate
yaṣṭavyam eveti manaḥ samādhāya sa sāttvikaḥ
12. abhisaṃdhāya tu phalaṃ dambhārtham api caiva yat
ijyate bharataśreṣṭha taṃ yajñaṃ viddhi rājasam

17.5 [Those] people, [who] endure[6] horrific austerity not [ordained by] the scriptures, possessed of ostentation and ego-sense, impelled by the force of desire and passion,
17.6 thoughtlessly oppressing the aggregation of elements abiding in [i.e., composing] the body, and [thereby] also [oppressing] Me abiding within the body—these know [to be] demonic [in their] intentions.
17.7 Even food, dear to all, is threefold. So are sacrifice, austerity, and charity. Hear this [now] about their distinction.
17.8 Foods [that] promote life, [the factor of] lucidity, strength, health, joy, and delight, [and that are] savory, rich-in-oil,[7] firm, and heart [-gladdening]—[these are] dear to the *sattva*-natured.
17.9 Foods [which are] pungent, sour, salty, hot, sharp, harsh, and burning—[these are] desired by the *rajas*-natured. [They] cause pain, grief, and disease.
17.10 And [food] which is spoiled, tasteless, putrid, stale, left over, and unclean—[this] is food agreeable to a *tamas*-natured [individual].[8]
17.11 The sacrifice that is offered observing the [scriptural] ordinance by [those who do] not hanker after [its] fruit [and who] concentrating the mind [know] "one should sacrifice"—that is *sattva*-natured.
17.12 But the sacrifice that is offered in expectation of the fruit [and] also for the purpose of ostentation—that, O Bharatashreshtha,[9] know [to be] *rajas*-natured.

6. The word *tapyante,* here rendered as "they endure," is formed from the root *tap,* meaning "to burn."
7. The term *snigdha,* here translated as "rich-in-oil," has also been rendered as "rich" (Edgerton 1944), "soft" (Radhakrishnan 1948), "greasy" (Hill 1928/1966), "fatty" (Bhaktivedanta Swami 1983), and "smooth" (Sargeant 1984). Nataraja Guru (1973) adopts "rich" and makes the following additional observation: "Some have made the mistake of translating [the plural] *snigdhāh* (rich) as meaning bland or tasteless. Such a meaning would only indicate a dietetic fad."
8. Sargeant (1984) has the following somewhat biased comment: "It is not difficult to detect in this and the preceding two stanzas the hand of the brāhman caste insisting on its superiority to an extent that is almost comic." Certainly the stanzas in question do not make a case for brahmanical superiority but rather one for a reasonable diet.
9. Bharatashreshtha is an epithet of Arjuna meaning "Best of the Bharatas."

विधिहीनमसृष्टान्नं मन्त्रहीनमदक्षिणम् ।
श्रद्धाविरहितं यज्ञं तामसं परिचक्षते ॥ १७—१३ ॥
देवद्विजगुरुप्राज्ञपूजनं शौचमार्जवम् ।
ब्रह्मचर्यमहिंसा च शारीरं तप उच्यते ॥ १७—१४ ॥
अनुद्वेगकरं वाक्यं सत्यं प्रियहितं च यत् ।
स्वाध्यायाभ्यसनं चैव वाङ्मयं तप उच्यते ॥ १७—१५ ॥
मनःप्रसादः सौम्यत्वं मौनमात्मविनिग्रहः ।
भावसंशुद्धिरित्येतत्तपो मानसमुच्यते ॥ १७—१६ ॥
श्रद्धया परया तप्तं तपस्तत्त्रिविधं नरैः ।
अफलाकाङ्क्षिभिर्युक्तैः सात्त्विकं परिचक्षते ॥ १७—१७ ॥
सत्कारमानपूजार्थं तपो दम्भेन चैव यत् ।
क्रियते तदिह प्रोक्तं राजसं चलमध्रुवम् ॥ १७—१८ ॥
मूढग्राहेणात्मनो यत्पीडया क्रियते तपः ।
परस्योत्सादनार्थं वा तत्तामसमुदाहृतम् ॥ १७—१९ ॥

13. vidhihīnam asṛṣṭānnaṃ mantrahīnam adakṣiṇam
    śraddhāvirahitaṃ yajñaṃ tāmasaṃ paricakṣate
14. devadvijaguruprājñapūjanaṃ śaucam ārjavam
    brahmacaryam ahiṃsā ca śārīraṃ tapa ucyate
15. anudvegakaraṃ vākyaṃ satyaṃ priyahitaṃ ca yat
    svādhyāyābhyasanaṃ caiva vāṅmayaṃ tapa ucyate
16. manaḥprasādaḥ saumyatvaṃ maunam ātmavinigrahaḥ
    bhāvasaṃśuddhir ity etat tapo mānasam ucyate
17. śraddhayā parayā taptaṃ tapas tat trividhaṃ naraiḥ
    aphalākāṅkṣibhir yuktaiḥ sāttvikaṃ paricakṣate
18. satkāramānapūjārthaṃ tapo dambhena caiva yat
    kriyate tad iha proktaṃ rājasaṃ calam adhruvam
19. mūḍhagrāheṇātmano yat pīḍayā kriyate tapaḥ
    parasyotsādanārthaṃ vā tat tāmasam udāhṛtam

17.13 The sacrifice [that is performed] lacking [proper scriptural] ordinance, without food-offering, lacking mantras, without remuneration [to the priest], devoid of faith—[that] is declared [to be] *tamas*-natured.

17.14 Worship of the gods, the twice-born,[10] the teachers, [and] the wise, [and also] purity, uprightness, chastity, and nonharming—[these are] called bodily austerity.

17.15 Speech [which] causes no disquiet, [is] truthful, pleasant, and beneficial, and also the practice of self-study (*svādhyāya*)—[that] is called austerity concerning speech.[11]

17.16 Serenity of mind, gentleness, silence, self-restraint, and the purification of [inner] states—that is called mental austerity.

17.17 This threefold austerity endured with supreme faith by men [who are] yoked and not hankering after the fruit [of their deeds]—[that] is declared [to be] *sattva*-natured.

17.18 Austerity which is performed for the sake of [obtaining] good treatment [from others], honor, and reverence out of ostentation—that is declared here [in this world to be] *rajas*-natured, fickle, [and] unsteady.

17.19 Austerity which is performed with the deluded notion (*graha*) of torturing oneself or for the sake of ruining another [person]—that is described [as] *tamas*-natured.

10. On the term *dvija* ("twice-born"), see note 2 for 1.7.

11. The Sanskrit text has *vān-mayam tapah,* which is literally "speech-formed austerity" and could also be translated as "vocal austerity."

दातव्यमिति यद्दानं दीयतेऽनुपकारिणे ।
देशे काले च पात्रे च तद्दानं सात्त्विकं स्मृतम् ॥ १७—२० ॥
यत्तु प्रत्युपकारार्थं फलमुद्दिश्य वा पुनः ।
दीयते च परिक्लिष्टं तद्दानं राजसं स्मृतम् ॥ १७—२१ ॥
अदेशकाले यद्दानमपात्रेभ्यश्च दीयते ।
असत्कृतमवज्ञातं तत्तामसमुदाहृतम् ॥ १७—२२ ॥
ॐ तत्सदिति निर्देशो ब्रह्मणस्त्रिविधः स्मृतः ।
ब्राह्मणास्तेन वेदाश्च यज्ञाश्च विहिताः पुरा ॥ १७—२३ ॥
तस्मादोमित्युदाहृत्य यज्ञदानतपःक्रियाः ।
प्रवर्तन्ते विधानोक्ताः सततं ब्रह्मवादिनाम् ॥ १७—२४ ॥
तदित्यनभिसंधाय फलं यज्ञतपःक्रियाः ।
दानक्रियाश्च विविधाः क्रियन्ते मोक्षकाङ्क्षिभिः ॥ १७—२५ ॥
सद्भावे साधुभावे च सदित्येतत्प्रयुज्यते ।
प्रशस्ते कर्मणि तथा सच्छब्दः पार्थ युज्यते ॥ १७—२६ ॥

20. dātavyam iti yad dānaṃ dīyate'nupakāriṇe
deśe kāle ca pātre ca tad dānaṃ sāttvikaṃ smṛtam
21. yat tu pratyupakārārthaṃ phalam uddiśya vā punaḥ
dīyate ca parikliṣṭaṃ tad dānaṃ rājasaṃ smṛtam
22. adeśakāle yad dānam apātrebhyaś ca dīyate
asatkṛtam avajñātaṃ tat tāmasam udāhṛtam
23. oṃ tat sad iti nirdeśo brahmaṇas trividhaḥ smṛtaḥ
brāhmaṇāś tena vedāś ca yajñāś ca vihitāḥ purā
24. tasmād oṃ ity udāhṛtya yajñadānatapaḥkriyāḥ
pravartante vidhānoktāḥ satataṃ brahmavādinām
25. tad ity anabhisaṃdhāya phalaṃ yajñatapaḥkriyāḥ
dānakriyāś ca vividhāḥ kriyante mokṣakāṅkṣibhiḥ
26. sadbhāve sādhubhāve ca sad ity etat prayujyate
praśaste karmaṇi tathā sacchabdaḥ pārtha yujyate

17.20 The gift that is given [because gifts ought] to be given [and is given] to [him from whom] no favor [can be expected], [and that is given in the proper] place [and at the right] time and to a worthy-recipient—that is held [to be] *sattva*-natured.

17.21 But [the gift] that is [given] for the sake of a favor or, again, [that] aims at the fruit [in the afterlife], and [that] is given reluctantly—that gift is held [to be] *rajas*-natured.

17.22 The gift that is given not at the [proper] place [and] time and to unworthy-recipients [and that is given with] disrespect [or] contemptuously—that is proclaimed [to be] *tamas*-natured.

17.23 OM TAT SAT[12]—this is held [to be] the triple designation of Brahman. By this were ordained of old the *brāhmanas*, the Vedas, and the sacrifices.

17.24 Therefore, uttering OM, the Brahman expounders always perform the rituals of sacrifice, charity, and austerity, [as] declared by prescription [in the sacred scriptures].

17.25 TAT—[those who] hanker after liberation perform varied rituals of sacrifice [and] austerity as well as rituals of charity, without aiming at the fruit [of their deeds].

17.26 SAT—this [word] is employed in [the sense of] "real" and in [the sense of "good." The word sat is also employed in [with respect to] praiseworthy actions, O son-of-Prithā.[13]

12. The literal meaning of the sacred utterance OM TAT SAT is "OM, That [is] real." "That" (TAT) is the transcendental Self, or Spirit. SAT is explained in 17.26.

13. On son-of-Prithā (Pārtha), see note 18 for 1.25.

यज्ञे तपसि दाने च स्थितिः सदिति चोच्यते ।
कर्म चैव तदर्थीयं सदित्येवाभिधीयते ॥ १७—२७ ॥
अश्रद्धया हुतं दत्तं तपस्तप्तं कृतं च यत् ।
असदित्युच्यते पार्थ न च तत्प्रेत्य नो इह ॥ १७—२८ ॥

27. yajñe tapasi dāne ca sthitiḥ sad iti cocyate
karma caiva tadarthīyaṃ sad ity evābhidhīyate
28. aśraddhayā hutaṃ dattaṃ tapas taptaṃ kṛtaṃ ca yat
asad ity ucyate pārtha na ca tat pretya no iha

17.27 SAT is called steadfastness in sacrifice, austerity, and charity. Also, action [performed] for that purpose is designated as SAT.

17.28 Whatever oblation is offered, [whatever] austerity is endured [and whatever] is done without faith—that is called *asat*, O son-of-Prithā, and [it is of] no [value] to us hereafter [or] here [in this world].

अर्जुन उवाच ।
संन्यासस्य महाबाहो तत्त्वमिच्छामि वेदितुम् ।
त्यागस्य च हृषीकेश पृथक्केशिनिषूदन ॥ १८—१ ॥
श्रीभगवानुवाच ।
काम्यानां कर्मणां न्यासं संन्यासं कवयो विदुः ।
सर्वकर्मफलत्यागं प्राहुस्त्यागं विचक्षणाः ॥ १८—२ ॥
त्याज्यं दोषवदित्येके कर्म प्राहुर्मनीषिणः ।
यज्ञदानतपःकर्म न त्याज्यमिति चापरे ॥ १८—३ ॥
निश्चयं शृणु मे तत्र त्यागे भरतसत्तम ।
त्यागो हि पुरुषव्याघ्र त्रिविधः संप्रकीर्तितः ॥ १८—४ ॥
यज्ञदानतपःकर्म न त्याज्यं कार्यमेव तत् ।
यज्ञो दानं तपश्चैव पावनानि मनीषिणाम् ॥ १८—५ ॥
एतान्यपि तु कर्माणि सङ्गं त्यक्त्वा फलानि च ।
कर्तव्यानीति मे पार्थ निश्चितं मतमुत्तमम् ॥ १८—६ ॥

arjuna uvāca

1. saṃnyāsasya mahābāho tattvam icchāmi veditum
   tyāgasya ca hṛṣīkeśa pṛthakkeśiniṣūdana

   śrībhagavān uvāca

2. kāmyānāṃ karmaṇāṃ nyāsaṃ saṃnyāsaṃ kavayo viduḥ
   sarvakarmaphalatyāgaṃ prāhus tyāgaṃ vicakṣaṇāḥ
3. tyājyaṃ doṣavadityeke karma prāhur manīṣiṇaḥ
   yajñadānatapaḥkarma na tyājyam iti cāpare
4. niścayaṃ śṛṇu me tatra tyāge bharatasattama
   tyāgo hi puruṣavyāghra trividhaḥ saṃprakīrtitaḥ
5. yajñadānatapaḥkarma na tyājyaṃ kāryam eva tat
   yajño dānaṃ tapaś caiva pāvanāni manīṣiṇām
6. etāny api tu karmāṇi saṅgaṃ tyaktvā phalāni ca
   kartavyānīti me pārtha niścitaṃ matam uttamam

CHAPTER 18

The Yoga of Renunciation and Liberation

Arjuna said:

18.1 I wish to know the truth about renunciation (*samnyāsa*), O mighty-armed [Krishna], and apart [from this], O Hrishīkesha,[1] about relinquishment (*tyāga*), O Keshinishūdana.[2]

The Blessed Lord said:

18.2 The casting-off of desire-born action—[this] the [wise] bards know as renunciation. The relinquishment of all actions' fruit—[this] the sages declare [to be] relinquishment.

18.3 "Action full-of-flaws[3] should be relinquished"—thus say some thoughtful [people]. "Acts [of] sacrifice, charity, and austerity should not be relinquished"—thus [say] others.

18.4 Hear [now] My conviction about that relinquishment, O Bharatasattama.[4] Relinquishment is declared [to be] threefold, O Purushavyāghra.[5]

18.5 Acts [of] sacrifice, charity, and austerity are not to be relinquished; verily, they ought to be performed. Sacrifice, charity, and austerity are purifiers for thoughtful [people].

18.6 But having relinquished [all] attachment and [actions'] fruits, even these actions should be performed—this is My decided ultimate (*uttama*) conviction (*mata*), O son-of-Prithā.[6]

1. On the epithet Hrishīkesha, see note 5 for 1.15.

2. The epithet Keshinishūdana ("Slayer of Keshin") refers to Krishna's killing of the demon Keshin. Sometimes the spelling *Keshinisūdana* is used.

3. The qualifying phrase "full-of-flaws" in Sanskrit is *doshavat*. The flaws (*dosha*) are all those mental qualities that make an action karmically inauspicious. Often the following five flaws or defects are mentioned as a group: lust (*kāma*), anger (*krodha*), greed (*lobha*), fear (*bhaya*), and delusion (*moha*).

4. Bharatasattama, modeled after Kurusattama (4.31), means "Foremost Bharata."

5. Purushavyāghra means literally "Man-Tiger."

6. On son-of-Prithā (Pārtha), see note 18 for 1.25.

नियतस्य तु संन्यासः कर्मणो नोपपद्यते ।
मोहात्तस्य परित्यागस्तामसः परिकीर्तितः ॥ १८—७ ॥
दुःखमित्येव यत्कर्म कायक्लेशभयात्त्यजेत् ।
स कृत्वा राजसं त्यागं नैव त्यागफलं लभेत् ॥ १८—८ ॥
कार्यमित्येव यत्कर्म नियतं क्रियतेऽर्जुन ।
सङ्गं त्यक्त्वा फलं चैव स त्यागः सात्त्विको मतः ॥ १८—९ ॥
न द्वेष्ट्यकुशलं कर्म कुशले नानुषज्जते ।
त्यागी सत्त्वसमाविष्टो मेधावी छिन्नसंशयः ॥ १८—१० ॥
न हि देहभृता शक्यं त्यक्तुं कर्माण्यशेषतः ।
यस्तु कर्मफलत्यागी स त्यागीत्यभिधीयते ॥ १८—११ ॥
अनिष्टमिष्टं मिश्रं च त्रिविधं कर्मणः फलम् ।
भवत्यत्यागिनां प्रेत्य न तु संन्यासिनां क्वचित् ॥ १८—१२ ॥
पञ्चैतानि महाबाहो कारणानि निबोध मे ।
सांख्ये कृतान्ते प्रोक्तानि सिद्धये सर्वकर्मणाम् ॥ १८—१३ ॥

7. niyatasya tu saṃnyāsaḥ karmaṇo nopapadyate
mohāt tasya parityāgas tāmasaḥ parikīrtitaḥ
8. duḥkham ity eva yat karma kāyakleśabhayāt tyajet
sa kṛtvā rājasaṃ tyāgaṃ naiva tyāgaphalaṃ labhet
9. kāryam ity eva yat karma niyataṃ kriyate'rjuna
saṅgaṃ tyaktvā phalaṃ caiva sa tyāgaḥ sāttviko mataḥ
10. na dveṣṭy akuśalaṃ karma kuśale nānuṣajjate
tyāgī sattvasamāviṣṭo medhāvī chinnasaṃśayaḥ
11. na hi dehabhṛtā śakyaṃ tyaktuṃ karmāṇy aśeṣataḥ
yas tu karmaphalatyāgī sa tyāgīty abhidhīyate
12. aniṣṭam iṣṭaṃ miśraṃ ca trividhaṃ karmaṇaḥ phalam
bhavaty atyāgināṃ pretya na tu saṃnyāsināṃ kvacit
13. pañcaitāni mahābāho kāraṇāni nibodha me
sāṃkhye kṛtānte proktāni siddhaye sarvakarmaṇām

18.7 For the renunciation of necessary action is inappropriate. Its relinquishment out of delusion is proclaimed [to be] *tamas*-natured.

18.8 Should [a *yogin*] relinquish action from fear of bodily affliction [or] pain (*duhkha*), [then,] performing [merely] *rajas*-natured relinquishment, he will, verily, not attain the fruit of [genuine] relinquishment.

18.9 [When] he performs necessary action that is indeed to be done, O Arjuna, and by relinquishing attachment and the fruit [of one's action]—the relinquishment is deemed [to be] *sattva*-natured.

18.10 The relinquisher [who is] suffused with *sattva*, [who is] intelligent, [and whose] doubt is severed—he does not hate uncongenial action, nor [is he] attached to congenial[7] [action].

18.11 For it is not possible for the body-wearer to relinquish actions entirely. Rather, he who relinquishes the fruit of action is styled a [true] "relinquisher."

18.12 Unwanted, wanted, and mixed[8]—threefold is the fruit of action of the departing nonrelinquishers. But [there is] none whatsoever for renouncers.[9]

18.13 Learn from Me, O mighty-armed [Arjuna], the [following] five causes [as] proclaimed in the Sāmkhya system[10] for the accomplishment of all actions.

7. Compare stanza 2.50 for the use of the word *kaushala* ("congenial") as "skill." Hill (1928/1966) translates this term as "fitting," while Bhaktivedanta Swami (1983) understands it as "auspicious."
8. These three categories are probably rebirth as a deity, as a demon, and as a human being.
9. According to Shankara, the nonrelinquishers comprise also the *karma-yogins,* whom he contrasts with the real *jnāna-yogins*, but the context suggests that here the word *samnyāsin* stands for *tyāgin.*
10. The term *kritānta* (*krita-anta*), here translated as "system," means literally "done end," standing for the final conclusion of something. Shankara relates *kritānta* to *vedānta,* arguing that Vedānta, which brings Self-knowledge, terminates all work. Abhinavagupta understands *kritānta* as a synonym for *siddhānta,* or established philosophical system. The five "causes" are explained in the next stanza.

अधिष्ठनं तथा कर्ता करणं च पृथग्विधम् ।
विविधाश्च पृथक्चेष्टा दैवं चैवात्र पञ्चमम् ॥ १८—१४ ॥
शरीरवाङ्मनोभिर्यत्कर्म प्रारभते नरः ।
न्याय्यं वा विपरीतं वा पञ्चैते तस्य हेतवः ॥ १८—१५ ॥
तत्रैवं सति कर्तारमात्मानं केवलं तु यः ।
पश्यत्यकृतबुद्धित्वान्न स पश्यति दुर्मतिः ॥ १८—१६ ॥
यस्य नाहंकृतो भावो बुद्धिर्यस्य न लिप्यते ।
हत्वापि स इमाँल्लोकान्न हन्ति न निबध्यते ॥ १८—१७ ॥
ज्ञानं ज्ञेयं परिज्ञाता त्रिविधा कर्मचोदना ।
करणं कर्म कर्तेति त्रिविधः कर्मसंग्रहः ॥ १८—१८ ॥
ज्ञानं कर्म च कर्ता च त्रिधैव गुणभेदतः ।
प्रोच्यते गुणसंख्याने यथावच्छृणु तान्यपि ॥ १८—१९ ॥

14. adhiṣṭhānaṃ tathā kartā karaṇaṃ ca pṛthagvidham
vividhāś ca pṛthakceṣṭā daivaṃ caivātra pañcamam
15. śarīravāṅmanobhiryatkarma prārabhate naraḥ
nyāyyaṃ vā viparītaṃ vā paścaite tasya hetavaḥ
16. tatraivaṃ sati kartāram ātmānaṃ kevalaṃ tu yaḥ
paśyaty akṛtabuddhitvān na sa paśyati durmatiḥ
17. yasya nāhaṃkṛto bhāvo buddhir yasya na lipyate
hatvāpi sa imāṃl lokān na hanti na nibadhyate
18. jñānaṃ jñeyaṃ parijñātā trividhā karmacodanā
karaṇaṃ karma karteti trividhaḥ karmasaṃgrahaḥ
19. jñānaṃ karma ca kartā ca tridhaiva guṇabhedataḥ
procyate guṇasaṃkhyāne yathāvac chṛṇu tāny api

18.14 The [physical] basis,[11] also the agent,[12] and the multifarious instruments,[13] and the various kinds of distinct activity, and fate[14] as the fifth.

18.15 Whatever action a man undertakes with body, speech [or] mind, [whether] proper or otherwise—these five are its causes.

18.16 This being so, he who sees himself merely as the agent due to incomplete wisdom—that dull-wit[15] does not see [the truth].

18.17 He whose [mental] state is not ego-driven,[16] whose wisdom-faculty is not defiled, though slaying [all] these worlds—he does not slay, nor is he bound.

18.18 Knowledge, [that which is] to-be-known,[17] and the knower are the threefold impulse to action. Instrument, action, and agent are the threefold nexus of action.

18.19 In the reckoning[18] of the primary-qualities, [according to] the distinction between the primary-qualities, knowledge, action, and agent are declared [to be] threefold. Hear about these rightly (*yathāvat*) as well.

11. The term *adhishthāna,* here rendered as "basis," is generally taken to be the physical body. Abhinavagupta begs to differ; he takes it to refer to the objects of the senses.

12. The "agent" (*kartri*) is the subject, the empirical self, or *jīvātman,* who sows and reaps good or bad karma.

13. The word *karana* ("instrument") denotes here the ten senses, or eleven senses if the lower mind (*manas*) is included.

14. The term *daiva* (lit. "divine") is here rendered in its common nominal meaning as "fate." We could also explain it as "divine providence." As Shankara explains, this term more particularly refers to the deities; thus, the Sun (Āditya) graces the eyes, and other deities govern the other sense organs.

15. The word *durmati,* which is translated here as "dull-wit," means literally "he whose intelligence is bad/poor." Sargeant (1984), amusingly, renders the word as "blockhead."

16. The Sanskrit text has *ahamkrita,* which means literally "I-made."

17. The term *jneya,* "that which is to-be-known," refers to any knowable object.

18. The Sanskrit text has *samkhyāna,* which the classical commentators straightforwardly equate with the Sāmkhya system but which probably has a more general meaning here.

सर्वभूतेषु येनैकं भावमव्ययमीक्षते ।
अविभक्तं विभक्तेषु तज्ज्ञानं विद्धि सात्त्विकम् ॥ १८—२० ॥
पृथक्त्वेन तु यज्ज्ञानं नानाभावान्पृथग्विधान् ।
वेत्ति सर्वेषु भूतेषु तज्ज्ञानं विद्धि राजसम् ॥ १८—२१ ॥
यत्तु कृत्स्नवदेकस्मिन्कार्ये सक्तमहैतुकम् ।
अतत्त्वार्थवदल्पं च तत्तामसमुदाहृतम् ॥ १८—२२ ॥
नियतं सङ्गरहितमरागद्वेषतः कृतम् ।
अफलप्रेप्सुना कर्म यत्तत्सात्त्विकमुच्यते ॥ १८—२३ ॥
यत्तु कामेप्सुना कर्म साहंकारेण वा पुनः ।
क्रियते बहुलायासं तद्राजसमुदाहृतम् ॥ १८—२४ ॥
अनुबन्धं क्षयं हिंसामनपेक्ष्य च पौरुषम् ।
मोहादारभ्यते कर्म यत्तत्तामसमुच्यते ॥ १८—२५ ॥
मुक्तसङ्गोऽनहंवादी धृत्युत्साहसमन्वितः ।
सिद्ध्यसिद्ध्योर्निर्विकारः कर्ता सात्त्विक उच्यते ॥ १८—२६ ॥

20. sarvabhūteṣu yenaikaṃ bhāvam avyayam īkṣate
avibhaktaṃ vibhakteṣu taj jñānaṃ viddhi sāttvikam
21. pṛthaktvena tu yaj jñānaṃ nānābhāvān pṛthagvidhān
vetti sarveṣu bhūteṣu taj jñānaṃ viddhi rājasam
22. yat tu kṛtsnavad ekasmin kārye saktam ahaitukam
atattvārthavad alpaṃ ca tat tāmasam udāhṛtam
23. niyataṃ saṅgarahitam arāgadveṣataḥ kṛtam
aphalaprepsunā karma yat tat sāttvikam ucyate
24. yat tu kāmepsunā karma sāhaṃkāreṇa vā punaḥ
kriyate bahulāyāsaṃ tad rājasam udāhṛtam
25. anubandhaṃ kṣayaṃ hiṃsām anapekṣya ca pauruṣam
mohād ārabhyate karma yat tat tāmasam ucyate
26. muktasaṅgo'nahaṃvādī dhṛtyutsāhasamanvitaḥ
siddhyasiddhyor nirvikāraḥ kartā sāttvika ucyate

18.20 [The knowledge] by which the one immutable state-of-existence is seen in all beings, undivided in the divided—that knowledge know as *sattva*-natured.

18.21 But [that] knowledge which recognizes through separateness various distinct states-of-being in all beings—that knowledge know as *rajas*-natured.

18.22 Again, [that knowledge] which clings to a single effect as if [it were] the whole, without [due] cause, without concern for reality, and [which is] slight—that is described as *tamas*-natured.

18.23 [That] action which is necessary [and which is] performed without attachment and without passion or aversion by [one who] craves not for the fruit [of his deeds]—that is called *sattva*-natured.

18.24 But [that] action which is performed with great strain, or else, out of ego-sense, by [one who] craves [to realize selfish] desires—that is named *rajas*-natured.

18.25 [That] action which is undertaken through delusion without regard to the consequence, [be it] loss or hurt, or to [one's] human-capacity—that is called *tamas*-natured.

18.26 The agent [who is] freed from attachment, [who is] not an "I-sayer," [who is] endowed with steadfastness and zeal, [and who is] unchanged in success or failure—[he] is called *sattva*-natured.

रागी कर्मफलप्रेप्सुर्लुब्धो हिंसात्मकोऽशुचिः ।
हर्षशोकान्वितः कर्ता राजसः परिकीर्तितः ॥ १८—२७ ॥
अयुक्तः प्राकृतः स्तब्धः शठो नैकृतिकोऽलसः ।
विषादी दीर्घसूत्री च कर्ता तामस उच्यते ॥ १८—२८ ॥
बुद्धेर्भेदं धृतेश्चैव गुणतस्त्रिविधं शृणु ।
प्रोच्यमानमशेषेण पृथक्त्वेन धनंजय ॥ १८—२९ ॥
प्रवृत्तिं च निवृत्तिं च कार्याकार्ये भयाभये ।
बन्धं मोक्षं च या वेत्ति बुद्धिः सा पार्थ सात्त्विकी ॥ १८—३० ॥
यया धर्ममधर्मं च कार्यं चाकार्यमेव च ।
अयथावत्प्रजानाति बुद्धिः सा पार्थ राजसी ॥ १८—३१ ॥
अधर्मं धर्ममिति या मन्यते तमसावृता ।
सर्वार्थान्विपरीतांश्च बुद्धिः सा पार्थ तामसी ॥ १८—३२ ॥
धृत्या यथा धारयते मनःप्राणेन्द्रियक्रियाः ।
योगेनाव्यभिचारिण्या धृतिः सा पार्थ सात्त्विकी ॥ १८—३३ ॥

27. rāgī karmaphalaprepsur lubdho hiṃsātmako'śuciḥ
harṣaśokānvitaḥ kartā rājasaḥ parikīrtitaḥ
28. ayuktaḥ prākṛtaḥ stabdhaḥ śaṭho naikṛtiko'lasaḥ
viṣādī dīrghasūtrī ca kartā tāmasa ucyate
29. buddher bhedaṃ dhṛteś caiva guṇatas trividhaṃ śṛṇu
procyamānam aśeṣeṇa pṛthaktvena dhanaṃjaya
30. pravṛttiṃ ca nivṛttiṃ ca kāryākārye bhayābhaye
bandhaṃ mokṣaṃ ca ya vetti buddhiḥ sā pārtha sāttvikī
31. yayā dharmam adharmaṃ ca kāryaṃ cākāryam eva ca
ayathāvat prajānāti buddhiḥ sā pārtha rājasī
32. adharmaṃ dharmam iti yā manyate tamasāvṛtā
sarvārthān viparītāṃś ca buddhiḥ sā pārtha tāmasī
33. dhṛtyā yathā dhārayate manaḥprāṇendriyakriyāḥ
yogenāvyabhicāriṇyā dhṛtiḥ sā pārtha sāttvikī

18.27 The agent [who is] passionate, craving for the fruit of action, greedy, of violent nature, impure, [and] subject to[19] elation [and] depression—[he] is declared [to be] *rajas*-natured.

18.28 The agent [who is] unyoked, uncultured, obstinate, deceitful, base, lazy, despondent, and "long-threaded"[20]—[he] is called *tamas*-natured.

18.29 Hear [now] of the threefold distinction of the wisdom-faculty (*buddhi*) and also of steadfastness [based on] the primary-qualities, [which I will] explain unreservedly and separately, O Dhanamjaya.[21]

18.30 The wisdom-faculty that knows activity and cessation, right [and] wrong [actions], fear [and] fearlessness, bondage [and] liberation—that, O son-of-Prithā, is *sattva*-natured.

18.31 The wisdom-faculty by which one knows the law (*dharma*) and lawlessness (*adharma*), as well as right and wrong incorrectly—that, O son-of-Prithā, is *rajas*-natured.

18.32 The wisdom-faculty that, enveloped in darkness, thinks [that] lawlessness is the law (*dharma*), and [that sees] all things [thus] reversed—that, O son-of-Prithā, is *tamas*-natured.

18.33 The steadfastness by which one "holds" [i.e., maintains] the activities of the mind, the life-force, and the senses through unswerving Yoga—that steadfastness, O son-of-Prithā, is *sattva*-natured.

19. The English phrase "subject to" corresponds to the Sanskrit *anvita* ("endowed with").
20. The phrase *dīrgha-sūtrin,* here rendered as "long-threaded," refers to someone who procrastinates.
21. On Dhanamjaya, see note 7 for 1.15.

यया तु धर्मकामार्थान्धृत्या धारयतेऽर्जुन ।
प्रसङ्गेन फलाकाङ्क्षी धृतिः सा पार्थ राजसी ॥ १८—३४ ॥
यया स्वप्नं भयं शोकं विषादं मदमेव च ।
न विमुञ्चति दुर्मेधा धृतिः सा पार्थ तामसी ॥ १८—३५ ॥
सुखं त्विदानीं त्रिविधं शृणु मे भरतर्षभ ।
अभ्यासाद्रमते यत्र दुःखान्तं च निगच्छति ॥ १८—३६ ॥
यत्तदग्रे विषमिव परिणामेऽमृतोपमम् ।
तत्सुखं सात्त्विकं प्रोक्तमात्मबुद्धिप्रसादजम् ॥ १८—३७ ॥
विषयेन्द्रियसंयोगाद्यत्तदग्रेऽमृतोपमम् ।
परिणामे विषमिव तत्सुखं राजसं स्मृतम् ॥ १८—३८ ॥

34. yayā tu dharmakāmārthān dhṛtyā dhārayate'rjuna
prasaṅgena phalākāṅkṣī dhṛtiḥ sā pārtha rājasī
35. yayā svapnaṃ bhayaṃ śokaṃ viṣādaṃ madam eva ca
na vimuñcati durmedhā dhṛtiḥ sā pārtha tāmasī.
36. sukhaṃ tv idānīṃ trividhaṃ śṛṇu me bharatarṣabha
abhyāsād ramate yatra duḥkhāntaṃ ca nigacchati
37. yat tad agre viṣam iva pariṇāme'mṛtopamam
tat sukhaṃ sāttvikaṃ proktam ātmabuddhiprasādajam
38. viṣayendriyasaṃyogād yat tad agre'mṛtopamam
pariṇāme viṣam iva tat sukhaṃ rājasaṃ smṛtam

18.34 But, O Arjuna, the steadfastness by which one "holds" [i.e., maintains the pursuit of] law, pleasure, [and] wealth (*artha*) with attachment [and] hankering after the fruit [of one's deeds]—that steadfastness, O son-of-Prithā, is *rajas*-natured.

18.35 [The steadfastness] by which a dull-minded [person] does not avoid sleep, fear, grief, despondency, and intoxication—that steadfastness, O son-of-Prithā, is *tamas*-natured.

18.36 But hear now from Me, O Bharatarshabha,[22] the threefold happiness. Wherein one rejoices after [extensive] practice and [by which] one reaches the end of [all] suffering,

18.37 which in the beginning is like poison [but which] when transformed [over time becomes] like nectar—that happiness is proclaimed [to be] *sattva*-natured, [which is] born from the serenity-grace (*prasāda*) of Self's wisdom (*buddhi*).

18.38 That which [arises] through the union of the senses [with their corresponding] objects, [which] is like nectar in the beginning [but] when transformed [over time becomes] like poison—that happiness is held [to be] *rajas*-natured.

22. On Bharatarshabha, see note 48 for 3.41.

यदग्रे चानुबन्धे च सुखं मोहनमात्मनः ।
निद्रालस्यप्रमादोत्थं तत्तामसमुदाहृतम् ॥ १८—३९ ॥
न तदस्ति पृथिव्यां वा दिवि देवेषु वा पुनः ।
सत्त्वं प्रकृतिजैर्मुक्तं यदेभिः स्यात्त्रिभिर्गुणैः ॥ १८—४० ॥
ब्राह्मणक्षत्रियविशां शूद्राणां च परंतप ।
कर्माणि प्रविभक्तानि स्वभावप्रभवैर्गुणैः ॥ १८—४१ ॥
शमो दमस्तपः शौचं क्षान्तिरार्जवमेव च ।
ज्ञानं विज्ञानमास्तिक्यं ब्रह्मकर्म स्वभावजम् ॥ १८—४२ ॥
शौर्यं तेजो धृतिर्दाक्ष्यं युद्धे चाप्यपलायनम् ।
दानमीश्वरभावश्च क्षत्रकर्म स्वभावजम् ॥ १८—४३ ॥
कृषिगोरक्ष्यवाणिज्यं वैश्यकर्म स्वभावजम् ।
परिचर्यात्मकं कर्म शूद्रस्यापि स्वभावजम् ॥ १८—४४ ॥
स्वे स्वे कर्मण्यभिरतः संसिद्धिं लभते नरः ।
स्वकर्मनिरतः सिद्धिं यथा विन्दति तच्छृणु ॥ १८—४५ ॥

39. yad agre cānubandhe ca sukhaṃ mohanam ātmanaḥ
nidrālasyapramādotthaṃ tat tāmasam udāhṛtam
40. na tad asti pṛthivyāṃ vā divi deveṣu vā punaḥ
sattvaṃ prakṛtijair muktaṃ yad ebhiḥ syāt tribhir guṇaiḥ
41. brāhmaṇakṣatriyaviśāṃ śūdrāṇāṃ ca paraṃtapa
karmāṇi pravibhaktāni svabhāvaprabhavair guṇaiḥ
42. śamo damas tapaḥ śaucaṃ kṣāntir ārjavam eva ca
jñānaṃ vijñānam āstikyaṃ brahmakarma svabhāvajam
43. śauryaṃ tejo dhṛtir dākṣyaṃ yuddhe cāpy apalāyanam
dānam īśvarabhāvaś ca kṣatrakarma svabhāvajam
44. kṛṣigorakṣyavāṇijyaṃ vaiśyakarma svabhāvajam
paricaryātmakaṃ karma śūdrasyāpi svabhāvajam
45. sve sve karmaṇy abhirataḥ saṃsiddhiṃ labhate naraḥ
svakarmanirataḥ siddhiṃ yathā vindati tac chṛṇu

18.39 [That] happiness which in the beginning and in the sequel deludes the self, stemming from sleep, indolence, and heedlessness—that is designated as *tamas*-natured.

18.40 [There] is no entity (*sattva*) on earth or again among the gods in heaven who is free from these three primary-qualities born of the Cosmos (*prakriti*).

18.41 The actions of priests, warriors, merchants, and serfs are apportioned, O Paramtapa,[23] [according] to the primary-qualities arising [in their] own-being.

18.42 Calm, restraint, austerity, purity, patience, and uprightness, [real] knowledge [and] worldly-knowledge, piety[24]—[these are] the behavior (*karman*) of a priest, born of [his] own-being.

18.43 Courage, vigor, steadfastness, resourcefulness, and also an unwillingness-to-flee in battle, generosity, and a regal disposition—[these are] the behavior of a warrior, born of [his] own-being.

18.44 Agriculture, cattle-tending, [and] trade—[these are] the behavior of a merchant, born of [his] own-being. Moreover, behavior of the nature of service is born of the own-being of a serf.

18.45 Content each in his own action, a man gains [spiritual] consummation. Hear [next] how he finds success [by being] content in [his] own [appropriate] action.

23. On Arjuna's epithet Paramtapa, see note 5 for 2.3.

24. The Sanskrit term *āstikya* is derived from *asti* ("it is") and denotes an attitude of affirmation toward the Vedic revelation or the existence of the Divine. For simplicity's sake, I have translated this term here as "piety."

यतः प्रवृत्तिर्भूतानां येन सर्वमिदं ततम् ।
स्वकर्मणा तमभ्यर्च्य सिद्धिं विन्दति मानवः ॥ १८—४६ ॥
श्रेयान्स्वधर्मो विगुणः परधर्मात्स्वनुष्ठितात् ।
स्वभावनियतं कर्म कुर्वन्नाप्नोति किल्बिषम् ॥ १८—४७ ॥
सहजं कर्म कौन्तेय सदोषमपि न त्यजेत् ।
सर्वारम्भा हि दोषेण धूमेनाग्निरिवावृताः ॥ १८—४८ ॥
असक्तबुद्धिः सर्वत्र जितात्मा विगतस्पृहः ।
नैष्कर्म्यसिद्धिं परमां संन्यासेनाधिगच्छति ॥ १८—४९ ॥
सिद्धिं प्रप्तो यथा ब्रह्म तथाप्नोति निबोध मे ।
समासेनैव कौन्तेय निष्ठा ज्ञानस्य या परा ॥ १८—५० ॥

46. yataḥ pravṛttir bhūtānāṃ yena sarvam idaṃ tatam
svakarmaṇā tam abhyarcya siddhiṃ vindati mānavaḥ
47. śreyān svadharmo viguṇaḥ paradharmāt svanuṣṭhitāt
svabhāvaniyataṃ karma kurvann āpnoti kilbiṣam
48. sahajaṃ karma kaunteya sadoṣam api na tyajet
sarvārambhā hi doṣeṇa dhūmenāgnir ivāvṛtāḥ
49. asaktabuddhiḥ sarvatra jitātmā vigataspṛhaḥ
naiṣkarmyasiddhiṃ paramāṃ saṃnyāsenādhigacchati
50. siddhiṃ prapto yathā brahma tathāpnoti nibodha me
samāsenaiva kaunteya niṣṭhā jñānasya yā parā

18.46 [He] from whom the activity of [all] beings [is derived], by whom all this is spread out—worshipping Him by [one's] own [allotted] action, a human [being] finds success.

18.47 Better is [one's] own-law imperfectly [carried out] than another's law well performed.[25] Performing the action necessitated by [one's] own-being, [the *yogin*] does not accumulate guilt.

18.48 One should not relinquish innate[26] action, even [if] defective, O son-of-Kuntī,[27] for all undertakings are veiled by flaws[28] as it were, [as] fire by smoke.

18.49 [He whose] wisdom-faculty is everywhere unattached, [whose] self is subdued, [with all] longing gone—he attains through renunciation the supreme perfection of action-transcendence.[29]

18.50 Learn from Me [now] briefly how, having attained perfection, [the *yogin*] reaches *brahman*, which is the highest way-of-life[30] of wisdom, O son-of-Kuntī.

25. This stanza reiterates the profound recommendation of stanza 3.35.
26. The Sanskrit word *sahaja,* here given as "innate," means literally "born with." Here it designates spontaneous action that arises from one's own-being (*svabhāva*).
27. On son-of-Kuntī (Kaunteya), see note 19 for 1.27.
28. On the term *dosha* ("fault/flaw/defect"), see note 3 for 18.3.
29. On "action-transcendence" (*naishkarmya*), see note 9 for 3.4.
30. The term *nishthā,* here rendered as "way-of-life," is often translated as "summit." But perhaps its usage in this stanza suggests that abiding in the world-ground (*brahman*) is a process rather than a state. This makes sense when one considers that for Krishna, mergence with the world-ground is not the ultimate spiritual attainment. See also 3.3 and 17.1.

बुद्ध्या विशुद्धया युक्तो धृत्यात्मानं नियम्य च ।
शब्दादीन्विषयांस्त्यक्त्वा रागद्वेषौ व्युदस्य च ॥ १८—५१ ॥
विविक्तसेवी लघ्वाशी यतवाक्कायमानसः ।
ध्यानयोगपरो नित्यं वैराग्यं समुपाश्रितः ॥ १८—५२ ॥
अहंकारं बलं दर्पं कामं क्रोधं परिग्रहम् ।
विमुच्य निर्ममः शान्तो ब्रह्मभूयाय कल्पते ॥ १८—५३ ॥
ब्रह्मभूतः प्रसन्नात्मा न शोचति न काङ्क्षति ।
समः सर्वेषु भूतेषु मद्भक्तिं लभते पराम् ॥ १८—५४ ॥
भक्त्या मामभिजानाति यावान्यश्चास्मि तत्त्वतः ।
ततो मां तत्त्वतो ज्ञात्वा विशते तदनन्तरम् ॥ १८—५५ ॥
सर्वकर्माण्यपि सदा कुर्वाणो मद्व्यपाश्रयः ।
मत्प्रसादादवाप्नोति शाश्वतं पदमव्ययम् ॥ १८—५६ ॥

51. buddhyā viśuddhayā yukto dhṛtyātmānaṃ niyamya ca
    śabdādīn viṣayāṃs tyaktvā rāgadveṣau vyudasya ca
52. viviktasevī laghvāśī yatavākkāyamānasaḥ
    dhyānayogaparo nityaṃ vairāgyaṃ samupāśritaḥ
53. ahaṃkāraṃ balaṃ darpaṃ kāmaṃ krodhaṃ parigraham
    vimucya nirmamaḥ śānto brahmabhūyāya kalpate
54. brahmabhūtaḥ prasannātmā na śocati na kāṅkṣati
    samaḥ sarveṣu bhūteṣu madbhaktiṃ labhate parām
55. bhaktyā mām abhijānāti yāvān yaś cāsmi tattvataḥ
    tato māṃ tattvato jñātvā viśate tad anantaram
56. sarvakarmāṇy api sadā kurvāṇo madvyapāśrayaḥ
    matprasādād avāpnoti śāśvataṃ padam avyayam

18.51 Yoked by [his] purified wisdom-faculty and restraining the self with steadiness, relinquishing objects [like] sound and so on, and casting off attachment (*rāga*) and aversion,

18.52 dwelling in solitude, eating lightly, controlling speech, body, [and] mind, ever intent on the Yoga of meditation, resorting to dispassion,

18.53 shunning the ego-sense, force, arrogance, desire, anger, [and] possessiveness, [being] peaceful, [and] without [the thought of] "mine"—he is fit to become the world-ground.

18.54 *Brahman*-become, [with] tranquil self—he does not grieve, nor hanker after [anything]. [Seeing] the same in all beings, he gains supreme devotion (*bhakti*) to Me.

18.55 Through devotion he really [comes to] know Me, how great [and] who I am. Then, having really known Me, he forthwith enters into that [My being].

18.56 Moreover, always performing all actions [and] taking-refuge in Me—he attains by My grace the eternal, immutable abode.

चेतसा सर्वकर्माणि मयि संन्यस्य मत्परः ।
बुद्धियोगमुपाश्रित्य मच्चित्तः सततं भव ॥ १८—५७ ॥
मच्चित्तः सर्वदुर्गाणि मत्प्रसादात्तरिष्यसि ।
अथ चेत्त्वमहंकारान्न श्रोष्यसि विनङ्क्ष्यसि ॥ १८—५८ ॥
यदहंकारमाश्रित्य न योत्स्य इति मन्यसे ।
मिथ्यैष व्यवसायस्ते प्रकृतिस्त्वां नियोक्ष्यति ॥ १८—५९ ॥
स्वभावजेन कौन्तेय निबद्धः स्वेन कर्मणा ।
कर्तुं नेच्छसि यन्मोहात्करिष्यस्यवशोऽपि तत् ॥ १८—६० ॥
ईश्वरः सर्वभूतानां हृद्देशेऽर्जुन तिष्ठति ।
भ्रामयन्सर्वभूतानि यन्त्रारूढानि मायया ॥ १८—६१ ॥
तमेव शरणं गच्छ सर्वभावेन भारत ।
तत्प्रसादात्परां शान्तिं स्थानं प्रप्स्यसि शाश्वतम् ॥ १८—६२ ॥

57. cetasā sarvakarmāṇi mayi saṃnasya matparaḥ
buddhiyogam upāśritya maccittaḥ satataṃ bhava
58. maccittaḥ sarvadurgāṇi matprasādāt tariṣyasi
atha cet tvam ahaṃkārān na śroṣyasi vinaṅkṣyasi
59. yad ahaṃkāram āśritya na yotsya iti manyase
mithyaiṣa vyavasāyas te prakṛtis tvāṃ niyokṣyati
60. svabhāvajena kaunteya nibaddhaḥ svena karmaṇā
kartuṃ necchasi yan mohāt kariṣyasy avaśo'pi tat
61. īśvaraḥ sarvabhūtānāṃ hṛddeśe'rjuna tiṣṭhati
bhrāmayan sarvabhūtāni yantrārūḍhāni māyayā
62. tam eva śaraṇaṃ gaccha sarvabhāvena bhārata
tat prasādāt parāṃ śāntiṃ sthānaṃ prapsyasi śāśvatam

18.57 Renouncing in thought all actions in Me, intent on Me, resorting to *buddhi-yoga*, [you should] be constantly Me-minded.

18.58 Me-minded, you will transcend all difficulties by My grace. But if out of ego-sense you will not listen [to Me], you will perish.[31]

18.59 Resorting to that ego-sense, you [might] think, "I will not fight!" [But] this resolve of yours [would be in] vain, [because] the Cosmos (*prakriti*) will compel you.

18.60 [That] which out of delusion (*moha*) you do not wish to do, even that you will [have to] do unwittingly, bound [as you are] by [your] own action born of [your] own-being, O son-of-Kuntī.

18.61 The Lord abides in the heart region of all beings, O Arjuna, whirling all [these] beings by [His] creative-power (*māyā*), [as if they were] mounted on a machine.

18.62 To Him alone go for refuge with all [your] being (*bhāva*), O descendant-of-Bharata! By His grace[32] you will attain supreme peace, the eternal abode.

31. The idea expressed here is that one can work either *for* or *against* the divine order. Which way a person will opt depends on the innate pattern that is the crystallization of the experience of many past embodiments. See 18.60.

32. The theism of the *Gītā* is nowhere more obvious than in the idea expressed here, that the devotee who goes for refuge to the Supreme Person qualifies for God's grace (*prasāda*).

इति ते ज्ञानमाख्यातं गुह्याद्गुह्यतरं मया ।
विमृश्यैतदशेषेण यथेच्छसि तथा कुरु ॥ १८—६३ ॥
सर्वगुह्यतमं भूयः शृणु मे परमं वचः ।
इष्टोऽसि मे दृढमिति ततो वक्ष्यामि ते हितम् ॥ १८—६४ ॥
मन्मना भव मद्भक्तो मद्याजी मां नमस्कुरु ।
मामेवैष्यसि सत्यं ते प्रतिजाने प्रियोऽसि मे ॥ १८—६५ ॥
सर्वधर्मान्परित्यज्य मामेकं शरणं व्रज ।
अहं त्वा सर्वपापेभ्यो मोक्षयिष्यामि मा शुचः ॥ १८—६६ ॥
इदं ते नातपस्काय नाभक्ताय कदाचन ।
न चाशुश्रूषवे वाच्यं न मां योऽभ्यसूयति ॥ १८—६७ ॥
य इदं परमं गुह्यं मद्भक्तेष्वभिधास्यति ।
भक्तिं मयि परां कृत्वा मामेवैष्यत्यसंशयः ॥ १८—६८ ॥

63. iti te jñānam ākhyātaṃ guhyād guhyataraṃ mayā
    vimṛśyaitad aśeṣeṇa yathecchasi tathā kuru
64. sarvaguhyatamaṃ bhūyaḥ śṛṇu me paramaṃ vacaḥ
    iṣṭo'si me dṛḍham iti tato vakṣyāmi te hitam
65. manmanā bhava madbhakto madyājī māṃ namaskuru
    mām evaiṣyasi satyaṃ te pratijāne priyo'si me
66. sarvadharmān parityajya mām ekaṃ śaraṇaṃ vraja
    ahaṃ tvā sarvapāpebhyo mokṣayiṣyāmi mā śucaḥ
67. idaṃ te nātapaskāya nābhaktāya kadācana
    na cāśuśrūṣave vācyaṃ na māṃ yo'bhyasūyati
68. ya idaṃ paramaṃ guhyaṃ madbhakteṣv abhidhāsyati
    bhaktiṃ mayi parāṃ kṛtvā mām evaiṣvyaty asaṃśayaḥ

18.63 Thus has knowledge more secret than [any other] secret been declared to you by Me. Reflecting on this completely, then do as you wish.

18.64 Hear again My supreme word, most secret of all. You are thus surely beloved of Me. Therefore, I will tell you [wherein lies your] welfare.

18.65 Be Me-minded, devoted to Me, sacrifice to Me, make reverence to Me—thus you will come to Me. I promise you truly, [for] you are dear to Me.

18.66 Relinquishing all *dharmas*, come to Me alone for shelter. I will release you from all sins. Do not grieve![33]

18.67 You [must] never reveal this to [anyone who does] not [practice] austerity, [who does] not worship [Me], nor to [one who does] not listen [to My teaching], nor to [one] who reviles Me.

18.68 He who will impart this supreme secret to devotees of Mine, showing highest devotion for Me, will undoubtedly come to Me.

33. Krishna does not contradict himself here by demanding the complete abandonment of all laws or duties (*dharma*), as realized with the renunciation of social life. *Parityajya,* like *tyajya,* means definitely renunciation in action, i.e., the relinquishing of selfish interests in the fruit of one's deeds. What is asked is that the true devotee should surrender to God completely and offer up all purposiveness (*samkalpa*). Hence a psychological, not a literal interpretation is required.

न च तस्मान्मनुष्येषु कश्चिन्मे प्रियकृत्तमः ।
भविता न च मे तस्मादन्यः प्रियतरो भुवि ॥ १८—६९ ॥
अध्येष्यते च य इमं धर्म्यं संवादमावयोः ।
ज्ञानयज्ञेन तेनाहमिष्टः स्यामिति मे मतिः ॥ १८—७० ॥
श्रद्धावाननसूयश्च शृणुयादपि यो नरः ।
सोऽपि मुक्तः शुभांल्लोकान्प्राप्नुयात्पुण्यकर्मणाम् ॥ १८—७१ ॥
कच्चिदेतच्छ्रुतं पार्थ त्वयैकाग्रेण चेतसा ।
कच्चिदज्ञानसंमोहः प्रनष्टस्ते धनंजय ॥ १८—७२ ॥
अर्जुन उवाच ।
नष्टो मोहः स्मृतिर्लब्धा त्वत्प्रसादान्मयाच्युत ।
स्थितोऽस्मि गतसंदेहः करिष्ये वचनं तव ॥ १८—७३ ॥

69. na ca tasmān manuṣyeṣu kaścin me priyakṛttamaḥ
bhavitā na ca me tasmād anyaḥ priyataro bhuvi
70. adhyeṣyate ca ya imaṃ dharmyaṃ saṃvādamāvayoḥ
jñānayajñena tenāham iṣṭaḥ syām iti me matiḥ
71. śraddhāvān anasūyaś ca śṛṇuyād api yo naraḥ
so'pi muktaḥ śubhāṃl lokān prāpnuyāt puṇyakarmaṇām
72. kaccid etac chrutaṃ pārtha tvayaikāgreṇa cetasā
kaccid ajñānasaṃmohaḥ pranaṣṭas te dhanaṃjaya

arjuna uvāca
73. naṣṭo mohaḥ smṛtirlabdhā tvatprasādān mayācyuta
sthito'smi gatasaṃdehaḥ kariṣye vacanaṃ tava

18.69 And among human-beings no one will do dearer service to Me than he; nor will [there ever] be on earth another dearer to Me than he.

18.70 And he who will study this lawful (*dharmya*) dialogue of ours, by him would I be desired through the sacrifice of knowledge; thus is My conviction.

18.71 And the man full-of-faith [who is] not scoffing [at Me], even if he should only hear [about this teaching], is released[34] [and] will attain the auspicious worlds of [those whose] actions are meritorious.

18.72 Has this been heard by you, O son-of-Prithā, with one-pointed mind? Has your confusion [caused by] ignorance been destroyed, O Dhanamjaya?[35]

Arjuna said:

18.73 Destroyed is [my] confusion [and] through your grace, O Acyuta,[36] I have obtained recollection.[37] I am resolved; [all] uncertainty is gone. I will do your bidding!

34. Here the intended "liberation" concerns only freedom from the coarsest level of existence. As Hill (1928/1966) rightly remarks: "[liberated] not, of course, from rebirth," because meritorious actions pertain at best to those who have entered the celestial realms, which ultimately must also be transcended.

35. Sanskrit favors passive sentence constructions, which, as in the present case, can be awkward in English, but I have refrained from rendering this verse in the active voice to give students of the *Gītā* a flavor of this scripture.

36. On the epithet Acyuta, see note 16 for 1.21.

37. Here the word *smriti* ("memory") stands for Arjuna's recollection of what constitutes true *dharma*. The use of the word "memory" is significant, because gnosis is not new knowledge but recognition (*pratyabhijñā*) of the eternal primal Truth. In his commentary, Abhinavagupta missed the opportunity of expounding on this teaching, which was so close to his heart. Radhakrishnan (1948) proffers the following pertinent remarks: "Freedom to choose rightly depends on moral training. Through sheer goodness we rise up to a liberty of spirit, which carries us out of the grossness to which the flesh is prone."

संजय उवाच ।
इत्यहं वासुदेवस्य पार्थस्य च महात्मनः ।
संवादमिममश्रौषमद्भुतं रोमहर्षणम् ॥ १८—७४ ॥
व्यासप्रसादाच्छ्रुतवानेतद्गुह्यमहं परम् ।
योगं योगेश्वरात्कृष्णात्साक्षात्कथयतः स्वयम् ॥ १८—७५ ॥
राजन्संस्मृत्य संस्मृत्य संवादमिममद्भुतम् ।
केशवार्जुनयोः पुण्यं हृष्यामि च मुहुर्मुहुः ॥ १८—७६ ॥
तच्च संस्मृत्य संस्मृत्य रूपमत्यद्भुतं हरेः ।
विस्मयो मे महान्राजन्हृष्यामि च पुनः पुनः ॥ १८—७७ ॥
यत्र योगेश्वरः कृष्णो यत्र पार्थो धनुर्धरः ।
तत्र श्रीर्विजयो भूतिर्ध्रुवा नीतिर्मतिर्मम ॥ १८—७८ ॥

saṃjaya uvāca
74. ity ahaṃ vāsudevasya pārthasya ca mahātmanaḥ
saṃvādam imam aśrauṣam adbhutaṃ romaharṣaṇam
75. vyāsaprasādāc chrutavān etad guhyam ahaṃ param
yogaṃ yogeśvarāt kṛṣṇāt sākṣāt kathayataḥ svayam
76. rājan saṃsmṛtya saṃsmṛtya saṃvādam imam adbhutam
keśavārjunayoḥ puṇyaṃ hṛṣyāmi ca muhur muhuḥ
77. tac ca saṃsmṛtya saṃsmṛtya rūpam atyadbhutaṃ hareḥ
vismayo me mahān rājan hṛṣyāmi ca punaḥ punaḥ
78. yatra yogeśvaraḥ kṛṣṇo yatra pārtho dhanurdharaḥ
tatra śrīr vijayo bhūtir dhruvā nītir matir mama

Samjaya said:

18.74 Thus have I heard this wondrous, hair-raising dialogue between the son-of-Vasudeva[38] and the son-of-Prithā, the great self.

18.75 By the grace of Vyāsa,[39] I heard this highest secret, the Yoga told directly[40] by Krishna Himself, the Lord of Yoga.

18.76 O king [Dhritarāshtra]! Recalling again and again[41] this wondrous, meritorious dialogue between Keshava[42] and Arjuna, I thrill-with-joy again and again.

18.77 And recalling again and again that most wondrous form of Hari,[43] my astonishment is great, O king, and I thrill-with-joy again and again.

18.78 Wherever Krishna, the Lord of Yoga, is [and] wherever the bow-bearer son-of-Prithā [Arjuna] is—there is fortune, victory, welfare, and sure guidance.[44] [This] is my conviction.

38. On son-of-Vasudeva, see note 58 for 10.37.

39. In this stanza, we again find Vyāsa writing himself into his own epic drama.

40. The Sanskrit text gives *sākshāt,* which means literally "before the eyes" and is rendered here as "directly."

41. The Sanskrit text gives *samsmritya samsmritya* (lit. "recalling recalling"), a duplication that suggests the repetition "again and again." See also 18.77.

42. On Keshava, see note 21 for 1.31.

43. Hari is another name of Krishna.

44. The term *nīti* can stand for personal or political guidance, or, as some translators have it, as statecraft.

Part Three
Word-for-Word Translation

yadeveha tadamutra

Whatever is here, that is there.

—*Katha-Upaniṣad* 2.1.10

Grammatical Note

INSTEAD OF VISARGA *ḥ*, which is written in the Devanagari (*devanāgarī*) script as a colon (:), I have used *s*, the grammatically correct stem. Thus *māmakāḥ* ("mine" in the plural) in verse 1.1 becomes *māmakās*, and the singular *yuyudhāno* (= Yuyudhānaḥ) of verse 1.4 becomes *yuyudhānas*. I have left case endings unmodified, such as the genitive plural of *pāṇḍuputrāṇām* in verse 1.3 or the dual of *sughoṣamaṇipuṣpakau* in verse 1.16. I have, however, adjusted euphonically required consonantal changes to the proper stem, such as *yady* (required by a following vowel) to *yadi*. The indeclinable words *tu* ("but"), *eva* ("indeed, verily"), and *hi* ("indeed, for") are frequently used as metric fillers or for emphasis. I have generally omitted them. Whenever it seemed useful, I have given grammatical hints (e.g., singular, dual, plural, genitive, feminine, etc.) for beginning Sanskrit students.

Those wanting to delve into the Sanskrit text of the *Gītā* will quickly appreciate that the syntax in Sanskrit is not well developed and that euphonic (good-sounding) and metric considerations come first. However, students will also realize that the use of case endings seldom leaves room for confusion.

Word-for Word Translation

CHAPTER I. THE YOGA OF ARJUNA'S DESPONDENCY

dhṛtarāṣṭra (dhṛtarāṣṭras) = Dhritarāshtra; uvāca = he said;
1.1: dharmakṣetre (dharma + kṣetre) = on the field (kṣetra) of the law; kurukṣetre (kuru + kṣetre) = on the field of the Kurus; samavetās (plural) = assembled; yuyutsavas (plural) = eager to fight; māmakās (plural) = mine; pāṇḍavās = Pāndavas; caiva (ca + eva) = and also; kim = what; akurvata = they did; saṃjaya = O Samjaya.

saṃjaya (saṃjayas) = Samjaya; uvāca = he said;
1.2: dṛṣṭvā = having seen, here: seeing; tu = but; pāṇḍavānīkam (pāndava + anīkam) = rank of the Pāndavas; vyūḍham = arrayed, lined up; duryodhanas = Duryodhana; tadā = then; ācāryam = preceptor; upasaṃgamya = approaching; rājā = king, prince; vacanam = word, saying; abravīt = he spoke.

1.3: paśyaitām (paśya + etām) = behold (paśya) this; pāṇḍuputrāṇām (pāṇḍu + putrāṇām) = of the Pāndu sons; ācārya = O preceptor; mahatīm = great; camūm = army; vyūḍhām = arrayed, lined up; drupadaputreṇa (drupada + putreṇa) = by the son of Drupada; tava = your; śiṣyeṇa = by disciple; dhīmatā = by wise.

1.4: atra = here; śūrās = heroes; maheṣvāsās (mahā = iṣu + āsās) = great arrow (iṣu) throwers, i.e., archers; bhīmārjunasamās (bhīma

+ arjuna + samās) (plural) = equal to Bhīma [and] Arjuna; yudhi = in battle; yuyudhānas = Yuyudhāna; virāṭas = Virāta; ca = and; drupadas = Drupada; ca = and; mahārathas (mahā + rathas) = great chariot.

1.5: dhṛṣṭaketus = Dhrishtaketu; cekitānas = Cekitāna; kāśirājas (kāśi + rājas) = king of the Kāshis; ca = and; vīryavān = valiant; purujit = Purujit; kuntibhojas = Kuntibhoja; ca = and; śaibyas = Shaibya; ca = and; narapuṃgavas (nara + puṃgavas) = man-bull, i.e., bull among men.

1.6: yudhamanyus = Yudhamanyu; ca = and; vikrāntas = courageous; uttamaujas = Uttamaujas; ca = and; vīryavān = valiant; saubhadras = son-of-Subhadrā; draupadeyās = sons-of-Draupadī; ca = and; sarva = all; eva = indeed; mahārathās = (mahā + rathās) = lit. great chariots, here: great chariot-warriors.

1.7: asmākaṃ = our, here: us; tu = also; viśiṣṭās (plural) = excellent; ye (plural); = who; tān = them, here: they; nibodha = you know!, here: learn!; dvijottama = (dvija + uttama) = O best of the twice-born; nāyakās = leaders; mama = of me, my; sainyasya = of army; saṃjñārtham (samjnā + artham) = [by] proper name; tān = them; bravīmi = I tell, name; te = to you.

1.8: bhavān = you (honorific), here: Yourself; bhīṣmas = Bhīshma; ca = and; karṇas = Karna; ca = and; kṛpas = Kripa; ca = and; samitiṃjayas (samitim + jayas) = victorious (jaya) in combat; aśvatthāmā = Ashvatthāmān; vikarṇas = Vikarna; ca = and; saumadattis = son-of-Somadatta; tathaiva (tathā + eva) = also, as well as; ca = and.

1.9: anye = others, here: other; ca = and; bahavas = many; śūrās = heroes; madarthe (mad + arthe) = for my sake; tyaktajīvitās (tyakta + jīvitās) = abandoned lives, here: [ready to] lay down [their] lives; nānāśastrapraharaṇās (nāna + śastra + praharaṇās) = various (nānā) assailing (praharaṇa) weapons; sarve = all; yuddhaviśāradās (yuddha + viśāradās) (plural) = skilled in battle.

1.10: aparyāptam = unlimited; tad = this; asmākam = our; balam = force; bhīṣmābhirakṣitam (bhīṣma + abhirakṣitam) = guarded by Bhīshma; paryāptam = limited; tu = but; idam = this; eteṣām = of them, their; balam = force; bhīmābhirakṣitam (bhīma + abhirakṣitam) = guarded by Bhīma.

1.11: ayaneṣu = in maneuvers; ca = and; sarveṣu = in all; yathābhāgam (yathā + bhāgam) = as (yathā) appointed; avasthitās (plural) = placed, positioned; bhīṣmam = Bhīshma; evābhirakṣantu (eva + abhirakṣantu) = verily . . . guard!; bhavantas = you [all]; sarva = all, here: everyone; eva = verily; hi = indeed, here: omitted.

1.12: tasya = of him, here: to him; saṃjanayan = generating, here: to give; harṣam = thrill, here: joy; kuruvṛddhas (kuru + vṛddhas) = aged Kuru; pitāmahas = grandfather; siṃhanādam (simha + nādam) = lion (siṃha) roar; vinadyocchais (vinadya + ucchais) (plural) = sounding (vinadya) on high; śaṅkham = conch; dadhmau = he blew; pratāpavān = powerfully.

1.13: tatas = thence, then; śaṅkhās = conchs; ca = and; bheryas = kettledrums; ca = and; paṇavānakagomukhās (paṇava + ānaka + gomukhās) = cymbals (paṇava), drums (ānaka), [and] "bull-mouths," i.e., trumpets; sahasaivābhyahanyanta (sahasā + eva + abhyahanyanta) = suddenly (sahasā) indeed (eva) [were] sounded, here: *eva* is omitted; sas = he, here: the; śabdas = sound, here: uproar; tumulas = tumultuous; 'bhavat (abhavat) = it was.

1.14: tatas = thence, then; śvetais (plural) = with white; hayais = with steeds; yukte = in yoked; mahati = in great; syandane = in chariot; sthitau (dual) = standing; mādhavas = Mādhava; pāṇḍavas = son-of-Pāndu; caiva (ca + eva) = and indeed, here: also; divyau (dual) = [two] divine; śaṅkhau (dual) = [two] conchs; pradadhmatus = they [both] blew.

1.15: pāñcajanyam = "of the five peoples" [the name of Krishna's conch]; hṛṣīkeśas (hṛṣī + keśas) = bristling hair [an epithet of Krishna]; devadattam = "god-given" [the name of Arjuna's conch]; dhanaṃjayas = Conqueror of Wealth (i.e., Arjuna); pauṇḍram = "[belonging to] the Pundras," the name of Bhīma's conch; dadhmau = he blew; mahāśaṇkham (mahā + śaṇkham) = great conch; bhīmakarmā (bhīma + karmā) (singular) = fearful (bhīma) deed, here: doer-of-fearful-deeds; vṛkodaras (vṛka + udaras) = wolf-bellied [an epithet of Bhīma].

1.16: anantavijayam (ananta + vijayam) = "endless victory" [the name of Yudhishthira's conch]; rājā = king, prince; kuntīputras (kuntī + putras) = son of Kuntī; yudhiṣṭhiras = Yudhishthira; nakulas = Nakula; sahadevas = Sahadeva; ca = and; sughoṣamaṇipuṣpakau (sughoṣa + manipuṣpakau) (dual) = "good sounding" [the name of Nakula's conch] and "gem flowered" [the name of Sahadeva's conch].

1.17: kāśyas = of the Kashīs, here: Kāshi-king; ca = and; parameṣvāsas (parama + iṣu + āsas) = supreme archer; śikhaṇḍī = Shikhandin; ca = and; mahārathas = great chariot, here: great chariot-warrior; dhṛṣṭadyumnas = Dhrishtadyumna; virāṭas = Virāta; ca = and; sātyakis = Sātyaki; cāparājitas (ca + aparājitas) = and unconquered.

1.18: drupadas = Drupada; draupadeyās = sons-of-Draupadī; ca = and; sarvaśas = all together; pṛthivīpate (pṛthivī + pate) = O lord (pati) of the earth; saubhadras = the son-of-Subhadrā [and epithet of Abhimanyu]; ca = and; mahābāhus (mahā + bāhus) = great armed, here: mighty-armed; śaṅkhān = conchs; dadhmus = they blew; pṛthakpṛthak = severally, here: each [his own].

1.19: sas = his, here: that; ghoṣas = uproar; dhārtarāṣṭrāṇām = of the sons-of-Dhritarāshtra; hṛdayāni = hearts; vyadārayat = it pierced; nabhas = sky; ca = and; pṛthivīm = earth; caiva (ca + eva) = and indeed, here: *eva* is omitted; tumulas = tumult, here: tumultuously; vyanunādayan = causing to resound, here: resound.

1.20: atha = now, then; vyavasthitān (plural) = arrayed, here: in array; dṛṣṭvā = having seen, here: beholding; dhārtarāṣṭrān = the sons-of-Dhritarāshtra; kapidhvajas (kapi + dhvajas) = ape (kapi) bannered; pravṛtte = in coming forth, here: omitted, implied in "at"; śastrasaṃpāte (śastra + saṃpāte) = at the clash of weapons (śastra); dhanus = bow; udyamya = raising, here: took up; pāṇḍavas = son-of-Pāndu (i.e., Arjuna).

1.21: hṛṣīkeśam (hṛṣī + keśam) = "bristling hair" [an epithet of Krishna]; tadā = then; vākyam = word; here: words; idam = this, here: these; āha = he said, here: addressed; mahīpate (mahī + pate) = O Lord (pati) of the earth; senayos (dual)= of [both] armies; ubhayos (dual)= of both; madhye = in the middle [between]; ratham = chariot; sthāpaya = you cause to stand!; here: you halt!; me = of me, my; 'cyuta (acyuta) = O Acyuta (i.e., Krishna).

1.22: yāvad = as much, until, here: so that; etān = these; nirīkṣe = I [may] see, here: I [may] survey; 'ham (aham) = I; yoddhukāmān (plural) = eager for battle (plural); avasthitān = assembled (plural); kais = with whom?; mayā = by me; saha = with; yoddhavyam = to be fought, here: must fight; asmin = in this; raṇasamudyame (raṇa + samudyame) = in enterprise of combat (raṇa).

1.23: yotsyamānān (plural) = ready to fight; avekṣe = I behold; 'ham (aham) = I; ya (for ye), (plural) = who; ete = these, here: those; 'tra (atra) = here; samāgatās (plural) = assembled; dhārtarāṣṭrasya = of son-of-Dhritarāshtra (i.e., Duryodhana); durbuddhes = of evil-minded; yuddhe = in battle; priyacikīrṣavas (priya + cikīrṣavas) = desirous to please (priya).

1.24: evam = thus; uktas = spoken, here: addressed; hṛṣīkeśas (hṛṣī + keśas) = Hrishīkesha (i.e. Krishna); guḍākeśena (guḍā + keśena) = by "balled hair" [an epithet of Arjuna]; bhārata = O descendant-of-Bharata; senayos = of [both] armies; ubhayos = of both; madhye = in the middle [between]; sthāpayitvā = having stopped, here: brought to a halt; rathottamam (ratha + uttamam) = [that] excellent (uttama) chariot.

1.25: bhīṣmadroṇapramukhatas (bhīṣma + droṇa + pramukhatas) = in front (pramukhatas) of Bhīshma [and] Drona; sarveṣām =

of all [these]; ca = and; mahīkṣitām (mahī + kṣitām) = rulers (kṣit) of the earth; uvāca = he said; pārtha = O son-of-Prithā (i.e., Arjuna); paśyaitān (paśya + etān) = you behold these!; samavetān (plural) = gathered, assembled; kurūn = Kurus; iti = thus (it is used to indicate a quotation).

1.26: tatrāpaśyat (tatra + apaśyat) = there (tatra) he saw; sthitān (plural) = standing; pārthas = son-of-Prithā (i.e., Arjuna); pitṛn = fathers; atha = then, here: omitted; pitāmahān = grandfathers; ācāryān = preceptors; mātulān = (maternal) uncles; bhrātṛn = brothers; putrān = sons; pautrān = grandsons; sakhīn = friends, comrades; tathā = as well as.

1.27: śvaśurān = fathers-in-law; suhṛdas = "good-hearted ones" [i.e., friends]; caiva (ca + eva) = and indeed, here: omitted; senayos (dual) = of [both] armies; ubhayos (dual) = of both; api = also, here: and; tān = them; samīkṣya = seeing; sas kaunteyas = he the son-of-Kuntī [i.e., Arjuna]; sarvān (plural) = all; bandhūn = relatives, kinsmen; avasthitān (plural) = standing [in array].

1.28: kṛpayā = with pity; parayāviṣṭas (parayā + āviṣṭas) = filled with (āviṣṭa) great, here: filled with deep; viṣīdan = despondent; idam = this; abravīt = he said, spoke; dṛṣṭvemān (dṛṣṭvā + imān) = having seen these; here: seeing these; svajanān (sva + janān) (plural) = own people; kṛṣṇa = O Krishna; yuyutsūn (plural) = eager to fight; samavasthitān (plural) = standing [before me].

1.29: sīdanti = they sit, here: they fail; mama = of me, my; gātrāṇi = limbs; mukham = mouth; ca = and; pariśuṣyati = it makes dry, here: is parched; vepathus = trembling; ca = and; śarīre = in the body; me = of me, my; romaharṣas (roma + harṣas) = bristling hair, here: hair is [caused to] bristle; ca = and; jāyate = it is born, here: it is caused.

1.30: gāṇḍīvam = [the name of Arjuna's bow]; sraṃsate = it drops, here: it slips; hastāt = from hand; tvac = skin; caiva (ca + eva) = and also; paridahyate = it burns, here: is completely (pari) afire; na ca = and not, here: also not; śaknomi = I am able; avasthātum = to stand; bhramatīva (bhramati + iva) = it roams as it were (iva), here: it seems to reel; ca = and; me = of me, my; manas = mind.

1.31: nimittāni = signs, omens; ca = and, here: moreover; paśyāmi = I see; viparītāni (plural) = adverse; keśava = O Keshava (i.e., Krishna); na = not; ca = and, read together: nor; śreyas = good; 'nupaśyāmi (anupaśyāmi) = [can] I foresee; hatvā = having slain, here: in slaying; svajanam (sva + janam) = own people; āhave = in combat.

1.32: na = not; kāṅkṣe = I hanker; vijayam = victory; kṛṣṇa = O Krishna; na = not; ca = and, read together: nor yet; rājyam = kingdom; sukhāni = pleasures; ca = and, here: or; kim = what?, here: of what?; nas = to us; rājyena = with kingdom; govinda = O Govinda; kim = what?, here: of what?; bhogais = with enjoyments, here: enjoyments; jīvitena = with life, here: life; vā = or.

1.33: yeṣām = of whom, here: for whose; arthe = for the sake; kāṅkṣitam = hankered, here: [we] hanker; nas = by us, here: we; rājyam = kingdom; bhogās = pleasures; sukhāni = enjoyments; ca = and; ta (te) = they; ime = these; 'vasthitās (avasthitās) (plural) = standing, here: stand; yuddhe = in combat, here: for combat; prāṇān = lives; tyaktvā = having abandoned, here: surrendering; dhanāni = wealth; ca = and.

1.34: ācāryās = preceptors; pitaras = fathers; putrās = sons; tathaiva (tathā + eva) = indeed as well as, here: *eva* is omitted; ca = and; pitāmahās = grandfathers; mātulās = (maternal) uncles; śvaśurās = fathers-in-law; pautrās = grandsons; śyālās = brothers-in-law; saṃbandhinas = relatives; tathā = as well as.

1.35: etān = them; na = not; hantum = to kill; icchāmi = I wish; ghnatas = slayers, here: [they should] slay; 'pi (api) = also, even if; madhusūdana (madhu + sūdana) = "slayer of Madhu" [i.e., Krishna]; api = also, even; trailokya (trai + lokya) = triple world; rājyasya = of rulership; hetos = of cause, here: for the sake of; kim = what?, here: how [much less]; nu = indeed, here: omitted; mahīkṛte (mahī + kṛte) = for the sake of the earth (mahī).

1.36: nihatya = killing, here: if we kill; dhārtarāṣṭrān = the sons-of-Dhritarāshtra; nas = us, ours; kā = what?; prītis = delight; syāt = could be; janārdana (jana + ardana) = "O agitator of people," O Janārdana (i.e., Krishna); pāpam = sin; evāśrayet (eva + āśrayet) = only it would cling; asmān = us; hatvaitān (hatvā + etān) = having slain these, here: should we slay those; ātatāyinas (plural) = whose-bows-are-strung.

1.37: tasmān = therefore; nārhās = (na + arhās) (plural) = not justified, not allowed; vayam = we; hantum = to kill; dhārtarāṣṭrān = the sons-of-Dhritarāshtra; svabāndhavān (sva + bāndhavān) (plural) = own kinsmen, here: own kin; svajanam (sva + janam) = own people; hi = for; katham = how?; hatvā = having slain, here: we were to slay; sukhinas = happy; syāma = we could be; mādhava = O Mādhava.

1.38: yadi = if; api = even; ete = these; na = not, here: cannot; paśyanti = they see; lobhopahatacetasas (lobha + upahata + cetasas) = [with their] minds corrupted by greed; kulakṣayakṛtam (kula + kṣaya + kṛtam) = the destruction of the family (kula) done, here: to destroy the family; doṣam = flaw, here: is flawed; mitradrohe (mitra + drohe) = treachery toward a friend; ca = and; pātakam = transgression.

1.39: katham = how?; na = not, here: should [we] not; jñeyam = to be known, here: to be wise; asmābhis = by us, here: we; pāpāt = from sin; asmān = from this; nivartitum = to turn away; kulakṣayakṛtam (kula + kṣaya + kṛtam) = destruction of the family done, here: in the destruction of the family; doṣam = flaw; prapaśyadbhis = by seeing, here: [we who] behold; janārdana (jana + ardana) = O Janārdana.

1.40: kulakṣaye (kula + kṣaye) = upon the destruction of the family; praṇaśyanti = they are lost, here: they collapse; kuladharmās (kula + dharmās) = the family laws; sanātanās (plural) = everlasting; dharme = in the law, here: when the law; naṣṭe = once perished; kulam = the family; kṛtsnam = whole; adharmas = lawlessness; 'bhibhavati (abhibhavati) = it is overcome, here: befalls; uta = and, also, here: omitted.

1.41: adharmābhibhavāt (adharma + abhibhavāt) = through the prevalence of lawlessness (adharma); kṛṣṇa = O Krishna; praduṣyanti = they are corrupted; kulastriyas (kula + striyas) = family women; strīṣu = in women; duṣṭāsu (plural, locative) = in defiled, here: once [the women] are defiled; vārṣṇeya = O Vārshneya [i.e., Krishna]; jāyate = it is born, here: it occurs; varṇasaṃkaras (varṇa + saṃkaras) = intermixing of the classes.

1.42: saṃkaras = intermixing; narakāyaiva (narakāya + eva) = to hell indeed, here: *eva* is omitted; kulaghnānām (kula + ghnānām) = family destroyers; kulasya = of the family, here: family; ca = and, here: also; patanti = they fall; pitaras = the ancestors; hy (hi) = indeed; eṣām = of these, here: their; luptapiṇḍodakakriyās (lupta = piṇḍa + udaka + kriyās) = ritual-offerings (kriyā) of rice-balls [and] water (udaka) [are] discontinued.

1.43: doṣais = by flaws; etais = by these; kulaghnānām (kula + ghnānām) = of the family wreckers; varṇasaṃkarakārakais (varṇa + saṃkara + kārakais) = by [those who] cause class intermixture, here: class minglers; utsādyante = they are destroyed; jātidharmās (jāti + dharmās) = the caste laws; kuladharmās (kula + dharmās) = the family laws; ca = and; śāśvatās (plural) = eternal.

1.44: utsannakuladharmāṇāṃ (utsanna + kula + dharmāṇām) = of destroyed (utsanna) family laws; manuṣyāṇām = of men, here: for the men; janārdana (jana +ardana) = O Janārdana; narake = in hell; niyatam = sure [some manuscripts have aniyatam, "indefinite" qualifying "abode"]; vāsas = abode; bhavatīti (bhavati + iti) = there is thus (iti); anuśuśruma = we have heard.

1.45: aho = ah!; bata = alas!; mahat = great; pāpam = sin; kartum = to do, here: [we are indeed determined] to commit; vyavasitās (plural) = determined; vayam = we; yad = which, here: as; rājyasukhalobhena (rājya + sukha + lobhena) = out of greed for royal pleasures; hantum = to slay; svajanam (sva + janam) = own people; udyatās (plural) = intent on, here: prepared to.

1.46: yadi = if; mām = me; apratīkāram = unresisting; aśastram = without weapon, here: unarmed; śastrapāṇayas (śastra + pāṇayas) = weapons in [their] hands, here: arms in hand; dhārtarāṣṭrā = the sons-of-Dhritarāshtra; raṇe = in combat; hanyus = they should slay; tad = this; me = to me; kṣemataram (kṣema + taram) = more (tara) tranquillity, here: more agreeable; bhavet = it would be.

1.47: evam = thus; uktvārjunas (uktvā + arjunas) = Arjuna having said, here: having [thus] spoken, Arjuna; saṃkhye = in [the midst of] conflict; rathopastha (ratha + upastha) [for ratha-upasthe] = chariot seat; upāviśat = he sat down, here: he sank down; visṛjya = casting down; saśaram = with (sa-) arrow; cāpam = bow; śokasaṃvignamānasas (śoka + saṃvigna + mānasas) = mind agitated with grief (śoka).

CHAPTER 2: THE YOGA OF KNOWLEDGE

saṃjaya (saṃjayas) = Samjaya; uvāca = he said;

2.1: tam = him; tathā = thus; kṛpayāviṣṭam (kṛpayā + aviṣṭam) = overcome (aviṣṭa) with pity; aśrupūrṇākulekṣaṇam (aśru + pūrṇa + ākula + īkṣaṇam) = downcast (ākula) eyes full (pūrṇa) of tears; viṣīdantam = despairing; idam = this; vākyam = word; uvāca = he said; madhusūdanas = Madhusūdana.

śrībhagavān (śrī + bhagavān) = Blessed Lord; uvāca = he said;

2.2: kutas = whence?; tvā = you, here: on you; kaśmalam = weakness; idam = this; viṣame = in difficulty; samupasthitam = approaching, here: comes; anāryajuṣṭam (anārya + juṣṭam) = befitting a non-ārya; asvargyam = nonheavenly, here: not-conducive-to-heaven; akīrtikaram (akīrti + karam) = causing disrepute (akīrti), here: brings disrepute; arjuna = O Arjuna.

2.3: klaibyam = unmanliness; mā = not; sma = indeed, here: omitted; gamas = you should [not] undergo, here: you should [not] adopt; pārtha = O son-of-Prithā (i.e., Arjuna); naitat (na + etad) = not this (etad); tvayi = in you, here: you; upapadyate

= it is fitting, here: becomes [you not]; kṣudram = base; hṛdayadaurbalyam (hṛdaya + daurbalyam) = faint-heartedness (from hṛdaya, "heart"); tyaktvottiṣṭha (tyaktvā + uttiṣṭha) = having abandoned [it], rise!, here: give up [this faint-heartedness and] rise!; paraṃtapa = O Paramtapa.

arjuna (arjunas) = Arjuna; uvāca = he said;

2.4: katham = how?; bhīṣmam = Bhīshma; aham = I; saṃkhye = in combat; droṇam = Droṇa; ca = and; madhusūdana = O Madhusūdana (i.e., Krishna); iṣubhis = with arrows; pratiyotsyāmi = I will fight, here: I [can] attack; pūjārhāvarisūdana (pūjā + arhau + arisūdana) (pūjā-arhau is in the dual) = reverence-worthy O Arisūdana.

2.5: gurūn = teachers; ahatvā = having slain, here: slay; hi = for; mahānubhāvān (mahā + anubhāvān) (plural) = greatly (mahā) dignified; śreyas = better; bhoktum = to eat; bhaikṣyam = alms-food; apīha (api + iha) = even here; loke = in the world; hatvārthakāmān (hatvā + artha + kāmān) (plural) = having slain desirous of gain, here: slay [though they are] desirous of gain; tu = but, though; gurūn = teachers; ihaiva (iha + eva) = here [on earth] indeed, here: *eva* is omitted; bhuñjīya = I should eat, I should enjoy; bhogān = pleasures; rudhirapradigdhān (rudhira + pradigdhān) (plural) = blood-smeared.

2.6: na = not, here: nor; caitad (ca + etad) = and this; vidmas = [do] we know; katarat (dual) = which?; nas = us, here: for us; garīyas = important; yad = which, here: whether; vā = or; jayema = we should be victorious; yadi = if; vā = or; nas = us; jayeyus = they should conquer; yān = whom, here: omitted; eva = indeed, here: omitted; hatvā = having slain; na = not; jijīviṣāmas = we desire to live; te = they; 'vasthitās (avasthitās) (plural) = arrayed; pramukhe = in the face, here: facing [us]; dhārtarāṣṭrās = the sons-of-Dhritarāshtra.

2.7: kārpaṇyadoṣopahatasvabhāvas (kārpaṇya + doṣa + upahata + sva + bhāvas) = own-being (svabhāva) corrupted [by the] fault (doṣa) of pity; pṛcchāmi = I ask; tvām = you; dharmasaṃmūḍhacetās (dharma + saṃmūḍha + cetās) (singular) = [my] mind confused (saṃmūḍha) [about] the law; yad = which; śreyas = better; syāt = it should be; niścitam = for certain; brūhi = you tell; tad = this, here: omitted; me = to me; śiṣyas = pupil; te = of you, your; 'ham (aham) = I; śadhi = you instruct [me]!; mām = me; tvām = you; prapannam = suppliant, here: approaching.

2.8: na = not, here: cannot; hi = indeed, for; prapaśyāmi = I see; mamāpanudyāt (mama + apanudyāt) = it should dispel, here: [what] would dispel; yad = which, here: what; śokam = grief; ucchoṣaṇam = drying up, here: dries up; indriyāṇām = of the senses; avāpya = attaining, here: win; bhūmau = on earth; asapatnam = unrivaled; ṛddham = prosperous; rājyam = rulership; surāṇām = of the deities; api = even; cādhipatyam (ca + ādhipatyam) = and sovereignty.

saṃjaya (saṃjayas) = Samjaya; uvāca = he said;

2.9: evam = thus; uktvā = having said, spoken, here: [thus] spoke; hṛṣīkeśam = Hrishīkesha [i.e., Krishna]; guḍākeśas (guḍā + keśa) = Gudākesha [i.e., Arjuna]; paraṃtapas = Paramtapa [i.e., Arjuna]; na = not; yotsya = I will [not] fight; iti = used to indicate a quotation; govindam = Govinda; uktvā = having said, here: having declared; tūṣṇīm = silently, here: silence; babhūva = he became, here: he lapsed into; ha = indeed, here: omitted.

2.10: tam = him; uvāca = he said, here: he spoke; hṛṣīkeṣas = Hrishīkesha; prahasan = laughingly; iva = as it were; bhārata = O descendant-of-Bharata; senayos = of [both] armies; ubhayos = of both, here: the two; madhye = in the middle, here: between; viṣīdantam = dejected; idam = this; vacas = word.

śrībhagavān (śrī + bhagavān) = Blessed Lord; uvāca = he said;

2.11: aśocyān (plural) = not to be grieved; anvaśocas = you have grieved, here: you grieve; tvam = you; prajñāvādān (prajñā + vādān) = wisdom (prajñā) words; ca = and [yet]; bhāṣase = you speak; gatāsūn (gata + asūn) (plural) = gone the life-breaths, i.e., dead; agatāsān (agata + asūn) (plural) = not gone the life-breaths, i.e., living; ca = and; nānuśocanti (na + anuśocanti) = they [do] not; paṇḍitās (plural) = the learned.

«tvam = you, here: your; mānuṣyeṇopahatāntarātmā (mānuṣyeṇa + upahata + antarātmā) = by humanness assailed (upahata) inner self, here: inner self assailed by what-is-all-too-human; viṣādamohābhībhavāt (viṣāda + moha + abhībhavāt) = by being overpowered by dejection (viṣāda) [and] delusion (moha); visaṃjñas = without understanding, here: lacks understanding; kṛpāgṛhītas (kṛpā + gṛhītas) = seized by pity (kṛpā); samavekṣya = seeing; bandhūn = kinsmen; abhiprapannān = fall into; mukham = face, here: jaws; antakasya = of death.»

2.12: na = not, here: never (in conjunction with jātu); tu = but, here: omitted; evāham (eva + aham) = verily I; jātu = ever; nāsam (na + āsam) = not was I; na = not; tvam = you; neme (na + ime) = not these; janādhipās (jana + adhipās) = rulers; na = not; caiva (ca + eva) = and also; na = not, here: nor; bhaviṣyāmas = we will be; sarve = all; vayam = we; atas param = henceforth.

2.13: dehinas = of the embodied one, here: of body-essence; 'smin (asmin) = in this; yathā = just as; dehe = in the body; kaumāram = childhood; yauvanam = youth; jarā = old age; tathā = thus, likewise, here: so too; dehāntaraprāptis (deha + antara + prāptis) = attainment of another (antara) body, here: obtains another body; dhīras = thoughtful; tatra = in this, here: by this; na = not; muhyati = he is confused.

2.14: mātrāsparśās (mātrā + sparśās) = material contacts (sparśa); tu = indeed; kaunteya = O son-of-Kuntī; śītoṣṇasukhaduḥkhadās (śīta + uṣṇa + sukha + duḥkha + dās) (plural) = bestowing (da) cold, heat (uṣna), pleasure [and] pain (duḥkha) (plural), here: give rise to . . . ; āgamāpāyinas (āgama + apāyinas) (plural) = coming [and] going, here: come and go; 'nityās (anityās) (plural) = impermanent; tān = them; titikṣasva = you endure!; bhārata = O descendant-of-Bharata.

2.15: yam = whom; hi = for; na = not; vyathayanti = they cause to tremble, here: they distress; ete = these; puruṣam = man; puruṣarṣabha (puruṣa + ṛṣabha) = O bull-man; samaduḥkhasukham (sama + duḥkha + sukham) = same [toward] pain (duḥkha) [and] pleasure; dhīram = wise one;

sas = he, here: the; 'mṛtatvāya (amṛtatvāya) = to immortality (amṛtatva), here: for immortality; kalpate = he is fit.

2.16: nāsatas (na + asatas) = not (na) of nonexistent (asat); vidyate = it is found, here: there is; bhāvas = being, here: coming-into-being; nābhāvas (na + abhāvas) = no (na) disappearance; vidyate = it is found, here: there is; satas = of existent (sat); ubhayos (dual) = of both; api = also, here: moreover; dṛṣṭas = seen; 'ntas (antas) = end; tu = indeed, here: omitted; anayos (dual) = of these [two]; tattvadarśibhis = by the seers-of-Reality.

2.17: avināśi = indestructible; tu = but, yet; tad = that; viddhi = know; yena = by which; sarvam = entire; idam = this; tatam = spread out; vināśam = destruction; avyayasyāsya = of the immutable; na kaścit = no one; kartum = to accomplish; arhati = he is able.

2.18: antavantas (plural) = finite; ime = these; dehās = bodies; nityasya = of eternal; uktās (plural) = are said; śarīriṇas = of the embodied; anāśinas = of the indestructible; 'prameyasya (aprameyasya) = of the incommensurable; tasmāt = therefore, hence; yudhyasva = you fight!; bhārata = O descendant-of-Bharata.

2.19: yas = who; enam = this; vetti = he knows, here: he thinks; hantāram = slayer; yas = who; caiman (ca + enam) = and (ca) this; manyate = he thinks; hatam = slain; ubhau (dual) = both; tau (dual) = they [both]; na = not; vijānītas (dual) = [both] know; nāyam (na + ayam) = not this; hanti = he slays, here: [does not] slay; na = not, here: nor; hanyate = he is slain.

2.20: na = not; jāyate = he is born; mriyate = he dies; vā = or, here: nor; kadācit = any time, here: ever; nāyam = not this; bhūtvā = having become, here: having-come-to-be; bhavitā = will be, will become; vā = or; na = not; bhūyas = again, here the whole phrase needs to be read: shall again cease-to-be; ajas = unborn; nityas = eternal; śāśvatas = everlasting; 'yam (ayam) = this; purāṇas = primordial; na = not; hanyate = it is slain; hanyamāne = when slain; śarīre = when body.

2.21: vedāvināśinam (veda + avināśinam) = knowledge (veda) [of the] indestructible, here: he knows the indestructible; nityam = eternal; yas = who; enam = this; ajam = unborn; avyayam = immutable; katham = how?; sas = he, here: the; puruṣas = man; pārtha = O son-of-Prithā; kam = whom?; ghātayati = he causes to slay; hanti = he slays; kam = whom?

2.22: vāsāṃsi = garments; jīrṇāni (plural) = worn-out; yathā = as; vihāya = discarding; navāni = new ones; gṛhnāti = he seizes; naras = man; 'parāṇi (aparāṇi) = others; tathā = so; śarīrāṇi = bodies; vihāya = discarding; jīrṇāni (plural) = worn-out; anyāni = others; saṃyāti = he enters; navāni = new ones; dehī = embodied [Self].

2.23: nainam = (na + enam) not this; chindanti = they cleave; śastrāṇi = weapons; nainam = (na + enam) not this; dahati = it burns; pāvakas = fire; na = not; cainam = (ca + enam) and this, here: *ca* is omitted; kledayanti = they cause to be wet, here: wet; āpas = waters, here: water; na = not; śoṣayati = it causes to dry, here: [does] dry; mārutas = wind.

2.24: acchedyas = uncuttable; 'yam (ayam) = this; adāhyas = unburnable; 'yam (ayam) = this; akledyas = unwettable; 'śoṣya (aśoṣya) = undryable; eva = indeed, verily, here: omitted; ca = and; nityas = eternal; sarvagatas = omnipresent; sthāṇus = stable; acalas = unmoving; 'yam (ayam) = this; sanātanas = everlasting.

2.25: avyaktas = unmanifest; 'yam (ayam) = this; acintyas = unthinkable; 'yam (ayam) = this; avikāryas = unchangeable; 'yam (ayam) = this; ucyate = it is said, it is called; tasmāt = hence; evam = thus; viditvainam (viditvā + enam) = having known this (enam), here: knowing this; nānuśocitum (na + anuśocitum) = not to grieve; arhasi = you should [not].

2.26: atha cainam (atha ca + enam) = now and this, here: moreover; nityajātam (nitya + ajātam) = eternally born; nityam = eternally; vā = or, here: and; manyase = you deem; mṛtam = dead, here: dying; tathāpi (tathā + api) = then even, here:

omitted; tvam = you; mahābāho (mahā + bāho) = O mighty-armed [Arjuna]; nainam (na + enam) = not this, here: for it; śocitum = to grieve; arhasi = you should.

2.27: jātasya = of born, here: of all-that-is-born; hi = for; dhruvas = certain; mṛtyus = death; dhruvam = certain; janma = birth; mṛtasya = of dead, here: of all-that-dies; ca = and; tasmāt = therefore; aparihārye = in [this] inevitable; 'rthe (arthe) = in [this] matter; na = not; tvam = you; śocitum = to grieve; arhasi = you should.

2.28: avyaktādini (avyakta + ādini) (plural) = unmanifest beginnings; bhūtāni = beings; vyaktamadhyāni (vyakta + madhyāni) (plural) = manifest middles, here: in [their] middle-states; bhārata = O descendant-of-Bharata; avyaktanidhanāni (avyakta + nidhanāni) (plural) = unmanifest ends; eva = indeed; tatra = in this, here: over this; kā = what [reason is there for]?; paridevanā = lamentation, here: lamenting.

2.29: āścaryavat = marvelous, here: as a marvel; paśyati = he sees; kaścid = someone; enam = this; āścaryavat = marvelous, here: as a marvel; vadati = he speaks; tathaiva (tathā eva) = similarly; cānyas (ca + anyas) = and another; āścaryavat = marvelous, here: as a marvel; cainam (ca + enam) = and this; anyas = other, another; śṛṇoti = he hears; śrutvāpi (śrutvā + api) = yet (api) having heard; enam = this; veda = he knows; na = no; caiva (ca + eva) = and verily; kaścid = anyone, here: [no] one.

2.30: dehī = embodied [Self], here: body-essence; nityam = eternally; avadhyas = inviolable; 'yam (ayam) = this; dehe = in body; sarvasya = of all; bhārata = O descendant-of-Bharata; tasmāt = therefore; sarvāṇi (plural) = all, here: any; bhūtāni = beings, here: being; na = not; tvam = you; śocitum = to grieve; arhasi = you can, you should.

2.31: svadharmam (sva + dharmam) = own law; api = also, even, here: further; cāvekṣya (ca + avekṣya) = and looking at, here: considering; na = not; vikampitum = to waver; arhasi = you can, you should; dharmyāt = than [a] lawful; hi = for; yuddhāt =

than a war; śreyas = better; 'nyat (anyat) = other; kṣatriyasya = for a warrior; na = not, here: nothing; vidyate = is found, here: there is.

2.32: yadṛcchayā = by chance; copapannam (ca + upapannam) = and occurring; svargadvāram (svarga + dvāram) = gate to heaven (svarga); apāvṛtam = open, here: opening; sukhinas (plural) = happy; kṣatriyās = warriors; pārtha = O son-of-Prithā; labhante = they attain, here: they encounter; yuddham = battle; īdṛśam = such.

2.33: atha = now; ced = if; tvam = you; imam = this; dharmyam = lawful; saṃgrāmam = combat; na = not; kariṣyasi = you will do, here: you will engage; tatas = thence, then; svadharmam (sva + dharmam) = own law; kīrtim = honor; ca = and; hitvā = having avoided, here: [by] disregarding; pāpam = sin; avāpsyasi = you will incur.

2.34: akīrtim = dishonor; cāpi (ca + api) = and also, here: furthermore; bhūtāni = beings; kathayiṣyanti = they will recount; te = of you, your; 'vyayām (avyayām) = forever; saṃbhāvitasya = for the honorable [man]; cākīrtis (ca + akīrtis) = and dishonor; maraṇāt = than death; atiricyate = it surpasses.

2.35: bhayāt = from fear; raṇāt = from combat; uparatam = withdrawn, here: withdrew; maṃsyante = they regard; tvām = you; mahārathās = great chariot-warriors; yeṣām = of whom; ca = and; tvam = you; bahumatas (bahu + matas) = great esteem; bhūtvā = having been, here: hold [you in]; yāsyasi = you will go, here: you will become; lāghavam = lightness, here: levity.

2.36: avācyavādān (avācya + vādān) = words (vāda) not to be spoken, here: abusive; ca = and; bahūn (plural) = many; vadiṣyanti = they will speak; tavāhitās (tava + ahitās) = your ill-wishers; nindantas (plural) = ridiculing, here: denouncing; tava = your; sāmarthyam = prowess; tatas = thence, then, here; than that; duḥkhataram (duḥkha + taram) = more painful (duḥkha); tu = indeed, but, here: omitted; kim = what?

2.37: hatas = slain; vā = or, here: omitted; prāpsyasi = you will attain, here: you will reach; svargam = heaven; jitvā = having conquered, here: [should you be] victorious; vā = or, here: omitted; bhokṣyase = you will enjoy; mahīm = earth; tasmāt = therefore; uttiṣṭha = you rise!; kaunteya = O son-of-Kuntī; yuddhāya = for battle; kṛtaniścayas (kṛta + niścayas) = done (kṛta) [with] conviction, here: resolute.

2.38: sukhaduḥkhe (sukha + duḥkhe) (dual) = pleasure and pain; same (dual) = same, alike; kṛtvā = having done, here: holding; lābhālābhau (lābha + alābhau) (dual) = profit and loss; jayājayau (jaya + ajayau) (dual) = victory and defeat; tatas = thence, then, here: thus; yuddhāya = for battle; yujyasva = you engage!, here: gird [yourself]!; naivam (na + evam) = not thus; pāpam = sin; avāpsyasi = you will incur.

2.39: eṣā = this; te = to you; 'bhihitā (abhihitā) (feminine) = declared, here: revealed; sāṃkhye = in Sāmkhya, here: according to; buddhis (feminine) = wisdom; yoge = in Yoga; tu = indeed; imām = this; śṛṇu = you hear!; buddhyā = by wisdom, here: by the wisdom-faculty; yuktas = yoked; yayā = by which; pārtha = O son-of-Prithā; karmabandham (karma + bandham) = action bond, here: binding [effect of] action; prahāsyasi = you will forsake, here: you will transcend.

2.40: nehābhikramanāśas (na + iha + abhikrama + nāśas) = not here (iha) an effort [comes to] destruction (nāśa), here: no effort is lost; 'sti (asti) = is; pratyavāyas = reverse, here: slipping-back; na = no; vidyate = is found, here: there is; svalpam = little; api = even; asya = of this; dharmasya = of law; trāyate = it rescues; mahatas = from great; bhayāt = from fear.

2.41: vyavasāyātmikā (vyavasāya + ātmikā) = [having] the essence of determination (vyavasāya); buddhis = wisdom, here: wisdom-faculty; ekeha (ekā + iha) = single here (iha); kurunandana = O delight of the Kurus [an epithet of Arjuna]; bahuśākhā (bahu + śākhās) = many branches, many-branched; hi = indeed, here: however; anantās (plural) = endless; ca = and;

buddhayas = wisdoms, here: wisdom-faculties; 'vyavasāyinām (avyavasāyinām) (plural) = of the irresolute, here: [of those who are] devoid of determination.

2.42: yām (feminine) = which, here: omitted; imām (feminine) = this, here: omitted; puṣpitām (feminine) = flowery; vācam (feminine) = speech; pravadanti = they say, here: they utter; avipaścitas = undiscerning ones; vedavādaratās (veda + vāda + ratas) = [people] delighting in the lore of the Vedas; pārtha = O son-of-Prithā; nānyat (na + anyat) = no other, here: nothing else; astīti (asti + iti) = there is thus, here: iti is used to indicate a quotation; vādinas (plural) = saying.

2.43: kāmātmānas (kāma + ātmānas) (plural) = [having] desire (kāma) as essence; svargaparā (svarga + parās) (plural) = intent on heaven; janmakarmaphalapradām (janma + karma + phala + pradām) = rebirth [is the] fruit (phala) of action; kriyāviśeṣabahulām (kriyā +viśeṣa + bahulām) = many (bahula) special rites (kriyā); bhogaiśvaryagatim (bhoga + aiśvarya + gatim) = enjoyment [and] lordship (aiśvarya) [as] aim, here: the attainment of enjoyment and lordship; prati = in regard to, here: for.

2.44: bhogaiśvaryaprasaktānām (bhoga + aiśvarya + prasaktānām) = of [those who are] attached to enjoyment and lordship; tayāpahṛtacetasām (tayā + apahṛta + cetasām) (plural) = of those [who have] carried-away minds; vyavasāyātmikā (vyavasāya + ātmikā) = of the essence (ātmikā) of determination; buddhis = wisdom, here: wisdom-faculty; samādhau = in ecstasy; na = not; vidhīyate = it is settled.

2.45: traiguṇyaviṣayās (traiguṇya + viṣayās) = the triad of primary-qualities [are] subjects, here: . . . is the subject-matter; vedās = Vedas; nistraiguṇyas = free of the triple primary-qualities; bhavārjuna (bhava + arjuna) = O Arjuna be [free]!; nirdvandvas = free of the pair-of-opposites, here: free of the pairs-of-opposites; nityasattvasthas (nitya + sattva + sthas) = always [in] sattva abiding, here: abide always in sattva!; niryogakṣemas (niryoga + kṣemas) = without [trying to] gain or keep [anything]; ātmavān = Self-possessed.

2.46: yāvān = as much; arthas = use; udapāne = in a [water] reservoir; sarvatas = all-round; saṃplutodake (saṃpluta + udake) = in water (udaka) flooded; tāvān = so much; sarveṣu = in all; vedeṣu = in the Vedas; brāhmaṇasya = for the brāhmaṇa; vijānatas = for the knowing.

2.47: karmaṇi = in action; evādhikāras (eva + adhikāras) = indeed, alone claim, here: [in action] alone [is your] rightful-interest (adhikāras); te = your; mā = not, never; phaleṣu = in fruits, here: fruit; kadācana = at any time; mā = not, nor; karmaphalahetus (karma + phala + hetus) = action fruit [as] motive; bhūs = it should be; mā = not, nor; te = your; saṅgas = attachment; 'stu (astu) = let be; akarmaṇi = in inaction, here: to inaction.

2.48: yogasthas (yoga + sthas) = Yoga fixed, here: steadfast in Yoga; kuru = do!, here: perform!; karmāṇi = in action; saṅgam = attachment; tyaktvā = having abandoned, here: abandoning; dhanaṃjaya = O Dhanamjaya; siddhyasiddhyos (siddhi + asiddhyos) (dual) = in success and failure; samas = same; bhūtvā = having been, here: remaining [the same]; samatvam = equanimity; yogas = Yoga; ucyate = is called.

2.49: dūreṇa = by far; hi = indeed; avaram = inferior; karma = action; buddhiyogāt (buddhi + yogāt) = than the Yoga [of] wisdom, here: *buddhi-yoga* retained in Sanskrit; dhanaṃjaya = O Dhanamjaya; buddhau = in wisdom, here: in the wisdom-faculty; śaraṇam = refuge; anviccha = you seek!; kṛpaṇās (plural) = pitiful; phalahetavas (phala + hetavas) (plural) = [whose] motives [is] the fruit.

2.50: buddhiyuktas (buddhi + yuktas) = buddhi yoked; jahātiha (jahāti + iha) = he leaves behind here; ubhe (dual) = both; sukṛtaduṣkṛte (sukṛta + duṣkṛte) (dual) = well-done and ill-done; tasmāt = therefore, hence; yogāya = to Yoga; yujyasva

= you yoke!, here: yoke yourself!; yogas = Yoga; karmasu = in actions; kauśalam = skill.

2.51: karmajam (karma + jam) = action-born; buddhiyuktās (buddhi + yuktās) = *buddhi* yoked; hi = indeed, here: omitted; phalam = fruit; tyaktvā = having abandoned, here: have renounced; manīṣiṇas (plural) = the wise; janmabandhavinirmuktās (janma + bandha + vinirmuktās) = [those who are] liberated [from] the bondage of birth [and death]; padam = region; gacchanti = they go; anāmayam = free from ill.

2.52: yadā = when; te = your; mohakalilam (moha + kalilam) = thicket of delusion (moha); buddhis = wisdom, here: wisdom-faculty; vyatitariṣyati = it will go beyond, here: has traversed; tadā = then; gantāsi = you will go, here: you will acquire; nirvedam = disinterest; śrotavyasya = of [what] will be heard; śrutasya = of [what] has been heard; ca = and.

2.53: śrutivipratipannā (śruti + vipratipannā) (feminine) = diverted by revealed-tradition (śruti); te = your; yadā = when; sthāsyati = it will stand; niścalā (feminine) = motionless; samādhau = in ecstasy; acalā (feminine) = unmoving, here: still; buddhis (feminine) = wisdom, here: wisdom-faculty; tadā = then; yogam = Yoga; avāpsyasi = you will attain.

2.54: sthitaprajñasya (sthita + prajñasya) = of [one who is] steadied (sthita) in gnosis; kā = what?; bhāṣā = speech, definition; samādhisthasya (samādhi + sthasya) = of [one who is] abiding (sthasya) in ecstasy; keśava = O Keshava; sthitadhīs (sthita + dhīs) = steadied in vision (dhī); kim = what? how?; prabhāṣeta = he might speak; kim = what? how?; āsīta = he might sit; vrajeta = he might move about; kim = what? how?

śrībhagavān (śrī + bhagavān) = Blessed Lord; uvāca = he said;
2.55: prajahāti = he relinquishes; yadā = when; kāmān (plural) = desires; sarvān = all; pārtha = O son-of-Prithā; manogatān (manas + gatān) (plural) = mind gone, here: that the mind; ātmani = in the self; evātmanā (eva + ātmanā) = indeed with the

self; tuṣṭas = contended, content; sthitaprajñas (sthita + prajñas) = steadied in gnosis; tadocyate (tadā + ucyate) = then he is called.

2.56: duḥkheṣvanudvignamanās (duḥkeṣu + anudvigna + manās) (singular) = in sorrows unagitated-minded, here: [whose] mind is unagitated in sorrow; sukheṣu = in pleasures, here: pleasure; vigataspṛhas (vigata + spṛhas) = gone (vigata) desire, here: devoid of longing; vītarāgabhayakrodhas (vīta + rāga + bhaya + krodhas) = free from passion (rāga), fear [and] anger; sthitadhīs (sthita + dhīs) = steadied in vision (dhī); munis = sage; ucyate = he is called.

2.57: yas = who; sarvatrānabhisnehas (sarvatra + anabhisnehas) = everywhere unattached, here: unattached all-round; tattat (tad + tad) = this [or] that; prāpya = encountering; śubhāśubham (śubha + aśubham) = auspious [or] inauspicious; nābhinandati (na abhinandati) = not rejoices, here: neither . . . ; na = not, here: nor . . . ; dveṣṭi = he dislikes; tasya = his; prajñā (feminine) = gnosis; pratiṣṭhitā (feminine) = established, here: well established.

2.58: yadā = when; saṃharate = he withdraws; cāyam (ca + ayam) = and this; kūrmas = tortoise; 'ṇgānīva (aṅgāni + iva) = the limbs as it were (iva), here: iva is translated as "as"; sarvaśas = wholly, here: from every side; indriyāṇīndriyārthebhyas (indriyāṇi + indriya + arthebhyas) = the senses (indriya) from the objects (artha) of the senses; tasya = his; prajñā (feminine) = gnosis; pratiṣṭhitā (feminine) = established, here: well-established.

2.59: viṣayās = objects; vinivartante = they disappear; nirāhārasya = of the non-eating; dehinas = of the embodied one; rasavarjam (rasa + varjam) = relish, taste (rasa) exepted; rasas = relish, taste; 'pyasya (api + asya) = also for him; param = the Supreme; dṛṣtvā = having seen, here: upon seeing; nivartate = it disappears.

2.60: yatatas = of the striving [man]; hi = yet; api = also, even; kaunteya = O son-of-Kuntī; puruṣasya = of the man; vipaścitas = of the discerning [man]; indriyāṇi = the senses; pramāthīni (plural) = agitated; haranti = they carry away; prasabham = forcibly; manas = mind.

2.61: tāni = these; sarvāṇi (plural) = all; saṃyamya = controlling; yuktas = yoked; āsīta = he should sit, here: let him sit; matparas (mad + paras) = intent (para) on me; vaśe = under control; hi = for; yasyendriyāṇi (yasya + indriyāṇi) = whose senses; tasya = his; prajñā (feminine) = gnosis; pratiṣṭhitā (feminine) = established, here: well established.

2.62: dhyāyatas = contemplating, here: when [a man] contemplates; viṣayān = objects; puṃsas = of a man, here: when a man; saṅgas = contact, here: direct-contact; teṣūpajāyate (teṣu + upajāyate) = in them is born, here: with them is born; saṇgāt = from direct-contact; saṃjāyate = it springs; kāmas = desire; kāmāt = from desire; krodhas = anger; 'bhijāyate (abhijāyate) = it is born, here: it is produced.

2.63: krodhāt = from anger; bhavati = it comes; saṃmohas = confusion; saṃmohāt = from confusion; smṛtivibhramas (smṛti + vibhramas) = memory (smṛti) wandering, here: disorder of the memory; smṛtibhramśāt (smṛti + bhramśāt) = from disorder of the memory (smṛti); buddhināśas (buddhi + nāśas) = the destruction (nāśas) of wisdom, here: the destruction of the wisdom-faculty; buddhināśāt (buddhi + nāśāt) = from the destruction of the wisdom-faculty; praṇaśyati = he is lost.

2.64: rāgadveṣaviyuktais (rāga + dveṣa + viyuktais) = with [being] disjoined from passion (rāga) [and] aversion (dveṣa); tu = but, here: omitted; viṣayān = objects; indriyais = with the senses; caran = moving; ātmavaśyais (ātma + vaśyais) = with self-restraints; vidheyātmā (vidheya + ātmā) = governed, here: well-governed (vidheya) self; prasādam = grace, serenity, here: serenity-grace; adhigacchati = he attains, here: he approaches.

2.65: prasāde = in serenity-grace, here: [on reaching] serenity-grace; sarvaduḥkhānām (sarva + duḥkhānām) = of all (sarva) sorrows, here: of all sorrow; hānis = cessation; asya = for him; 'pajāyate (apajāyate) = it arises; prasannacetasas (prasanna + cetasas) = of the clear minded; hi = indeed, here: omitted; āśu = at once; buddhis = wisdom, here: wisdom-faculty; paryavatiṣṭhate = it is firmly grounded.

2.66: nāsti (na + asti) = not is, here: there is no; buddhis = wisdom, here: wisdom-faculty; ayuktasya = for the unyoked; na = no; cāyuktasya (ca + ayuktasya) = and for the unyoked; bhāvanā = meditation, contemplation, here: becoming-whole [from the grammatical root *bhū*, "to become"]; na = not; cābhāvayatas (ca + abhāvayatas) = and for the non-meditating, here: for the [one who does] not become-whole; śāntis = peace; aśāntasya = of the unpeaceful [man]; kutas = whence; sukham = joy, happiness.

2.67: indriyāṇām = of the senses; hi = indeed, here: omitted; caratām (plural) = roaming; yad = which, when; manas + mind; 'nuvidhīyate (anuvidhīyate) = it is governed; tad = that, then; asya = of him, his; harati = it carries away; prajñām = gnosis; vāyus = wind; nāvam = boat; ivāmbhasi (iva + ambhasi) = like [the wind] on the sea.

2.68: tasmāt = hence; yasya = whose; mahābāho (mahā + bāhu) = O mighty-armed [Arjuna]; nigṛhītāni (plural) = withdrawn; sarvaśas = everywhere, here: all-round; indriyāṇīndriyārthebhyas (indriyāṇi + indriya + arthebhyas) = the senses from the objects of the senses; tasya = his; prajñā (feminine) = gnosis; pratiṣṭhitā (feminine) = established, here: well-established.

2.69: yā (feminine) = what, which; niśā (feminine) = night; sarvabhūtānām (sarva + bhūtānām) = of all beings; tasyām = in this; jāgarti = he is wakeful; saṃyamī = the self-controlled; yasyām = in what, in which; jāgrati = he is awake; bhūtāni = beings; sā = she [i.e., niśā], here: that; niśā (feminine) = night; paśyatas = of the seeing; munes = of the sage.

2.70: āpūryamāṇam = begin full, here: full; acalapratiṣṭham (acala + pratiṣṭham) = having unmoving ground; samudram = ocean;

āpas = waters; praviśanti = they enter; yadvat = just as; tadvat = just so, here: so; kāmās = desires; yam = whom, here: him who; praviśanti = they enter; sarve = [they] all; sas = he; śāntim = peace; āpnoti = he attains; na = not; kāmakāmī (kāma + kāmī) = the desirer (kāmin) of desires.

2.71: vihāya = abandoning; kāmān = desires; yas = who; sarvān = all; pumān (singular) = the man; carati = he moves about; niḥspṛhas = devoid of longing; nirmamas = devoid [of the thought of] mine; nirahaṃkāras = devoid of I-maker, here: without ego-sense; sas = he; śāntim = peace; adhigacchati = he attains, here: he approaches.

2.72: eṣā = this; brāhmī = brahmic; sthitis = state; pārtha = O son-of-Prithā; naināṃ (na + enām) = not this, here: no [longer]; prāpya = attaining; vimuhyati = he is deluded; sthitvāsyām (sthitvā + asyām) = having stationed in it, here: abiding therein; antakāle = at the end-time; 'pi (api) = also; brahmanirvāṇam (brahma + nirvāṇam) = extinction in brahman, here: extinction in the world-ground (brahman); ṛcchati = he attains.

CHAPTER 3: THE YOGA OF ACTION

arjunas = Arjuna; uvāca = he said;

3.1: jyāyasī (feminine) = superior; ced = if; karmaṇas = than action, here: to action; te = your, here: you; matā (feminine) = opinion; buddhir = wisdom; janārdana = O Janārdana; tad = that, then; kim = why?; karmaṇi = in action, here: into deed; ghore = in dreadful; māṃ = me; niyojayasi = you urge; keśava = O Keshava.

3.2: vyāmiśreṇaiva (vyāmiśreṇa + iva) = with mixed as it were, here: ambiguous; vākyena = with speech; buddhim = wisdom, here: wisdom-faculty; mohayasīva (mohayas + iva) = you confuse as it were, here: you apparently confuse; me = my; tad = this, that; ekam = one; vada = you tell!; niścitya = for sure; yena =

by which; śreyas = the good; 'ham (aham) = I [shall attain]; āpnuyām = I should [be able to] attain.

śrībhagavān (śrī + bhagavān) = Blessed Lord; uvāca = he said;

3.3: loke = in world; 'smin (asmin) = in this; dvividhā = twofold; niṣṭhā = way-of-life; purā = long ago; proktā (feminine) = proclaimed; mayānāgha (mayā + anāgha) = by me (mayā), O Anagha; jñānayogena = by the Yoga of Knowledge; sāṃkhyānām = for the Sāmkhyas; karmayogena = by Karma-Yoga; yoginām = for the yogins.

3.4: na = not; karmaṇām = of actions; anārambhān = by the non-initiation; naiṣkarmyam = action-transcendence; puruṣas = man; 'śnute (aśnute) = he enjoys, here: [does] he enjoy; na = not, here: nor; ca = and, here: omitted; saṃnyasanāt = by renunciation; eva = alone; siddhim = perfection; samādhigacchati = he comes near, here: [does] he approach.

3.5: na = not, here: nor; hi = for; kaścid = anyone; kṣaṇam = a moment; api = even; jātu = ever; tiṣṭhati = he stays, he remains, here: remain; akarmakṛt = without performing (kṛt) action; kāryate = he is caused to perform; hi = indeed; avaśas = unwittingly; karma = action; sarvas = all, here: every [being]; prakṛtijais = by [the primary-qualities] born of the Cosmos (prakṛti); guṇais = by the primary-qualities.

3.6: karmendriyāṇi = the action senses; saṃyamya = controlling, restraining; yas = who; āste = he sits; manasā = with the mind; smaran = remembering; indriyārthān = sense objects; vimūḍhātmā (vimūḍha + ātmā) = confounded self; mithyācāras (mithyā + ācāras) = [having] false conduct, here: hypocrite; sas = he; ucyate = he is called.

3.7: yas = who; tu = but; indriyāṇi = the senses; manasā = with the mind; niyamyārabhate (niyamya + ārabhate) = controlling [the senses] he embarks; 'rjuna (arjuna) = O Arjuna; karmendriyais = with the action senses; karmayogam = Karma-Yoga; asaktas = unattached; sas = he; viśiṣyate = distinguished, here: [more] excellent.

3.8: niyatam = necessary; kuru = do!; karma = action; tvam = you; karma = action; jyāyas = superior; hi = for; akarmaṇas = than inaction, here: to inaction; śarīrayātrāpi (śarīra + yātrā + api) = body process even, here: even [your] body's processes; ca = and, here: omitted; te = your; na = not; prasidhyet = it should be accomplished, here: it can be accomplished; akarmaṇas = by inaction.

3.9: yajñārthāt (yajña + arthāt) = by having sacrifice (yajña) as goal, here: intended as sacrifice; karmaṇas = by action; 'nyatra (anyatra) = otherwise, here: save [when this action]; lokas = world; 'yam (ayam) = this; karmabandhanas (karma + bandhanas) = bound [by] action; tadartham (tad + artham) = that purpose; karma = action; kaunteya = O son-of-Kuntī; muktasaṅgas (mukta + saṅgas) = devoid (mukta) of attachment; samācara = engage!

3.10: sahayajñās (saha + yajñās) = together with sacrifices, here: together with sacrifice; prajās = creatures; sṛṣṭvā = having created, here: emanating; purovāca (purā + uvāca) = anciently said, here: of old said; prajāpatis = Prajāpati; anena = by this; prasaviṣyadhvam = may you bring forth!; eṣa = this; vas (plural) = your; 'stu (astu) = may it be; iṣṭakāmadhuk (iṣṭa + kāma + dhuk) = [what is] desired (iṣṭa) wish-fulfilling cow.

3.11: devān = deities; bhāvayatānena (bhāvayata + anena) = with this (anena) may you sustain; te = they; devās = deities; bhāvayantu = may they sustain; vas (plural) = of you; parasparam = one another; bhāvayantas (plural) = sustaining; śreyas = the good, here: the good; param = supreme; avāpsyatha (second person) = you shall obtain.

3.12: iṣṭān (plural) = desired; bhogān = foods, here: food; hi = for; vas = to you; devās = deities; dāsyante = they will give; yajñabhāvitas (yajña + bhāvitas) = sustained by sacrifice; tais = by these; dattān = gifts; apradāyaibhyas (apradāya + ebhyas) = not given to them; yas = who; bhuṅkte = he enjoys; stenas = thief; eva = only, here: but; sas = he.

3.13: yajñaśiṣṭāśinas (yajña + śiṣṭa + āśinas) = consuming the sacrificial (yajña) leavings; santas = good [men]; mucyante = they are released; sarvakilbiṣais (sarva + kilbiṣais) = from all guilt (kilbiṣa); bhuñjate = they eat; te = they; tu = but; agham = wickedness; pāpās = [they are] evil; ye = who; pacanti = they cook; ātmakāraṇāt (ātma + kāraṇāt) = out of self-cause, here: for their own sake.

3.14: annāt = from food; bhavanti = they come-into-being; bhūtāni = beings; parjanyāt = from rain; annasaṃbhavas (anna + saṃbhavas) = food produced [by rain]; yajñāt = from sacrifice; bhavati = it comes-into-being; parjanyas = rain; yajñas = sacrifice; karmasamudbhavas (karma + samudbhavas) = born (samudbhavas) [from ritual] action.

3.15: karma = action; brahmodbhavam (brahma + udbhavam) = arising (udbhavam) [from] the world-ground, here: arises . . . ; viddhi = you know!; brahmākṣarasamudbhavam (brahma + akṣara + samudbhavam) = the world-ground (brahman) is born (samudbhavam) [from] the Imperishable; tasmāt = therefore; sarvagatam = omnipresent; brahma = the world-ground; nityam = ever; yajñe = in sacrifice; pratiṣṭhitam = established.

3.16: evam = thus; pravartitam = rotating; cakram = wheel; nānuvartayatīha (na + anuvartayati + iha) = not he causes-to-turn, here: he does not turn; yas = who; aghāyus (agha + āyus) = a wicked life; indriyārāmas (indriya + ārāmas) = sensual delight; mogham = in vain; pārtha = O son-of-Prithā; sas = he; jīvati = he lives.

3.17: yas = who; tu = yet; ātmaratis (ātma + ratis) = enjoyment in the self; eva = only; syāt = he should be; ātmatṛptas (ātma + tṛptas) = satisfied with the self; ca = and; mānavas = human, here: human-being; ātmani = in the self; eva = only; ca = and; saṃtuṣṭas = content; tasya = for him; kāryam = to be done; na = not, here: nothing; vidyate = is found, there is.

3.18: naiva (na + eva) = not indeed, here: indeed no; tasya = for him; kṛtenārthas (kṛtena + arthas) = with [what is] done purpose (artha), here: purpose in any [action] done; nākṛteneha (na + akṛtena + iha) = with [what is] not done (akṛtena) here (iha); kaścana = anything, here: any; na = and; cāsya (ca + asya) = and of him (asya), here: and he; sarvabhūteṣu (sarva + bhūteṣu) = in all beings, here: on any being; kaścid = any; arthavyapāśrayas (artha + vyapāśrayas) = purpose (artha) dependence, here: dependence [for any] purpose.

3.19: tasmāt = therefore; asaktas = unattached; satatam = always; kāryam = to be done; karma = action; samācara = you perform!; asaktas = unattached; hi = for; ācaran = performing; karma = action; param = the Supreme; āpnoti = attains; pūruṣas = the man.

3.20: karmaṇaiva (karmaṇā + eva) = by action indeed (eva); hi = for, here: omitted; saṃsiddhim = perfection, here: consummation; āsthitā (plural) = attained; janakādayas (janaka + ādayas) = Janaka and others; lokasaṃgraham (loka + saṃgraham) = maintenance [of] the world (loka), here: world's welfare; evāpi (eva + api) = only also, here: even [considering] only; saṃpaśyan = considering; kartum = to act; arhasi = you should be able, here: you ought to.

3.21: yadyad (yad + yad) = whatever; ācarati = he does; śreṣṭhas = the best; tattat (tad + tad) = this [and] that, here: that; evetaras (eva + itaras) = verily (eva) other; janas = people; sas = he; yad = what, here: whatever; pramāṇam = measure, here: standard; kurute = he makes, here: he sets; lokas = the world; tad = that; anuvartate = it follows.

3.22: na = not, here: no; me = for me; pārthāsti (pārtha + asti) = O son-of-Prithā there is (asti); kartavyam = to be done; triṣu = in three; lokeṣu = in worlds; kiṃcana = anything; nānavāptam (na +anavāptam) = not ungained, here: nor [anything] ungained; avāptavyam = to be gained; varta (for varte) = I engage; eva ca = nevertheless, here: and yet; karmaṇi = in action.

3.23: yadi = if; hi = for; aham = I; na = not; varteyam = I should engage; jātu = ever, here: at all; karmaṇi = in action; atandritas

= untiringly; mama = my; vartmānuvartante (vartma + anuvartante) = they follow (anuvartante) [my] track; manuṣyās = humans; pārtha = O son-of-Prithā; sarvaśas = wholly, here: everywhere.

3.24: utsīdeyus = they would perish; ime = these; lokās = worlds; na = not; kuryām = to act, here: to perform; karma = action; ced = if; aham = I; saṃkarasya = of chaos; ca = and; kartā = the maker, here: the author; syām = I should be, here: I would be; upahanyām = I should destroy, here: I would destroy; imās = these; prajās = creatures.

3.25: saktās (plural) = attached; karmaṇi = in action; avidvāṃsas (plural) = the unwise; yathā = just as; kurvanti = they perform; bhārata = O descendant-of-Bharata; kuryāt = he should do; vidvān = the wise one; tathāsaktas (tathā + asaktas) = thus unattached; cikīrṣus = desiring to do, here: desiring to accomplish; lokasaṃgraham = the world's welfare.

3.26: na = not; buddhibhedam (buddhi + bhedam) = buddhi breach (bheda); janayet = he should not generate, here: let not [the wise] generate; ajñānām (plural) = of the ignorant; karmasaṅginam (karma + saṅginam) (plural) = of the action-attached; joṣayet = he should cause to rejoice; sarvakarmāṇi (sarva +karmāṇi) = all actions; vidvān = the wise [man]; yuktas = yoked; samācaran = performing.

3.27: prakṛtes = of the Cosmos; kriyamāṇāni = being performed (plural); guṇais = by the primary-qualities; karmāṇi = actions; sarvaśas = wholly, here: everywhere; ahaṃkāravimūḍhātmā (ahaṃkāra + vimūḍha + ātmā) = [he whose] self is deluded (vimūḍha) by the ego-sense; kartāham (kartā + aham) = I [am] the doer; iti = used to indicate a quotation; manyate = he thinks.

3.28: tattvavid (tattva + vid) = the reality (tattva) knower; tu = but; mahābāho (mahā + bāho) = O mighty-armed [Arjuna]; guṇakarmavibhāgayos (guṇa + karma +vibhāgayos) (dual) =

apportionment of the primary-qualities and actions; guṇās = the primary-qualities; guṇeṣu = in the primary-qualities, here: upon the primary-qualities; vartanta (for vartante) = they function, here: they are; iti = thus, here: used to indicate a quotation; matvā = having thought, here: realizing; na = not; sajjate = he is attached.

3.29: prakṛtes = of the Cosmos; guṇasaṃmūḍhās (guṇa + saṃmūḍhās) = [those who are] fooled by the primary-qualities (guṇa); sajjante = they are attached; guṇakarmasu (guṇa + karmasu) = in the actions (karma) of the primary-qualities, here: to the actions . . . ; tān = them, here: those; akṛtsnavidas (akṛtsna + vidas) = the knowers (vid) of the non-Whole; mandān (plural) = dull-witted; kṛtsnavid (kṛtsna + vid) = knower of the Whole (kṛtsna); na = not; vicālayet = he should not cause to waver, here: he should not upset.

3.30: mayi = in me; sarvāṇi = all; karmāṇi = actions; saṃnyasyādhyātmacetasā (saṃnyasya + adhyātma + cetasā) = renouncing [with] the mind [turned toward] the inner self, here: [toward] the basis-of-self; nirāśīs = without hope; nirmama = without [the sense of] mine; bhūtvā = having become; yudhyasva = you fight!; vigatajvaras (vigata = jvaras) = gone the fever, here: the fever-of-anxiety departed.

3.31: ye (plural) = who; me = my; matam = doctrine, here: teaching; idam = this; nityam = ever; anutiṣṭhanti = they practice; mānavās = humans, here: human-beings; śraddhāvantas (plural) = possessing faith, here: firm-in-faith; 'nasūyantas (anasūyantas) (plural) = uncomplaining; mucyante = they are liberated; te = they; 'pi (api) = too; karmabhis = from actions.

3.32: ye = who (plural); tvetad (tu + etad) = but (tu) this; abhyasūyantas = complaining (plural); nānutiṣṭhanti (na + anutiṣṭhanti) = not they practice; me = my; matam = teaching; sarvajñānavimūḍhān (sarva + jñāna + vimūḍhān) (plural) = fooled (vimūḍha) by all knowledge; tān = them; viddhi = you know!; naṣṭān (plural) = lost; acetasas (plural) = mindless.

3.33: sadṛśam = in accordance with; ceṣṭate = he behaves; svasyās = of own, here: with [his] own; prakṛtes = of nature; jñānavān = the knowledge-possessed one, here: the knowledgeable [man]; api = even; prakṛtim = nature; yanti = they follow; bhūtāni = beings; nigrahas = restraint, here: repression; kim = what?; kariṣyati = it will accomplish.

3.34: indriyasyendriyasyārthe (indriyasya + indriyasya + arthe) = toward the object (artha) of [their] respective senses; rāgadveṣau (rāga + dveṣau) (dual) = passion and hatred; vyavasthitau (dual) = are seated, here: directed; tayos (dual) = of these; na = not, here: none; vaśam = power; āgacchet = one should come; tau = both; hyasya (hi + asya)= his (asya) indeed; paripanthinau (dual) = waylayers.

3.35: śreyān = better; svadharmas (sva + dharmas) = own law; viguṇas = deficient, here: imperfectly; paradharmāt (para + dharmāt) = than another`s (para) law; svanuṣṭhitāt (su + anuṣṭhitāt) = than well (su) performed; svadharme (sva + dharme) = in own-law; nidhanam = death; śreyas = better; paradharmas (para + dharmas) = another's law (dharma); bhayāvahas (bhaya + āvahas) = fear instilling.

arjunas = Arjuna; uvāca = he said;
3.36: atha = now; kena = by what?; prayuktas = impelled; 'yam (ayam) this; pāpam = sin; carati = he commits, here: to commit; pūruṣas = man; anicchan = unwittingly; api = even; vārṣṇeya = O descendant-of-Vrishni; balāt = by force; iva = as it were, here: as though; niyojitas = urged, commanded, here: constrained.

śrībhagavān (śrī + bhagavān) = Blessed Lord; uvāca = he said;
3.37: kāmas = desire; eṣa = this; krodhas = anger; eṣa = this; rajoguṇasamudbhavas (rajas + guṇa + samudbhavas) = born of (samudbhava) the primary-quality of activity (rajas), here: born of rajo-guna; mahāśanas (mahā + āśanas) = greatly consuming, here: all-devouring; mahāpāpmā (mahā + pāpmā) = greatly evil; viddhi = you know!; enam = this; iha = here; vairiṇam = the enemy.

«arjunas = Arjuna; uvāca = he said;
bhavatyeṣa (bhavati + eṣa) = this (eṣa) becomes, here: this arises; katham = how?; kṛṣṇa = O Krishna; katham = how?; caiva (ca + eva) = and indeed, here: omitted; vivardhate = it increases; kimātmakas (kim + ātmakas) = what [is its] essence?; kimācārastanmamācakṣya (kim + ācāras + tan + mama + ācakṣya) = what [is its] character? This (tad) tell me (mama); pṛcchatas = the asking one, here: who asks.

śrībhagavān (śrī + bhagavān) = Blessed Lord; uvāca = he said; eṣa = this; sūkṣmas = subtle; paras = supreme; śatrurdehinām (śatrus + dehinām) = the foe of the embodied one, here: . . . of the body-essences; indriyais = with the senses; saha = together with; sukhatantras = (sukha + tantras) = depending on pleasure, here: web of pleasure; ivāsinas (iva + āsinas) = being seated as it were (iva), here: . . . seemingly; mohayan = deluding; pārtha = O son-of-Prithā; tiṣṭhati = it stands, here: it persists.

kāmakrodhamayas (kāma + krodha + mayas) = made (maya) of desire [and] anger; ghoras = terrible; stambhaharṣasamudbhavas (stambha + harṣa + samudbhavas) = born of paralyzing (stambha) exhilaration, here: causing . . . ; ahaṃkāras = the ego-sense; 'bhimānātmā (abhimāna + ātmā) = of the essence (ātman) of infatuation; dustaras = difficult-to-transcend; pāpakarmabhis (pāpa + karmabhis) = by sinful (pāpa) actions.

harṣamasya (harṣam + asya) = exhilaration of him (asya); nivartyaiṣa (nivartya + eṣa) = this (eṣa) is depriving, here: it deprives; śokamasya (śokam + asya) = grief of him; dadāti = it gives; ca = and; bhayam = fear; cāsya (ca + asya) = and of him; karotyeṣa (karoti + eṣa) = this makes, here: it brings; mohayaṃstu (mohayan + tu) = stupefying indeed; muhurmuhus (muhus + muhus) = again and again.

sas = he, here: omitted; eṣa = this; kaluṣas = turbid; kṣudraśchidraprekṣī (kṣudraś + chidra + prekṣī) = peeping into keyholes; dhanaṃjaya = O Dhanamjaya; rajas = activity, here: rajas; pravṛttas = propelled; mohātmā (moha + ātmā) = [of] the essence (ātman) of delusion; manuṣyāṇām = of human-beings; upadravas = distress. »

3.38: dhūmenāvriyate (dhūmena + āvriyate) = by smoke (dhūma) [fire] is enveloped; vahnis = fire; yathādarśas (yathā + darśas) = just as a mirror; malena = by dust; ca = and; yathā = just as; albenāvṛtas (albena + āvṛtas) = it is concealed by a membrane; garbhas = embryo; tathā = so; tenedam (tena + idam) = this [world [is covered] by that (tad) [desire]; āvṛtam = covered over.

3.39: āvṛtam = covered over; jñānam = knowledge; etena = by this; jñāninas = of the knower; nityavairiṇā (nitya + vairiṇā) = by the perpetual (nitya) enemy; kāmarūpeṇa = by the desire-formed [enemy], here: in the form of desire; kaunteya = O son-of-Kuntī; duṣpūreṇānalena (duṣpūreṇa + analena) = by the difficult-to-fill (duṣpūra) fire, here: by the insatiable fire; ca = and, here: omitted.

3.40: indriyāṇi = the senses; manas = the [lower] mind; buddhis = wisdom-faculty; asyādhiṣṭhānam (asya + adhiṣṭhānam) = its (asya) foundation, here: its hiding-places; ucyate = is called; etais = through these; vimohayati = it fools; eṣa = this, here: omitted; jñānam = knowledge; āvṛtya = concealing; dehinam = of the embodied one, here: of the body-essence.

3.41: tasmāt = therefore; tvam = you; indriyāṇi = the senses; ādau = at first; niyamya = controlling, restraining; bharatarṣabha = O Bharatarshabha; pāpmānam = evil; prajahi = you kill!, here: you strike down!; hi = indeed, here: omitted; enam = this; jñānavijñānanāśanam (jñāna + vijñāna + nāśanam) = destroying (nāśana) knowledge [and] world-knowledge (vijñāna).

3.42: indriyāṇi = the senses; parāṇi (plural) = superior; āhus = they say; indriyebhyas = than the senses, here: to the senses; param = higher, superior; manas = the mind; manasas = than the mind; tu = but, here: omitted; parā = higher, superior; buddhis = wisdom-faculty; yas = who, what; buddhes = than the wisdom-faculty, here: to the wisdom-faculty; paratas = superior; tu = indeed, here: verily; sas = he.

3.43: evam = thus; buddhes = than the wisdom-faculty, here: to the wisdom-faculty; param = superior; buddhvā = having awakened; saṃstabhyātmānam (saṃstabhya + ātmānam) = stabilizing the self (ātman); ātmanā = by the self; jahi = you slay!; śatrum = enemy; mahābāho (mahā + baho) = O mighty-armed [Arjuna]; kāmarūpam (kāma + rūpam) = desire-formed, here: in the form of desire; durāsadam = difficult-(dur)-to-conquer.

CHAPTER 4: THE YOGA OF WISDOM

śrībhagavān (śrī + bhagavān) = Blessed Lord; uvāca = he said;
4.1: imam = this; vivasvate = to Vivasvat; yogam = Yoga; proktavān = proclaiming, here: proclaimed; aham = I; avyayam = immutable; vivasvān = Vivasvat; manave = to Manu; prāha = he told; manus = Manu; ikṣvākave = to Ikshvāku; 'bravīt (abravīt) = he declared.

4.2: evam = thus; paraṃparāprāptam (paraṃparā + prāptam) = received (prāpta) from one to another (by succession); imam = this; rājarṣayas (rāja + ṛṣayas) = the royal seers; vidus = they knew; sas = he; kāleneha (kālena + iha) = with time here (iha); mahatā = with great, here: with long; yogas = Yoga; naṣṭas = lost; paraṃtapa = O Paramtapa.

4.3: sas = he, here: omitted; evāyam (eva + ayam) = verily this; mayā = by me; te = to you; 'dya (adya) = today; yogas = Yoga; proktas = proclaimed, here: I proclaim; purātanas = ancient; bhaktas = devotee; 'si = (asi) you are; me = my; sakhā = friend; ceti (ca + iti) = and thus, here: *iti* is omitted; rahasyam = secret; hi = for, indeed, here: verily; etad = this; uttamam = foremost, unexcelled.

arjunas = Arjuna; uvāca = he said;
4.4: aparam = later; bhavatas = of you (honorific form); janma = birth; param = earlier; janma = birth; vivasvatas = of Vivasvat; katham = how?; etad = this; vijānīyām = I should understand;

tvam = you; ādau = in the beginning; proktavān = proclaiming, here: proclaimed; iti = thus, here: omitted.

śrībhagavān (śrī + bhagavān) = Blessed Lord; uvāca = he said;
4.5: bahūni = many; me = my; vyatītāni (plural) = gone, here: past; janmāni = births; tava = your; cārjuna (ca + arjuna) = and O Arjuna; tāni = them; aham = I; veda = I know; sarvāṇi (plural) = all; na = not; tvam = you; vettha = you [do not] know; paraṃtapa = O Paramtapa.

4.6: ajas = unborn; 'pi (api) = even; san = being (participle); avyayātmā (avyaya + ātmā) = immutable self; bhūtānām = of beings; īśvaras = lord; 'pi (api) = even; san = being (participle); prakṛtim = nature; svām = [my] own; adhiṣṭhāya = governing; saṃbhavāmi = I-come-to-be; ātmamāyayā (ātma + māyayā) = by the creative-power (māyā) of myself (ātman).

4.7: yadā yadā = whenever; hi = for; dharmasya = of the law; glānis = diminution; bhavati = there is; bhārata = O descendant-of-Bharata; abhyutthānam = upswing; adharmasya = of lawlessness; tadātmānam (tadā + ātmānam) = then myself; sṛjāmi = I create; aham = I.

4.8: paritrāṇāya = for the protection; sādhūnām = of good (people); vināśāya = for the destruction; ca = and; duṣkṛtām = of wrongdoers; dharmasaṃsthāpanārthāya (dharma + saṃsthāpana + arthāya) = for the sake (artha) of establishing the law; saṃbhavāmi = I come-into-being; yuge yuge = from age to age.

4.9: janma = birth; karma = action; ca = and; me = my; divyam = divine; evam = thus; yas = who; vetti = knows; tattvatas = really; tyaktvā = having abandoned, here: abandoning; deham = the body; punarjanma = rebirth; naiti (na + eti) = not goes, here: never [again] undergoes; mām = to me; eti = he goes, here: he comes; sas = he; 'rjuna (arjuna) = O Arjuna.

4.10: vītarāgabhayakrodhās (vīta + rāga + bhaya + krodhās) (plural) = free from (vīta) passion, fear (bhaya), [and] anger; manmayā (mad + mayā) (plural)= filled (maya) by me; upāśritās (plural)

= resorting, here: = [they] resort; mām = to me; bahavas (plural) = many; jñānatapasā (jñāna + tapasā) = by the austerity of knowledge; pūtā = purified; madbhāvam (mad + bhāvam) = my state-of-existence; āgatās (plural) = have come, here: [they] come.

4.11: ye (plural) = who; yathā = just as; mām = to me; prapadyante = they resort; tāṃs (tān) = them; tathaiva (tathā + eva) = thus verily, here: so; bhajāmi = I love; aham = I; mama = my; vartmānuvartante (vartma + anuvartante) = they follow [my] track; manuṣyās = humans; pārtha = O son-of-Prithā; sarvaśas = everywhere.

4.12: kāṅkṣantas (plural) = hankering; karmaṇām = of actions, here: in [ritual] actions; siddhim = success; yajanta (for yajante) = they sacrifice; iha = here; devatās = deities; kṣipram = swiftly; hi = for; mānuṣe = in the human [world]; loke = in the world; siddhis (feminine) = success; bhavati = there is, here: comes; karmajā (feminine) = action-born, here: born of [ritual] action.

4.13: cāturvarṇyam = quartet-of-classes; mayā = by me; sṛṣṭam = created; guṇakarmavibhāgaśas (guṇa + karma + vibhāgaśas) = primary-qualities and actions apportioned; tasya = of this; kartāram = the doer, here: the author; api = although; mām = me; viddhi = you know!; akartāram = the nondoer; avyayam = immutable.

4.14: na = not; mām = me; karmāṇi = actions; limpanti = they defile; na = not, here: no; me = my, here: for me; karmaphale (karma + phale) = in the fruit (phala) of action, here: for action's fruit; spṛhā = hankering; iti = thus; mām = me; yas = who; 'bhijānāti (abhijānāti) = he recognizes; karmabhis = by actions; na sas = he is not; badhyate = he is [not] bound.

4.15: evam = thus; jñātvā = having known, here: knowing; kṛtam = performed; karma = action; pūrvais = by the ancients; api = too; mumukṣubhis = by the [ones who are] desirous-of-liberation; kuru = you perform!; karmaiva (karma + eva) = action indeed;

tasmāt = therefore; tvam = you; pūrvais = by the ancients; pūrvataram (pūrva + taram) = of old; kṛtam = done.

4.16: kim = what?; karma = action; kim = what?; akarmeti (akarma + iti) = inaction, *iti* is used to indicate a quotation; kavayas = bards; 'pi (api) even; atra = about this; mohitās (plural) = bewildered, confused; tat = that; te = to you; karma = action; pravakṣyāmi = I shall declare; yad = which; jñātvā = having known; mokṣyase = you will be freed; 'śubhāt (aśubhāt) = from ill.

4.17: karmaṇas = of action; hi = indeed; api = also, here: omitted; boddhavyam = to be known, here: one ought to understand; boddhavyam = here: one ought to understand; ca = and; vikarmaṇas = of wrong-action; akarmaṇas = of inaction; ca = and; boddhavyam = here: one ought to understand; gahanā (feminine) = impenetrable; karmaṇas = of action; gatis (feminine) = course.

4.18: karmaṇi = in action; akarma = inaction; yas = who; paśyet = he should see, here: he sees; akarmaṇi = in inaction; ca = and; karma = action; yas = who; sas = he; buddhimān = wise, here: wisdom-endowed; manuṣyeṣu = among humans; sas = he; yuktas = yoked; kṛtsnakarmakṛt (kṛtsna + karma + kṛt) = performing (kṛt) whole (kṛtsna) action.

4.19: yasya = whose; sarve = all, here: every; samārambhās = enterprises, here: enterprise; kāmasaṃkalpavarjitās (kāma = saṃkalpa + varjitās) (plural) = free (varjita) from desire and motive; jñānāgnidagdhakarmāṇam (jñāna + agni + dagdha + karmāṇam) = [he whose] action is burned (dagdha) in the fire (agni) of knowledge; tam = him; āhus = they call; paṇḍitam = learned; budhās (plural) = the wise.

4.20: tyaktvā = having relinquished; karmaphalāsaṅgam (karma + phala + āsaṇgam) = attachment (āsaṅga) to the fruit (phala) of action; nityatṛptas (nitya-tṛptas) = ever content; nirāśrayas = independent; karmaṇi = in action; abhipravṛttas = engaged; 'pi (api) = though; naiva (na + eva) = not verily, here: *eva* is omitted; kiṃcid [together with na] = nothing; karoti = he acts, here: does [not] act; sas = he.

4.21: nirāśīs = hopeless, here: hoping-for-nothing; yatacittātmā (yata + citta + ātmā) = restrained (yata) [in] thought (citta) [and] self; tyaktasarvaparigrahas (tyakta + sarva + parigrahas) = abandoned (tyakta) all possession, here: abandoning all possessions; śārīram = body; kevalam = only; karma = action; kurvan = performing; nāpnoti (na + āpnoti) = not he attains, here: he [does] not incur; kilbiṣam = guilt.

4.22: yadṛcchālābhasaṃtuṣtas (yadṛcchā + lābha + saṃtuṣtas) = content (saṃtuṣṭa) [with what is] chance (yadṛcchā) obtained; dvandvātītas (dvandva + atītas) = transcending the pairs-of-opposites; vimatsaras = without envy; samas = the same; siddhāvasiddhau (siddhau + asiddhau) = in success [and] failure; ca = and; kṛtvāpi (kṛtvā + api) = having done even, here: though performing; na = not; nibadhyate = he is [not] bound.

4.23: gatasaṅgasya (gata + saṅgasya) = for [him whose] attachment is gone (gata); muktasya = for the liberated one; jñānāvasthitacetasas (jñāna + avasthita + cetasas) = [whose] mind is established (avasthita) [in] knowledge; yajñāyācaratas (yajñāya + ācaratas) = performing for sacrifice (yajña); karma = action; samagram = entirely; pravilīyate = it is dissolved.

4.24: brahmārpaṇam (brahma + arpaṇam) = the world-ground [is] the offering; brahma = the world-ground; havis = the oblation; brahmāgnau (brahma + gnau) = the world-ground in the fire (agni); brahmaṇā = by the world-ground; hutam = offered; brahmaiva (brahma + eva) = the world-ground verily (eva); tena = by him; gantavyam = to be reached; brahmakarmasamādhinā (brahma + karma + samādhinā) = by concentration (samādhi) [upon] action [which is] the world-ground.

4.25: daivam = divine, here: god-related; evāpare = (eva + apare) verily some (apare); yajñam = sacrifice; yoginas = yogins; paryupāsate (plural) = they conduct; brahmāgnāvapare (brahma + agnau + apare) = into the fire (agni) of the world-ground some others (apare), here: others . . . ; yajñam = sacrifice; yajñenaivopajuhvati (yajñena + eva + upajuhvati) (plural) = by means of sacrifice indeed they offer, here: *eva* is omitted.

4.26: śrotrādīnīndriyāṇi (śrotra + ādīni + indriyāṇi) = hearing [and] the other senses; anye = others; saṃyamāgniṣu (saṃyama + agniṣu) = in the fires of restraint (saṃyama), here: in the fire . . . ; juhvati (plural) = they offer; śabdādīn (śabda + ādīn) = sound (śabda) etc.; viṣayān = objects; anya (for anye) = others; indriyāgniṣu (indriya + agniṣu) = in the fires of the senses (indriya), here: the fire . . . ; juhvati (plural) = they offer.

4.27: sarvāṇīndriyakarmāṇi (sarvāṇi + indriya + karmāṇi) = all sense actions; prāṇakarmāṇi (prāṇatkarmāṇi) = actions of the life-force (prāṇa); cāpare (ca + apare) = and others, here: still others; ātmasaṃyamayogāgnau (ātma + saṃyama + yoga + agnau) = in the fire (agni) of the Yoga of self-restraint (ātma-saṃyama); juhvati (plural) = they offer; jñānadīpite (jñāna + dīpite) = in being kindled (dīpita) by knowledge, here: kindled by. . . .

4.28: dravyayajñās (dravya + yajñās) = material-objects (dravya) [as] sacrifices, here: . . . sacrifice; tapoyajñās (tapas + yajñās) = sacrifices of austerity (tapas), here: . . . sacrifice; yogayajñās (yogayajñās) = sacrifices of Yoga, here: . . . sacrifice; tathāpare (tathā + apare) = thus some, here: some [again]; svādhyāyajñānayajñās (svādhyāya + jñāna + yajñās) (plural) = knowledge (jñāna) [gained from] study [as] sacrifices, here: . . . sacrifice; ca = and; yatayas = ascetics; saṃśitavratās (saṃśita + vratās) = [ascetics of] severe vows.

4.29: apāne = in the out-breath; juhvati (plural) = they offer; prāṇam = life-force; prāṇe = in the in-breath; 'pānam (apānam) = the out-breath; tathāpare (tathā + apare) = thus others, here: yet others; prāṇāpānagatī (prāṇa + apāna + gatī) (dual) = the flows [of] the in-breath [and] out-breath, here: the flow . . . ; ruddhvā = having controlled, here: controlling; prāṇāyāmaparāyaṇās (prāṇāyāma + parāyaṇās) (plural) = here: intent on breath control.

4.30: apare = others; niyatāhārās (niyata + āhārās) = [those who are] restricting the diet; prāṇān = breaths; prāṇeṣu = into breaths; juhvati (plural) = they offer; sarve = all ; 'pi (api) = also, here: omitted; ete = these; yajñavidas (yajña + vidas) = knowers (vid) of the sacrifice; yajñakṣapitakalmaṣās (yajña + kṣapita + kalmaṣās) = [those whose] defilements (kalmaṣa) are removed by sacrifice.

4.31: yajñaśiṣṭāmṛtabhujas (yajña + śiṣta + amṛta + bhujas) = enjoying (bhujas) the nectarine (amṛta) sacrifical remains (śiṣṭa); yānti = they go, here: they enter; brahma = the world-ground; sanātanam = everlasting; nāyam (na + ayam) = not this; lokas = world; 'sti (asti) = it is; ayajñasya = for the nonsacrificer; kutas = how [much less]?; 'nyas (anyas) = other; kurusattama (kuru + sattama) = O Kurusattama.

4.32: evam = thus; bahuvidhās (bahu + vidhās) (plural) = manifold; yajñās (plural) = the sacrifices; vitatās (plural) = spread out; brahmaṇas = of the world-ground; mukhe = in the face, here: in the presence; karmajān (karma + jān) (plural) = born of action (karma); viddhi = you know!; tān = them, here: these; sarvān (plural) = all; evam = thus; jñātvā = having known, here: knowing; vimokṣyase = you will be released.

4.33: śreyān = better; dravya + mayāt = than [that which consists of] material (dravya); yajñāt = than [material] sacrifice; jñānayajñas (jñāna + yajñas) = sacrifice of knowledge; paraṃtapa = O Paramtapa; sarvam = all; karmākhilam (karma + akhilam) = action completely; pārtha = O son-of-Prithā; jñāne = in knowledge; parisamāpyate = it is fully (parisam-) contained, here: is consummated.

4.34: tad = this, that; viddhi = you know!, here: you [learn to] know!; praṇipātena = by bowing, here: by reverence; paripraśnena = by inquiry; sevayā = by service; upadekṣyanti = they will teach; te = to you, here: you; jñānam = knowledge; jñāninas = the knowers; tattvadarśinas (tattva + darśinas) = [those who] behold reality.

4.35: yad = which; jñātvā = having known; na = not; punas = again; moham = confusion; evam = thus; yāsyasi = you will go, here: you will [not]succumb; pāṇḍava = O son-of-Pāndu; yena = by which; bhūtāni = beings; aśeṣeṇa = without remainder, entirely, here: all; drakṣyasi = you will behold; ātmani = in the self; atha = then also, here: then; mayi = in me.

4.36: api = even; ced = if; asi = you are; pāpebhyas = among evil ones, here: sinners; sarvebhyas = among all; pāpakṛttamas (pāpa + kṛt + tamas) = the most sin-doing one, here: the most sinful; sarvam = all; jñānaplavenaiva (jñāna + plavena + eva) = with the raft (plava) of knowledge indeed (eva); vṛjinam = of crookedness; saṃtariṣyasi = you will cross.

4.37: yathaidhāṃsi (yathā + edhāṃsi) (plural) = as (yathā) fuel (edhas); samiddhas = kindled; 'gnis (agnis) = fire; bhasmasāt = to ashes; kurute = it makes, here: it reduces; 'rjuna (arjuna) = O Arjuna; jñānāgnis (jñāna + agnis) = the fire of knowledge; sarvakarmāṇi (sarva + karmāṇi) = all actions; bhasmasāt = to ashes; kurute = it reduces; tathā = so.

4.38: na = not, here: no; hi = for; jñānena = with knowledge, here: knowledge; sadṛśam = equal, like; pavitram = purifier; iha = here; vidyate = is found, here: there is; tad = that, this; svayam = [him]self; yogasaṃsiddhas (yoga + saṃsiddhas) = perfected [in] Yoga; kālenātmani (kālena + ātmani) = in time (kāla) in [him] self; vindati = he finds, here: he will find.

4.39: śraddhāvāṃl (śraddhāvān) = the faith-filled; labhate = he attains; jñānam = knowledge; tatparas (tad + paras) = intent on that; saṃyatendriyas (saṃyata + indriyas) = restrained sense, here: . . . senses; jñānam = knowledge; labdhvā = having attained; parām = supreme; śāntim = peace; acireṇādhigacchati (acireṇa + adhigacchati) = quickly (acireṇa) he attains, here: he will quickly attain.

4.40: ajñas = ignorant, unknowing; cāśraddadhānas (ca + aśraddadhānas) = and without faith; ca = and; saṃśayātmā (saṃśaya + ātmā) = [he who is] of doubting self; vinaśyati = he will perish; nāyam (na + ayam) = not this, here: *na* is translated as "no"; lokas = world; 'sti (asti) = it is; na = not, here: either; paras = beyond, here: the next; na = not, here: or; sukham = happiness; saṃśayātmanas (saṃśaya + ātmanas) = for the doubting self.

4.41: yogasaṃnyastakarmāṇam (yoga + saṃnyasta + karmāṇam) = [he who has] renounced action through Yoga; jñānasaṃchinnasaṃśayam (jñāna + saṃchinna + saṃśayam) = [whose] doubt is dispelled (saṃchinna) by knowledge; ātmavantam (ātma + vantam) = self-possessed; na = not; karmāṇi = actions; nibadhnanti = they bind; dhanaṃjaya = O Dhanamjaya.

4.42: tasmāt = therefore; ajñānasaṃbhūtam (ajñāna + saṃbhūtam) = born of ignorance; hṛtstham (hṛt + stham) = seated [in] the heart; jñānāsinātmanas (jñāna + āsinā + ātmanas) = with the sword of knowledge (jñāna) of the self; chittvainam (chittvā + enam) = having cut this (enam); saṃśayam = doubt; yogam = Yoga; ātiṣṭhottiṣṭha (ātiṣṭha + uttiṣṭha) = you resort! (ātiṣṭha), you arise!; bhārata = O descendant-of-Bharata.

CHAPTER 5: THE YOGA OF THE RENUNCIATION OF ACTION

arjunas = Arjuna; uvāca = he said;

5.1: saṃnyāsam = renunciation; karmaṇām = of actions; kṛṣṇa = O Krishna; punas = again; here: then again; yogam = Yoga; ca = and; śaṃsasi = you praise; yad = which; śreyas = better; etayos = of the two; ekam = [which] one; tad = this, that; me = to me, here: me; brūhi = you tell!; suniścitam = for certain.

śrībhagavān (śrī + bhagavān) = Blessed Lord; uvāca = he said;

5.2: saṃnyāsas = renunciation; karmayogas (karma + yogas) = Yoga of Action; ca = and; niḥśreyasakarau (niḥśreyasa + karau) (dual) = greatest-fortune (niḥśreyasa) making, here: leading to . . . ; ubhau (dual) = both; tayos (dual) = of these; tu = but;

karmasaṃnyāsāt (karma + saṃnyāsāt) = than renunciation [of] action; karmayogas = Karma-Yoga; viśiṣyate = it is distinguished, here: it is better.

5.3: jñeyas = to be known; sas = he; nityasaṃnyāsī (nitya + saṃnyāsī) = eternal renouncer, here: perpetual . . . ; yas = who; na = not; dveṣṭi = he hates; na = not, here: or; kāṅkṣati = he hankers; nirdvandvas = without the pairs-of-opposites; hi = for; mahābāho (mahā + bāho) = mighty-armed [Arjuna]; sukham = easily; bandhāt = from bondage; pramucyate = he is released.

5.4: sāṃkhyayogau (dual) = Sāmkhya and Yoga; pṛthak = distinct, different; bālās = simpletons; pravadanti = they declare; na = not; paṇḍitās (plural) = the learned; ekam = one; apyāsthitas (api + āsthitas) = even (api) resorting; samyañc = properly; ubhayos (dual) = of both; vindate = he finds, here: there is; phalam = fruit.

5.5: yad = which; sāṃkhyais = by the Sāmkhyas; prāpyate = it is attained; sthānam = state; tad = this, that; yogais = by the Yogas (i.e., yogins); api = also; gamyate = it is gone to, it is reached; ekam = one; sāṃkhyam = Sāmkhya; ca = and; yogam = Yoga; ca = and; yas = who; paśyati = he sees; sas = he; paśyati = he sees.

5.6: saṃnyāsas = renunciation; tu = but; mahābāho (mahā + bāho) = mighty-armed [Arjuna]; duḥkham = suffering, difficult; āptum = to attain; ayogatas = without Yoga; yogayuktas (yoga + yuktas) = yoked [in] Yoga; munis = sage; brahma = world-ground; nacireṇādhigacchati (na + cireṇa + adhigacchati) = he attains (adhigacchati) in not (na) a long time (cireṇa), here: he approaches quickly.

5.7: yogayuktas (yoga + yuktas) = yoked [in] Yoga; viśuddhātmā (viśuddha + ātmā) = [who has] purified the self; vijitātmā (vijita + ātmā) = [who has] subdued the self; jitendriyas (jita + indriyas) = [who has] conquered the senses; sarvabhūtātmabhūtātmā (sarva + bhūta + ātma + bhūta + ātmā) = [he whose] self has become (bhūta) the self of all (sarva) beings (bhūta); kurvan = doing, performing; api = even though; na = not; lipyate = he is defiled.

5.8: naiva (na + eva) = not indeed, here: *na* goes with the next word; kiṃcid = anything, here: na kiṃcid "nothing"; karomīti (karomi + iti) = I do thus, here: *iti* is used to indicate a quotation; yuktas = yoked; manyate = he thinks, reflects; tattvavid (tattva + vid) = knower (vid) of reality; paśyan = seeing; śṛṇvan = hearing; spṛśan = touching; jighran = smelling; aśnan = eating; gacchan = walking; svapan = sleeping; śvasan = breathing.

5.9: pralapan = talking; visṛjan = excreting; gṛhṇan = grasping; unmiṣan = opening; nimiṣan = closing; api = also, here: and; indriyāṇīndriyārtheṣu (indriyāṇi + indriya + artheṣu) = senses in the objects (artha) of the senses; vartanta (for vartante) = they exist, they abide; iti = here: used to indicate a quotation; dhārayan = maintaining.

5.10: brahmaṇi = in the world-ground, here: to the world-ground; ādhāya = placing, here: assigning; karmāṇi = actions; saṅgam = attachment; tyaktvā = having abandoned; karoti = he acts; yas = who; lipyate = he is defiled; na = not; sas = he; pāpena = by sin; padmapattram (padma + pattram) = lotus leaf; ivāmbhasā (iva + ambhasā) = like, as (iva) by water.

5.11: kāyena = with the body; manasā = with the mind; buddhyā = with the wisdom-faculty; kevalais (plural) = with merely; indriyais (plural) = with senses; api = even, here: and even; yoginas = the yogins; karma = action; kurvanti = they perform; saṅgam = attachment; tyaktvātmaśuddhaye (tyaktvā + ātma + śuddhaye) = having abandoned [attachment] for self-purification.

5.12: yuktas = yoked; karmaphalam (karma + phalam) = fruit (phala) of action; tyaktvā = having abandoned, here: having relinquished; śāntim = peace; āpnoti = he attains; naiṣṭhikīm = final, ultimate; ayuktas = unyoked; kāmakāreṇa (kāma +

kāreṇa) = by action [resulting from] desire, here: acting from desire; phale = to the fruit; saktas = attached; nibadhyate = he is bound.

5.13: sarvakarmāṇi (sarva + karmāṇi) = all actions; manasā = with the mind; saṃnyasyāste (saṃnyasya + āste) = renouncing he sits, here: ... sitting; sukham = happily; vaśī = the ruler; navadvāre (nava + dvāre) = in nine-gated; pure = in city; dehī = the embodied one, here: body-essence; naiva (na + eva) = not verily, here: verily neither; kurvan = acting, here: he acts; na = not, here: nor; kārayan = causing-to-act, here: causes-to-act.

5.14: na = not, here: neither; kartṛtvam = agency; na = not, here: nor; karmāṇi = actions; lokasya = of the world; sṛjati = he creates; prabhus = the lord; na = not, here: nor; karmaphalasaṃyogam (karma + phala + saṃyogam) = union (saṃyoga) [between] action [and its] fruit; svabhāvas (sva + bhāvas) = own-being; tu = but, here: omitted; pravartate = it proceeds, here: it stimulates-to-action.

5.15: nādatte (na + ādatte) = he takes on; kasyacid = of anyone; pāpam = sin, sinful; na = not, here: omitted; caiva (ca + eva) = and verily, here: or; sukṛtam = good; vibhus = all-pervading; ajñānenāvṛtam (ajñānena + āvṛtam) = covered by ignorance (ajñāna); jñānam = knowledge; tena = by it, here: thereby; muhyanti = they are deluded; jantavas = creatures, people.

5.16: jñānena = by knowledge; tu = but; tad = this, that; ajñānam = ignorance; yeṣām (plural) = of whom, here: for those; nāśitam = destroyed; ātmanas = of the self; teṣām = of them, here: their; ādityavat (āditya + vat) = like (vat) the sun; jñānam = knowledge; prakāśayati = it illumines; tad = this, that; param = supreme.

5.17: tadbuddhayas (tad + buddhayas) = [those who have their] wisdom-faculties [focused on] that; tadātmānas (tad + ātmānas) = [those who have their] selves [immersed in] that; tanniṣṭhās (tad + niṣṭhās) = [those who have] that [as their] basis; tatparāyaṇās (tad + parāyaṇās) = [those who have] that [as their] supreme-goal (para + ayaṇa); gacchanti = they go; apunarāvṛttim (apunas + āvṛttim) = not again (apunas) [to experience] return, here: rebirth; jñānanirdhūtakalmaṣās (jñāna + nirdhūta + kalmaṣās) = defilements (kalmaṣa) cast off [by means of] knowledge.

«smarantas = remembering; 'pi (api) = though; muhus = repeatedly; tu = but, here: omitted; etad = this; spṛśantas = touching, here: coming-in-touch; 'pi (api) = although; svakarmaṇi (sva + karmaṇi) = own action; saktās (plural) = attached; api = although; na = not; sajjanti = they adhere; paṇke = in puddle; ravikarās (ravi + karās) = sun rays; iva = like. »

5.18: vidyāvinayasaṃpanne (vidyā + vinaya + saṃpanne) = in [one] endowed with understanding (vidyā) [and] culturedness (vinaya); brāhmaṇe = in a brāhmaṇa; gavi = in cow; hastini = in elephant; śuni = in dog; caiva (ca eva) = and indeed, here: and even; śvapāke (śva + pāke) = in dog-cooker; ca = and, here: or; paṇḍitās (plural) = the learned; samadarśinas (sama + darśinas) (plural) = seeing the same (sama).

5.19: ihaiva (iha + eva) = here verily, here: even here; tais = by those; jitas = conquered, here: have conquered; sargas = creation; yeṣām (plural) = of whom, here: whose; sāmye = in sameness; sthitam = established; manas = mind; nirdoṣam = devoid-of-fault; hi = indeed, here: omitted; samam = the same; brahma = world-ground; tasmāt = hence; brahmaṇi = in the world-ground; te = they; sthitās = established.

5.20: na = not; prahṛṣyet = he should rejoice; priyam = cherished; prāpya = attaining, here: on gaining; nodvijet (na + udvijet) = he should not become agitated, here: nor should he . . . ; prāpya = on gaining; cāpriyam (ca + apriyam) = and noncherished; sthirabuddhis (sthira + buddhis) = [with] steadied wisdom-faculty; asaṃmūḍhas = devoid-of-confusion; brahmavid (brahma + vid) = knower (vid) of *brahman;* brahmaṇi = in world-ground; sthitas = established.

5.21: bāhyasparśeṣu = in external contacts, here: to external contacts; asaktātmā (asakta + ātmā) = unattached self; vindati = he finds; ātmani = in self; yad = who; sukham = joy; sas = he; brahmayogayuktātmā (brahma + yoga + yukta + ātmā) = self yoked (yukta) in Yoga [to] the world-ground; sukham = joy; akṣayam = immutable; aśnute = he attains.

5.22: ye (plural) = who, which; hi = for; saṃsparśajās (saṃsparśa + jās) (plural) = [those] born (ja) of contact, here: contact-born; bhogās = pleasures; duḥkhayonayas (duḥkha + yonayas) = wombs (yoni) of suffering; eva = indeed; te = they; ādyantavantas (ādi + anta + vantas) (plural) = having a beginning [and] end; kaunteya = O son-of-Kuntī; na = not, here: does not; teṣu = in them; ramate = he delights; budhas = sage.

5.23: śaknotīhaiva (śaknoti + iha + eva) = he is able (śaknoti) here verily; yas = who; soḍhum = to bear; prāk = before; śarīravimokṣaṇāt (śarīra + vimokṣaṇāt) = by release [from] the body; kāmakrodhodbhavam (kāma + krodha + udbhavam) = arising [from] desire [and] anger; vegam = shock; sas = he; yuktas = yoked; sas = he; sukhī = happy; naras = man.

5.24: yas = who; 'ntaḥsukhas (antas + sukhas) = inner (anta) joy; 'ntarārāmas (antara + ārāmas) = inner rejoicing (ārāma); tathāntarjyotis (tathā + antas + jyotis) = thus inner light (jyoti), here: *tathā* is translated as "and hence"; eva = indeed; yas = who; sas = he; yogī = yogin; brahmanirvāṇam (brahma + nirvāṇam) = extinction [in] the world-ground; brahmabhūtas (brahma + bhūtas) = having become (bhūta) the world-ground; 'dhigacchati (adhigacchati) = he approaches.

5.25: labhante = they obtain, here: they reach; brahmanirvāṇam (brahma + nirvāṇam) = extinction [in] world-ground; ṛṣayas = seers; kṣīṇakalmaṣās (kṣīṇa + kalmaṣās) (plural) = [whose] defilements [are] dwindled (kṣīṇa); chinnadvaidhā (chinna + dvaidhā) (plural) = [whose] dualities [are] destroyed; yatātmānas (yata + ātmānas) = [whose] selves [are] controlled;

sarvabhūtahite (sarva + bhūta + hite) = in the good of all (sarva) beings; ratās = [those who] delight.

5.26: kāmakrodhaviyuktānām (kāma + krodha + viyuktānām) = for [those who are] freed from desire [and] anger; yatīnām = for the ascetics; yatacetasām (yata + cetasām) (plural) = for [those whose] mind is controlled; abhitas = close; brahma-nirvāṇam (brahma + nirvāṇam) = extinction [in] world-ground; vartate = it exists; viditātmanām (vidita + ātmanām) = for [those by whom] the self is known, here: for the self-knowing [ascetics].

5.27: sparśān = contacts; kṛtvā = having made, here [together with the next word]: shutting out; bahis = outside, here: [shutting] out; bāhyān (plural) = external; cakṣus = eye; caivāntare (ca + eva + antare) = and indeed in the middle, here: *eva* is omitted; bhruvos = of the brows (dual); prāṇāpānau (prāṇa + apānau) = in-breath and out-breath (dual); samau (dual) = evenly; kṛtvā = having made, here: making; nāsābhyantaracāriṇau (nāsā + abhyantara + cāriṇau) (dual) = moving in the nose, here: move [evenly] in the nose.

5.28: yatendriyamanobuddhis (yata + indriya + manas + buddhis) = [with] controlled senses, mind, [and] wisdom-faculty; munis = the sage; mokṣaparāyaṇas (mokṣa + parāyaṇas) = intent on liberation; vigatecchābhayakrodhas (vigata + icchā + bhaya + krodhas) = [he who is] devoid of longing, fear [and] anger; yas = who; sadā = ever; mukta = liberated; eva = truly; sas = he.

5.29: bhoktāram = enjoyer; yajñatapasām (yajña + tapasām) = of sacrificial austerities; sarvalokamaheśvaram (sarva + loka + mahā + īśvaram) = the great (mahā) lord (īsvara) of all the worlds; suhṛdam (su + hṛdam) = good-hearted, here: kind-hearted [friend]; sarvabhūtānām (sarva + bhūtānām) = of all beings; jñātvā = having known, here: knowing; mām = me; śāntim = peace; ṛcchati = he attains.

śrībhagavān (śrī + bhagavān) = Blessed Lord; uvāca = he said;

6.1: anāśritas = independent, here: regardless; karmaphalam (karma + phalam) = fruit (phala) [of] action; kāryam = to be done; karma = action; karoti = he performs; yas = who; sas = he; saṃnyāsī = renouncer; ca = and; yogī = yogin; ca = and; na = not; niragnis = without fire; na = not, here: omitted; cākriyas (ca + akriyas) = and inactive.

6.2: yam = whom, which; saṃnyāsam = renunciation; iti = thus, here: used to indicate a quotation; prāhus = they say, here: they call; yogam = Yoga; tam = this, that; viddhi = you know!; pāṅḍava = O son-of-Pāndu; na = not; hi = indeed; asaṃnyastasaṃkalpas (asaṃnyasta + saṃkalpas) = without renounced [selfish] motive, here: without renouncing motive; yogī = yogin; bhavati = he becomes; kaścana = anyone, [with the preceding na]: no one.

6.3: āruruksos = for [one] desiring-to-ascend; munes = for a sage; yogam = Yoga; karma = action; kāraṇam = cause, here: means; ucyate = it is said [to be]; yogārūḍhasya (yoga + ārūḍhasya) = for [one who] has ascended [to the apex of] Yoga; tasyaiva (tasya + eva) = for him verily, here: *eva* is omitted; śamas = quiescence; kāraṅam = cause, here: means; ucyate = it is said.

6.4: yadā = when; hi = indeed; nendriyārtheṣu (na + indriya + artheṣu) = not to the sense objects, here: neither . . . ; na = not, here: nor; karmasu = to actions; anuṣajjate = he clings; sarvasaṃkalpasaṃnyāsī (sarva + saṃkalpa + saṃnyāsī) = renouncing all [selfish] motive; yogārūḍhas (yoga + ārūḍhas) = [the sage who] has ascended in Yoga; tadocyate (tadā + ucyate) = then he is called, then he is said [to be].

6.5: uddharet = he should uplift, here: he should raise; ātmanātmānam (ātmanā + ātmānam) = the self by the self; nātmānam (na +ātmānam) = not the self; avasādayet = he should [let it] sink; ātmaiva (ātmā + eva) = the self indeed; hi

= for; ātmanas = of the self; bandhus = friend; ātmaiva (ātmā + eva) = the self indeed; ripus = enemy; ātmanas = of the self.

6.6: bandhus = friend; ātmātmanas (ātmā + ātmanas) = the self of the self; tasya = of him; yenātmaivātmanā (yena + ātmā + eva + ātmanā) = by whom the self [is] verily [conquered] by the self; jitas = conquered; anātmanas = of the nonself, here: of [one who is] bereft-of-self; tu = but; śatrutve = in enmity; vartetātmaiva (varteta + ātmā + eva) = the self verily would exist (varteta), here: the self is . . . , *eva* is omitted; śatruvat (śatru + vat) = like (vat) an enemy.

6.7: jitātmanas (jita + ātmanas) = of conquered self, here: of the self-conquered; praśāntasya = of the tranquil; paramātmā (parama + ātmā) = supreme self; samāhitas = concentrated; śītoṣṅasukhaduḥkheṣu (śīta + uṣṅa + sukha + duḥkheṣu) = in hot (uṣṇa), cold (śīta), pleasure, [and] pain (duḥkha); tathā = thus, here: as well as; mānāpamānayos (māna + apamānayos) (dual) = in honor and dishonor.

6.8: jñānavijñānatṛptātmā (jñāna + vijñāna + tṛpta + ātmā) = [he whose] self is satisfied (tṛpta) with knowledge [and] worldly-knowledge (vijñāna); kūṭasthas (kūṭa + sthas) = [who is] summit (kūṭa) abiding; vijitendriyas (vijita + indriyas) = [with his] senses conquered; yuktas = yoked; iti = thus, here: omitted; ucyate = he is called, here: he is said [to be]; yogī = yogin; samaloṣṭāśmakāñcanas (sama + loṣṭa + aśma + kāñcanas) = [for whom] a clod-of-earth (loṣṭa), a stone (aśma), [and a piece of] gold (kāñcana) [are] the same.

6.9: suhṛnmitrāryudāsīnamadhyasthadveṣyabandhuṣu (suhṛd + mitra + ari + udāsīna + madhya + stha + dveṣya + bandhuṣu) = toward companions (bandhu), good-hearted (su-hṛd) friends (mitra), enemies (ari), indifferent (udāsīna) [people], "middle-standing" (madhya-stha) [i.e., neutral people], [and] hateful [people]; sādhuṣu = toward good [people]; api = also; ca = and; pāpeṣu = toward sinful [people]; samabuddhis (sama + buddhis) = [he whose] wisdom-faculty [is] the same [in regard to, or toward]; viśiṣyate = he is distinguished.

6.10: yogī = yogin; yuñjīta = he should yoke [himself]; satatam = continually; ātmānam = self, himself; rahasi = in solitude, here: in privacy; sthitas = established, here: remaining; ekākī = solitary, alone; yatacittātmā (yata+ citta + ātmā) = [he whose] mind [and] self are restrained; nirāśīs = free-from-hope; aparigrahas = without grasping.

6.11: śucau = in pure; deśe = in place; pratiṣṭhāpya = establishing; sthiram = stable; āsanam = seat; ātmanas = for himself; nātyucchritam (na + atyucchritam) = not too high; nātinīcam (na + atinīcam) = not too low; cailājinakuśottaram (caila + ajina + kuśa + uttaram) = [having for a] covering (uttara) cloth (caila), deerskin (ajina), [or] kuśa-grass.

6.12: tatraikāgram (tatra + eka + agram) = there one-pointed; manas = mind; kṛtvā = having made, here: making; yatacittendriyakriyas (yata + citta + indriya + kriyas) = [having] the activity [of] mind [and] senses controlled (yata); upaviśyāsane (upaviśya + āsane) = sitting on the seat (āsana); yuñjyād = he should yoke [himself]; yogam = Yoga; ātmaviśuddhaye (ātma + viśuddhaye) = for self-purification.

6.13: samam = even; kāyaśirogrīvam (kāya + śiras + grīvam) = trunk (kāya), head, [and] neck; dhārayan = holding; acalam = motionless; sthiras = steady; saṃprekṣya = gazing; nāsikāgram (nāsikā + agram) = tip (agra) of the nose (nāsikā); svam = own, here: his; diśas = directions, here: round about; cānavalokayan (ca + anavalokayan) = and without looking.

6.14: praśāntātmā (praśānta + ātmā) = [with] tranquil self; vigatabhīs = devoid of fear; brahmacārivrate (brahmacāri + vrate) = in vow of chastity; sthitas = steadfast; manas = mind; saṃyamya = controlling, here: controlled; maccittas (mad + cittas) = me-minded, mind on me; yuktas = yoked; āsīta = he should sit; matparas (mad + paras) = intent on me.

6.15: yuñjan = yoking; evam = thus; sadātmānam (sadā + ātmānam) = ever [yoking] himself; yogī = yogin; niyatamānasas (niyata + mānasas) = of restrained mind; śāntim = peace; nirvāṇaparamām (nirvāṇa + paramām) = supreme extinction; matsaṃsthām (mad + saṃsthām) = established (stha), here: [having its] subsistence in me; adhigacchati = it goes, here: it approaches.

6.16: nātyaśnatas (na + atyaśnatas) = not for [one who is] eating too much, here: not for overeater; tu = but; yogas = Yoga; 'sti (asti) = it is; na = not, here: nor; caikāntam (ca + ekāntam) = and [one who is] absolutely, here: and [him who eats] not at all; anaśnatas = non-eating [i.e., fasting], here: [who] eats not; na = not, here: nor; cātisvapnaśīlasya (ca + atisvapna + śīlasya) = and (ca) for [one who has] the habit (śīla) of excessive (ati) sleep, here: ca is translated as "yet"; jāgratas = for [one who is constantly] awake; naiva (na + eva) = not even, here: nor even; cārjuna (ca + arjuna) = and O Arjuna.

6.17: yuktāhāravihārasya (yukta + āhāra + vihārasya) = of [him who is] yoked in food (āhāra) [and] recreation (vihāra); yuktaceṣṭasya (yukta + ceṣṭasya) = of [him whose] activities (ceṣṭa) are yoked, here: . . . disciplined; karmasu = in actions; yuktasvapnāvabodhasya (yukta + svapna + avabodhasya) = of [him who is] yoked [in] sleeping [and] waking; yogas = Yoga; bhavati = it becomes, it is, here: omitted; duḥkhahā (duḥkha + hā) = dispelling suffering, here: it dispels sufferings.

6.18: yadā = when; viniyatam = restrained; cittam = mind; ātmani = in self; evāvatiṣṭhate (eva + avatiṣṭhate) = alone it abides; niḥspṛhas = devoid-of-longing; sarvakāmebhyas (sarva + kāmebhyas) = for all desires; yuktas = yoked; iti = thus, here: used to indicate a quotation: then; ucyate = he is called; tadā = then.

6.19: yathā = as; dīpas = lamp; nivātasthas (nivāta + sthas) = standing [in a] windless (nivāta); neṅgate (na + iṅgate) = it flickers (iṅgate) not; sopamā (sas + upamā) = that simile; smṛtā = remembered, here: recalled; yoginas = of yogin; yatacittasya (yata + cittasya) = of yoked mind; yuñjatas =

of practicing, here: he practices; yogam = Yoga; ātmanas = of self.

6.20: yatroparamate (yatra + uparamate) = where it is curbed, here: when it is curbed; cittam = mind; niruddham = controlled; yogasevayā (yoga + sevayā) = by the service of Yoga; yatra = where, when; caivātmanātmānam (ca + eva + ātmanā + ātmānam) = and the self by the self, here: *eva* is omitted; paśyan = beholding, here: is beheld; ātmani = in the self; tuṣyati = he is content.

6.21: sukham = joy, happiness; ātyantikam = utmost; yad = which; tad = this, that; buddhigrāhyam (buddhi + grāhyam) = grasped by the wisdom-faculty; atīndriyam (ati + indriyam) = extrasensory; vetti = he knows; yatra = where, when; na = not; caivāyam (ca + eva + ayam) = and even (eva) this; sthitas = standing [still]; calati = he moves; tattvatas = from reality (tattva).

6.22: yam = which; labdhvā = having attained; cāparam (ca + aparam) = and other; lābham = gain; manyate = he thinks; nādhikam (na + adhikam) = no greater; tatas = thence, then, here: than that; yasmin = in which; sthitas = abiding; na = not; duḥkhena = by suffering; guruṅāpi (guruṅā + api) = by heavy even (api); vicālyate = he is shaken.

6.23: tam = this, that; vidyāt = let it be known, here: he should know; duḥkhasaṃyogaviyogam (duḥkha + saṃyoga + viyogam) = disunion (viyoga) of the union (saṃyoga) with suffering; yogasaṃjñitam (yoga + saṃjñitam) = called (saṃjñitam) yoga; sas = he; niścayena = with determination; yoktavyas = to be practiced; yogas = Yoga; 'nirviṇṇacetasā (anirviṇṇa + cetasā) = with undejected mind.

6.24: saṃkalpaprabhavān (saṃkalpa + prabhavān) = arising from motive (saṃkalpa); kāmān = desires; tyaktvā = having abandoned, here: abandoning; sarvān (plural) = all; aśeṣatas = entirely; manasaivendriyagrāmam (manasā + eva + indriya +

grāmam) = verily (eva) the host (grāma) of senses by the mind; viniyamya = restraining; samantatas = completely.

6.25: śanais śanais = gradually; uparamet = he should be quiet, here: he should come to rest; buddhyā = by the wisdom-faculty; dhṛtigṛhītayā (dhṛti + gṛhītayā) = by holding steadfast (dhṛti); ātmasaṃstham (ātma + saṃstham) = self-settled, here: settled in the self; manas = mind; kṛtvā = having made, here: making; na = not; kiṃcid = anything; api = even, here: omitted; cintayet = he should think.

6.26: yatas yatas [duplication for emphasis] = whenever, here: wherever; niścarati = it roves about; manas = mind; cañcalam = fickle; asthiram = unsteady; tatas tatas = thence, then, here: from there; niyamyaitad (niyamya + etad) = restraining it; ātmani = in the self; eva = verily, indeed, here: omitted; vaśam = control; nayet = he should lead, here: he should bring [it under control].

6.27: praśāntamanasam (praśānta + manasam) = tranquil mind; hi = for; enam = him, here: that; yoginam = yogin; sukham = joy; uttamam = foremost, unexcelled; upaiti = it goes, here: it comes; śāntarajasam (śānta + rajasam) = appeased (śānta) passion; brahmabhūtam (brahma + bhūtam) = become (bhūta) [one with] the world-ground; akalmaṣam = undefiled, here: free-from-defilement.

6.28: yuñjan = yoking; evam = thus; sadātmānam (sadā + ātmānam) = always (sadā) the self; yogī = yogin; vigatakalmaṣas (vigata + kalmaṣas) = gone [all] defilement, here: [he whose] defilements are gone; sukhena = with joy, with ease; brahmasaṃsparśam (brahma + saṃsparśam) = contact (saṃsparśa) with the world-ground; atyantam = endless; sukham = joy; aśnute = he attains.

6.29: sarvabhūtastham (sarva + bhūta + stham) = abiding (stham) in all beings; ātmānam = the self; sarvabhūtāni (sarva + bhūtāni) = all beings; cātmani (ca + ātmani) = and in the self; īkṣate = he sees; yogayuktātmā (yoga + yukta + ātmā) = [he whose] self is yoked (yukta) [through] Yoga; sarvatra = everywhere; samadarśanas (sama + darśanas) = same vision, here: beholds the same.

6.30: yas = who; mām = me; paśyati = he sees; sarvatra = everywhere; sarvam = all; ca = and; mayi = in me; paśyati = he sees; tasyāham (tasya + aham) = of him (tasya) I; na = not; praṇaśyāmi = I am lost; sas = he; ca = and; me = to me; na = not, here: with ca, "nor"; praṇaśyati = he is lost.

6.31: sarvabhūtasthitam (sarva + bhūta + sthitam) = established in all beings, here: abiding in all beings; yas = who; mām = me; bhajati = he worships; ekatvam = oneness; āsthitas = established; sarvathā = in whatever way, howsoever; vartamānas = existing, here: he exists; 'pi (api) = indeed, even; sas = he; yogī = yogin; mayi = in me; vartate = he dwells.

6.32: ātmaupamyena (ātmā + aupamyena) = self identity; sarvatra = everywhere; samam = same; paśyati = he sees; yas = who; 'rjuna (arjuna) = O Arjuna; sukham = joy; vā = or; yadi = if, whether; vā = or; duḥkham = suffering; sas = he, here: omitted; yogī = yogin; paramas = supreme; matas = is deemed.

arjunas = Arjuna; uvāca = he said;

6.33: yas = who; 'yam (ayam) = this; yogas = Yoga; tvayā = by you; proktas = proclaimed; sāmyena = through sameness; madhusūdana (madhu + sūdana) = O Madhusūdana; etasyāham (etasya + aham) = of this I (aham); na = not, here: cannot; paśyāmi = I see; cañcalatvāt = because of fickleness (calatva); sthitim = state; sthirām = steady.

6.34: cañcalam = fickle; hi = indeed; manas = mind; kṛṣṇa = O Krishna; pramāthi = impetuous; balavat = strong; dṛḍham = firm, here: obstinate; tasyāham (tasya + aham) = of it (tasya) I; nigraham = control; manye = I think; vāyos = of the wind; iva = like; suduṣkaram = very (su-) difficult-to-achieve.

śrībhagavān (śrī + bhagavān) = Blessed Lord; uvāca = he said;

6.35: asaṃśayam = undoubtedly; mahābāho (mahā + bāho) = O mighty-armed [Arjuna]; manas = mind; durnigraham = difficult-to-restrain; calam = fickle; abhyāsena = by practice; tu = but; kaunteya = O son-of-Kuntī; vairāgyeṇa = by dispassion; ca = and; gṛhyate = it is seized, here: it can be seized.

6.36: asaṃyatātmanā (asaṃyata + ātmanā) = by uncontrolled self, here: [he whose] self is unsubdued; yogas = Yoga; duṣprāpas = difficult to obtain; iti = thus, here: this; me = my; matis = conviction; vaśyātmanā (vaśya + ātmanā) = by self [under] control; tu = but; yatatā = by striving; śakyas = possible; 'vāptum (avāptum) = to attain; upāyatas = by [appropriate] means.

arjunas = Arjuna; uvāca = he said;

6.37: ayatis = undisciplined one; śraddhayopetas (śraddhayā + upetas) = endowed with faith (śraddhā), here: arrived at faith; yogāt = from Yoga; calitamānasas (calita + mānasas) = deviated mind; aprāpya = not attaining; yogasaṃsiddhim (yoga + saṃsiddhim) = consummation of Yoga; kām = what?; gatim = course; kṛṣṇa = O Krishna; gacchati = he goes, here: does he go.

«lipsamānas = desirous; satām = of the virtuous ones; mārgam = road; pramūḍhas = confused; brahmaṇas = of the world-ground, here: to . . . ; pathi = on the path; anekacittas (aneka + cittas) = disunited mind; vibhrāntas = distracted; mohasya = of delusion; eva = verily, here: omitted; vaśam = control, here: power; gatas = gone, here: come under. »

6.38: kaccid = from *kad*, "what?," combined with *na*, this expression often means "I hope not"; nobhayavibhraṣṭas (na + ubhaya + vibhraṣṭas) = not unsuccessful in both (ubhaya); chinnābhram (chinna + abhram) = riven cloud (abhra); iva = like; naśyati = he perishes; apratiṣṭhas = lack-of-foundation, here: without a stand; mahābāho (mahā + bāho) = O mighty-armed [Arjuna]; vimūḍhas = deluded; brahmaṇas = of the world-ground, here: to the world-ground; pathi = on the path.

6.39: etad = this; me = my, of mine; saṃśayam = doubt; kṛṣṇa = O Krishna; chettum = to cut, here: to dispel; arhasi = you can; aśeṣatas = completely; tvad = you; anyas = other; saṃśayasyāsya (saṃśayasya + asya) = of doubt (saṃśaya) of it, here: this doubt; chettā = cutter, here: to dispel; na = not; hi = indeed, here: omitted; upapadyate = he comes, exists, here: he steps forward.

śrībhagavān (śrī + bhagavān) = Blessed Lord; uvāca = he said;
6.40: pārtha = O son-of-Prithā; naiveha (na + eva + iha) = not verily here [on earth], here: neither (na) here, *eva* is omitted; nāmutra (na + amutra) = not thither, here: nor above; vināśas = destruction; tasya = for him; vidyate = it exists, here: there is; na = not, no; hi = for, because; kalyāṇakṛt (kalyāṇa + kṛt) = doer (kṛt) of good; kaścid = anyone; durgatim = misfortune, here: bad (dus-) course (gati); tāta = O son; gacchati = he goes, here: he takes.

6.41: prāpya = attaining, reaching; puṇyakṛtān (puṇya + kṛtān) = of the doers of virtuous [deeds]; lokān = the worlds; uṣitvā = having dwelled; śāśvatīs (plural) = endless; samās = years; śucīnām = of pure [people]; śrīmatām = of auspicious [people]; gehe = into the home; yogabhraṣṭas = fallen from Yoga, here; failed in Yoga; 'bhijāyate (abhijāyate) = is born.

6.42: athavā = or else; yoginām = of yogins; eva = indeed, here: omitted; kule = in family; bhavati = he comes, here: he is born; dhīmatām = of wise [yogins]; etad = this, here: omitted; hi = indeed, here: yet; durlabhataram (durlabha + taram) = more difficult to attain, here: very difficult to obtain; loke = in world; janma = birth; yad = which, here: omitted; īdṛśam = such.

6.43: tatra = there; tam = him, that; buddhisaṃyogam (buddhi + saṃyogam) = union with the wisdom-faculty; labhate = he achieves; paurvadehikam (paurva + dehikam) = previous embodiment; yatate = he strives; ca = and; tatas = thence, then, here: omitted; bhūyas = again, here: once again; saṃsiddhau = in consummation, here: for consummation; kurunandana (kuru + nandana) = O Kurunandana.

6.44: pūrvābhyāsena (pūrva + abhyāsena) = by previous practice; tenaiva (tena + eva) = by it verily, here: omitted; hriyate = he is carried; hi = indeed, here: omitted; avaśas = against will; 'pi (api) = even; sas = he; jijñāsus = desirous to know; api = even; yogasya = of Yoga; śabdabrahmātivartate (śabda + brahma + ativartate) = he transcends (ativartate) the sonar (śabda) world-ground.

6.45: prayatnāt = with effort; yatamānas = striving; tu = but; yogī = yogin; saṃśuddhakilbiṣas (saṃśuddha + kilbiṣas) = cleansed of guilt (kilbiṣa); anekajanmasaṃsiddhas (aneka + janma + saṃsiddhas) = perfected (saṃsiddha) [through] many (aneka) a birth; tatas = thence, then; yāti = he goes; parām = supreme; gatim = course.

6.46: tapasvibhyas = than ascetics; 'dhikas (adhikas) = greater; yogī = yogin; jñānibhyas = than knowers; 'pi (api) = even; matas = thought to be, is deemed; 'dhikas (adhikas) = greater; karmibhyas = than performers-of-ritual-action; cādhikas (ca + adhikas) = and greater; yogī = yogin; tasmāt = therefore; yogī = yogin; bhavārjuna (bhava + arjuna) = O Arjuna, you be!

6.47: yoginām = of yogins; api = even, moreover; sarveṣām = of all; madgatenāntarātmanā (mad + gatena + antara + ātmanā) = with inner (antara) self absorbed (gata) in me; śraddhāvān = faithful one; bhajate = he worships; yas = who; mām = me; sas = he; me = to me; yuktatamas (yukta + tamas) = most yoked; matas = is deemed.

CHAPTER 7: THE YOGA OF WISDOM AND KNOWLEDGE

śrībhagavān (śrī + bhagavān) = Blessed Lord; uvāca = he said;

7.1: mayyāsaktamanās (mayi + āsakta + manās, singular) = mind attached in me (mayi), here: . . . to me; pārtha = O son-of-Prithā; yogam = Yoga; yuñjan = yoked, engaged; madāśrayas (mad + āśrayas) = [having] me as refuge; asaṃśayam = without doubt; samagram = entirely, fully; mām = me; yathā = as what, how?; jñāsyasi = you will know, here: you may know; tad = that, here: how; śṛṇu = you hear!

7.2: jñānam = knowledge; te = to you; 'ham (aham) = I; savijñānam (sa + vijñānam) = with worldly knowledge; idam = this; vakṣyāmi = I will tell; aśeṣatas = completely without reserve; yad = which; jñātvā = having known, here: knowing; neha (na + iha) = not here, here: nothing (with anyad) here (iha); bhūyas = more; 'nyad (anyad) = other; jñātavyam = to be known; avaśiṣyate = it remains.

7.3: manuṣyāṇām = of humans; sahasreṣu = in, among thousands; kaścid = anyone; yatati = he strives; siddhaye = for perfection (siddhi); yatatām = of the striving ones; api = even; siddhānām = of adepts; kaścid = anyone; mām = me; vetti = he knows; tattvatas = from reality, here: truly.

7.4: bhūmis = earth; āpas = water; 'nalas (analas) = fire; vāyus = air; kham = ether, space; manas = mind; buddhis = wisdom-faculty; eva =only, here: omitted; ca = and; ahaṃkāras = ego-sense; itīyam (iti + iyam) = thus (iti) this; me = my; bhinnā = divided, division; prakṛtis = nature; aṣṭadhā = eightfold.

7.5: apareyam (aparā + iyam) = lower this (iyam); itas = than this; tu = but; anyām = other (feminine); prakṛtim = nature; viddhi = you know!; me = my; parām = higher; jīvabhūtām (jīva + bhūtām) = consisting of life, here: life element; mahābāho (mahā + bāho) = O strong-armed [Arjuna]; yayedam (yayā + idam) = by which this; dhāryate = is supported; jagat = world, universe.

7.6: etad = this; yonīni = wombs, here: womb; bhūtāni = beings; sarvāṇīti (sarvāṇi + iti) = all thus, here: *iti* is omitted; upadhāraya = you understand!; aham = I; kṛtsnasya = of the whole; jagatas = of the universe; prabhavas = origin; pralayas = dissolution, here: end; tathā = as well as, here: and.

7.7: mattas = than me; parataram = higher; nānyat (na + anyat) = not other; kiṃcid = something, here: with *na*, "nothing";

asti = it is; dhanaṃjaya (dhanaṃ + jaya) = O Dhanamjaya; mayi = in me; sarvam = all; idam = this; protam = strung; sūtre = on a thread; maṇigaṇās (maṇi + gaṇās) = jewel clusters; iva = like.

7.8: rasas = essence, flavor; 'ham (aham) = I; apsu = in waters; kaunteya = O son-of-Kuntī; prabhāsmi (prabhā + asmi) = radiance I am; śaśisūryayos (śaśi + sūryayos) (dual) = of sun and moon; praṇavas = humming sound, here: retained in Sanskrit; sarvavedeṣu (sarva + vedeṣu) = in all the Vedas; śabdas = sound; khe = in ether, space, here: of space; pauruṣam = manhood; nṛṣu = in men, here: of men.

7.9: puṇyas = virtuous, here: pure; gandhas = fragrance; pṛthivyām = in earth, here: of earth; ca = and; tejas = glow; cāsmi (ca + asmi) = and I am; vibhāvasau = in flame, here: of fire; jīvanam = life; sarvabhūteṣu (sarva + bhūteṣu) = in all (sarva) beings, here: of all beings; tapas = austerity; cāsmi (ca + asmi) = and I am; tapasviṣu = in ascetics, here: of ascetics.

7.10: bījam = seed; mām = me; sarvabhūtānām (sarva + bhūtānām) = of all beings; viddhi = you know!; pārtha = O son-of-Prithā; sanātanam = eternal; buddhis = wisdom-faculty; buddhimatām (buddhi + matām) (plural) = of the wisdom-endowed; asmi = I am; tejas = glow, radiance; tejasvinām = of radiant ones; aham = I.

7.11: balam = power; balavatām = of powerful ones; cāham (ca + aham) = and I; kāmarāgavivarjitam (kāma + rāga + vivarjitam) = devoid (vivarjita) of desire [and] passion; dharmāviruddhas (dharma + aviruddhas) = law unopposed, here: not opposed to the law; bhūteṣu = in beings; kāmas = desire; 'smi (asmi) = I am; bharatarṣabha (bharata + ṛṣabha) = O Bharatarshabha.

7.12: ye (plural) = which, who, here: left untranslated; caiva (ca + eva) = and verily, here: moreover; sāttvikās (plural) = luminous; bhāvās = states; rājasās (plural) = dynamic; tāmasās (plural) = obscuring; ca = and; ye (plural) = which, who, here: omitted; mattas = from me; eveti (eva + iti) = verily thus, here: *iti* is omitted; tān = them, here: those; viddhi = you know!; na = not; tu = but, yet; aham = I; teṣu = in them; te = they; mayi = in me.

7.13: tribhis = by three; guṇamayais (guṇa + mayais) = by the primary-qualities formed; bhāvais = by states-of-existence; ebhis = by these; sarvam = all, here: entire; idam = this; jagat = universe; mohitam = deluded; nābhijānāti (na + abhijānāti) = it [does] not recognize; mām = me; ebhyas = from these, than these, here: them; param = higher, here: beyond; avyayam = immutable.

7.14: daivī = divine; hi = for; eṣā = this; guṇamayī (guṇa + mayī) = formed by the primary-qualities; mama = my; māyā = creative-power; duratyayā = difficult-to-transcend; mām = [to] me; eva = verily, here: alone; ye (plural) = which, who; prapadyante = they resort; māyām = creative-power; etām = this; taranti = they transcend; te = they.

7.15: na = not; mām = [in] me; duṣkṛtinas = wrongdoers; mūḍhās (plural) = confounded; prapadyante = they resort; narādhamās (nara + adhamās) = lowest of men; māyayāpahṛtajñānās (māyayā + apahṛta + jñānās) (plural) = [those] deprived (apahṛta) of knowledge by creative-power; āsuram = demonic; bhāvam = condition; āśritās = [those who] have recourse.

7.16: caturvidhās = fourfold, here: four kinds; bhajante = they worship; mām = me; janās = people; sukṛtinas = good-doing; 'rjuna (arjuna) = O Arjuna; ārtas = afflicted; jijñāsus = desirous-of-knowledge; arthārthī (artha + arthī) = [he whose] object is the welfare [of the world]; jñānī = knower; ca = and; bharatarṣabha (bharata + ṛṣabha) = O Bharatarshabha.

7.17: teṣām = of these; jñānī = knower; nityayuktas (nitya + yuktas) = ever yoked; ekabhaktis (eka + bhaktis) = single devotion; viśiṣyate = he is excellent; priyas = dear; hi = because; jñāninas = of the knower, here: to the knower; 'tyartham (atyartham) = exceedingly; aham = I; sas = he; ca = and; mama = of me, here: to me; priyas = dear.

7.18: udārās (plural) = exalted; sarva = all; evaite (eva + ete) = indeed these; jñānī = knower; tu = but; ātmaiva (ātmā + eva) = self indeed; me = my; matam = is deemed, here: I deem; āsthitas = established; sas = he; hi = for; yuktātmā (yukta + ātmā) = [who is of] yoked self; mām = [in] me; evānuttamām (eva + anuttamām) = alone (eva) supreme; gatim = course.

7.19: bahūnām = of many; janmanām = of births; ante = at the end; jñānavān = knowledge-endowed; mām = [to] me; prapadyate = he resorts; vāsudevas (vāsudevas) = son-of-Vasudeva [i.e., Krishna]; sarvam = all; iti = thus; sas = he; mahātmā (mahā + ātmā) = great soul; sudurlabhas = difficult-to-find.

7.20: kāmais = by desires; tais tais = by these and those, here: by whatever; hṛtajñānās (hṛta + jñānās) = [those who are] deprived of knowledge; prapadyante = they resort; 'nyadevatās (anya + devatās) = other deities; taṃ tam = this or that; niyamam = rule, obligation; āsthāya = having recourse; prakṛtyā = by nature; niyatās (plural) = constrained; svayā = by own, here: by their own.

7.21: yas yas = whoever, whichever; yām yām = whatever; tanum = body, form; bhaktas = devotee; śraddhayārcitum (śraddhayā + ārcitum) = to worship (ārcitum) with faith; icchati = he desires; tasya tasyācalām (tasya + tasya + acalām) = of him whosoever immovable (acālam), here: immovable [faith] of his; śraddhām = faith; tām = that; eva = indeed, here: very; vidadhāmi = [do] I grant; aham = I.

7.22: sas = he; tayā = by that; śraddhayā = by faith; yuktas = yoked; tasyārādhanam (tasya + ārādhanam) = of this reverence, here: to reverence that; īhate = he seeks; labhate = he obtains; ca = and; tatas = thence, then; kāmān = desires; mayaiva (mayā + eva) = by me verily; vihitān = ordained, here: dispensed; hi = indeed; tān = them, here: left untranslated.

7.23: antavat = having an end, here: finite; tu = but; phalam = fruit; teṣām = of them; tad = this, that; bhavati = it becomes, here: is; alpamedhasām (alpa + medhasām) (plural) = of little intelligence; devān = deities; devayajas (deva + yajas) (plural) = deity worshippers; yānti = they go; madbhaktās (mad + bhaktās) = my devotees; yānti = they go, here: they come; mām = [to] me; api = however.

7.24: avyaktam = unmanifest; vyaktim = manifestation; āpannam = fallen into; manyante = they think; mām = me; abuddhayas (plural) = unwise; param = higher; bhāvam = state-of-existence; ajānantas (plural) = ignorant; mamāvyayam (mama + avyayam) = my immutable; anuttamam = unsurpassed.

7.25: nāham (na + aham) = not I; prakāśas = visible-light; sarvasya = of all, here: to all; yogamāyāsamāvṛtas (yoga + māyā + samāvṛtas) = veiled (samāvṛtas) [by] the creative-power [of my] Yoga; mūḍhas = deluded; 'yam (ayam) = this; nābhijānāti (na + abhijānāti) = not knows; lokas = universe; mām = me; ajam = unborn; avyayam = immutable.

7.26: vedāham (veda + aham) = know I; samatītani (samatītāni) (plural) = passed, here: past; vartamānāni (plural) = existing, here: present; cārjuna (ca + arjuna) = and O Arjuna; bhaviṣyāṇi (plural) = those-to-come; ca = and; bhūtāni = beings; mām = me; tu = but; veda = he knows; na kaścana = no one.

7.27: icchādveṣasamutthena (icchā + dveṣa + samutthena) = by rising [from] longing (icchā and aversion; dvandvamohena (dvandva + mohena) = by the delusion of the pairs-of-opposites (dvandva); bhārata = O descendant-of-Bharata; sarvabhūtāni (sarva + bhūtāni) = all beings; saṃmoham = confusion; sarge = in [this] creation; yānti = they go; here: they succumb; paraṃtapa = O Paramtapa.

7.28: yeṣām = of whom; tu = but; antagatam (anta + gatam) = end-gone, here: has come to an end; pāpam = evil; janānām = of men; puṇyakarmaṇām (puṇya + karmaṇām) = of [those] of meritorious actions, here: [those who perform] meritorious actions; te = they; dvandvamohanirmuktās (dvandva + moha + nirmuktās) (plural) = released from the delusion of the pairs-of-opposites; bhajante = they worship; mām = me; dṛḍhavratās (dṛḍha + vratās) (plural) = [who are of] steadfast vows.

7.29: jarāmaraṇamokṣāya (jarā + maraṇa + mokṣāya) = toward release from old age [and] death; mām = me; āśritya = taking recourse; yatanti = they strive; ye (plural) = which, who; te = they; brahma = world-ground; tad = this, that; vidus = they know; kṛtsnam = wholly; adhyātmam = basis-of-self; karma = action; cākhilam (ca + akhilam) = and entire.

7.30: sādhibhūtādhidaivam (sa + ādhibhūta + adhidaivam) = with basis-of-beings [and] divine-basis; mām = me; sādhiyajñam (sa + adhiyajñam) = with basis-of-sacrifice; ca = and; ye (plural) = which, who; vidus = they know; prayāṇakāle (prayāṇa + kāle) = at going-forth time; 'pi (api) = also; ca = and; mām = me; te = they; vidus = they know; yuktacetasas (yukta + cetasas) (plural) = [those who are] yoked-minded.

CHAPTER 8: THE YOGA OF THE IMPERISHABLE ABSOLUTE

arjunas = Arjuna; uvāca = he said;

8.1: kim = what?; tad = this, that; brahma = world-ground; kim = what?; adhyātmam = basis-of-self; kim = what?; karma = action; puruṣottama = O Purushottama; adhibhūtam = elemental-basis; ca = and; kim = what?; proktam = proclaimed; adhidaivam = divine-basis; kim = what?; ucyate = it is said.

8.2: adhiyajñas = sacrificial-basis; katham = how?; kas = who; 'tra (atra) = here; dehe = in body; 'smin (asmin) = in this; madhusūdana = O Madhusūdana; prayāṇakāle (prayāṇa + kāle) = at going-forth time; ca = and; katham = how?; jñeyas = to be known; 'si (asi) = you are; niyatātmabhiḥ (niyata + ātmabhis) (plural) = by [those who are of] restrained self.

śrībhagavān (śrī + bhagavān) = Blessed Lord; uvāca = he said;

8.3: akṣaram = imperishable; brahma = left untranslated;

paramam = supreme; svabhāvas (sva + bhāvas) = own-being; 'dhyātmam (adhyātmam) = basis-of-self; ucyate = it is said; bhūtabhavodbhavakaras (bhūta + bhāva + udbhavakaras) = originating the state-of-existence of beings; visargas = creativity; karmasaṃjñitaḥ (karma + saṃjñitas) = designated as action.

8.4: adhibhūtam = elemental-basis; kṣaras = perishable; bhāvas = state-of-existence; puruṣas = spirit; cādhidaivatām (ca + adhidaivatām) = and divine-basis; adhiyajñas = sacrificial-basis; 'ham (aham) = I [am]; evātra (eva + atra) = verily here, here: *eva* is omitted; dehe = in body; dehabhṛtam (deha-bhṛtām) = O body-wearer, here: O body-wearers; vara = O best [of].

8.5: antakāle (anta + kāle) = at going-forth time; ca = and; mām = me; eva = verily, indeed, here: alone; smaran = remembering; muktvā = having released; kalevaram = body; yas = who; prayāti = he goes forth; sas = he; madbhāvam (mad + bhāvam) = my state-of-existence; yāti = he goes; nāsti = not is, here: [there] is no; atra = here, here: of this; saṃśayas = doubt.

8.6: yaṃ yam = whatever; vāpi (vā + api) = or also, here: *vā* is omitted; smaran = remembering; bhāvaṃ = state-of-existence; tyajati = he abandons; ante = in the end; kalevaram = body; taṃ tam = [to] that; evaiti (eva + eti) = verily he goes; kaunteya = O son-of-Kuntī; sadā = always; tadbhāvabhāvitas (tad + bhāva + bhāvitas) = caused-to-become (bhāvitas) that state-of-existence, here: forced to become . . . .

8.7: tasmāt = therefore; sarveṣu kāleṣu = at all times; mām = me; anusmara = you remember!; yudhya = you fight!; ca = and; mayi = in me, here: on me; arpitamanobuddhis (arpita + manas + buddhis) = mind [and] wisdom-faculty fixed; mām = me; evaiṣyasi (eva + eṣyasi) = verily you will come; asaṃśayas = undoubtedly.

8.8: abhyāsayogayuktena (abhyāsa + yoga + yuktena) = by [consciousness] yoked by the Yoga of practice; cetasā = mind; nānyagāminā (na + anya + gāminā) = by not going elsewhere (anya), here: not going astray; paramam = supreme; puruṣam =

spirit; divyam = divine; yāti = he goes; pārthānucintayan (pārtha + anucintayan) = O son-of-Prithā [i.e., Arjuna] contemplating.

8.9: kavim = bard; purāṇam = ancient; anuśāsitāram = governor; aṇos = than small; aṇiyāmsam = smaller; anusmaret = he should remember, here: he remembers; yas = who; sarvasya = of all; dhātāram = supporter; acintyarūpam (acintya + rūpam) = inconceivable (acintya) form; ādityavarṇam (āditya + varṇam) = sun-colored; tamasas = of darkness, here: darkness; parastāt = beyond.

8.10: prayaṇakāle (prayaṇa + kāle) = at going-forth time; manasācalena (manasā + acalena) = with unmoving mind; bhaktyā = by devotion; yuktas = yoked; yogabalena (yoga + balena) = with power of Yoga; caiva (ca + eva) = and verily, here: *eva* is omitted; bhruvos = of eyebrows; mādhye = in middle, here: to the middle; prāṇam = life-force; aveśya = causing to enter, here: directing; saṃyak = properly; sas = he; tam = that; param = supreme; puruṣam = spirit; upaiti = he goes, here: he comes; divyam = divine.

8.11: yad = which; akṣaram = imperishable; vedavidas = Veda-knowers; vadanti = they speak; viśanti = they enter; yad = which; yatayas = ascetics; vītarāgas = devoid of passion; yad = which; icchantas = desiring; brahmacaryam = chastity; caranti = they pursue; tat = that; te = to you; pādam = state; saṃgraheṇa = briefly; pravakṣye = I will declare.

8.12: sarvadvārāṇi (sarva + dvārāṇi) = all gates; samyamya = controlling; manas = mind; hṛdi = in heart; nirudhya = confining; ca = and; mūrdhni = in head; ādhāyātmanas (ādhāya + ātmanas) = placing [the life-force] of self, here: placing one's; prāṇam = life-force; asthitas = established; yogadhāraṇām (yoga + dhāraṇām) = [in] concentration of Yoga.

8.13: om = the sacred syllable; iti = thus, here: used to indicate a quotation; ekākṣaram (eka + akṣaram) = monosyllable; brahma = here: Brahman; vyāharan = reciting; mām = me; anusmaran = remembering; yas = who; prayāti = goes forth, here: departs [i.e., dies]; tyajan = abandoning; deham = body; sas = he; yāti = he goes; paramām = supreme; gatim = course.

8.14: ananyacetās (ananya + cetās) = [whose] mind [does not go] elsewhere, here: [who is of] undiverted mind; satatam = always; yas = who; mām = me; smarati = he remembers; nityaśas = constantly; tasyāham (tasya + aham) = of him I [am]; sulabhas = easy to reach, here: easily attained; pārtha = O son-of-Prithā; nityayuktasya (nitya + tasya) = of [him who is] continually yoked; yoginas = of the yogin.

8.15: mām = me; upetya = coming; punarjanma = rebirth; duḥkhālayam = abode of suffering (duḥkha); aśāśvatam = impermanent; nāpnuvanti (na + apnuvanti) = they [do] not incur, here: they [do] not undergo; mahātmānas (mahā + ātmānas) = great selves; saṃsiddhim = consummation; paramām = supreme; gatās (plural) = gone, here: having gone.

8.16: ābrahmabhuvanāllokās (ā + brahma + bhuvanāt + lokās) = worlds (loka) up to (ā) the realm (bhuvana) of Brahma; punarāvartinas (punar + āvartinas) (plural) = again evolutions, here: repeatedly evolve; 'rjuna (arjuna) = O Arjuna; mām = [to] me; upetya = coming, here: having come; tu = but, however; kaunteya = O son-of-Kuntī; punarjanma = rebirth; na = not; vidyate = it exists, here: there is.

8.17: sahasrayugaparyāntam (sahasra + yuga + paryantam) = extending to a thousand ages, here: lasts a thousand ages; ahar = day; yad = which; brahmaṇas = of Brahma; vidus = they know; rātrim = night; yugasahasrāntam (yuga + sahasra + antām) = ending [after] a thousand ages, here: ends after a thousand ages; te = they, here: these; 'horātravidas (ahas + rātra + vidas) (plural) = knowers of day [and] night; janās (plural) = people.

8.18: avyaktād = from the unmanifest; vyaktayas (plural) = manifest; sarvās = all; prabhavanti = they originate, here: they spring forth; aharāgame (ahan + āgame) = at the coming of day; rātryāgame (rātri + āgame) = at the coming of night; pralīyante

= they merge, they dissolve; tatraivāvyaktasaṃjñake (tatra + eva + avyakta + saṃjñake) = indeed (eva) into that (tatra) [state] designated (saṃjñaka) [as] unmanifest.

8.19: bhūtagrāmas (bhūta + grāmas) = aggregation of being; sas = he, here: this; evāyam (eva + ayam) = verily this, here: this same; bhūtvā bhūtvā = having come into being [again and again], here: [which] comes-into-being again and again; pralīyate = it merges, it dissolves; rātryāgame (rātri + āgame) = at the coming of night; 'vaśas (avaśas) = involuntarily; pārtha = O son-of-Prithā; prabhavati = it arises, here: it springs forth; aharāgame (ahan + āgame) = at the coming of day.

8.20: paras = higher, beyond; tasmāt = than this, than that; tu = but; bhāvas = state-of-existence; 'nyas (anyas) = other, here: another; 'vyaktas (avyaktas) = unmanifest; 'vyaktāt (avyaktāt) = than unmanifest; sanātanas = everlasting; yas = who, which; sas = he, it; sarveṣu = in all, here: of all; bhūteṣu = in beings, here: of [all] beings; naśyatsu = in perishings, here: on the destruction; na = not; vinaśyati = he is destroyed.

8.21: avyaktas = unmanifest; 'kṣara (akṣara) = imperishable; iti = thus, here: omitted; uktas = is; tam = that, here: him; āhus = they call; paramām = supreme; gatim = course; yam = which; prāpya = having attained, here: when attained; na = not; nivartante = they return; tad = that, this; dhāma = abode; paramam = supreme; mama = my.

8.22: puruṣas = spirit; sas = he, here: this; paras = supreme; pārtha = O son-of-Prithā; bhaktyā = through devotion; labhyas = attainable; tu = but, here: omitted; ananyayā = not [directed] to another; yasyāntaḥsthāni (yasya + antas + sthāni) = abiding within (antas) whose [being]; bhūtāni = beings; yena = by whom; sarvam = all, here: entire; idam = this [universe]; tatam = spread out.

8.23: yatra = where, when; kāle = in time; tu = but; anāvṛttim = no-return; āvṛttim = return; caiva (ca + eva) = and verily, here: or; yoginas = yogins; prayātās (plural) = gone forth; yānti =

they go; tam = that; kālam = time; vakṣyāmi = I will declare; bharatarṣabha = O Bharatarshabha.

8.24: agnis = fire; jyotis = luminosity; ahas = day; śuklas = bright; ṣaṇmāsās (ṣaṇ + māsās) = six months; uttarāyaṇam (uttara + ayanam) = northern course; tatra = in this, here: in them; prayātās (plural) = going forth; gacchanti = they go; brahma = Brahman; brahmavidas (brahma + vidas) = Brahman knowers; janās (plural) = people.

8.25: dhūmas = smoke; rātris = night; tathā = likewise, here: and; kṛṣṇas = black, here: dark [fortnight]; ṣaṇmāsās (ṣaṇ + māsās) = six months; dakṣiṇāyanam (dakṣiṇā + ayanam) = southern course; tatra = in this, here: in them; cāndramasam = lunar; jyotis = luminosity; yogī = yogin; prāpya = having attained, here: he attains; nivartate = he returns.

8.26: śuklakṛṣṇe (śukla + kṛṣṇa) = bright and dark; gatī (dual) = courses; hi = verily; ete (feminine dual) = these two; jagatas = of the universe, here: in the universe; śāśvate (dual) = eternal; mate (dual) = are considered; ekāya = by one; yāti = he goes; anāvṛttim = non-return; anyayāvartate (anyayā + āvartate) = by other [there is] return, here: by the other, he returns; punas = again.

8.27: naite (na + ete) (dual) = not these; sṛtī (dual) = pathways; pārtha = O son-of-Prithā; jānan = knowing; yogī = yogin; muhyati = is deluded; kaścana = whatsoever; tasmāt = therefore, hence; sarveṣu = at all; kāleṣu = at times; yogayuktas (yoga + yuktas) = yoked in Yoga; bhavārjuna (bhava + arjuna) = O Arjuna, you be!

8.28: vedeṣu = in Vedas, here: to Vedas; yajñeṣu = in sacrifices, here: to sacrifices; tapaḥsu = in austerities, here: to austerities; caiva (ca + eva) = and indeed, here: or; dāneṣu = in gifts, here: to gifts; yat = which, here: whatever; puṇyaphalam (puṇya + phalam) = meritorious fruit; pradiṣṭam = prescribed, here: assigned; atyeti = he transcends; tat = this, that; sarvam

= all, entire; idam = this; viditvā = having known, here: knowing; yogī = yogin; param = supreme; sthānam = state; upaiti = he goes, here: he reaches; cādyam (ca + ādyam) = and primal.

CHAPTER 9: THE YOGA OF THE ROYAL WISDOM AND THE ROYAL SECRET

śrībhagavān (śrī + bhagavān) = Blessed Lord; uvāca = he said;

9.1: idam = this; tu = but; te = to you; guhyatamaṃ = most secret; pravakṣyāmi = I will declare; anasūyave = to the uncomplaining, here: nongrumbling; jñānam = knowledge; vijñānasahitam (vijñāna + sahitam) = together (sahita) with discrimination, here: world-knowledge; yad = which; jñātvā = having known, here: knowing; mokṣyase = you shall be freed; 'śubhāt (aśubhāt) = from inauspicious [karma].

9.2: rājavidyā (rāja + vidyā) = royal science; rājaguhyam (rāja + guhyam) = royal secret; pavitram = purifier; idam = this; uttamam = unexcelled, foremost; pratyakṣāvagamam (pratyakṣa + avagamanam) = evident [to one's] understanding; dharmyam = lawful; susukham (su + sukham) = very easy; kartum = to do, here: to apply; avyayam = immutable.

9.3: aśraddadhānās = [those who] have no faith; puruṣās = men; dharmasyāsya (dharmasya + asya) = of this (asya) law; paraṃtapa = O Paramtapa; aprāpya = not having reached, here: without reaching; mām = me; nivartante = they return; mṛtyusaṃsāravartmani (mṛtyu + saṃsāra + vartmani) = in the course of the death (mṛtyu) cycle, here: to the course . . . .

9.4: mayā = by me; tatam = spread out; idam = this; sarvam = all, entire; jagat = universe; avyaktamūrtinā (avyakta + mūrtinā) = by unmanifest form; matsthāni (mad + sthāni) = me-abiding, here: abide in me; sarvabhūtāni (sarva + bhūtāni) = all beings; na = not; cāham (ca + aham) = I am; teṣvavasthitas (teṣu +

avasthitas) = in them abiding, here: [I do not] subsist in them.

9.5: na = not; ca = and; matsthāni (mad + sthāni) = me-abiding, here: [they do not] abide in me; bhūtāni = beings; paśya = behold; me = my; yogam = Yoga; aiśvaram = lordly; bhūtabhṛt (bhūta + bhṛt) = being-bearing, here: sustains beings; na = not; ca = and; bhūtasthas (bhūta + sthas) = being-abiding, here: abiding in beings; māmātmā (māma + ātmā) = myself; bhūta = bhavanas (bhūta + bhāvanas) = causes beings (bhūta) to be.

«sarvagas (sarva + gas) = all-going, here: omnipresent; sarvas = all, here: whole; cādyas (ca + ādyas) = and primordial; sarvakṛtsarvadarśanas (sarva + kṛt + sarva + darśanas) = all-doing [and] all-seeing; sarvajñas (sarva + jñas) = all-knowing; sarvadarśī (sarva + darśī) = seer of all; ca = and; sarvātmā (sarva + ātmā) = self of all; sarvatomukhas (sarvatas + mukhas) = facing (mukhas) everywhere.»

9.6: yathākāśasthitas (yathā + ākāśa + sthitas) = as space abiding, here: abides in space; nityam = always, ever; vāyus = wind; sarvatragas (sarvatra + gas) = all-going, here: everywhere; mahān = great, here: mighty; tathā = thus, here: so; sarvāṇi (plural) = all; bhūtāni = beings; matsthānīti (mad + sthāni + iti) = me-abiding, here: abide in me, *iti* is used to indicate a quotation; upadhāraya = understand.

«evam = thus; hi = indeed; sarvabhūteṣu (sarva + bhūteṣu) = in all beings; carāmyanabhilakṣitas (carāmi + anabhilakṣitas) = I move unrecognized; bhūtaprakṛtimāt (bhūta + prakṛtimāt) = by the nature of beings; sthāya = adopting; sahaiva (saha + eva) = with, *eva* is omitted; ca = and; vinaiva (vinā + eva) = without, *eva* is omitted; ca = and.»

9.7: sarvabhūtāni (sarva + bhūtāni) = all beings; kaunteya = O son-of-Kuntī; prakṛtim = nature; yānti = they go, here: they come; māmikām = my; kalpakṣaye (kalpa + kṣaye) = at the end of an aeon; punas = again; tāni = them; kalpādau (kalpa + ādau) = at the beginning of an aeon; visṛjāmi = I emit; aham = I.

9.8: prakṛtiṃ = nature; svam = own; avastabhya = supported; visṛjāmi = I emit; punas punas = again [and] again; bhūtagramam (bhūta + gramam) = aggregation of beings; imam = this; kṛtsnam = whole; avaśaṃ = powerless; prakṛtes = of nature; vaśāt = by the power.

9.9: na = not; ca = and; mām = me; tāni = these; karmāṇi = actions; nibadhnanti = they bind; dhanaṃjaya = O Dhanamjaya; udāsīnavad (udāsīna + vat) = like (vat) a disinterested [person]; āsīnam = sitting, seated, here: I behave; asaktaṃ = unattached; teṣu = in these; karmasu = in actions.

9.10: mayādhyakṣena (mayā + adhyakṣena) = by my supervision, here: under my supervision; prakṛtis = nature; sūyate = it produces; sacarācaram (sacara + acaram) = moving [and] unmoving; hetunānena (hetunā + anena) = for this (anena) reason; kaunteya = O son-of-Kuntī; jagat = universe; viparivartate = it revolves.

9.11: avajānanti = they scorn; mām = me; mūḍhās = fools; manuṣīm = human; tanum = body; āśritam = assumed; param = higher; bhāvam = state-of-existence; ajānantas = ignored; mama = of my; bhūtamaheśvaram (bhūta + mahā + īśvaram) = [as] the great lord (īśvara) of beings.

9.12: moghāśā (mogha + āśā) = vain hopes; moghakarmaṇas (mogha + karmaṇas) = vain actions; moghajñānavicetasas (mogha + jñāna + vicetasas) = vain knowledge [of those] bereft-of-sense (vicetasas); rākṣasīm = monstrous; āsurīm = demoniacal; caiva (ca + eva) = and indeed, here: *eva* is omitted; prakṛtim = nature; mohinīm = delusive; śritās = [those who] resort.

9.13: mahātmanas (mahā + ātmanas) = great selves; tu = but; mām = me; pārtha = O son-of-Prithā; daivīm = divine; prakṛtim = nature; āśritās (plural) = taking refuge; bhajanti = they worship; ananyamanasas (ananya + manasas) = [those whose] minds [are] not elsewhere (ananya); jñātvā = having known, here: knowing; bhūtādim (bhūta + ādim) = beginning (ādi) of beings; avyayam = immutable.

9.14: satatam = always; kīrtayantas (plural) = glorifying; mām = me; yatantas (plural) = striving; ca = and; dṛḍhavratas (dṛḍha + vratās) = steadfast [in their] vows; namasyantaśca (namasyantas + ca) (plural) = and (ca) bowing down; mām = to me; bhaktyā = with devotion; nityayuktās (nitya + yuktās) = [those who are] ever yoked; upāsate = they worship.

9.15: jñānayajñena (jñāna + yajñena) = by sacrifice of knowledge; cāpi (ca + api) = and also, here: *api* is omitted; anye = others; yajantas = [they who are] worshipping, here: offering; mām = me; upāsate = they worship; ekatvena = by unity, here: unity; pṛthaktvena = by diversity, here: in diversity; bahudhā = manifold; viśvatomukham (viśvatas + mukham) = facing everywhere.

9.16: aham = I; kratus = rite; aham = I; yajñas = sacrifice; svadhāham (svadhā + aham) = oblation I; aham = I; auṣadham = herb; mantras = mantra; 'ham (aham) = I; aham = I; evājyam (eva + ājyam) = indeed clarified-butter, here: *eva* is left untranslated; aham = I; agnis = fire; aham = I; hutam = offering.

9.17: pitāham (pitā + aham) = father I; asya = of this; jagatas = of the universe; mātā = mother; dhātā = supporter; pitāmahas (pitā + mahas) = grandsire; vedyam = to-be-known; pavitram = purifier; omkāras (om + kāra) = om-maker, here: the syllable om; ṛk = praise [referring to the *Rig-Veda*]; sāma (sāman) = chant [referring to the *Sāma-Veda*]; yajus = sacrifice [referring to the *Yajur-Veda*]; eva = indeed, here: omitted; ca = and.

9.18: gatis = course; bhārtā = sustainer; prabhus = lord; sākṣī = witness; nivāsas = home; śaraṇam = refuge; suhṛt (su + hṛt) = good heart, friend; prabhavas = origin; pralayas = dissolution; sthānam = state, here: [middle-]state; nidhānam = receptacle; bījam = seed; avyayam = immutable.

9.19: tapāmi = I burn; aham = I; aham = I; varṣam = rain; nigṛhnāmi = I hold back; utsṛjāmi = I pour forth; ca = and; amṛtam = immortal, immortality; caiva (ca + eva) = and, here: *eva* is omitted; mṛtyuśca (mṛtyus + ca) = and (ca) death; sat = existent; asaccāham (asat + ca + aham) = nonexistent and I [am]; arjuna = O Arjuna.

9.20: traividyā (trai + vidyā) = triple science; mām = me; somapās (soma + pās) = soma drinkers; pūtapāpās (pūta + pāpās) (plural) = purged of sins, here purged of sin; yajñais = with sacrifices; iṣṭvā = having worshipped; svargatim (svar + gatim) = course [to] heaven; prārthayante = they wish; te = they; puṇyam = meritorious; āsādya = attaining; surendralokam (surendra + lokam) = world (loka) of the lord-of-gods; aśnanti = they eat, they enjoy, here: they taste; divyān (plural) = divine; divi = in heaven; devabhogān = (deva + bhogān) gods' pleasures.

9.21: te = they; taṃ = this, that; bhuktvā = having enjoyed; svargalokam (svarga + lokam) = world of heaven; viśalam = wide; kṣiṇe = with exhausted ; puṇye = with merit; martyalokam (martya + lokam) = world of mortals (martya); viśanti = they enter; evam = thus; trayīdharmam (trayī + dharmam) = triple law; anuprapannās (plural) = following; gatāgatam (gata + agatam) = going [and] coming; kāmakāmās (kāma + kāmās) (plural) = desiring [objects of] desire; labhante = they gain.

9.22: ananyās (plural) = none other, here: with undiverted [mind]; cintayantas (plural) = reflecting; mām = me; ye (plural) = who; janās (plural) = people; paryupāsate = they worship; teṣām = of them, here: for those; nityābhiyuktānām (nitya + abhiyuktānām) = of [those who are] ever yoked; yogakṣemam (yoga + kṣemam) = security in Yoga; vahāmi = I bring; aham = I.

9.23: ye (plural) = who; 'py (api) = also, even [those]; anyadevatābhaktās (anya + devatā + bhaktās) (plural) = devoted to other deities; yajante = they worship; śraddhayānvitās (śraddhayā + anvitās) (plural) = endowed with faith (śraddhā); te = they; 'pi (api) = also, here: omitted; mām = me; eva = verily; kaunteya = O son-of-Kuntī; yajanti = they worship;

avidhipūrvakam (a + vidhi + pūrvakam) = not according to [established] ordinance (vidhi).

9.24: aham = I; hi = for; sarvayajñānām (sarva + yajñānām) = of all sacrifices; bhoktā = enjoyer (bhoktṛ); ca = and; prabhus = lord; eva = indeed; ca = and; na = not; tu = but; mām = me; abhijānanti = they know; tattvenātas (tattvena + atas) = in truth hence; cyavanti = they fall; te = they.

9.25: yānti = they go; devavratās (deva + vratās) (plural) = god-vowed; devān = [to] the gods; pitṝn = [to] the ancestors; yānti = they go; pitṛvratās (pitṛ + vratās) (plural) = ancestor-vowed; bhūtāni = lower-beings; yānti = go; bhūtejyās (bhūta + ijyās) = [those who] worship lower-beings; yānti = go; madyājinas (mad + yājinas) (plural) = me-sacrificing, here: [those who] sacrifice to me; 'pi (api) = but; mām = me.

9.26: pattram = leaf; puṣpam = flower; phalam = fruit; toyam = water; yas = who; me = to me; bhaktyā = with devotion; prayacchati = he offers; tad = this, that; aham = I; bhaktyupahṛtam (bhakti + upahṛtam) = offered with devotion, here: an offering out of devotion; aśnāmi = I eat; prayatātmanas (prayata + ātmanas) = from exerting self, here: with an exerting self.

9.27: yad = which, here: whatever; karoṣi = you do; yad = which, here: whatever; aśnāsi = you eat; yad = which, here: whatever; juhoṣi = you offer [in sacrifice]; dadāsi = you give; yad = which, here: whatever; yad = which, here: whatever; tapasyasi = austerities-you-perform; kaunteya = O son-of-Kuntī; tad = this, that; kuruṣva = you do!; madarpaṇam (mad + arpaṇam) = me-offering, here: an offering to me.

9.28: śubhāśubhaphalais (śubha + aśubha + phalais) = with auspicious [or] inauspicious fruits, here: [whose] fruits are . . . ; evam = thus; mokṣyase = you will be freed; karmabandhanais = from the bonds of action; saṃnyāsayogayuktātmā (saṃnyāsa + yoga + yukta + ātmā) = self yoked in Yoga [and] renunciation; vimuktas = released; mām = me; upaiṣyasi = you will come.

9.29: samas = same; 'ham (aham) = I; sarvabhūteṣu (sarva + bhūteṣu) = in all beings; na = not, here: none; me = of me, here: to me; dveṣyas = disliked, here: hateful; 'sti (asti) = it is; na = not, here: nor; priyas = dear; ye (plural) = who; bhajanti = they worship; tu = but; mām = me; bhaktyā = with devotion; mayi = in me; te = they; teṣu = in them; cāpi (ca + api) = and also; aham = I.

9.30: api = even; ced = if; sudurācāras (su + dur + ācāras) = [someone of] very bad conduct; bhajate = he worships; mām = me; ananyabhāk (ananya + bhak) = devoted to no other; sādhus = good; eva = verily; sas = he; mantavyas = should be considered; samyag = rightly; vyavasitas = resolved; hi = for; sas = he.

9.31: kṣipram = swiftly; bhavati = he becomes; dharmātmā (dharma + ātmā) = law[ful] self, here: self [established in] the law; śaśvacchāntim (śaśvat + śāntim) = everlasting peace; nigacchati = he attains; kaunteya = O son-of-Kuntī; pratijānīhi = you understand!; na = no; me = of me, of mine; bhaktas = devotee; praṇaśyati = he is lost.

9.32: mām = [in] me; hi = for; pārtha = O son-of-Prithā; vyapāśritya = taking refuge; ye (plural) = who; 'pi (api) = even; syus = be they; pāpayonayas (pāpa + yonayas) = [from] evil wombs; striyas = women; vaiśyas = merchans; tathā = also, here: and even; śudras = serfs; te = they; 'pi (api) = also; yānti = they go; parām = supreme; gatim = course.

9.33: kim = what?; punas = again, here: how much more so?; brāhmaṇās = priests, here: retained in Sanskrit; puṇyās = meritorious; bhaktās = devoted; rājarṣayas (rāja + ṛṣayas) = royal seers; tathā = thus, here: and; anityam = transient; asukham = joyless; lokam = world; imam = this; prāpya = attaining, here: attained; bhajasva = you worship!; mām = me.

9.34: manmanā (mad + manā) (singular) = me-minded; bhava = you be!; madbhaktas (mad + bhaktas) = me-devoted, here: my devotee; madyājī (mad + yājī) = me-sacrificing, sacrificing to me, here: my sacrificer; mām = me; namaskuru (namas + kuru) = you make obeisance!; mām = [to] me; evaiṣyasi (eva + eṣyasi)

= verily you will go, here: verily you will come; yuktvaivam (yuktvā + evam) = having yoked thus; ātmānam = [your]self; matparāyaṇas (mad + parāyaṇas) = me-intended, intent on me.

CHAPTER 10: THE YOGA OF [DIVINE] MANIFESTATION

śrībhagavān (śrī + bhagavān) = Blessed Lord; uvāca = he said;
10.1: bhūyas = again, here: moreover; eva = verily, here: omitted; mahābaho (mahā + baho) = O mighty-armed [Arjuna]; śṛṇu = you hear!; me = of me, here: my; paramaṃ = supreme; vācas = word; yad = which; te = to you; 'ham (aham) = I; prīyamāṇāya = to dear one, here: to [you who are my] beloved [friend]; vakṣyāmi = I will declare; hitakāmyayā (hita + kāmyayā) = out of a desire for [your] welfare.

10.2: na = not, here: neither; me = of me, here: my; vidus = they know; suragaṇās (sura + gaṇās) = hosts of gods; prabhavam = origin; na = not, here: nor; maharṣayas (mahā + ṛṣayas) = great seers; aham = I; ādis = beginning; hi = for; devānām = of gods; maharṣīnām (mahā + ṛṣīnām) = of great seers; ca = and; sarvaśas = everywhere.

10.3: yas = who; mām = me; ajam = unborn; anādim = beginningless; ca = and; vetti = he knows; lokamaheśvaram (loka + mahā + īśvaram) = great lord of the world; asaṃmūḍhas = bewildered; sas = he; martyeṣu = among mortals; sarvapāpais (sarva + pāpais) = from all sins; pramucyate = he is released.

10.4: buddhis = [control of the] wisdom-faculty; jñānam = knowledge; asaṃmohas = nonbewilderment; kṣamā = patience; satyam = truthfulness; damas = restraint; śamas = tranquillity; sukham = pleasure; duḥkham = pain; bhavas = becoming; 'bhavas (abhavas) = nonbecoming; bhayam = fear; cābhayam (ca + abhayam) = and fearlessness; eva = verily, here: also; ca = and.

10.5: ahiṃsā = nonharming; samatā = sameness; tuṣṭis = contentment; tapas = austerity; dānam = gift, charity; yaśas = dignity; 'yaśas (ayaśas) = indignity; bhavanti = they arise; bhāvās = states-of-existence; bhūtānām = of beings; mattas = from me; eva = indeed; pṛthagvidhās (pṛthag + vidhās) (plural) = [having] diverse forms, here: [in all their] diversity.

10.6: maharṣayas (mahā + ṛṣayas) = great seers; sapta = seven; pūrve = in the past, here: of old; catvāras = four; manavas = Manus; tathā = as also; madbhāvās (mad + bhāvās) (plural) = my states, here: my state-of-existence; manasās (plural) = from [my] mind, here: of [my] mind; jātās (plural) = born; yeṣām (plural) = of whom, here: from them [sprung]; lokas = world; imās = these; prajās = creatures.

10.7: etām = this; vibhūtim = power-of-manifestation; yogam = Yoga; ca = and; mama = my; yas = who; vetti = he knows; tattvatas = in truth, really; sas = he; 'vikampena (avikampena) = by unshaking; yogena = by Yoga; yujyate = he is yoked; nātra (na + atra) = not here, here: on this [there is] no; saṃśayas = doubt.

10.8: aham = I; sarvasya = of all; prabhavas = origin; mattas = from me; sarvam = all, here: everything; pravartate = it happens, here: it emerges; iti = thus; matvā = having considered, here: considering; bhajante = they worship; mām = me; budhās (plural) = the wise; bhāvasamanvitās (bhāva + samanvitās) (plural) = endowed with [the appropriate] state-of-existence.

10.9: maccittās (mad + cittās) (plural) = me-minded; madgataprāṇās (mad + gata + prāṇās) (plural) = the life-force gone into me, here: . . . dissolved in me; bodhayantas (plural) = enlightening; parasparam = each other; kathayantas (plural) = talking; ca = and; mām = [of] me; nityam = always, constantly; tuṣyanti = they are content; ca = and; ramanti = they rejoice; ca = and.

10.10: teṣām = of them, here: to these; satatāyuktānām (satatā + yuktānām) = of [those who are] ever yoked, here: to the ever yoked; bhajatām = of worshippers, here: worship [me]; prītipūrvakam (prīti + pūrvakam) = with delight (prīti);

dadāmi = I give; buddhiyogam (buddhi + yogam) = Yoga of wisdom, here: retained in Sanskrit; tam = that; yena = by which; mām = me; upayānti = they go, here: they approach; te = they.

10.11: teṣām = for those; evānukampārtham (eva + anukampā + artham) = verily compassion purpose, here: out of compassion, with *eva* omitted; aham = I; ajñānajam (ajñāna + jam) = nescience-born; tamas = darkness; nāśayāmi = I destroy, I dispel; ātmabhāvasthas (ātma + bhāva + sthas) = abiding (stha) in [my] self's (ātma) state-of-existence; jñānadīpena (jñāna + dīpena) = by the lamp of knowledge; bhāsvatā = by the bright.

arjunas = Arjuna; uvāca = he said;

10.12: param = supreme; brahma = brahman; param = supreme; dhāma = abode; pavitram = purifier; paramam = supreme; bhavān = you (honorific); puruṣam = spirit; śāsvatam = eternal; divyam = divine; ādidevam = primordial god; ajam = unborn; vibhum = all-pervading.

10.13: āhus = they say, they speak; tvām = [of] you; ṛṣayas = seers; sarve = all; devarṣis (deva + ṛṣis) = divine seer; nāradas = Nārada; tathā = thus, here: and also; asitas devalas = Asita Devala; vyāsas = Vyāsa; svayam = yourself; caiva (ca + eva) = and thus, here: and [you tell me] so; bravīṣi = you tell; me = to me.

10.14: sarvam = all; etad = this; ṛtam = true; manye = I think, I deem; yad = which, here: that; mām = me; vadasi = you speak, here: you tell; keśava = O Keśava; na = not, her: neither; hi = indeed; te = [of] you; bhagavan = O blessed one; vyaktim = manifestation, here: manifest [form]; vidus = they know; devās = gods; na = not, here: nor; dānavās = demons.

10.15: svayam = yourself; evātmanātmānam (eva + ātmanā + ātmānam) = verily by [your] self [you know] [your]self; vettha = you know; tvam = you; puruṣottama = O Supreme Spirit; bhūtabhāvana (bhūta + bhāvana) = generating welfare, here:

generating beings; bhūteśa (bhūta + īśa) = O lord of being; devadeva (deva + deva) = O god of gods; jagatpate (jagat + pate) = O ruler (pati) of the universe.

10.16: vaktum = to tell; arhasi = you are able, here: you should [tell]; aśeṣeṇa = without remainder, entirely, here: without reservation; divya = divine; hi = indeed, here: left untranslated; ātmavibhūtayas (ātma + vibhūtayas) = [your] self's powers-of-manifestation; yābhis (plural) = by which; vibhūtibhis = by powers-of-manifestation; lokān = worlds; imān = these; tvam = you; vyāpya = having pervaded, here: pervading; tiṣṭhasi = you abide.

10.17: katham = how?; vidyām = knowledge; aham = I; yogin = O yogin; tvām = you; sadā = always; paricintayan = reflecting; keṣu keṣu = in whatever, in what various; ca = and; bhāveṣu = in states-of-existence; cintyas = to be thought, here: ought [I] to think; 'si (asi) = you are; bhagavan = O blessed one; mayā = by me, here: do I?

10.18: vistareṇātmanas (vistareṇa + ātmanas) = extensively of [your] self; yogam = Yoga; vibhūtim = power-of-manifestation; ca = and; janārdana = O Janārdana; bhūyas = again; kathaya = you tell!; tṛptis = satiation, here: satiated; hi = for; śṛṇvatas = of hearing; nāsti (na + asti) = it is not (na), here: I am not; me = for me, here: I; 'mṛtam (amṛtam) = immortal, nectar.

śrībhagavān (śrī + bhagavān) = Blessed Lord; uvāca = he said;

10.19: hanta = lo!; te = to you; kathayiṣyāmi = I will tell; divyās (plural) = divine; hi = indeed; ātmavibhūtayas (ātma + vibhūtayas) = [your] self's powers-of-manifestation; prādhānyatas (plural) = principal; kuruśreṣṭha (kuru + śreṣṭha) = O best of the Kurus; nāsti (na + asti) = not is, here: there is no; antas = end; vistarasya = of extent, here: to the extent; me = of me, my.

10.20: aham = I; ātmā = self; guḍākeśa (guḍā + keśa) = O Gudākesha; sarvabhūtāśayasthitas (sarva + bhūta + āśaya + sthitas) =

abiding (sthita) [in] the resting-place (āśaya) of all beings; aham = I; ādis = beginning; ca = and; madhyam = middle; ca = and; bhūtānām = of beings; antas = end; eva = verily, here: omitted; ca = and.

10.21: ādityānām = of Ādityas; aham = I; viṣṇus = Vishnu; jyotiṣām = of luminaries; ravis = sun; aṃśumān = radiant; marīcis = Marīci; marutām = of Maruts; asmi = I am; nakṣatrāṇām = of lunar mansions; aham = I; śaśī = moon.

10.22: vedānām = of Vedas; sāmavedas = *Sāma-Veda*; 'smi (asmi) = I am; devānām = of gods; asmi = I am; vāsavas = Vāsava; indriyāṇām = of [or among] senses; manas = mind; cāsmi (ca + asmi) = and I am; bhūtānām = of [or among] beings; asmi = I am; cetanā = sentience.

10.23: rudrāṇām = of [or among] Rudras; śamkaras = Shamkara; cāsmi (ca + asmi) = and I am; vitteśas (vitta + īśas) = lord of riches; yakṣarakṣasām (yakṣa + rakṣasām) = of [or among] and I am; merus = Meru; śikhariṇām = of [or among] mountain-peaks; aham = I.

10.24: purodhasām = of [or among] domestic-priests; ca = and; mukhyam = chief; mām = me; viddhi = you know!; pārtha = O son-of-Prithā; bṛhaspatim = Brihaspati; senānīnām = of [or among] commanders; aham = I; skandas = Skanda; sarasām = of [or among] watery-expanses; asmi = I am; sāgaras = ocean.

10.25: maharṣīṇām (mahā + ṛṣīṇām) = of [or among] great seers; bhṛgus = Bhrigu; aham = I; girām = of [or among] utterances; asmi = I am; ekam = single; akṣaram = syllable; yajñānām = of [or among] sacrifices; japayajñas (japa + yajñas) = recitation sacrifice; 'smi (asmi) = I am; sthāvarāṇām = of [or among] immovables; himālayas = Himalaya.

10.26: aśvatthas = ashvattha tree; sarvavṛkṣāṇām (sarva + vṛkṣāṇām) = of [or among] all trees; devarṣīṇām (deva + ṛṣīṇām) = of [or among] divine seers; ca = and; nāradas = Nārada;

gandharvāṇām = of [or among] Gandharvas; citrarathas = Citraratha; siddhānām = of [or among] adepts; kapilas = Kapila; munis = sage.

10.27: uccaiḥśravasam = Uccaihshravas; aśvānām = of [or among] horses; viddhi = you know!; mām = me; amṛtodbhavam (amṛta + udbhavam) = born from nectar; airāvatam = Airāvata; gajendrāṇām = of [or among] elephants; narāṇām = of [or among] men; ca = and; narādhipam (nara + adhipam) = man-ruler, human ruler.

10.28: āyudhānām = of [or among] weapons; aham = I; vajram = thunderbolt; dhenūnām = of [or among] cows; asmi = I am; kāmadhuk (kāma + dhuk) = wish-fulfilling cow; prajanas = procreating; cāsmi (ca + asmi) = and I am; kandarpas = Kandarpa; sarpāṇām = of [or among] serpents; asmi = I am; vāsukis = Vāsuki.

10.29: anantas = Ananta; cāsmi (ca + asmi) = and I am; nāgānām = of [or among] serpents, here: the Nāgas; varuṇas = Varuna; yādasām = of [or among] water-dwellers; aham = I; pitṛṇām = of [or among] ancestors; aryamā = Aryaman; cāsmi (ca + asmi) = and I am; yamas = Yama; saṃyamatām = of [or among] subjugators; aham = I.

10.30: prahlādas = Prahlāda; cāsmi (ca + asmi) = and I am; daityānām = of [or among] the Daityas; kālas = time; kalayatām = of [or among] reckoners; aham = I; mṛgāṇām = of [or among]; ca = and; mṛgendras (mṛga + indras) = lord of beasts; 'ham (aham) = I; vainateyas = Vainateya; ca = and; pakṣiṇām = of [or among] birds.

10.31: pavanas = wind; pavatām = of [or among] purifying [things]; asmi = I am; rāmas = Rāma; śastrabhṛtām = of [or among] weapon-bearers; aham = I; jhaṣāṇām = of [or among] water-monsters; makaras = crocodile; cāsmi (ca + asmi) = and I am; śrotasām = of [or among] streams; asmi = I am; jāhnavī = Jānhavī.

10.32: sargāṇām = of creations; ādis = beginnning; antas = end; ca = and; madhyam = middle; caivāham = and verily I; arjuna = O Arjuna; adhyātmavidyā (adhyātma + vidyā) = science (vidyā) of the basis-of-self; vidyānām = of sciences; vādas = speech; pravadatām = of [or among] speakers; aham = I.

10.33: akṣaraṇam = of [or among] letters; akāras (a + kāras) = letter *a*; 'smi (asmi) = I am; dvandvas = dvandva (dual compound); sāmāsikasya = of the system-of-compounds; ca = and; aham = I; evākṣayas (eva + akṣayas) = verily (eva) indestructible; kālas = time; dhātāham (dhātā + aham) = I supporter; viśvatomukhas (viśvatas + mukhas) = facing everywhere.

10.34: mṛtyus = death; sarvaharas (sarva + haras) = all-seizing; cāham (ca + aham) = and I; udbhavas = origin; ca = and; bhaviṣyatām = of future-events; kīrtis = fame; śrīs = fortune; vāk = speech; ca = and; nārīṇām (pural) = of [or among] feminine [words]; smṛtis = memory; medhā = intelligence; dhṛtis = steadfastness; kṣamā = patience.

10.35: bṛhatsāma (bṛhat + sāma) = great chant; tathā = also, here: again; sāmnām = of [or among] chants; gāyatrī = gāyatrī [meter]; chandasām = of [or among] meters; aham = I; māsānām = of [or among] months; mārgaśīrṣas (mārgas + śīrṣas) = deer-headed (from mŕgas); 'ham (aham) = I; ṛtūnām = of [or among] seasons; kusumākaras (kusumas + ākaras) = flower mine.

10.36: dyūtam = gambling; chalayatām = of tricksters; asmi = I am; tejas = splendor; tejasvinām (plural) = of the splendid; aham = I; jayas = victory; 'smi (asmi) = I am; vyavasāyas = resolution; 'smi (asmi) = I am; sattvam = sattva; sattvavatām (plural) = of the sattva endowed; aham = I.

10.37: vṛṣṇīnām = of [or among] the Vrishnis; vāsudevas = Vāsudeva; 'smi (asmi) = I am; pāṇḍavānām = of [or among] the sons-of-Pāndu; dhanaṃjayas = Dhanamjaya; munīnām = of [or among] sages; api = even, indeed, here: omitted; aham = I; vyāsas =

Vyāsa; kavīnām = of [or among] bards; uśanā = Ushanas; kavis = bard.

10.38: daṇḍas = rod-of-punishment; damayatām = of chastisers; asmi = I am; nītis = statecraft; asmi = I am; jigīṣatām = of [those who are] eager-for-conquest; maunam = silence; caivāsmi (ca + eva + asmi) = and verily I am; guhyānām = of secrets; jñānam = knowledge; jñānavatām (plural) = of the knowledge endowed; aham = I.

«oṣadhīnām = of [or among] herbs; yavas = barley; cāsmi (ca + asmi) = and I am; dhātūnām = of [or among] metals; asmi = I am; kāñcanam = gold; saurabheyas = Saurabheya; gavām = of [or among] cows; asmi = I am; snehānām = of [or among] fats; sarpis = butter; api = even, indeed, here: omitted; aham = I; sarvāsām = of [or among] all; tṛṇajatīnām (tṛṇa + jatīnām) = of [or among] categories of grasses; darbhas = darbha [grass]; 'ham (aham) = I; pāṇḍunandana (pāṇḍu + nandana) = O delight-of-Pāndu. »

10.39: yad = which; cāpi (ca + api) = and also; sarvabhūtānām (sarva + bhūtānām) = of all beings, here: in all . . . ; bījam = seed; tad = this, that; aham = I; arjuna = O Arjuna; na = not, here: no; tad = this, that; asti = it is, here: there is; vinā = without, here: apart; yat = which; syāt = it should be, here: it can exist; mayā = by me, here: from me; bhūtam = being; carācaram (cara + acaram) = moving [or] unmoving.

10.40: nāntas (na + antas) = no end; 'sti (asti) = it is, here: there is; mama = my; divyānām (plural) = divine; vibhūtīnām = powers-of-manifestation; paraṃtapa = O Paramtapa; eṣas = this, here: the [extent]; tūddeśatas (tu + uddeśatas) = indeed by-way-of-example, here: *tu* is omitted; proktas = proclaimed; vibhūtes = of power-of-manifestation; vistaras = extent; mayā = by me, here: turned into active voice.

10.41: yad yad = whatever; vibhūtimat = powerful, here: power-charged; sattvam = entity; śrīmad = prosperous; ūrjitam =

vigorous; eva = indeed, here: omitted; vā = or; tad tad = here: that; evāvagaccha (eva + avagaccha) = verily, you recognize!, here: you [must] recognize; tvam = you; mama = my; tejoṃśasaṃbhavam (tejas + aṃśa + saṃbhavam) = fragmentary (aṃśa) birth [of my] splendor.

10.42: athavā = but; bahunaitena (bahunā + etena) = with this (etena) much, here: with so many [details]; kim = what?; jñātena = with knowing, here: to know; tavārjuna (tava + arjuna) = of you, O Arjuna; viṣṭabhyāham (viṣṭabhya + aham) = establishing I, here: having established I [abide]; idam = this; kṛtsnam = whole [universe]; ekāṃśena (eka + aṃśena) = with a single (eka) fragment; sthitas = abiding, here: [I] abide; jagat = universe.

CHAPTER 11: THE YOGA OF THE VISION OF [THE LORD'S] ALL-FORM

arjunas = Arjuna; uvāca = he said;

11.1: madanugrahāya (mad + anugrahāya) = as a favor (anugraha) to me; paramam = supreme; guhyam = secret; adhyātmasaṃjñitam (adhyātma + saṃjñitam) = basis-of-self called; yad = which; tvayoktam (tvayā + uktam) = by you uttered, here: you have uttered; vacas = word, speech; tena = by this; mohas = confusion; 'yam (ayam) = this; vigatas = gone, here: dispelled; mama = my, of mine.

11.2: bhavāpyayau (bhava + apyayau) (dual) = becoming and dissolution, here: emergence and . . . ; hi = for; bhūtānām = of beings; śrutau (dual) = having heard [about the two], here: I have heard; vistaraśas = in detail; mayā = by me; tvattas = from you; kamalapattrākṣa (kamala + pattra + akṣa) = O lotus-petal-eyed, here: O lotus-eyed; māhātmyam = glory; api = also; cāvyayam (ca + avyayam) = and immutable, here: as well as . . .

11.3: evam = thus; etad = this; yathāttha (yathā + āttha) = as you tell, here: as you have described; tvam = you; ātmānam = self, yourself; parameśvara (parama + īśvara) = O supreme lord;

draṣṭum = to see; icchāmi = I desire; te = your; rūpam = form; aiśvaram = lordly; puruṣottama (puruṣa + uttama) = O Supreme Spirit.

11.4: manyase = you think; yadi = if; tad = this, that; śakyam = possible; mayā = by me, for me; draṣṭum = to see; iti = thus, here: that; prabho = O Lord; yogeśvara (yoga + īśvara) = O Lord of Yoga; tatas = thence, then; me = to me; tvam, here: omitted = you; darśayātmānam (darśaya + ātmānam) = cause me to see [your]self, here: reveal to me to see [your]self; avyayam = immutable.

śrībhagavān (śrī + bhagavān) = Blessed Lord; uvāca = he said;

11.5: paśya = you behold!; me = my; pārtha = O son-of-Prithā; rūpāni = forms; śataśas = hundredfold; 'tha (atha) = also, here: omitted; sahasraśas = thousandfold; nānāvidhāni (nānā + vidhāni) = [of] varied kinds; divyāni (plural) = divine; nānāvarṇākṛtīni (nānā + varṇa + ākṛtīni) = diverse colors [and] shapes, here: many-colored and many-shaped; ca = and.

11.6: paśyādityān (paśya + ādityān) = you behold! the Ādityas; vasūn = Vasus; rudrān = Rudras; aśvinau (dual) = [two] Ashvins; marutas = Maruts; tathā = as well as, as also; bahūni = many; adṛṣṭapurvāṇi (adṛṣṭa + purvāṇi) (plural) = unseen before, here: not seen before; paśyāścaryāṇi (paśya + āścaryāṇi) = you behold! wonders; bhārata = O descendant-of-Bharata.

11.7: ihaikastham (iha + eka + stham) = here [as] one abiding; jagat = universe; kṛtsnam = whole; paśyādya (paśya + ādya) = you behold now!; sacarācaram (sacara + acaram) = moving [and] unmoving; mama = my; dehe = in body; guḍākeśa (guḍā + keśa) = O Gudākesha; yad = which, here: whatever; cānyad (ca + anyad) = and other, here and [whatever] else; draṣṭum = to see; icchasi = you desire.

11.8: na = not; tu = yet; mām = me; śākyase = you are able, here: you will be able; draṣṭum = to see; anenaiva (anena + eva) = with this verily, here: omitted; svacakṣuṣā (sva + cakṣuṣā) (singular) = with [your] own eye; divyam = divine; dadāmi = I give, here:

I will give; te = to you; cakṣus = eye; paśya = you behold!; me = my; yogam = Yoga; aiśvaram = lordly.

saṃjaya (saṃjayas) = Samjaya; uvāca = he said;
11.9: evam = thus; uktvā = having spoken; tatas = thence, then; rājan = O king; mahāyogeśvaras (mahā + yoga + īśvaras) = great Lord of Yoga; haris = Hari; darśayam āsa = he revealed; pārthāya = to son-of-Prithā; paramam = supreme; rūpam = form; aiśvaram = lordly.

11.10: anėkavaktranayanam (aneka + vaktra + nayanam) = many mouths [and] eyes [I have made this and all subsequent phrases plural]; anekādbhūtadarśanam (aneka + adbhūta + darśanam) = many wondrous appearances; anekadivyābharaṇam (aneka + divya + ābharaṇam) = many divine ornaments; divyānekodyatāyudham (divya + aneka + udyata + āyudham) = divine many upraised weapons.

11.11: divyamalyāmbaradharam (divya + mālya + ambara + dharam) = wearing divine garlands [and] garments; divyagandhānulepanam (divya + gandha + anulepanam) = anointed with divine fragrances; sarvāścaryamayam (sarva + āścarya + mayam) = consisting of (maya) all marvels, here: all-wonderful; devam = god; anantam = infinite; viśvatomukham (viśvatas + mukham) = facing everywhere, here: omnipresent.

11.12: divi = in sky; sūryasahasrasya (sūrya + sahasrasya) = of a thousand suns (sūrya); bhavet = it would be; yugapad = at once, simultaneously; utthitā = risen, here: were to arise; yadi = if; bhās (feminine) = splendor; sadṛśī = equal to, like; sā = she [i.e., bhās], here: this; syād = it would be; bhāsas = of splendor; tasya = of this, here: of that; mahātmanas (mahā + ātmanas) = of the great self.

11.13: tatraikastham (tatra + eka + stham) = abiding (stha) therein [as] one; jagat = universe; kṛtsnam = whole; pravibhaktam = divided; anekadhā = manifold; apaśyad = he saw; devadevasya (deva + devasya) = of the God of gods; śarīre = in body; pāṇḍavas = son-of-Pāndu; tadā = then.

11.14: tatas = thence, then; sas = he; vismayāviṣṭas (vismaya + āviṣṭas) = filled with astonishment (vismaya); hṛṣṭaromā (hṛṣṭa + romā) = [he whose] hair is bristling; dhanaṃjayas (dhanam + jayas) = Dhanamjaya; praṇamya = bowing; śirasā = with head; devam = god; kṛtāñjalis (kṛta + añjalis) = made saluting [gesture], here: doing añjali; abhāṣata = he spoke.

arjunas = Arjuna; uvāca = he said;

11.15: paśyāmi = I see, I behold; devān = gods; tava = of you; deva = O god; dehe = in body; sarvān (plural) = all; tathā = thus, here: and; bhūtaviśeṣasaṃghān (bhūta + viśeṣa + saṃghān) (plural) = kinds (viśeṣa) of beings assembled; brahmāṇam = Brahma; īśam = lord; kamalāsanastham (kamala + āsana + stham) = stationed on a lotus seat, here: seated on . . . ; ṛṣīn = seers; ca = and; sarvān = all; uragān (ura + gān) = earth-goers [i.e., serpents]; ca = and; divyān (plural) = divine.

11.16: anekabāhūdaravaktranetram (aneka + bāhu + udara + vaktra + netram) = many arms, bellies, mouths, [and] eyes; paśyāmi = I behold; tvā = you; sarvatas = everywhere; 'nantarūpam (ananta + rūpam) = endless form; nāntam (na + antam) = no end; na = no; madhyam = middle; na punas = not again, here: and also no; tavādim (tava + ādim) = of you beginning; paśyāmi = I see [in you]; viśveśvara (viśva + īśvara) = O All-Lord; viśvarūpa (viśva + rūpa) = O All-Form.

11.17: kirīṭinam = diadem; gadinam = mace; cakriṇam = discus; ca = and; tejorāśim (tejas + rāśim) = mass of brilliance (tejas); sarvatas = everywhere, here: all-around; dīptimantam = flaming; paśyāmi = I behold; tvām = you; durnirīkṣyam = hard-to-see; samantāt = completely; dīptānalārkadyutim (dīpta + anala + arka + dyutim) = blazing radiance (dyuti) of sun (arka) fire (anala); aprameyam = immeasurable.

11.18: tvam = you; akṣaram = imperishable; paramam = supreme; veditavyam = to be known, here: [ought] to be known; tvam = you; asya = of this; viśvasya = of all; param = supreme; nidhānam = receptacle; tvam = you; avyayas = immutable; śāśvatadharmagoptā (śāśvata + dharma + goptā) = guardian of the eternal law; sanātanas = everlasting; tvam = you; puruṣas = spirit; matas = thought, opinion, conviction; me = of me, my.

11.19: anādimadhyāntam (anādi + madhya + antam) = without (an-) beginning, middle [and] end; anantavīryam (ananta + vīryam) = [of] infinite vitality (vīrya); anantabāhum (ananta + bāhum) = [having] infinite arms; śaśisūryanetram (śaśi + sūrya + netram) = [having] sun [and] moon (śaśi) for eyes; paśyāmi = I behold; tvā = you; dīptahutāśavaktram (dīpta + huta + aśa + vaktram) = [with] blazing oblation-devouring (huta-aśa) mouth (vaktra); svatejasā (sva + tejasā) = with own brilliance; viśvam = everything, all; idam = this; tapantam = burning up.

11.20: dyāvāpṛthivyos (dyāvā + pṛthivyos) (dual) = of sky [and] of nature, here: between heaven and earth; idam = this; antaram = between; hi = indeed, here: left untranslated; vyāptam = pervaded; tvayaikena (tvayā + ekena) = by you alone; diśas (plural) = quarters; ca = and; sarvās (plural) = all; dṛṣṭvādbhutam (dṛṣṭvā + adbhutam) = having seen [this] wondrous, here: seeing . . . ; rūpam = form; idam = this; tavogram (tava + ugram) = of you terrifying; lokatrayam (loka + trayam) = triple world; pravyathitam = trembling, here: it shudders; mahātman (mahā + ātman) = O great self.

11.21: amī (plural) = yonder; hi = indeed, here: left untranslated; tvām = you; surasaṃghās (sura + saṃghās) = hosts of gods; viśanti = they enter; kecid = some; bhītās (plural) = terrified; prāñjalayas (plural) = with salutation [gestures]; gṛṇanti = they praise; svastīti (svasti + iti) = hail, *iti* is used to indicate a quotation; uktvā = having said, here: crying out; maharṣisiddhasaṃghās (mahā + ṛṣi + siddha + saṃghās) = hosts of great seers [and] perfected ones, here: multitude . . . ; stuvanti = they praise; tvā = you; stutibhis = with hymns-of-praise; puṣkalābhis (plural) = with plenteous.

11.22: rudrādityas (rudra + ādityas) = Rudras [and] Ādityas; vasavas = Vasus; ye (plural) = who; ca = and; sādhyās = Sādhyas; viśve (plural) = Vishvedevas; 'śvinau (aśvinau) (dual) = [two] Ashvins; marutas = Maruts; coṣmapās (ca + ūṣmapās) = and quaffers-of-steam; ca = and; gandharvayakṣāsurasiddhasaṃghās (gandharva + yakṣa + asura + siddha + saṃghās) = hosts of Gandharvas, Yakshas, Asuras, and perfected ones; vīkṣante = they behold; tvā = you; vismitās (plural) = astounded; caiva (ca + eva) = and verily, here: *eva* is omitted; sarve = all.

11.23: rūpam = form; mahat = great; te = of you; bahuvaktranetram (bahu + vaktra + netram) = [having] many mouths [and] eyes; mahābaho (mahā + baho) = O mighty-armed [Krishna]; bahubahūrupādam (bahu + bāhu + ūru + pādam) = [having] many arms (bāhu), thighs, [and] feet; bahūdaram (bahu + udaram) = [having] many bellies; bahudaṃṣṭrākarālam (bahu + daṃṣṭrā + karālam) = [having] many formidable fangs; dṛṣṭvā = having seen, here: beholding; lokās = worlds; pravyathitās (plural) = trembling, here: they shudder; tathāham (tathā + aham) = thus I, here: so [do] I.

11.24: nabhaḥspṛśam (nabhas + spṛśam) = sky touching; dīptam = blazing; anekavarṇam (aneka + varṇam) = [having] many colors; vyattānanam (vyātta + ānanam) = gaping mouth; dīptaviśālanetram (dīpta + viśāla + netram) = blazing vast eyes; dṛṣṭvā = having seen, here: seeing; hi = indeed, here: left untranslated; tvām = you; pravyathitāntarātmā (pravyathita + antas + ātmā) = quaking inner self; dhṛtim = fortitude; na = not, no; vindāmi = I find; śamam = tranquillity; ca = and, here: or; viṣṇo = O Vishnu.

11.25: daṃṣṭrākarālāni (daṃṣṭrā + karālāni) = [having] formidable fangs; ca = and; te = of you; mukhāni = mouths; dṛṣṭvaiva (dṛṣṭvā + eva) = having seen verily, here: and seeing; kālānalasaṃnibhāni (kāla + anala + saṃnibhāni) (plural) = resembling fire [at the end of] time; diśas (plural) = quarters; na = not; jāne = I know; na = not; labhe = I obtain, here: I find; ca = and; śarma = shelter (sharman); prasīda = you be gracious!; deveśa (deva + īśa) = O Lord of gods; jagannivāsa (jagat + nivāsa) = O Home of the universe.

11.26: amī = those, here: these; ca = and; tvām = you; dhṛtarāṣṭrasya = of Dhritarāshtera; putrās = sons; sarve = all;

sahaivāvanipālasaṃghais (saha + eva + avani + pāla + saṃghais) = verily (eva) together with (saha) hosts of protectors of the earth (avani) [i.e., kings], here: *eva* is omitted; bhīṣmas = Bhīshma; droṇas = Drona; sūtaputras (sūta + putras) = son of the charioteer [i.e., Karna]; tathāsau (tathā + asau) = thus that, here: left untranslated; sahāsmadīyais (saha + asmadīyais) = with our; api = also, here: and also; yodhamukhyais (yodha + mukhyais) = with leading warriors.

11.27: vaktrāṇi = mouths; te = your; tvaramāṇās = swiftly; viśanti = they enter; daṃṣṭrākarālāni (daṃṣṭrā + karālāni) = [with] formidable fangs (daṃṣṭrā); bhayānakāni = fear-instilling; kecid = some; vilagnās = clinging, here: sticking; daśanāntareṣu (daśana + antareṣu) = in between teeth; saṃdṛśyante = they are seen; cūrṇitais = with pulverized; uttamāṇgais (uttama + aṇgais) = with highest limbs [i.e., heads].

«nānārūpais (nānā + rūpais) = by various forms, here: by various kinds [of men]; puruṣairvadhyamānās (puruṣais + vadhyamānās) = by men slain; viśanti = they enter; te = they; vaktram = mouth; acintyarūpam (acintya + rūpam) = inconceivable form; yaudhiṣṭhirās = followers-of-Yudhishthira; dhārtarāṣṭrās = followers-of-Dhritarāshtra; ca = and; yodhās (plural) = fighting; śāstrais = by weapons; kṛttās (plural) = cut down; vividhais = by diverse; sarvaiva (sarva + eva) = all verily, here: all surely; tvad = your; tejasā = by glow, radiance; nihatās (plural) = destroyed, annihilated; nūnam = now, presently; ete = these; tathā = thus; hīme (hi + ime) = verily these, here: omitted; tvad = your; śarīram = body; praviṣṭās (plural) = entered, here: they enter.»

11.28: yathā = as; nadīnām = rivers; bahavas = many; 'mbuvegās (ambu + vegās) = water torrents; samudram = ocean; evābhimukhās (eva + abhimukhās) (plural) = verily are facing, here: [flow] headlong toward; dravanti = they flow; tathā = thus, here: so; tavāmī (tava + amī) = your those, here: your these [heroes]; naralokavīrās (nara + loka + vīrās) = heroes [in] the world of men; viśanti = they enter; vaktrāṇi = mouths; abhivijvalanti (plural) = flaming.

11.29: yathā = as; pradīptam = blazing; jvalanam = flame; pataṅgās = moths; viśanti = they enter; nāśāya = for destruction; saṃṛddhavegās (saṃṛddha + vegās) = profuse streams; tathaiva (tathā + eva) = thus verily, here: so, *eva* is omitted; nāśāya = for destruction; viśanti = they enter; lokās = world; tavāpi (tava + api) = your indeed, here: *api* is omitted; vaktrāṇi = mouths; saṃṛddhavegās (saṃṛddha + vegās) = profuse streams.

11.30: lelihyase = you lick up; grasamānas = devouring; samantāt = completely, entirely; lokān = worlds; samagrān = all; vadanais = with mouths; jvaladbhis = flaming; tejobhis (plural) = with brilliances, here: with brilliance; apūrya = filling; jagat = universe; samagram = entire; bhāsas = rays; tavogrās (tava + ugrās) = your dreadful; pratapanti = they blaze forth; viṣṇo = O Vishnu.

11.31: ākhyāhi = you tell!; me = to me; kas = who?; bhavān = you [honorific]; ugrarūpas (ugra + rūpas) = [being of] dreadful form; namas = salutation; 'stu (astu) = it may be; te = to you; devavara (deva + vara) = O best of gods; prasīda = you be gracious!; vijñātum = to know; icchāmi = I wish; bhavantam = you [honorific]; ādyam = at first, in the beginning; na = not; hi = indeed, here: left untranslated; prajānāmi = I comprehend; tava = of you, your; pravṛttim = creativity.

śrībhagavān (śrī + bhagavān) = Blessed Lord; uvāca = he said;
11.32: kālas = time; 'smi (asmi) = I am; lokakṣayakṛt (loka + kṣaya + kṛt) = wreaker (kṛt) of the world's destruction; pravṛddhas = mighty; lokān = worlds; samāhartum = to annnihilate; iha = here; pravṛttas = engaged; ṛte = except; 'pi (api) = indeed, here: left untranslated; tvā = [for] you; na = not; bhaviṣyanti = they will [not;] be; sarve = all; ye (plural) = who, here: these; 'vasthitās (avasthitās) = arrayed; pratyanīkeṣu (pratya + nīkeṣu) = in opposing armies; yodhās = warriors.

11.33: tasmāt = therefore; tvam = you; uttiṣṭha = you arise!; yaśas = glory; labhasva = you gain!, here: you win!; jitvā = having conquered, here: conquering; śatrūn = enemies; bhuṅkṣva

= you enjoy!; rājyam = kingdom; samṛddham = prosperous; mayaivaite (mayā + eva + ete) = by me verily they, here: *eva* is omitted; nihatās (plural) = slain; pūrvam = previously, here: already; eva = here: omitted; nimittamātram (nimitta + mātram) = mere (mātra) instrument; bhava = you be!; savyasācin (savya + sācin) = [he who is] skilled (sācin) with the left hand [i.e., ambidextrous], O Savyasācin.

11.34: droṇam = Drona; ca = and; bhīṣmam = Bhīshma; ca = and; jayadratham = Jayadratha; ca = and; karṇam = Karna; tathānyān (tathā + anyān) = as well as (tathā) others (plural); api = also; yodhavīrān (yodha + vīrān) = warrior heroes; mayā = by me; hatān (plural) = slain; tvam = you; jahi = you strike!; mā = not; vyathiṣṭhās = you hesitate; yudhyasva = you fight!; jetāsi = you will conquer; raṇe = in battle; sapatnān = rivals.

saṃjaya (saṃjayas) = Samjaya; uvāca = he said;
11.35: etad = this, here: these; śrutvā = having heard, here: hearing; vacanam = word, here: words; keśavasya = of Keshava; kṛtāñjalis (kṛta + añjalis) = made salutation + the añjali [gesture]; vepamānas = trembling; kirīṭī = Kirītī; namaskṛtvā (namas + kṛtvā) = salutation having been made, here: saluting; bhūya = again; evāha (eva + āha) = verily he said, here: *eva* is omitted; kṛṣṇaṃ = Krishna; sagadgadaṃ = stammering; bhītabhītas (bhītas + bhītas) = very frightened; praṇamya = bowing-down.

arjunas = Arjuna; uvāca = he said;
11.36: sthāne = rightly; hṛṣīkeśa (hṛṣī + keśa) = O Hrishikesha; tava = of you, your; prakīrtyā = with praise; jagat = universe; prahṛṣyati = it rejoices; anurajyate = it is enraptured; ca = and; rakṣāṃsi = Rakshasas; bhītāni (plural) = terrified; diśas = quarters, directions; dravanti = they flee; sarve = all; namasyanti = they salute; ca = and; siddhasaṃghās (siddha + saṃghās) = hosts of perfected ones.

11.37: kasmāt = why?; ca = and; te = to you; na = not; nameran = should they salute; mahātman (mahā + ātman) = great self; garīyase = heavier, greater; brahmaṇas = than Brahma; 'pi (api)

= also, even; ādikartre (ādi + kartre) = primordial creator; ananta = infinite; deveśa (deva + īśa) = O Lord of gods; jagan (jagat + nivāsa) = O Home of the universe; tvam = you; akṣaram = imperishable; sad = existence; asat = nonexistence; tatparam (tad + param) = beyond that (tad); yad = which.

11.38: tvam = you; ādidevas (ādi + devas) = primordial god; puruṣas = spirit; purāṇas = ancient; tvam = you; asya = of this; viśvasya = of all; param = supreme; nidhānam = receptacle; vettāsi (vettā + asi) = knower you are; vedyam = to be known; ca = and; param = supreme; ca = and; dhāma = abode; tvayā = by you; tatam = spread out; viśvam = all; anantarūpa (ananta + rūpa) = O infinite form;

11.39: vāyus = Vāyu; yamas = Yama; 'gnis (agnis) = Agni; varuṇas = Varuna; śaśāṇkas = rabbit[-marked], i.e., moon; prajāpatis (prajā + patis) = Prajāpati; tvam = you; prapitāmahas = great-grandsire; ca = and; namo namas (namas + namas) = salutation, salutation; te = to you; 'stu (astu) = may it be; sahasrakṛtvas (sahasra + kṛtvas) = thousandfold; punas = again; ca = and; bhūyas = again; 'pi (api) = also, here: and; namo namas (namas + namas) = salutation, salutation; te = to you.

11.40: namas = salutation; purastād = from in front; atha = now, here: and; pṛṣṭhatas = from behind; te = to you; namas = salutation; 'stu (astu) = may it be; te = to you; sarvatas = all-around; eva = verily, here: omitted; sarva = O all; anantavīryāmitavikramas (ananta + vīrya + amita + vikramas) = infinite vitality [and] immeasurable might; tvam = you; sarvam = all; samāpnoṣi = you complete; tatas = thence, then; 'si (asi) = you are; sarvas = all.

11.41: sakheti (sakhā + iti) = friend, here: *iti* is used to indicate a quotation; matvā = having thought, here: thinking; prasabham = importunately; yad = what, here: that; uktam = said; he = hey; kṛṣṇa = Krishna!; he = hey; yādava = Yādava!; he = hey; sakheti (sakhā + iti) = friend!, here: *iti* is used to indicate a quotation; ajānatā = by [being] ignorant; mahimānam =

majesty; tavedam (tava + idam) = your this; mayā = by me; pramādāt = out of heedlessness; praṇayena = with fondness; vāpi (vā + api) = or even, here: perhaps.

11.42: yad = what, here: that; cāvahāsārtham (ca + avahāsa + artham) = and [for] the purpose (artha) [of] jesting, here: in jest; asatkṛtas (asat + kṛtas) = badly treated, here: disrespect; 'si (asi) = you are; vihāraśayyāsanabhojaneṣu (vihāra + śayya + āsana + bhojaneṣu) = at play, reposing, sitting [or] eating; ekas = alone; 'tha (atha) = now; vāpi (vā + api) = or also; acyuta = O Acyuta; tatsamakṣam (tad + samakṣam) = before the eyes, here: in the presence [of others]; tad = that, here: left untranslated; kṣāmaye = I ask pardon; tvām = [from] you; aham = I; aprameyam = immeasurable, here: unfathomable.

11.43: pitāsi (pitā + asi) = father you are; lokasya = of world; carācarasya (cara + acarasya) = of moving [and] unmoving; tvam = you; asya = of this; pūjyas = worship-worthy; ca = and; gurus = teacher; garīyān = heavier, greater, very venerable; na = not, here: none; tvatsamas (tvad + samas) = your equal; 'sti (asti) = he is; abhyadhikas = greater; kutas = how?; 'nyas (anyas) = other, here: anything; lokatraye (loka + traye) = in the triple world; 'pi (api) = even, also, here: left untranslated; apratimaprabhāva (apratima + prabhāva) = O [you of] matchless might.

11.44: tasmāt = therefore; praṇamya = bowing-down; praṇidhāya = bending-low; kāyam = body; prasādaye = I seek [your] indulgence; tvām = you; aham = I; īśam = lord; īḍyam = to be praised, praiseworthy; piteva (pitā + iva) = father as it were; putrasya = of son; sakheva (sakhā + iva) = friend as it were; sakhyus = of friend; priyas = dear, here: lover; priyāyārhasi (priyāya + arhasi) = to a beloved you can, here: . . . you should; deva = O god; soḍhum = to bear.

«divyāni = divine; karmāṇi = actions; tavādbhūtāni (tava + adbhūtāni) (plural) = your wondrous; pūrvāṇi (plural) = ancient, here: ancient; pūrve = of old; 'pi (api) = also, here: left untranslated; ṛṣayas = seers; smaranti = they recall; nānyas (na +

anyas) = no other; 'sti (asti) = there is; kartā = creator; jagatas = of universe; tvam = you; ekas = one; dhātā = originator; vidhātā = dispenser; ca = and; vibhus = almighty; bhavas = becoming; ca = and.

tavādbhūtam (tava + adbhūtam) = your wonder; kim = what?; nu = indeed; bhavet = could there be; asahyam = irresistible, here: impossible; kim = what?; vā = or; śakyam = able to; paratas = superior, here: further; kīrtayiṣye = I will praise, here: I could praise; kartāsi (kartṛ + asi) = you are maker; sarvasya = of all; yatas = from which, here: since; svayam = [your]self; vai = indeed, here: left untranslated; vibho = O almighty; tatas = thence, then; sarvam = all; idam = this; tvam = you; eva = verily.

atyadbhutam = exceedingly wondrous; karma = action; na = not, no; duṣkaram = difficult; te = for you; karmopamānam (karmas + upamānam) = parallel [to] work, here: . . . to deeds; na = not, no; hi = for; vidyate = is found, there is; te = to your; na = not, no; te = to your; guṇānām = of qualities; parimāṇam = measure; asti = it is; na = not, no; tejasas = of brilliance; nāpi (na + api) = not even, here: or; balasya = of strength; narddhes (na + ṛddhes) = not of prosperity, here: or to [your] prosperity.»

11.45: adṛṣṭapūrvam (adṛṣṭa + pūrvam) = seen previously; hṛṣitas = thrilled; 'smi (asmi) = I am; dṛṣṭvā = having seen; bhayena = with fear; ca = and, here: but; pravyathitam = distressed; manas = mind; me = my; tad = this, that; eva = verily, here: left untranslated; me = to me; darśaya = you show!; deva = O god; rūpam = form; prasīda = you be gracious!; deveśa (deva + īśa) = O lord of gods; jagannivāsa (jagat + nivāsa) = O home of the universe.

11.46: kirīṭinam = crown; gadinam = mace; cakrahastam (cakra + hastam) = discus in hand; icchāmi = I desire, I wish; tvām = you; draṣṭum = to see; aham = I; tathaiva (tathā + eva) = thus verily, here: even as; tenaiva (tena + eva) = with that verily, here: that, *eva* is left untranslated; rūpeṇa = with form; caturbhujena (catur + bhujena) = with four arms; sahasrabāho (sahasra

+ bāho) = O thousand-armed; bhava = you be!, here: you assume!; viśvamūrte (viśva + mūrte) = O all-form.

śrībhagavān (śrī + bhagavān) = Blessed Lord; uvāca = he said

11.47: mayā = by me, here: my; prasannena = by being gracious, here: out of kindness; tavārjunedam (tava + arjuna + idam) = for you, O Arjuna, this; rūpam = form; param = supreme; darśitam = shown; ātmayogāt (ātma + yogāt) = by self's Yoga; tejomayam (tejas + mayam) = brilliance-made, here: brilliant; viśvam = all[-comprising]; anantam = infinite; ādyam = primordial; yad = which, here: this; me = of mine; tvadanyena (tvad + anyena) = by you [and none] other, here: . . . by anyone; na = not; dṛṣṭapūrvam (dṛṣṭa + pūrvam) = seen previously, seen before.

11.48: na = not, here: neither; vedayajñādhyayanais (veda + yajña + ādhyayanais) = by Vedas, sacrifices, studies; na = not, here: nor; dānais = by gifts, by charity; na = not, here: nor; ca = and, here: omitted; kriyābhis = by rituals; na = not, here: nor; tapobhis = by austerities; ugrais = terrible, here: fierce; evaṃrūpas (evam + rūpas) = thus-formed; śakya = able to, here: can; aham = I; nṛloke (nṛ + loke) = in human world; draṣṭum = to see, here: be seen; tvadanyena (tvad + anyena) = by other than you, here: by anyone [but] you; kurupravīra (kuru + pravīra) = O Kurupravīra.

11.49: mā = not; te = of you; vyathās = you should quake, here: you [need not] tremble; mā = not; ca = and, here: omitted; vimūḍhabhāvas (vimūḍha + bhāvas) = bewildered state-of-existence, here: . . . condition; dṛṣṭvā = having seen, here: seeing; rūpam = form; ghoram = horrifying; īdṛś = such, here: that; mamedam (mama + idam) = of mine this [form]; vyapetabhīs (vyapeta + bhīs) = freed from fear; prītamanās (prīta + manās) (singular) = glad-minded; punas = again; tvam = you; tad = this, that; eva = verily, here: very; me = of me; rūpam = form; idam = this, here: the; prapaśya = behold!

saṃjayas = Samjaya; uvāca = he said;

11.50: iti = thus, here: omitted; arjunam = Arjuna; vāsudevas (vāsu + devas) = Vāsudeva; tathoktvā (tathā + uktvā) = thus having spoken; svakam = own; rūpam = form; darśayām āsa = he revealed; bhūyas = again; āśvāsayām āsa = he comforted; ca = and; bhītam = terrified; enam = this, here: the [terrified]; bhūtvā = having become, here: having assumed; punas = again; saumyavapus (saumya + vapus) = pleasant body; mahātmā (mahā + ātmā) = great self.

arjunas = Arjuna; uvāca = he said;
11.51: dṛṣṭvedam (dṛṣṭvā + idam) = having seen this, here: beholding; mānuṣam = human; rūpam = form; tava = of you; saumyam = pleasant; janārdana (jana + ardana) = O Janārdana; idānīm = now; asmi = I am; saṃvṛttas = composed; sacetās (sa + cetās) = with thoughts, here: with consciousness; prakṛtim = [normal] nature; gatas = gone, here: returned.

śrībhagavān (śrī + bhagavān) = Blessed Lord; uvāca = he said;
11.52: sudurdarśam (su + durdarśam) = very (su) difficult seeing, here: very-difficult-to-see; idam = this; rūpam = form; dṛṣṭavān asi = you have seen; yad = which; mama = of me, my; devās = gods; api = also, even; asya = of this; rūpasya = of form; nityam = forever; darśanakāṅkṣiṇas (darśana + kāṅkṣiṇas) (plural) = [those who] hanker after a glimpse.

11.53: nāham (na + aham) = not I; vedais = by Vedas; na = not, here: nor; tapasā = by austerity; na = not, here: nor; dānena = by charity; na = not, here: nor; cejyayā (ca + ijyayā) = and by sacrifice; śakye = I am able, I can; evaṃvidhas (evam + vidhas) = such mode, here: in the shape; draṣṭum = to see, here: [I cannot] be seen; dṛṣṭavān asi = you have seen; mām = me; yathā = as, here: omitted.

11.54: bhaktyā = by devotion; tu = but; ananyayā = by no (an-)other; śakye = I am able, here: I can; aham = I; evaṃvidhas (evam + vidhas) = such mode, here: in this shape; 'rjuna (arjuna) = O Arjuna; jñātum = to know, here: can be known; draṣṭum = to see, here: can be seen; ca = and; tattvena = in reality; praveṣṭum = to enter, here: can be entered into; ca = and; paraṃtapa (param + tapa) = O Paramtapa.

11.55: matkarmakṛt (mad + karma + kṛt) = doing (kṛt) my action, here: [he who] does my work; matparamas (mad + paramas) = [he who has] me [as his] supreme [intent]; madbhaktas (mad + bhaktas) = [he who] is devoted to me; saṅgavarjitas (saṅga + varjitas) = attachment abandoned; nirvairas = free-from-enmity; sarvabhūteṣu (sarva + bhūteṣu) = in [or toward] all beings; yas = who; sas = he; mām = me; eti = he goes; pāṇḍava = O son-of-Pāndu.

CHAPTER 12: THE YOGA OF DEVOTION

arjunas = Arjuna; uvāca = he said;

12.1: evam = thus; satatayuktās (plural) = ever yoked; ye (plural) = who; bhaktās (plural) = devoted, here: devotees; tvām = you; paryupāsate (plural) = they worship; ye (plural) = who; cāpi (ca + api) = and also, here: or; akṣaram = imperishable; avyaktam = unmanifest; teṣām = of them; ke (plural) = which?; yogavittamās (yoga + vit + tamās) = the best knowers of Yoga.

śrībhagavān (śrī + bhagavān) = Blessed Lord; uvāca = he said;

12.2: mayi = in me, on me; āveśya = fixing; manas = mind; ye (plural) = who; mām = me; nityayuktās (nitya + yuktās) = ever yoked; upāsate = they worship; śraddhayā = with faith; parayopetās (parayā + upetās) = endowed (upeta) with supreme; te = they, here: those; me = of me, here: I [deem]; yuktatamās (yukta + tamās) = most yoked; matās = are deemed, here: I deem.

12.3: ye (plural) = who; tu = but; akṣaram = imperishable; anirdeśyam = indefinable; avyaktam = unmanifest; paryupāsate (plural) = they worship; sarvatragam (sarvatra + gam) = all-going, here: omnipresent; acintyam = inconceivable; ca = and; kūṭastham (kūṭas + stham) = summit-abiding; acalam = unmoving; dhruvam = firm.

12.4: saṃniyamyendriyagrāmam (saṃniyamya + indriya + grāmam) = restraining the host (grāma) of senses; sarvatra = everywhere,

here: in everything; samabuddhayas (sama + buddhayas) (plural) = same wisdom-faculties, here: [their] wisdom-faculty the same; te = they; prāpnuvanti = they attain; mām = me; eva = verily; sarvabhūtahite (sarva + bhūta + hite) = for the welfare of all beings; ratās (plural) = delighting.

12.5: kleśas = pain, struggle; 'dhikataras (adhikataras) = greater; teṣām = of them, here: of those; avyaktāsaktacetasām (avyakta + āsakta + cetasām) (plural) = of [those whose] mind is attached to the unmanifest; avyaktā (feminine) = unmanifest; hi = indeed, for; gatis = path, course; duḥkham = painful, troubled; dehavadbhis = by embodied [beings]; avāpyate = it is reached.

12.6: ye (plural) = who; tu = but; sarvāṇi = all; karmāṇi = actions; mayi = in me; saṃnyasya = renouncing; matparās (mat + parās) = intent on me; ananyenaiva (ananyena + eva) = by no other verily, here: *eva* is omitted; yogena = by Yoga; mām = me; dhyāyantas = contemplating; upāsate = they worship.

12.7: teṣām = of them, here: of those; aham = I; samuddhartā = uplifter; mṛtyusaṃsārasāgarāt (mṛtyu + saṃsāra + sāgarāt) = from the ocean of the cycle of death (mṛtyu); bhavāmi = I become; na cirāt = before long; pārtha = O son-of-Prithā; mayi = in me; āveśitacetasām (āveśita + cetasām) (plural) = fixed mind.

12.8: mayi = in me; eva = verily, here: alone; manas = mind; ādhatsva = you place!; mayi = in me; buddhim = wisdom-faculty; niveśaya = you settle!; nivasiṣyasi = you will dwell; mayi = in me; eva = verily, here: alone; ata ūrdhvam = henceforth; na = not, no; saṃśayas = doubt.

12.9: atha = now; cittam = mind; samādhātum = to concentrate; na = not; śaknoṣi = you are able; mayi = in me; sthiram = firmly; abhyāsayogena (abhyāsa + yogena) = by the Yoga of practice, here: through Yoga practice; tatas = thence, then; mām = me; icchāptum (iccha + āptum) = you seek to attain!; dhanaṃjaya (dhanam + jaya) = O Dhanamjaya.

12.10: abhyāse = in practice, here: to practice; 'pi (api) = even, here: if; asamarthas = unable; 'si (asi) = you are; matkarmaparamas (mat + karma + paramas) = my supreme (parama) work; bhava = you be!; madartham (mad + artham) = [for] my sake; api = even; karmāṇi = actions; kurvan = doing, performing; siddhim = perfection; avāpsyasi = you will attain.

12.11: athaitad (atha + etad) = now this; api = even; aśaktas = unable; 'si (asi) = you are; kartum = to do; madyogam (mad + yogaṁ) = my Yoga; āśritas = resorting; sarvakarmaphalatyāgam (sarva + karma + phala + tyāgam) = relinquishing all actions's fruit; tatas = thence, then; kuru = you do! you perform!; yatātmavān (yata + ātmavān) = controlled self.

12.12: śreyas = better; hi = indeed, for; jñānam = knowledge; abhyāsāt = than practice; jñānāt = than knowledge; dhyānam = meditation; viśiṣyate = it is preferred, it is superior to; dhyānāt = from meditation; karmaphalatyāgas (karma + phala + tyāgas) = relinquishing the fruit of action; tyāgāt = by relinquishing; śantis = peace; anantaram = immediate.

12.13: adveṣṭā = nonhater, here: no hatred; sarvabhūtānām (sarva + bhūtānām) = of [toward] all beings, here: for any being; maitras = friendly; karuṇas = compassionate; eva = verily, here: left untranslated; ca = and; nirmamas = devoid of (nir-) "mine"; nirahaṃkāras = free from (nir-) I-maker, here: without ego-sense; samaduḥkhasukhas (sama + duḥkha + sukhas) = same in pleasure [and] pain; kṣamī = patient.

12.14: saṃtuṣṭas = content; satatam = ever; yogī = yogin; yatātmā (yata + ātmā) = controlled self, here: self-controlled; dṛḍhaniścayas (dṛḍha + niścayas) = firm resolve; mayi = in me; arpitamanobuddhis (arpita + manas + buddhis) = offered up mind and wisdom-faculty; yas = who; madbhaktas (mad + bhaktas) = devoted to me; sas = he; me = to me; priyas = dear.

12.15: yasmāt = from whom; nodvijate (na + udvijate) = it shrinks not; lokas = world; lokāt = from world; nodvijate (na + udvijate) =

it shrinks not; ca = and; yas = who; harṣāmarṣabhayodvegais (harṣa + āmarṣa + bhaya + udvegais) (plural) = from exultation, anger, fear, [and] agitation; muktas = released, here: free; yas = who; sas = he; ca = and; me = to me; priyas = dear.

12.16: anapekṣas = impartial; śucis = pure; dakṣas = skilled; udāsīnas = indifferent; gatavyathas (gata + vyathas) = disquiet gone; sarvārambhaparityāgī (sarva + ārambha + parityāgī) = [he who has] relinquished all undertaking; yas = who; madbhaktas (mad + bhaktas) = devoted to me; sas = he; me = to me; priyas = dear.

12.17: yas = who; na = not; hṛṣyati = he rejoices; na = not; dveṣṭi = he hates; na = not; śocati = he grieves; na = not; kāṅkṣati = he hankers after; śubhāsubhaparityāgī (śubha + aśubha + parityāgī) = he who has] relinquished pleasant [and] unpleasant; bhaktimān = devotee, filled with devotion; yas = who; sas = he; me = to me; priyas = dear.

12.18: samas = same; śatrau = toward enemy; ca = and; mitre = toward friend; ca = and; tathā = thus; mānāvamānayos (mānāva + mānayos) (dual) = honor [and] dishonor; śītoṣṇasukhaduḥkheṣu (śīta + uṣṇa + sukha + duḥkheṣu) = in cold [and] heat, pleasure [and] pain; samas = same; saṅgavivarjitas (saṅga + vivarjitas) = devoid of attachment (saṅga).

12.19: tulyanindāstutis (tulya + nindā + stutis) = equal blame [and] praise; maunī = silent; saṃtuṣṭas = content; yena = by which, here: omitted; kenacid = with whatever; aniketas = homeless; sthiramatis (sthira + matis) = [who is of] steady mind; bhaktimān = devotee, filled with devotion; me = to me; priyas = dear; naras = man.

12.20: ye (plural) = who; tu = but; dharmyāmṛtam (dharmya + amṛtam) = lawful nectar-of-immortality; idam = this; yathoktam (yathā + uktam) = as declared; paryupāsate (plural) = they worship; śraddadhānās = [those who] have faith;

matparamās (mat + paramās) = [those who make] me [their] supreme; bhaktās = [those who] are devoted; te = they; 'tīva (atīva) = exceedingly; me = to me; priyās (plural) = dear.

CHAPTER 13: THE YOGA OF THE DISTINCTION BETWEEN THE FIELD AND THE FIELD-KNOWER

arjunas = Arjuna; uvāca = he said;

13.0: prakṛtim = Cosmos; puruṣam = Spirit; caiva (ca + eva) = and indeed, here: *eva* is left untranslated; kṣetram = field; kṣetrajñam (kṣetra + jñam) = field-knower; eva = indeed, here: omitted; ca = and; etad = this; veditum = to know; icchāmi = I desire; jñānam = knowledge; jñeyam = what-is-to-be-known, i.e., the object of knowledge; ca = and; keśava = O Keshava [i.e., Krishna].

śrībhagavān (śrī + bhagavān) = Blessed Lord; uvāca = he said;

13.1: idam = this; śarīram = body; kaunteya = O son-of-Kuntī [i.e., Arjuna]; kṣetram = field; iti = here: used to indicate a quotation; abhidhīyate = it is designated; etad = this; yas = who; vetti = he knows; tam = that; prāhus = they say; kṣetrajñas (kṣetra + jñas) = field-knower; iti = here: used to indicate a quotation; tadvidas (tad + vidas) (plural) = knowers of that (tad), here: . . . it.

13.2: kṣetrajñam (kṣetra + jñam) = field-knower; cāpi (ca + api) = and also; mām = me; viddhi = you know!; sarvakṣetreṣu (sarva + kṣetreṣu) = in all fields; bhārata = O descendant-of-Bharata; kṣetrakṣetrajñayos (kṣetra + kṣetra + jñayos) (dual) = of field and field-knower; jñānam = knowledge; yad = which; tad = this, that; jñānam = knowledge; matam = is deemed, here: I deem; mama = of me, here: I.

13.3: tad = this, that; kṣetram = field; yad = which, here: what; ca = and; yādṛś = like what; ca = and; yadvikāri (yad + vikāri) = which [or what] form; yatas = whence; ca = and; yad = which; sas = he; ca = and; yas = who; yatprabhāvas (yad + prabhāvas)

= which [or what] might; ca = and; tad = this, that; samāsena = briefly; me = of [or from] me; śṛṇu = you hear!

13.4: ṛṣibhis = by seers; bahudhā = manifold, here: in many ways; gītam = sung; chandobhis = by hymns; vividhais = by various; pṛthak = distinctly; brahmasūtrapadais (brahma + sūtra + padais) = with aphoristic (sūtra) expressions about the world-ground; caiva (ca + eva) = and indeed, here: and also; hetumadbhis (plural) = with well-reasoned; viniścitais (plural) = with conclusive.

13.5: mahābhūtāni (mahā + bhūtāni) = great elements; ahaṃkāras = I-maker [i.e., ego-sense]; buddhis = wisdom-faculty; avyaktam = unmanifest; eva = indeed, here: *eva* is omitted; ca = and; indriyāṇi = senses; daśaikam (daśa + ekam) = ten [plus] one [i.e., eleven]; ca = and; pañca = five; cendriyagocarās (ca + indriya + gocarās) = and cow-pastures (gocara) of the senses.

13.6: icchā = desire; dveṣas = hatred, aversion; sukham = pleasure; duḥkham = pain; saṃghātas = confusion; cetanā = consciousness; dhṛtis = holding; etad = this; kṣetram = field; samāsena = in brief; savikāram (sa + vikāram) = with (sa) modification, here: with modifications; udāhṛtam = described.

13.7: amānitvam = lack-of-pride; adambhitvam = unpretentiousness; ahiṃsā = nonharming; kṣāntis = patience; ārjavam = uprightness; ācāryopāsanam (ācārya + upāsanam) = reverence for the preceptor; śaucam = purity; sthairyam = steadiness; ātmavinigrahas (ātma + vinigrahas) = self-restraint.

13.8: indriyārtheṣu (indriya + artheṣu) = toward sense objects; vairāgyam = dispassion; anahaṃkāras = absence-of-ego-sense; eva = indeed; ca = and; janmamṛtyujarāvyādhiduḥkhadoṣānu darśanam (janma + mṛtyu + jarā + vyādhi + duḥkha + doṣa + anudarśanam) = insight into the defects (doṣa) of birth, death, old age, illness, and suffering.

13.9: asaktis = nonattachment; anabhiṣvaṅgas = absence-of-clinging; putradāragṛhādiṣu (putra + dāra + gṛha + ādiṣu) = toward son, wife, home, and the like (ādi); nityam = constant; ca = and; samacittatvam (sama + cittatvam) = same-mindedness; iṣṭāniṣṭopapattiṣu (iṣṭa + aniṣṭa + upapattiṣu) = in desirable [and] undesirable happenings.

13.10: mayi = in me; cānanyayogena (ca + ananya + yogena) = by no other Yoga; bhaktis = devotion; avyabhicāriṇī = unswerving; viviktadeśasevitvam (vivikta + deśa + sevitvam) = resorting (sevitva) to an solitary place (deśa); aratis = dislike; janasaṃsadi (jana + saṃsadi) = in company of people (jana).

13.11: adhyātmajñānanityatvam (adhyātma + jñāna + nityatvam) = constancy (nityatva) of the knowledge of the basis-of-self; tattvajñānārthadarśanam (tattva + jñāna + artha + darśanam) = insight (darśana) into the purpose (artha) of the knowledge of reality (tattva); etad = this; jñānam = knowledge; iti = thus, here: this; proktam = proclaimed; ajñānam = ignorance; yad = which, what; atas = hence, here: omitted; 'nyathā (anyathā) = otherwise.

13.12: jñeyam = object-of-knowledge; yad = which; tad = this, that; pravakṣyāmi = I will declare; yad = which; jñātvāmṛtam (jñātvā + amṛtam) = having known [he attains to] immortality, here: knowing . . . ; aśnute = attains; anādimat = beginningless; param = supreme; brahma = world-ground; na = not, here: neither; sat = existence; tad = this, that; nāsat (na + asat) = not nonexistence, here: nor . . . ; ucyate = it is called.

13.13: sarvatas = everywhere; pāṇipādam (pāṇi + pādam) = hand [and] foot, here: hands and feet; tad = this, that; sarvatas = everywhere; 'kṣiśiromukham (akṣi + śiras + mukham) = eye, head, mouth, here: eyes, heads, and mouths; sarvatas = everywhere; śrutimat = having hearing, here: ears; loke = in world; sarvam = all; avṛtya = enveloping; tiṣṭhati = it is present.

13.14: sarvendriyaguṇābhāsam (sarva + indriya + guṇa + ābhāsam) = appearance of all sense qualities, here: appearing . . . ; sarvendriyavivarjitam (sarva + indriya + vivarjitam) = devoid of all senses; asaktam = unattached; sarvabhṛt (sarva + bhṛt) = all-supporting; caiva (ca + eva) = and even, here: and yet; nirguṇam = beyond (nir-) the primary-qualities; guṇabhoktṛ (guṇa + bhoktṛ) = enjoyer of primary-qualities; ca = and.

13.15: bahis = outside, without; antas = within; ca = and; bhūtānām = of beings; acaram = unmoving; caram = moving; eva = verily, here: yet; ca = and; sūkṣmatvāt = because of subtleness; tad = this, that; avijñeyam = not-to-be-known, here: cannot be known; dūrastham (dūra + stham) = far-abiding, here: standing afar; cāntike (ca + antike) = and in the vicinity, here: near; ca = and; tad = this, that.

13.16: avibhaktam = undivided; ca = and; bhūteṣu = in beings; vibhaktam = divided; iva = as it were, here: seemingly; ca = and; sthitam = abiding, here: it abides; bhūtabhartṛ (bhūta + bhartṛ) = supporter of beings; ca = and; tad = this, that; jñeyam = to be known; grasiṣṇu = devourer; prabhaviṣṇu = generator; ca = and.

13.17: jyotiṣām = of lights; api = also; tad = thiat, that; jyotis = light; tamasas = of darkness; param = beyond; ucyate = it is called; jñānam = knowledge; jñeyam = what-is-to-be-known [i.e., object of knowledge]; jñānagamyam (jñāna + gamyam) = accessible (gamya) to knowledge; hṛdi = in heart; sarvasya = of all; viṣṭhitam = seated.

13.18: iti = thus; kṣetram = field; tathā = thus, likewise; jñānam = knowledge; jñeyam = what-is-to-be-known; coktam (ca + uktam) = and is called, explained; samāsatas = briefly; madbhaktas (mad + bhaktas) = my devotee; etad = this; vijñāya = knowing; madbhāvāyopapadyate (mad + bhāvāya + upapadyate) = my state-of-existence he approaches.

13.19: prakṛtim = Cosmos; puruṣam = Spirit; caiva (ca + eva) = and verily, here: *eva* is left untranslated; viddhi = you know!; anādī = beginningless; ubhau (dual) = both; api = also; vikārān = modifications; ca = and; guṇān = primary-qualities; caiva (ca + eva) = and verily, here: *eva* is omitted; viddhi = you know!; prakṛtisaṃbhavān (prakṛti + saṃbhavān) (plural) = arising from Cosmos, here: arise . . . .

13.20: kāryakāraṇakartṛtve (kārya + kāraṇa + kartṛtve) = in regard to the agency [underlying] instruments (kāraṇa) [and] effects (kārya); hetus = cause; prakṛtis = comos; ucyate = it is called; puruṣas = spirit; sukhaduḥkhānām (sukha + duḥkhānām) = of pleasure [and] pain; bhoktṛtve = in [inasmuch as it is] enjoyership; hetus = cause; ucyate = it is called.

13.21: puruṣas = spirit; prakṛtisthas (prakṛti + sthas) = abiding [in] the Cosmos; hi = verily, here: left untranslated; bhuṅkte = it enjoys, it experiences; prakṛtijān (prakṛiti + jān) = cosmos-born; guṇān = primary-qualities; kāraṇam = cause, instrument; guṇasaṅgas (guṇa + saṅgas) = attachment to the primary-qualities; 'sya (asya) = of this, here: of its; sadasadyonijanmasu (sat + asat + yoni + janmasu) (plural) = in births [into] good [and] bad wombs (yoni), here: birth in . . . .

13.22: upadraṣṭānumantā (upadraṣṭā + anumantā) = supervisor [and] permitter; ca = and; bhartā = supporter; bhoktā = enjoyer; maheśvaras (mahā + īśvaras) = great lord; paramātmeti (parama + ātma + iti) = supreme self thus (iti), here: *iti* is used to indicate a quotation; cāpi (ca + api) = and also; uktas = is called; dehe = in body; 'smin (asmin) = in this; puruṣas = Spirit; paras = supreme, highest.

13.23: yas = who; evam = thus; vetti = he knows; puruṣam = spirit; prakṛtim = cosmos; ca = and; guṇais = with primary-qualities; saha = together with; sarvathā = in whatever way; vartamānas = existing, here: he exists; 'pi (api) = also, even, here: omitted; na = not; sas = he; bhūyas = again; 'bhijāyate (abhijāyate) = he is born.

13.24: dhyānenātmani (dhyānena + ātmani) = through meditation in the self; paśyanti = they perceive; kecid = some; ātmānam = self; ātmanā = by the self; anye = others; sāṃkhyena = by Sāmkhya; yogena = by Yoga; karmayogena (karma + yogena) = by Karma-Yoga; cāpare (ca + apare) = and others.

13.25: anye = others; tu = indeed, but; evam = thus, here: of this; ajānantas = ignorant; śrutvānyebhyas (śrutvā + anyebhyas) =

having heard from others, here: hearing from others; upāsate = they worship; te = they; 'pi (api) = also, too; cātitaranti (ca + atitaranti) = and they transcend; eva = verily, here: omitted; mṛtyum = death; śrutiparāyaṇās (śruti + parāyaṇās) = being dedicated to what they hear (śruti) [i.e., to revelation].

13.26: yāvat = inasmuch, here: omitted; saṃjāyate = it is born; kiṃcid = whatever; sattvam = being; sthāvarajaṅgamam (sthāvara + jaṇgamam) = motionless [or] moving; kṣetrakṣetrajñasaṃyogāt (kṣetra + kṣetra + jña + saṃyogāt) = from the union (saṃyoga) of the field and field-knower; tad = this, that; viddhi = you know!; bharatarṣabha (bharata +ṛṣabha) = O Bharatarshabha.

13.27: samam = same; sarveṣu = in all; bhūteṣu = in being; tiṣṭhantam = standing, present; parameśvaram (parama + īśvaram) = supreme lord; vinaṣyatsu = in perishings, here: upon perishing; avinaśyantam = not perishing; yas = who; paśyati = he sees; sas = he; paśyati = sees.

13.28: samam = same; paśyan = seeing; hi = for; sarvatra = everywhere; samavasthitam = abiding; īśvaram = lord; na = not, here: cannot; hinasti = he hurts; ātmanātmānam (ātma + na + ātmānam) = [him]self (ātmānam) by [him]self; tatas = thence, hence; yāti = he treads; parām = supreme, highest; gatim = course.

13.29: prakṛtyaiva (prakṛtyā + eva) = by cosmos indeed (eva), here: *eva* is omitted; ca = and; karmāṇi = actions; kriyamāṇāni (plural) = performed; sarvaśas = exclusively; yas = who; paśyati = he sees; tathātmānam (tathā + ātmānam) = thus the self; akartāram = nondoer, here: it is inactive; sas = he; paśyati = sees.

13.30: yadā = when; bhūtapṛthagbhāvam (bhūta + pṛthag + bhāvam) = diverse states-of-existence (bhāva) of beings; ekastham (eka + stham) = abiding (stha) in one; anupaśyati = he perceives; tatas = thence, here: from that; eva = indeed, here: omitted; ca = and; vistāram = spreading-forth; brahma = world-ground; saṃpadyate = he attains; tadā = then.

13.31: anāditvān = from beginnningless, here: because . . . beginningless; nirguṇatvāt = because [it is] beyond the primary-qualities; paramātmāyam (parama + ātmā + ayam) = this supreme self; avyayas = immutable; śarīrasthas (śarīra + sthas) = abiding in body; 'pi (api) = even, here: although; kaunteya = O son-of-Kuntī; na = not, here: neither; karoti = it acts; na = not, here: nor; lipyate = it is defiled.

13.32: yathā = as; sarvagatam (sarva + gatam) = omnipresent; saukṣmyāt = because of subtleness; ākāśam = ether-space; nopalipyate (na + upalipyate) = not polluted; sarvatrāvasthitas (sarvatra + avasthitas) = abiding everywhere; dehe = in body; tathātmā (tathā + ātmā) = thus, so the self; nopalipyate (na + upalipyate) = it is not polluted.

13.33: yathā = as; prakāśayati = it illuminates; ekas = one, singly; kṛtsnam = whole; lokam = world; imam = this; ravis = sun; kṣetram = field; kṣetrī = field-owner; tathā = thus, so; kṛtsnam = whole; prakāśayati = it illuminates; bhārata = O descendant-of-Bharata.

13.34: kṣetrakṣetrajñayos (kṣetra + kṣetra + jñayos) (dual) = of the field and the field-knower; evam = thus; antaram = distinction, difference; jñānacakṣuṣā (jñāna + cakṣuṣā) = by the eye of knowledge; bhūtaprakṛtimokṣam (bhūta + prakṛti + mokṣam) = liberation from the elemental (bhūta) cosmos; ca = and; ye (plural) = who; vidus = they know; yānti = they go; te = they; param = highest, supreme.

CHAPTER 14: THE YOGA OF THE DISTINCTION BETWEEN THE TRIPLE QUALITIES

śrībhagavān (śrī + bhagavān) = Blessed Lord; uvāca = he said;
14.1: param = highest; bhūyas = again; pravakṣyāmi = I will proclaim; jñānānām = of knowledges, here: kinds-of-knowledge; jñānam = knowledge; uttamam = foremost, unexcelled; yad = which; jñātvā = having known, here: knowing; munayas = sages; sarve

= all; parām = highest; siddhim = perfection; itas = hence; gatās (plural) = gone, here: have gone.

14.2: idam = this; jñānam = knowledge; upāśritya = resorting; mama = of me, my; sadharmyam = identity; āgatās (plural) = come; sarge = at [new] creation; 'pi (api) = even; nopajāyante (na + upajāyante) = they are not born; pralaye = at dissolution; na = not, here: nor; vyathanti = they [need not] tremble; ca = and, here: omitted.

14.3: mama = of me, my; yonis = womb; mahat = great; brahma = world-ground; tasmin = in it; garbham = fetus; dadhāmi = I plant; aham = I; saṃbhavas = birth; sarvabhūtānām = of all beings; tatas = thence, here: from that; bhavati = it becomes, here: it comes; bhārata = O descendant-of-Bharata.

14.4: sarvayoniṣu = in all wombs; kaunteya = O son-of-Kuntī; mūrtayas = forms; saṃbhavanti = they arise; yās (plural) = which; tāsām = of them; brahma = world-ground; mahat = great; yonis = womb; aham = I; bījapradas = seed given, here: [who] gives the seed; pitā = father.

14.5: sattvam = here: retained in Sanskrit; rajas = here: retained in Sanskrit; tamas = here: retained in Sanskrit; iti = thus, here: left untranslated; guṇās = primary-qualities; prakṛtisaṃbhavās = born of the cosmos; nibadhnanti = they fasten; mahābāho = O mighty-armed [Arjuna]; dehe = in body, here: to body; dehinam = embodied [self], here: body-essence; avyayam = immutable.

14.6: tatra = therein, here: of these; sattvam = here: retained in Sanskrit; nirmalatvāt = because of immaculateness; prakāśakam = illuminating; anāmayam = without ill; sukhasaṅgena (sukha + saṅgena) = by attachment to joy (sukha); badhnāti = it binds; jñānasaṅgena (jñāna + saṅgena) = by attachment to knowledge; cānagha (ca + anagha) = and O Anagha.

14.7: rajas = here: retained in Sanskrit; rāgātmakam (rāga + ātmakam) = nature of passion (rāga); viddhi = you know!;

tṛṣṇasaṅgasamudbhavam (tṛṣṇa + saṅga + samudbhavam) = produced from thirst [and] attachment; tad = this, that; nibadhnāti = it binds; kaunteya = O son-of-Kuntī; karmasaṅgena (karma + saṅgena) = by attachment to action; dehinam = embodied, here: body-essence.

14.8: tamas = here: retained in Sanskrit; tu = but; ajñānajam (ajñāna + jam) = born of ignorance; viddhi = you know!; mohanam = deluding; sarvadehinām (sarva + dehinām) = all embodied ones, here: all body-essences; pramādālasyanidrābhis (pramāda + ālasya + nidrābhis) = by heedlessness, indolence [and] sleep; tad = this, that; nibadhnāti = it binds; bhārata = O descendant-of-Bharata.

14.9: sattvam = here: retained in Sanskrit; sukhe = in [to] joy; sañjayati = it attaches; rajas = here: retained in Sanskrit; karmāṇi = in [to]; bhārata = O descendant-of-Bharata; jñānam = knowledge; āvṛtya = veiling; tu = but; tamas = here: retained in Sanskrit; pramāde = in [to] heedlessness; sañjayati = it attaches; uta = indeed, here: omitted.

14.10: rajas = here: retained in Sanskrit; tamas = here: retained in Sanskrit; cābhibhūya = and overpowering, here: are overpowered; sattvam = here: retained in Sanskrit; bhavati = it becomes; bhārata = O descendant-of-Bharata; rajas = here: retained in Sanskrit; sattvam = here: retained in Sanskrit; tamas = here: retained in Sanskrit; caiva (ca + eva) = and verily, here: and thus also; tamas = here: retained in Sanskrit; sattvam = here: retained in Sanskrit; rajas = here: retained in Sanskrit; tathā = thus, as well as.

14.11: sarvadvāreṣu (sarva + dvāreṣu) = in [at] all gates; dehe = in body; 'smin (asmin) = in this; prakāśas = luminosity; upajāyate = it is born, here: it appears; jñānam = knowledge; yadā = when; tadā = then; vidyāt = it should be known, here: he should know; vivṛddham = increased; sattvam = here: retained in Sanskrit; iti = thus, here: left untranslated; uta = indeed, here: left untranslated.

14.12: lobhas = greed; pravṛttis = activity; ārambhas = undertaking; karmāṅām = of actions; aśamas = unrest; spṛhā = desire; rajasi = in rajas, here: from rajas; etāni = these; jāyante = they are born, they arise; vivṛddhe = upon increasing, here: when it increases; bharatarṣabha (bharata + ṛṣabha) = O Bharatarshabha.

14.13: aprakāśas = lack-of-luminosity; 'pravṛttis (apravṛttis) = inactivity; ca = and; pramādas = heedlessness; mohas = delusion; eva = verily, here: also; ca = and; tamasi = in tamas, here: from tamas; etāni = these; jāyante = they are born, they arise; vivṛddhe = upon increasing, here: when it increases; kurunandana (kuru + nandana) = Kurunandana.

14.14: yadā = when; sattve = in sattva, here: when sattva; pravṛddhe = upon increasing, here: it has increased; tu = but; pralayam = dissolution; yāti = he goes; dehabhṛt (deha + bhṛt) = body-wearer; tadottamavidām (tadā + uttama + vidām) (genitive plural) = then of the foremost knowers [or of the knowers of the supreme]; lokān = worlds; amalān (plural) = undefiled; pratipadyate = he enters.

14.15: rajasi = in rajas, here: when rajas; pralayam = dissolution; gatvā = having gone, here: he meets with; karmasaṅgiṣu (karma + saṅgiṣu) (plural) = in [or among] action-attached; jāyate = he is born; tathā = thus, similarly; pralīnas = he is dissolved; tamasi = in tamas, here: when tamas; mūḍhayoniṣu (mūḍha + yoniṣu) = in wombs [of the] deluded; jāyate = he is born.

14.16: karmaṇas = of action; sukṛtasyāhus (su + kṛtasya + āhus) = well-done (sukṛta) they say; sāttvikam = sattvic, sattva-natured; nirmalam = undefiled; phalam = fruit; rajasas = of rajas; tu = but; phalam = fruit; duḥkham = suffering; ajñānam = ignorance; tamasas = of tamas; phalam = fruit.

14.17: sattvāt = from sattva; saṃjāyate = it is born, here: it arises; jñānam = knowledge; rajasas = from rajas; lobhas = great; eva = verily, here: omitted; ca = and; pramādamohau (pramāda + mohau) = heedlessness and delusion; tamasas = from tamas;

bhavatas (dual) = they arise; 'jñānam (ajñāna) = ignorance; eva = verily, here: omitted; ca = and, here: as well as.

14.18: ūrdhvam = upward; gacchanti = they go; sattvasthā (sattva + sthā) = sattva abiding, here: abides in sattva; madhye = in middle; tiṣṭhanti = they stay; rājasās (plural) = rajasic; jaghanyaguṇavṛttisthās (jaghanya + guṇa + vṛtti + sthās) = [those who are] established (stha) in the lowest (jaghanya) mode of the primary-qualities; adhas = downward; gacchanti = they go; tāmasās (plural) = tamasic.

14.19: nānyam (na + anyam) = not other, here: no other; guṇebhyas = than the primary-qualities; kartāram = agent; yadā = when; draṣṭānupaśyati (draṣṭā + anupaśyati) = the seer sees; guṇebhyas = than the primary-qualities; ca = and; param = highest, here: beyond; vetti = he knows; madbhāvam (mad + bhāvam) = my state-of-existence; sas = he; 'dhigacchati (adhigacchati) = he attains.

14.20: gunān = primary-qualities; etān = these; atītya = transcending; trīn = three; dehī = embodied, here: body-essence; dehasamudbhavān (deha + samudbhavān) = sources of body; janmamṛtyujarāduḥkhais (janma + mṛtyu + jarā + duḥkhais) = from birth, death, old age, [and] suffering; vimuktas = freed; 'mṛtam (amṛtam) = immortal, immortality; aśnute = he attains, he gains.

arjunas = Arjuna; uvāca = he said;

14.21: kais = by what?; liṅgais = by signs; trīn = three; guṇān = primary-qualities; etān = these; atītas = transcending, here: he-who-transcends; bhavati = he becomes, here: he is; prabho = O lord; kimācāras (kim + ācāras) = what conduct?; katham = how?; caitān (ca + etān) = and these; trīn = three; guṇān = primary-qualities; ativartate = he passes beyond, here: [does] he pass beyond.

śrībhagavān (śrī + bhagavān) = Blessed Lord; uvāca = he said;

14.22: prakāśam = illumination; ca = and; pravṛttim = activity; ca = and; moham = delusion; eva = verily, here: left untranslated; ca

= and; pāṇḍava = O son-of-Pāndu; na = not; dveṣṭi = he hates; saṃpravṛttāni = occurrences, here: [when they] arise; na = not; nivṛttāni = cessations, here: [when they] cease; kāṅkṣati = he hankers after.

14.23: udāsīnavad (udāsīna + vat) = like (-vat) [someone who is] indifferent; āsīnas = seated; guṇais = by the primary-qualities; yas = who; na = not; vicālyate = he is perturbed; guṇās = primary-qualities; vartanta (for vartante) = they revolve; iti = thus, here: used to indicate a quotation; eva = verily, thus; yas = who; 'vatiṣṭhati (avatiṣṭhati) = he stands, here: stands-aloof; neṅgate (na + iṅgate) = he stirs not, here: does not stir.

14.24: samaduḥkhasukhas (sama + duḥkha + sukhas) = same [in] pleasure (sukha) [and] pain; svasthas (sva + sthas) = self-abiding, self-reliant; samaloṣṭāśmakāñcanas (sama + loṣṭa + aśma + kāñcanas) = same [toward] a clod-of-earth, stone, [or] gold; tulyapriyāpriyas (tulya + priya + apriyas) = equal [-minded] [toward] dear [or] unpleasant; dhīras = steadfast; tulyanindātmasaṃstutis (tulya + nindā + ātma + saṃstutis) = equal[-minded] [toward] praise of [him]self [or] blame (tulya), here: equal[-minded] [toward] blame or praise [showered on] him.

14.25: mānāvamānayos (mānāva + mānayos) (dual) = in honor [and] dishonor; tulyas = equal[-minded]; tulyas = equal [-minded]; mitrāripakṣayos (mitra + ari + pakṣayos) (dual) = toward the sides of friend [or] enemy; sarvārambhaparityāgī (sarva + ārambha + parityāgī) = renouncer of all undertakings; guṇātītas (guṇa + atītas) = transcending the primary-qualities, here: [one who has] transcended . . . ; sas = he; ucyate = he is called.

14.26: mām = me; ca = and; yas = who; 'vyabhicāreṇa (avyabhicāreṇa) = with unfailing; bhaktiyogena (bhakti + yogena) = with the Yoga of devotion; sevate = he serves; sas = he; guṇān = primary-qualities; samitītyaitān (samitītya + etān) = having transcended these; brahmabhūyāya (brahma + bhūyāya) (dative) = for becoming the world-ground; kalpate = he is fit.

14.27: brahmaṇas = of world-ground; hi = for; pratiṣṭhāham (pratiṣṭhā + aham) = I (aham) [am] the foundation; amṛtasyāvyayasya (amṛtasya + avyayasya) = of the immortal [and] immutable; ca = and; śāśvatasya = of everlasting; ca = and; dharmasya = of law; sukhasyaikāntikasya (sukhasya + ekāntikasya) = of joy (sukha) of singular (ekāntika); ca = and.

CHAPTER 15: THE YOGA OF THE SUPREME PERSON

śrībhagavān (śrī + bhagavān) = Blessed Lord; uvāca = he said;
15.1: ūrdhvamūlam (ūrdhva + mūlam) = above the root (mūla), here: roots above; adhaḥśakham (adhas + śakham) = below the branch, here: branches below; aśvattham = here: retained in Sanskrit; prāhus = they say; avyayam = immutable; chandāṃsi = hymns; yasya = whose; parṇāni = leaves; yas = who; tam = that; veda = he knows; sas = he; vedavid (veda + vid) = Veda-knower.

15.2: adhas = below; cordhvam (ca + ūrdhvam) = and above; prasṛtās (plural) = spreading out; tasya = of it, its; śākhās = branches; guṇapravṛddhās (guṇapravṛddhās) = nourished by the primary-qualities; viṣayapravālās (viṣaya + pravālās) = objects [as] twigs; adhas = below; ca = and; mūlāni = roots; anusaṃtatāni (plural) = stretched out, here: they proliferate; karmānubandhīni (karma + anubandhīni) (plural) = action-linked; manuṣyaloke (manuṣya + loke) = in human world.

15.3: na = not; rūpam = form; asyeha (asya + iha) = of it here; tathopalabhyate (tathā + upalabhyate) = it is thus perceived; nāntas (na + antas) = not end, here: nor [its] end; na = not, here: nor; cādis (ca + ādis) = and beginning; na = not, here: nor; ca = and; saṃpratiṣṭhā = foundation; aśvattham = here: retained in Sanskrit; enam = this; suvirūḍhamūlam (su + virūḍha + mūlam) = well (su-) developed root, here: . . . roots; asaṅgaśastreṇa (asaṅga + śastreṇa) = with weapon (śastra) of nonattachment; dṛḍhena = with firm, solid; chittvā = having cut, here: having felled.

15.4: tatas = thence, then; padam = state; tad = this, that; parimārgitavyam = to be tracked; yasmin = in which, here: from which; gatās = [those who are] gone, here: [those who have] reached; na = not; nivartanti = they return; bhūyas = again; tam = that; eva = verily; cādyam (ca + ādyam) = and beginning, here: and primordial; puruṣam = spirit; prapadye = I-go-for-refuge; yatas = whence; pravṛttis = creativity; prasṛtā (feminine) = flowed forth; purāṇī = ancient.

15.5: nirmāṇamohās (nirmāṇa + mohās) = [those who are] without (nir-) pride [and] delusion; jitasaṅgadoṣās (jita + saṅga + doṣās) = [those who have] vanquished the blemish of attachment; adhyātmanityās (adhyātma + nityās) = [those who are] ever [abiding in] the basis-of-self; vinivṛttakāmās (vinivṛtta + kāmās) = [those who have] stilled desires (kāma); dvandvais = from pairs-of-opposites; vimuktās = [those who are] freed; sukhaduḥkhasaṃjñais (sukha + duḥkha + saṃjñais) = from [those who are] known [as] pleasure [and] pain; gacchanti amūḍhās = [those who are] undeluded they go (gacchanti); padam = state; avyayam = immutable; tad = this, that.

15.6: na = not; tad = this, that; bhāsayate = it illuminates; sūryas = sun; na = not, here: nor; śaśāṅkas = moon [lit. "hare-marked," corresponding to the "man in the moon" motif]; na = nor; pāvakas = fire; yad = which; gatvā = having gone, here: once reached; na = not; nivartante = they return; tad = this, that; dhāma = abode; paramam = supreme; mama = of me, my.

15.7: mamaivāṃśas (mama + eva + aṃśas) = only (eva) a fragment of myself (mama); jīvaloke (jīva + loke) = in the world [of] living; jīvabhūtas (jīva + bhūtas) = living element [or being], here: life-principle; sanātanas = everlasting; manaḥśaṣṭhānīndriyāṇi (manas + śaṣṭhāni + indriyāṇi) = mind [as] sixth sense (indriya); prakṛtisthāni (prakṛti + sthāni) (plural) = abiding [in] cosmos; karṣati = it attracts.

15.8: śarīram = body; yad = which, here: whatever; avāpnoti = he attains, here: he takes on; yad = which, here: whatever; cāpi (ca + api) = and also, here: *api* is omitted; utkrāmatīśvaras (utkrāmati + īśvaras) = the lord rises (utkrāmati); gṛhitvaitāni (gṛhitvā + etāni) = having seized these; saṃyāti = it carries; vāyus = wind; gandhān = scents; ivāśayāt (iva + āśayāt) = from place-of-origin [to place] as it were, here: even as [the wind] from place-of-origin [*āśaya* denotes a scent's resting place, such as a flower].

15.9: śrotram = hearing; cakṣus = eye, here: seeing; sparśanam = touch; ca = and; rasanam = taste; ghrāṇam = smell; eva = verily, here: omitted; ca = and, here: as well as; adhiṣṭhāya = employing; manas = mind; cāyam (ca + ayam) = and this; viṣayān = objects; upasevate = it indulges.

15.10: utkrāmantam = rising, here: it rises; sthitam = staying, abiding, here: it abides; vāpi (vā + api) = or also, here: *api* is omitted; bhuñjānam = enjoying, here: it enjoys; vā = or; guṇānvitam (guṇa + anvitam) = endowed with primary-qualities; vimūḍhās (plural) = deluded; nānupaśyanti (na + anupaśyanti) = they see not; paśyanti = they see; jñānacakṣuṣas (jñāna + cakṣuṣas) (plural) = knowledge-eyed.

15.11: yatantas (plural) = striving; yoginas = yogins; cainam (ca + enam) = and this, here: and [they behold] him; paśyanti = they behold; ātmani = in the self; avasthitam = established; yatantas (plural) = striving; 'pi (api) = but; akṛtātmānas (akṛta + ātmānas) (plural) = [those who are of] unperfected self; nainam (na + enam) = not this, here: [they see] him not; paśyanti = they behold, they see; acetasas (plural) = unintelligent.

15.12: yad = which; ādityagatam (āditya + gatam) = gone to the sun, here: entered the sun; tejas = brilliance; jagat = universe; bhāsayate = it illuminates; 'khilam (akhilam) = entire; yad = which; candramasi = in the moon; yad = which; cāgnau (ca + agnau) = and in fire; tad = this, that; tejas = brilliance; viddhi = you know!; māmakam = mine.

15.13: gām = earth [lit. "she who is walked upon"]; āviśya = entering, here: penetrating; ca = and; bhūtāni = beings; dhārayāmi = I support; aham = I; ojasā = with vitality; puṣṇāmi = I cause-to-thrive, here: I nourish; cauṣadhīs (ca + auṣadhīs) = and herbs; sarvās (plural) = all; somas = here: retained in Sanskrit; bhūtvā = having become, here: becoming; rasātmakas (rasa + ātmakas) = of the nature (ātmaka) of ambrosia, here: . . . of ambrosial-rain.

15.14: aham = I; vaiśvānaras = lit. "pertaining to all men," the digestive fire, here: retained in Sanskrit [from viśva "all" + nara "men"]; bhūtvā = having become, here: becoming; prāṇinām = of breathing [beings], here: living [beings]; deham = [in] body; āśritas = resorted, here: situated; prāṇāpānasamāyuktas (prāṇa + apāna + samāyuktas) = conjoined with in-breath [and] outbreath; pacāmi = I cook; annam = food; caturvidham = fourfold.

15.15: sarvasya = of all; cāham (ca + aham) = and I; hṛdi = in heart; saṃniviṣṭas = lodged; mattas = from me; smṛtis = memory; jñānam = knowledge; apohanam = reasoning; ca = and; vedais = by Vedas; ca = and; sarvais = by all; aham = I; eva = verily, here: left untranslated; vedyas = to be known; vedāntakṛt (vedānta + kṛt) = maker of Veda's end; vedavid (veda + vid) = knower of Vedas; eva = verily, here: also; cāham (ca + aham) = and I.

15.16: dvau (dual) = two; imau (dual) = these two; puruṣau (dual) = two spirits; loke = in world; kṣaras = perishable; cākṣaras (ca + akṣaras) = and imperishable; eva = verily, here: omitted; ca = and; kṣaras = perishable; sarvāṇi (plural) = all; bhūtāni = beings; kūṭasthas (kūṭa + sthas) = summit-abiding; 'kṣaras (akṣaras) = imperishable; ucyate = it is called.

15.17: uttamas = foremost, unexcelled; puruṣas = spirit; tu = but; anyas = other; paramātmeti (parama + ātmā + iti) = thus (iti) the supreme self, here: *iti* is used to indicate a quotation; udāhṛtas = named; yas = who; lokatrayam (loka + trayam) = triple world; āviśya = entering, here: penetrating; bibharti = he supports; avyayas = immutable; īśvaras = lord.

15.18: yasmāt = because, since; kṣaram = perishable; atītas = transcended; 'ham (aham) = I; akṣarāt = than the imperishable; api = even; cottamas (ca + uttamas) = and unexcelled, here: and higher; atas = thence, therefore; 'smi (asmi) = I am; loke = in world; vede = in Veda; ca = and; prathitas = extolled; puruṣottamas (puruṣa + uttamas) = Supreme Spirit.

15.19: yas = who; mām = me; evam = thus; asaṃmūḍhas = undeluded; jānāti = he knows; puruṣottamam (puruṣa + uttamam) = Supreme Spirit; sas = he; sarvavid (sarva + vid) = all-knowing; bhajati = he worships; mām = me; sarvabhāvena (sarva + bhāvena) = with all being; bhārata = O descendant-of-Bharata.

15.20: iti = thus; guhyatamam (guhya + tamam) = most secret; śāstram = teaching; idam = this; uktam = it is spoken, here: was declared; mayānagha (mayā + anagha) = by me, O Anagha; etad = this; buddhvā = having known, here: knowing; buddhimān = wise; syāt = he should be, here: he will be; kṛtakṛtyas (kṛta + kṛtyas) = work done (kṛta), here: work-fulfilled; ca = and; bhārata = O descendant-of-Bharata.

CHAPTER 16: THE YOGA OF THE DISTINCTION BETWEEN THE DIVINE AND DEMONIAC DESTINY

śrībhagavān (śrī + bhagavān) = Blessed Lord; uvāca = he said;

16.1: abhayam = fearlessness; sattvasaṃśuddhis (sattva + saṃśuddhis) = purity of sattva; jñānayogavyavasthitis (jñāna + yoga + vyavasthitis) = steadfastness in the Yoga of knowledge; dānam = gift, charity; damas = restraint; ca = and; yajñas = sacrifice; ca = and; svādhyāyas = self-study; tapas = austerity; ārjavam = uprightness;

16.2: ahiṃsā = nonharming; satyam = truthfulness; akrodhas = absence-of-anger; tyāgas = relinquishment; śantis = peace; apaiśunam = nonslandering; dayā = kindness; bhūteṣu = in [toward] beings; aloluptvam = nongreediness; mārdavam = gentleness; hrīs = modesty; acāpalam = absence-of-haste;

16.3: tejas = vigor; kṣamā = patience; dhṛtis = fortitude; śaucam = purity; adrohas = absence-of-malice; nātimānitā (na + atimānitā) = not excessive-pride, here: no . . . ; bhavanti = they become, they are; saṃpadam = destiny; daivīm = divine; abhijātasya = of [someone] born; bhārata = O descendant-of-Bharata.

16.4: dambhas = ostentation; darpas = arrogance; 'timānas (atimānas) = excessive-conceit; ca = and; krodhas = anger; pāruṣyam = harshness; eva = verily, here: left untranslated; ca = and, here: as well as; ajñānam = ignorance; cābhijātasya (ca + abhijātasya) = and of [someone] born; pārtha = O son-of-Prithā; saṃpadam = destiny; āsurīm = demonic.

16.5: daivī = divine; saṃpad = destiny; vimokṣāya = to liberation; nibandhāyāsurī (nibandhāya + asurī) = to bondage the demonic; matā (feminine) = is considered; mā = not; śucas = you grieve!; saṃpadam = destiny; daivīm = divine; abhijātas = born; 'si (asi) = you are; pāndava = O son-of-Pāndu.

16.6: dvau (dual) = two; bhūtasargau (bhūta + sargau) (dual) = [two] creations [of] beings, here: [two types of] beings have been created; loke = in world; 'smin (asmin) = in this; daivas = divine; āsuras = demonic; eva = verily, here: also; ca = and; daivas = divine; vistaraśas = extensively; proktas = proclaimed; āsuram = demonic; pārtha = O son-of-Prithā; me = of me, from me; śṛṇu = you hear!

16.7: pravṛttim = activity; ca = and; nivṛttim = cessation; ca = and; janās = people; na = not; vidus = they know; āsurās (plural) = demonic; na = not; śaucam = purity; nāpi (na + api) = not also, here: neither; cācāras (ca + ācāras) = and good-conduct, here: nor . . . ; na = not, here: nor; satyam = truthfulness; teṣu = in them; vidyate = it is found.

16.8: asatyam = untruthfulness, here: without truth; apratiṣṭham = unfounded, unsettled, here: without foundation; te = they; jagat = universe; āhus = they say; anīśvaram = ungodly, here: without a lord; aparasparasaṃbhūtam (aparaspara + saṃbhūtam) = not produced one by another, here: not produced in sequence; kim anyat = what else?; kāmahaitukam (kāma + haitukam) = caused by desire.

16.9: etām = this; dṛṣṭim = view; avaṣṭabhya = holding; naṣṭātmanas (naṣṭa + ātmanas) = lost selves; 'lpabuddhayas (alpa + buddhayas) (plural) = [having] little wisdom; prabhavanti = they arise, they come forth; ugrakarmāṇas (ugra + karmāṇas) (plural) = [doing] cruel actions; kṣayāya = for destruction; jagatas = of universe; 'hitās (ahitās) = enemies.

16.10: kāmam = desire; āśritya = resorting, here: depending; duṣpūram = insatiable; dambhamānamadānvitas (dambha + māna + mada + anvitas) = possessed (anvita) of ostentation, pride, [and] intoxication; mohāt = through delusion; gṛhitvāsadgrāhān (gṛhitvā + asat + grāhān) = having held untrue conceptions, here: holding . . . ; pravartante = they practice; 'śucivratās (aśuci + vratās) = impure vows.

16.11: cintām = worry, care, here: cares; aparimeyām (feminine) = innumerable; ca = and; pralayāntām (pralaya + antām) (feminine) = ending with dissolution (pralaya); upāśritās (plural) = dependent, here: obsessed with; kāmopabhogaparamās (kāma + upabhoga + paramās) (plural) = [having] gratification of desires [as] supreme; etāvat = so much, here: this [is all]; iti = thus, here: used to indicate a quotation; niścitās (plural) = convinced.

16.12: āśāpāśaśatais (āśā + pāśa + śatais) = by hundreds of cords of hope; baddhās (plural) = bound; kāmakrodhaparāyaṇās (kāma + krodha + parāyaṇās) = addicted to desire [and] anger (krodha); īhante = they seek; kāmabhogārtham (kāma + bhoga + artham) = purpose (artha) [of] gratifying (bhoga) desires; anyāyenārthasaṃcayān (anyāyena + artha + saṃcayān) (plural) = by other [i.e., unjust] [means] accumulating riches.

16.13: idam = this; adya = today; mayā = by me; labdham = gained; imam = this; prāpsye = I will fulfill; manoratham (manas +

ratham) = fancy [lit. "mind chariot"]; idam = this; astīdam (asti + idam) = it is this; api = also; me = of me, mine; bhaviṣyati = it will be; punas = again, here: also; dhanam = wealth.

16.14: asau = that; mayā = by me; hatas = slain; śatrus = enemy; haniṣye = I will slay; cāparān (ca + aparān) (plural) = and others; api = also; īśvaras = lord; 'ham (aham) = I; aham = I; bhogī = enjoyer; siddhas = perfected-one; 'ham (aham) = I; balavān = mighty; sukhī = happy.

16.15: āḍhyas = wealthy; 'bhijanavān (abhijanavān) = well-born; asmi = I am; kas = who?; 'nyas (anyas) = other, here: else; 'sti (asti) = he is; sadṛśas = equal, like; mayā = by me; yakṣye = I will sacrifice; dāsyāmi = I will give, here: I will be charitable; modiṣya (for modiṣye) = I will rejoice; iti = thus, here: used to indicate a quotation; ajñānavimohitās (ajñāna + vimohitās) (plural) = [those who are] deluded by ignorance.

16.16: anekacittavibhrāntās (aneka + citta + vibhrāntās) (plural) = [those who are] led astray by many (aneka) thoughts; mohajālasamāvṛtās (moha + jāla + samāvṛtās) (plural) = [those who are] entangled in a net (jāla) of delusion; prasaktās (plural) = attached, here: addicted; kāmabhogeṣu (kāma + bhogeṣu) = to enjoyments of desires, here: to gratification . . . ; patanti = they fall; narake = into hell; 'śucau (aśucau) = into impure.

16.17: ātmasaṃbhāvitās (ātma + saṃbhāvitās) (plural) = self-conceited; stabdhās (plural) = obstinate; dhanamānamadānvitās (dhana + māna + mada + anvitās) (plural) = full of intoxication (mada) [and] pride of wealth; yajante = they sacrifice, here: they perform; nāmayajñais (nāma + yajñais) = with nominal sacrifices; te = they; dambhenāvidhipūrvakam (dambhena + avidhi + pūrvakam) = with ostentation (dambha) [and] without (a-) following (pūrvaka) [proper] rules.

16.18: ahaṃkāram = ego-sense; balam = force; darpam = arrogance; kāmam = desire; krodham = anger; ca = and; saṃśritās (plural) = clinging; mām = me; ātmaparadeheṣu (ātma + para + deheṣu)

= in self [and] other bodies, here: in [their] own [and] other bodies; pradviṣantas (plural) = [those who] hate; 'bhyasūyakās (abhyasūyakās) (plural) = [those who are] indignant, envious, here: detractors.

16.19: tān = them, here: these; aham = I; dviṣatas (plural) = [those who hate], here: haters; krūrān (plural) = cruel; saṃsāreṣu = in cycles, here: into the cycle; narādhamān (nara + adhamān) (plural) = lowest of men; kṣipāmi = I hurl; ajasram = incessantly; aśubhān (plural) = [those who are] inauspicious; āsurīṣu = in demonic; eva = verily, here: left untranslated; yoniṣu = in wombs.

16.20: āsurīm = demonic; yonim = womb; āpannā = attaining, here: falling; mūḍhās (plural) = deluded; janmani janmani = in birth after birth; mām = me; aprāpyaiva (aprāpya + eva) = not reaching verily; kaunteya = O son-of-Kuntī; tatas = thence; yānti = they go, they tread; adhamām (feminine) = lowest; gatim = course.

16.21: trividham = threefold; narakasyedam (narakasya + idam) = of hell this; dvāram = gate; nāśanam = destruction; ātmanas = of self; kāmas = desire; krodhas = anger; tathā = thus, as well as; lobhas = greed; tasmāt = therefore; etad = this; trayam = triad; tyajet = one should abandon.

16.22: etais = from these; vimuktas = released; kaunteya = O son-of-Kuntī; tamodvārais (tamas + dvārais) = from darkness (tamas) gates; tribhis = from three; naras = man; ācarati = he pursues; ātmanas = of self, here: for [him]self; śreyas = best; tatas = thence; yāti = he goes, he treads; parām (feminine) = supreme; gatim = course.

16.23: yas = who; śāstravidhim (śāstra + vidhim) = scriptural (śāstra) ordinance; utsṛjya = discarding; vartate = he turns, he follows; kāmakāratas (kāma + kāratas) = desire-making, here: prompting of desires; na = not; sas = he; siddhim = perfection; avāpnoti = reaches; na = not, here: nor; sukham = joy; na = not, here: nor; parām (feminine) = supreme; gatim = course.

16.24: tasmāt = therefore; śāstram = scripture; pramāṇam = standard; te = of you, here: you; kāryākāryavyavasthitau (kāryā + akārya + vyavasthitau) (dual) = to-be-done and not-to-be-done, here: right and wrong; jñātvā = having known, here: knowing; śāstravidhānoktam (śāstra + vidhāna + uktam) = said [or prescribed] (ukta) by scriptural injunction; karma = action; kartum = to do, to perform; ihārhasi (iha + arhasi) = here you are able, here you should [perform].

CHAPTER 17: THE YOGA OF DISTINCTION BETWEEN THE TRIPLE FAITH

arjunas = Arjuna; uvāca = he said;

17.1: ye (plural) = who; śāstravidhim = scriptural (śāstra) ordinance; utsṛjya = discarding; yajante = they worship, here: they perform; śraddhayānvitās = with faith (śraddhā) endowed; teṣām = them; niṣṭhā (feminine) = way-of-life; tu = but, indeed, here: left untranslated; kā (feminine) = what?; kṛṣṇa = O Krishna; sattvam = retained in Sanskrit; āho = is it so, here: represented by a question mark; rajas = retained in Sanskrit; tamas = retained in Sanskrit.

śrībhagavān (śrī + bhagavān) = Blessed Lord; uvāca = he said;

17.2: trividhā (feminine) = threefold; bhavati = it becomes, it is; śraddhā = faith; dehinām (plural) = of embodied-ones, here: of body-essences; sā = she [i.e., śraddhā], here: the; svabhāvajā (feminine) = born of own-being; sāttvikī = sattva-natured; rājasī = rajas-natured; caiva (ca + eva) = and verily, here: both left untranslated; tāmasī = tamas-natured; ceti (ca + iti) = and thus, here: or, with *iti* being omitted; tām (feminine) = of this; śṛṇu = you listen!, you hear!

17.3: sattvānurūpā (sattva + anurūpā) (feminine) = corresponding, here: it corresponds to; sarvasya = of all, here: of every [being]; śraddhā = faith; bhavati = it becomes, it is; bhārata = O descendant-of-Bharata; śraddhāmayas (śraddhā + mayas) = made of faith; 'yam (ayam) = this; puruṣas = spirit; yas = who;

yacchraddhas (yad + śraddhas) = which having-faith, here: whatever [his] faith; sas = he; eva = verily; sas = he.

17.4: yajante = they worship; sāttvikās (plural) = sattva-natured; devān = gods; yakṣaraksāṃsi = Yakshas [and] Rakshasas; rājasās (plural) = rajas-natured; pretān = the departed; bhūtagaṇān (bhūta + gaṇān) = hosts of elementals (bhūta); cānye (ca + anye) = and others; yajante = they worship; tāmasās (plural) = tamas-natured; janās (plural) = people.

17.5–17.6: aśāstravihitam (aśāstra + vihitam) = not ordained by scripsture, here: . . . by the scriptures; ghoram = horrific; tapyante = they endure; ye (plural) = who; tapas = austerity; janās (plural) = people; dambhāhaṃkārasaṃyuktas (dambha + ahaṃkāra + saṃyuktās) = connected with ostentation [and] ego-sense, here: possessed of . . . ; kāmarāgabalānvitās (kāma + rāga + bala + anvitās (plural) = endowed with the force (bala) [of] desire [and] passion, here: filled with . . . ; karśayantas (plural) = causing-to-plow, here: oppressing; śarīrastham (śarīra + stham) = abiding (stha) in body; bhūtagrāmam (bhūta + grāmam) = aggregate of elements; acetasas = unthinking, thoughtlessly; mām = me; caivāntaḥśarīrastham (ca + eva + antas + śarīra + stham) = and (ca) verily (eva) abiding (stha) within (antas) the body, here: *eva* is translated as "also"; tān = them; viddhi = you know!; āsuraniścayān (āsura + niścayān) (plural) = [having] demonic intention.

17.7: āhāras = food; tu = indeed, here: omitted; api = also, even; sarvasya = of all, here: to all; trividhas = threefold; bhavati = it becomes, it is; priyas = dear; yajñas = sacrifice; tapas = austerity; tathā = thus, here: so; dānam = gift, charity; tesām = of them; bhedam = distinction; imam = this; śṛṇu = you hear!, you listen!

17.8: āyuḥsattvabalārogyasukhaprītivivardhanās (āyus + sattva + bala + ārogya + sukha + prīti + vivardhanās) (plural) = promoting (vivardhana) life (āyu), essence (sattva), strength (bala), health (ārogya), joy (sukha), [and] delight (prīti); rasyās (plural) = savory; snigdhās (plural) = rich-in-oil; sthirās (plural) =

firm; hṛdyās (plural) = heart[-gladdening]; āhārās = foods; sāttvikapriyās (sāttvika + priyās) (plural) = dear to sattva-natured.

17.9: kaṭvamlalavaṇātyuṣṇatīkṣṇarukṣavidāhinas (kaṭu + amla + lavaṇa + atyuṣṇa + tīkṣṇa + rūkṣa + vidāhinas) (plural) = pungent, sour, salty, hot, sharp, harsh [and] burning; āhārās (plural) = foods; rājasasyeṣṭās (rājasasya + iṣṭās) (plural) = coveted by rajas-natured; duḥkhaśokāmayapradās (duḥkha + śoka + āmaya + pradās) (plural) = causing pain, grief, [and] disease, here: [they] cause . . .

17.10: yātayāmam = spoiled; gatarasam (gata + rasam) = tasteless [lit. "gone taste"]; pūti = putrid; paryuṣitam = stale; ca = and; yad = which; ucchiṣṭam = left over; api = also, here: omitted; cāmedhyam (ca + amedhyam) = and unclean; bhojanam = food; tāmasapriyam (tāmasa + priyam) = dear (priya) to a tamas-natured [individual].

17.11: aphalākāṅkṣibhis (aphala + ākāṅkṣibhis) = [those who do] not (a-) hanker after the fruit; yajñas = sacrifice; vidhidṛṣṭas (vidhi + dṛṣṭas) (singular) = observing [scriptural] ordinance; yas = who, which; ijyate = it is offered; yaṣṭavyam = to be sacrificed; eveti (eva + iti) = verily, thus, here: *eva* is omitted and *iti* is used to indicate a quotation; manas = mind; samādhāya = concentrating; sas = he, here: that; sāttvikas = sattva-natured.

17.12: abhisaṃdhāya = having in view, here: in expectation; tu = but; phalam = fruit; dambhārtham (dambha + artham) = [for] purpose (artha) of ostentation; api = also; caiva (ca + eva) = and verily, here: *eva* is omitted; yad = which; ijyate = it is offered; bharataśreṣṭha (bharata + śreṣṭha) = O Bharatashreshtha; tam = that; yajñam = sacrifice; viddhi = you know!; rājasam = rajas-natured.

17.13: vidhihīnam (vidhi + hīnam) = lacking (hīna) ordinance; asṛṣṭānnam (asṛṣṭa + annam) = not (a-) offered food; mantrahīnam (mantra + hīnam) = lacking (hīna) mantras; adakṣiṇam = without (a-) remuneration; śraddhāvirahitam (śraddhā + virahitam) = devoid of faith; yajñam = sacrifice; tāmasam = tamas-nature; paricakṣate = it is declared.

17.14: devadvijaguruprājñapūjanam (deva + dvija + guru + prājña + pūjanam) = worship (pūjana) [of] gods, twice-born, teachers, the wise; śaucam = purity; ārjavam = uprightness; brahmacaryam (brahma + caryam) = chastity [lit. "brahmic conduct"]; ahiṃsā = nonharming; ca = and; śarīram = body, bodily; tapas = austerity; ucyate = it is called.

17.15: anudvegakaram (anudvega + karam) = causing (kara) no (an-) disquiet, here: [which] causes . . . ; vākyam = speech; satyam = truthfulness, truthful; priyahitam (priya + hitam) = dear [or pleasant] [and] beneficial (hita); ca = and; yad = which; svādhyāyābhyasanam (svādhyāya + abhyasanam) = practice (abhyasana) of self-study; caiva (ca + eva) = and indeed, here: and also; vāṅmayam (vāc + mayam) = speech formed, here: concerning (maya) speech; tapas = austerity; ucyate = it is called.

17.16: manaḥprasādas (manas + prasādas) = serenity (prasāda) of mind; saumyatvam = gentleness; maunam = silence; ātmavinigrahas (ātma + vinigrahas) = self-restraint; bhāvasaṃśuddhis (bhāva + saṃśuddhis) = purification (saṃśuddhi) of states; iti = thus, here: omitted; etad = this; tapas = austerity; mānasam = mental; ucyate = it is called.

17.17: śraddhayā = with faith; parayā = with supreme; taptam = endured; tapas = austerity; tad = this, that; trividham = threefold; narais = by men; aphalākāṅkṣibhis (aphala + ākāṅkṣibhis) = not (a-) hankering after the fruit; yuktais (plural) = by yoked; sāttvikam = sattva-natured; paricakṣate = it is declared.

17.18: satkāramānapūjārtham (satkāra + māna + pūjā + artham) = for the sake (artha) of good treatment (sat + kāra), honor, reverence (pūjā); tapas = austerity; dambhena = with ostentation, here: out of ostentation; caiva (ca + eva) = and verily, here: *eva* is omitted; yad = which; kriyate = it is done, it is performed; tad

= this, that; iha = here; proktam = proclaimed; rājasam = rajas-natured; calam = fickle; adhruvam = unsteady.

17.19: mūḍhagrāheṇātmanas (mūḍha + grāheṇa + ātmanas) = with deluded notion (grāha) of self; yad = which; pīḍayā = with torture, here: of torturing; kriyate = it is done, it is performed; tapas = austerity; parasyotsādanārtham (parasya + utsādana + artham) = for the sake (artha) of ruining (utsādana) another; vā = or; tad = this, that; tāmasam = tamas-natured; udāhṛtam = described.

17.20: dātavyam = [ought] to be given; iti = thus, here: used to indicate a quotation; yad = which; dānam = charity, gift; dīyate = it is given; 'nupakāriṇe (anupakāriṇe) (singular) = to [him from whom] no (an-) favor [can be expected]; deśe = in place, here: at . . . ; kāle = in time, here: at . . .; ca = and; pātre (singular) = to worthy-recipient; ca = and; tad = this, that; dānam = charity, gift; sāttvikam = sattva-natured; smṛtam = remembered, here: held.

17.21: yad = which; tu = but; pratyupakārārtham (pratyupakāra + artham) = for sake (artha) of favor; phalam = fruit; uddiśya = aiming, here: [that] aims; vā = or; punas = again; dīyate = it is given; ca = and; parikliṣṭam = reluctantly; tad = this, that; dānam = charity, gift; rājasam = rajas-natured; smṛtam = remembered, here: held.

17.22: adeśakāle (adeśa + kāle) = not (a-) in [proper] place [and] time; yad = which; dānam = charity, gift; apātrebhyas (plural) = to unworthy-recipients; ca = and; dīyate = it is given; asatkṛtam (asat + kṛtam) = badly treated, here: disrespect; avajñātam = contemptuously; tad = this, that; tāmasam = tamas-natured; udāhṛtam = described.

17.23: oṃ = retained in Sanskrit; tad = this, that, here: retained in Sanskrit; sat = existence, real, here: retained in Sanskrit; iti = thus, here: used to indicate quotation; nirdeśas = designation; brahmaṇas = of Brahman; trividhas = threefold, triple; smṛtas = remembered, here: held; brāhmaṇās = priests, here: retained in Sanskrit; tena = by this; vedās = Vedas; ca = and; yajñās = sacrifices; ca = and; vihitās = ordained; purā = of old.

17.24: tasmāt = therefore; om = retained in Sanskrit; iti = thus, here: used to indicate a quotation; udāhṛtya = uttering; yajñadānatapaḥkriyās (yajña + dāna + tapas + kriyās) = rituals (kriyā) of sacrifice, charity [and] austerity; pravartante = they perform; vidhānoktās (vidhāna + uktās) = declared by prescription; satatam = always; brahmavādinām (brahma + vādinām) = Brahman expounders.

17.25: tad = this, that; iti = thus, here: used to indicate a quotation; anabhisaṃdhāya = without (an-) aiming at; phalam = fruit; yajñatapaḥkriyās (yajña + tapas + kriyās) = rituals of sacrifice [and] austerity; dānakriyās (dāna + kriyās) = rituals of charity; ca = and, here: as well as; vividhās (plural) = varied; kriyante = they do, they perform; mokṣakāṅkṣibhis (mokṣa + kāṅkṣibhis) = by [those] hankering after liberation.

17.26: sadbhāve (sat + bhāve) = in [the sense of] real; sādhubhāve (sādhu + bhāve) = in [the sense of] good; ca = and; sat = existence, real; iti = used to indicate a quotation; etad = this; prayujyate = it is employed; praśaste = in [respect to] praiseworthy; karmaṇi = in [respect to] actions; tathā = thus, here: also; sacchabdas (sat + śabdas) = word *sat*; pārtha = O son-of-Prithā; yujyate = it is employed.

17.27: yajñe = in sacrifice; tapasi = in austerity; dāne = in charity; ca = and; sthitis = steadfastness; sat = retained in Sanskrit; iti = used to indicate a quotation; cocyate (ca + ucyate) = and it is called; karma = action; caiva (ca + eva) = and verily, here: also; tad = this, that; arthīyam = for purpose; sat = retained in Sanskrit; iti = used to indicate a quotation; evābhidhīyate (eva + abhidhīyate) = verily it is designated, here: *eva* is omitted.

17.28: aśraddhayā = without (a-) faith; hutam = oblation; dattam = offered; tapas = austerity; taptam = endured; kṛtam = done; ca

= and; yad = which, here: whatever; asat = retained in Sanskrit; iti = thus, here: used to indicate a quotation; ucyate = it is called; pārtha = O son-of-Prithā; na = not, here: no; ca = and; tad = this, that; pretya = having gone, the hereafter; nas = of us, to us; iha = here.

CHAPTER 18: THE YOGA OF RENUNCIATION AND LIBERATION

arjunas = Arjuna; uvāca = he said;

18.1: saṃnyāsasya = of renunciation, here: about . . . ; mahābaho (mahā + baho) = O mighty-armed [Krishna]; tattvam = truth; icchāmi = I wish; veditum = to know; tyāgasya = of relinquishment, here: about . . . ; ca = and; hṛśīkeśa (hṛśī + keśa) = O Hrishīkesha; pṛthak = apart [from this]; keśiniṣūdana (keśi + niṣūdana) = O Keshinishūdana.

śrībhagavān (śrī + bhagavān) = Blessed Lord; uvāca = he said;

18.2: kāmyānām = of desiderative, here: of desire-born; karmaṇām = of action; nyāsam = casting-off; saṃnyāsam = renunciation; kavayas = bards; vidus = they know; sarvakarmaphalatyāgam (sarva + karma + phala + tyāgam) = relinquishment (tyāga) of all action's fruit; prāhus = they declare; tyāgam = relinquishment; vicakṣaṇās (plural) = clear-eyed, here: sages.

18.3: tyājyam = to be relinquished; doṣavat = full-of-flaws; iti = thus, here: used to indicate a quotation; eke (plural) = some; karma = action; prāhus = they declare; manīṣiṇas (plural) = thoughtful [people]; yajñadānatapaḥkarma (yajña + dāna + tapas + karma) = acts [of] sacrifice, charity, austerity; na = not; tyājyam = to be relinquished; iti = thus, here: used to indicate a quotation; cāpare (ca + apare) = and others.

18.4: niścayam = conviction; śṛṇu = you hear!, you listen!; me = of me, my; tatra = in that; tyāge = in [regard to] relinquishment, here: about relinquishment; bharatasattama (bharata + sattama) = O Bharatasattama; tyāgas = relinquishment; hi = indeed, here: omitted; puruṣavyāghra (puruṣa + vyāghra) = O man-tiger; trividhas = threefold; saṃprakīrtitas = declared.

18.5: yajñadānatapaḥkarma (yajña + dāna + tapas + karma) = acts [of] sacrifice, charity, [and] austerity; na = not; tyājyam = to be relinquished; kāryam = to be performed; eva = verily; tad = this, that; yajñas = sacrifice; dānam = charity; tapas = austerity; caiva (ca + eva) = and verily, here: *eva* is omitted; pāvanāni = purifiers; manīṣiṇām (plural) = of thoughtful [people], here: for . . .

18.6: etāni = these; api = even; tu = but; karmaṇi = actions; saṅgam = attachment; tyāktvā = having relinqished; phalāni = fruits; ca = and; kartavyānīti (kartavyāni + iti) (plural) = to be performed; me = of me, my; pārtha = O son-of-Prithā; niścitam = conclusive, decided; matam = opinion, conviction; uttamam = unexcelled, here: ultimate.

18.7: niyatasya = of obligatory, here: of necessary; tu = but; saṃnyāsas = renunciation; karmaṇas = of action; nopapadyate (na + upapadyate) = it is not appropriate, here: it is inappropriate; mohāt = from delusion; tasya = of it; parityāgas = relinquishment; tāmasas = tamas-natured; parikīrtitas = proclaimed.

18.8: duḥkham = suffering, pain; iti = thus, here: omitted; eva = verily, here: omitted; yad = which, here: omitted; karma = action; kāyakleśabhayāt (kāya + kleśa + bhayāt) = due to fear (bhaya) [of] bodily (kāya) affliction (kleśa); tyajet = he should abandon; sas = he; kṛtvā = having done, here: performing; rājasam = rajas-natured; tyāgam = relinquishment; naiva (na + eva) = not verily; tyāgaphalam (tyāga + phalam) = fruit [of] relinquishment; labhet = he should attain, he would, here: he will attain.

18.9: kāryam = to be done; iti = thus, here: omitted; eva = indeed; yad = which, here: that; karma = action; niyatam = necessary; kriyate = he does, he performs; 'rjuna (arjuna) = O Arjuna; saṅgam = attachment; tyāktvā = having relinquished, here:

relinquishing; phalam = fruit; caiva (ca + eva) = and also; sas (masculine) = he, here: it; tyāgas = relinquishment; sāttvikas = sattva-natured; matas = deemed.

18.10: na = not; dveṣṭi = he hates; akuśalam = uncongenial; karma = action; kuśale = congenial; nānuṣajjate (na + anuṣajjate) = he is not attached, here: nor is he attached; tyāgī = relinquisher; sattvasamāviṣṭas (sattva + samāviṣṭas) = suffused with sattva; medhāvī = intelligent; chinnasaṃśayas (chinna + saṃśayas) = severed doubt.

18.11: na = not; hi = for; dehabhṛtā (deha + bhṛtā) = body-wearer; śakyam = possible; tyaktum = to relinquish; karmāṇi = actions; aśeṣatas = entirely; yas = who; tu = rather; karmaphalatyāgī (karma + phala + tyāgī) = relinquisher [of] action's fruit; sas = he; tyāgīti (tyāgī + iti) = relinquisher thus, here: *iti* is used to indicate a quotation; abhidhīyate = he is designated.

18.12: aniṣṭam = unwanted; iṣṭam = wanted; miśram = mixed; ca = and; trividham = threefold; karmaṇas = of action; phalam = fruit; bhavati = it becomes, it is; atyāginām (a + tyāginām) = of non-relinquishers; pretya = departing [i.e., dying]; na = not, here: none; tu = but; saṃnyāsinām = of renouncers; kvacit = any whatsoever.

18.13: pañcaitāni (pañca + etāni) = these (etāni) five, here: the [following] five; mahābaho (mahā + baho) = O mighty-armed [Arjuna]; karaṇāni = causes; nibodha = you learn!; me = from me; sāṃkhye = in Sāmkhya; kṛtānte (kṛta + ante) = in conclusion, here: in system; proktāni (plural) = proclaimed; siddhaye = for accomplishment; sarvakarmaṇām (sarva + karmaṇām) = of all actions.

18.14: adhiṣṭhānam = [physical] basis; tathā = also; kartā = agent; karaṇam = instrument; ca = and; pṛthagvidham (pṛthag + vidham) = various kind, here: various kinds; vividhās (plural) = multifarious; ca = and; pṛthakceṣṭā (pṛthak + ceṣṭā) = distinct activity; daivam = fate; caivātra (ca + eva + atra) = and indeed here, here: *evātra* is omitted; pañcamam = fifth.

18.15: śarīravāṅmanobhis (śarīra + vāc +manobhis) = with body, speech, [or] mind; yad = which, here: whatever; karma = action; prārabhate = he undertakes; naras = man; nyāyyam = proper; vā = or; viparītam = reverse, here: otherwise; vā = or; pañcaite (pañca + ete) = these five; tasya = of it; hetavas = causes.

18.16: tatraivam (tatra + evam) = in this thus, here: this [being] so; sati = being; kartāram = agent; ātmānam = [him]self; kevalam = alone, here: merely; tu = indeed, here: left untranslated; yas = who; paśyati = he sees; akṛtabuddhitvāt (akṛta + buddhitvāt) = due to incomplete (akṛta) wisdom; na = not; sas = he, here: that; paśyati = sees; durmatis = dull-wit.

18.17: yasya = whose; nāhaṃkṛtas (na + ahaṃ + kṛtas) = not I-made, here: not ego-driven; bhāvas = state; buddhis = wisdom-faculty; yasya = whose; na = not; lipyate = it is defiled; hatvāpi (hatvā + api) = though (api) having slain, here: though slaying; sas = he; imān = these; lokān = worlds; na = not; hanti = he slays; na = not, here: nor; nibadhyate = he is bound.

18.18: jñānam = knowledge; jñeyam = to be known; parijñātā = knower; trividhā (feminine) = threefold; karmacodanā (karma + codanā) = impulse [to] action; karaṇam = instrument; karma = action; karteti (kartā + iti) = agent thus; trividhas = threefold; karmasaṃgrahas (karma + saṃgrahas) = nexus [of] action.

18.19: jñānam = knowledge; karma = action; ca = and; kartā = agent; ca = and; tridhaivas = threefold; guṇabhedatas (guṇa + bhedatas) = from the division of the primary-qualities; procyate = it is declared; guṇasaṃkhyāne (guṇa + saṃkhyāne) = in reckoning of the primary-qualities; yathāvat = duly, rightly; śṛṇu = you hear!; tāni = these; api = also, as well.

18.20: sarvabhūteṣu (sarva + bhūteṣu) = in all beings; yenaikam (yena + ekam) = by which one; bhāvam = state-of-existence; avyayam = immutable; īkṣate = he sees; avibhaktam = undivided; vibhakteṣu = in divided; tad = this, that; jñānam = knowledge; viddhi = you know!; sāttvikam = sattva-natured.

18.21: pṛthaktvena = by separateness; tu = but; yad = which; jñānam = knowledge; nānābhāvān (nānā + bhāvān) = various states-of-existence; pṛthagvidhān (pṛthag + vidhān) = several kinds; vetti = [which] knows, here: [which] recognizes; sarveṣu = in all; bhūteṣu = in beings; tad = this, that; jñānam = knowledge; viddhi = you know!; rājasam = rajas-natured.

18.22: yad = which; tu = but, here: again; kṛtsnavat = like whole, here: as if [it were] whole; ekasmin = in one; kārye = in [what is] to be done, here: effect; saktam = attached; ahaitukam = without (a-) [due] cause; atattvārthavat (atattva + arthavat) = without (a-) concern for reality (tattva); alpam = small, slight; ca = and; tad = this, that; tāmasam = tamas-natured; udāhṛtam = described.

18.23: niyatam = necessary; saṅgarahitam (saṅga + rahitam) = without (rahita) attachment; arāgadveṣatas (arāga + dveṣatas) = without (a-) passion (rāga) [or] aversion; kṛtam = done; aphalaprepsunā (aphala + prepsunā) = by [one who] craves not (a-) the fruit; karma = action; yad = which; tad = this, that; sāttvikam = sattva-natured; ucyate = it is called.

18.24: yad = which; tu = but; kāmepsunā (kāma + īpsunā) = by [one who] craves desires; karma = action; sāhaṃkāreṇa (sa + ahaṃkāreṇa) = with (sa) ego-sense; vā = or; punas = again, here: [or] else; kriyate = he performs; bahulāyāsam (bahula + āyāsam) = [with] great strain; tad = this, that; rājasam = rajas-natured; udāhṛtam = described.

18.25: anubandham = consequence; kṣayam = loss; hiṃsām = hurt; anapekṣya = disregarding, here: without regard to; ca = and; pauruṣam = human-capacity; mohāt = out of delusion; ārabhyate = it is undertaken; karma = action; yad = which; tad = this, that; tāmasam = tamas-nature; ucyate = it is called.

18.26: muktasaṅgas (mukta + saṅgas) = freed from attachment; 'nahaṃvādī (anaham + vādī) = not (an-) I-sayer; dhṛtyutsāhasamanvitas (dhṛti + utsāha + samanvitas) = endowed with steadfastness (dhṛti) [and] zeal; siddhyasiddhyos (siddhi + asiddhyos) (dual) = in success and failure; nirvikāras = unchanged; kartā = agent; sāttvika = sattva-nature; ucyate = he is called.

18.27: rāgī = passionate; karmaphalaprepsus (karma + phala + prepsus) = craving for the fruit of action; lubdhas = greedy; hiṃsātmakas (hiṃsā + ātmakas) = [of] violent nature; 'śucis (aśucis) = impure; harṣaśokānvitas (harṣa + śoka + anvitas) = endowed with elation [and] grief, here: subject to elation and depression (śoka); kartā = agent; rājasas = rajas-natured; parikīrtitas = proclaimed.

18.28: ayuktas = unyoked; prakṛtas = uncultured; stabdhas = obstinate; śathas = deceitful; naikṛtikas = base; 'lasas (alasas) = lazy; viṣādī = despondent; dīrghasūtrī (dīrgha + sūtrī) = long-threaded; ca = and; kartā = agent; tāmasa = tamas-nature; ucyate = he is called.

18.29: buddhes = of wisdom-faculty; bhedam = distinction; dhṛtes = of steadfastness; caiva (ca + eva) = and also; guṇatas = [based on] primary-qualities; trividham = threefold; śṛṇu = you hear!; procyamānam = explaining, here: [I will] explain; aśeṣeṇa = unreservedly; pṛthaktvena = separately; dhanaṃjaya (dhanam + jaya) = O Dhanamjaya.

18.30: pravṛttim = activity; ca = and; nivṛttim = cessation; ca = and; kāryākārye (kārya + akārye) (dual) = right and wrong; bhayābhaye (bhaya + abhaye) (dual) = fear and fearlessness; bandham = bondage; mokṣam = liberation; ca = and; yā (feminine) = which; vetti = it knows; buddhis = wisdom-faculty; sā = she [i.e., buddhi]; pārtha = O son-of-Prithā; sāttvikī (feminine) = sattva-natured.

18.31: yayā (feminine) = by which; dharmam = law; adharmam = anomie, lawlessness; ca = and; kāryam = right; cākāryam (ca + akāryam) = and wrong; eva = verily, here: left untranslated; ca = and, here: as well as; ayathāvat = incorrectly; prajānāti = it knows; buddhis = wisdom-faculty; sā = she [i.e., buddhi]; pārtha = O son-of-Prithā; rājasī (feminine) = rajas-natured.

18.32: adharmam = lawlessness; dharmam = law; iti = thus, here: used to indicate a quotation; yā (feminine) = which; manyate = it thinks; tamasāvṛtā (tamasā + āvṛtā) (feminine) = enveloped by darkness (tamas); sarvārthān (sarva + arthān) = all things; viparītān (plural) = reversed; ca = and; buddhis = wisdom-faculty; sā = she [i.e., buddhi]; pārtha = O son-of-Prithā; tāmasī (feminine) = tamas-natured.

18.33: dhṛtyā = by steadfastness; yayā (feminine) = by which; dhārayate = she [i.e., dhṛti] holds; manaḥprāṇendriyakriyās (manas + prāṇa + indriya + kriyās) = activities (kriyā) of mind, life-force, [and] senses; yogenāvyabhicāriṇyā (yogena + avyabhicāriṇyā) = through unswerving Yoga; dhṛtis = steadfastness; sā = she [i.e., dhṛti]; pārtha = O son-of-Prithā; sāttvikī = sattva-natured.

18.34: yayā (feminine) = by which; tu = but; dharmakāmārthān (dharma + kāma + arthān) (plural) = law, desire, wealth; dhṛtyā = with steadfastness; dhārayate = it holds; 'rjuna (arjuna) = O Arjuna; prasaṅgena = with attachment; phalākāṅkṣī (phala + ākāṅkṣī) = hankering after the fruit; dhṛtis = steadfastness; sā = she [i.e. dhṛti]; pārtha = O son-of-Prithā; rājasī (feminine) = rajas-natured.

18.35: yayā (feminine) = by which; svapnam = sleep; bhayam = fear; śokam = grief; viṣādam = despondency; madam = intoxication; eva = verily, here: omitted; ca = and; na = not; vimuñcati = he abandons, here: he avoids; durmedhā = dull-minded; dhṛtis = steadfastness; sā = she [i.e., dhṛti]; pārtha = O son-of-Prithā; tāmasī (feminine) = tamas-natured.

18.36: sukham = pleasure, here: happiness; tu = but; idānīm = now; trividham = threefold; śṛṇu = you hear!; me = from me; bharatarṣabha (bharata + ṛṣabha) = O Bharatarshabha; abhyāsāt ramate = he rejoiced from practice, here: . . . after practice; yatra = where, here: wherein; duḥkhāntam (duḥkha + antam) = end of suffering; ca = and; nigacchati = he goes, he reaches.

18.37: yad = which; tad = this, that, here: left untranslated; agre = in the beginning; viṣam = poison; iva = like; pariṇāme = upon transformation, here: when transformed; 'mṛtopamam (amṛta + upamam) = resembling nectar (amṛta), here: like nectar; tad = this, that; sukham = pleasure, here: happiness; sāttvikam = sattva-natured; proktam = proclaimed; ātmabuddhiprasādajam (ātma + buddhi + prasāda + jam) = born (ja) from the serenity-grace (prasāda) of self's wisdom (buddhi).

18.38: viṣayendriyasaṃyogāt (viṣaya + indriya + saṃyogāt) = union [of] objects [and] senses; yad = which; tad = this, that; agre = in the beginning; 'mṛtopamam (amṛta + upamam) = resembling nectar, here: like nectar; pariṇāme = upon transformation, here: when transformed; viṣam = poison; iva = like; tad = this, that; sukham = pleasure, here: happiness; rājasam = rajas-natured; smṛtam = remembered, here: held.

18.39: yad = which; agre = in the beginning; cānubandhe (ca + anubandhe) = and upon consequence, here: and in the sequel; ca = and; sukham = pleasure, here: happiness; mohanam = deluding, here: it deludes; ātmanas = of self; nidrālasyapramādottham (nidrā + ālasya + pramāda + uttham) = arising from sleep, indolence, [and] heedlessness; tad = this, that; tāmasam = tamas-natured; udāhṛtam = described.

18.40: na = not, here: no; tad = this, that; asti = it is, there is; pṛthivyām = on earth; vā = or; divi = in heaven; deveṣu = among gods; vā = or; punas = again; sattvam = being; prakṛtijais (prakṛti + jais) = from [guṇas] born of the Cosmos; muktam = freed, free from; yad = which; ebhis = by these; syāt = it may be; tribhis = from three; guṇais = from primary-qualities.

18.41: brāhmaṇakṣatriyaviśām (brāhmaṇa + kṣatriya + viśām) = of brāhmanas (priests), warriors, [and] merchants; śūdrānām = of serfs; ca = and; paraṃtapa (param + tapa) = O Paramtapa; karmāṇi = actions; pravibhaktāni (plural) = apportioned; svabhāvaprabhāvais (svabhāva + prabhāvais) = by arising [in their] own-being; guṇais = by primary-qualities.

18.42: śamas = calm; damas = restraint; tapas = austerity; śaucam = purity; kṣāntis = patience; ārjavam = uprightness; eva = verily, here: omitted; ca = and; jñānam = knowledge; vijñānam = [worldly-]knowledge; āstikyam = piety; brahmakarma (brahma + karma) = activity (karman) of a brāhmaṇa, here: behavior (karman) . . . ; svabhāvajam (sva + bhāva + jam) = born [of his] own-nature.

18.43: śauryam = courage; tejas = brilliance, here: vigor; dhṛtis = steadfastness; dākṣyam = resourcefulness; yuddhe = in battle; cāpi (ca + api) = and also; apalāyanam = non-fleeing, here: unwillingness-to-flee; dānam = generosity; īśvarabhāvas (īśvara + bhāvas) = lordly state-of-existence, here: regal disposition; ca = and; kṣātram = military, here: warrior; karma = action, here: behavior; svabhāvajam (sva + bhāva + jam) = born (ja) [of his] own-being.

18.44: kṛṣigaurakṣyavāṇijyam (kṛṣi + gaurakṣya + vāṇijyam) = agriculture (kṛṣi, for kṛṣikā), cattle-tending, [and] trade; vaiśyakarma (vaiśya + karma) = merchant activity, here: behavior of a merchant; svabhāvajam (sva + bhāva + jam) = born [of his] own-being; paricaryātmakam (paricaryā + ātmakam) = [of] the nature (ātmaka) of service; karma = action, here: behavior; śūdrasyāpi (śūdrasya + api) = of a serf moreover; svabhāvajam (sva + bhāva + jam) = born [of his] own-being.

18.45: sve sve = each [his] own; karmaṇi = actions; abhiratas = content; saṃsiddhim = consummation; labhate = he attains; naras = man; svakarmaniratas (sva + karma + niratas) = content in own action; siddhim = success; yathā = just as, here: how; vindati = he finds; tad = this, that; śṛṇu = you hear!

18.46: yatas = from whom; pravṛttis = activity; bhūtānām = of beings; yena = by whom; sarvam = all; idam = this; tatam = spread out; svakarmaṇā (sva + karmaṇā) = by own action; tam = that, here: him; abhyarcya = worshiping; siddhim = success; vindati = he finds; mānavas = human.

18.47: śreyān = better; svadharmas (sva + dharmas) = own-law; vigunas = imperfectly; paradharmāt (para + dharmāt) = than another's law; svanuṣṭhitat (su + anuṣṭhitat) = than well-performed; svabhāvaniyatam (sva + bhāva + niyatam) = necessitated by own-being; karma = action; kurvan = performing; nāpnoti (na + āpnoti) = he accumulates not (na); kilbiṣam = guilt.

18.48: sahajam = innate; karma = action; kaunteya = O son-of-Kuntī; sadoṣam = defective; api = even; na = not; tyajet = he should relinquish; sarvārambhās (sarva + ārambhās) = all undertakings; hi = for; doṣeṇa = with flaw, here: by flaws; dhūmenāgnis (dhūmena + agnis) = fire with smoke; ivāvṛtās (iva + āvṛtās) (plural) = veiled as it were.

18.49: asaktabuddhis (asakta + buddhis) = unattached wisdom-faculty; sarvatra = everywhere; jitātmā (jita + ātmā) = subdued self; vigataspṛhas (vigata + spṛhas) = gone longing; naiṣkarmyasiddhim (naiṣkarmya + siddhim) = action-transcendence (naiṣkarmya) perfection; paramām = supreme; saṃnyāsenādhigacchati (saṃnyāsena + adhigacchati) = through renunciation he attains.

18.50: siddhim = perfection; prāptas = having attained; yathā = just as, here: how; brahma = Brahman; tathāpnoti (tathā + āpnoti) = thus he attains; nibodha = you learn!; me = from me; samāsenaiva (samāsena + eva) = briefly verily, here: *eva* is omitted; kaunteya = O son-of-Kuntī; niṣṭhā = way-of-life; jñānasya = of knowledge; yā (feminine) = which; parā (feminine) = highest [qualifying *niṣṭhā*].

18.51: buddhyā = by wisdom-faculty; viśuddhayā (feminine) = by pure; yuktas = yoked; dhṛtyātmānam (dhṛtyā + ātmānam) = self with steadiness (dhṛti); niyamya = restraining; ca = and; śabdādīn (śabda + ādīn) (plural) = sound and so on; viṣayān = objects; tyaktvā = having relinquished, here: relinquishing; rāgadveṣau (rāga + dveṣau) (dual) = attachment and aversion; vyudasya = casting off; ca = and.

18.52: viviktasevī (vivikta + sevī) = dwelling in solitude; laghvāśī (laghu + āśī) = eating lightly; yatavākkāyamānasas (yata + vāk

+ kāya + mānasas) = controlled speech, body, [and] mind, here: controlling . . . ; dhyānayogaparas (dhyāna + yoga + paras) = intent on Yoga [of] meditation; nityam = ever; vairāgyam = dispassion; samupāśritas = resorting.

18.53: ahaṃkāram (aham + kāram) = ego-sense; balam = force; darpam = arrogance; kāmam = desire; krodham = anger; parigraham = possessiveness; vimucya = shunning; nirmamas = without (nir-) "mine"; śāntas = peaceful; brahmabhūyāya (brahma + bhūyāya) = for becoming the world-ground; kalpate = he is fit.

18.54: brahmabhūtas (brahma + bhūtas) = *brahman*-become; prasannātmā (prasanna + ātmā) = tranquil self; na = not; śocati = he grieves; na = not, here: nor; kāṅkṣati = he hankers; samas = the same; sarveṣu = in all; bhūteṣu = in beings; madbhaktim (mad + bhaktim) = devotion to me; labhate = he gains; parām = supreme.

18.55: bhaktyā = through devotion; mām = me; abhijānāti = he knows; yāvān = how great (yāvat); yas = who; cāsmi (ca + asmi) = and I am; tattvatas = really; tatas = thence, then; mām = me; tattvatas = really; jñātvā = having known; viśate = he enters; tadanantaram (tad + anantaram) = forthwith.

18.56: sarvakarmāṇi (sarva + karmāṇi) = all actions; api = also, moreover; sadā = always; kurvāṇas = performing; madvyapāśrayas (mad + vyapāśrayas) = taking-refuge in me; matprasādāt (mat + prasādāt) = by my grace; avāpnoti = he attains; śāśvatam = eternal; padam = place, abode; avyayam = immutable.

18.57: cetasā = with the mind, here: in thought; sarvakarmāṇi (sarva + karmāṇi) = all actions; mayi = in me; saṃnyasya = renouncing; matparas (mat + paras) = intent on me; buddhiyogam (buddhi + yogam) = Yoga of the wisdom-faculty, here: retained in Sanskrit; upāśritya = resorting; maccittas (mat + cittas) = me-minded; satatam = constantly; bhava = you be!

18.58: maccittas (mat + cittas) = me-minded; sarvadurgāni (sarva + durgāni) = all difficulties; matprasādāt (mat + prasādāt) = by my grace; tariṣyasi = you will overcome, here: you will transcend; atha = now, here: but; ced = if; tvam = you; ahaṃkārān (aham + kārāt) = by ego-sense, here: out of . . . ; na = not; śroṣyasi = you will hear, here: you will listen; vinaṅkṣyasi = you will perish.

18.59: yad = which, here: that; ahaṃkāram (aham + kāram) = ego-sense; āśritya = resorting; na = not; yotsya = I will fight; iti = thus, here: used to indicate a quotation; manyase = you think; mithyaiṣas (mithyā + eṣas) = [in] vain this; vyavasāyas = resolve; te = of you; prakṛtis = Cosmos; tvām = you; niyokṣyati = it will compel.

18.60: svabhāvajena (sva + bhāva + jena) = by [action] born of own-being; kaunteya = O son-of-Kuntī; nibaddhas = bound; svena = by own; karmaṇā = by action; kartum = to do; necchasi (na + icchasi) = not you wish; yad = which; mohāt = from delusion, here: out of . . . ; kariṣyasi = you will do; avaśas = unwittingly; 'pi (api) = even; tad = this, that.

18.61: īśvaras = lord; sarvabhūtānām (sarva + bhūtānām) = of all beings; hṛddeśe (hṛd + deśe) = in heart space, here: in heart region; 'rjuna (arjuna) = O Arjuna; tiṣṭhati = he abides; bhrāmayan = whirling; sarvabhūtāni (sarva + bhūtāni) = all beings; yantrārūḍhāni (yantra + ārūḍhāni) (plural) = mounted on a machine; māyayā = creative-power.

18.62: tam = to him; eva = alone; śaraṇam = refuge; gaccha = you go!; sarvabhāvena (sarva + bhāvena) = with all being; bhārata = O descendant-of-Bharata; tatprasādāt (tat + prasādāt) = through his grace; param = supreme; śāntim = peace; sthānam = condition, abode; prāpsyasi = you will attain; śāśvatam = eternal.

18.63: iti = thus; te = to you; jñānam = knowledge; ākhyātam = declared; guhyāt = than secret; guhyataram (guhya + taram) = more secret; mayā = by me; vimṛśyaitad (vimṛśya + etad) =

reflecting [on] this; aśeṣena = completely; yathecchasi (yathā + icchasi) = as you wish; tathā = thus, here: then; kuru = you do!

18.64: sarvaguhyatamam (sarva + guhya + tamam) = most secret [of] all; bhūyas = again; śṛṇu = you hear!; me = of me, my; paramam = supreme; vacas = word; iṣṭas = desired, here: beloved; 'si (asi) = you are; me = of me, by me; dṛḍham = firm, surely; iti = thus, here: this; tatas = thence, here: therefore; vakṣyāmi = I tell; te = your; hitam = welfare.

18.65: manmanā (man + manā) = me-minded; bhava = you be!; madbhaktas (mad + bhaktas) = devoted to me; madyājī (mad + yājī) = sacrificing to me; mām = to me; namaskuru (namas + kuru) = you make reverence!; mām = to me; evaiṣyasi (eva + eṣyasi) = thus you will go, here: you will come; satyam = truly; te = to you; pratijāne = I promise; priyas = dear; 'si (asi) = you are; me = to me.

18.66: sarvadharmān (sarva + dharmān) = all laws, here: all dharmas; parityajya = relinquishing; mām = to me; ekam = alone; śaraṇam = refuge; vraja = you go!, here: you come; aham = I; tvā = to you; sarvapāpebhyas (sarva + pāpebhyas) = from all sins; mokṣayiṣyāmi = I will release; mā = not; śucas = grieve.

18.67: idam = this; te = to you; nātapaskāya (na + atapaskāya) = not [here: never] to [him who has] no austerity; nābhaktāya (na + abhaktāya) = not to [him who does] not worship; kadācana = together with na: never; na = not; cāśuśrūṣave (ca + aśuśrūṣave) = and [who does] not (a-) listen [to the teaching]; vācyam = to be said, here: [you] reveal; na = not, here: nor; ca = and; mām = me; yas = who; 'bhyasūyati (abhyasūyati) = he reviles.

18.68: yas = who; idam = this; paramam = supreme; guhyam = secret; madbhakteṣu (mad + bhakteṣu) = to devotees of mine; abhidhāsyati = he will impart; bhaktim = devotion; mayi = to me; parām = highest, supreme; kṛtvā = having done, here: showing; mām = to me; evaiṣyati (eva + eṣyati) = verily he will go, here: verily he will come; asaṃśayas = undoubtedly.

18.69: na = not; ca = and; tasmāt = therefore; manuṣyeṣu = among humans; kaśćid = anyone; me = to me; priyakṛttamas (priya + kṛt + tamas) = doing dearer [service]; bhavitā = he will be; na = not; ca = and; me = to me; tasmāt = therefore, here: than this, than he; anyas = other, here: another; priyataras (priya + taras) = dearer; bhuvi = on earth.

18.70: adhyeṣyate = he will study; ca = and; yas = who; imam = this; dharmyam = lawful; saṃvādam = dialogue; āvayos (dual) = between us, here: of ours; jñānayajñena (jñāna + yajñena) = by the knowledge [of] sacrifice; tenāham (tena + aham) = by him I; iṣṭas = desired; syām = I would be; iti = thus; me = of me, my; matis = conviction.

18.71: śraddhāvān = full-of-faith; anasūyas = scoffing; ca = and; śṛṇuyāt = he should hear; api = even, here: even if; yas = who; naras = man; sas = he; 'pi (api) = even, here: only; muktas = released; śubhān (plural) = auspicious; lokān = worlds; prāpnuyāt = he should attain, here: he will attain; puṇyakarmaṇām (puṇya + karmaṇām) = of [those whose] actions [are] meritorious.

18.72: kaccid = [from kad + cid in the sense of "has it?"], here: has [this]?; etad = this; śrutam = heard; pārtha = O son-of-Prithā; tvayaikāgreṇa (tvayā + ekāgreṇa) = by you with one-pointed; cetasā = with mind; kaccid = has it?; ajñānasaṃmohas (ajñāna + saṃmohas) = confusion of ignorance; praṇaṣṭas = destroyed; te = your; dhanaṃjaya (dhanam + jaya) = O Dhanamjaya.

arjunas = Arjuna; uvāca = he said;

18.73: naṣṭas = destroyed; mohas = delusion; smṛtis = recollection; labdhā = gained, obtained; tvatprasādān (tvat + prasādān) = by your grace; mayācyuta (mayā + acyuta) = by me, O Acyuta; sthitas = settled, here: resolved; 'smi (asmi) = I am; gatasaṃdehas (gata + saṃdehas) = gone uncertainty; kariṣye = I will do; vacanam = word, here: bidding; tava = your.

saṃjayas = Samjaya; uvāca = he said;

18.74: iti = thus; aham = I; vāsudevasya (vāsu + devasya) = son-of-Vasudeva [Krishna]; pārthasya = of son-of-Prithā [Arjuna]; ca = and; mahātmanas (mahā + ātmanas) = great self; saṃvādam = dialogue; imam = this; aśrauṣam = I have heard; adbhutam = wondrous, marvelous; romaharṣaṇam (roma + harṣaṇam) = hair-raising.

18.75: vyāsaprasādāt (vyāsa + prasādāt) = by Vyāsa's grace; śrutavān = hearing, here: I have heard; etad = this; guhyam = secret; aham = I; param = highest; yogam = Yoga; yogeśvarāt (yoga + īśvarāt) = by lord [of] Yoga; kṛṣṇāt = by Krishna; sākṣāt = directly; kathayatas = narrating, here: told; svayam = [him]self.

18.76: rājan = O king; saṃsmṛtya saṃsmṛtya = recalling again and again; saṃvādam = dialogue; imam = this; adbhutam = wondrous; keśavārjunayos (keśava + arjunayos) (dual) = between Keshava [Krishna] and Arjuna; puṇyam = meritorious; hṛṣyāmi = thrill-with-joy; ca = and; muhus muhus = again and again.

18.77: tad = this, that; ca = and; saṃsmṛtya saṃsmṛtya = recalling again and again; rūpam = form; atyadbhutam = most wondrous; hares = of Hari [i.e., Krishna]; vismayas = astonishment; me = my; mahān = great; rājan = O king; hṛṣyāmi = I thrill-with-joy; ca = and; punas punas = again and again.

18.78: yatra = where, here: wherever; yogeśvaras (yoga + īśvaras) = Lord [of] Yoga; kṛṣṇas = Krishna; yatra = wherever; pārthas = son-of-Prithā; dhanurdharas (dhanur + dharas) = bow-bearing [archer]; tatra = there; śrīs = fortune; vijayas = victory; bhūtis = welfare; dhruvā = sure; nītis = guidance; matis = conviction; mama = my.

Select Bibliography

Editions, Translations, and Studies

Ādidevānanda, Svāmī, ed. and trans. n.d. *Śrī Rāmānuja Gītā Bhāṣya*. Mylapore: Sri Ramakrishna Math.

Arnold, Edwin, trans. 1899. *Bhagavadgita*. New York: Dover Publications, repr. 1993.

Belvalkar, Shripad Krishna, ed. 1968 (2nd ed.). *The Bhagavadgītā*. Poona: Bhandarkar Oriental Research Institute. Critical Edition used for the present translation.

———, ed. 1947 (1st ed.). *The Bhagavadgītā*. Poona: Bhandarkar Oriental Research Institute.

Bhaktivedanta, Swami A. C., trans. 1983. *The Bhagavad Gītā As It Is*. Los Angeles: Bhaktivedanta Book Trust.

Bolle, Kees W., trans. 1979. *The Bhagavadgītā: A New Translation*. Berkeley: University of California Press.

Buitenen, J. A. B. van, trans. 1981. *The Bhagavadgītā in the Mahābhārata: A Bilingual Edition*. Chicago: University of Chicago Press.

Callewaert, W. M., and Shilanand Hemraj. 1983. *Bhagavadgītānuvāda: A Study in Transcultural Translation*. Ranchi: Satya Bharati Publications.

Chidbhavananda, Swami, trans. 1991. *Bhagavad Gita*. Tirupparaithurai: Sri Ramakrishna Tapovanam.

Chinmayananda, Swami, trans. 2000. *The Bhagavad Geeta*. Langhorn, Pa.: Chinmaya Publications. Complete DVD set.

Deshpande, Rangnath Ramakrishna, trans. 1947. *Shrimad Bhagavad-Gita*. 4 vols. Aundh: Swadhyaya Mandal.

Deutsch, Eliot, trans. *The Bhagavad-Gītā*. With introduction and critical essays. New York: Holt, Rinehart & Winston, 1968.

Edgerton, Franklin, trans. 1925, 1944. *The Bhagavad Gita*. New York: Harper Torchbooks, 1964.

Gandhi, M. K. 1948. *Discourses on the Gita*. Ahmedabad: Navajivan Publishing House.

Gauchhwal, B. S. 1967. *The Concept of Perfection in the Teachings of Kant and the Gītā*. Delhi: Motilal Banarsidass.

Gotshalk, Richard, trans. 1985. *Bhagavad Gītā: Translation and Commentary*. Delhi: Motilal Banarsidass.

Hill, W. Douglas P., trans. 1928. *The Bhagavadgītā: An English Translation and Commentary*. 2nd ed. Oxford: Oxford University Press, 1953, 1966.

Katz, Ruth Cecily. 1989. *Arjuna in the Mahabharata: Where Krishna Is, There Is Victory*. Foreword by Daniel H. H. Ingalls. Columbia, S.C.: University of South Carolina Press.

Kaveeshwar, G. W. 1971. *The Ethics of the Gītā*. Foreword by S. Radhakrishnan. Delhi: Motilal Banarsidass.

Marjanovic, Boris, trans. 2006. *Abhinavagupta's Commentary on the Bhagavad-Gita: Gītārtha-Samgraha*. Portland, Ore.: Rudra Press.

Mascaró, Juan, trans. 1962. *The Bhagavad Gita*. London: Penguin Books.

Nataraja Guru, trans. 1973. *The Bhagavad Gītā: A Sublime Hymn of Dialectics Composed by the Antique Sage-Bard Vyāsa*, 2nd ed. New Delhi: R & K Publishing House.

Parrinder, Geoffrey. 1974. *Upanishads, Gita and Bible*. New York: Harper Torchbooks.

Prabhavananda, Swami, and Christopher Isherwood, trans. 1947. *Bhagavad-Gita: The Song of God*. Introduction by Aldous Huxley. London: Phoenix House.

Prem, Krishna, trans. 1938. *The Yoga of the Bhagavat Gita*. London: Stuart & Watkins, 1969.

Radhakrishnan, Sarvepalli, trans. 1948. *The Bhagavadgītā*. London: George Allen & Unwin.

Rama, Swami, trans. 1985. *Perennial Psychology of the Bhagavad Gita*. Honesdale, Pa.: Himalayan International Institute of Yoga Science and Philosophy of the USA.

Robinson, Catherine A. 2006. *Interpretations of the Bhagavad-Gītā and Images of the Hindu Tradition: The Song of the Lord*. London: Routledge.

Rosen, J. 2000. *Gita on the Green: The Mystical Tradition behind Bagger Vance*. New York: Continuum.

Sadale, G. S., ed. 1935. *The Bhagavad-Gītā: With Eleven Commentaries*. Bombay: Gujarati Printing Press.

Sargeant, Winthrop, trans. *The Bhagavad Gita*. Foreword by Christopher Chapple. Albany, N.Y.: SUNY Press, 1994. Rev. ed. by C. Chapple.

Satwalekar, Shripad Damodar. 1961. *Shrimad Bhagawad-Gita: With a Commentary Explaining the Object of Human Life*. Pardi: Swadhyaya Mandal.

Sharma, Arvind. 1986. *The Hindu Gītā: Ancient and Classical Interpretations of the Bhagavadgītā*. La Salle, Ill.: Open Court Publishing.

Sharpe, Eric J. 1985. *The Universal Gītā: Western Images of the Bhagavad Gītā—A Bicentenary Survey.* La Salle, Ill.: Open Court Publishing.

Telang, K. T., trans. 1908. *The Bhagavadgītā with the Sanatsujātīya and the Anugītā.* Delhi: Motilal Banarsidass, 1965.

Tilak, B. G., trans. 1965. *Gita Rahasya.* Poona: J. S. Tilak & S. S. Tilak.

Tripurari, Swami B. V., trans. 2001. *The Bhagavad Gita: Its Feeling and Philosophy.* San Rafael, Calif.: Mandala Publishing Group.

Venkatesananda, Swami, trans. 1972. *The Song of God.* Chiltern Farm, P.O. Elgin, South Africa.

Warrier, A. G. Krishna, trans. n.d. *Srīmad Bhagavad Gītā Bhāṣya of Śrī Śaṃkarācārya.* Madras: Sri Ramakrishna Math.

Wilkins, Sir Charles, trans. 1785. *Bhagvat Geeta: Dialogues of Kreeshna and Arjoon.* London: Nourse.

Yogananda, Paramahansa, trans. 1995. *God Talks with Arjuna: The Bhagavad Gita.* 2 vols. Los Angeles: Self-Realization Fellowship.

Zaehner, R. C., trans. 1966. *The Bhagavad-Gītā.* Oxford: Clarendon Press, 1969.

Other Publications

Aśvaghoṣa. 1907. *The Awakening of Faith in the Mahayana Doctrine—The New Buddhism,* trans. Timothy Richard. London: Charles Skilton Ltd., 1961.

———. 1967. *The Awakening of Faith, Attributed to Aśvaghosha,* trans. with commentary by Yoshito S. Hakeda. New York: Columbia University Press.

Aurobindo, Sri. 1959. *The Foundations of Indian Culture.* Pondicherry: Sri Aurobindo Ashram.

Chapple, Christopher Key. 1986. *Karma and Creativity.* Albany, N.Y.: SUNY Press.

Dandekar, R. N. "Indian Mythology," in vol. 2 of Haridas Bhattacharyya (ed.), *The Cultural Heritage of India,* 6 vols. Hollywood: Vedanta Press, 2002.

Daniélou, Alain. 1991. *The Myths and Gods of India* (3d ed.). Rochester, Vt.: Inner Traditions International.

Dasgupta, Surendranath. 1952. *A History of Indian Philosophy,* vol. 2. Cambridge: Cambridge University Press.

Feuerstein, Georg. 2010. *Encyclopedia of Yoga and Tantra.* Boston: Shambhala Publications.

———. 2008. *The Yoga Tradition: Its History, Literature, Philosophy, and Practice,* 3rd ed. Prescott, Ariz.: Hohm Press.

———. 2007. *Yoga Morality: Ancient Teachings at a Time of Global Crisis.* Prescott, Ariz.: Hohm Press.

———. 2003. *The Deeper Dimension of Yoga: Theory and Practice.* Boston: Shambhala Publications.

———, and Brenda Feuerstein. 2007. *Green Yoga*. Eastend, Saskatchewan: Traditional Yoga Studies.

———, et al. 1995. *In Search of the Cradle of Civilization: New Light on Ancient India.* Wheaton, Ill.: Quest Books.

Frawley, David. 1991. *Gods, Sages and Kings.* Salt Lake City, Utah: Passage Press.

Gonda, Jan. 1993 (reprint). *Aspects of Early Viṣṇuism.* Delhi: Motilal Banarsidass.

———. 1970. *Viṣṇuism and Śivaism: A Comparison.* London: Athlone Press.

Jaiswal, Suvira. 1981. 2d rev. ed. *The Origin and Development of Vaiṣṇavism: Vaiṣṇavism from 200 B.C. to A.D. 500.* New Delhi: Munshiram Manoharlal.

Kern, Hendrik. 1963. *Saddharma-Pundarīka or The Lotus of the True Law.* New York: Dover Publications. First published in 1884 as vol. 21 of the *Sacred Books of the East* series edited by F. Max Müller.

Kak, Subhash. 2003. "The Date of the Mahabharata War." www.scribd.com/doc/6403178/The-Date-of-the-Mahabharata-War.

———. 1994. *The Astronomical Code of the Ṛgveda.* New Delhi: Aditya Prakashan.

Kane, P. V. 1994. *History of Dharmasastra.* Vol. 5, Part 2. Poona: Bhandarlear Oriental Research Institute.

Matsubara, Mitsunori. 1994. *Pāñcarātra Saṃhitās and Early Vaiṣṇava Theology.* Delhi: Motilal Banarsidass.

Nicolas, Antonio de, trans. 1990. *The Bhagavad Gītā.* York Beach, Maine: Nicolas Hays.

———. 1976. *Avatāra: The Humanization of Philosophy Through the Bhagavad Gītā.* New York: Nicolas Hays.

Possahl, G., ed. 1982. *Harappan Civilization: A Contemporary Perspective.* Warminster: Aris & Phillips.

Rao, S. S. 1999. *The Lost City of Dvāraka.* New Delhi: Aditya Prakashan.

Renfrew, Colin. 1987. *Archaeology & Language.* Cambridge, N.Y.: University of Cambridge.

Schrader, F. Otto. 1916. *Introduction to the Pāncarātra and the Ahirbudhnya-Samhitā.* Adyar: Adyar Library and Research Centre.

Sharma, Aravind. 1979.

Siddhantashastree, Rabindra Kumar. 1975. *Śaivism through the Ages.* New Delhi: Motilal Manoharlal.

———. 1985. *Vaiṣṇavism through the Ages.* New Delhi: Munshiram Manoharlal.

Upadhyaya, K. N. 1971. *Early Buddhism and the Bhagavadgita.* Delhi: Motilal Banarsidass.

Yukteswar, Sri. 1984. *The Holy Science.* Los Angeles: Self-Realization Fellowship.

Glossary of Select Terms in the *Bhagavad-Gītā*

The meanings given are those used in the translation of the *Bhagavad-Gītā* in Part Two (unless the word is left untranslated). Glossary terms are alphabetized according to the English alphabet, not the Sanskrit. Abbreviations in the glossary are as follows:

adj. = adjective
cf. = Latin, "compare"; that is, "see, by way of comparison"
fem. = feminine noun
fut. part. = future participle, a verb form (absent in English) conveying an action that is about to occur
masc. = masculine noun
neutr. = neuter noun
past part. = passive past participle

abhāva (masc.): nonbecoming. Cf. *bhava*.
abhaya (neutr.): fearlessness. Cf. *bhaya*.
abhyāsa (masc.): practice. See also *vairāgya*.
abhyāsa-yoga (masc.): Yoga of practice.
acāpala (neutr.): absence-of-haste.
ācārya (masc.): preceptor. Cf. *guru*.
ācāryopāsana (neutr.): reverence for the preceptor.
adambhitva (neutr.): unpretentiousness.
adbhūta (adj.): wondrous.
adharma (masc.): anomie. Cf. *dharma*.
adhibhūta (masc.): basis-of-beings.
adhidaiva (masc.): divine-basis.
adhikāra (masc.): rightful-interest.
ādhipatya (neutr.): sovereignty.
adhiṣṭhāna/adhishthāna (neutr.): basis.
adhiyajña (masc.): basis-of-sacrifice.
adhyakṣa/adhyaksha (neutr.): supervision.
adhyātman (masc.): basis-of-self.
adroha (masc.): absence-of-malice.
agha (neutr./adj.): wickedness; wicked

agra (neutr.): beginning; tip [of nose].
ahaṃkāra (masc.): "I-maker," the ego-sense. Cf. *anahaṃkāra*.
ahaṃkṛta (adj.): ego-driven.
ahaṃvādin (masc.): "I-sayer."
āhāra (masc.): food; diet. Cf. *nirāhāra*. See also *anna; bhojana*.
ahiṃsā (fem.): nonharming.
aiśvara/aishvara (adj.): lordly.
aiśvarya/aishvarya (masc.): lordship.
aja (adj.): unborn.
ajñāna (masc./adj.): ignoramus; ignorant.
ākāṅkṣa/ākānksha (masc.): hankering.
akarman (neutr.): inaction. Cf. *karman*.
akārya (fut. part.): what-is-not-to-be-done; wrong. Cf. *kārya*.
ākāśa/ākāsha (masc.): ether-space.
akīrti (fem.): disrepute; dishonor. Cf. *kīrti*.
akrodha (masc.): absence-of-anger. Cf. *krodha*.
akṛtsna-vid/akritsna-vid (masc.): knower of the non-Whole. Cf. *kṛtsna-vid*.
akṣara/akshara (neutr./adj.): imperishable. Cf. *kṣara*.
alasa (adj.): lazy.
ālasya (neutr.): indolence.
aloluptva (neutr.): non-greediness.
alpa (adj.): slight.
amānitva (neutr.): lack-of-pride.
amedhya (adj.): unclean.
amla (adj.): sour.
amṛta (adj.): immortal, nectarine. See also *amṛtatva*.
amṛtatva (neutr.): immortality. See also *amṛta*.
aṃśa/amsha (masc.): fragment.
anabhiṣvaṅga/anabhishvanga (masc.): absence-of-clinging.
anahaṃkāra (masc.): absence-of-ego-sense. Cf. *ahaṃkāra*.
anapekṣa/anapeksha (masc.): [that which is] without expectation.
anasūya (adj.): non-grumbling.
anāvṛtti (fem.): [path of] no-return. Cf. *āvṛtti*.
anirdeśya/anirdeshya (adj.): indefinable.
aniṣṭa/anishta (adj.): unwanted. Cf. *iṣṭa*.
anīśvara/anīshvara (masc./adj.): [that which is] without a lord, lordless. Cf. *īśvara*.
anitya (adj.): transient.
añjali/anjali (masc.): the gesture of folded hands.
anna (neutr.): food. See also *āhāra; bhojana*.
anta (masc.): end.
antakāla (masc.): end time, i.e., final hour
anubandha (masc.): consequence, sequel.
anugraha (masc.): grace, favor.
anukampā (fem.): compassion.
anumantṛ (masc.): permitter.
apaiśuna/apaishuna (neutr.): non-slandering.
apamāna (masc.): dishonor.
apāna (neutr.): out-breath. Cf. *prāṇa*.
aparigraha (masc./adj.): non-grasping.
aprakāśa/aprakāsha (masc.): lack-of-luminosity. Cf. *prakāśa*.
aprameya (neutr.): incommensurable.
apravṛtti (fem.): inactivity. Cf. *pravṛtti*.

apuṇya (neutr./adj.): demerit, demeritorious. Cf. *puṇya*.
ārāma (masc.): delight
ārjava (masc.): uprightness.
ārogya (neutr.): health.
artha (masc.): thing, matter, topic, goal, use.
ārūḍha (past part.): ascended.
ārurukṣu/ārurukshu (adj.): desiring-to-ascend.
asakta (past part.): unattached. Cf. *sakta*.
asakti (fem.): nonattachment.
aśama/ashama (masc.): unrest. Cf. *śama*.
āsana (neutr.): seat.
asat (masc./adj.): nonexistence; bad. Cf. *sat*.
āśaya/āshaya (masc.): resting-place.
āścarya/āshcarya (neutr./adj.): wonder, marvelous.
āśraya/āshraya (masc.): refuge.
asukha (adj.): joyless. Cf. *sukha*; *duḥkha*
asura (masc.): antigod, demon. Cf. *sura*.
aśvattha/ashvatta (masc.): pipal tree.
atimāna (masc.): pride.
atīndriya (adj.): extrasensory.
ātman (masc.): self. Cf. *brahman*. See also *paramātman*.
ātmavinigraha (masc.): self-restraint.
atyuṣṇa/atyushna (adj.): hot.
auṣadha/aushadha (neutr.): herb.
āvṛtti (fem.): [path of] return. Cf. *anāvṛtti*.
avyakta (neutr./past part.) unmanifest. Cf. *vyakta*.
avyaya (neutr./adj.): immutable.
āyāsa (masc.): strain.
ayaśa/ayasha (masc.): indignity. Cf. *yaśa*.
ayukta (past part.): unyoked, i.e., undisciplined. Cf. *yukta*.
āyus (masc.): life.
bala (neutr.): power, force, strength.
bandha (masc.): bondage.
bandhu (masc.): friend.
bhaikṣya/bhaikshya (neutr.): alms-food.
bhakta (masc.): devotee.
bhakti (fem.): devotion.
bhakti-yoga (masc.): Yoga of devotion.
bhartṛ/bhartri (masc.): sustainer.
bhava (masc.): becoming. Cf. *abhāva*.
bhāva (masc.): mode-of-existence, disposition.
bhaya (neutr.): fear. Cf. *abhaya*.
bheda (masc.): breach. See *buddhi-bheda*.
bhoga (masc.): enjoyment, pleasure.
bhojana (neutr.): food. See also *āhāra; anna*.
bhoktṛ/bhoktri (masc.): enjoyer.
bhrū (fem.): eyebrow.
bhūmi (fem.): earth.
bhūta (masc./neutr.): being, lower-being, element, elemental.
bhūteśa/bhūtesha (masc.): lord of beings.
bhūti (fem.): welfare.
bīja (neutr.): seed. See also *garbha*.
Brahma (masc.): the creator-god.
brahma-bhūta (past part. [having] become the world-ground.
brahmacarya (neutr.): chastity (lit. "brahmic conduct").
brahman (neutr.): World-ground. Cf. *ātman*. When written Brahman, the word refers to the Absolute.

brahma-nirvāṇa (neutr.): extinction in the world-ground.
brāhmaṇa (masc.): priest; the priestly estate.
buddhi (fem.): wisdom, wisdom-faculty. Cf. *jñanā; prajñā.*
buddhi-bheda (masc.): *buddhi*-breach.
buddhi-yoga (masc.): Yoga of wisdom.
budha (masc.): wise one.
cakra (neutr.): wheel.
cañcalatva (neutr.): fickleness.
cātur-vārṇya (neutr.): quartet-of-classes.
cetanā (fem.): consciousness.
cetas (neutr.): mind.
cintā (fem.): care, worry.
citta (neutr.): mind, attention, thought.
codanā (fem.): impulse.
daiva (adj.): divine, god-related.
dakṣa/daksha (adj.): skilled.
dākṣya/dākshya (neutr.): resourcefulness.
dama (masc.): restraint.
dambha (masc.): ostentation.
dāna (neutr.): charity, generosity.
daṇḍa (masc.): rod-of-punishment.
darpa (masc.): arrogance.
darśana/darshana (neutr.): vision, insight.
datta (masc./adj.): gift, given.
dayā (fem.): compassion. See also *karuṇā.*
deha (masc./neutr.): body. See also *śarīra.*
dehabhṛt/dehabhrit (masc.): body-wearer. See also *dehin.*
dehin (masc.): embodied [self], body-essence. See also *dehabhṛt; śarīrin.*
deśa/desha (masc.): place.
deva (masc.): god. See also *sura.*
devavrata (masc.): god-vowed.
dhāman (neutr.): abode.
dhanurdhara (masc.): bow-bearer.
dhāraṇā (fem.): concentration.
dharma (masc.): law, lawfulness. See also *dharmakṣetra; jātidharma; kuladharma.* Cf. *adharma.*
dharmakṣetra/dharmakshetra (neutr.): field of the law. See also *dharma; kṣetra.*
dharmya (adj.): lawful.
dhātṛ/dhātri (masc.): supporter.
dhṛti/dhriti (fem.): steadfastness, fortitude.
dhyāna (neutr.): meditation.
dīrghasūtrin (masc.): long-threaded [person], i.e., procrastinator.
doṣa/dosha (masc./neutr.): flaw, defect.
duḥkha (masc.): pain, suffering. Cf. *sukha.*
durmati (masc.): dull-wit.
durmedha (adj.): dull-minded.
dvandva (masc.): pair-of-opposites. Cf. *nirdvandva.*
dvāra (neutr.): gate.
dveṣa/dvesha (masc.): aversion, hatred. Cf. *rāga.*
dvija (masc.): twice-born.
ekāgra (adj.): one-pointed.
ekatva (neutr.): oneness, unity. Cf. *pṛthaktva.*
gahana (adj.): impenetrable
garbha (masc.): fetus. See also *bīja.*
gatarasa (adj.): tasteless.
gati (fem.): course.
ghora (adj.): fierce.
glāni (fem.): diminution.
gocara (masc.): cow-pasture, i.e., sensory world.
goptṛ (masc.): guardian.

gorakṣya/gorakshya (neutr.): tending cattle.
grāma (masc.): aggregation.
guhya (neutr.): secret. See also *rahasya.*
guṇa (masc.): quality, primary-quality. See also *rajas; sattva; tamas.*
guru (masc.): teacher.
hāni (fem.): cessation.
harṣa/harsha (masc.): thrill, joy, exultation, elation.
hetu (masc.): motive, cause, reason.
hita (neutr.): welfare.
hṛd (neutr.): heart.
hṛdayadaurbalya (neutr.): faint-heartedness.
hṛdaya/hridaya (adj.): heart [-gladdening].
hrī (fem.): modesty.
huta (neutr.): offering.
icchā (fem.): longing, will.
indriya (neutr.): instrument, meaning sense. See also *karmendriya.*
iṣṭa/ishta (past part.): wanted. Cf. *aniṣṭa.*
īśvara/īshvara (masc.): lord. Cf. *anīśvara.*
īśvarabhāva/ īshvarabhāva (masc.): regal disposition.
jagat (neutr.): universe.
janādhipa (masc.): ruler.
janman (neutr.): birth. See also *punarjanman.*
jarā (fem.): old age.
jāta (past part.): born, all-that-is-born. Cf. *mṛta.*
jātidharma (masc.): caste law. See also *dharma.*
jaya (masc.): victory.
jīvabhūta (masc.): life-element.
jñāna/jñāna (neutr.): knowledge. Cf. *prajñā; vijñāna.*
jñānavat (adj.): knowledgeable.
jñāna-yoga (masc.): Yoga of knowledge.
jñānin (masc.): knower.
jñeya (fut. part.): what-is-to-be-known, i.e., the object.
kāla (masc.): time.
kalevara (neutr.): body.
kalmaṣa/kalmasha (masc.): defilement.
kalpa (masc.): aeon.
kāma (masc.): desire.
karaṇa (neutr.): instrument.
kāraṇa (neutr.): cause, instrument, means, sake.
karman (neutr.): karma, action, behavior. Cf. *akarman; vikarman.*
karmasagraha (masc.): nexus of action.
karma-yoga (masc.): Yoga of [self-transcending] action.
karmendriya (neutr.): action sense, i.e., conative sense (as opposed to *jñānendriya,* which is not found in the *Gītā*). See also *indriya.*
karmin (masc.): performer-of-[ritual]-action.
karpaṇya (neutr.): pity. See also *kṛpā.*
kartṛ/kartri (masc.): doer, agent.
karuṇā (fem.): compassionate. See also *dayā.*
kārya (fut. part.): [what is] to be done, right, effect. Cf. *akārya.*
kaṭu (adj.): pungent.
kauśala/kaushala (neutr.): skill.
kavi (masc.): bard.
kāya (masc.): body.
kilbiṣa/kilbisha (neutr.): guilt.
kīrti (fem.): honor. Cf. *akīrti.*
klaibya (neutr.): unmanliness.
kleśa/klesha (masc.): struggle.
kratu (masc.): rite.

kriyā (fem.): ritual, activity.
krodha (masc.): anger. Cf. *akrodha.*
kṛpā/kripā (fem.): pity. See also *kārpaṇya.*
kṛṣi/krishi (fem.): agriculture.
kṛtsna/kritsna (adj.): whole.
kṛtsna-vid (masc.): knower of the Whole. Cf. *akṛtsna-vid*
kṣamā/kshamā (fem.): patience.
kṣaṇa/kshana (neutr.): moment.
kṣara/kshara (adj.): perishable. Cf. *akṣara*
kṣatriya/kshatriya (masc.): warrior.
kṣema/kshīma (masc.): tranquillity, security.
kṣetra/kshetra (neutr.): field. See also *dharmakṣetra; kurukṣetra.*
kṣetrajña/kshetrajna (masc.): field-knower.
kṣīṇa/kshīna (past part.): exhausted.
kula (masc.): family.
kuladharma (masc.): family law. See also *dharma.*
kurukṣetra/kurukshetra (neutr.): field of the Kurus. See also *kṣetra.*
kuṭastha (masc.): [he who is] summit-abiding.
lābha (neutr.): gain.
lāghava (neutr.): levity, contempt.
laghvāśin/laghvāshin (adj.): eating little.
lavaṇa (adj.): salty.
liṅga (neutr.): sign.
lobha (masc.): greed.
loka (masc.): realm, world. See also *trailokya.*
lokasaṃgraha (masc.): maintenance/welfare of the world.
mahābhūta (masc.): great element.
mahāratha (masc.): great chariot, a supreme warrior.
mahātman (masc.): great self.
māhātmya (neutr.): glory.
maheshvara (masc.): Great Lord.
māna (masc./neutr.): honor. Cf. *apamāna.*
manas (neutr.): mind.
manoratha (masc.): mind chariot, i.e., fancy, fantasy.
mantra (neutr.): [sacred] word.
manuṣya/manushya (masc./adj.): human.
maraṇa (neutr.): death. Cf. *mṛtyu; prāṇa.*
mārdava (neutr.): gentleness.
mata (neutr./past part.): opinion, conviction.
mati (fem.): opinion.
mātrāsparśa/mātrāsparsha (masc.): material contact. See also *sparśa.*
mauna (neutr.): silence.
māyā (fem.): creative-power.
medhā (fem.): intelligence.
miśra/mishra (adj.): mixed.
mithyācāra (masc.): [he who has] false conduct, hypocrite.
mogha (adj.): vain.
moha (masc.): delusion, confusion. Cf. *saṃmoha.*
mokṣa/moksha (masc.): liberation.
mṛta (past part.): dead, all-that-dies. Cf. *jāta.*
mṛtyu/mrityu (masc.): *death*. Cf. *maraṇa.*
mūḍha (part part.): confounded, deluded.
mukta (past part.): liberated.
muni (masc.): sage.
mūrti (fem.): form.
nabhas (neutr.): world-sky.
naikṛtika/naikritika (adj.): base.
naiṣkarmya/naishkarmya (neutr.): action-transcendence.
namas (neutr.): salutation.
nara (masc.): man.
naraka (masc.): hell. Cf. *svarga.*

nāśa/nāsha (masc.): destruction.
nāsikāgra (neutr.): tip of the nose.
nidhāna (neutr.): receptacle.
nidrā (fem.): sleep. See also *svapna.*
nigraha (masc.): repression.
niḥspṛha (adj./masc.): free-from-desire.
nimitta (neutr.): sign, omen, instrument.
nirahaṃkāra (adj./masc.): free-from-ego-sense.
nirāhāra (masc.): non-eating. Cf. *āhāra.*
nirāśis/nirāshis (adj./fem.): without hope.
nirāśraya/nirāshraya (adj.): independent.
nirdvandva (masc.): without the pairs-of-opposites. Cf. *dvandva.*
nirguṇa (adj.): beyond the primary-qualities.
nirmalatva (neutr.): immaculateness.
nirmama (masc./adj.): without ego-sense.
nirvāṇa (masc.): extinction. See also *brahmanirvāṇa.*
niścaya/nishcaya (masc.): conviction.
niṣṭhā/nishthā (fem.): way-of-life.
nīti (fem.): statecraft, guidance.
nitya (adj.): eternal. Cf. *anitya.*
nityatva (neutr.): constancy.
nivāsa (masc.): home, abode.
nivṛtti/nivritti (fem.): cessation. Cf. *pravṛtti.*
niyata (adj.): allotted, necessary, restrained.
ojas (neutr.): vitality.
oṃkāra (masc.): *oṃ* maker, the syllable OṂ/AUṂ.
paṇḍita (masc.): learned (person), scholar.
pada (neutr.): state.
pāpa (neutr.): sin, evil.
para (masc.): highest, supreme.
paramātman (masc.): supreme Self. See also *ātman.*
parigraha (masc.): possessiveness.
pariṇāma (masc.): change, transformation.
paripraśna/pariprashna (masc.): inquiry.
paritrāṇa (neutr.): protection.
pāruṣya/pārushya (neutr.): harshness.
paryuṣita/paryushita (adj.): stale.
pātaka (neutr.): transgression.
pauruṣa/paurusha (neutr.): human-capacity.
phala (neutr.): fruit.
pitṛ/pitri (masc.): ancestor.
prabhava (masc.): origin. Cf. *pralaya.*
prabhaviṣṇu/prabhavishnu (masc.): generator.
prabhu (masc.): lord.
prajñā/prajnā (fem.): gnosis, wisdom. Cf. *jñāna.*
prakāśa/prakāsha (masc.): visible-light, luminosity. Cf. *aprakāśa.*
prākṛta/prākrita (adj.): uncultured.
prakṛti/prakriti (fem.): nature, Cosmos.
pralaya (masc.): dissolution. Cf. *prabhava.*
pramāda (masc.): heedlessness.
pramāṇa (neutr.): measure, standard.
prāṇa (masc.): life, breath, in-breath, vital-force. Cf. *apāna, maraṇa.*
praṇava (masc.): humming-sound, i.e. the syllable OṂ.
prāṇāyāma (masc.): breath control.
praṇipāta (masc.): prostration, reverence.
prasāda (masc.): serenity, grace.
pravṛtti/pravritti (fem.): creativity, activity. Cf. *apravṛtti; nivṛtti.*
prayāṇa (neutr.): going-forth, i.e., death.

preta (masc.): departed, i.e., deceased person.
prīti (fem.): delight.
priyahita (adj.): beneficial.
pṛthaktva/prithaktva (neutr.): diversity. Cf. *ekatva*.
pūjā (fem.): reverence.
pūjya (adj.): venerable.
punarjanman (neutr.): rebirth. See also *janman*.
puṇya (neutr./adj.): merit, meritorious. Cf. *apuṇya*.
purāṇa (adj.): ancient, primordial.
puruṣa/purusha (masc.): man, Spirit.
pūruṣa/pūrusha (masc.): man.
puruṣottama/purushottama (masc.): Supreme Spirit.
pūti (adj.): putrid.
rāga (masc.): passion. Cf. *dveṣa*.
rahasya (neutr.): secret. See also *guhya*.
rājavidyā (fem.): royal science.
rājaguhya (neutr.): royal secret.
rajas (neutr.): primary-quality of dynamism, activity. Cf. *sattva, tamas*. See also *guṇa*.
rājasa (adj.): *rajas*-natured, dynamic. Cf. *sāttvika; tāmasa*.
rājarṣi/rājarishi (masc.): royal seer.
rasa (neutr.): ambrosia, essence.
rasya (adj.): savory.
ṛta/rita (adj./neutr.): true, truth.
rūkṣa/rūksha (adj.): harsh.
rūpa (neutr.): form.
śabda/shabda (masc.): sound.
sādharmya (neutr.): identity.
sādhu (masc.): good. Cf. *sat*.
sāgara (masc.): ocean.
sahaja (adj.): innate.
sākṣin/sākshin (masc.): witness.
sakta (past part.): attached. Cf. *asakta*.
sama (adj.): same.
śama/shama (masc.): tranquillity. Cf. *aśama*.
samacittatva (neutr.): same-mindedness.
samādhi (masc.): ecstasy, concentration.
samatā (fem.): sameness.
samatva (neutr.): equanimity.
saṃbhava (masc.): birth, origin, source.
saṃdeha (masc.): uncertainty.
saṃghāta (masc.): confusion.
saṃkalpa (masc.): motive.
saṃkara (masc.): confusion, chaos.
sāṃkhya (masc.): Sāmkhya, a philosophical teaching.
saṃkhya (neutr.): combat. Cf. *yuddha*.
saṃmoha (masc.): confusion, delusion. Cf. *moha*.
saṃnyāsa (masc.): renunciation.
saṃnyāsin (masc.): renouncer.
saṃpad (fem.): endowment.
saṃsāra (masc.): cycle.
saṃśaya/samshaya (masc.): doubt.
saṃsiddhi (fem.): perfection, accomplishment, consummation. See also *siddhi*.
saṃvāda (masc.): dialogue.
saṃyamin (masc.): he who is [self-] controlled.
saṃyoga (masc.): union. Cf. *viyoga*.
sanātana (adj.): everlasting.
saṅga (masc.): attachment.
śānti/shānti (fem.): peace.
śaraṇa/sharana (neutr.): refuge.
śarīra/sharīra (masc.): body. See also *deha*.
śarīrin/sharīrin (adj.): embodied. See also *dehin*.
sarvagata (adj.): omnipresent.
sarvavid (adj./masc.): all-knowing, all-knower.

Index

bards, 139, 299
behavior, 309
of enlightened being, 269
Belvalkar, Shripad Krishna, xi, 71, 241n46
bhagavad, meaning of, 9n1
Bhagavad-Gītā, 3, 6, 9, 12, 24, 52, 58–59
and *Mahābhārata*, 13
as traditional literature, 56
as Upanishad, 135n6
colophons of, 56–57
date of, 14, 16
imitations, 67–68
its influence on Buddhism, 69–70
Kashmiri recension of, 67
quoted, 25
symbolic interpretation of,
translations of, 71–75.
vocabulary and style, 16–17
Bhāgavata-Purāna, 24–25, 64–65
Bhāgavatism, 24, 42, 56, 61, 62, 64–65
bhakta, 135n5
bhakti, 66, 315
Bhaktisāra, 66
Bhaktivedanta, A. C. Swami (Prabhupada), 65, 68, 72
Bhakti-Yoga, 247, 249, 251
Bharata (king), 105n40
Bhārata (Arjuna), 101, 103, 147
Bhārata, 4, 50
Bharata war, x, 10–11, 13–14, 16, 36, 44, 49, 54
Bharatarshabha (Arjuna), 133
Bhārgavas, 24
Bhāskara, 81n3
bhāva, 137, 177, 205n4, 279
bhāvanā, 115n61
bhaya, 111, 299n3
Bhīma (Bhīmasena), 11, 13, 29, 32, 36, 79, 81, 83
biography of, 33–34
Bhīshma, 6, 8, 30–31, 35, 49, 81, 81n3, 83n14,
Bhīshmaka, 26
bhoga, 123n23
Bhrigu (sage), 24, 211, 217n62
bhūta, 105n38, 197n28
birth, 135, 137, 175, 255, 265, 269, 285
blame
and praise, 251, 271
body, 97, 99, 121, 267, 277, 291, 315
abandoned in *videha-mukti,* 137
as field, 253
cosmic, 223
of God, 117n66, 175n18,
retained in *jīvan-mukti,* 117n66
body-essence, 97, 103, 131, 150, 265, 269, 289
body-wearer, 181, 267, 269, 301
Bolle, Kees, 72
bondage, 281, 307
Brahma, 24, 29, 52, 65–66, 105n40, 203n2, 213n39, 237
as Prajāpati, 121n20
Day and Night of, 185
Brahma-Gītā, 68
Brahman, 167, 185, 187, 205, 295, 313. *See also* world-ground
brahman
nature of, 181
brāhmana, 153, 199
Brāhmanas, 56, 58
Brahmānda-Purāna, 25
brahma-nirvāna, 69, 117, 155, 159n11
Brāhmanism, 57–58
brahma-shirāstra, 29
Brahma-Sūtra, 253n5
brahmic state, 117
Brahmin (Brāhmana), 107
breath, 85n15, 155, 277
breath control, 143
Brihadāranyaka-Upanishad, 11, 117n64, 143n31
Brihaspati, 211

brihatī (meter), 215n52
brilliance of God, 233, 241, 277
Buddha, 38, 40, 70
buddhi, x–xi, 105n37, 107n46, 111n53, 113n57, 115, 283
buddhi-bheda, 127n37
buddhi-breach, 127
buddhi-nāsha, 113n57
Buddhism, 40, 69–70, 155n7, 165n18,
buddhi-yoga, 109, 205, 317
Buitenen, J. A. B. van, 72

Caitanya, 69
calm, 309
carācara, 257n20
cares, 283
caste laws, 91
caste system, 40
cattle-tending, 309
causes
 five, 301n10
Cekitāna, 79
cessation (of action), 159n7, 307
chance, 103, 141
Chāndogya-Upanishad, 11, 22, 64, 143n27, 273n1
chant, 215
chaos, 127
charity, 54, 185, 243, 281, 291, 293, 295, 297, 299
chastity
 vow of, 159
Choudhury, Makhan Lal Roy, 68
Christian theology, 129n42
chronology, 18–21
churning of the world ocean, 39
Citrāngadā, 30
Citraratha, 213
classes
 actions of, 309
 of Hinduism, 79n2, 89n29, 139
cleanliness, 159n10
cold and heat, 157, 251
compassion, 95n9, 205
conceit, 281
concentration, 141, 249, 291
concentrations
 of Yoga, 185
confusion, 113, 145, 255
conscience, 129n43
consciousness, 255
contemplation, 61, 149n2
control
 of self, 165
Cosmos, 253, 259, 317. *See also* universe, world
courage, 309
course
 lowest, 285
 northern, 187
 southern, 189
 supreme, 175, 185, 199, 285
creation, 153
creativity
 of Divine, 181
crocodile, 215

Daitya race, 39, 215
daiva, 303n14
Daniélou, Alain, 40
darbha, 217
darshana, 223, 255n12
Dasgupta, Surendranath, 66
death, 177, 215, 223n11, 227n18, 249, 255
 as end-time, 117,
 as "going-forth," 179n24, 181, 183
 cycle of, 191
 in performance of own-law, 129,
 survival of, 97n21
deceit, 285, 307
deerskin, 159
defilements, 153, 155, 163
 defined, 157
dehabhrit, 97n16

dosha, 299n3
doshavat, 299n3
doubt, 147, 301
Draupadī (queen), 11–12, 28, 79
Drishtadyumna, 79, 83
Drona, 6, 29–30, 32–34, 37, 49, 85, 93, 229, 235
Drumila (king), 205n7
Drupada (king), 11, 13, 30, 79, 81, 83
dualism, 175n18
dualities, 155
duhkha, 105, 111, 251, 301
Durmarshana, 34
durmati, 303n15
Durvāsas, 28
Duryodhana, 14, 29, 35, 49
  quoted, 79, 81
Dushshāsana, 5, 34
duty, 89n30, 121n16, 125n29
Dvaita, 175n18
dvandva, 97, 107n45, 215
dvāpara-yuga, 52–53
dvāra, 185n13
Dvārakā, 17, 23, 26–27
dvija, 79n2
Dwarka, 17, 23–24
Dyutimān (king), 35

earth, 173
Eckhart, 57
ecstasy, 107, 115n62, 117n63
Edgerton, Franklin, 45, 72
effort, 105, 169, 199
ego-sense, 105n38, 117, 127, 131, 171, 249, 255, 285, 305
ekāntins, 62
elementals, 289
elements, 171, 255
embryo, 133
enjoyment, 87, 123n23, 125, 153
envy, 141
equality, 165n14
equanimity, 107n46, 109
evil, 131, 133, 177
exile, 10, 14, 36, 49
existence
  conditioned, 41
existent, 99
extinction, 155, 159
  in world ground, 69, 117, 155. See also *brahma-nirvāna*
extrasensory, 161
exultation, 251
eye, divine, 223, 275n8
eyebrows
  middle of, 155, 183

failure, 141
  or success, 305
faith, 45, 129, 145, 147, 165, 169, 289, 297
  austerity and, 293
family, 89, 91, 167
  law, 91
fasting, 161
fate, 303
fear, 103, 111, 129, 137, 159, 251, 307, 309
  Arjuna's, 241
fearlessness, 281, 307
Feuerstein, Georg, 11n2, 17, 117n64
field
  defined, 253, 255
field-knower
  defined, 253
food, 123, 291
force, 285, 315
fortitude, 229, 281
fortune, 323
fragment
  divine, 219, 275
Frank, Otto, 68
Frawley, David, 54
friend, 135, 251, 271
fruit of action, 107, 199, 249, 291, 299, 301, 307

law, 95, 129, 137, 191, 199, 271, 307, 309
desire not opposed to, 173
guardian of, 225
triple, 197
lawlessness, 89, 137, 307
laws
abandoning all, 319n33
of caste, 91
of family, 91
learned one, 105n36, 107n46, 113n57, 117n66, 119n10, 141
life 12, 43, 64, 155, 281, 295, 307, 321n34
span of, 167n20
life-element, 181n5, 275
life-force, 143, 185, 205, 307
light
inner, 155
lobha, 299n3
loka-samgraha, 125n31
longing, 117, 177
lord, 283
lucidity, 291
Lunar Dynasty, 12, 191n2

Mādhava (Krishna), 81, 81n4
Madhu, 25, 81n4
Madhusūdana (Krishna), 81n4
Mādhva, 44, 175n18
Mādrī, 29
Mahābhārata, ix, 1–8, 10, 12, 22, 40, 49–52, 68, 103n32
and Vedas, 51
Mahadyogin, 66
Mahānārāyana-Upanishad, 61
maha-rathāh, 79n1
Mahāyāna-Shraddhā-Utpatti, 69
maheshvara, 193n16
Maitrāyanīya-Upanishad, 66
Maitreya, 49
manas, 121n15, 209n20, 275n6
Mandara (mount), 39
manifest, 101, 187
Manipushpaka (conch), 83
manoratha, 283n4
mantra, 195, 293
Manu, 39, 51, 54, 135, 153n4
Manus
four, 203
mānushya, 97
Manu-Smriti, 54
manvantara, 52
Marīci, 209
Marjanovic, Boris, 67
Maruts, 209, 221, 227
marvel, 101
Mascaró, Juan, 72–73
mātrā, 97n17
Matsubara, Mitsunori, 63
Matsya, 38–39
Matsyagandhī, 48
mauna, 111n55
māyā, 137, 175, 317
meditation, 249, 259, 315
memory, 255n11, 277. *See also* remembering
disorder of, 113
merit, 197
Meru (mount), 8, 211, 225n14
Mīmāmsā, 54
mind, 163, 183, 209n20, 249, 255, 275, 315
as one of the hiding-places, 133
confused about the law, 95
disunited, 167
fickleness of, 165
onepointedness of, 159
remembering objects with, 121n15
Sanskrit equivalents for, 75
the senses and, 115
mithyā-ācāra, 121n14
modesty, 281
moha, 299n3, 317
moksha, 97n21
moksha-shāstra, 12

monotheism, 60–65
morality, 12
motive, 157, 163
Müller, F. Max, 72
muni, 111n55
mūrti, 62
mystery, 221
mystical vision, 64
mythology, 40

nabhas, 229n25
Nāgas, 33, 213
naishkarmya, 119n9, 141n20
nakshatra, 209n18
Nakula, 11, 29, 31, 83
  biography, 34–35
Nāmm, 66
Nāra, 65
Nārada (sage), 26, 30, 205, 213
Naraka (demon), 26
Nara-Simha, 38–39
Nārayāna, 61, 65
Nārayanīya, 61, 63–64
nature
  lower, 193
nectar of immortality, 39, 251
Neo-Hinduism, 58–59
New Testament, 59
Nikhilananda, Swami, 223n11
nirāhāra, 113n56
Niramitra, 34
nirvāna, 69, 159
nishthā, 119. 289n1, 313n29
nīti, 323n44
nivritti, 281n3
niyata, 121n16
  nominal, 285
nonattachment, 255, 273
nondoer, 139
nondualism, 67, 139n15
nonexistent, 99
nonharming, 62, 255, 281, 293
nonviolence, 44
nose
  tip of, 159
obedience, 129n43
objects, 113, 121, 129, 143, 150, 157,
    255, 273, 309
  oblation, 227
old age, 177, 255, 269
om tat sat, 295
om, 185, 195, 211n30, 295
omniscience, 51
One, 261
oneness, 163
Oppenheimer, J. Robert, 223n11
order
  cosmic, 103n33
origin, 205, 215
origination
  dependent, 155n7
ostentation, 281, 283, 291, 293
Otto, Rudolf, 227n18
overeating, 161
overpopulation, 23
own-being, 74. *See also svabhāva*

pada, 185n12
Padma-Purāna, 68
pain, 255, 291, 301
  and pleasure, 97, 105, 157, 203, 249,
    259, 271, 275
pairs-of-opposites, 97, 107, 141, 149,
    177, 275
Pāncajanya (conch), 83
Pāncāla, 30
Pāncālī (queen), 11, 31, 33–35
Pāncarātra, 16, 44, 60–65, 67, 70
Pāncarātra-Samhitās, 62–63
Pāndava (Arjuna), 145
Pāndavas
  explained, 217n61
  vs. Kauravas (Kurus), 3, 9–10, 15
Pāndeya (sons-of-Pāndu), 79
pandita, 97, 141
Pāndu (king), 10–11, 28, 35, 49

About the Translators

GEORG FEUERSTEIN, PhD, is one of the leading voices of the East/West dialogue, and since the late 1960s has made many significant contributions to our understanding of India's spiritual heritage, notably Hindu Yoga.

He has authored more than fifty books, including *The Encyclopedia of Yoga and Tantra, The Yoga Tradition, Yoga Morality, The Yoga-Sūtra of Patanjali, The Deeper Dimension of Yoga, Wholeness or Transcendence?,* and *Tantra: Path of Ecstasy*. Among his forthcoming works is an English translation of the *Goraksha-Paddhati,* an ancient text on Hatha-Yoga, with a detailed commentary.

Although he no longer teaches publicly, he designed and currently tutors several distance-learning courses on Yoga philosophy and history offered by Traditional Yoga Studies (www.traditionalyogastudies.com).

For many years he has been a practitioner of Vajrayāna Buddhist Yoga, and since 2004 has lived in semiretirement in Canada.

BRENDA FEUERSTEIN, Georg's wife and collaborator, is the director of Traditional Yoga Studies and a teacher of Yoga based on the teachings of Buddhism. She is a former music teacher and health and fitness consultant. She has a strong interest in ecological issues and coauthored with Georg the books *Green Yoga* and *Green Dharma*. She recently released a CD on the practice of Yoga Sleep (Yoga-Nidrā). Other sound recordings are in progress. Brenda Feuerstein's works include a commentary on the *Yoga-Sūtra* from a woman's perspective.